THE MASTER ARCHITECT SERIES

# TAESUN HONG

## YKH ASSOCIATES

images
Publishing

# Contents

- 8 **Preface**
  Dr. Menas C. Kafatos
- 10 **Foreword**
  Prof. Junggon Kim
- 12 **Arche | Techne**
  William Bingham
- 14 **More with Less**
  Prof. Paul C.H. Lim
- 18 **Taesun Hong: Profile of a Master Architect**
  Hudson A. Matz
- 26 **Architecture Considered as Music**
  Taesun Hong

## NEW INSTRUMENT
- 32 Sebyeol Brewery
- 52 Hillmaru Country Club & Golf Hotel

## REPETITION
- 66 NEFS Headquarters
- 78 Buphwajungsa Temple
- 94 Ilyang DHL Korea Headquarters
- 104 Gimpo BOHM Officetel
- 110 Yangpyeongdong Mixed-Use Building
- 118 Busan Marine Terrace Resort

## VOID
- 132 Vinyl C Headquarters
- 146 Inje Residence
- 156 YKH Associates Headquarters
- 168 Vixen Headquarters
- 182 Trendex Headquarters
- 190 Paju Lotte Premium Outlet

## SENSE OF SURPRISE

- 200 Yeoju Residence
- 212 Seoul Performing Arts Center
- 226 Lotte Department Store Roof Garden
- 236 The Great Wall Apartment Factory
- 246 Nine Dragon Housing Complex
- 258 Buyeo Lotte Premium Outlet

## RHYTHM AND DYNAMICS

- 266 Lotte Underground Path & Plaza
- 272 Oak Valley Resort
- 282 Jeju Seogwipo VIP Institute Hotel Residence
- 294 Oyala Convention & Observatory

## CIRCULATION AND CONNECTION

- 302 Gyeonghui-dang Mixed-Use
- 312 Daejeon Hyundai Premium Outlet
- 322 Gimpo Hyundai Premium Outlet
- 328 Heyri "The Step" Plaza

## SCALE AND PROPORTION

- 336 Namsan Lotte Castle Iris Mixed-Use
- 340 SK Namsan Leaders' View Mixed-Use
- 344 Jamsil Posco the Starpark Residence
- 348 Yoido Richensia Mixed-Use Residence
- 354 Goheung Stella Resort
- 362 Yeosu The Ocean Resort

## APPENDIX

- 370 Chronological List of Other Works
- 387 YKH Associates Profile
- 390 Awards and Publications
- 394 Project Credits
- 399 Acknowledgments

# Preface

Dr. Menas C. Kafatos

This monograph of the work by master architect Taesun Hong is truly inspirational. It brings together architecture as a living art that stands alongside—and on its own at the same time—other great achievements of the human spirit.

Taesun Hong, as a gifted architect, musician, and as a person appreciating the greatness that the best of humanity brings to us, has put together an amazing collection of images, written descriptions, and compositions that allow the viewer to enter the world of architecture, the world of music, the world of art. Far from being a static account of architecture, the vision of Taesun Hong is as dynamic, flowing, energetic, and artistic as are his professional architectural works. The ancient Pythagoreans saw unity in both the physical, the artistic and the mathematical realms. In a sense, the works of Taesun Hong fit the ancient philosophical visions and are also very modern. To put it simply: they span time.

One can indeed follow the words, the terms that he uses, such as Proportion, Dynamics, Composition, Repetition, Harmony, Texture, Instrument, Scale, and so many others. But more than just follow, the reader, the observer, looking at the architectural works and designs, ends up by participating in the architectural dance that this great architect has created and is creating as a living art. The architectural compositions are not just building, they are flowing, they are in harmony with nature, they fit the landscapes in which they are found.

As a physicist, I notice with delight that the art of Taesun Hong (because what he creates is truly art) also fits the modern vision of the quantum universe. It may sound strange, but the unity expressed in his works also fits the quantum universe. The creator and the spectator become one through the mediation of the architectural compositions, the buildings, the designs. Geometry seems to be obvious and also subtle, mathematical proportions are intriguing and provide the harmony that delights the vision of the spectator, the vision of the observer. As such, the art of the architecture becomes a quantum creation. It becomes a mathematical harmony, an artistic harmony. It is after all the mathematics of the quantum world that a professional quantum physicist perceives. It is the mathematics of musical compositions that a musician utilizes even if the result is music.

Through the works of Taesun Hong, one can perhaps understand how the great architectural compositions of the past have an enduring value. Can the Parthenon just be a creation in ancient Athens? Can the Pyramid of Cheops just be a creation in ancient Egypt? In the same way, are the musical compositions of Bach, Mozart, or Beethoven just the creations of specific persons? Or are they lasting eternal works of creation? Space and time are integrated with harmony, compositions, flowing patterns, they are integrated with mathematical harmony and enduring patterns. These patterns flow and interlock like multidimensional structures in an Escher drawing. They are in this world and also out of this world.

In the end, one appreciates that at the foundations of Taesun Hong's works one discovers the philosophy of art, the philosophy of mathematics, the philosophy of science, and the philosophy of—above all—nature.

**Dr. Menas C. Kafatos** is the Fletcher Jones Endowed Chair Professor of Computational Physics at Chapman University in California, United States. Known quantum physicist and cosmologist, he is also an artist, a philosopher, and the author of many scientific articles and books (included on *New York Times*' Best Sellers list). He is a Foreign Member of the Korean Academy of Science and Technology.

# Foreword

Prof. Junggon Kim

Taesun Hong's featured projects in this book display two main design philosophies. The first is designing with a sense of locality; local building materials are found where the surrounding environment and the site connect. Understanding an urban site, being honest in material representation and its regulations to maximize space efficiency are all important factors of Taesun Hong's design. The machinery of architecture—a design concept pioneered in modernism and minimalism—is exposed in the elevations and plans of his designs, and is capable of being rendered well only by an experienced architect's touch. The clear expression of formative simplicity and material details is revealed without filtration, expressing movement within each drawing and the project itself.

The second design philosophy is using these techniques to generate timeless aesthetics. The projects' forms are geometric, monochrome, and abstract regular rhythms exhibit a preference for rational and classical box-shaped architectures. The resulting form is an abstraction free of ornamentation, exhibiting the exposed material unapologetically. Rather than blending materials into the geometries of the building, their full visual demonstration creates a new subject itself on the surface of the project.

For example, the achromatic bricks and colored concrete used in the YKH Associates Headquarters and the Sebyeol Brewery are not used on the buildings' exteriors as decorative detailing, but are instead a material study exhibition. This practice contrasts the common urban landscape of development, as most buildings utilize materials in a series or blend to support the overall form and/or function of the building. Using simple geometry to highlight materiality is an example of minimalism, as its omission of ornamentation or detailing focuses on its individual visual representation.

In projects with restrictive urban site plans such as the NEFS Headquarters, using minimalist design concepts to maximize floor efficiency is especially beneficial. Contrasting the common urban, the use of long, narrow stone cladding expresses a Hellenic rhythm of overall proportion and repetition, presenting a form that balances tranquility and grandeur in a visually chaotic downtown Seoul.

Kenneth Frampton referred to the definition of tectonics as a perceptual aesthetic order in which the presence of architecture is realized by structures, materials, and methods of production. Since it is based on the premise of realization, it comprehensively reveals the relationship between materiality and structure, the method of transferring strength and integrating materials, and the physical land on which the project is built.

Tectonics reflects culture and place, but it can be interpreted as a framework for traditions by new means and materials, rather than references to or imitations of history. Here, structures and materials have architectural properties that are represented by structural order through segmentation and coupling.

The Yangpeongdong Mixed-Use Building, Ilyang DHL Korea Headquarters, and Inje Residence are examples of integrating structural order through the interaction of revealing, concealing, dividing, and combining materials. Like the careful detailing of Ludwig Mies van der Rohe, Taesun Hong's structural order appears to be a fundamental skeleton of the plane in an attempt to create fine spatial and material composition. Oftentimes, the structural order is revealed in the exterior of the building while the repetition of lattice modules and unit spaces are expressed in the plan.

As the late Donald Judd suggested, parts of the building are perceived as a whole, not by formal relationships. Taesun Hong's architecture prioritizes the effective use of materiality through a project's representation instead of adhering to fleeting design norms, resulting in a consistently classic and timeless aesthetic.

**Prof. Junggon Kim** is a Professor at Konkuk University in Seoul, Korea. He completed a Bachelor of Architectural Engineering from Seoul National University (SNU) and a Master of Architecture from SNU and University of Pennsylvania. He also completed a Ph.D in Architecture from SNU. Junggon Kim is a registered architect of the Korean Institute of Registered Architects (KIRA) and is also a member of the American Institute of Architects (AIA).

# Arche | Techne

William Bingham

Architecture is the integration of art and science, and it has both intangible and tangible dimensions—Arche (idea) and Techne (form). It combines the implicit and the explicit into a structure that is created by the architect. When we look at the architecture of Taesun Hong, we see how he has managed the transformation of idea into form. So, it is the very nature of his work that his merging of art and science serves to shape and benefit human lives. Taesun Hong operates in the space that exists between the Arche and the Techne.

Taesun Hong and his architecture are the subjects of this book. Architecture for him represents the way that art and science are combined to shape our experience of the world. To understand Taesun Hong's work, it is necessary to examine his process and the sources of his inspiration. For him architecture represents a way of thinking that begins with a creative impulse and becomes complete with the built work. What Taesun Hong has been able to accomplish is to orchestrate the many forces that come into play in the design process, giving order to his architecture. His art is his work.

The art in architecture emerges out of the "Poetics of Space," and this poetic content has the power to influence human lives. In order to understand the way that Taesun Hong works, the art of his architecture needs to be explored. The source of his inspiration is found in music and the way that it weaves together complex variations. The paradigm of music and its creation presents us with the compositional nature of his process. In the way that idea and reality become combined, Taesun Hong explores the implicit and explicit dimensions of architecture, the space between the two is where his works find their beginning.

In examining his work, it is clear that Taesun Hong is dedicated to the art of architecture and the psychological impact that it has over us. Within this context, we can begin to explore the content of his work and the way that it has influence over the built environment. The nature of his work grows out of the way that architecture and music share common roles in shaping experience, giving expression to the world around us. Music is the way that Taesun Hong is able to describe his work, but the truth is that music has a strong influence over us in a way that architecture does as well.

Taesun Hong's process emerges out of an understanding that there is a poetic potential that architecture employs to create a multidimensional environment that merges the tangible with the intangible. The impact of his work results from his integration of idea and reality to produce experience. In this scenario, his designs create a sense of place, and serve to enrich human lives. Architecture for Taesun Hong is more than the prosaic enclosure of space—it shapes experience. Experience is the interlocuter between implicit and explicit realities.

It has been my pleasure to have served with him in a team structure where all of the team members have been vital to the process. Ultimately, the success of Taesun Hong's work resides in his mastery of the architectural process.

**William Bingham** is a design researcher at HIDDEN LINE and an adjunct professor in design at University of New Mexico.

# More with Less
Prof. Paul C.H. Lim

I remember watching Taesun Hong tirelessly and passionately working on his studio project when I was an undergraduate at Yale. For someone who was an economics major, visiting him late at night in his studio on York Street at Yale School of Architecture was truly a unique experience. Equally as unique was the perspective on architecture Taesun Hong shared with me on one of those visits. He was trying to find a solution to a problem while making his project unique vis-à-vis other students. I asked him, "Why architecture? Do you actually love this profession?" I said that because I had known about his music background, and at Oberlin College he was a music student, not pre-architecture. His answer was as pithy as it was poignant: He got into architecture because it makes human behavior possible, thus architecture was equally as important as food and clothing for humans to not merely survive, but also to thrive. In other words, architecture enables humans to truly flourish.

He added his principle of architectural search as "More with Less," and "Less is More." He told me that architecture is "learning of all possible building technologies, historical precedents, and finally putting all that knowledge into one's subconsciousness; and when the time for creation comes, with a simple stroke of the brush, one's potent creative energies explode into a format that is as minimal as possible but expresses a number of things." Taesun Hong loved Louis I. Kahn's Yale Center for British Art in New Haven for this very reason, and he reiterated to me a number of times that this is architecture at its best because it is "simple but contains everything."

Now, as I write these words, more than thirty years have passed. And I am simultaneously astounded and unsurprised as I look at his fabulous architecture now. Astounded because to articulate a lofty ideal and theory is one thing, but to have the privilege and fortuitous coalescence of circumstances is another. Taesun Hong has managed to put his theory into praxis. Yet I am unsurprised because I knew that his drive and tireless pursuit of his ideal would eventually lead to a "harvest" of buildings and architectural presences throughout the world that beautifully reflects his desires for true human flourishing and enhancing the beauty, truth, and goodness of the ecosystems where his projects are located. I am, by no means, an architectural historian or expert, but because I know how he has pursued his craft for over thirty years—designing every type of architecture from a high-rise to a small house for more than 500 projects built or unbuilt—I can now see the manifestation of his mantra blueprint, "More with Less." His architecture, from a layman's perspective, is very simple but potent, with multiple layers of meaning. In other words, in terms of artistic/architectural hermeneutics, his "texts" of designs and buildings as they blend with the surrounding ecosystems are inclusionary and inviting, rather than fixed and bounded. He has tried to solve the problems of many clients and the results were deeply satisfactory—this is a crucial part of the transaction of architectural design and execution. The client does not have to know every aspect of Taesun Hong's implied values—socioeconomic, emotional, historical, and above all musical sensibilities—yet the product that is delivered for them has to speak unequivocally to move them to satisfaction and augmentation of the desire to spend more—not less—time there, *inter alia*. Working in underdeveloped countries, for example, Taesun Hong has functioned with a very limited budget to achieve all those values, and for him, this has provided a long arc of vision for maximizing values for the limited resources we all have to share on a global scale of building things, places, and institutions. Over time, he has refined a way to build simply while creating beautiful places for *all*.

As a gifted artist and musician, Taesun Hong tries to layer his artistic sensibilities on every move; his works are subtle but powerful, just like the beautifully written scores by the French composer Erik Satie. Just as ancient Koreans have found a depth in architecture when their resources were limited, what is evident in his architecture is the power of strong negative space. In his YKH Associates Headquarters and the Trendex Headquarters, he used rising staircases as a theme—this theme is mysterious yet hopeful: reaching the sky as a user experiences a sense of "hope." It is fundamentally a very simple way of providing means of egress for a building but his gesture is more than that. One experiences "sense of light" and "sense of restfulness." Once a user reaches the top, there is a roof garden with a view. He has created this wonderful space with half the cost for that of Inje Residence in Gangwon-do,

South Korea, and has still overcome the innate issues of its site; to resolve the adjacency of the neighborhood ancestral tomb and a ruin-like structure, he looked to the old Korean architectural idea of "courtyard" but with an added value of creating views of the Seoraksan Mountain above the skyline of the residence's roof structure. He used very natural materials such as tile, stone, and wood: materials typically regarded as "timeless." It impresses me that this 4,306-square-foot (400-square-meter) house was built at a cost of under US$1 million. Taesun Hong told me that he harnessed geothermal energy by digging 505 feet (154 meters) into the ground to obtain nature's heat and redirected and repurposed it. More than ten years have passed, the building still functions beautifully, and it ages amazingly with natural scent and color just like an aged Burgundy wine.

Taesun Hong's concept of "more with less" is evident in the Sebyeol Brewery project in Paju-si, South Korea. He used a color pigment and local pinewood to create a new texture of concrete—of course with a very limited budget. With a rigorous search for an innate beauty of materials, he explored a way for visitors to experience a beer-making process and upgrade it to a "soul-searching" experience. As a visitor, one first samples the beer—the result of rigorous process of time and effort of the beer maker—in the naturally lit blue hall of the first floor and slowly makes their way up to the second floor to watch the entire beer-making process; the journey culminates at the exterior courtyard to experience nature's offerings, whether sunlight, rain, or snow. When one is in this courtyard the beer experience transforms itself into a true creation of nature. The "blue" aura of place that is created with a minimal gesture and methodology is so "pure" and "strong."

As a successor of a famed architectural firm, Taesun Hong has adopted Minoru Yamasaki's ideal of and commitment to public "good." Just as Yamasaki endeavored to create a public sphere in front of the World Trade Center in the 1970s, Taesun Hong is attempting to create a sense of surprise and, at the same time, an "oasis" in the heart of Seoul. For the Gyeonghui-dang Mixed-Use project, he tried to create another "Spanish Steps"—a public corridor to reconnect with history and nature. This beautiful project is also achieved under considerable budgetary constraints. All visitors to and citizens of Seoul now have a place to contemplate, play, and enjoy. I believe Taesun Hong's architecture is a *tour de force*, a result of countless hours of piano practicing, many strokes of the paint brush, and wields the powerful potency of experiencing different cultures; it is finally a fermentation of his knowledge of East and West, ancient and contemporary, baroque and avant-garde.

Although I am not sure whether *all* the readers of this book and viewers of architectural images herein will be enamored with them, I am sure of one thing: this book will generate conversation. If an inert building garners sufficient interest from people to become the object of conversation—public and private—as well as providing shelters, idea banks, and sites of cultural and economic productions, then the architect of such buildings, in this case Taesun Hong, deserves to become a focal point of discussion, which is precisely what this book is designed to do.

Taesun, you've come a long way, dear *hyung*! May many more people find the warmth and inviting spirit of your buildings every time they enter them.

**Prof. Paul C.H. Lim** (PhD, Cambridge) is an award-winning historian of early modern Europe. He currently teaches intellectual and religious history at Vanderbilt University. His book, *Mystery Unveiled: The Crisis of the Trinity in Early Modern England* (Oxford, 2012) won the Roland H. Bainton Prize in 2013 as the best book in history/theology by the Sixteenth Century Society and Conference. He has delivered papers and lectures at Oxford, Cambridge, St. Andrews, Harvard, Yale, Princeton, Penn, Dartmouth, Cornell, and UChicago, as well as in Sri Lanka, India, Cambodia, Switzerland, France, Ethiopia, Kenya, China, Japan, and South Korea.

# Taesun Hong
## Profile of a Master Architect

Hudson A. Matz

It is a humid May afternoon in Seoul, South Korea. Taesun Hong, design director and founder of YKH Associates, quietly inspects a study model from across his office's conference table. We're sitting in his firm's recently completed fourth-floor office, a building he himself had just finished giving me the tour of despite his tight schedule. As we wait for the sandwiches that he's ordered from the building's first-floor café, Taesun Hong jokes how his few black hairs have started turning gray. Between the elephant ladder leaning against his office's immense bookshelf and the grand piano placed beside his desk, you can tell Taesun Hong is an architect who doesn't sacrifice his autonomy in his busy routine.

Despite spending the past month researching his full body of work from both YKH Associates and Yamasaki Associates, Taesun Hong has an assortment of design magazines that he's featured in laid out across the table. I'm more than familiar with the design competitions he's won across South Korea and Asia, but I leaf through them anyway. The opening slide of his "Music & Architecture" presentation is displayed on his office conference monitor, a design theory topic that I imagine he's lectured about dozens of times in his years as an adjunct professor at Konkuk University in Seoul. To understand his origins and life as an architect, Taesun Hong says you need to understand him as a musician first.

### Early Beginnings

Taesun Hong was born November 6, 1964 and raised in Seoul. He remembers himself growing up as a fiercely competitive boy, wanting to stand out among his three siblings to parents who were rarely home. He credits his mother, an award-winning embroiderer, and father, a police officer with an intense passion for calligraphy, for his creativity and interest in fine arts.

When he was eight years old, Taesun Hong began playing the piano just so he could compete with his neighbor, a child protégée named Park Yongchul. Taesun Hong recalls how envious he was that the boy could produce such beautiful music with such small, delicate hands. Even after Park Yongchul moved away to Daegu, Taesun Hong had developed a passionate relationship with music. Through a childhood and adolescence marred by instability, immigration, and high expectation, Taesun Hong continued to express himself through his music and, eventually, through architecture.

Shortly after Taesun Hong's birth, his father left the Korean police department to work for the Korean Central Intelligence Agency in Tokyo. Seeing the poverty in the country and fearing the impending collapse of South Korea's military dictator Park Chung-hee's regime, Taesun Hong's father began making arrangements to move the family out of Korea to the United States. Between 1972 and 1978, Taesun Hong and his siblings relocated four times within Seoul before immigrating to Detroit, Michigan, in 1980. His mother and father had moved to the United States two years prior to establish permanent residency for their children. After years of living with their grandmother, the children were granted emergency visas in the week following the assassination of President Park Chung-hee. Taesun Hong still remembers the surreal experience vividly. Other sixteen-year-old boys spent that summer playing soccer or chasing girls. Taesun Hong, on the other hand, had to haul himself and his siblings through a collapsing country's capital city, through an occupied airport, and onto a plane bound for the United States (a country they'd never previously visited). He remembers feeling like he was the star of a Hollywood action movie.

## Education

Despite being a standout student in Korea, Taesun Hong's limited English made his transition to American high school brutal. In his first year, Taesun Hong remembers having to memorize entire books to prepare for exams, sometimes writing down entire chapters if he couldn't understand what the questions were specifically asking for. Eventually, his parents decided to try sending the kids to Cranbrook Schools, a nearby boarding school (designed by Eliel Saarinen) in Bloomfield Hills. Because of their poor English test scores, Taesun Hong and his siblings were initially turned away, but after the private school interviewed each child and heard the pleas of his parents, Taesun Hong became the family's lone attendee.

In 1981, he was one of few Asian boys in his class at Cranbrook. Despite having grown more confident in English, the advanced literature courses he had to take at Cranbrook were overwhelming. Understanding texts like Faulkner's *The Sound and the Fury* and being forced to participate in a Harkness-style discussion were simply beyond his capabilities. "I remember asking my father to send me those books in Korean so I could at least understand the content," laughs Taesun Hong.

Even though he spent many sleepless nights trying to catch up on homework while learning English, Taesun Hong found a few happy moments with his music and fine art classes. Playing piano at Cranbrook while also taking lessons with a piano teacher from Royal Oak, Michigan, he found himself dreaming of life as a pianist more and more. Infusing the style of piano he'd grown up playing in Korea with Shostakovich, Ravel, and Debussy had substantially expanded his musical comprehension. Regardless of the immense stress and isolation he felt in Bloomfield Hills, Taesun Hong still feels honored that he had the opportunity to attend Cranbrook because of his growth as a pianist. Thus, as an eighteen-year-old, Taesun Hong chose to attend Oberlin College, a small college in Ohio with one of the best music departments in the country, over the University of Michigan, which had a top-ranked medical program. To soothe his parent's fears, he told them he was still pursuing a pre-medical degree; he just wanted to leave Michigan.

As expected, Taesun Hong found the music facilities and program at Oberlin exceptional. During his freshman year, he was placed in a dorm called the 'Asia House,' which was a residential hall that accommodated a student body focused on Southeast Asian studies. Taesun Hong remembers becoming close friends with his dormmates because of their shared love for music and art. One of his favorite professors, a visiting scholar named Yoshinobu Taniguchi, who was a master of Shakuhachi (an ancient Japanese bamboo flute), was his neighbor. Being surrounded by students and faculty with whom he could relate to was a huge positive for him during his time at Oberlin. Similar to his time at Cranbrook, Taesun Hong immersed himself in fine art courses. It was here that he took a sculpting class with Ms. Athena Tacha, a professor and friend who suggested Taesun Hong take courses in architecture.

One teacher, a visiting professor from Peabody named Julian Martin, made a longstanding impression on him. Taesun Hong remembers him being an incredibly talented pianist, possessing more skill and knowledge than any other instructor he'd had before. However, after a few sessions of practicing with him, Martin told Taesun Hong that his fundamental skills were not good enough to consider a career as a pianist. Naturally, he was devastated, and became extremely depressed. Trying to prove to both Martin and himself that he had the abilities, Taesun Hong locked himself in one of Oberlin's music rooms for hours a day, practicing. Later, Taesun Hong found out that very same room was designed by none other than Minoru Yamasaki, his future employer and firm's namesake.

Needless to say, a career in architecture hadn't ever occurred to Taesun Hong. There were no architects in his family, and growing up in a struggling post-war Korea had limited his architectural exposure. After the great sacrifices his parents had endured to get them to the United States, becoming anything but a doctor would have been a disappointment. However, while he pursued a degree in Biology as a pre-med student, Taesun Hong quietly continued his love affair of studying and playing the piano, graduating with a minor in Piano Performance and Studio Art. Despite having the interest and intelligence to go to medical school, he found out during an internship he might not have the stomach for it.

The summer before graduation, Taesun Hong found work as a research assistant at Harvard Medical School's McLean Hospital. Using rats as test subjects, he helped study the relationship between alcohol and testosterone levels in males. Because of the volume of blood needed for the study, Hong was required to provide gallons of fresh blood on a weekly basis. He spent his summer in a dimly lit basement, responsible for killing and draining the blood of thousands of rats using a miniature guillotine device. He recalls how disturbing the experience was, going days without eating because of the trauma. By the end of the study, Taesun Hong had developed serious reservations about going to med school. Despite this, Taesun Hong graduated from Oberlin College in 1987 with a pre-medical track degree in Biology and a minor in Fine Arts.

Not knowing what lay ahead, Taesun Hong interviewed for an analyst position at Goldman Sachs in New York City while also taking the MCAT, and GMAT over the period of a couple months. After making it to the final round, Taesun Hong was invited to apply again the next year.

## Becoming an Architect

It was at this time when his former teacher, Ms. Athena Tacha, reached out to Taesun Hong and insisted he should look at the architectural field as a possible career path. She believed his background in math and fine art would be the perfect foundation for at least a summer design studio. With his curiosity piqued, Taesun Hong began investigating various architecture programs and firms. After finding the Career Discovery program at Harvard's Graduate School of Design, he decided to test the waters and apply. Not having the financial support of his family, he found a job as a computer programmer in New York City and saved money until he could move to Boston and pay his full tuition.

Taesun Hong remembers his time in Boston fondly. He became completely immersed in the world of architecture. Between 1987 and 1988, Hong was eagerly reading architectural magazines and visiting various famous buildings when he wasn't in the studio at Harvard's Graduate School of Design. Because of his experience working with computers and CAD software, he got an internship working at the Boston-based firm Leers Weinzapfel Associates in September 1988. At the time, few architecture companies were ready to invest in drawing software. He worked at Leers Weinzapfel Associates for a year in preparation for applying to graduate school. Working closely under partner Andrea Leers, Taesun Hong's fascination with architecture metastasized. He remembers Leers's kindness and intellectual generosity, introducing him to various architects, like Tadao Ando, who were goliaths in the field despite learning architecture much later. Leers introduced him to the works of Louis I. Kahn, specifically his Kimbell Art Museum and Yale Center for British Art. Taesun Hong remembers, "Bold, efficient, timeless architecture was rooted into my early years thanks to Kahn."

Because Leers and Ando were professors at Yale University at the time, Hong knew that pursuing a Master of Architecture there would be the most impactful for him as an architect. In the fall of the 1988, Taesun Hong moved to New Haven, Connecticut, to begin pursuing a Master of Architecture at Yale University.

Having the opportunity to attend desk critiques and reviews from starchitects like Frank Gehry, Zaha Hadid, Tadao Ando, and Cesar Pelli were incredible for Taesun Hong's development. However, the severity of some critiques shocked him: he vividly remembers professors telling students to just quit architecture altogether. Even after winning the student design competition at Yale his first year, Taesun Hong was still extremely self-conscious due to his limited architectural education and knowledge.

Due to the Eurocentric focus of architecture programs in the 1980s, Hong realized there was a cultural void in his internal architectural references. So, in 1989, Taesun Hong decided to attend a study abroad program in Florence, Italy, through Syracuse University. He was thrilled to be in a city overflowing with culture and architecture and being at the heart of the European Renaissance. Despite being mugged on the bus and losing his father's 35mm Leica M2 camera, Hong still remembers the city very fondly. "The city was a total gem and, now when I think about it, it was probably the best time of my life." Touring the city with other students, he was introduced to various chiantis and pastas. He even attended culinary classes through the Syracuse program, registering under the pseudonym 'Tevius Maximus Hong.' After his semester in Florence, Taesun Hong realized there was more architecture and culture to see on the continent, opting to stay a while longer. He traveled across Italy, then went to Spain, France, Prague, and even Budapest, sketching the whole time.

When he returned to Yale, he found the content in his architecture courses was much easier to relate to. He started to understand European precedents thoroughly and was now able to apply foreign architectural concepts and ornamentation into his own designs. He recalls being especially influenced by the work of the late Michael Sorkin, an outspoken advocate of the "six senses of architecture" philosophy. This helped Hong push himself into relating architecture to music for the first time in college.

Taesun Hong graduated from Yale in May of 1992. He returned to his family in Michigan over the summer after having found his job prospects in New York City were limited by his lack of extensive work experience and the recent recession. Wanting to stay local and be more independent, he decided to join the small Troy-based firm Pallos Architects as a partner. The founder, Tom Pallos, had worked for Yamasaki Associates, but had left to start his own firm. Working at Pallos & Hong Architects while living with his parents, Taesun Hong was living paycheck to paycheck.

In September of 1992, he got a call from Kip Serota, a principal at Yamasaki Associates and a former colleague of Tom's. They were entering a design competition in Incheon, Korea, for a bus terminal complex, and, knowing of Taesun Hong's background, Serota wanted him on their design team. Taesun Hong accepted the project—with a modest payment of $5,000—and commuted to Rochester Hills, Michigan, to Yamasaki's office. After his design won the competition, Taesun Hong received a senior designer position by Yamasaki's Senior Partner, William Ku. Having the opportunity to return to Korea for work and because his practice with Pallos & Hong Architects was no longer viable, Taesun Hong accepted the position and joined Yamasaki Associates in January of 1993.

## YKH Associates

Working with William Ku over the course of the next decade, Taesun Hong helped Yamasaki Associates win various design competitions and commissions in Korea, China, Japan, Vietnam, Dubai, and Equatorial Guinea. After winning the Parkview competition in Seoul in January of 2000, Taesun Hong decided to create an autonomous branch of the firm in Seoul, called Yamasaki Korea. William Ku was unable to allocate money to him due to the financial situation of the firm, so Hong opened the branch by raising approximately $1 million on his own. When the Michigan headquarters closed its doors in 2009, Taesun Hong's branch was the last in operation. With the permission of William Ku, Taesun Hong changed the firm's name to Yamasaki, Ku, Hong (YKH) Associates.

In our various conversations, Taesun Hong has reaffirmed multiple times that architecture is more akin to music than to the visual arts. Taesun Hong doesn't necessarily want his architecture to be visually shocking and stand out like Frank Gehry or Zaha Hadid's works. Often advocating "form follows function," Taesun Hong isn't as concerned with the general shape of his building as much as its effectiveness in creating a place for enhancing one's life. Taesun Hong remarks, "Too many architects get their egos involved in projects when it's not really about them. I don't need an 'ism' in my work. Every site is different and has a unique set of concepts waiting to be pulled out.

"Good architecture is something you shouldn't experience only once. You should be able to see it twenty years later and it still be beautiful, if not more so. Like classical music, time should only complement these expressions as the user themself has grown and matured. Like Louis I. Khan, designing with a sense of timelessness should be the goal of any architect with the future in mind.

"I love my profession and I am grateful to those who worked with me to create moments of excitement. My journey has not ended, but just started," concludes Taesun Hong.

**Hudson A. Matz** has been an intern at YKH Associates. He is a recent B.S. Architecture graduate of University of Michigan's Taubman College and is Architectural Designer at Stantec in San Francisco.

# Architecture Considered as Music

Taesun Hong

I see architecture as music. My work has been inspired by music. I studied physics, chemistry, and biology in college but if I were to choose one subject that has influenced my architectural design process the most, it would definitely be "music."

The word "music" is derived from the ancient Greek term *mousiki*, which originally referred to the "(art) of the muses," the latter being a term used to represent the ancient Greek goddesses of literature (including poetry), science, and the arts (especially music and song). Music can also be described as the art of expressing emotion by voice, with sound and rhythm being the most important factors. It is also the knowledge of how sounds combine in a way that leads to pleasure and affects the mind, for example to generate an emotional response.

Aficionados and experts alike have described music as being able to cause a knowledge of human existence and the ability to heal the soul. Thinkers, such as the Greek philosopher Aristotle (384–322 BC) viewed music as one of the branches of mathematics, and the Islamic philosopher and polymath Avicenna (AD 980–1037) from Persia, who mentioned music in mathematics in *The Book of Healing*, accepted this opinion, too. Unlike mathematics, however, all musical features are not certain and unchangeable. Instead, as the musical composer's ability and aesthetic is directly involved in music, thus it's also called an art. Today, music is an extensive science *and* art that has various and specialized parts, and voice is called music only once it's able to create a link between minds and when it is not limited by an abstract parameter. This aspect of architecture can be understood—felt, rather—at the mental or spiritual level as one perceives architecture from his or her own special angle. There have been many classic examples throughout the architectural timeline when this aspect can be sensed, that is, "felt." Violet Page aptly noted: "Music and architecture have the common property of putting us inside a sensorial whole different from that we ordinarily live in."

## Common Elements

I have studied these two art forms for a long time now, so have observed some profound similarities between architecture and music. To my mind, there are several musical terms that refer to both architecture and music.

The common elements include *scale*, which is essentially the physical or auditory magnitude of a design. Scales are chosen to generate a contrast or reference between the volume of forms.

The *rhythm* is the arranged system of things that have a regulated pattern, generating an expression. Rhythm is most derived and constructed from mathematical sequences. Rhythm is a strong, regularly repeated pattern. Rhythm in music is patterns of sounds in relation to a beat, whereas repetition of elements, openings, shapes, or structural bays establish regular or irregular rhythm in architecture.

Like rhythm, *repetition* relies on a mathematical, usually algebraic, series, which is relayed via reoccurring actions, events, or forms that are consistent.

*Texture* highlights the feel, appearance, or consistency of a surface or a substance. In music it refers to layers of sounds and rhythms produced in different instruments; in architecture texture appears in different materials used in the architectural construction. Texture, both in music and architecture, helps in understanding emotional and physical spaces. For example, differently textured surfaces can help in recognizing different physical and emotional spaces in a building. Similarly, differently sounding music also can help in recognizing different spaces within music.

The element of *harmony* is an orderly or pleasing combination of elements in a whole. In music, it is said to be a balance between sound and composition and in architecture it is a balance of elements together.

*Proportion* is the dimensional relation of one with the other. It is also the relation of part with the whole. Proportion in music is distance between notes or intervals. Also, it is the relation between intensities of various sound frequencies. Proportion in architecture is meant to be the relationship between elements together.

*Dynamics* govern the motivating or driving forces, physical or moral. It is the quality of action in music. It means how loud or quiet the music is. Dynamics in architecture is expressed through a sense of energetic movement and action. It is better understood through the building's façades or mass.

Moreover, a *sense of surprise* describes the impressive feeling after experiencing the range that extends from a narrow space to a wider space; similar to the musical strengths of *piano* (soft) and *forte* (loud).

In both art forms, the *void* (or rest) is expressed as a vacuum, negative space, visually or audibly. Expressions created by voids completely rely on a previous relationship to existing, positive masses.

*Circulation* and *connection*, of course, each define the movement through a system, much like how one space or sound connects to another.

And finally, work produced with *instruments* (visual and auditory materiality) is how a design is constructed based on its component's qualities/character. Even if the general form of the design doesn't change, its overall expression will if its component's mediums do, such as replacing stone with brick; using notes from a cello instead of a violin.

The experience of a wonderful building might in some way equate with the experience of a remarkable piece of music. The whole artistic experience is the change of perception. Music, too, has the same effect. After listening to a great piece of music it may remind one of some feeling or events experienced in the past and may also remind one of the spaces within which that event had taken place. All arts deal with space and time. Music and architecture have both passed through stages of tangible and intangible development in response to their time.

As abstract art forms that are based on rhythm, proportion, and harmony, architecture and music share a clear cultural lineage. This is how music and architecture is blended together and is able to be felt physically and understood spiritually.

While it is very well known that architects and musical composers have sought to identify distinctive resemblances between architecture and music, it has also been a significant topic within the realms of thinkers, writers, and artists alike, across many disciplines. The German writer Johann Wolfgang von Goethe is attributed as citing the metaphor "architecture is frozen music;" a similar sentiment shared by the German poet Friedrich Schlegel, who is attributed as saying "music is architecture in a fluid state and architecture is frozen music." The German philosopher and educator Friedrich Wilhelm Joseph von Schelling's interpretation was that "architecture is music in space, as it were a frozen music." Le Corbusier is known to have looked to music for inspiration: "Music, like architecture, is time and space." Frank Lloyd Wright explained, "It is perfectly true that music and architecture flower from the same stem […[ My father […] taught me to see a great symphony as an edifice, an edifice of sound." Louis I. Kahn had said that "When I see a plan, I must see the plan as if it were a symphony, of the realm in spaces in the construction of light." And the Renaissance architect Leon Battista Alberti is cited as saying "music and geometry are fundamentally one and the same; music is geometry translated into sound, and that in music the very same harmonies are audible which inform the geometry of the building" and that "the same characteristics that please the eye also please the ear."

**Pursuit of Happiness**

What is then the objective for pursuing "architecture" or "music"? I think the answer is "pursuing happiness." It's akin to finding a good bottle of wine. The fine wine's well-balanced proportions, textures, and harmonies are consistent with Goethe's realistic and harmonious archaic experience in Italy. I believe, after all, that the greatest similarities between architecture and music is that they are each a representation of the search for happiness and hope.

Taesun Hong, *Layering 1* (2021), pen and pencil

A **new instrument** is how a design is constructed based on its components' qualities/character. Even if the general form of the design doesn't change, its overall expression will—if its components' mediums do (i.e., replacing stone with bricks, using notes from a cello instead of a violin).

# SEBYEOL BREWERY
Paju-si, Gyeonggi-do, South Korea | 2019

Sebyeol Brewery is in Paju-si, a quiet suburban town 12 miles (20 kilometers) northwest of Seoul. The clients requested that the building's design both responds to the natural environment as well as integrates a social venue space to become a social and cultural center. Therefore, the design of this building considers a few different design prompts: The perception of the building's scale with the immediate rural environment; the interrelationship between interior activity and outside nature; and the interactive conditions between manufacturing space and human live space. In response to this environment, the scale and the preconception of industrial buildings needed to be reinterpreted.

The formwork that generated the façade acts as the main transitional element to reflect nature and to house the function of this architecture, in effect to reconcile it with nature. For this transition, different textures and the degree of roughness are used and positioned sequentially from outside to inside. Especially, the rough and natural treatment of the exterior wall is composed of organic material with inorganic concrete to perceive reminiscence of nature. The medium textured and chiseled surface of the concrete wall is designed for the inside transitional area, such as the space between the first- and second-floor area and the entranceway. The fine, smooth, blue-dyed concrete is exposed for all the interior space to interact with the natural and artificial lighting.

The distinctiveness of the façade design and method of construction was studied, investigated, and tested. This textured exterior wall is composed of three layers: the 5.9-inch (150-millimeter) insulation is laminated and sandwiched in between 7.9-inch (200-millimeter) reinforced dyed-concrete and 11-inch (280-millimeter) exterior façade cast concrete. The outer layer of concrete is cast by reusing local pinewood, and the bark was left embedded in the concrete surface for the texture. All the concrete used was dyed with cobalt-blue pigment, which allows the color to dissipate over time. This textured exterior wall was designed to perceive the different ambiance of daylight to create unique shadows to be projected so that people can observe and experience the time changes over the course of the day. After the sun sets and there's complete darkness, the light-revealing design at the bottom edge of the wall (at ground level) illuminates and reflects the wall texture.

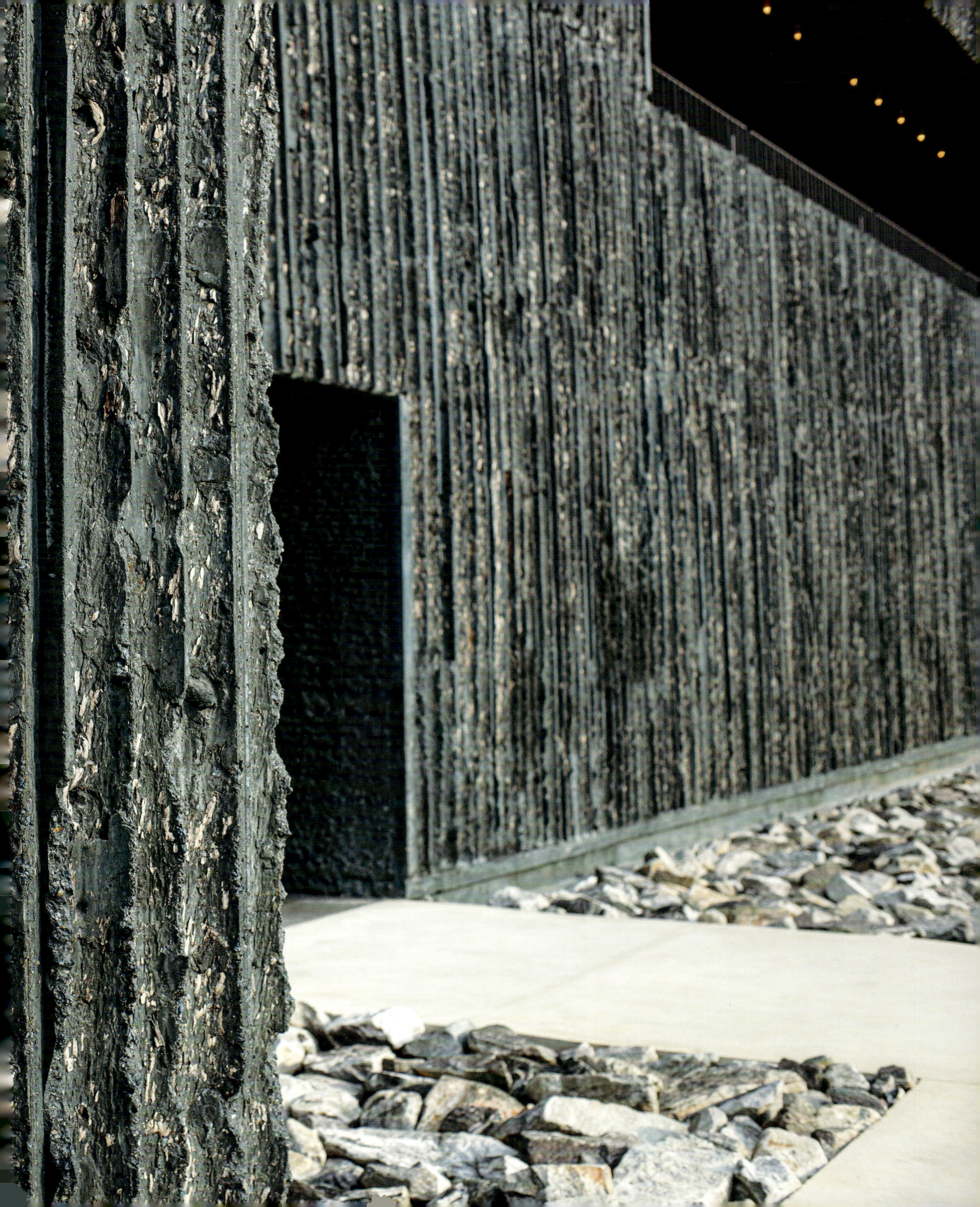

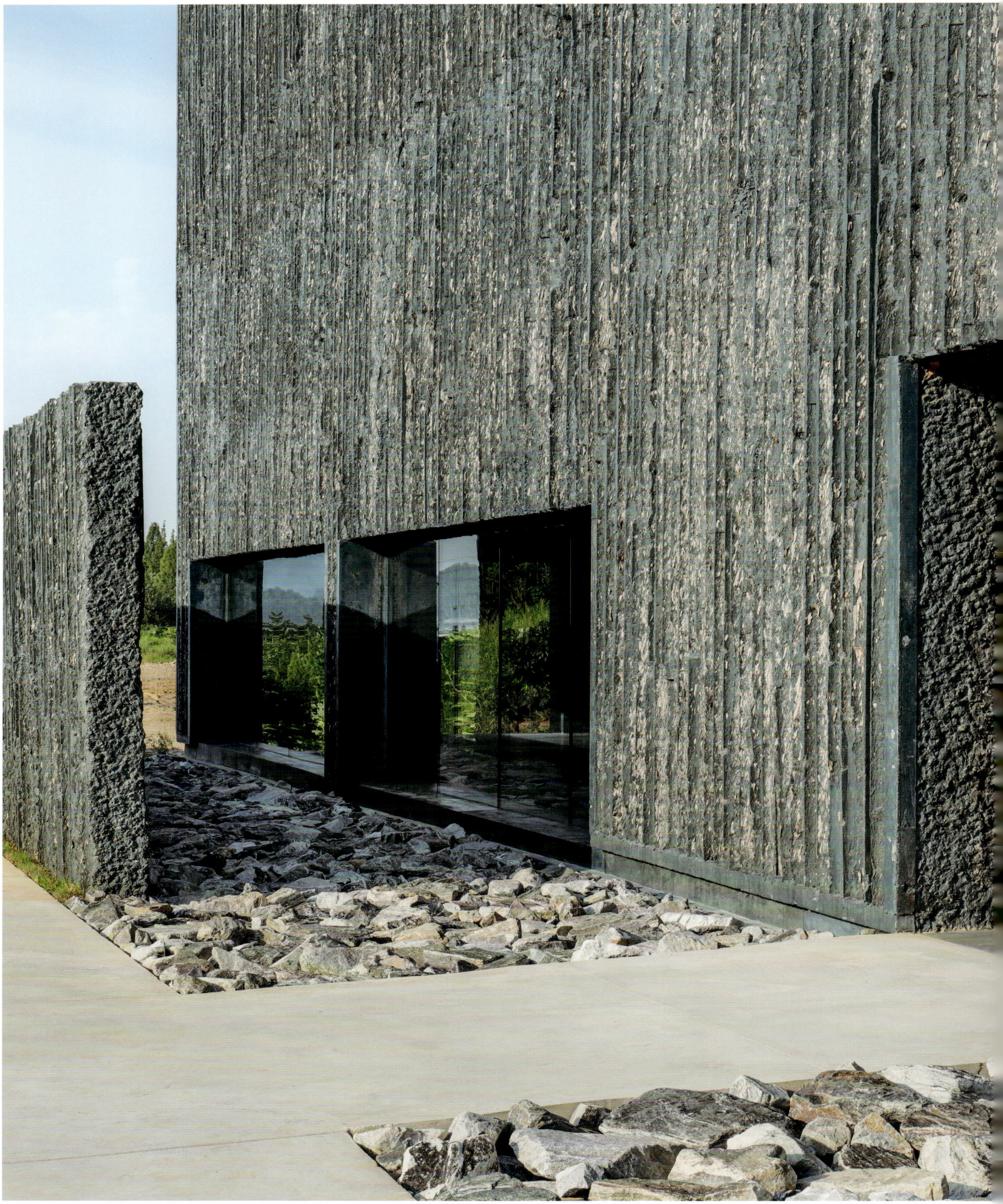

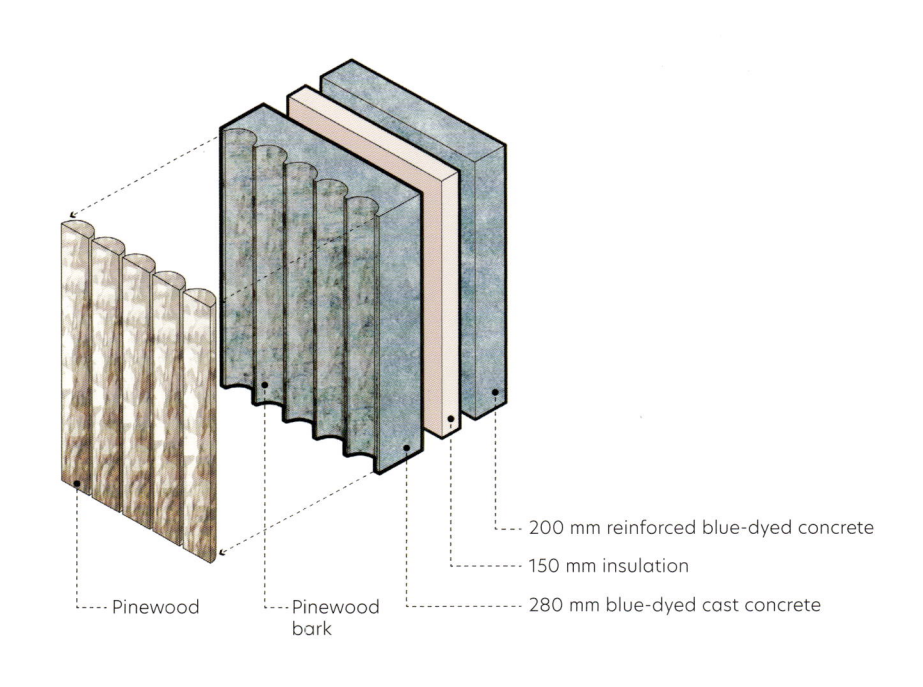

- - - 200 mm reinforced blue-dyed concrete
- - - 150 mm insulation
- - - 280 mm blue-dyed cast concrete

Pinewood

Pinewood bark

SEBYEOL BREWERY

40  NEW INSTRUMENT

SEBYEOL BREWERY

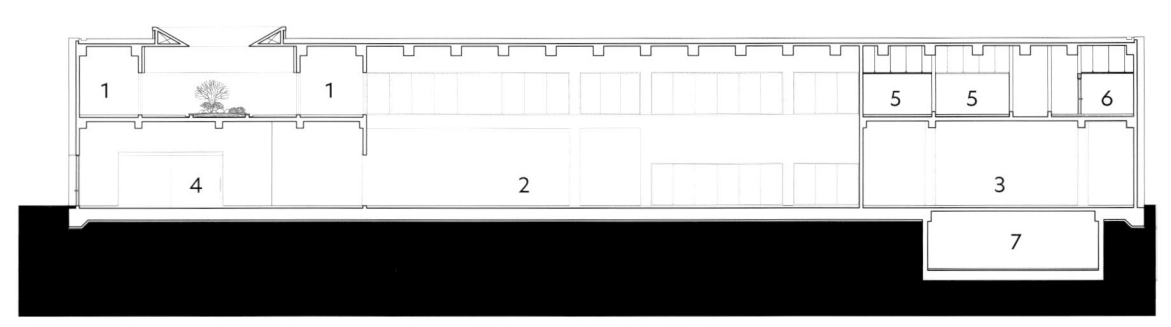

Section 1

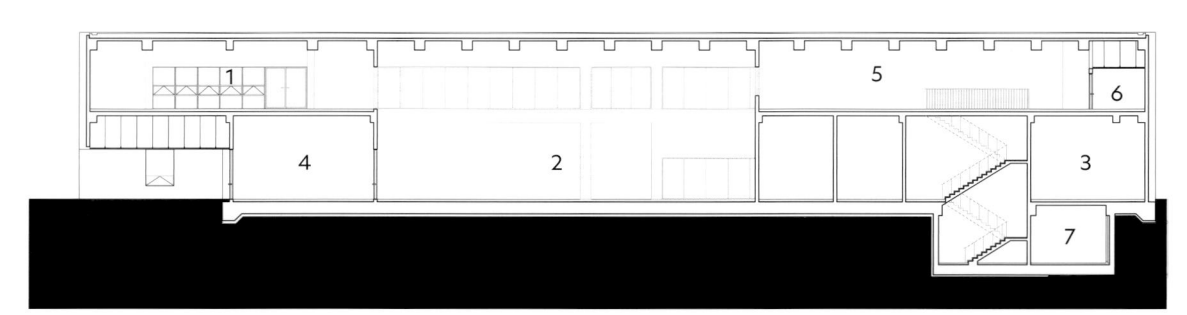

| | |
|---|---|
| 1 | Tasting room |
| 2 | Brewery |
| 3 | Malt warehouse |
| 4 | Storeroom |
| 5 | Restroom |
| 6 | Fitting room |
| 7 | Reservoir |

Section 3

| | |
|---|---|
| 1 | Tasting room |
| 2 | Brewery |
| 3 | Malt warehouse |
| 4 | Keg wash room |
| 5 | Office |
| 6 | Fitting room |
| 7 | Water tank |

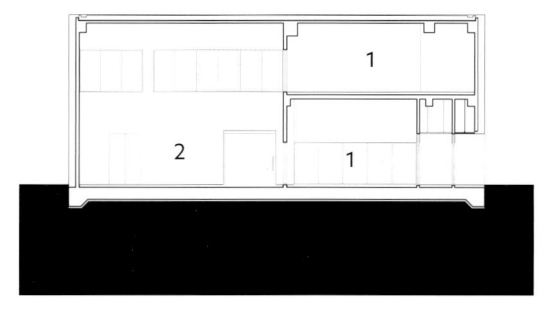

Section 2

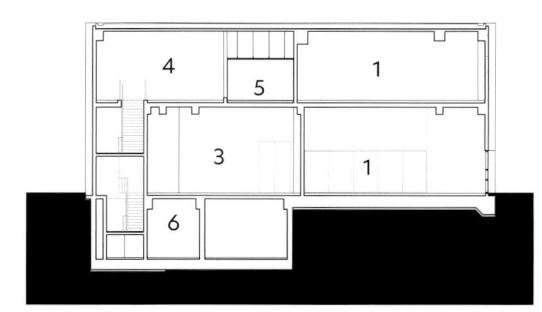

Section 4

| | |
|---|---|
| 1 | Tasting room |
| 2 | Brewery |
| 3 | Malt warehouse |
| 4 | Office |
| 5 | Restroom |
| 6 | Water tank |

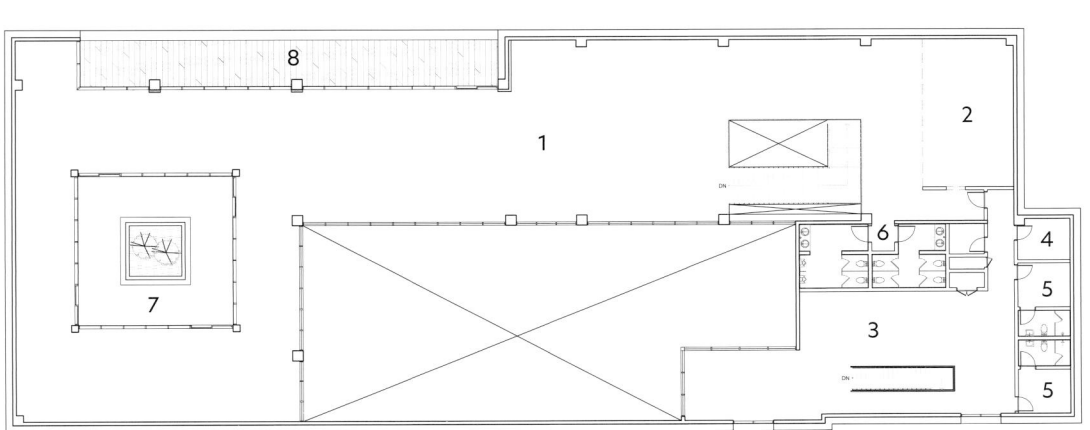

Second-floor plan

1. Tasting room
2. Kitchen
3. Office
4. Storeroom
5. Staff locker room
6. Restroom
7. Courtyard open to above
8. Balcony

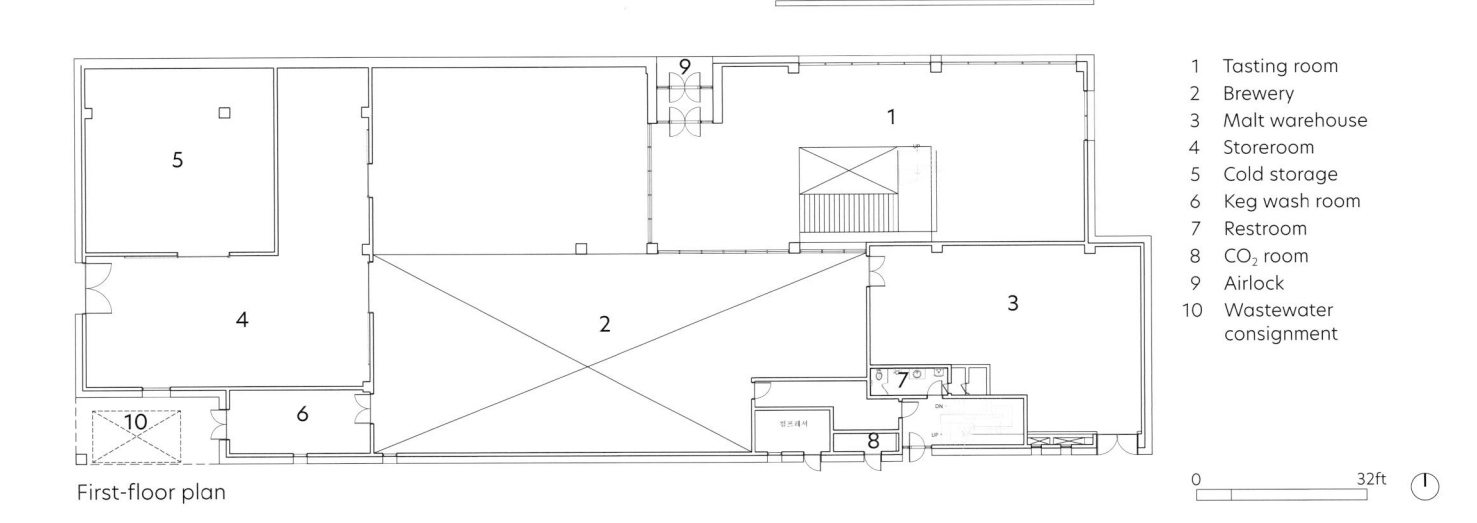

First-floor plan

1. Tasting room
2. Brewery
3. Malt warehouse
4. Storeroom
5. Cold storage
6. Keg wash room
7. Restroom
8. $CO_2$ room
9. Airlock
10. Wastewater consignment

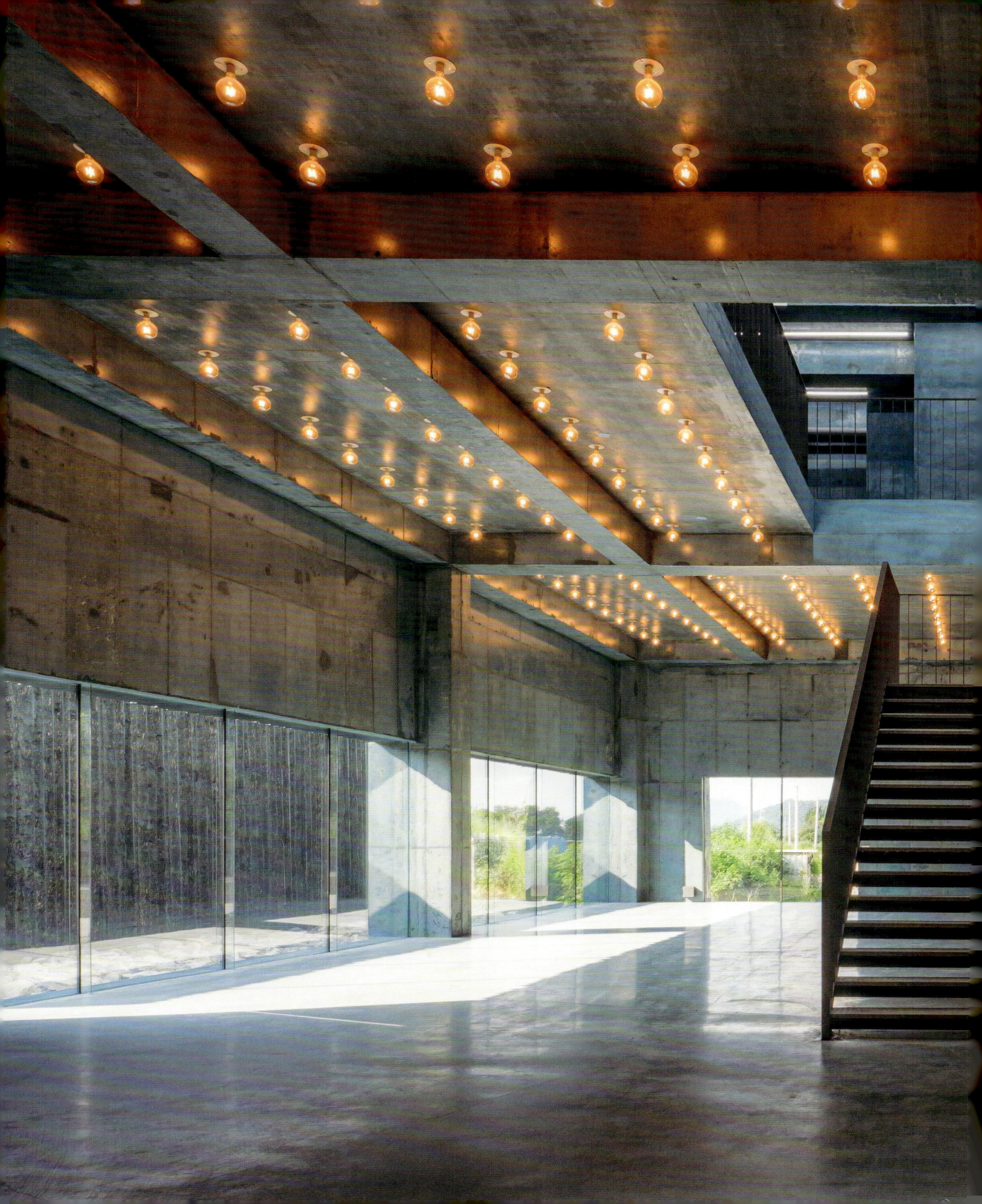

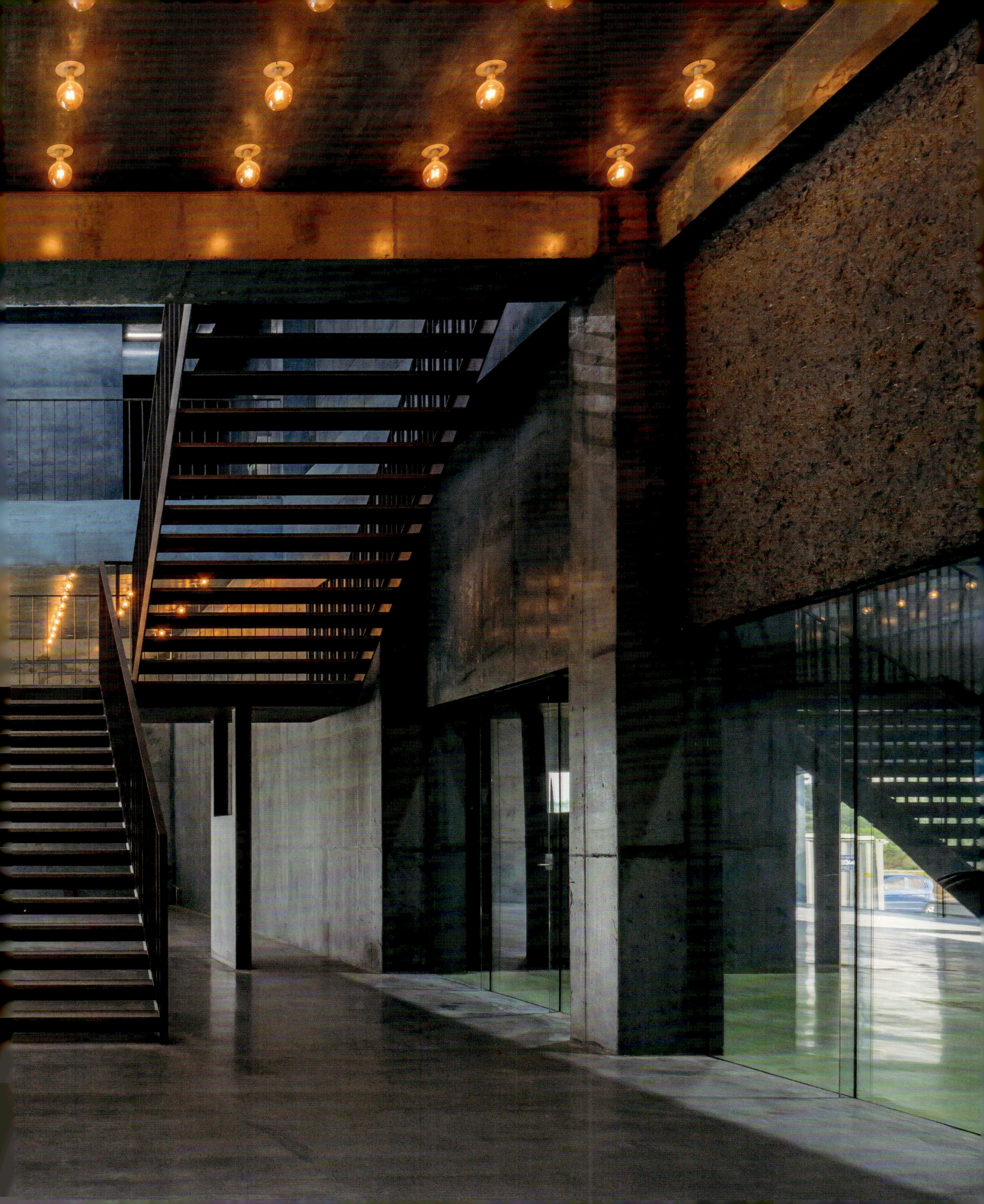

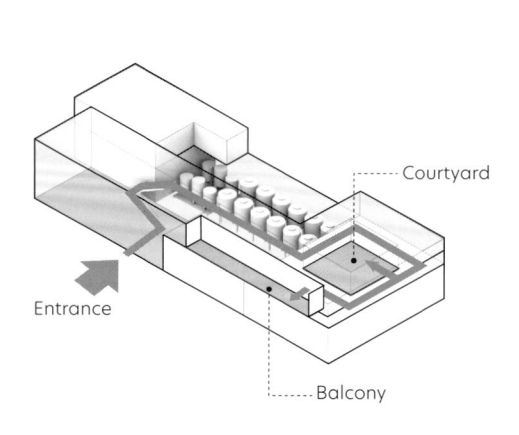

Office · · · · · · · · · · · · · · · · · · · · · · · · Brewery

Pub · · · · · · · · · · · · · · · · · · · · · · · · Pub

Courtyard

Entrance

Balcony · · · · · · · · · · · · · · · · · · · · · · · · Storage

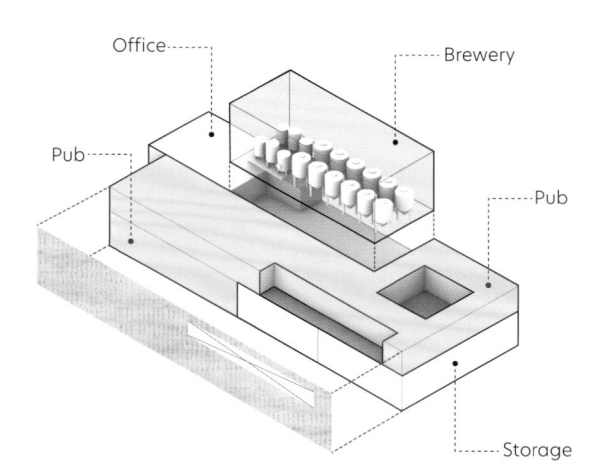

46   NEW INSTRUMENT

The layout of the program is communicated by the varying change in scale and materiality throughout the space. By extruding the social area one level above the glass-framed brewing station, the manufacturing center itself becomes an exhibition piece that enhances function of the new beer showcase. Despite being programmatically separated, the void that is formed in the floor of the second level draws the focus of the entire sampling area, spatially and socially connecting the two, thus integrating the two differently scaled spaces. Here, tasters can watch the beer-making process from above while still having access to the open balcony and food courts in the connected open courtyard. Because of these openings in the façade, natural sunlight flows into this well integrated interior space.

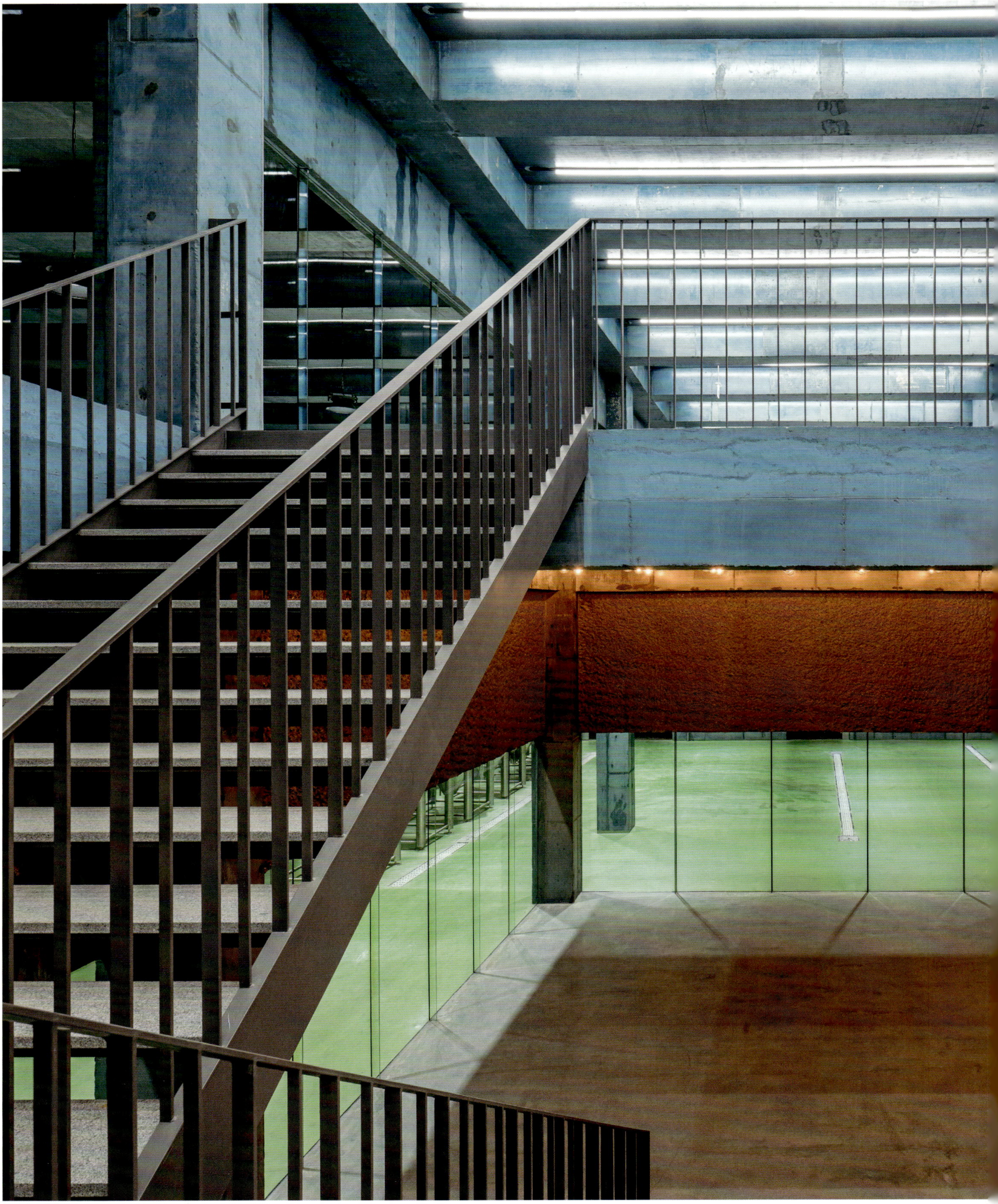

SEBYEOL BREWERY

Void space in this building has an important role in creating a visual connection among the functions of the building, the user's experience, and the sight of nature. To minimize disrupting the façade, we designed the building's program to have the brewing operations located at the northern end while social activity and spatial circulation take place at the southern end. Accordingly, the openings are reserved for the social sections as the natural sunlight is maximized due to the building's solar orientation.

The entryway is led by the deep opening and is relatively small in comparison to the building's scale. From that space, the blue light that is reflected from the blue-dyed concrete illuminates to give the visitor recognition. At the east side of the site stands a cobalt-blue formwork wall to sever the interior lobby space from the exterior parking lot area. This allows the lobby space to extend outside, allowing light to flow in from the window. Thus, visitors can experience the materiality and depth of three different walls.

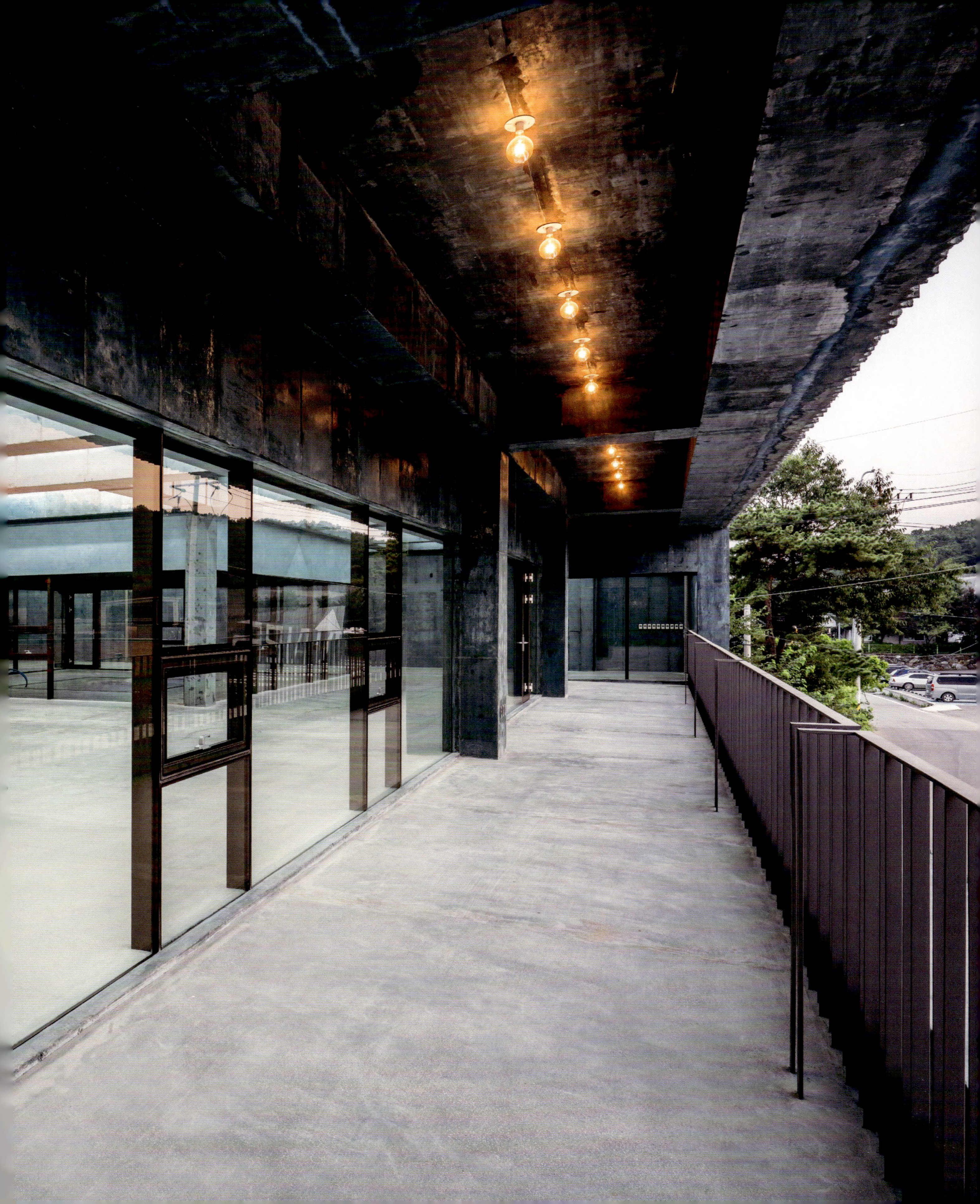

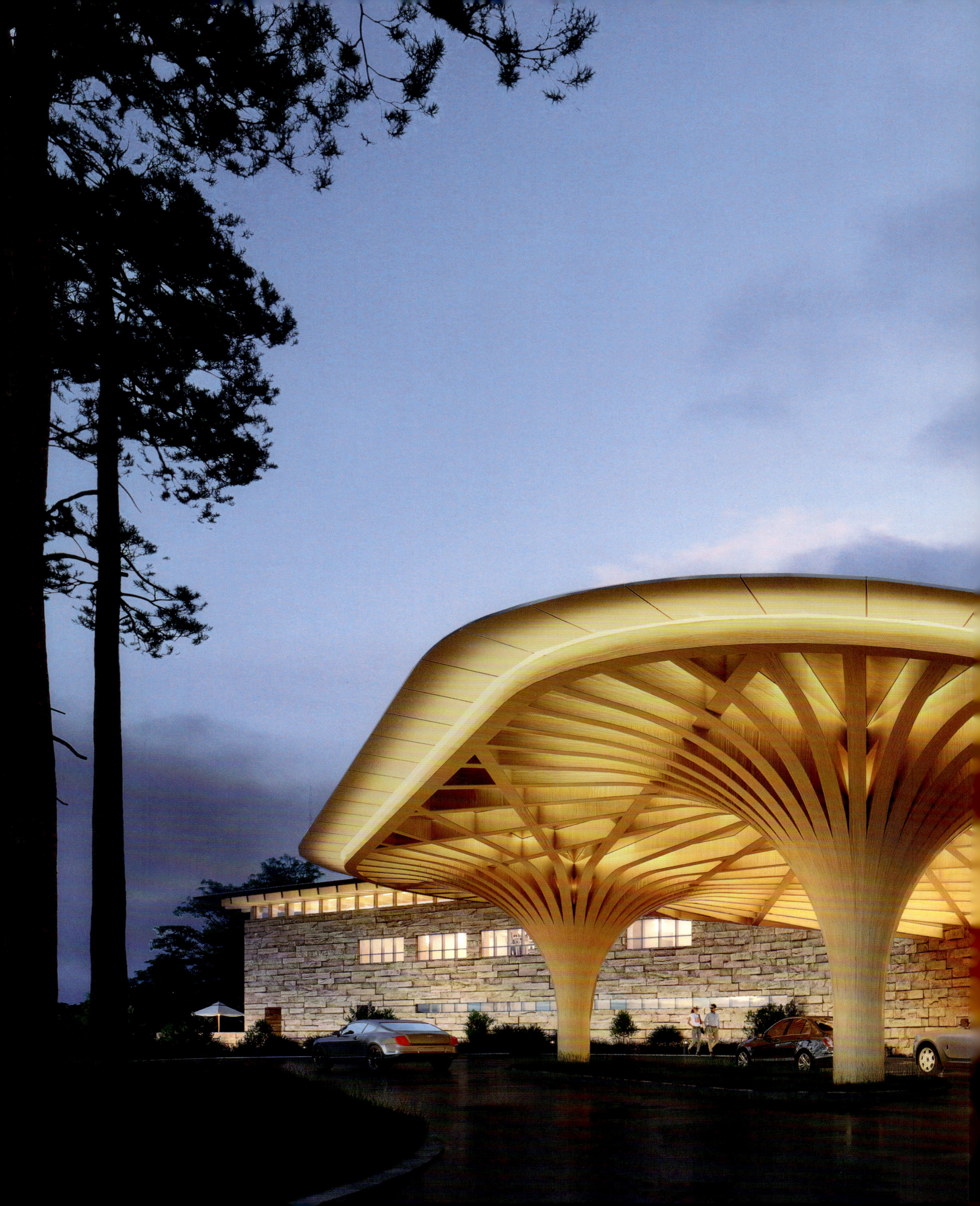

# HILLMARU COUNTRY CLUB & GOLF HOTEL

Pocheon-si, Gyeonggi-do, South Korea | 2015

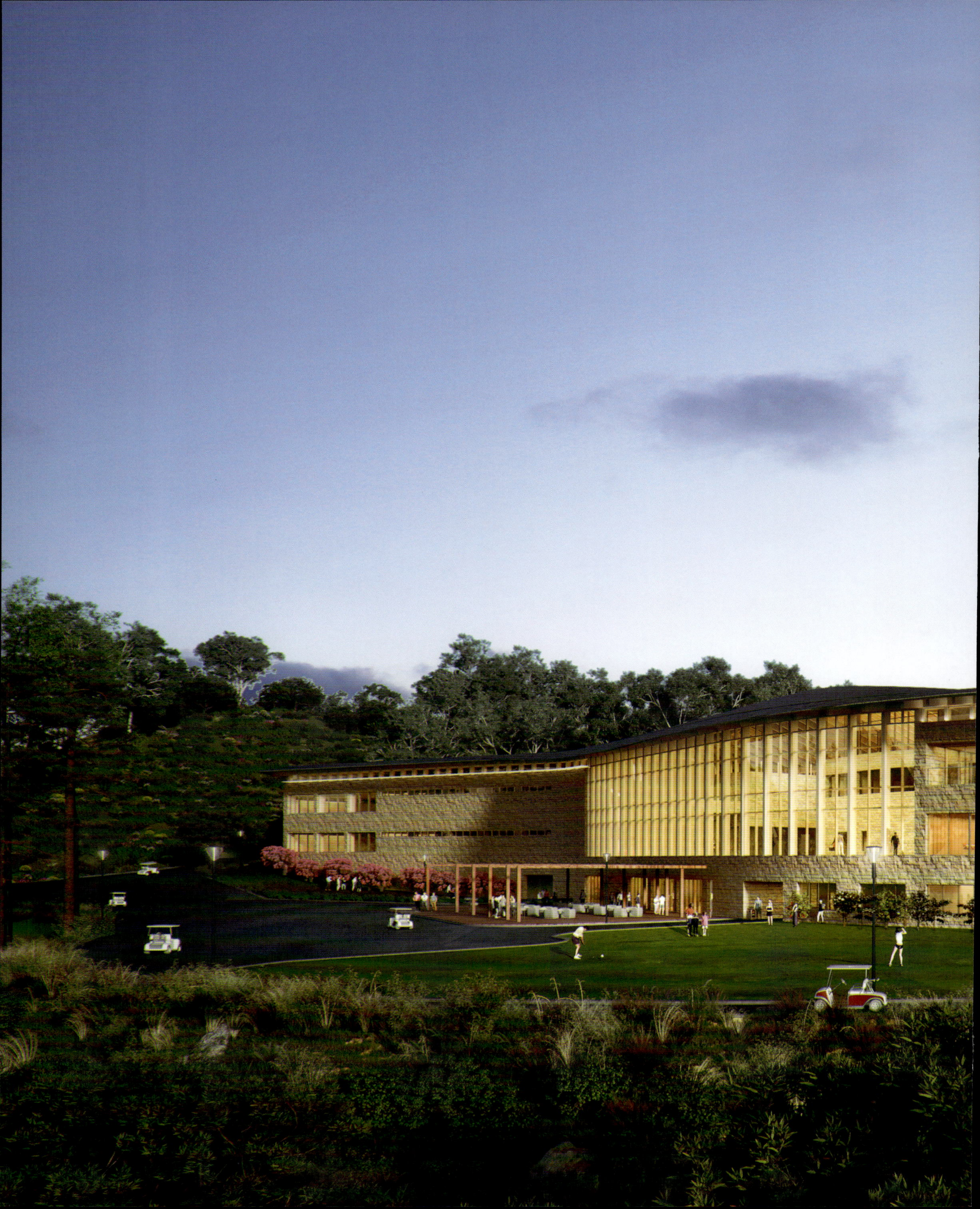

The Pocheon Hillmaru Country Club is located outside the rural town of Pocheon-si, South Korea. The owner asked us to develop a programmatic design that is both environmentally conscious and efficiently satisfies the athletic requirements of a 700-acre (283-hectare), 54-hole golf course.

Due to its size and expected number of visitors per day, the clubhouse accommodates approximately 1,000 private lockers, 200 electric cart storage spaces, and a luxury restaurant for up to 300 patrons. Additionally, the lobby space has a large atrium and a canopy that spans over the four-lane drop-off zone. We developed numerous potential siting plans that utilize these programmatic requirements in dynamic ways.

The central lobby hosts the largest space in the facility, dividing the restaurant, office, and locker room areas into separate zones. These locker room sections are divided to accommodate members, VIPs, and exclusive VIPs. Each section has its own relaxation/recovery area, hot tubs, and ice baths, with full views of the courses. Statistics indicated that more than two-thirds of golf members are male, thus we designed a section of the second-floor female locker area to be adapted into an extra locker room space for males, if needed. After finding ways to optimize the total training space, we found that locker width of 19.7 inches (500 millimeters) was most efficient.

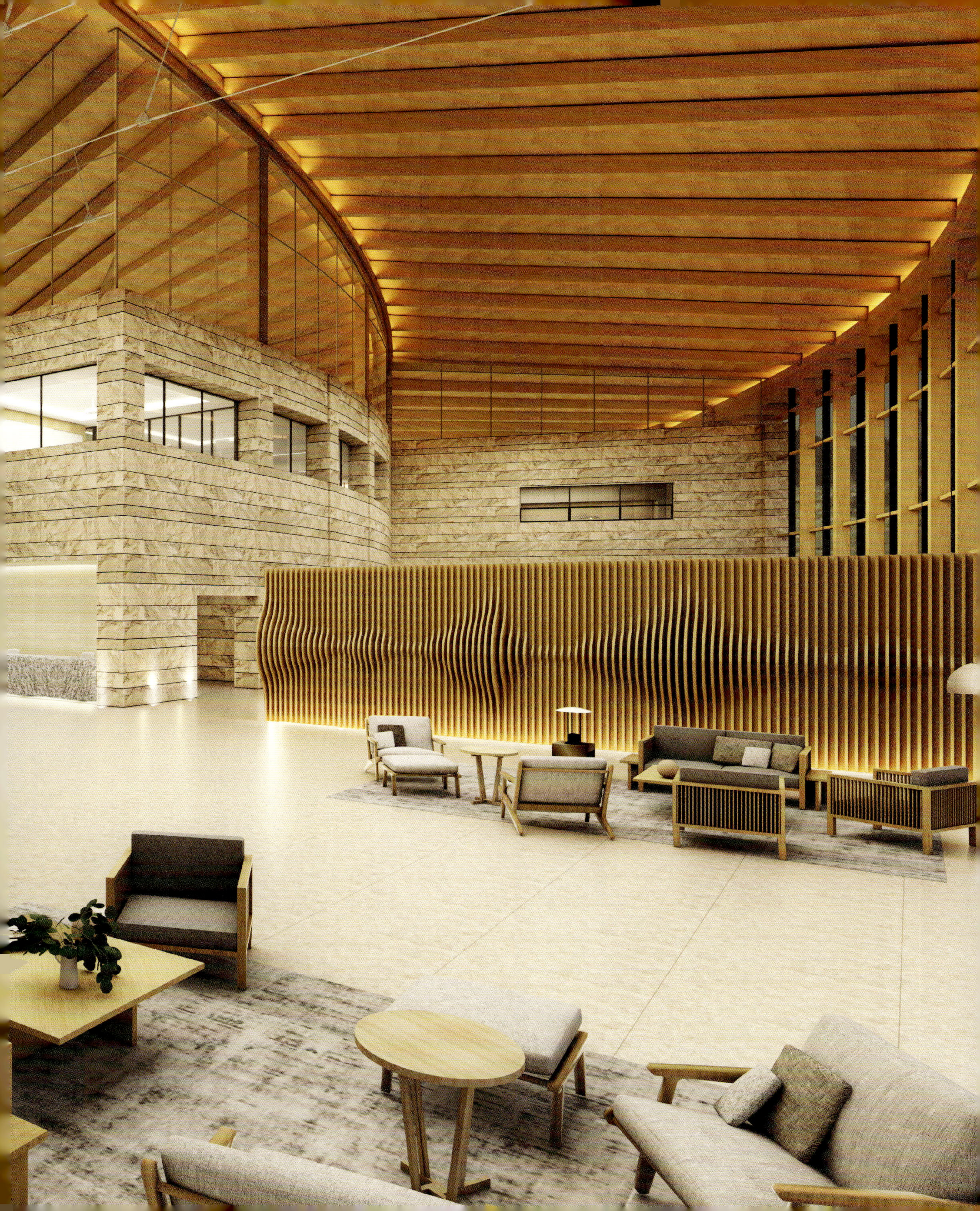

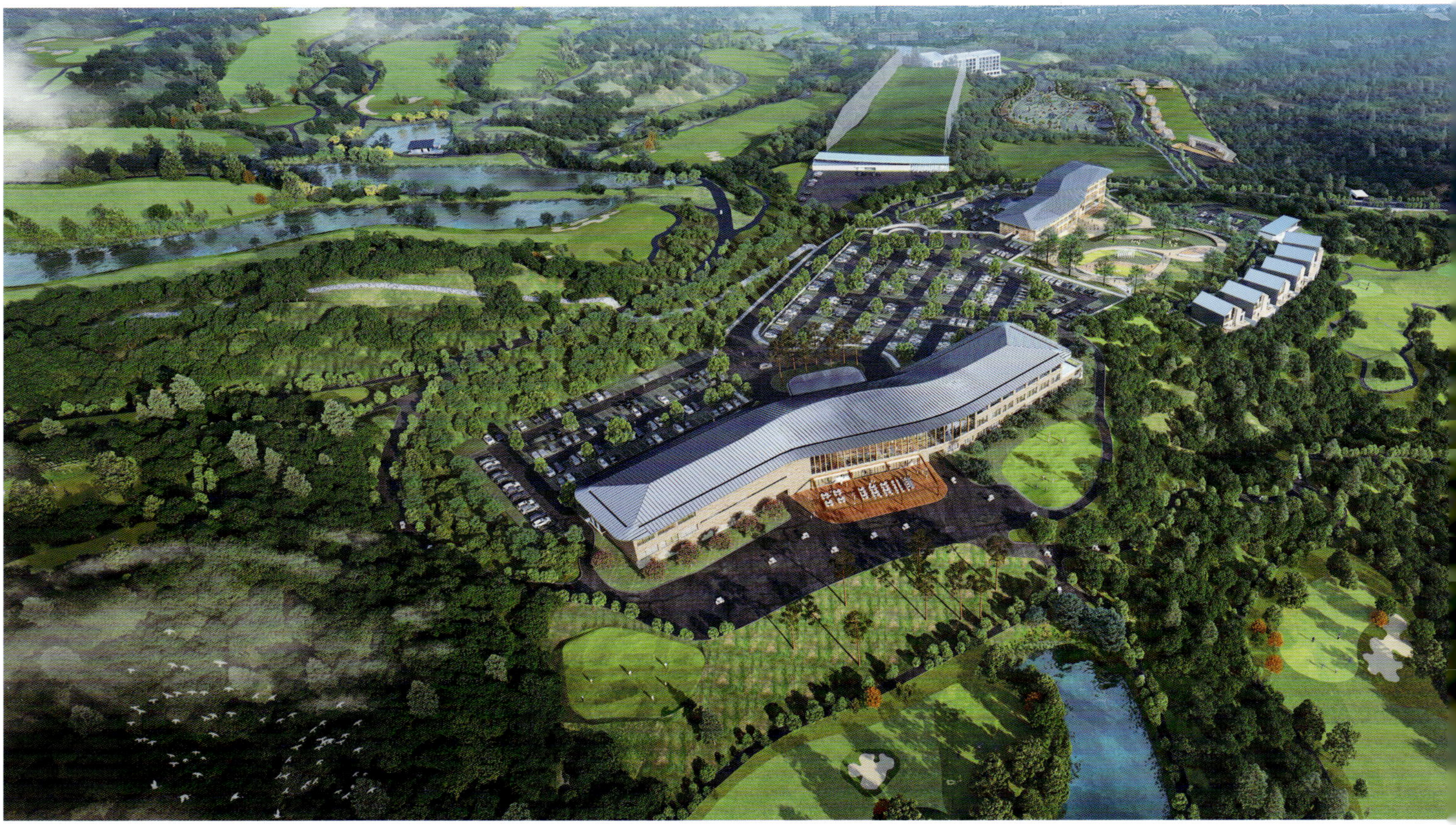

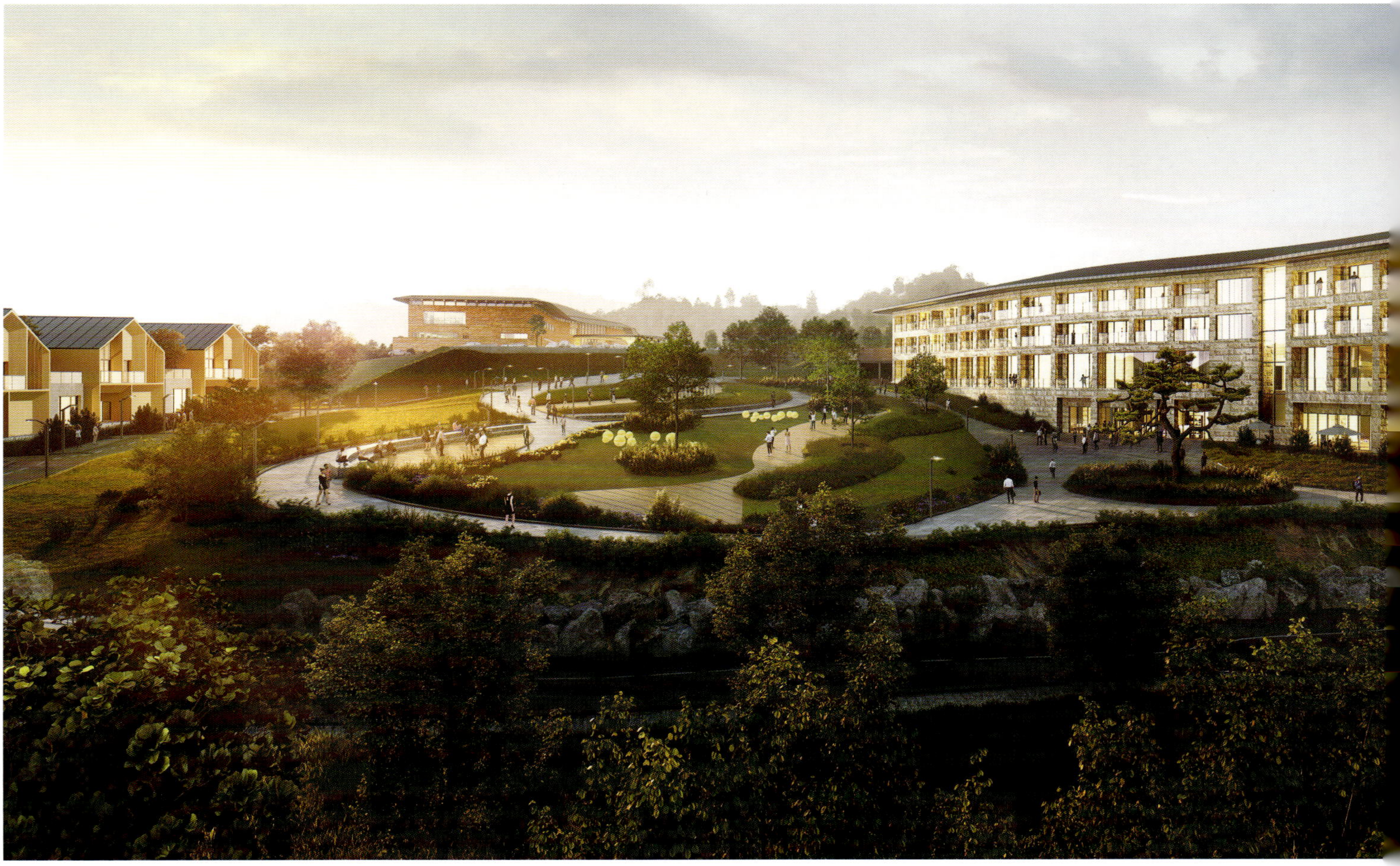

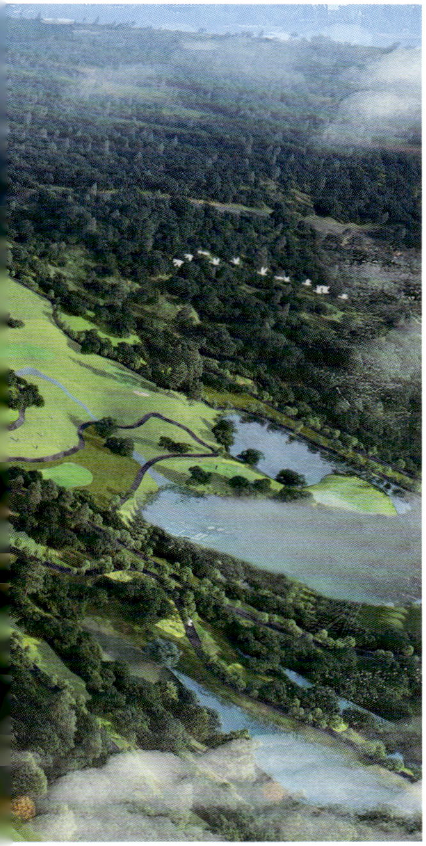
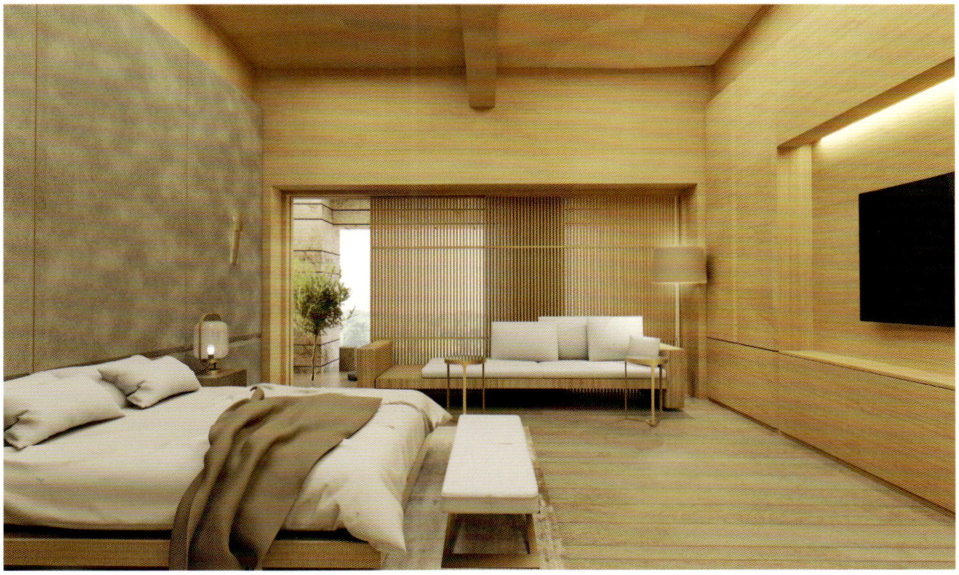
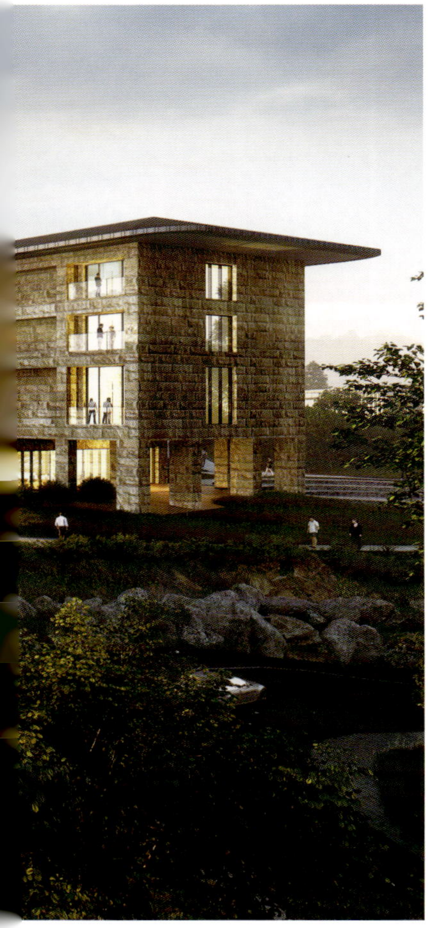
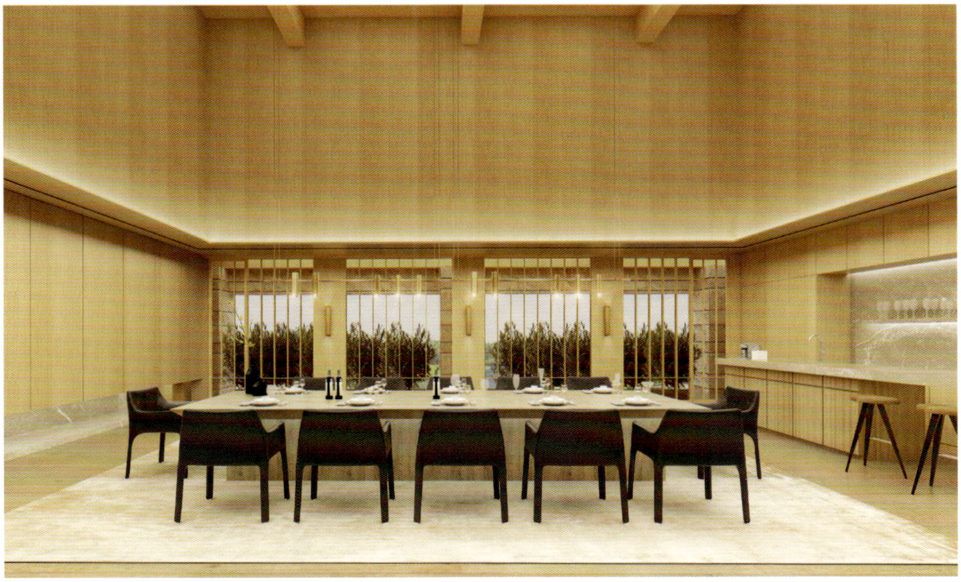
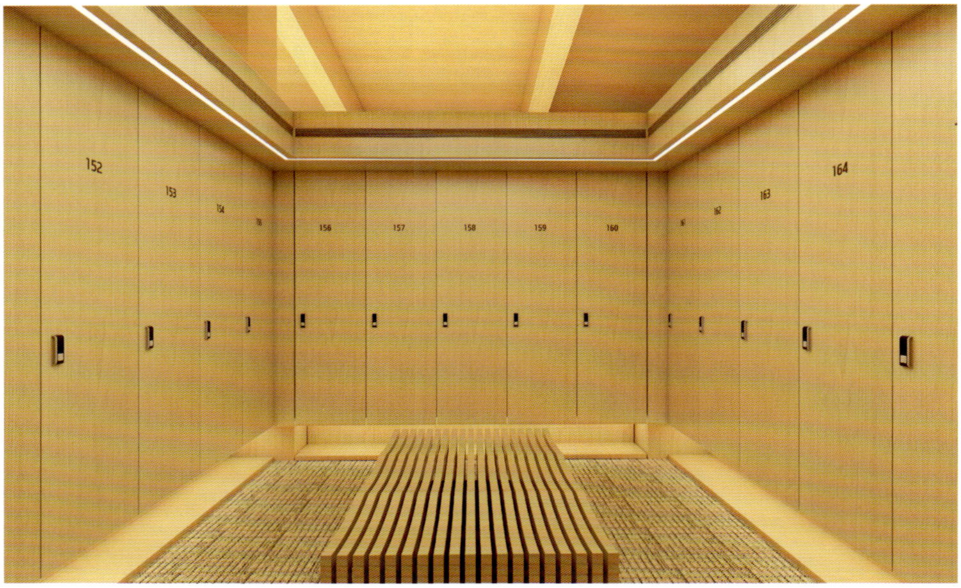
152
153
154
156
157
158
159
160
162
163
164

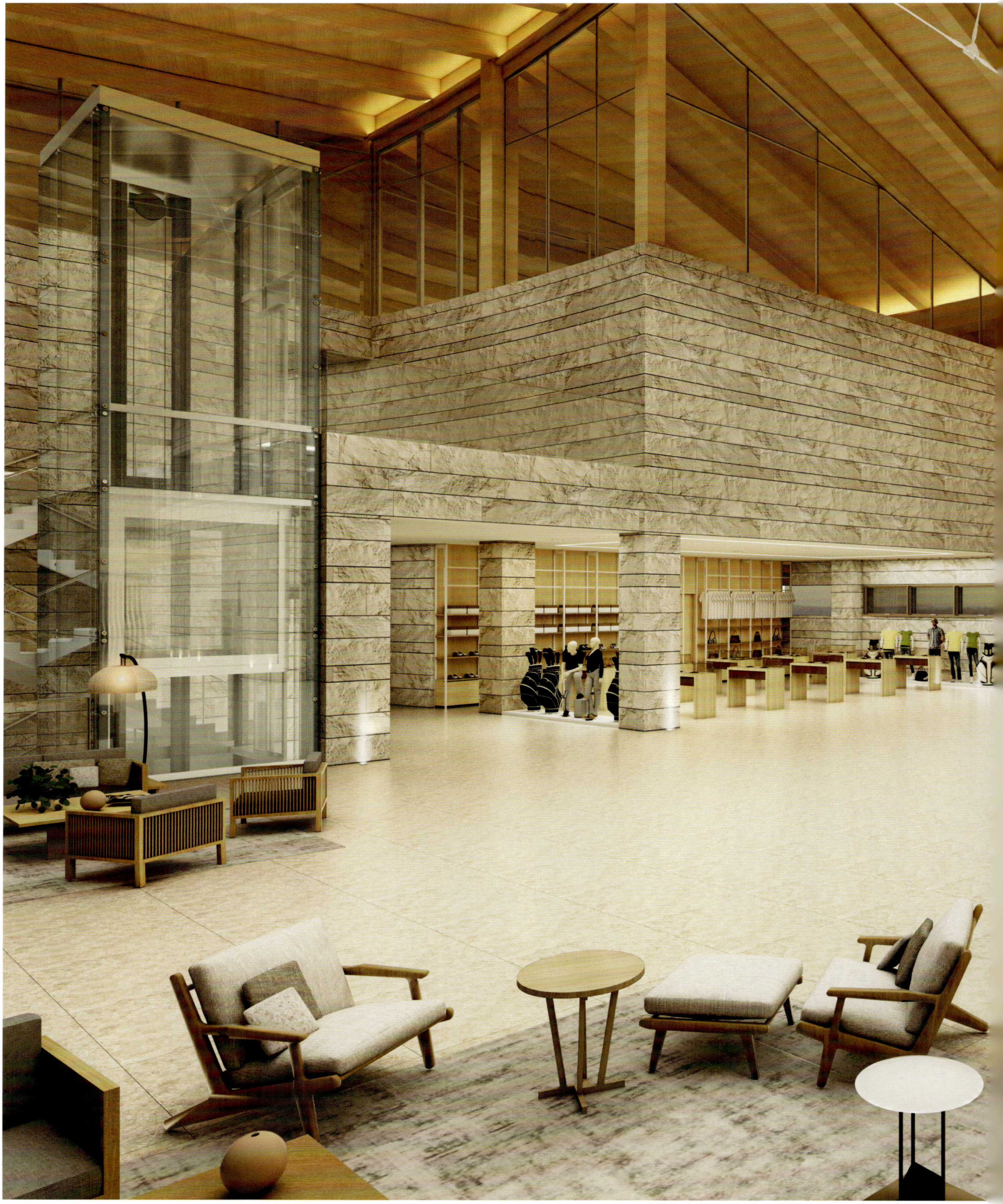

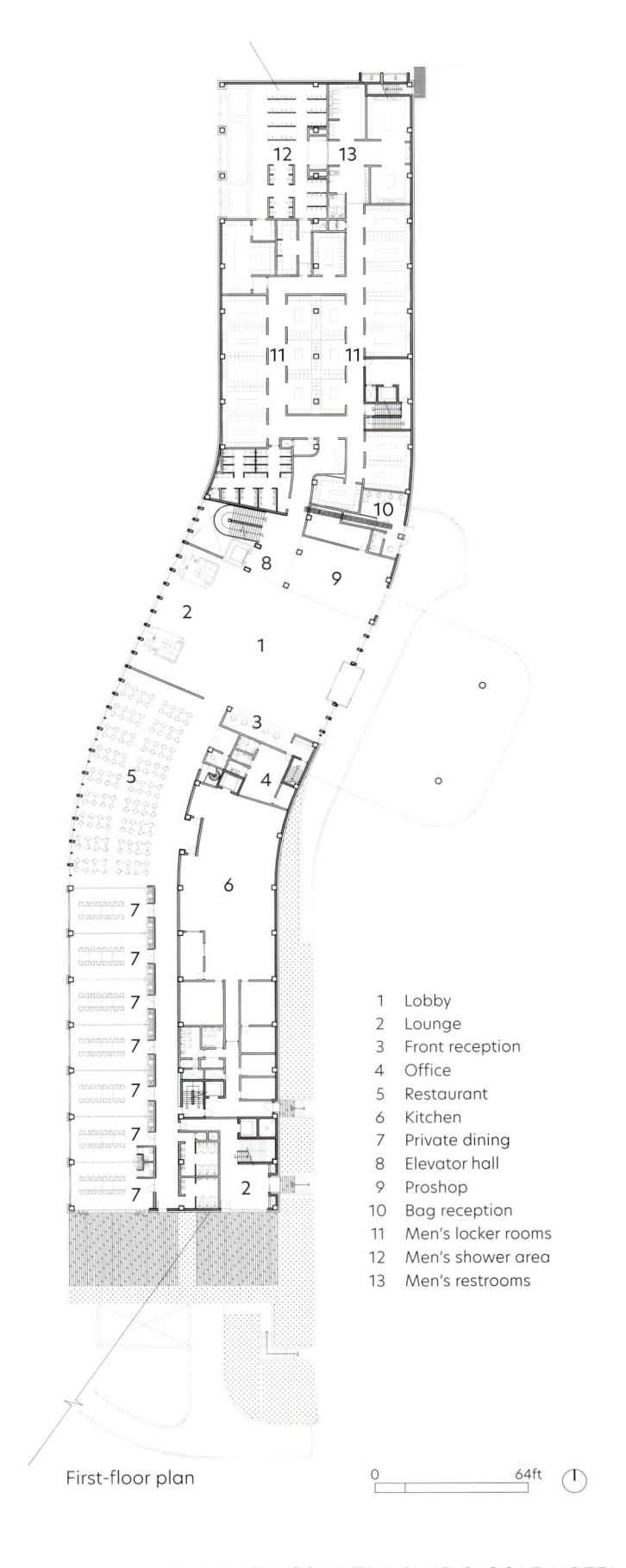

1 Lobby
2 Lounge
3 Front reception
4 Office
5 Restaurant
6 Kitchen
7 Private dining
8 Elevator hall
9 Proshop
10 Bag reception
11 Men's locker rooms
12 Men's shower area
13 Men's restrooms

First-floor plan

0  64ft

HILLMARU COUNTRY CLUB & GOLF HOTEL

Aesthetically, we attempted to integrate a traditional Korean design precedent into this contemporary golfing facility. A Blumer-Lehmann Glulam structure was used for the whale-like form roof structures. The roof structure has a sloped 9.84-foot (3-meter) overhang, a design detail common in traditional Korean roof structures. The clubhouse's roof is sheathed with a zinc metal and its exterior wall has a stone-clad finish. Within the building, the beams, eaves, and rafters all utilize laminated wood.

The spatial construction of the club's restaurant area is extremely adaptable. We installed folding doors at various points in the room's layout to change the size and privacy of a party's dining experience.

In the luxury hotel area, a total of thirty-six rooms are provided, varying from single-bed, two-bed, four-bed, and eight-bed suites.

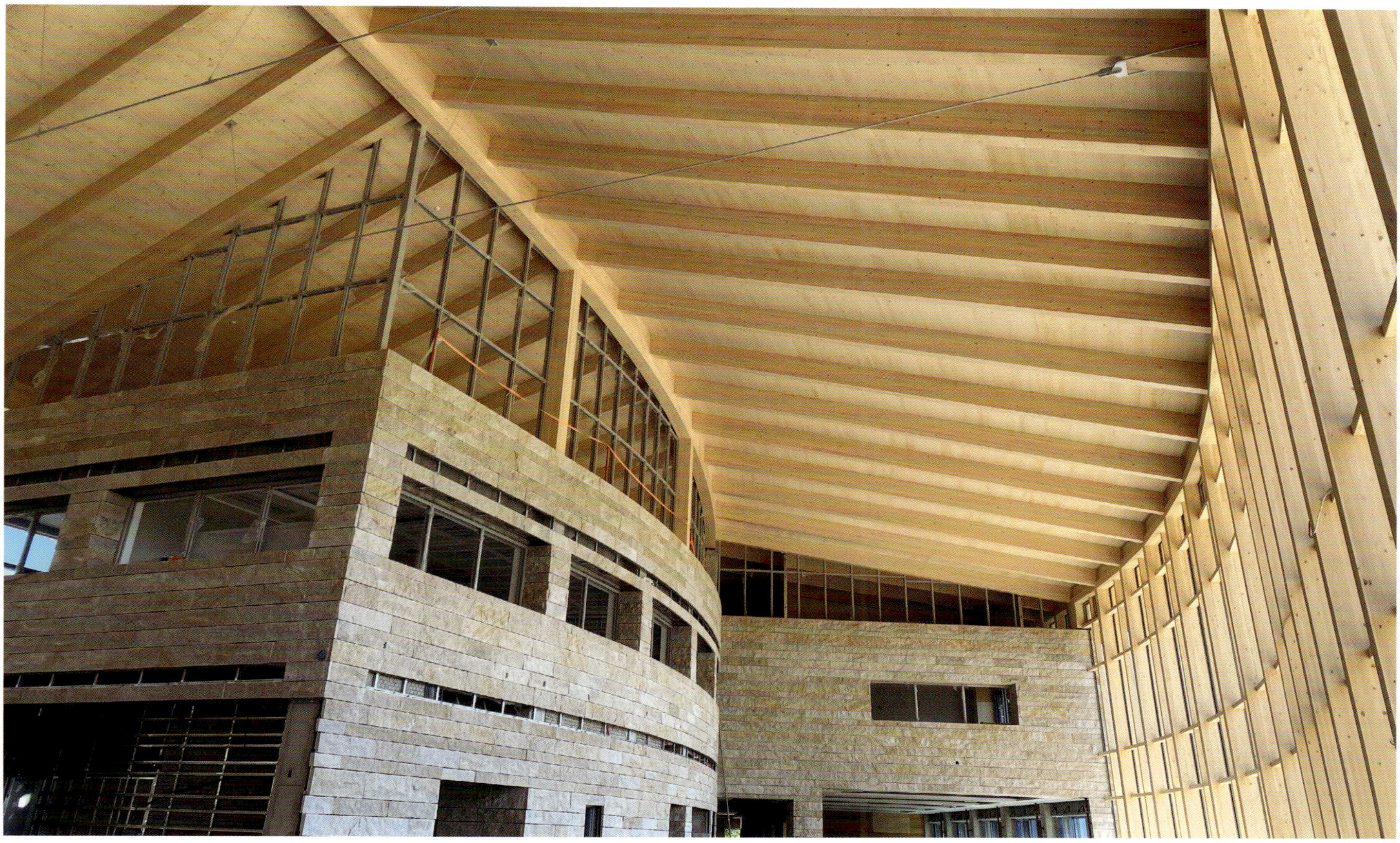

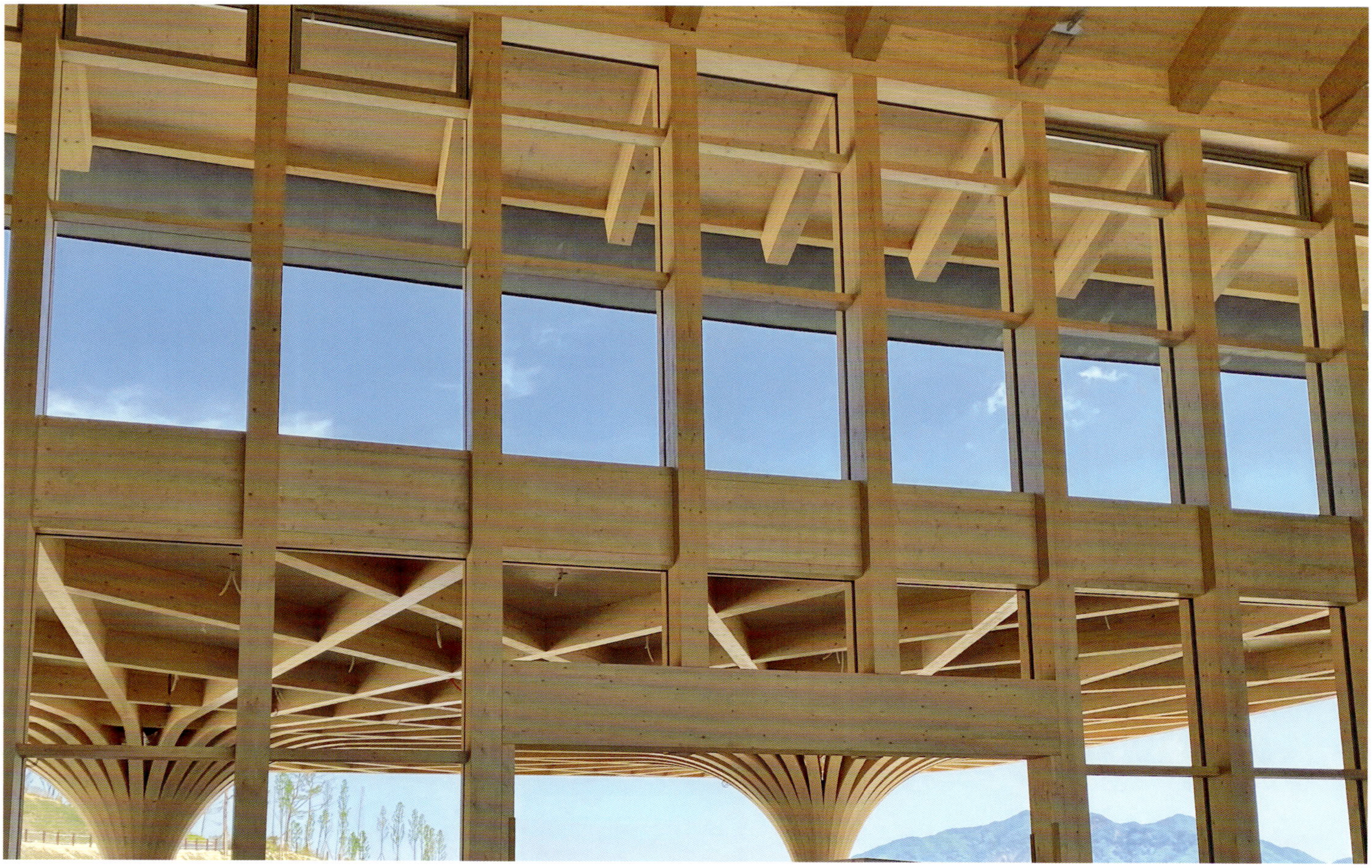

Taesun Hong, *Quantum Leap* (1981), lithograph

**Repetition** is essentially a recurring action, event, or form that has consistency. Like rhythm, repetition in architecture relies on a mathematical—usually algebraic—series.

# NEFS HEADQUARTERS

Gangnam-gu, Seoul, South Korea | 2020

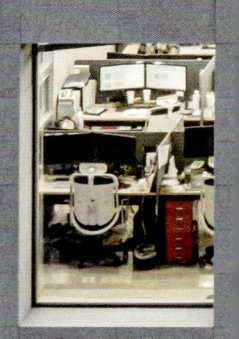

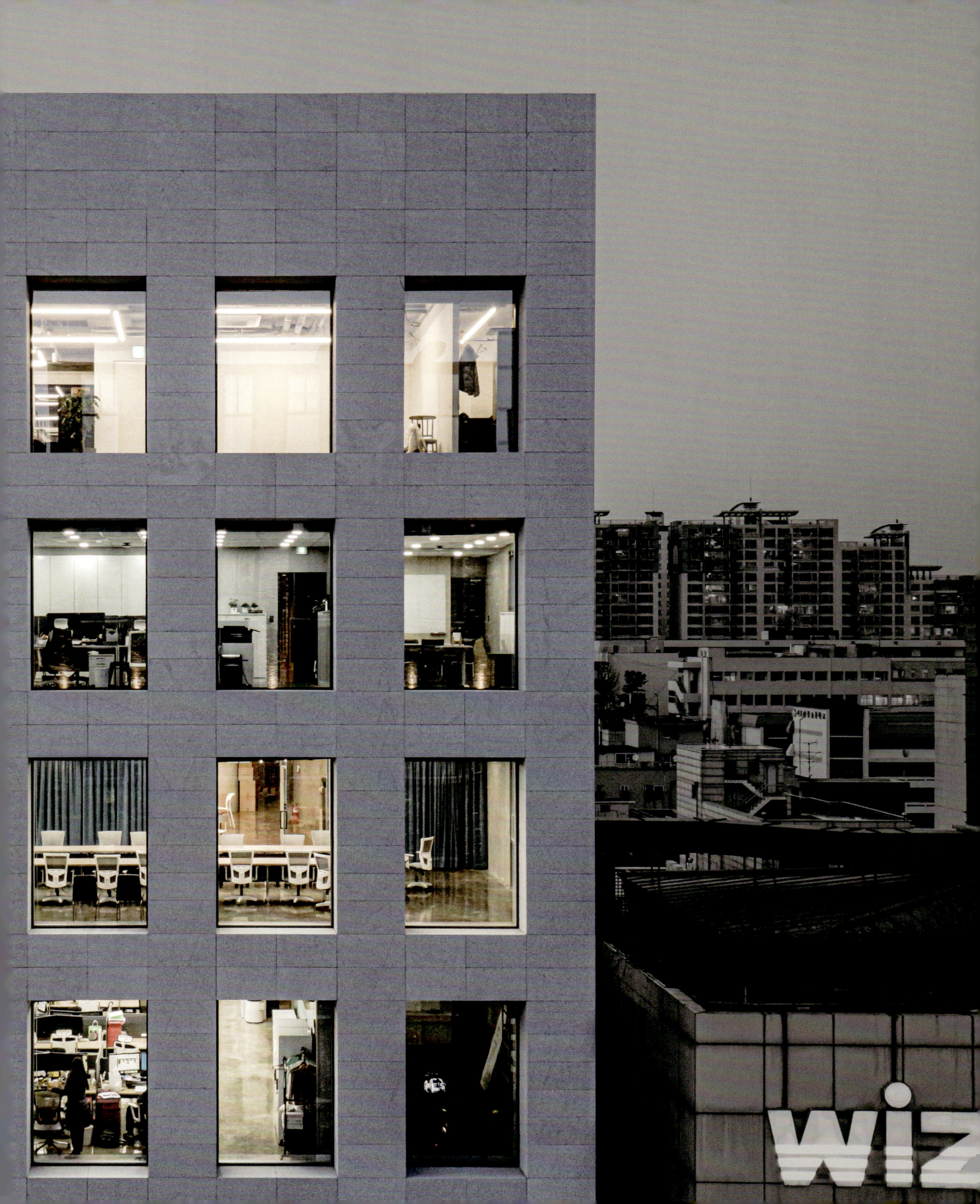
wiz

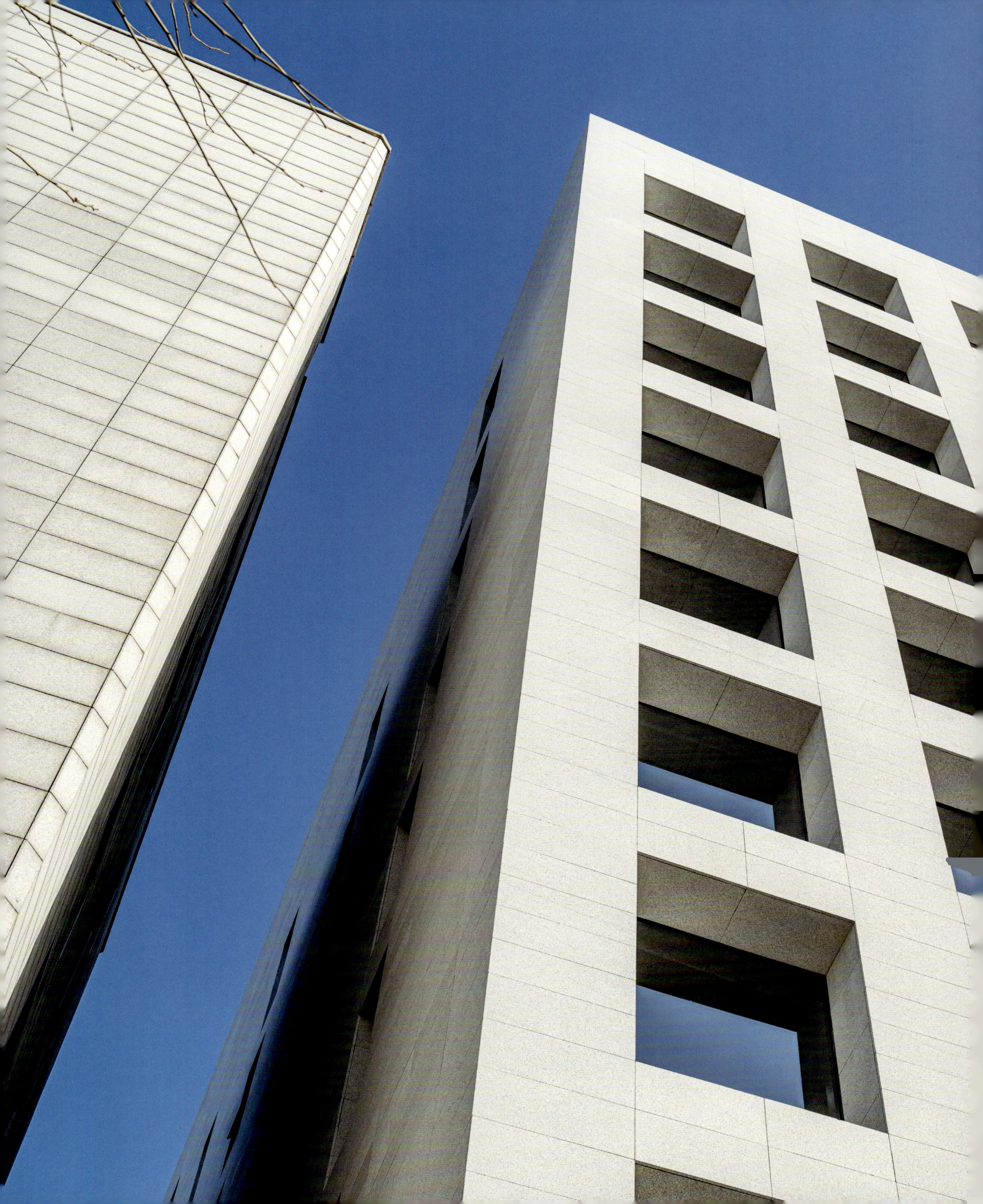

NEFS Headquarters is in Bongeunsa-ro, Gangnam-gu, one of the most commercially vibrant streets in Seoul. While not being involved initially, we were later commissioned to redesign the proposed building after our design was significantly more cost-effective in the construction cost estimate. In collaboration with an engineering team, we developed a clean, orthogonal façade through the "subtraction" scheme as the main design concept. The façade consists of honed finished white granite and reflective glass that allow the building to subtly emerge from its neighboring mixed-use buildings.

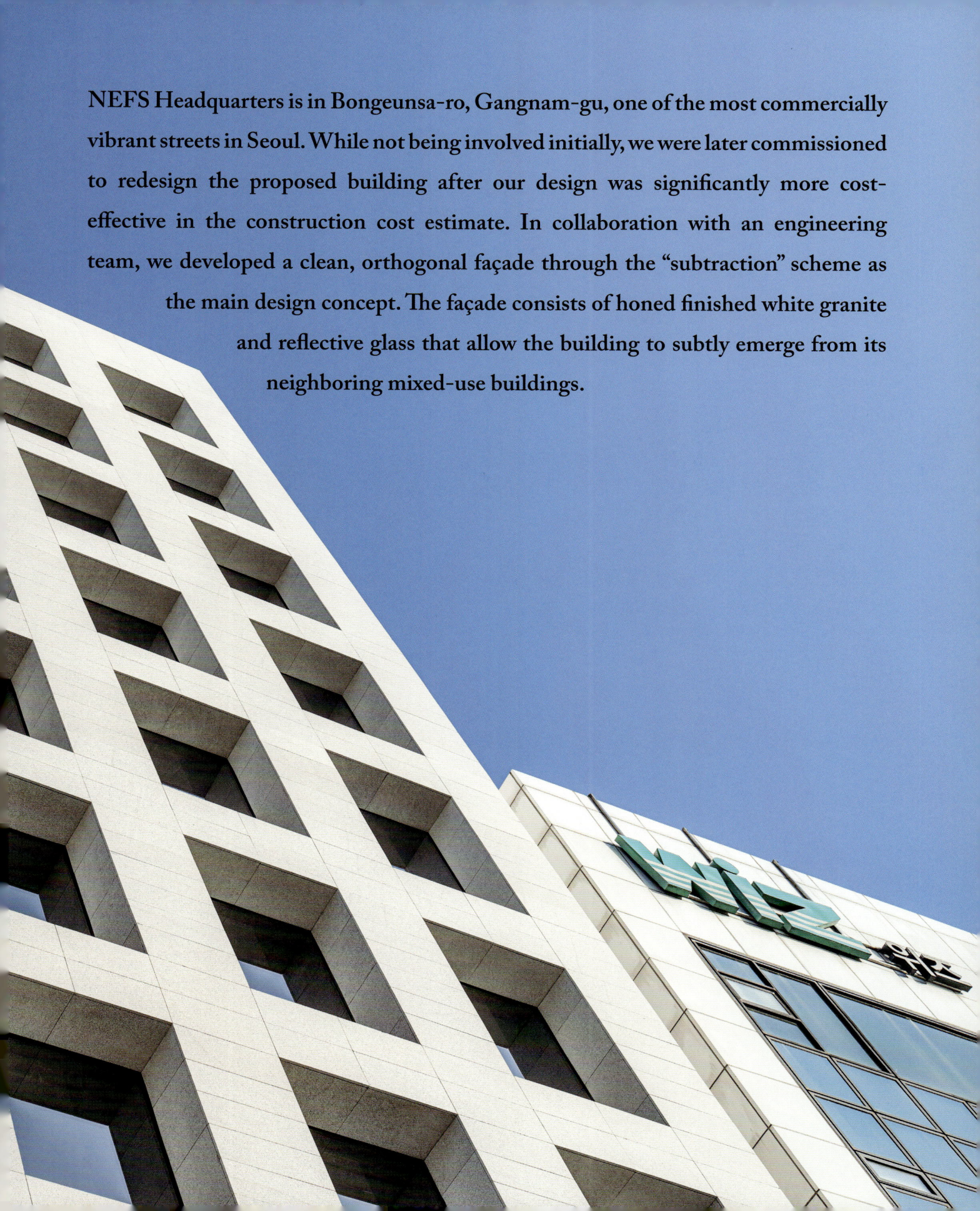

The simple rectangular and monolithic volume of the building minimizes the perimeter of the building from its T-shaped site. Its prime rectangular volume gently sits between the neighboring buildings, effectively using artless compositions, minimal ornamentation, and neutral colors and materials to serenely respond to its heterogeneous surroundings. This mixed-use building brings a visually calming presence to its urban context, a region that suffers from a patchwork of architectural styles due to the recent acceleration of development in this neighborhood.

As a result of these efforts, a compact noble building is animated by deep light through purely formed set-back windows, humanized by tactile comfort through visually soft materiality and distinguished by sensory richness through its serene architectural proportion. The openings facing the main street are designed with fixed-glass windows to extrude the usable office space out of each level, giving the occupants the perception of added mentally occupiable space. The thickness of the façades provides a depth that creates a changing play of light and shadow. The placement of operable windows provides natural air-flow ventilation.

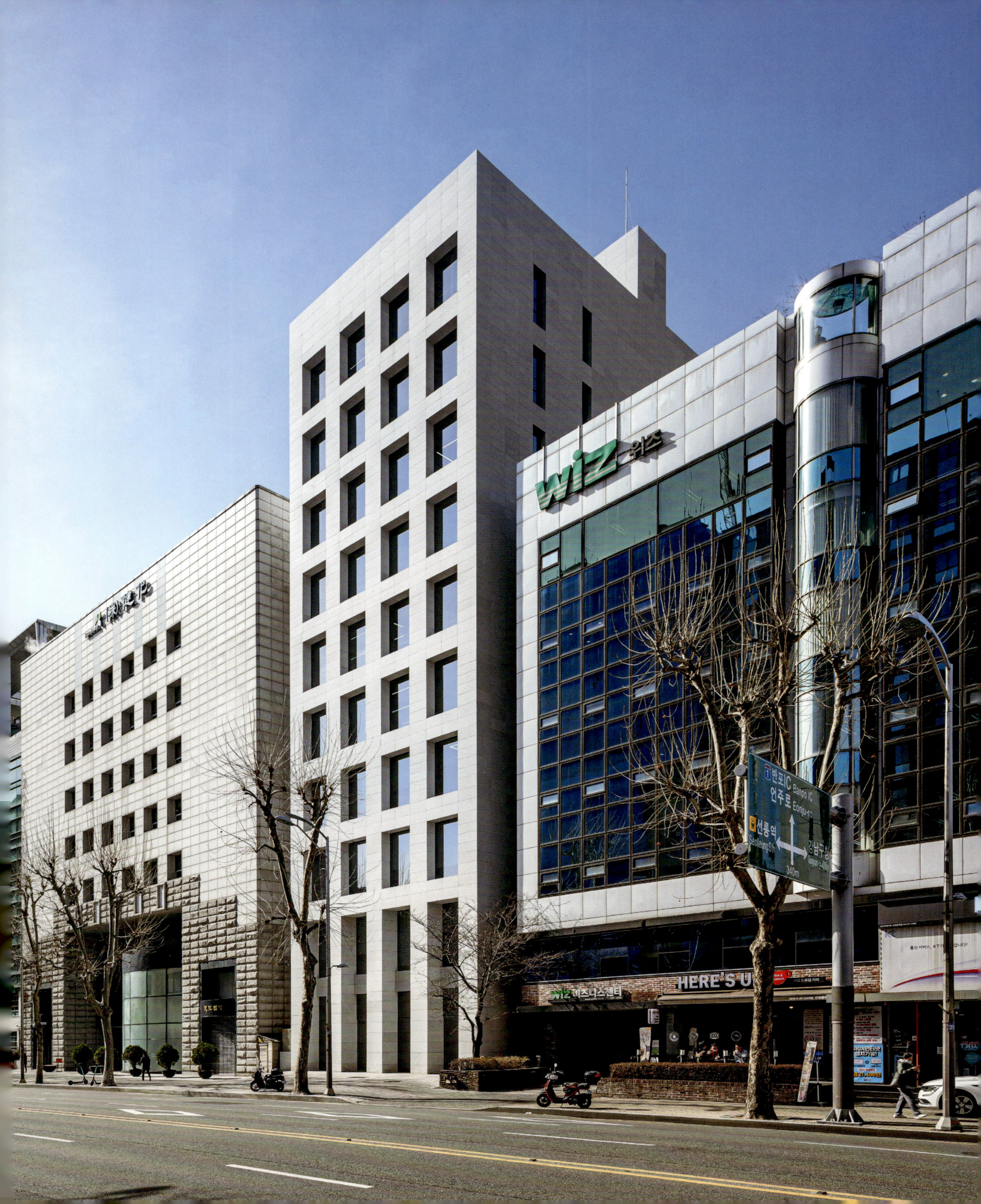
wiz
위즈

REPETITION

NEFS HEADQUARTERS 73

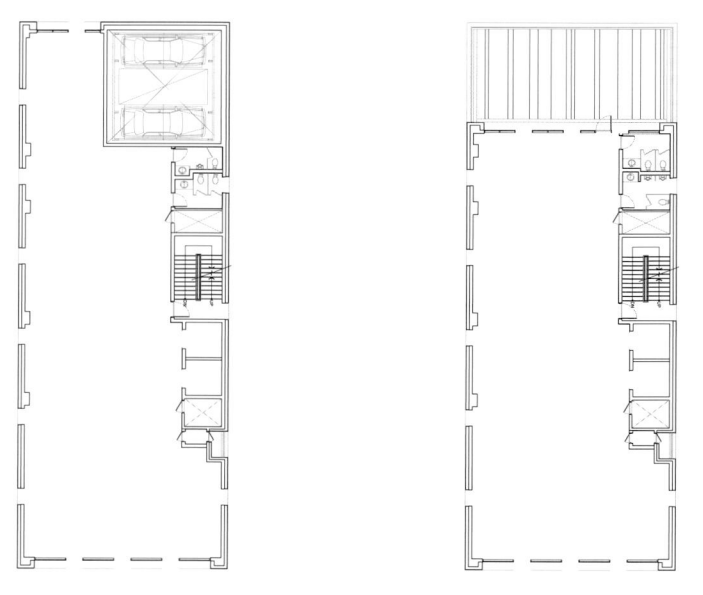

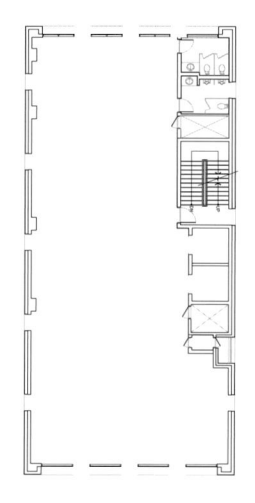

Typical (fourth to eighth) floor plan

Ninth-floor plan

Tenth-floor plan

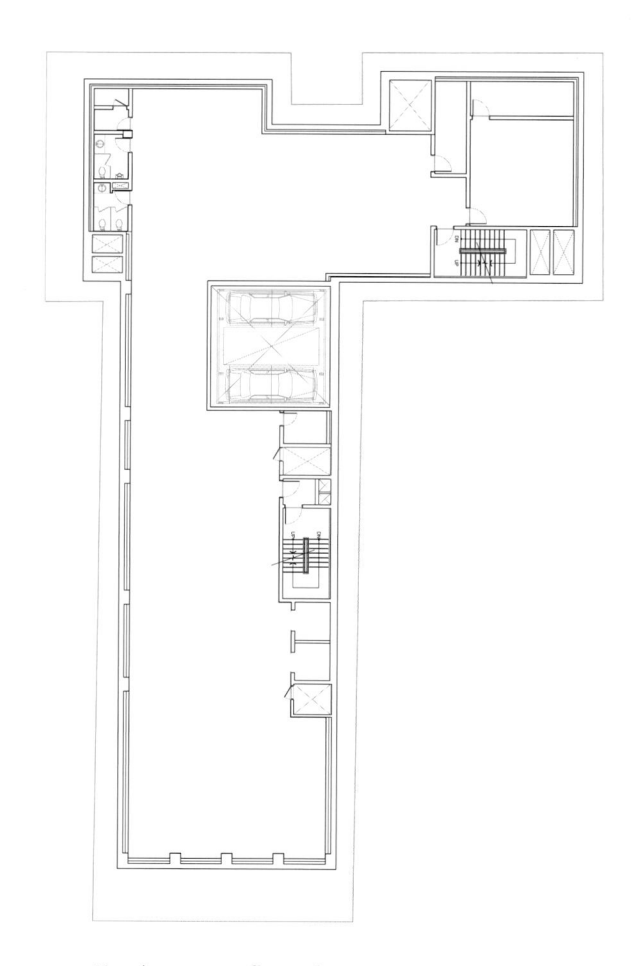

First basement floor plan

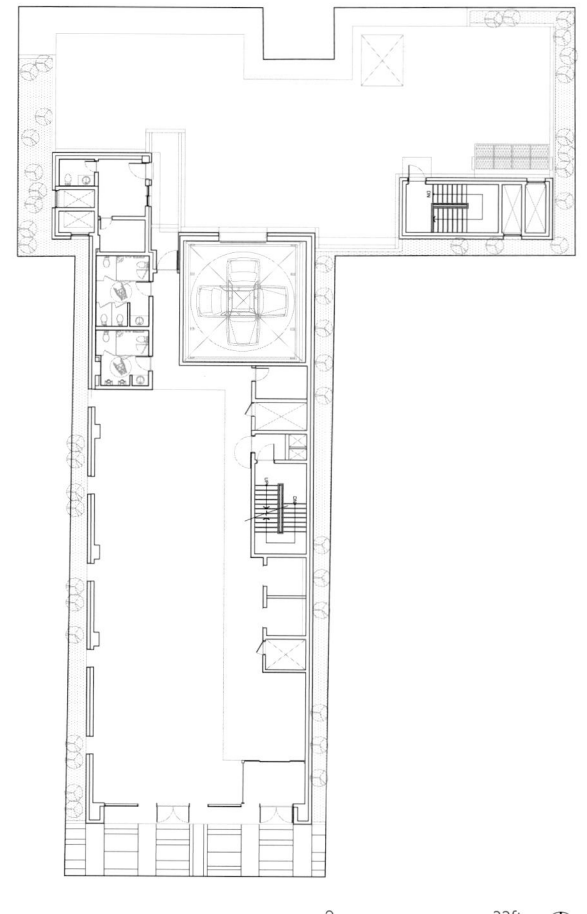

First-floor plan

0    32ft

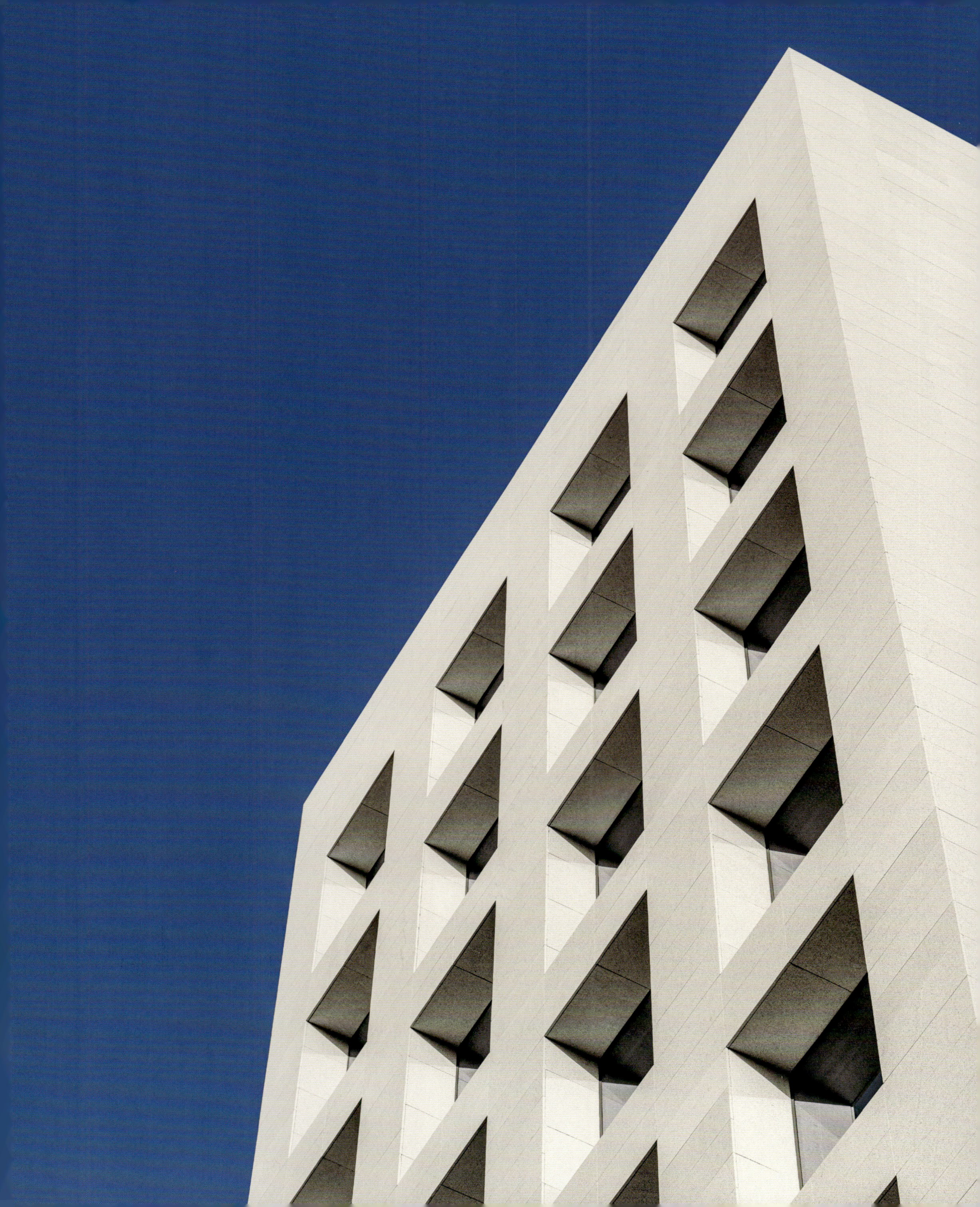

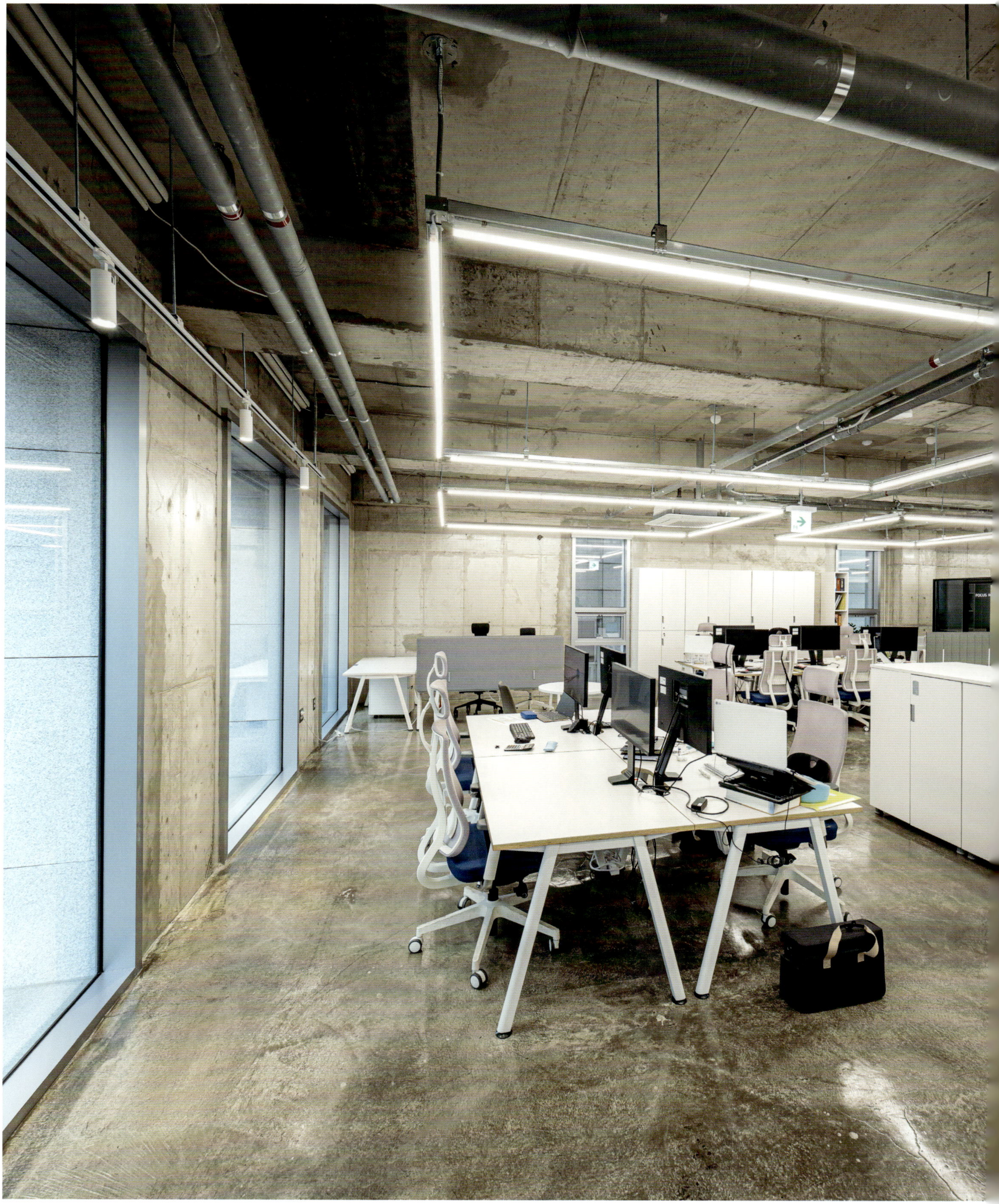

Similar strategy flows from the exterior to the interior spaces, creating a column-free-void on each floor to enhance the open implementation of space. By utilizing the same neutral material finishes for the inner and outer spaces, natural circulation into and out of the building is encouraged.

The two basement levels, ground level, and second floor are reserved for commercial use while floors three through ten are used as office space. On the top floor, the office program is interrupted by an open courtyard, bringing light from the rooftop garden into the office space. This calming transition to the outdoors offers a surreal contrast to the offices' urban landscape view. This relationship is analogous to the calming presence of the NEFS building façade's soft materiality and orderly sequence in comparison to the surrounding buildings' saturated and chaotic ones.

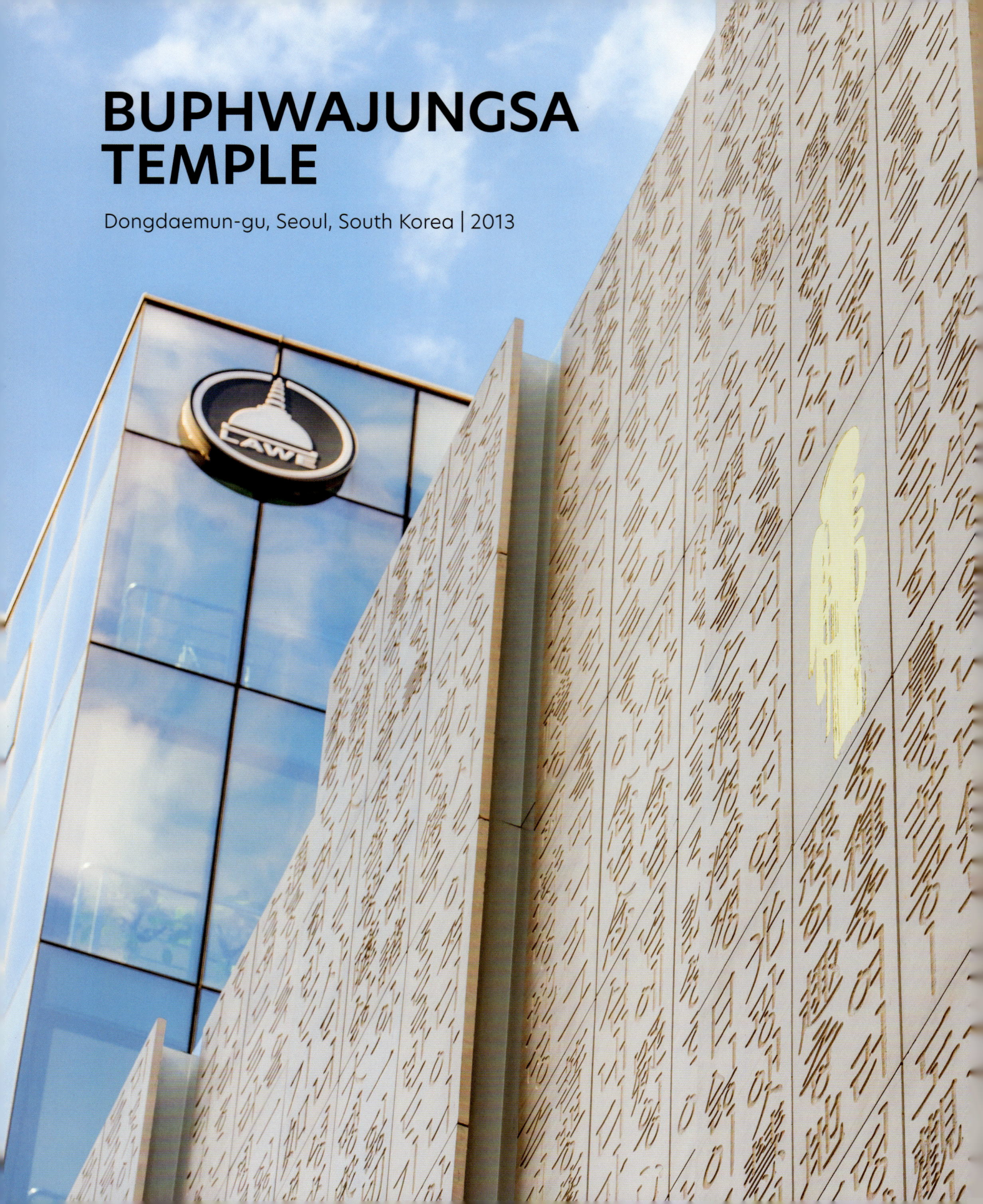

# BUPHWAJUNGSA TEMPLE

Dongdaemun-gu, Seoul, South Korea | 2013

In the heart of Seoul, the remodeled Buphwajungsa Temple is a modern, physical interpretation of traditional Buddhist philosophies. Initially approved by the local authority per building code, the temple required a complete re-design of its façade and interior concept. Our scheme was selected and satisfied the temple's needs despite the limited budget. With the given program setting, the exterior design and materials were planned and chosen to correspond to its spatial concepts to reflect its Buddhist values. The building's prayer spaces are separated into public, semipublic, and private zones. Instead of abiding by the conventional Buddhist temple typology, the project is designed to respond to the volumes generated from the surrounding urban fabric. The temple's redesign integrates the existing modern structures with a contemplative and introverted sacred inner space, revealing its delicate spiritual nature.

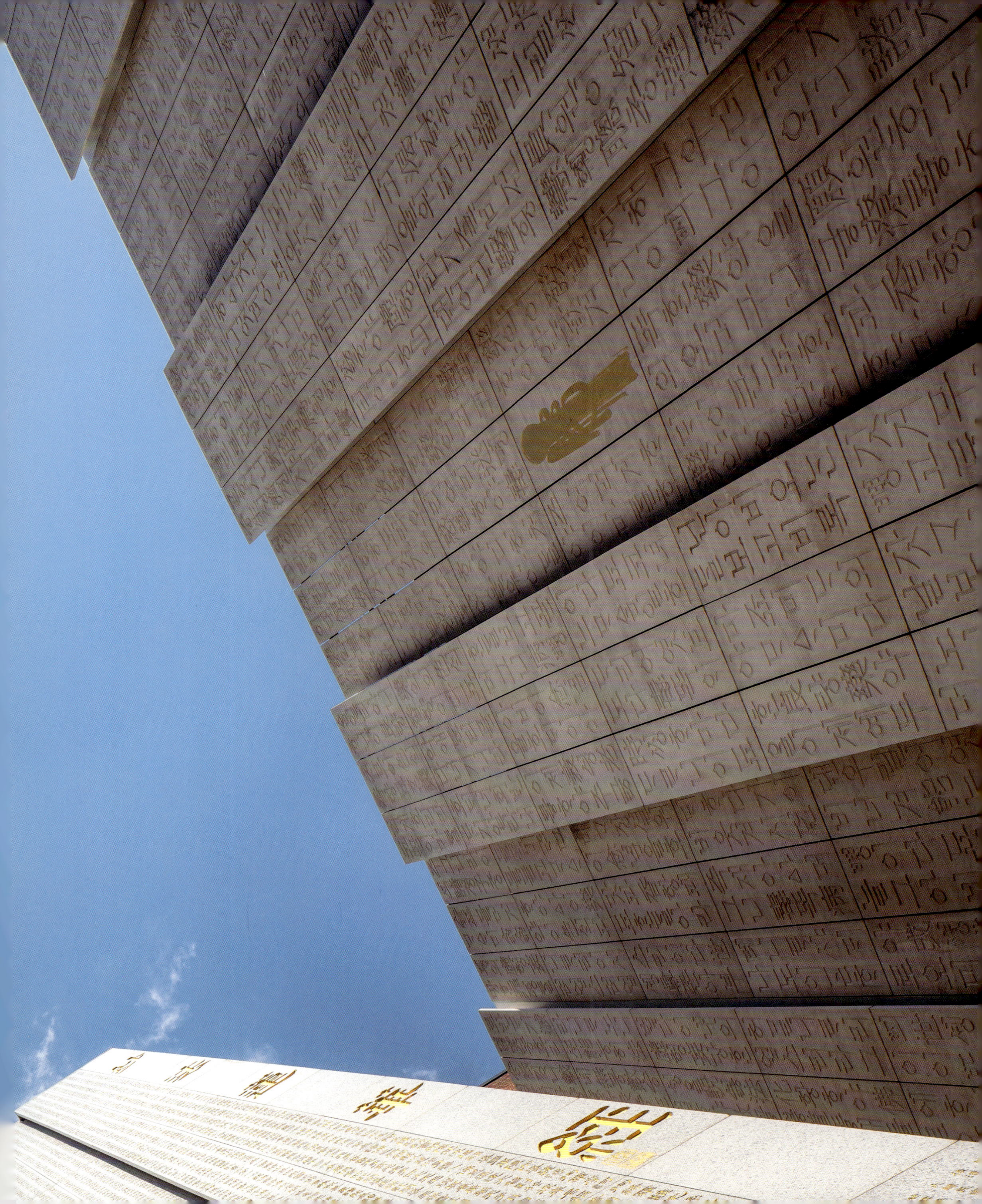

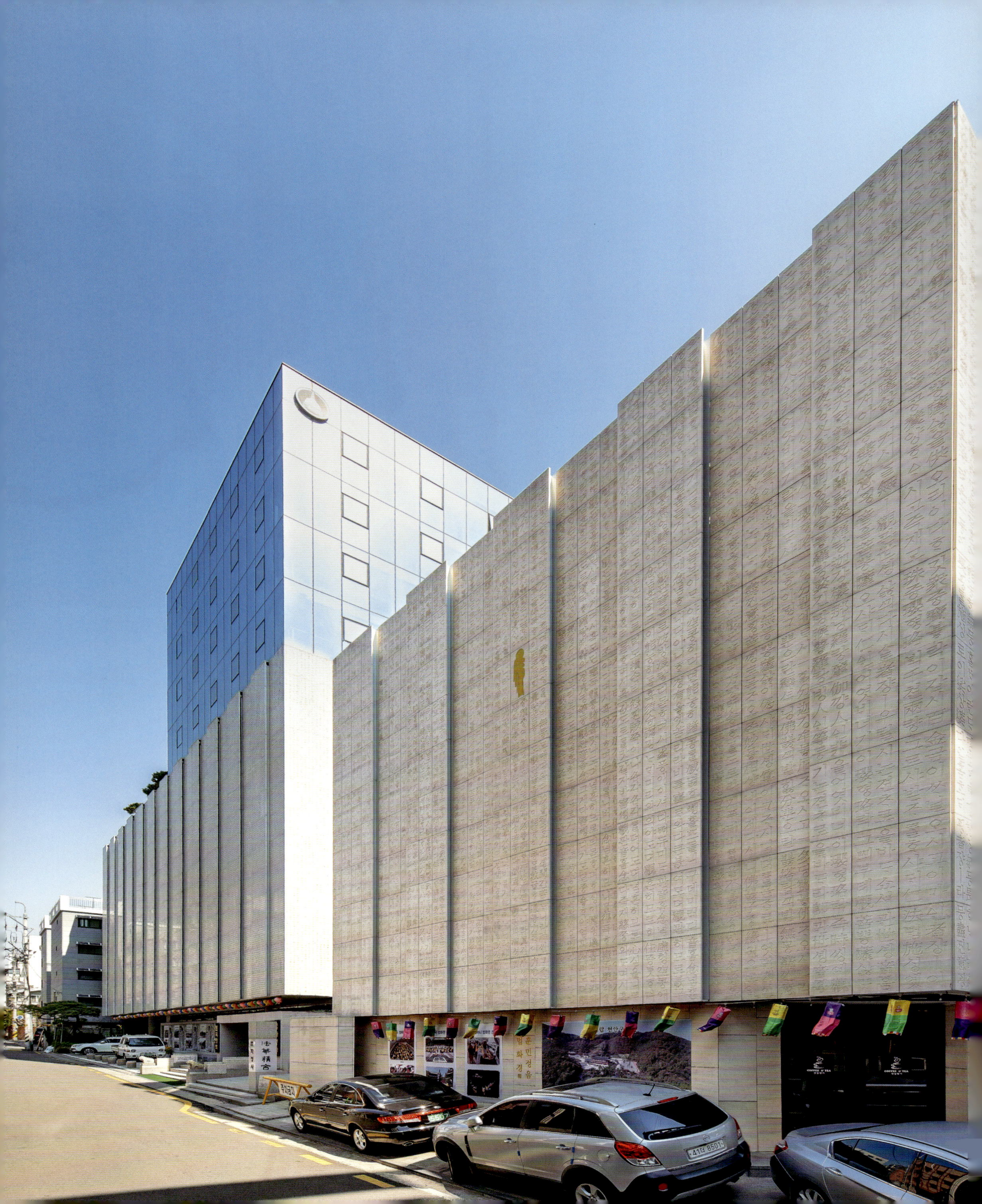

For the public zone, where different types of Buddha halls are located, the exterior design of the façade is enveloped by a local gray granite stone panel wall. Each wall panel is inscribed with forty-eight Chinese characters of "Lotus Sutra" scripture. (In ancient times, illuminated Sutra transcription, called Sagyeong, was the only way to spread the Buddhist teachings to the public.) By displaying Sagyeong Sutra on the temple's exterior, the façade itself becomes an exhibition of traditional Buddhist art and practice.

Transcribing onto the wall panels was also a method of fundraising for the temple's construction. The stone wall façade is divided into 1,800 stone panels, each sized at 49 x 20 x 2 inches (1,250 x 500 x 50 millimeters). The bulk of the stone panels were built with the assistance of 1,453 private donations and were inscribed with a donor's name on the back of the panel, allowing the building's construction cost to be met through people's merit.

For the most private zone of the building, the residences of the head and visiting monks are clad in reflecting glass to indirectly express the fundamental Buddhist concept of Nirvana. The term is used to describe the ultimate goal of the Buddhist path to achieve "nothingness/emptiness," so accurately representing it through the medium of architecture was crucial. From the exterior view, the use of the reflective glass is to mirror the existing nature (sky) and denote "self-realization of being" through the building façade.

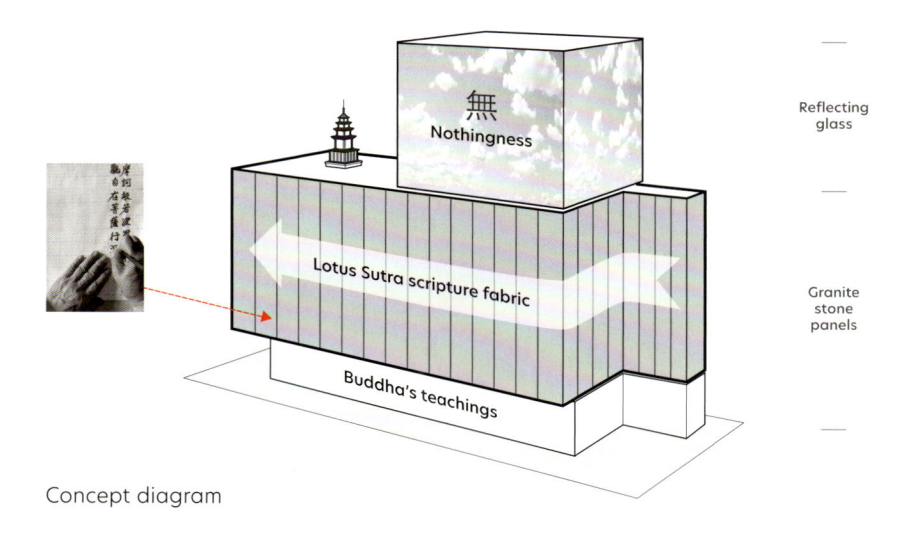

Concept diagram

Building diagram

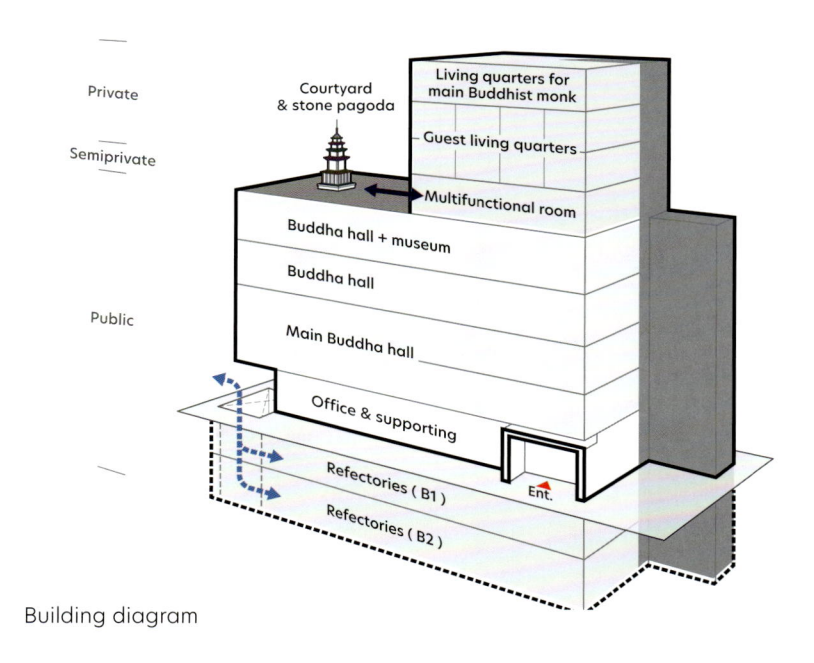

**84** REPETITION

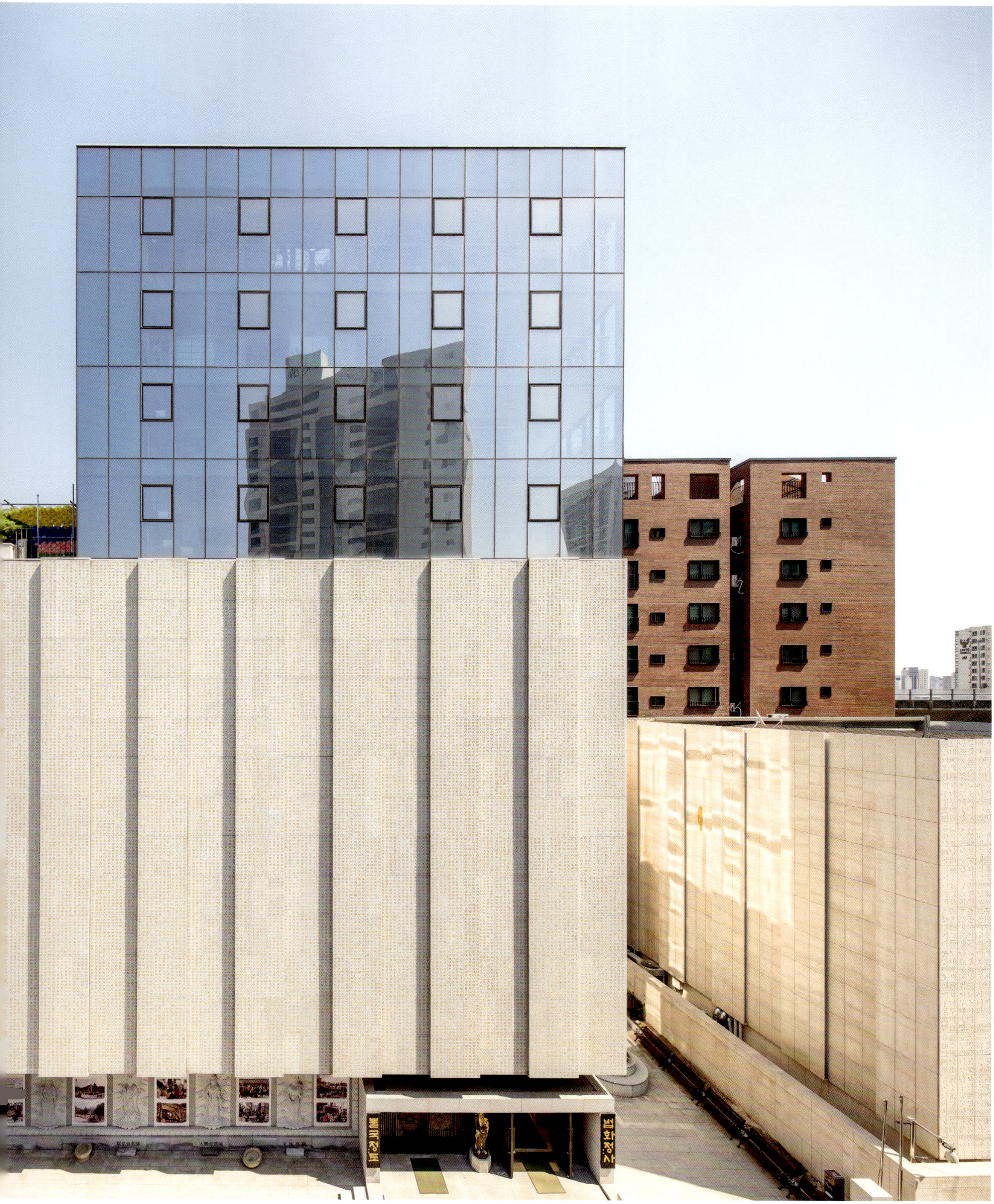
불국정토
법화정사

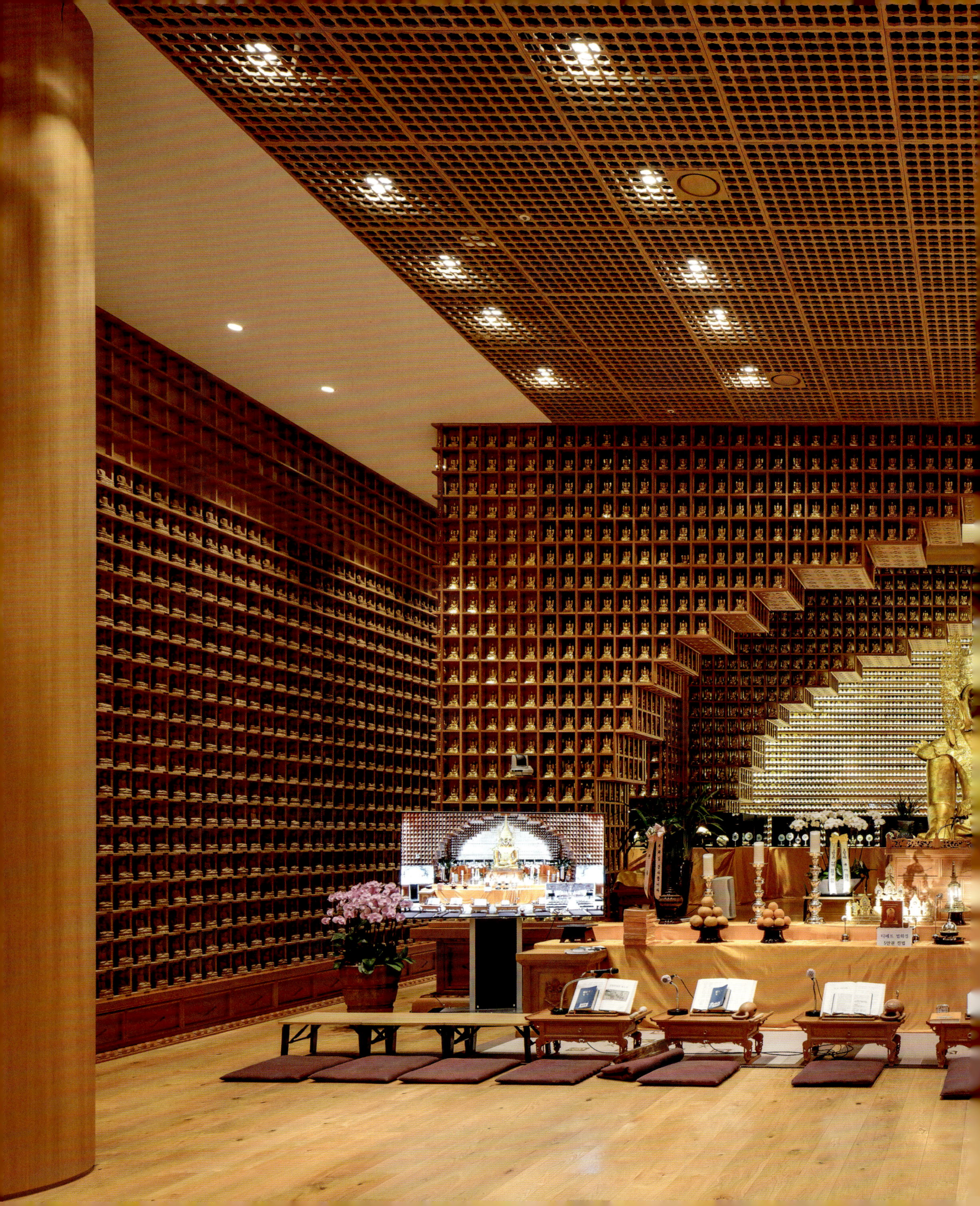

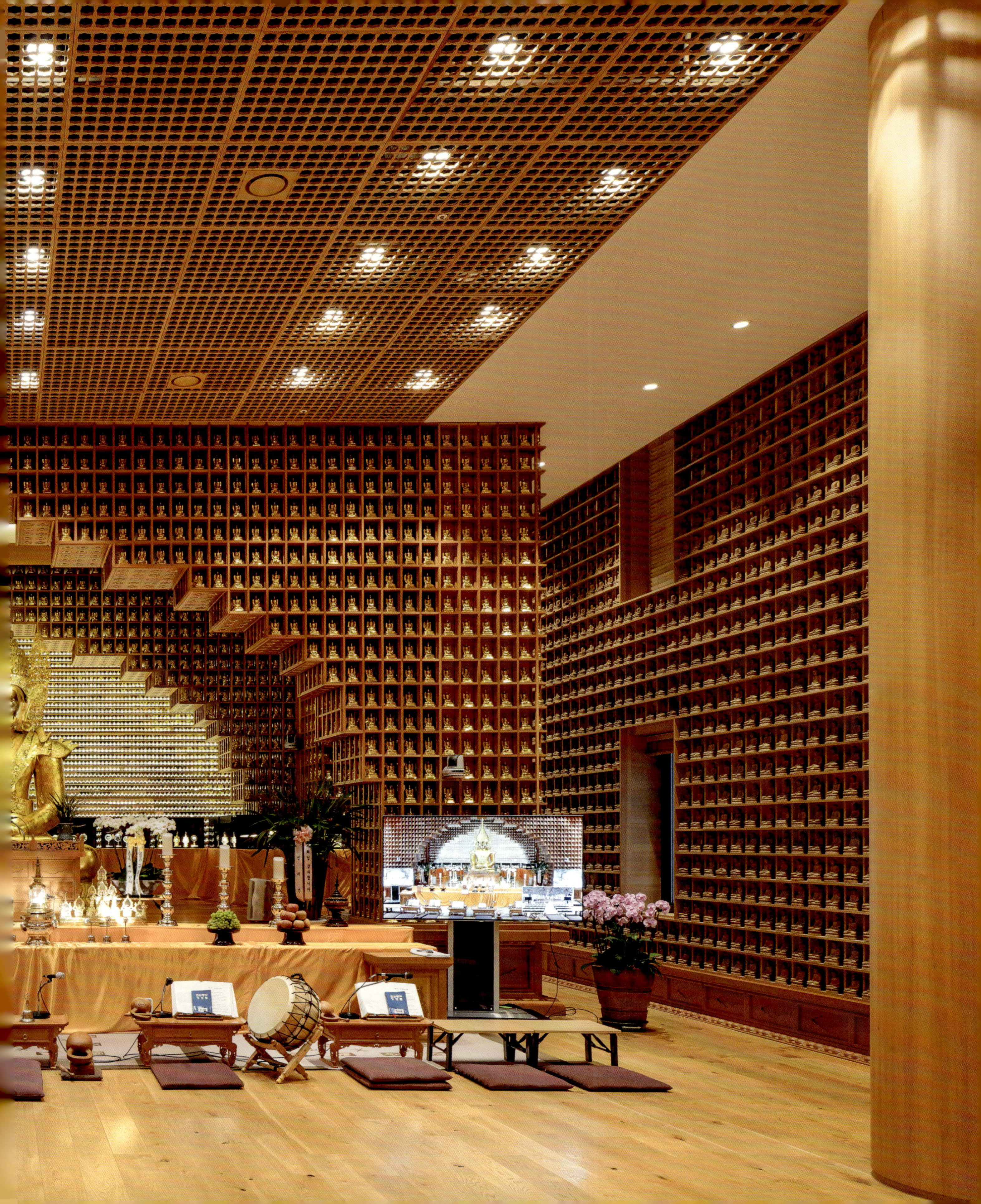

The design of the main sanctuary, found at the center of Buddha Hall, was inspired by the form of traditional Buddhist temples in Myanmar. The golden, 16-foot-tall (5-meter-tall) statue of Buddha (donated by the most noted Myanmar Buddhist Temple) sits alone as the focus of the shrine. Surrounding this statue are 10,000 smaller, handmade Buddha statues on a wooden modular shelving system that informs the space of the room. The interaction between the grid layout and the materiality of the Buddha status and the wooden shelves creates a wall pattern where each volumetric modular casing is projected. The sanctuary space is designed not only to satisfy religious needs in a modern and functional way, but to dramatically represent its symbolic significance as well.

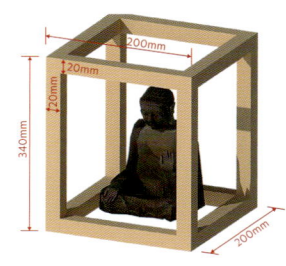

Modular Buddha statue casing

Precedent: Myanmar temple shape

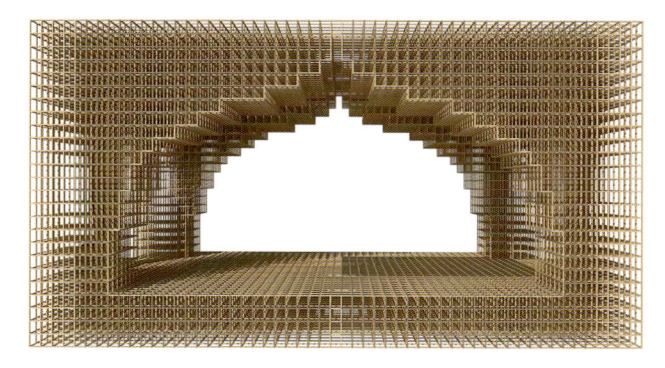

Interior main Buddha Hall sanctuary concept (second to third floors)

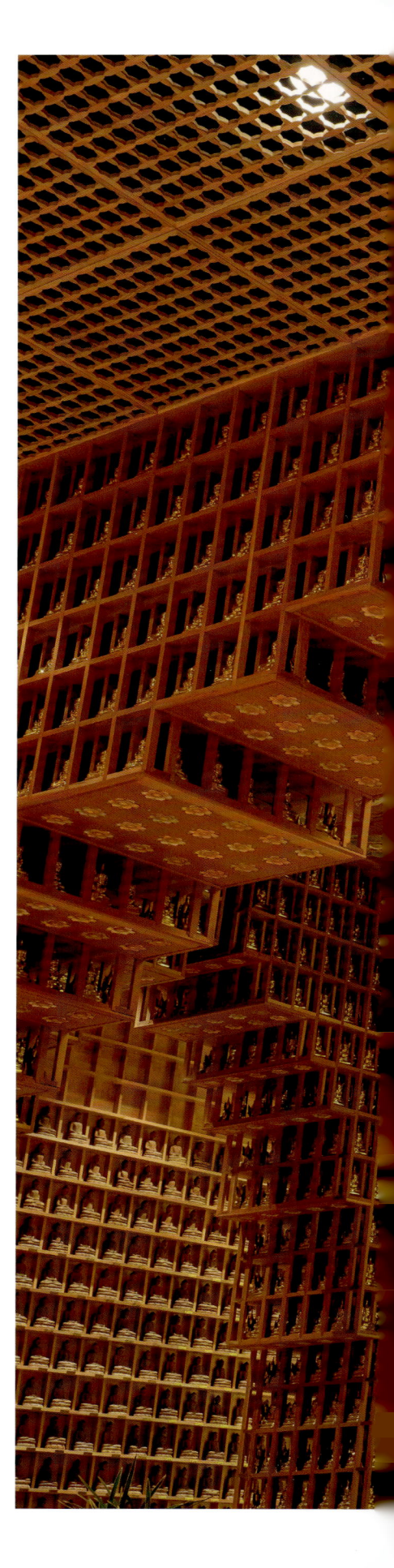

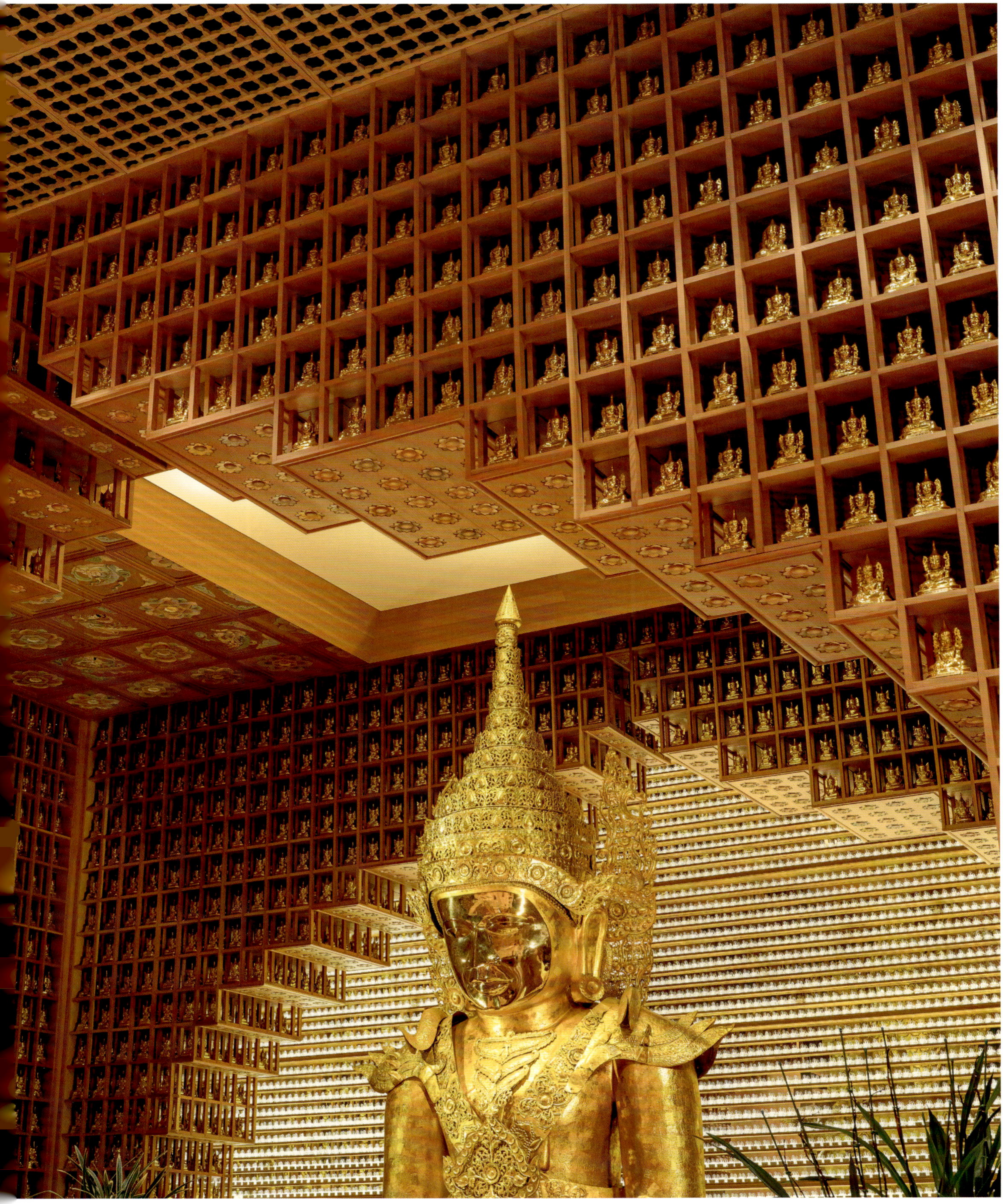

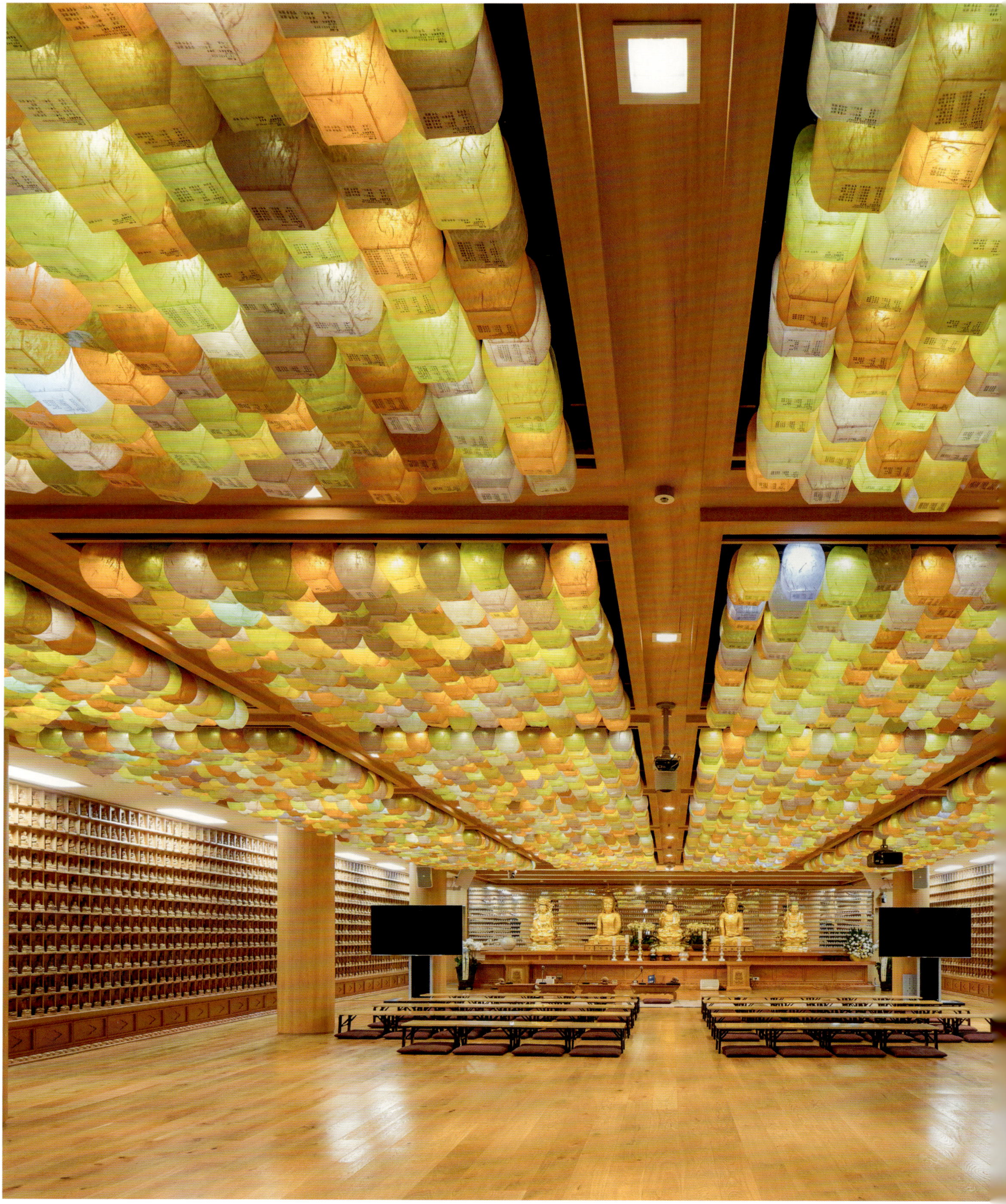

Lotus lanterns are widely used for the celebration of Buddhism for their historic representation of purity and enlightenment. For the Heaven's Sanctuary on the fourth floor, the lanterns that signify the lotus are designed with a plastic form (rather than the traditional way of using a rice paper) for the entire ceiling space. For the individual act of commemoration, each lantern is hung with the name of the congregant who leaves offerings of gratitude. The lanterns feature illumination with several different colors and operate with an automated system that allows for individual lantern height adjustment.

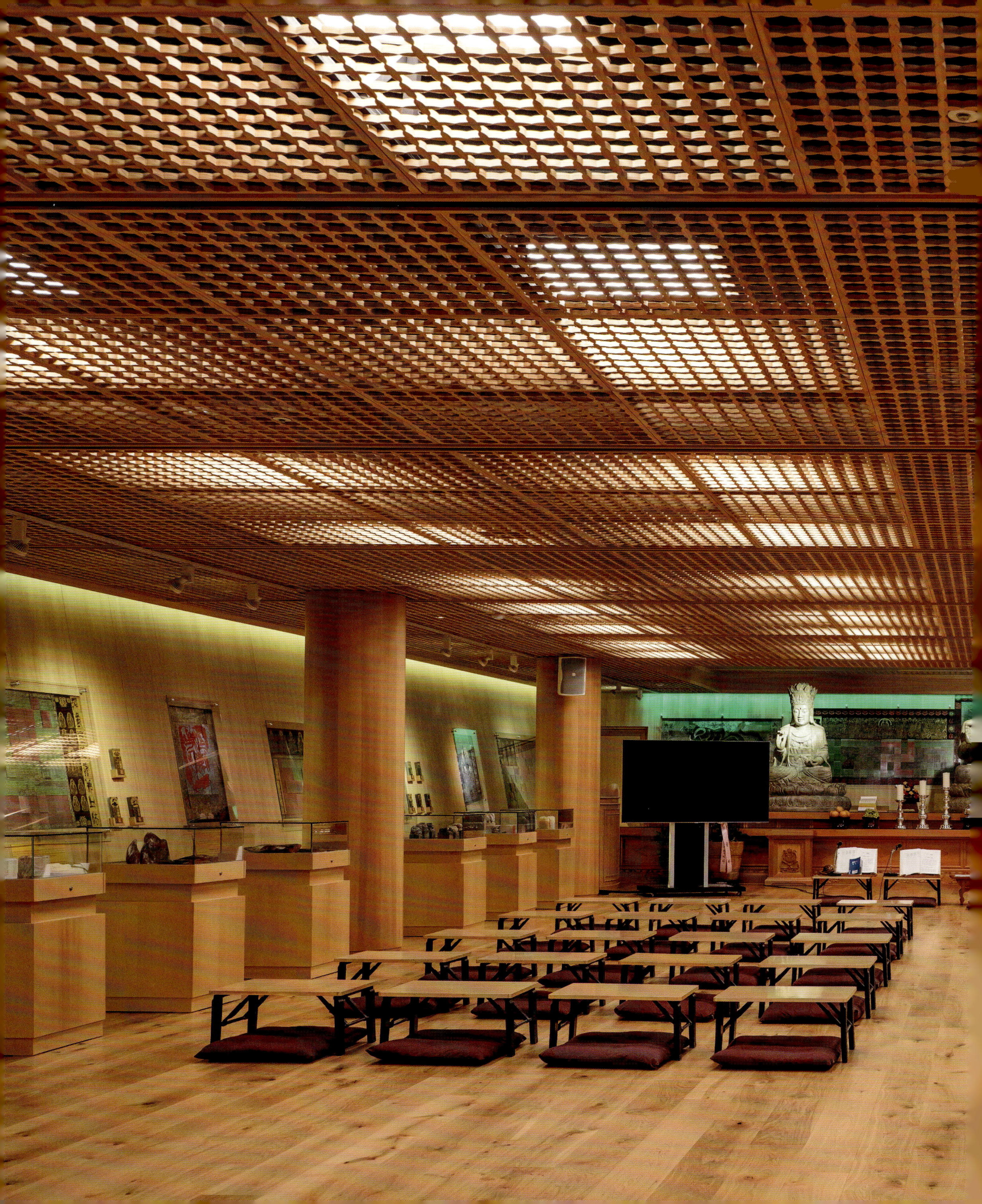

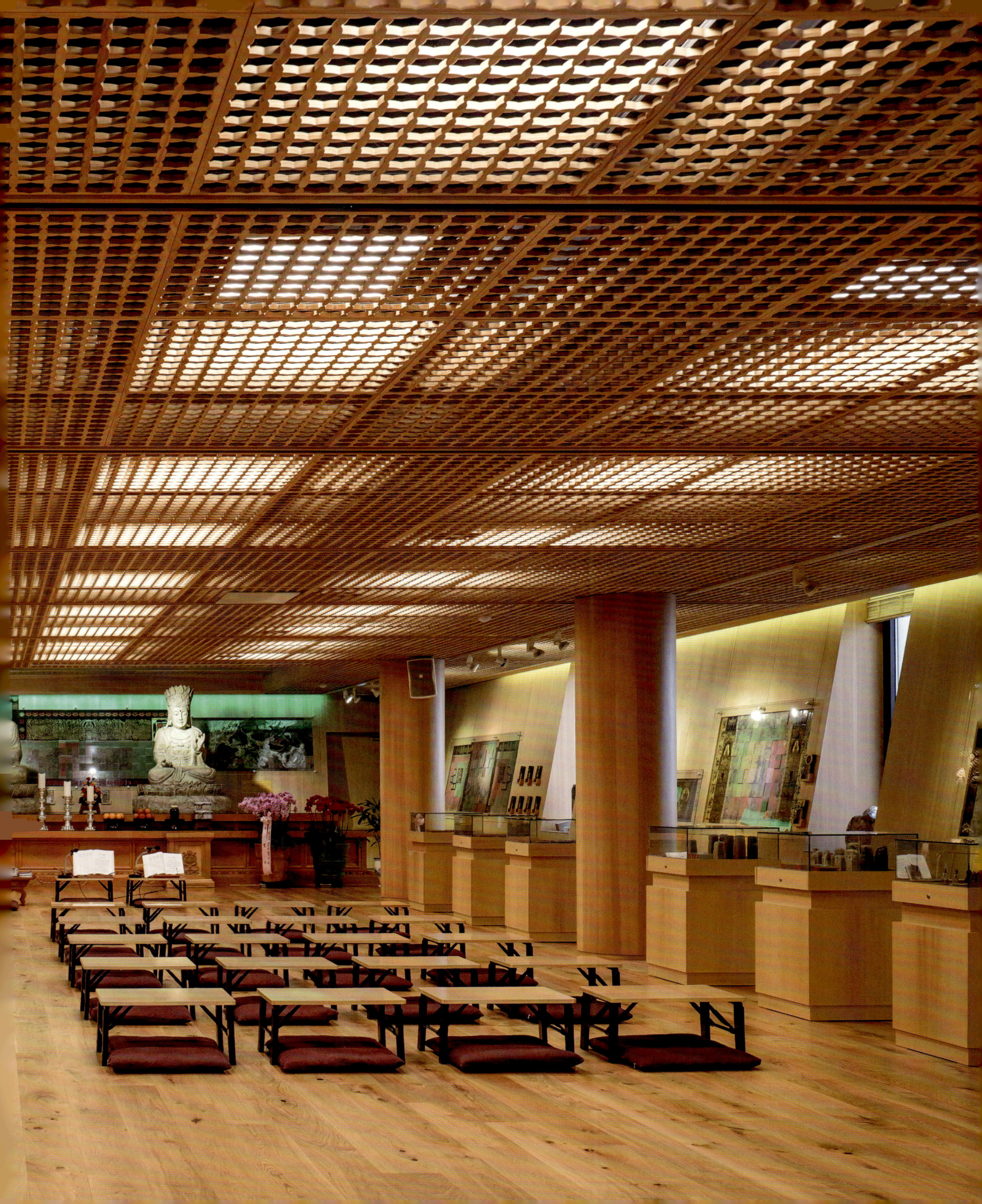

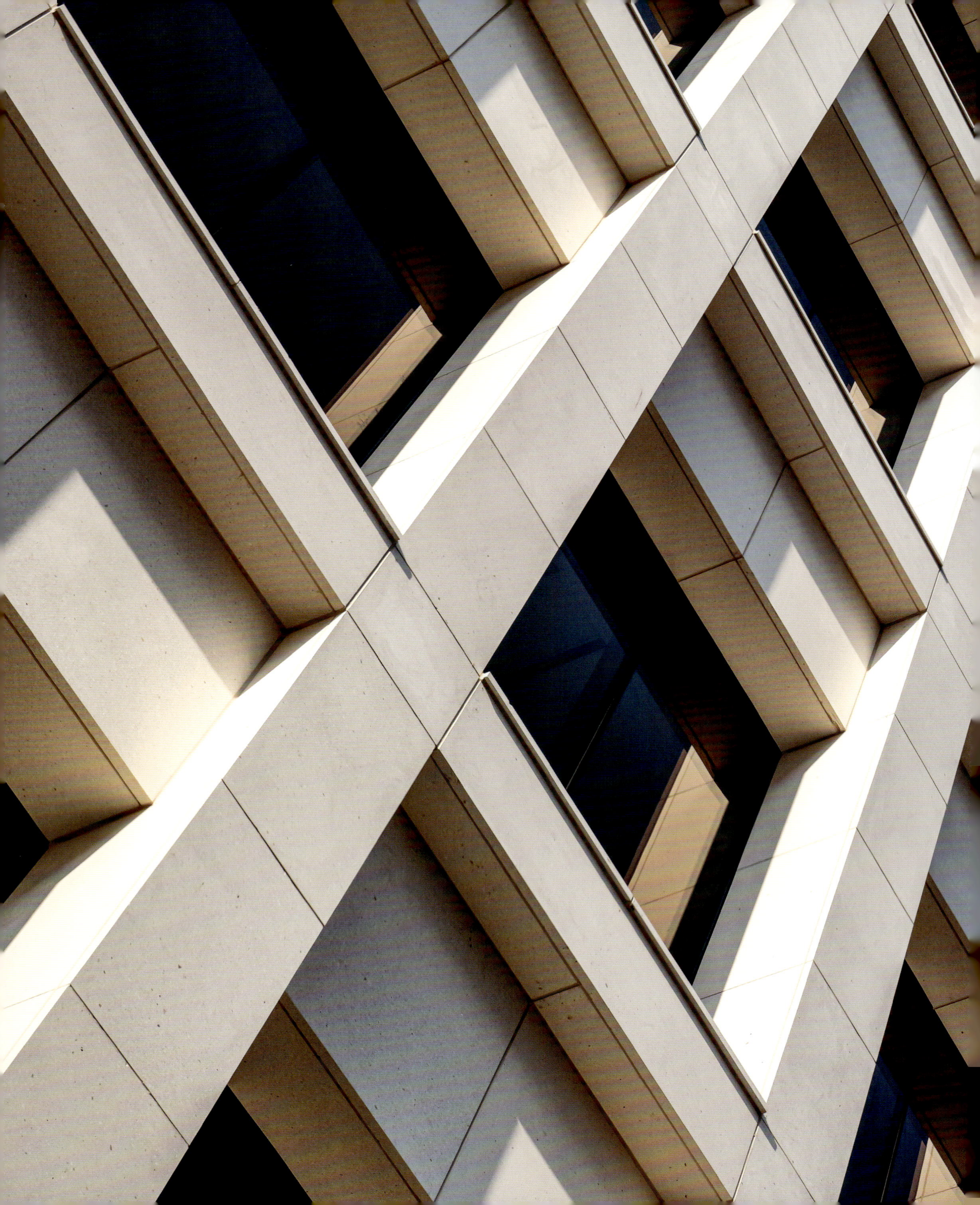

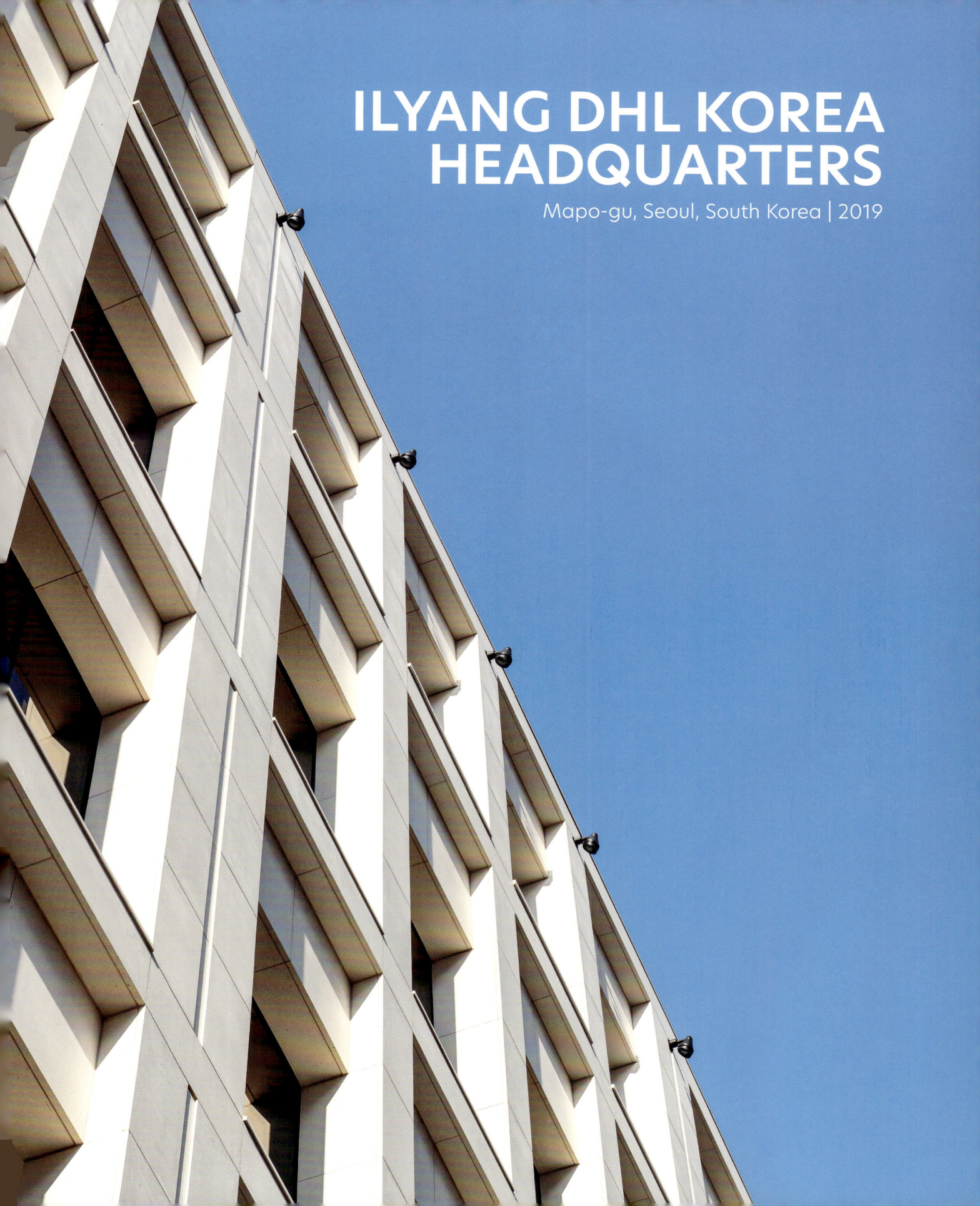

# ILYANG DHL KOREA HEADQUARTERS

Mapo-gu, Seoul, South Korea | 2019

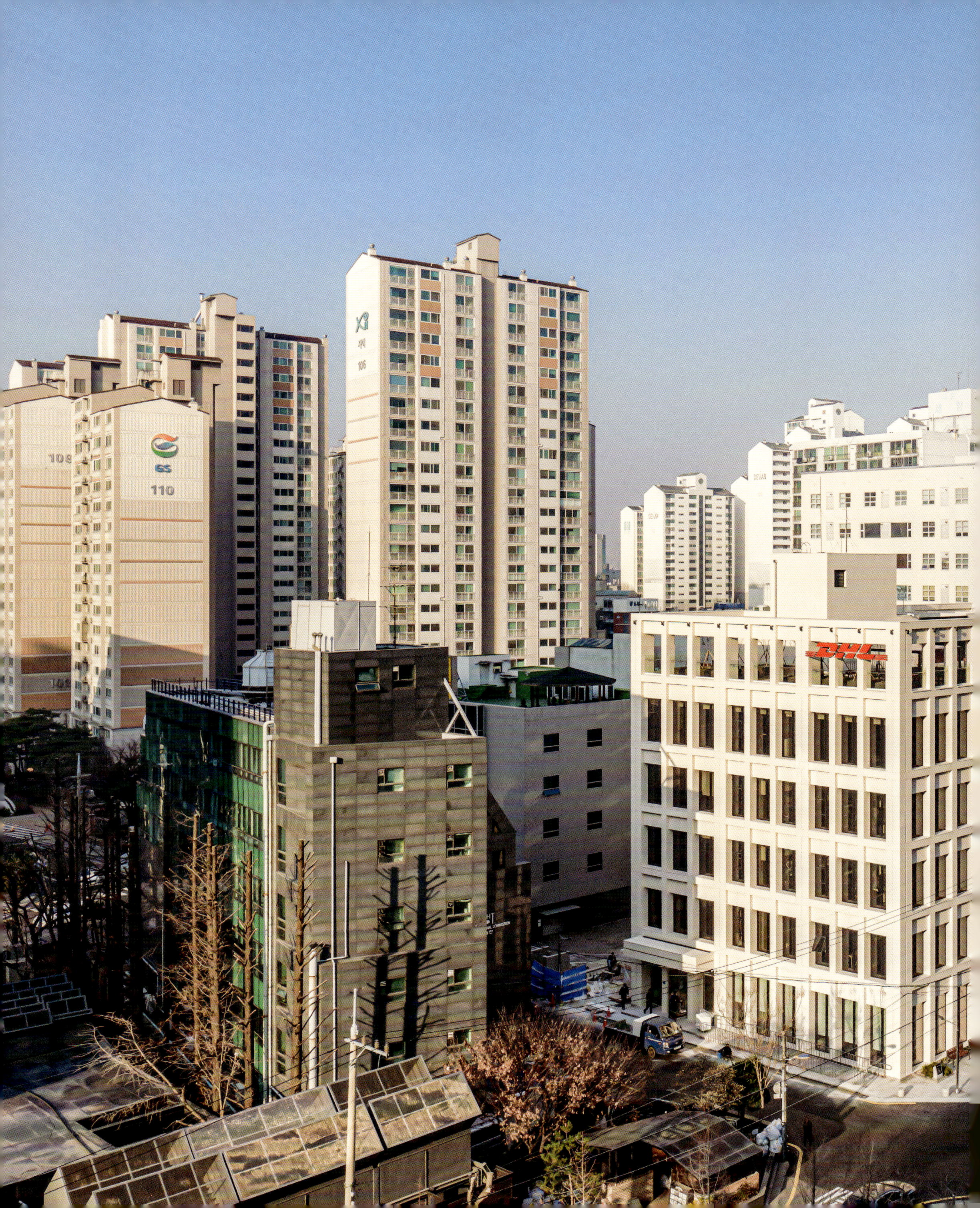

The Ilyang DHL Korea headquarters building is located near the Gongdeok Transit Station in downtown Seoul. The overall mass is a cuboid, which allows the design to maximize the available site space and harmonize with its surrounding environment. In response to the geometries generated from the tree line at Gyeongui Line Forest Park across the street, the building's façade imitates the repetitive vertical forms. This results in an exterior that attempts to fuse a vertical biological form with minimal design aesthetics.

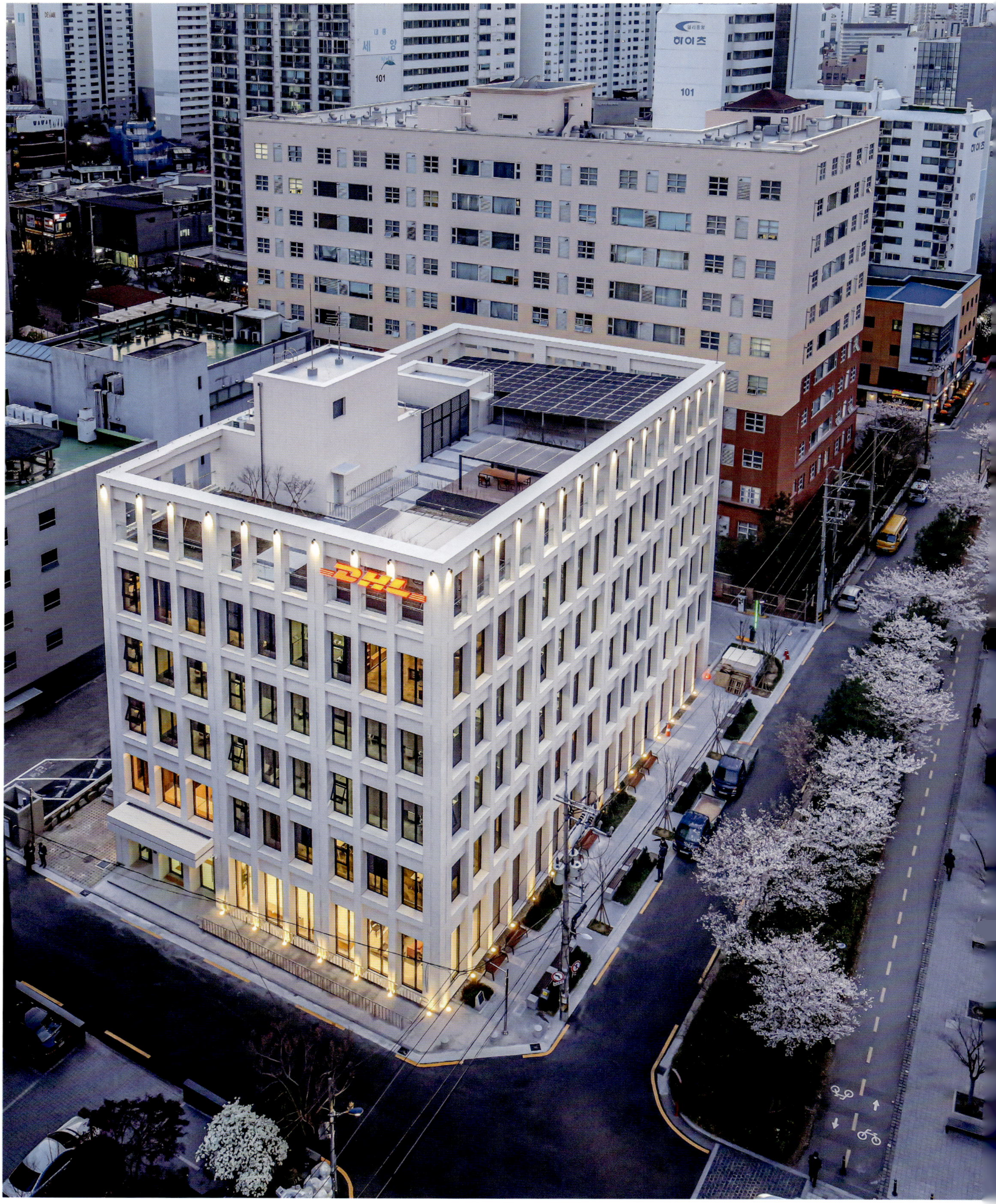

The neighboring Gyeongui Line Forest Park is an urban greenspace spanning 3.9 miles (6.3 kilometers), connecting the Hyochang-dong and Yeonnam-dong districts. While the park operates as a connection for pedestrians, it is also a greenspace where workers can go to relax and socialize. This is a critical element in attempting to create a workplace that promotes a work-and-rest area.

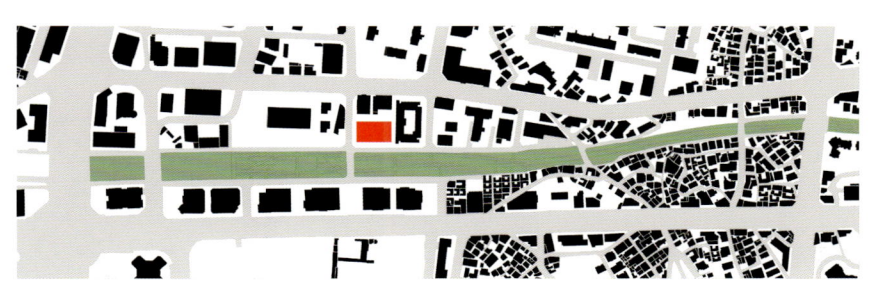

Site plan

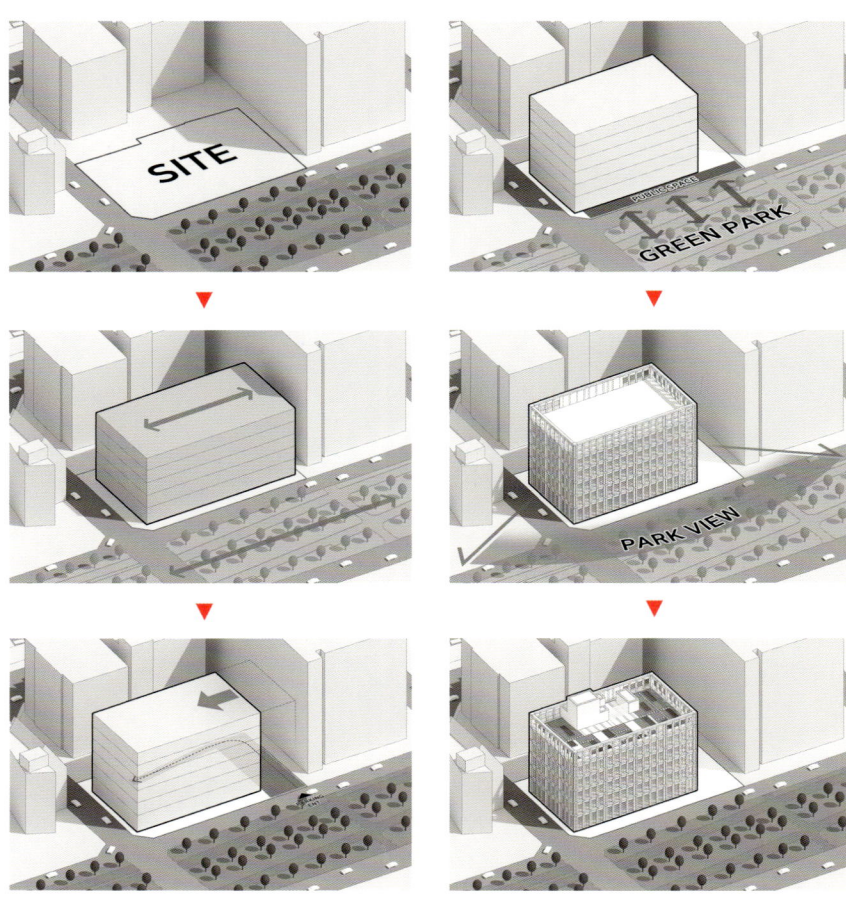

Site diagram

ILYANG DHL KOREA HEADQUARTERS

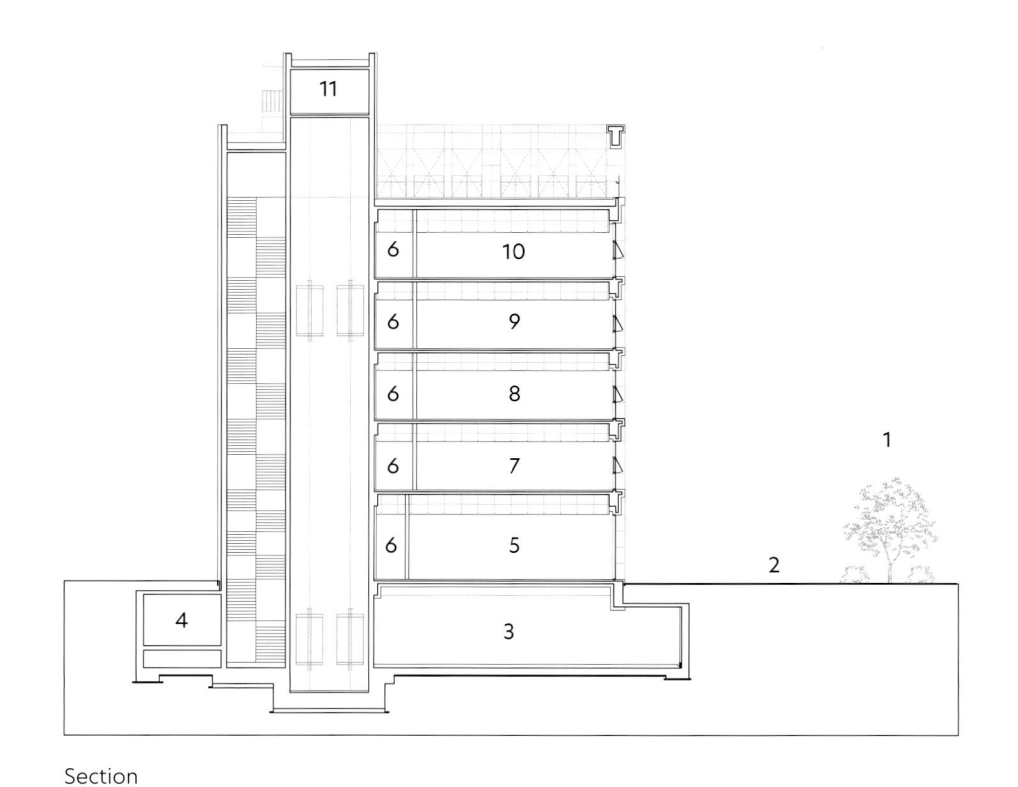

1. Gyeongui Line Forest Park
2. 6M street
3. Basement parking
4. Ramp
5. Mixed-use facility
6. Corridor
7. Lounge
8. Commercial headquarters
9. Financial headquarters
10. Office
11. Elevator mechanical room

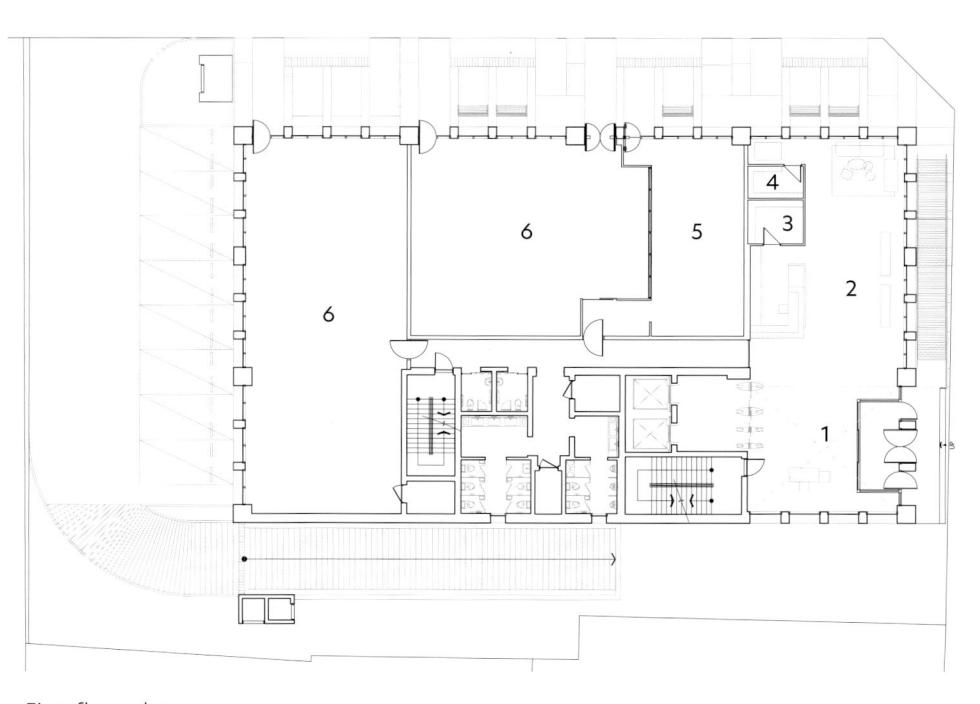

Section

1. Lobby
2. Business facilities
3. Cargo storage
4. Mail box
5. Retail store
6. Café

First-floor plan

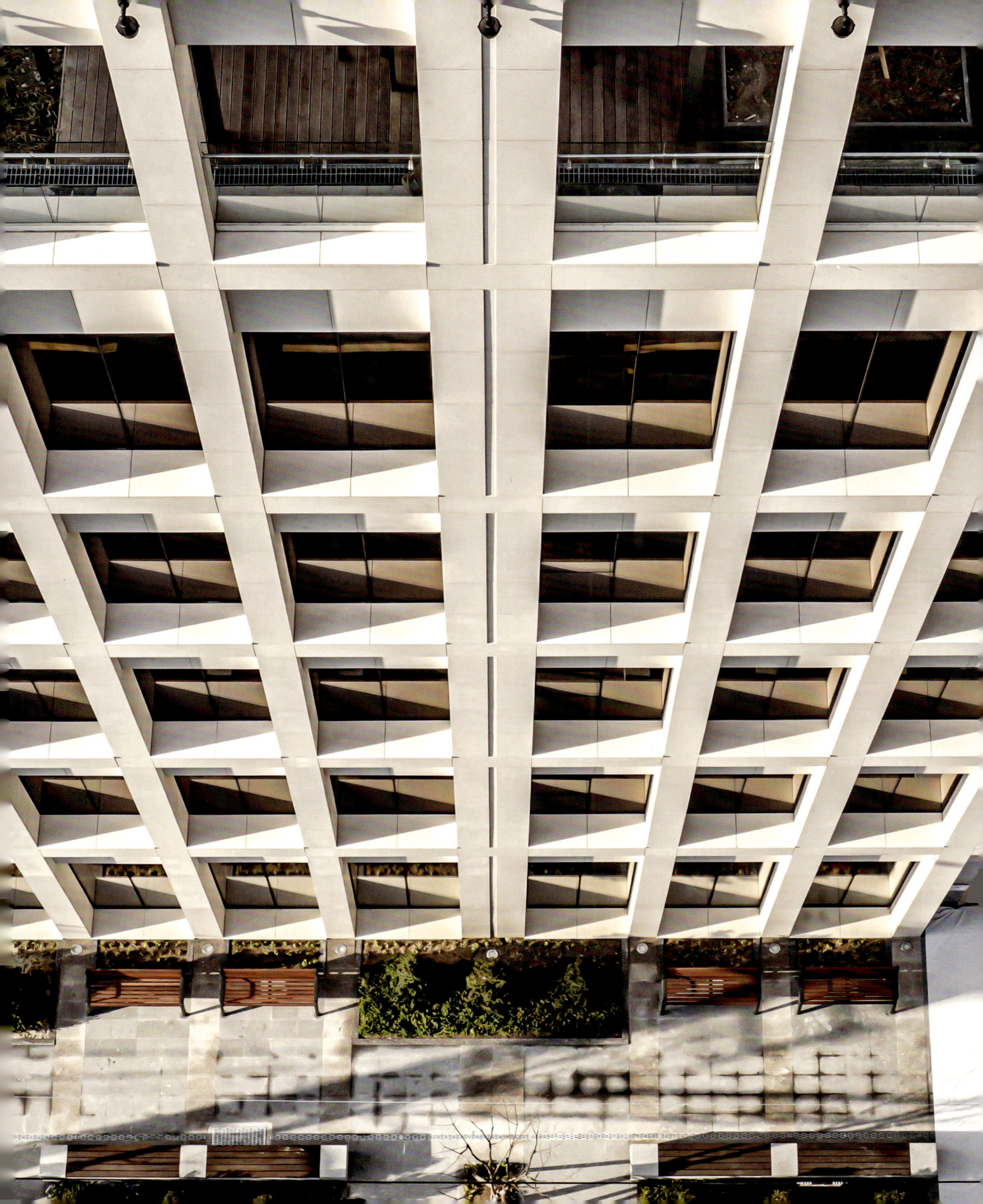

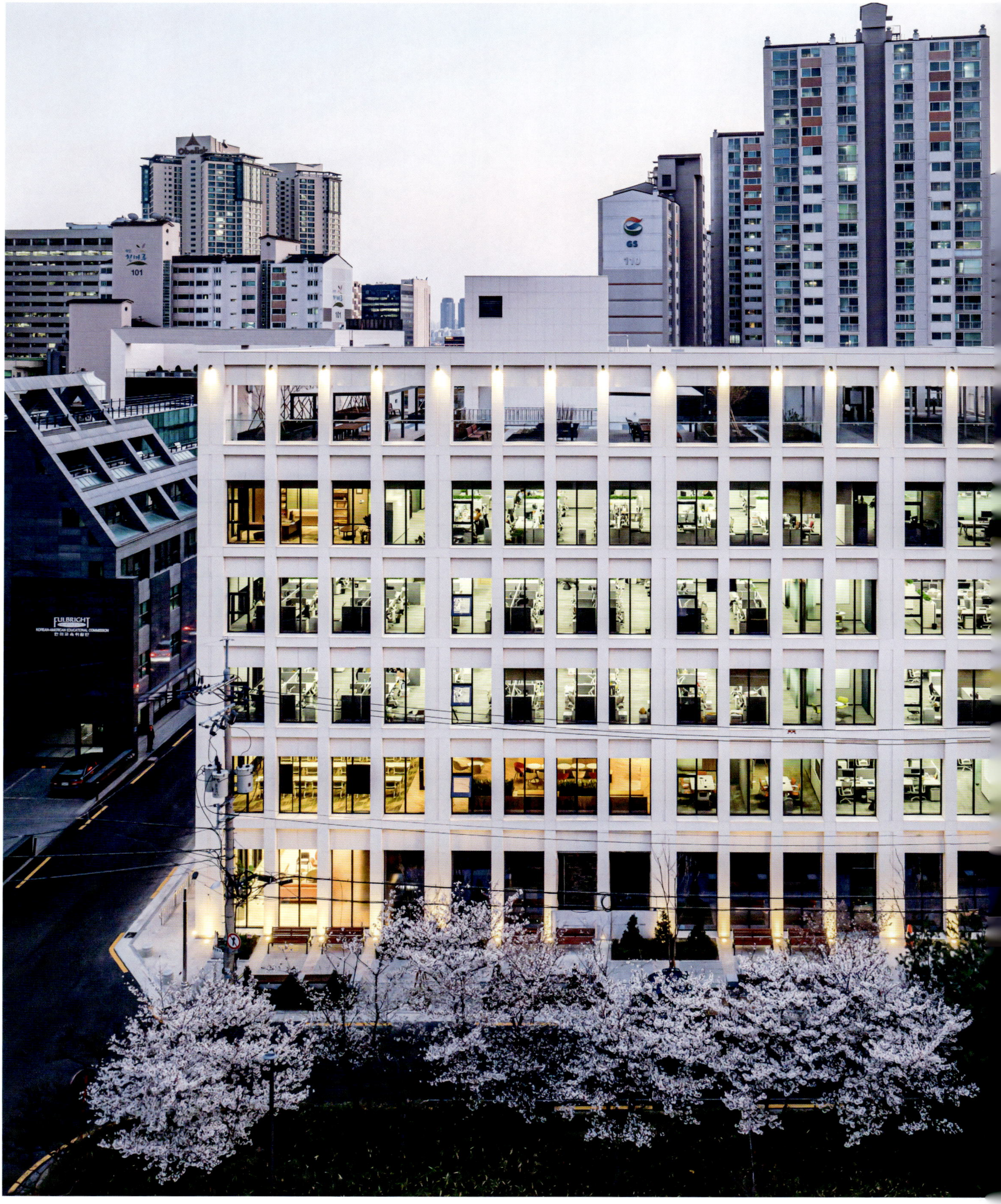

FULBRIGHT
KOREAN-AMERICAN EDUCATIONAL COMMISSION
GS

To maximize the circulation and square footage of the office's interior space, our design incorporates post-tension bows and load-bearing walls, removing the need of columns from the interior footprint. These additions also allowed us to achieve a taller ceiling and floor height.

After testing various types of stone tiles, the use of artificial marble was perfect in terms of enhancing the building's durability and reducing pollution. Due to the design and materiality, the building stands at the site with a presence of maturity and permanence.

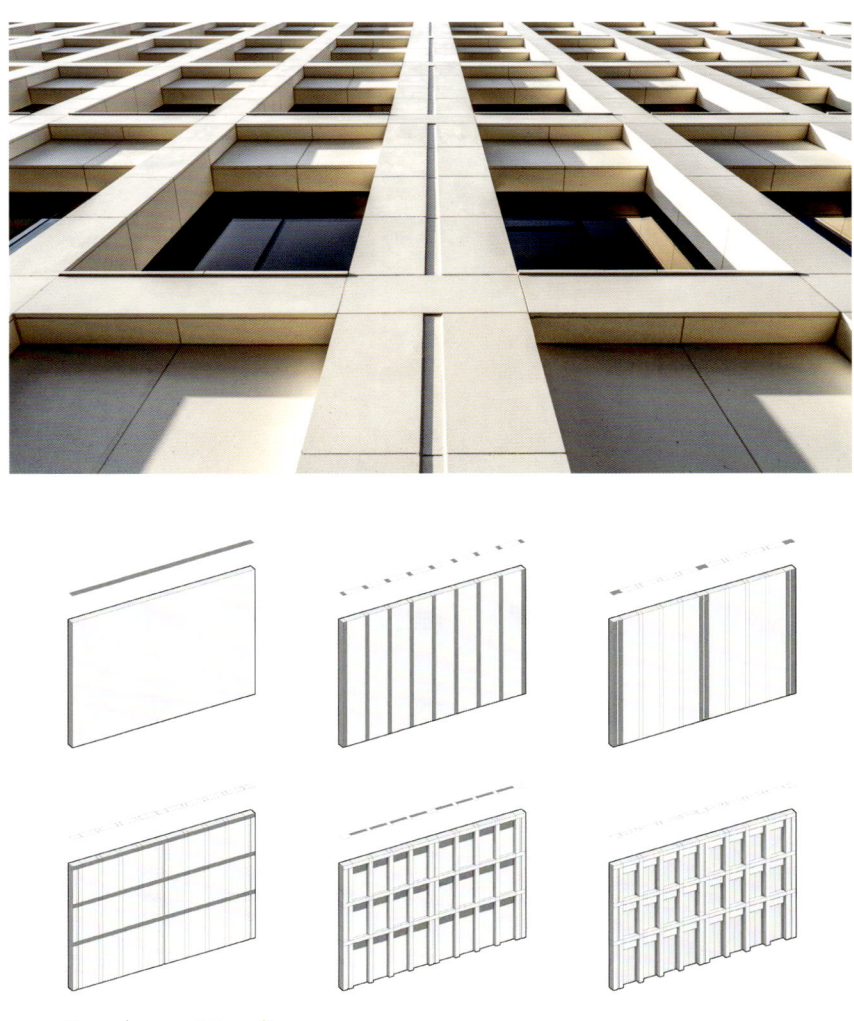

Façade repetition diagram

ILYANG DHL KOREA HEADQUARTERS

# GIMPO BOHM OFFICETEL
Gimpo-si, Gyeonggi-do, South Korea | 2018

TIRE PRO
KUMHO TIRE
타이어 프로
김포대로점 987-2902
타이어는 금호타이어
타이어 휠 얼라인먼트 밸런스
KUMHO TIRE
타이어프로 김포대로점
987-2902
겨울용 타이어
(Winter)
예약판매실시
국산차타이어
수입차
OPEN

ES 이에스 종합건설 (주) 996-3941.
(주)은성개발 983-6458
MERITZ 메리츠화재
청년PT24시헬스 031-984-1244 2F 3F
HYUNDAI

The Gimpo BOHM officetel is a mixed-use commercial center located in the Pungmu district of Gimpo-si, South Korea. The brick exterior, a traditional material that is enhanced by the polished dark glass and unique void formations, is designed to give a strong timeless, bold impression. The rough, warm, and colorful exterior is contrasted with a soft, smooth, and cool interior. These moments of internal and external space meet in the quad courtyard in the center of the building, adding vitality to the space.

The courtyard lies at the bottom of a spanning vertical void, receiving sunlight and fresh air down through the building's center. The presence of officetel's positive and negative spaces and its unique color scheme allow the building to emerge from its environment to become a local landmark, drawing attention to both its own commercial stores and the local businesses in the surrounding area.

To visually separate the commercial zone from the office zone in the front elevation, we adjusted the dimensions of the repeating square voids that hold the windows. The first two levels are stretched to communicate horizontality while the upper levels are pinched to communicate verticality. To increase the accessibility and circulation of retail space on the first two floors, we opened the walls so pedestrians are able to pass through our building seamlessly from the sidewalk. This change also connected the exterior public space to the building's central core void, attracting more observers and daily routes through the the officetel.

The client, a prominent developer in Incheon-si, was interested in creating potential development prototypes that would be unique and cost-effective. While originally skeptical, the owner agreed to the brick cladding after seeing our previous projects utilizing the material, such as the Brooklyn townhouses and loft. By using the services of local businesses, we managed to optimize the construction cost, allowing us to focus on the building's detailing and glass quality. We found that the moments of repetition in the materiality, sections, and program of this project successfully express how "repetition" can enhance architecture and the experience of the people who interact with it.

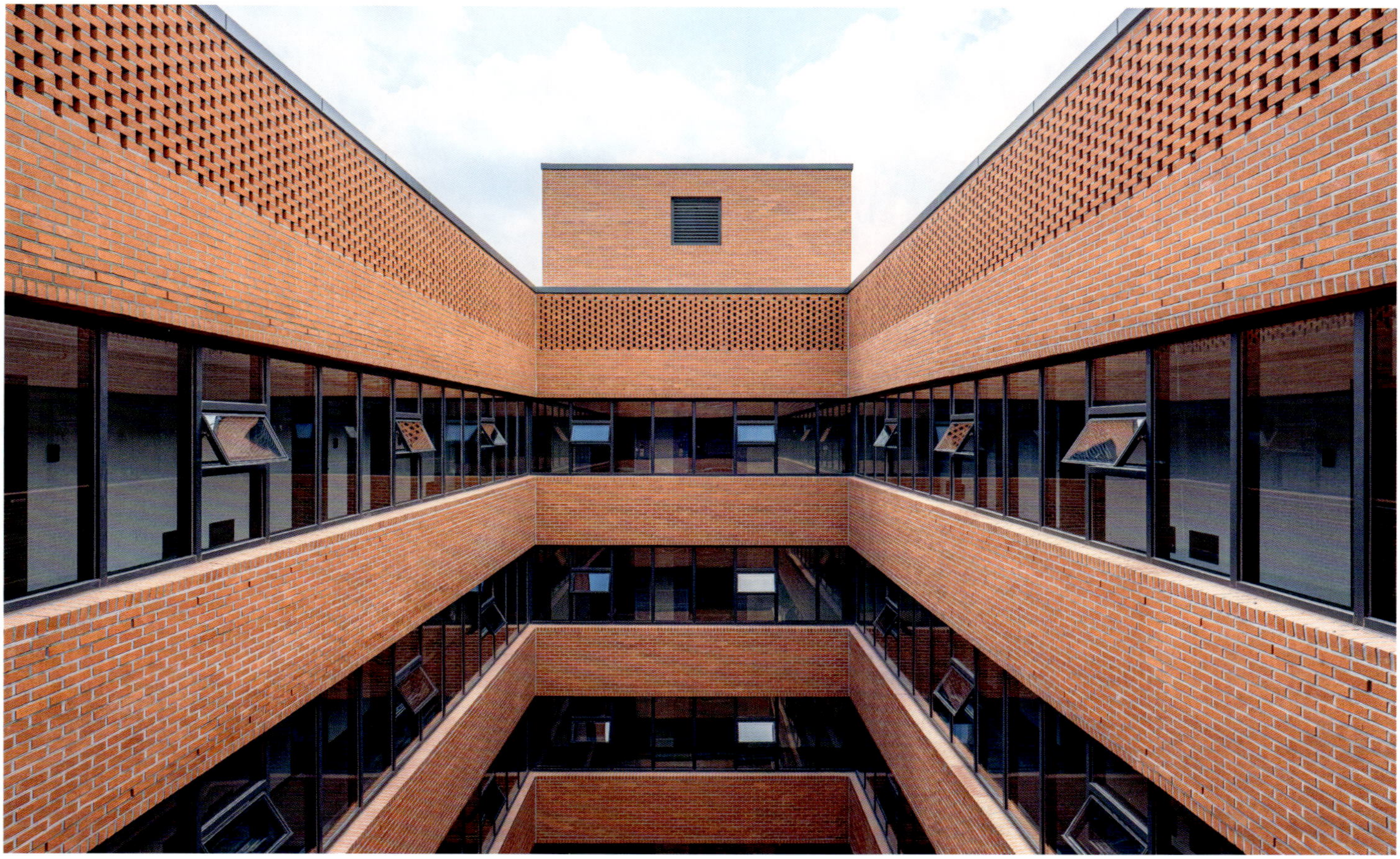

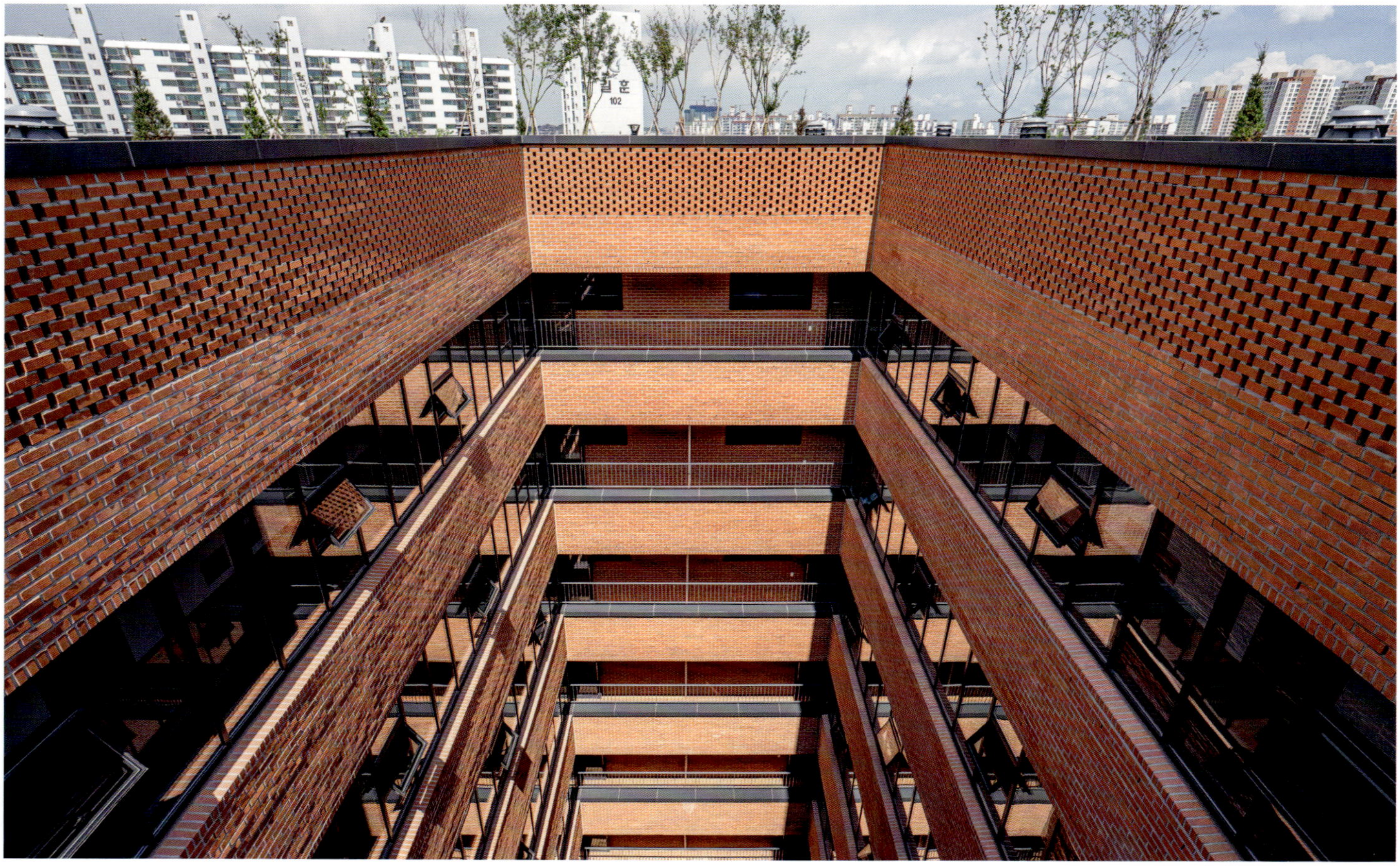
102

# YANGPYEONGDONG MIXED-USE BUILDING

Yeongdeungpo-gu, Seoul, South Korea | 2020

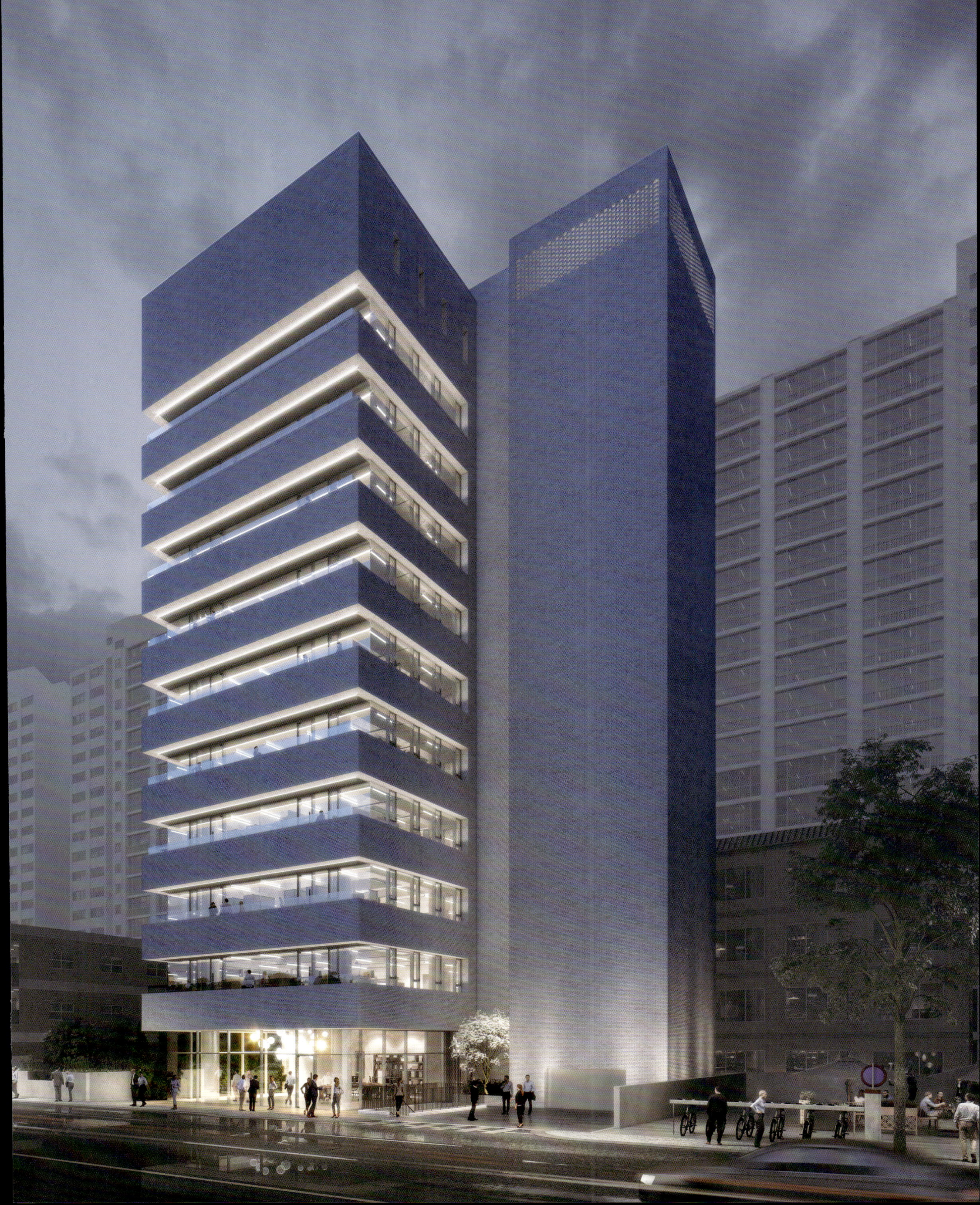

This is a twelve-story mixed-use development in Seoul's Yeongdeungpo-gu district. Originally, the client wanted to renovate the existing building and facilitate an addition. However, to enhance spatial and budgetary efficiencies, we created a new and more optimized modern design. This project's design focus centered on the relationships of positive and negative spaces generated from the repetition of slabs. Like the expressions conveyed by the minimalist artist Donald Judd in his sculptural works, the building's stacked masses generate a gesture of static movement. This acceleration in the physical medium was kept grounded by an inserted solid extrusion next to the project.

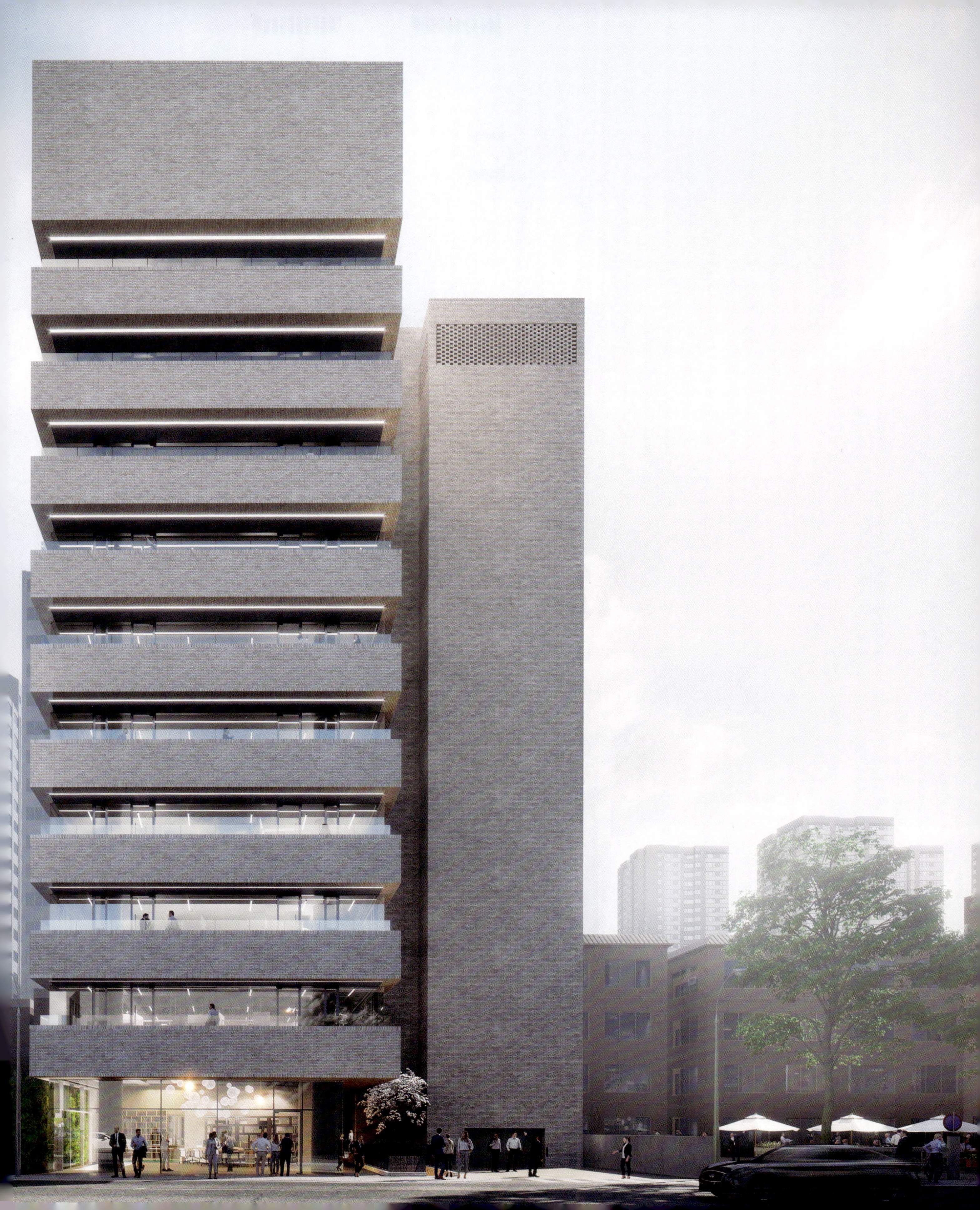

To unify the repeated volumes, their voids, and the rectangular form, the materiality of white aged brick was implemented throughout the building's exterior. Because of its incorporation of voided planes into its form, this building is an example of a monolithic structure with unique qualities of elevation and verticality.

The building's programs were divided into commercial, office, and residential units: the first floor housed a commercial storefront, the top two levels operate as apartment residences, and the levels in between serve as office spaces. To increase the flow of daylight into the building's lower retail sections, we implemented a sunken plaza. Due to the client's request to keep parking outside the building, the proposed large-scale underground garage concept was substituted with an efficient machine parking system that operates besides the main structure. This enables the storage to both hold more vehicles while also being an integral segment of the building's overall composition.

First-floor plan

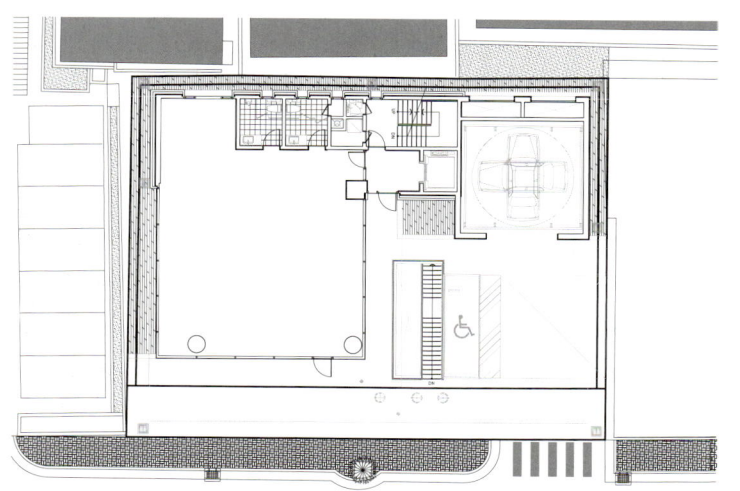

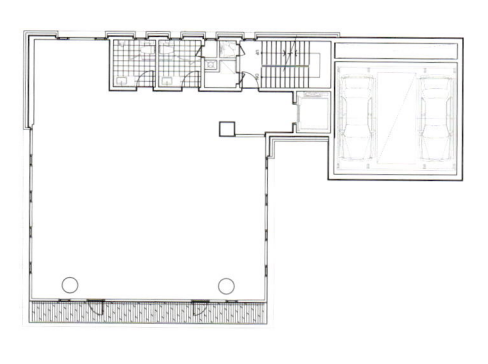

Typical floor plan   0 ——— 32ft

YANGPYEONGDONG MIXED-USE BUILDING   **115**

Section

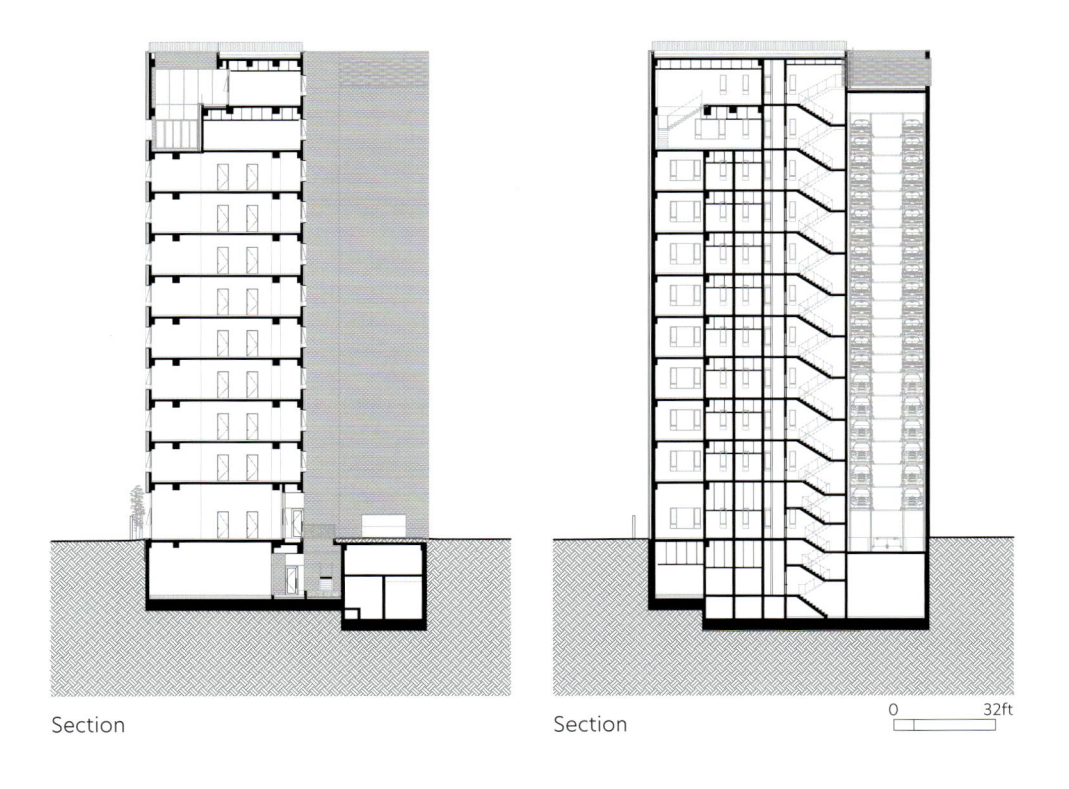

Section

0   32ft

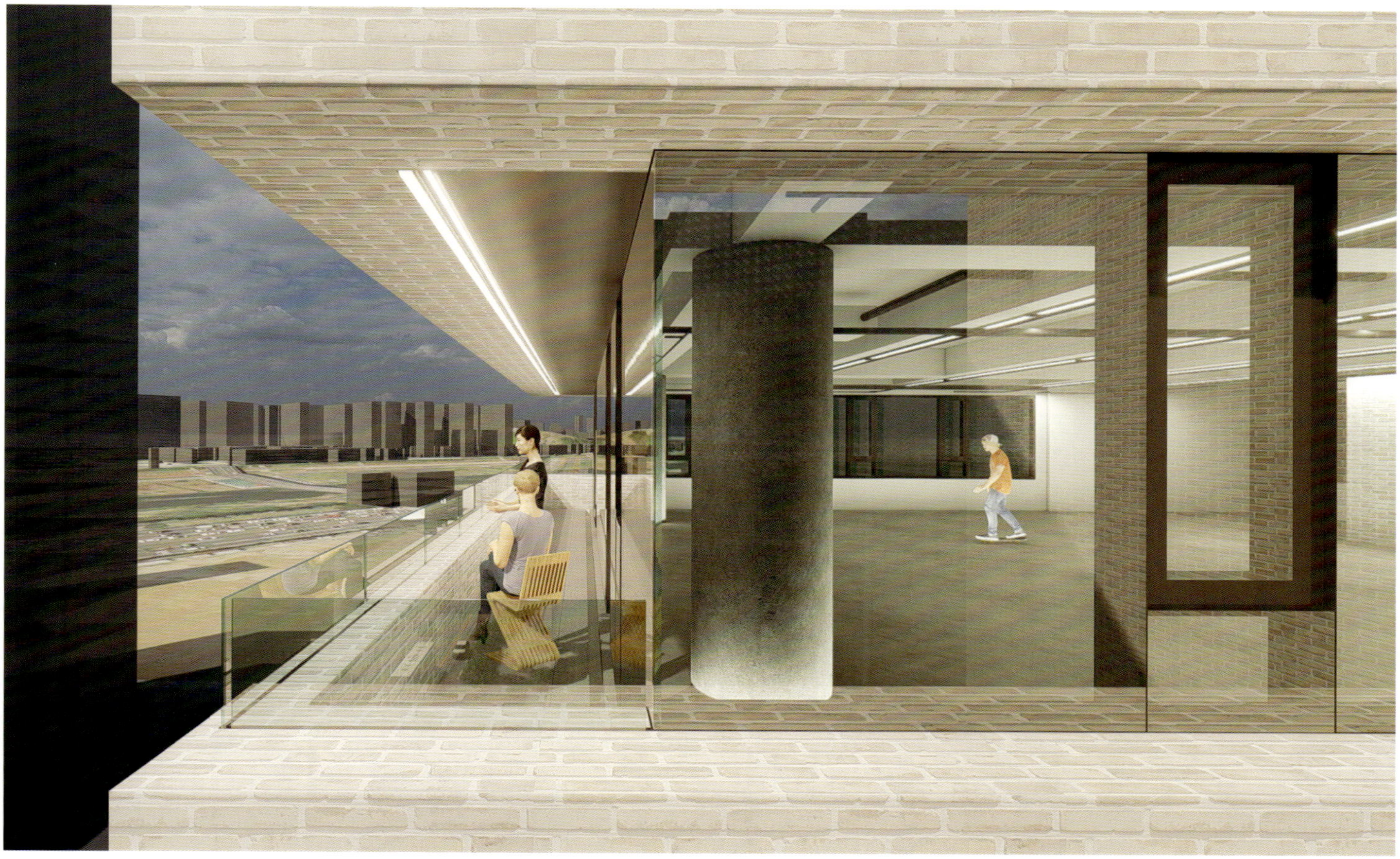

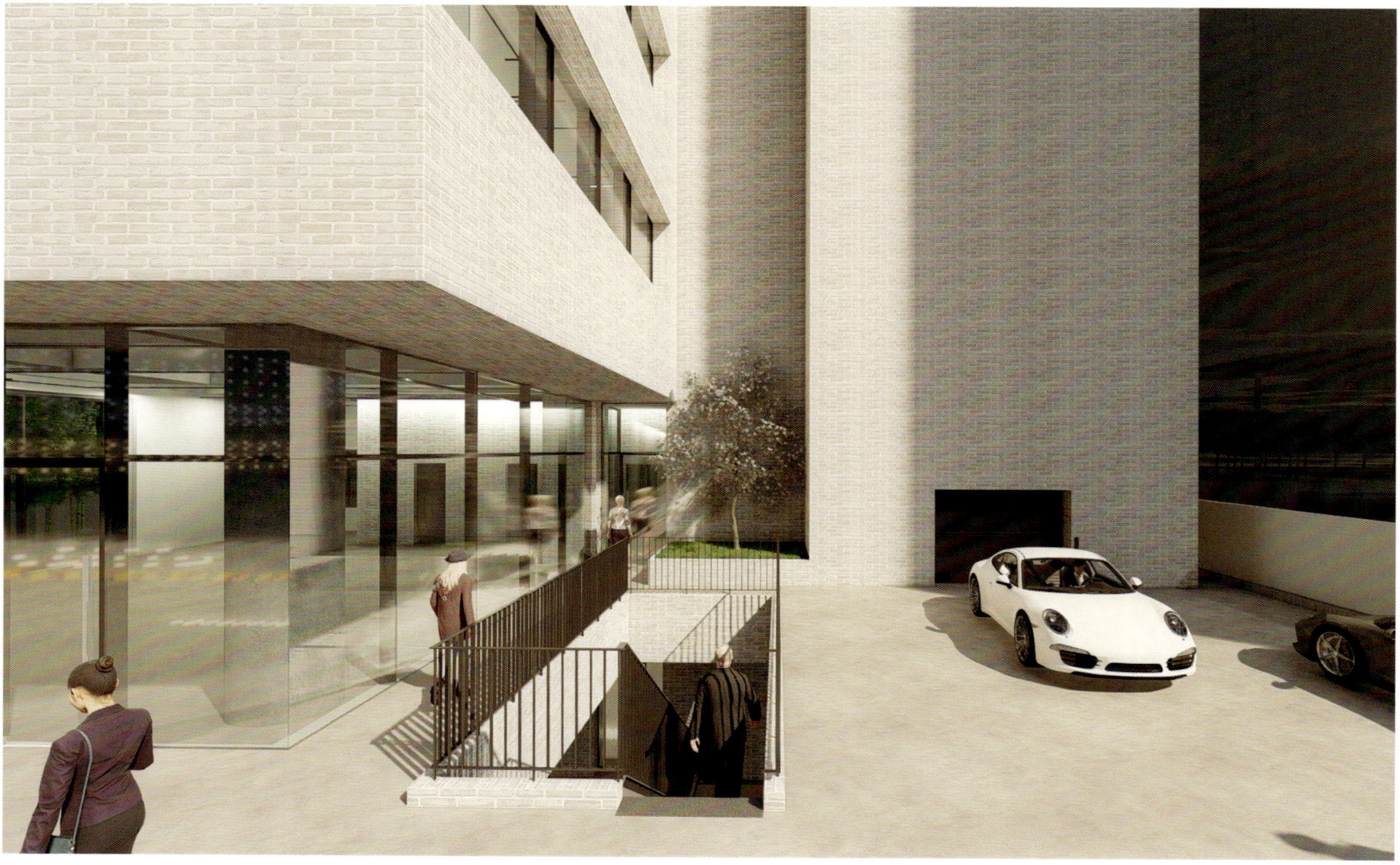

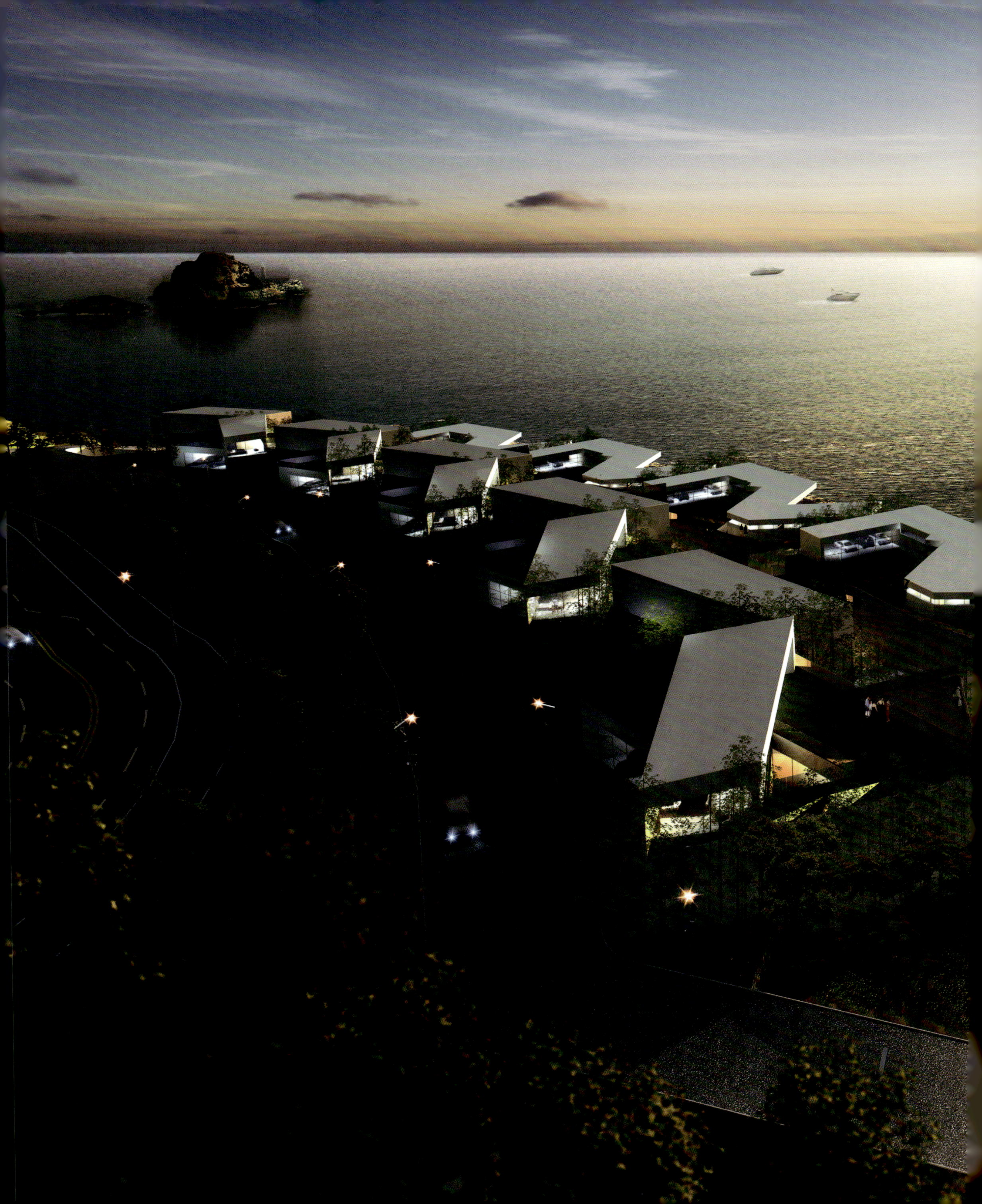

# BUSAN MARINE TERRACE RESORT

Nam-gu, Busan, South Korea | 2010

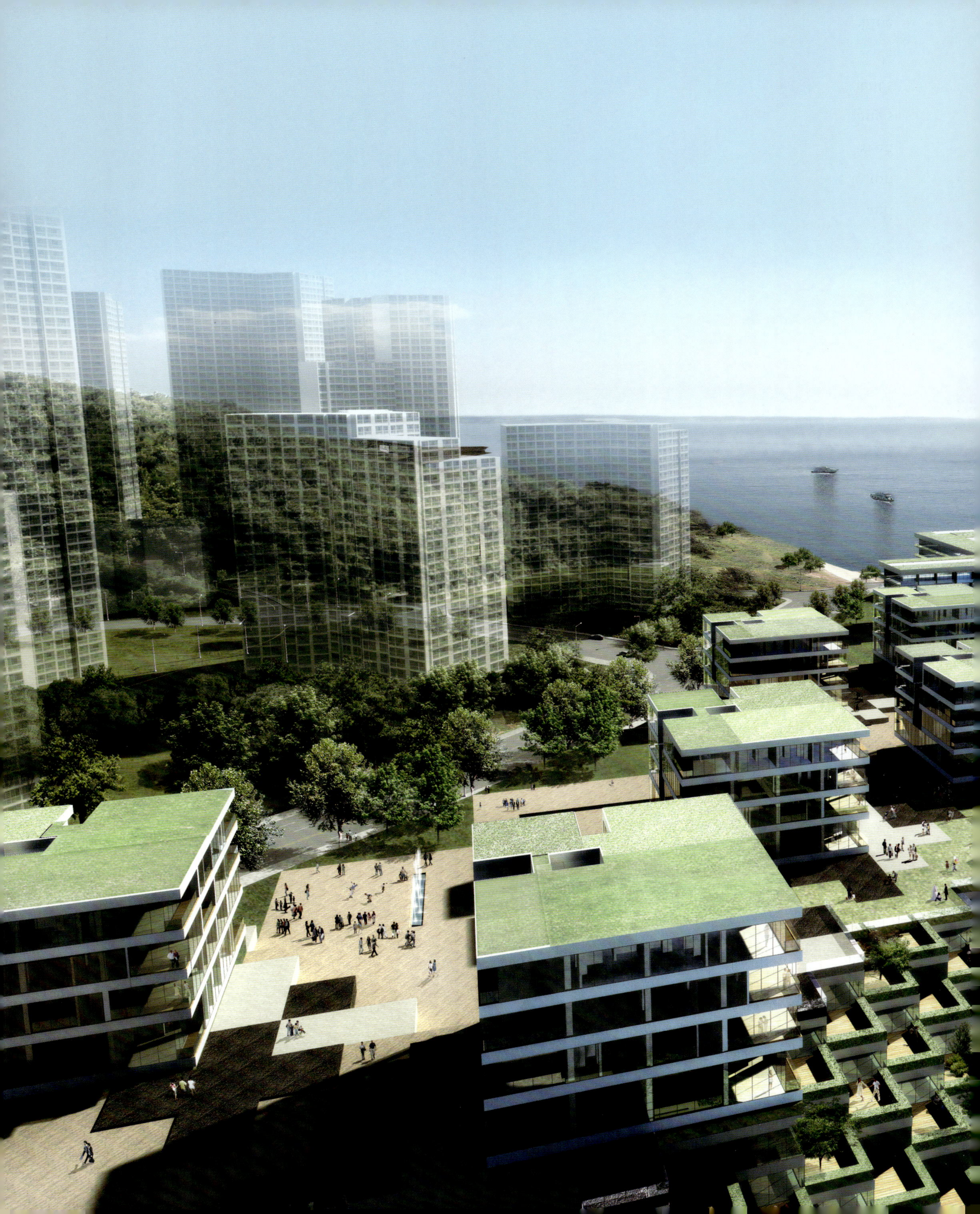

Overseeing Oryuk Island and its recently completed marina, the site of the Busan Marine Terrace Resort is located along the top of a spectacular sea cliff edge. The objective of this invitational design competition was to explore innovative ways in which this unique environment could enhance the privacy and viewing experience of a potential luxury condominium and/or boutique hotel complex. By actively adopting a dense, urban-terrace design concept throughout the site, our design earned first place in this design competition.

122  REPETITION

The unique topography of the site offered us the opportunity to explore a variety of designs and their respective advantages when implementing the platforms. Because of the terrace's relationship to the cliff, the residents can experience an undisturbed view of the sea as well as an open residential park in between the villa towers and cliffside housing. We created a private residential community by isolating a detached villa zone, providing increased security for the inhabitants.

Due to the size density of the project, one of the biggest challenges was making sure every room in all 117 residential units was provided with an operable sea view. By utilizing a staggered level system, our final layout successfully provides each unit with a full sea view with no interference between adjacent units.

For this site we experimented with the idea of a "super terrace," a series of small, closed terraces that form a single, communal exterior space. This super terrace not only maximizes the sea viewing experience for residents of this resort, but also allows it to become a social event.

The resort is divided into three clusters: Block A provides private and exclusive detached housing units within walking distance to the nearby marina; Block B provides semiprivate multihousing units with large bonus terraces; and Block C provides public boutique hotel rooms that are accessible to the adjacent park. The planning and layout of each section delivers a hierarchy within the site, creating a solution for the multiphased development within the project's budget.

And while the square footage and density of the resort is immense, the use of multilayered villas, condominiums, and terraces results in a luxury complex that is extremely efficient, beautiful, and eco-friendly.

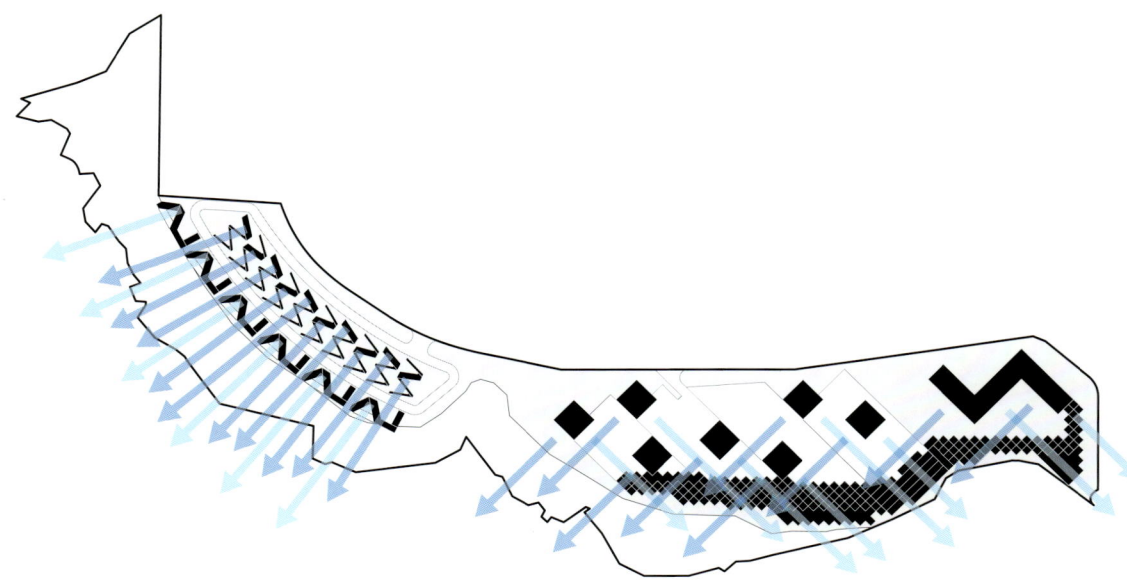

All accommodation is designed to maximize the views

**124** REPETITION

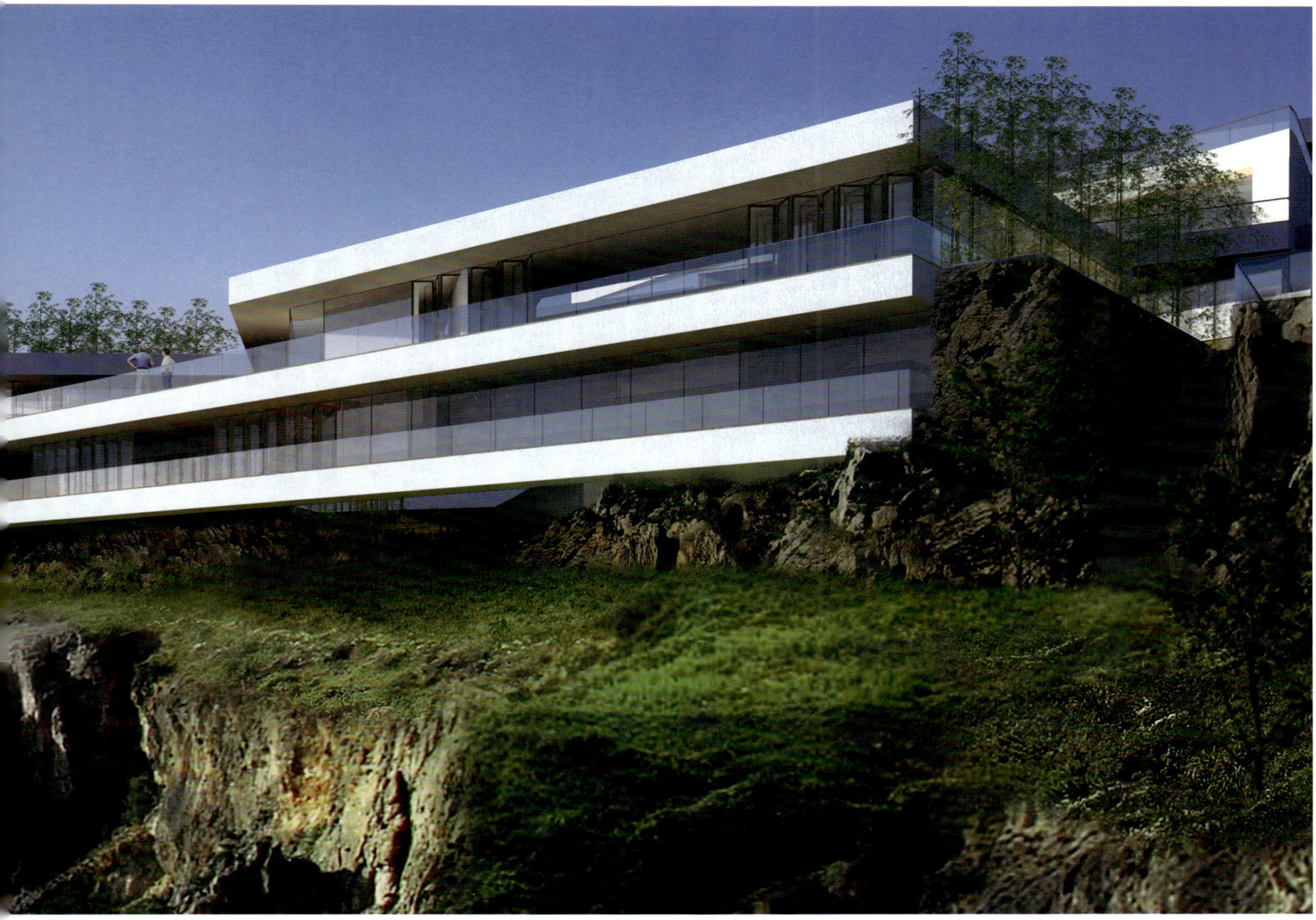

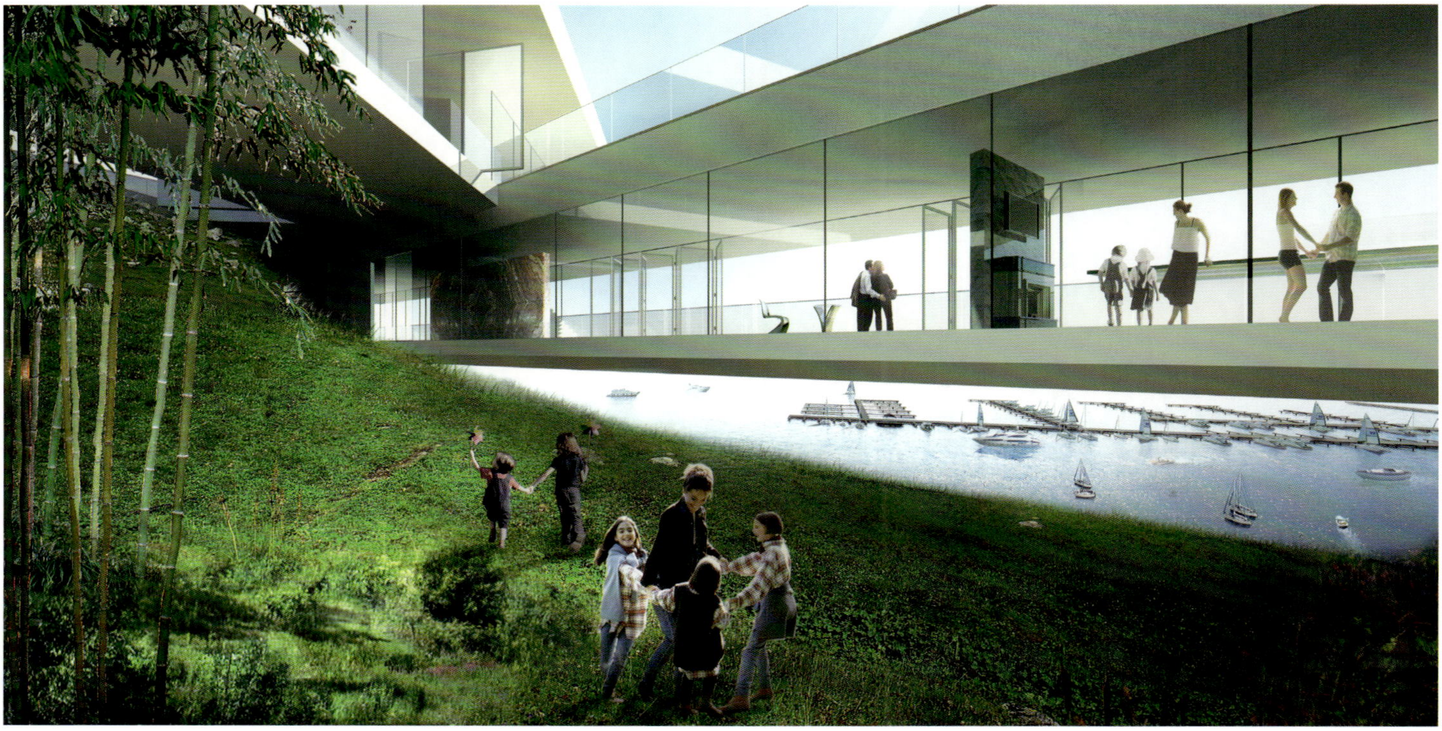

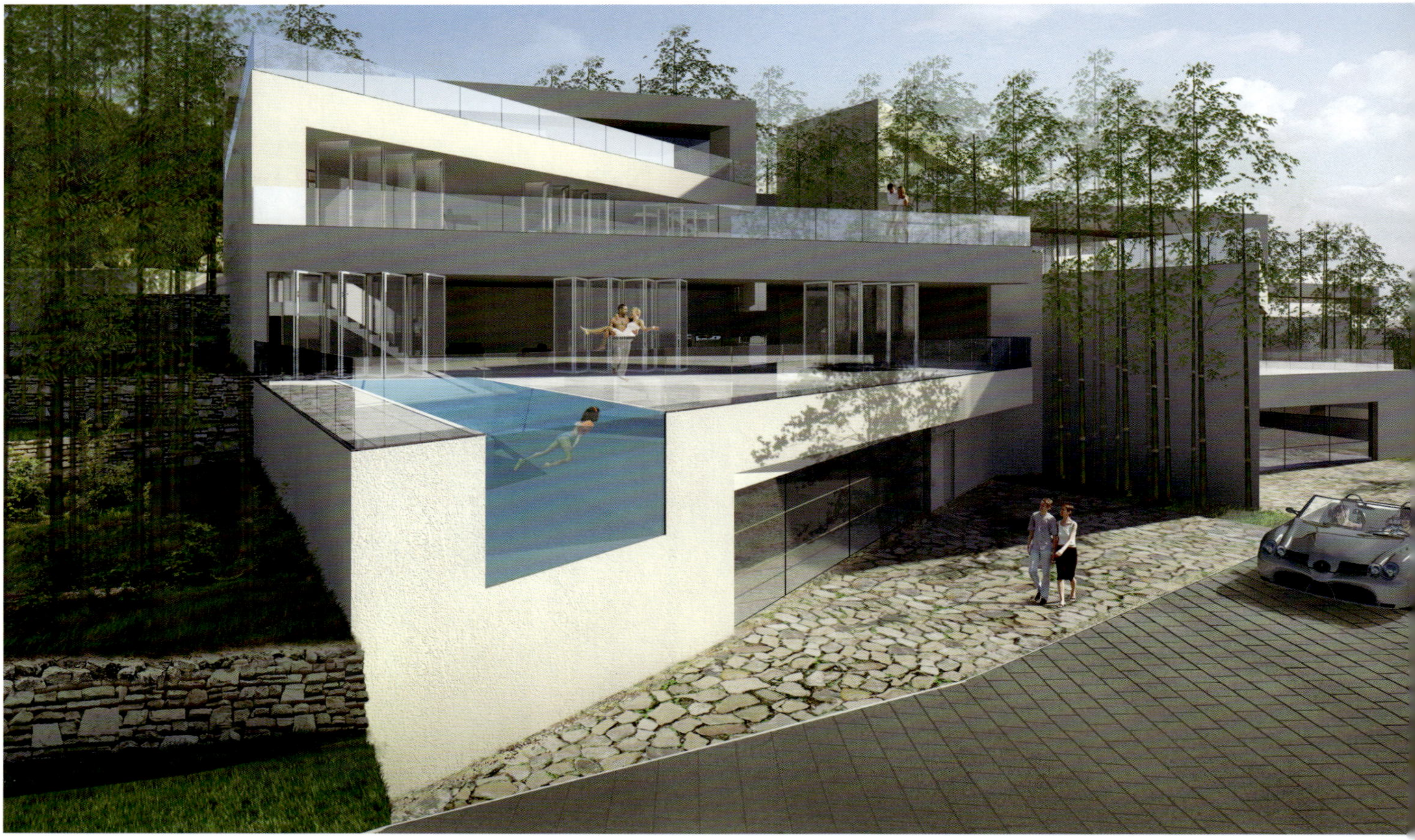

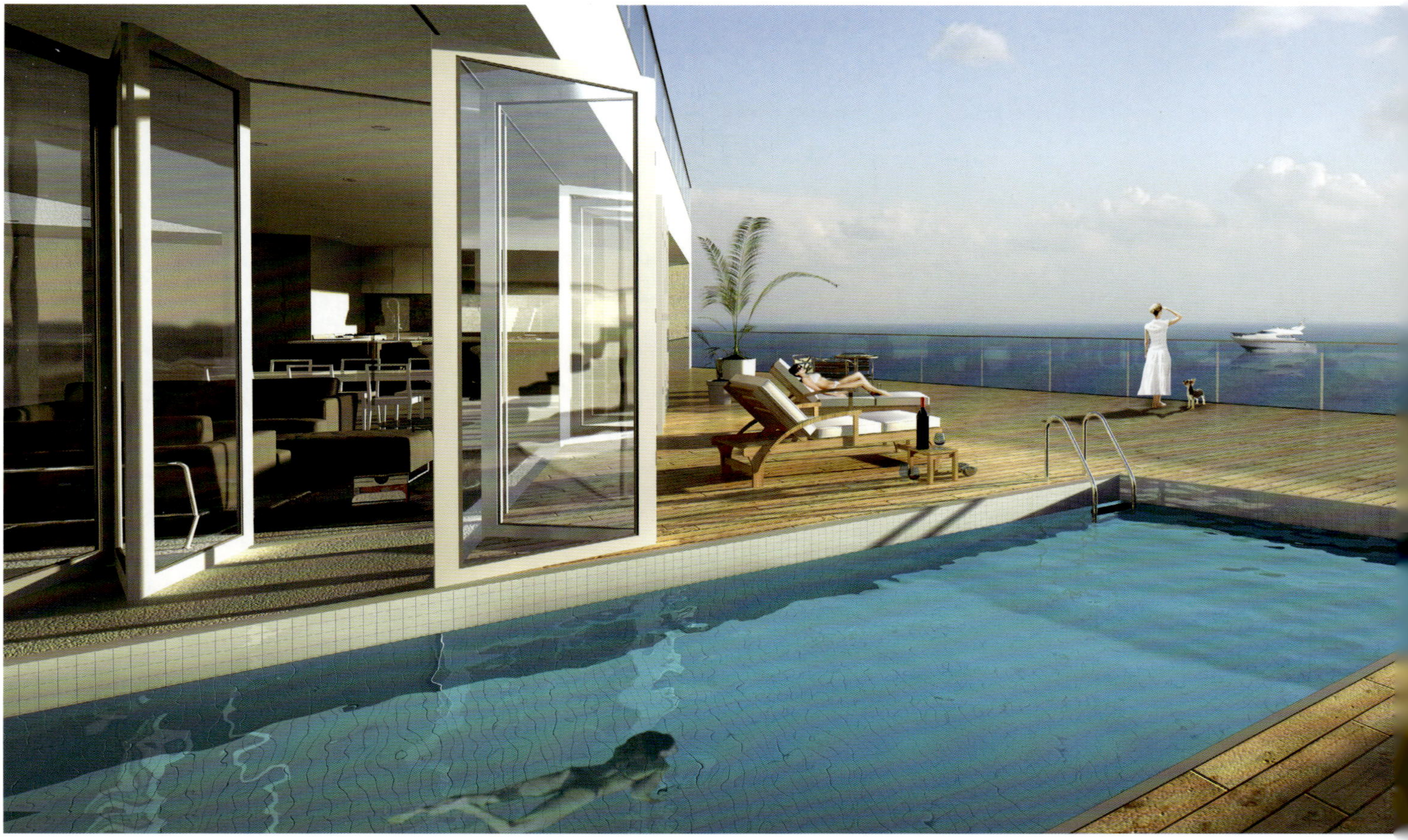

Chateau W-Peaks (2 Generation, 2 Entry House) and Villa Bar View (Entertainment House) comprise the single detached units. Casa Cristallo (Crystal Cube Tower) and the House of Hanging Garden (Terrace House) comprise the cluster housing zone as well.

Chateau W-Peaks, the cluster of private units located in Block A of the resort, comprises three floors of living space and one floor of parking. These luxury, detached villas take advantage of the site's elevation as they sit along the clifftop facing the western horizon. Due to the considerable topography, we elevated the second row of villas above the coastal properties, allowing them to operate independently. Despite their proximity, their orientation and use of solid walls at specific moments guarantees each villa's privacy. Each property utilizes green roofs to have bonus space for terraces or outdoor recreational activities.

Villa Bar View is located along the southern cliff of the seaside resort's site. This villa is designed for people who are looking for a true-entertaining house. Being designed specifically for entertainment and spectacle, this villa features a 131-foot-long (40-meter-long) bar zone containing a performance hall/gallery space, wine bar, gymnasium, infinity pool, and a sauna. This room floats above the living room's open deck, an area that has a garden, a firepit, and a trail down to the private dock. A glass folding door between the interior space and the villa's terrace adds spatial flexibility to this design. On the opposite side, the villa's ground level has five parking spaces that directly access the northern road.

Casa Cristallo comprises six, multiunit towers located just above the House of the Hanging Garden modular unit array at the top of Block B. By rotating each tower 45 degrees and placing each core in the north corner, the rooms in every unit have an unobscured sea view. Each building's core contains the stairs and elevator shafts, which are isolated from the units to minimize noise generated from the core area. The programmatic layout of each two-storey unit is optimized so the living and dining spaces have the most window room.

The House of Hanging Garden cluster is a series of modular units, rotated 45 degrees, which together form the terraced housing system. Each room facing the sea view has a 21 x 21 foot (6.4 x 6.4 meter) modular terrace from the unit below, potentially doubling the total space of each unit. Whether the clients choose to landscape their terrace as a private garden or open deck, they still have access to their own private outside ocean view.

The public boutique hotel—hosting 111 suite rooms and 29 terraced suites—is located in the easternmost part of the resort in Block C. The hotel's terraced suites are sited in the same series as the cluster housing zone, effectively preserving, and maximizing, the views to the ocean. Due to its membership spa, fitness center, outdoor pool, golf practice range, and multipurpose convention facility (specialized for weddings), the hotel operates as the social and recreational epicenter of the resort.

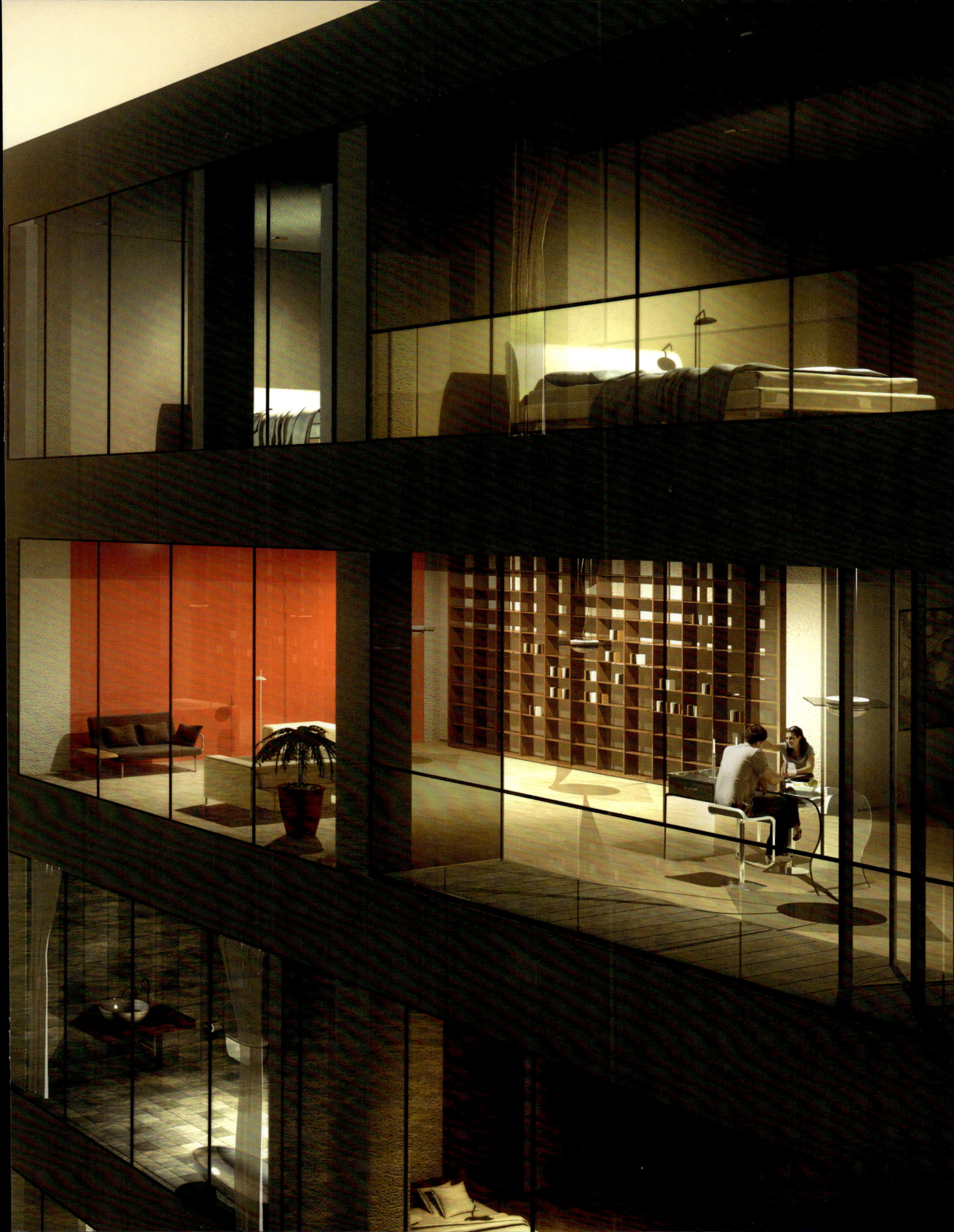

Taesun Hong, *Quantum Leap III* (1984), charcoal

A design that incorporates a **void**, i.e., a vacuum or negative space, can be expressed visually or audibly. Expression created by a void relies completely on a previous relationship to an existing positive mass.

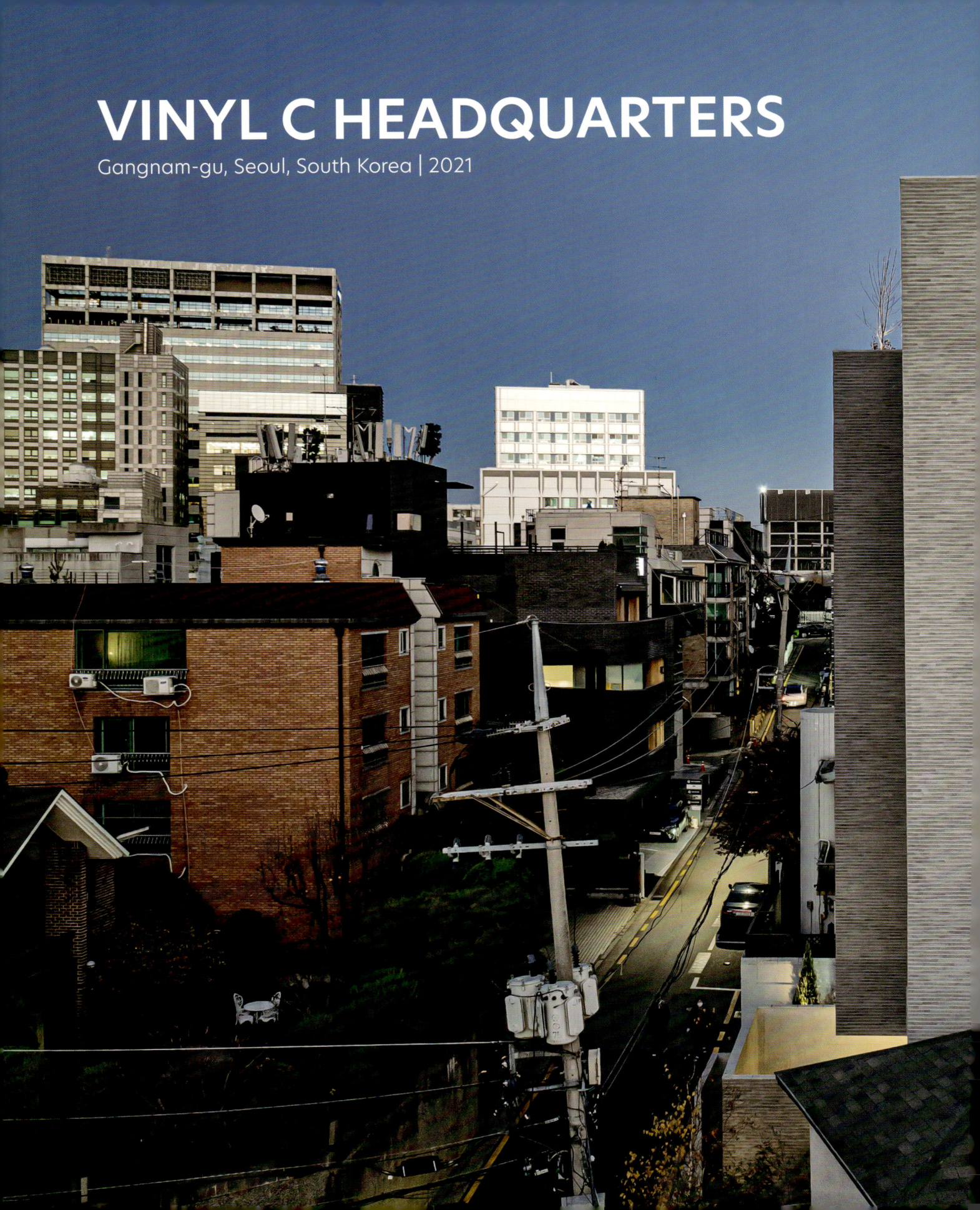

# VINYL C HEADQUARTERS

Gangnam-gu, Seoul, South Korea | 2021

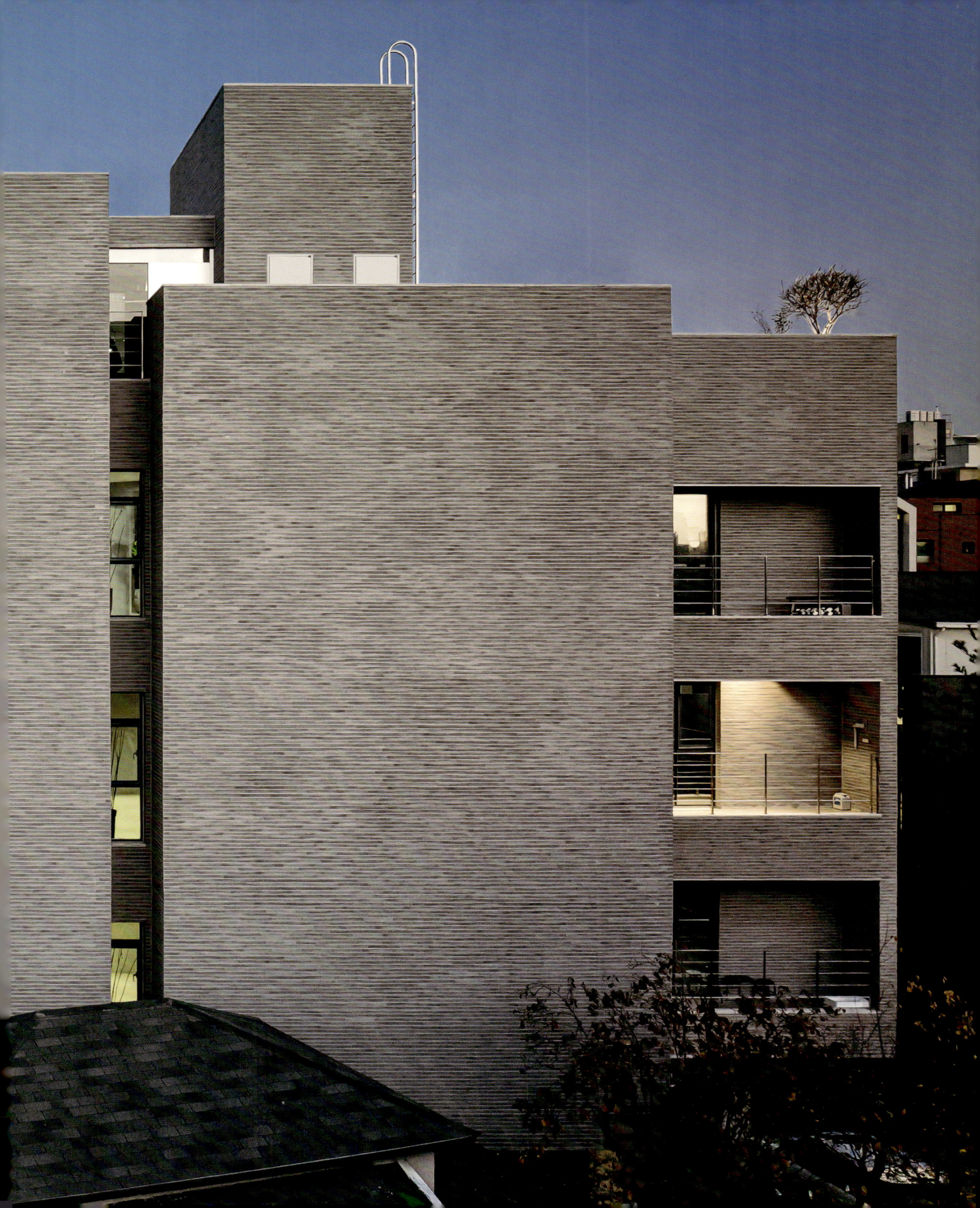

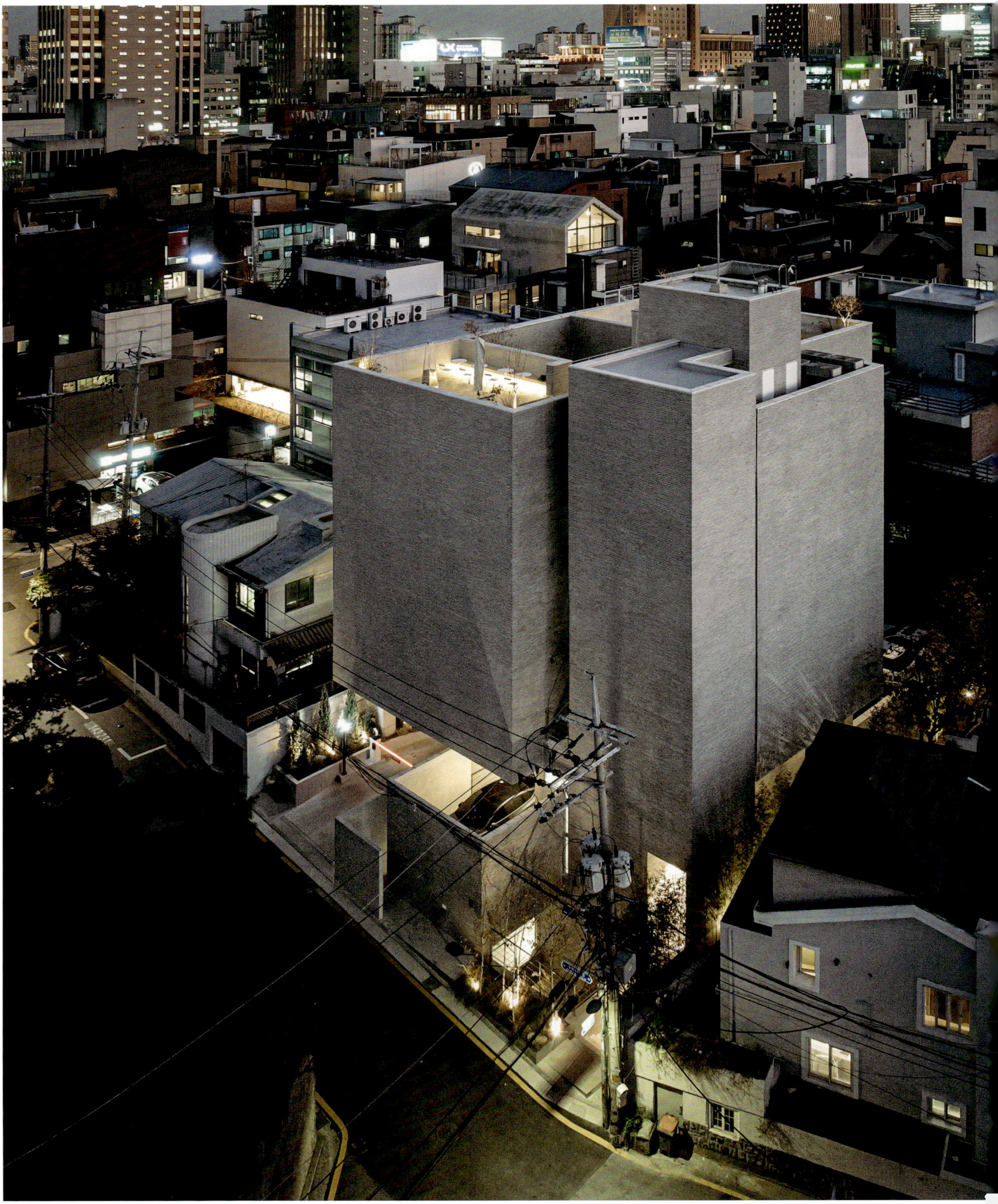

VINYL C HEADQUARTERS   135

Vinyl C is one of the frontier UI/UX design companies in the country, based in Gangnam-gu, Seoul, Korea. As per the client's vision, to provide a simple but explicit headquarters solution for users, we engaged their needs and their minimum requirements for their office program.

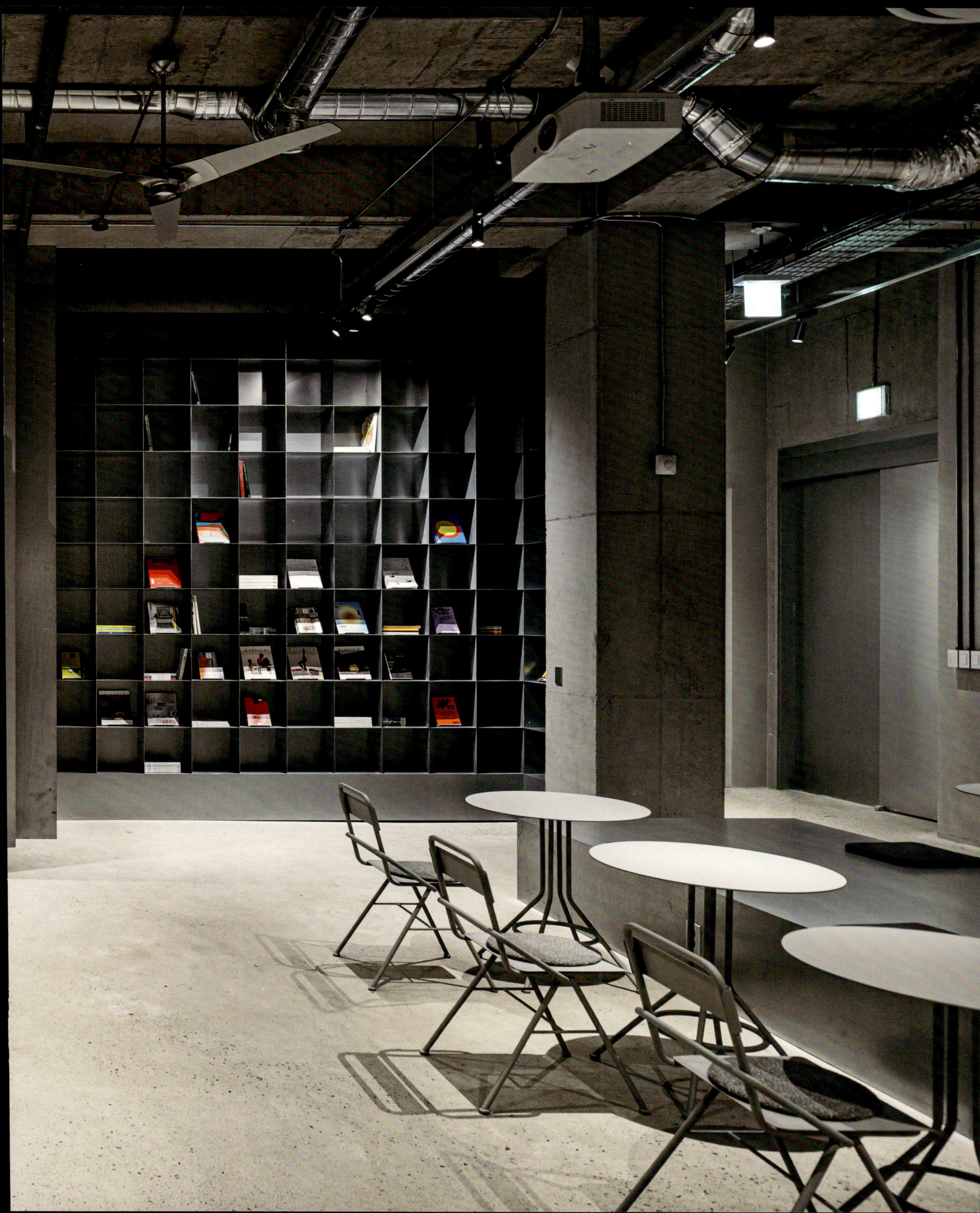

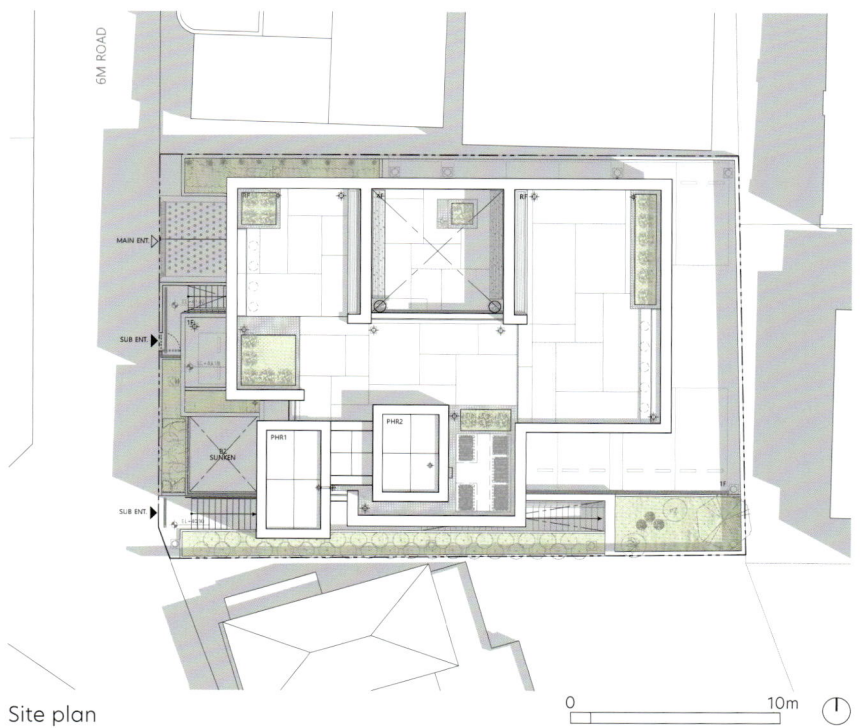

Site plan

138  VOID

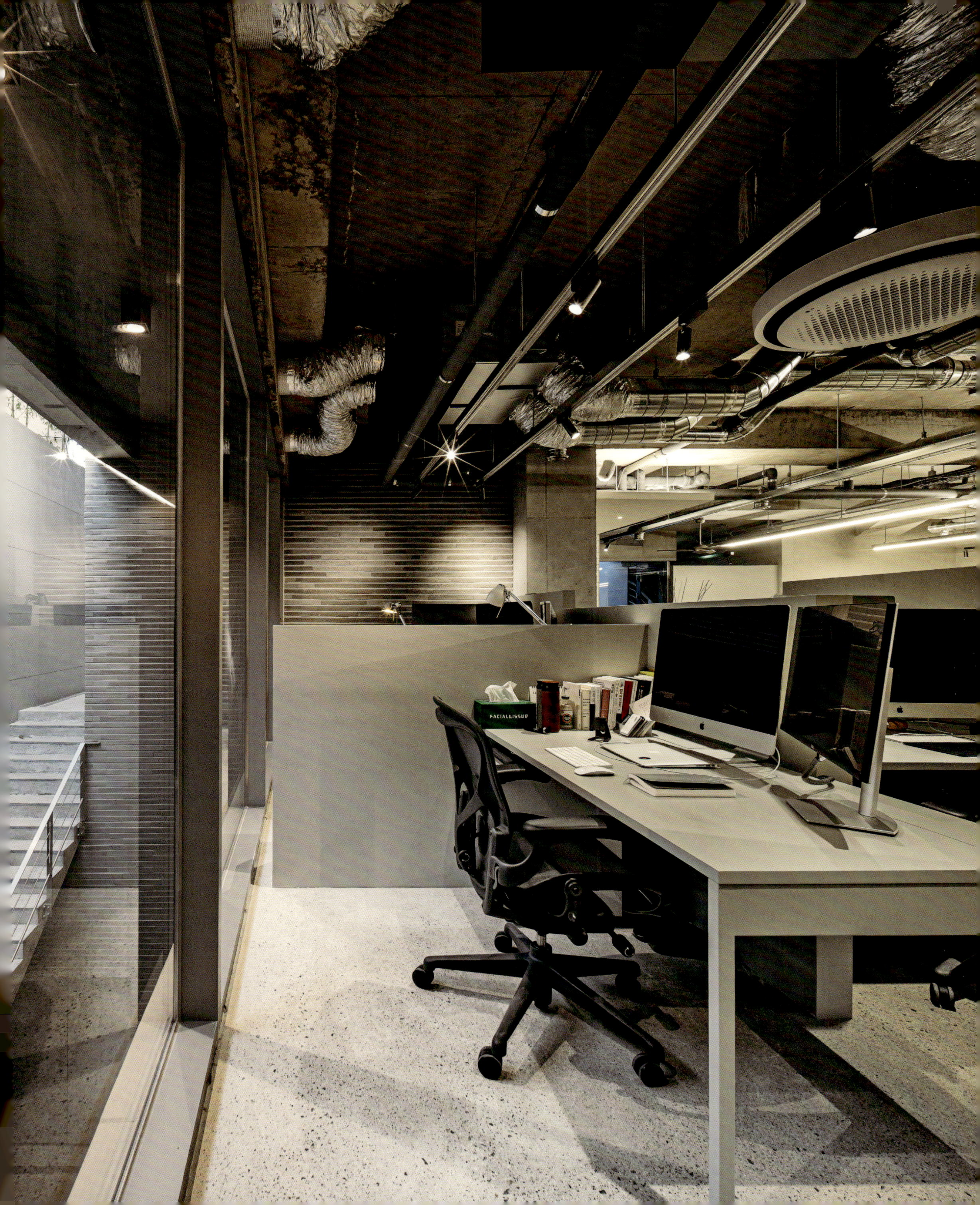

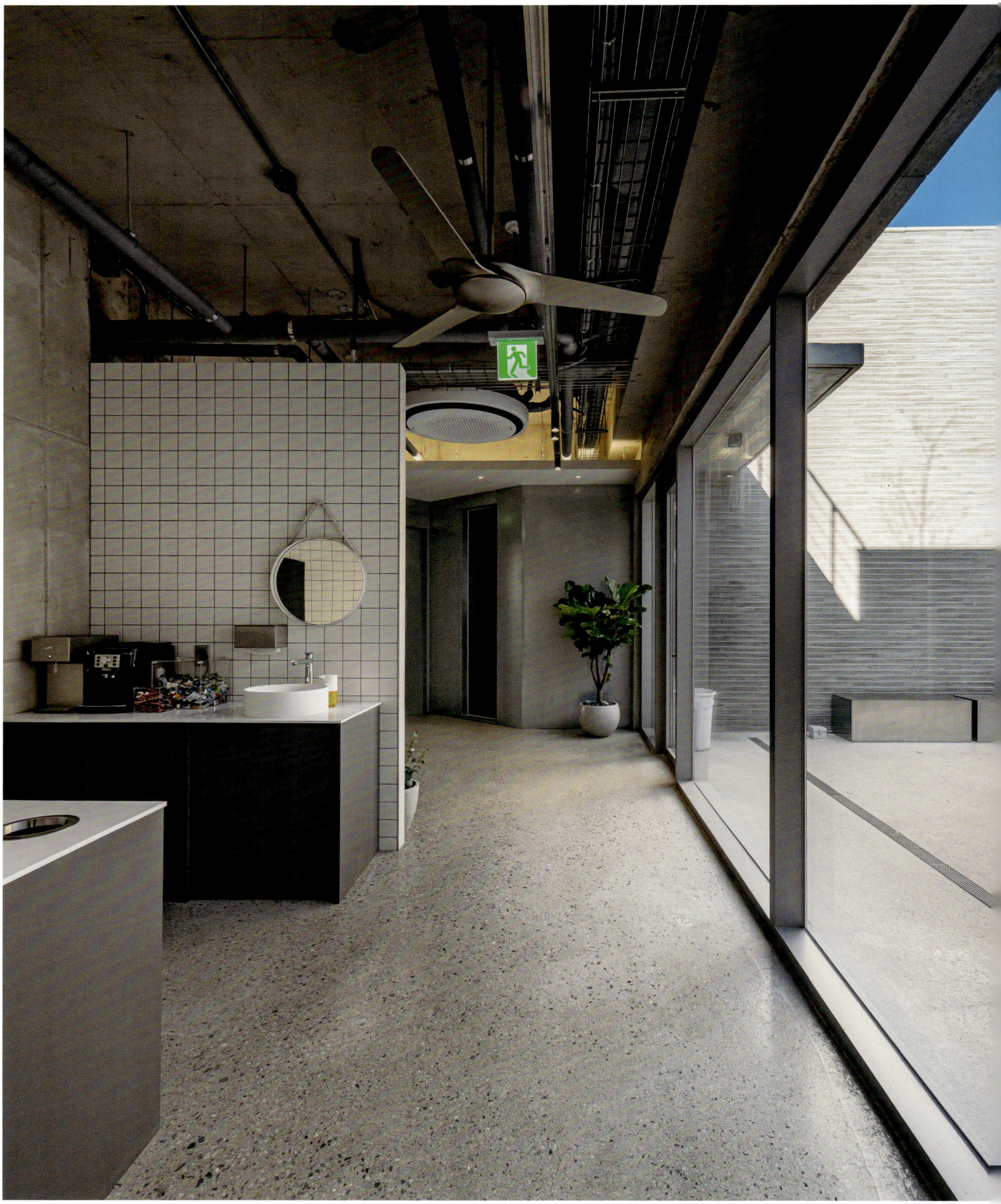

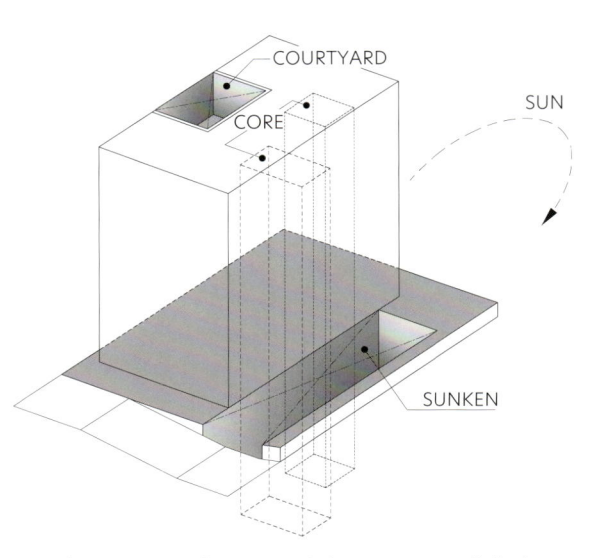

A sunken courtyard program brings more sunlight into the building

VINYL C HEADQUARTERS **141**

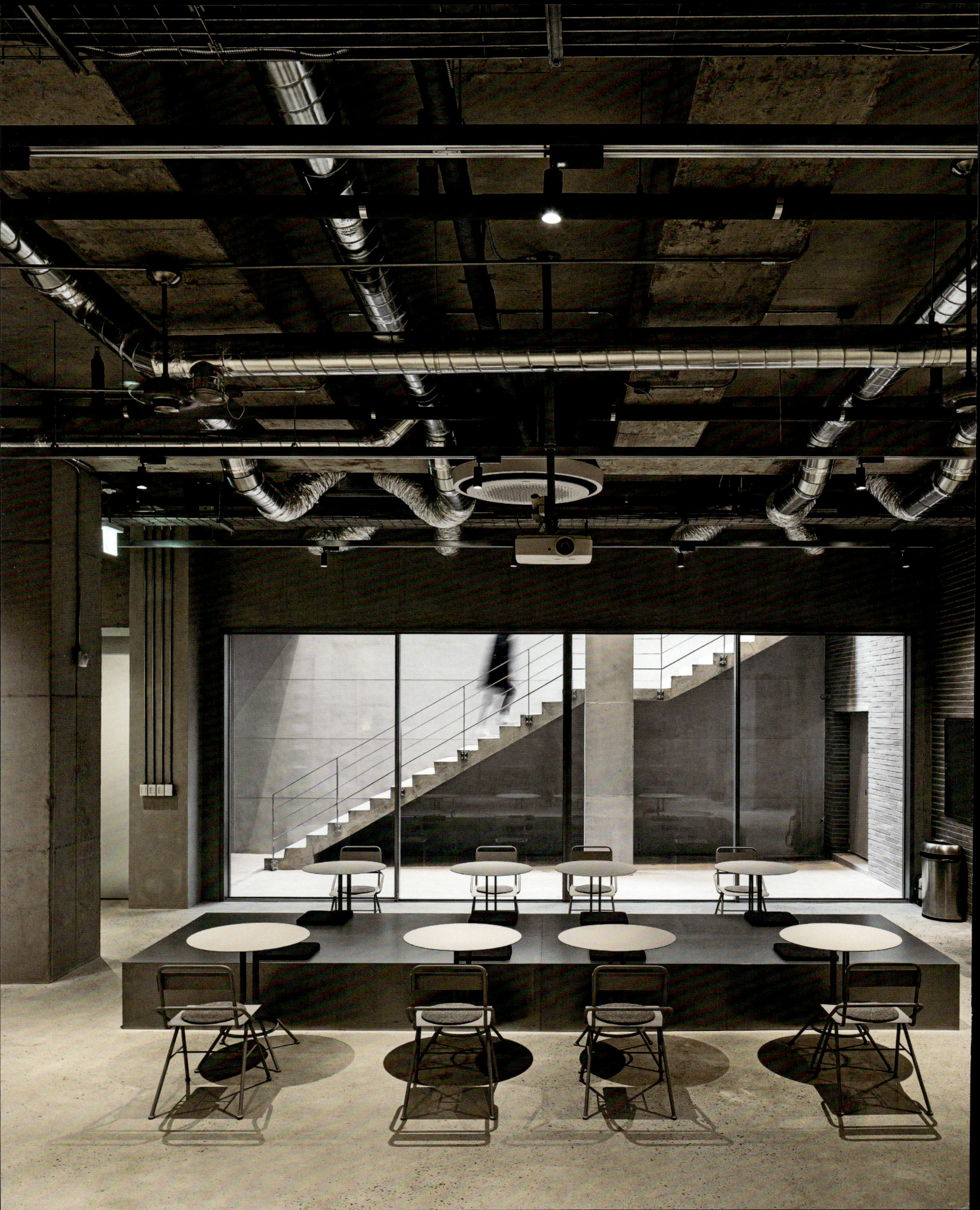

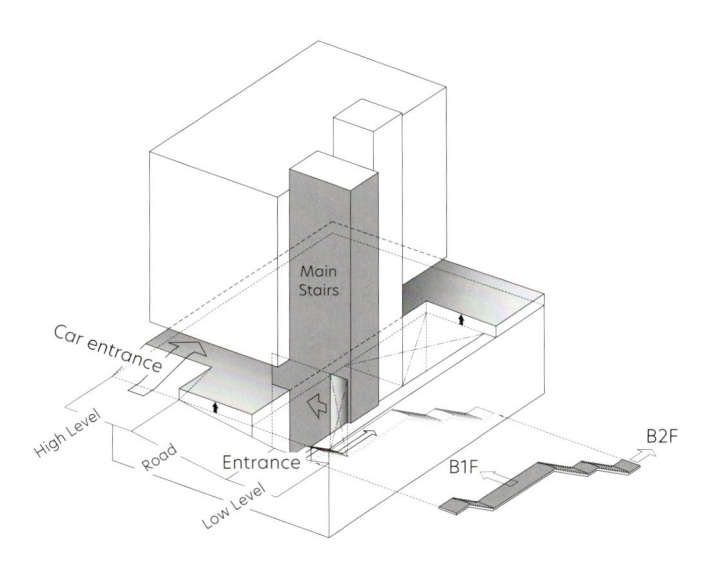

Lifting up the ground level to create higher basement spaces, including entrances to cars, pedestrian, and basement levels.

VINYL C HEADQUARTERS  **143**

Like all other projects in Gangnam-gu, we had to satisfy the minimum requirements for the required parking and maximum allowable building areas. We decided to locate all the required parking on the ground level. We provided 120 working stations for the employees on the second, third, and B1 levels and make the fourth (top floor) for conference use and for the CEO's office. We also located the conference hall and gym on the B2 level.

Our aim for this project was to achieve a pure monolithic figure from the road and accentuate the entrance by a protruding rectangular entry mass, thus hiding the parking on the ground level. A sunken courtyard is also located on the B2 level, which is connected by the outdoor stair, bringing in daylight and fresh air intake. White brick tiles that match the reinforced concrete are used to clad the building and to unify the building masses.

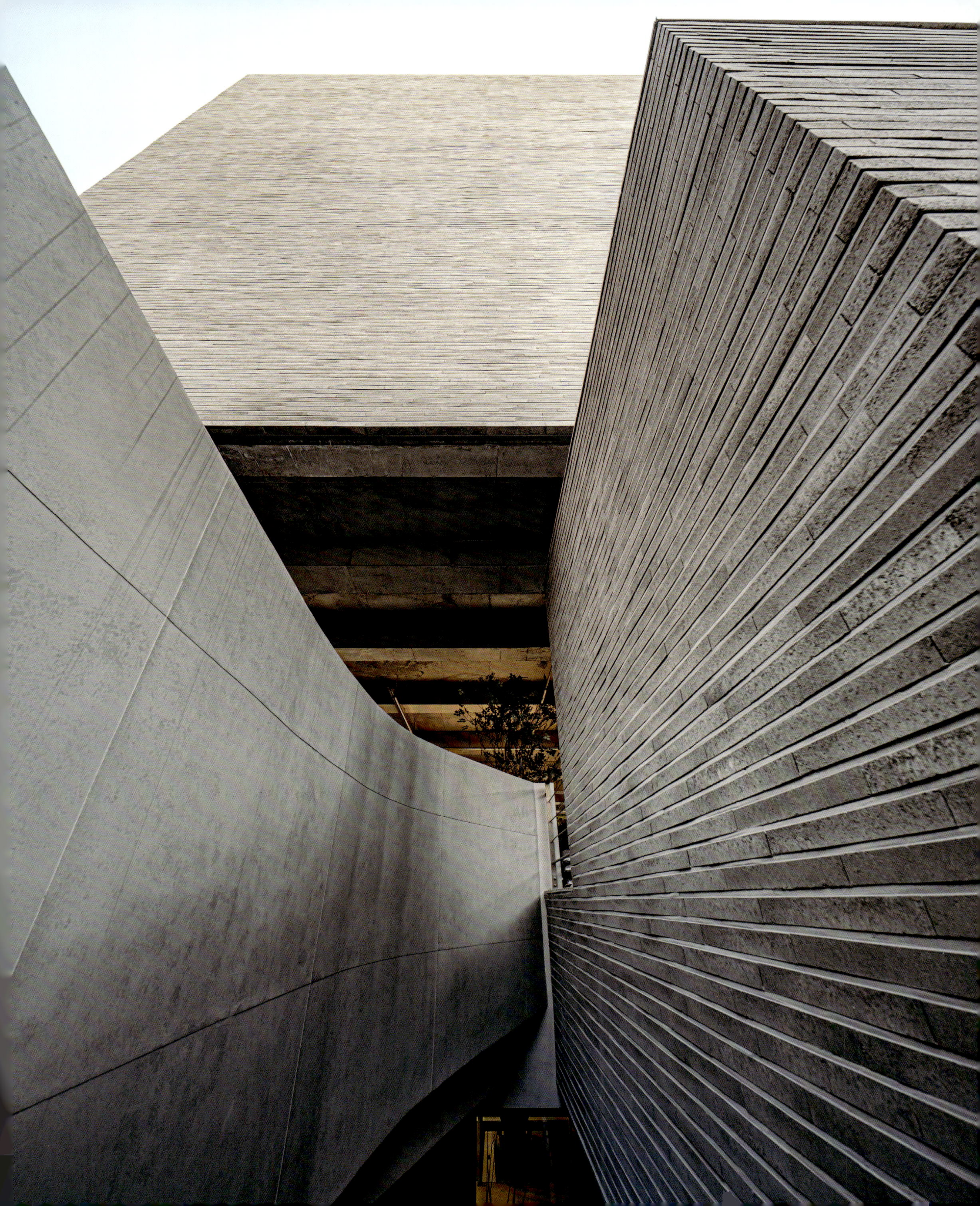

# INJE RESIDENCE

Inje-gun, Gangwon-do, South Korea | 2014

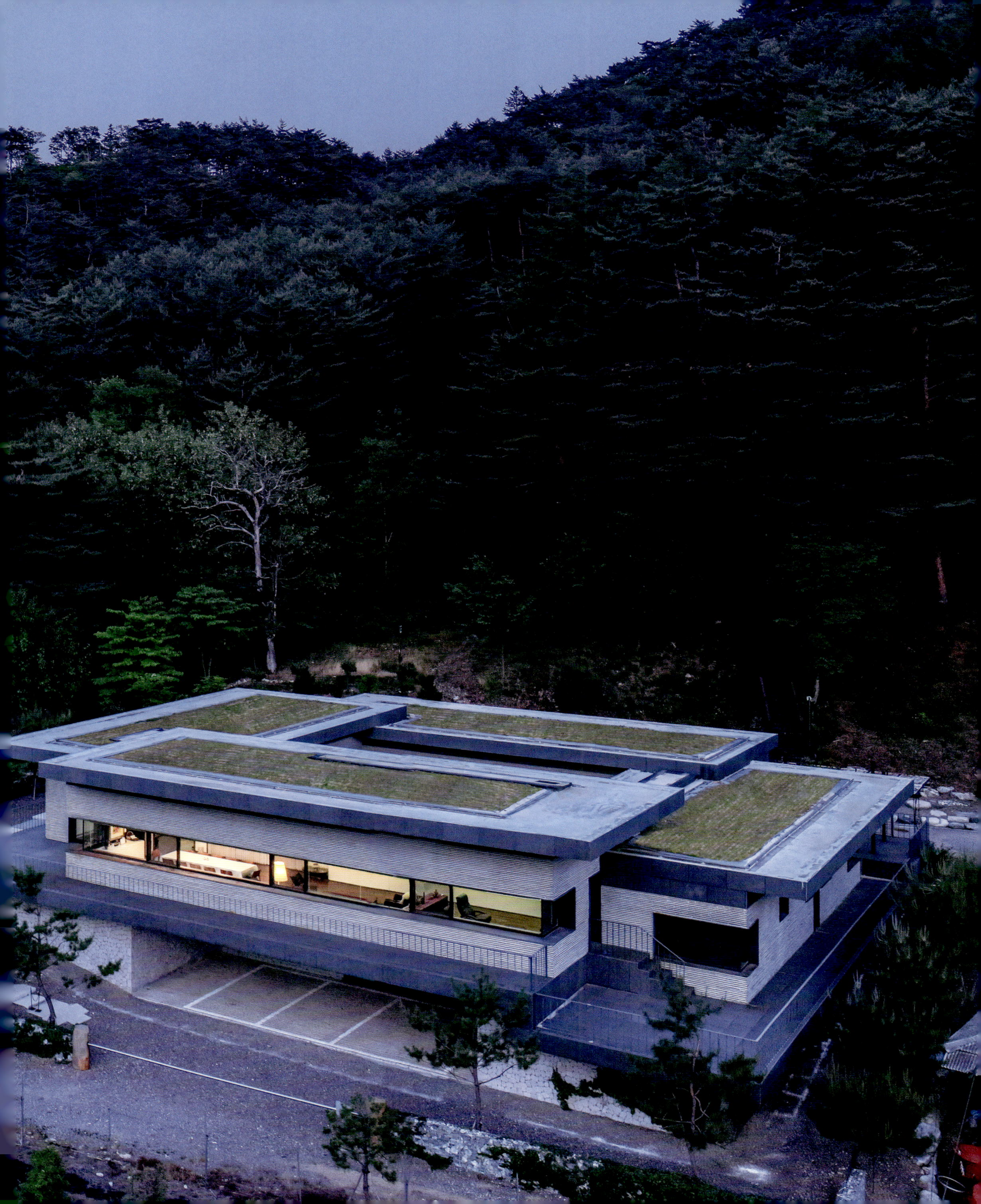

Located in the foothills of Seoraksan Mountain, one of the main challenges of designing this villa was successfully responding to the context of its site. Due to the extreme topography of this hillside location, the solution was to adapt an ancient Korean traditional interior courtyard design, anchoring the focus of the home inward. Then, four volumes are extruded from the hill's surface and given the programs: master suite wing, living and dining wing, kitchen and amenity wing, and guest and gallery wing. The inward view of this courtyard not only accommodates various family activities, but also provides a mountain view through the center opening of the courtyard, which enhances a quiet and contemplative aura and avoids the unpleasant view of a neighborhood ancestral tomb and the adjacent hut.

Site condition

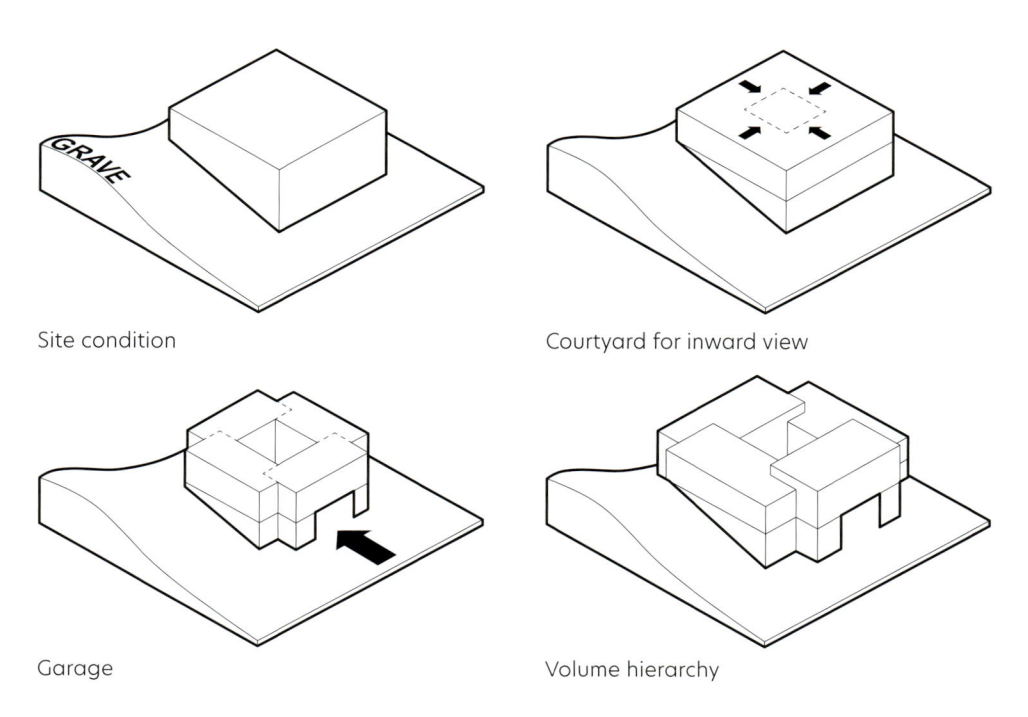

Courtyard for inward view

Garage

Volume hierarchy

150   VOID

The four volumes are positioned at different levels in response to the sloped site, arranged in a volumetric hierarchy. Each of these volumes, or wings, hold various residential spaces that face the courtyard and bleed into each other, with the corridors acting as mediators between the outdoor and indoor spaces. As these four integrated volumes are positioned at different heights, various levels of openings are subsequently deployed. For this construction, continuous wall girders with horizontal beams are used to open walls. The larger windows reduce the separation between zones, admit more natural light, and allow more flexibility in the entrance spaces. Each opening frames out a new boundary and adds new relationships to the outdoor space.

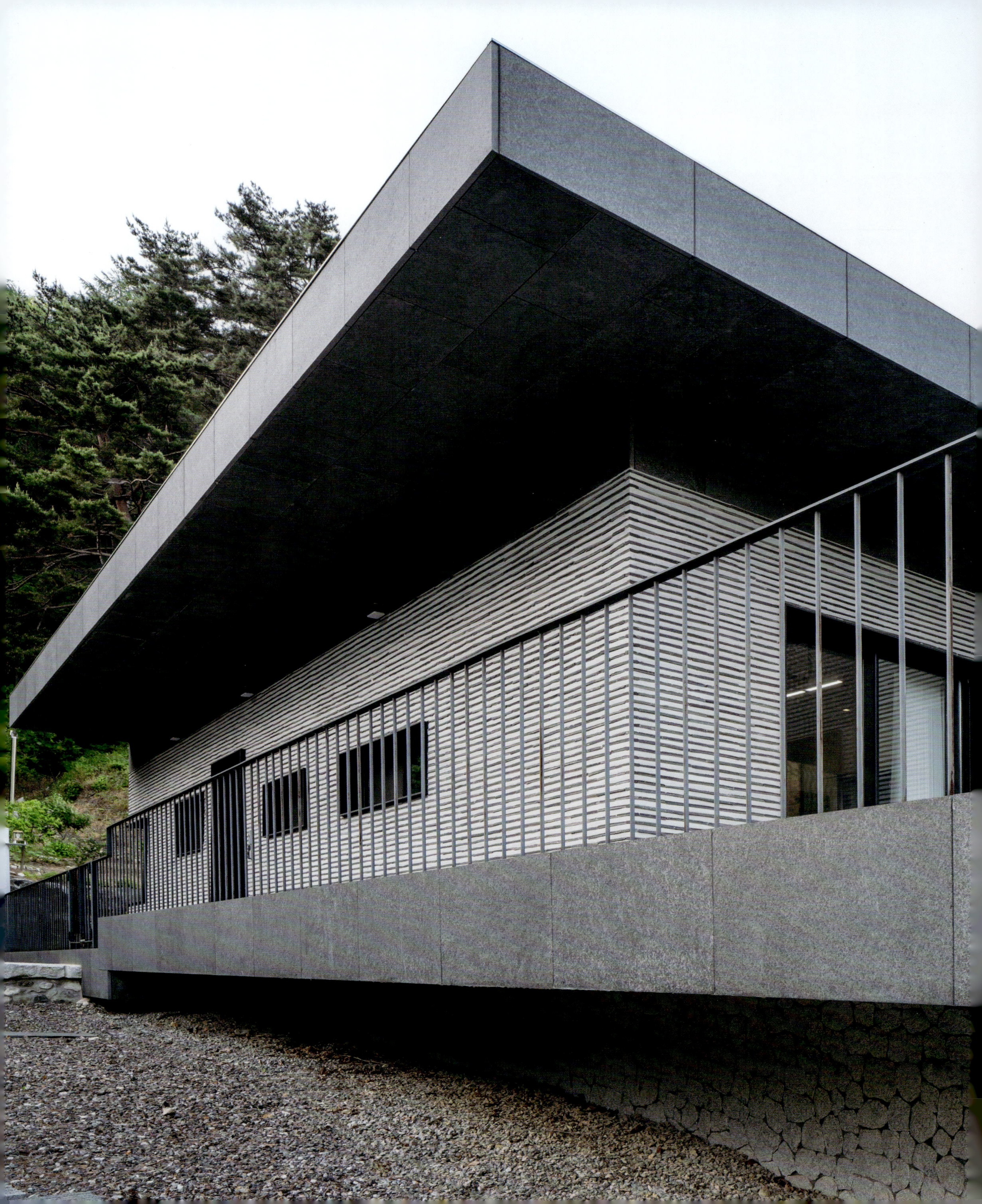

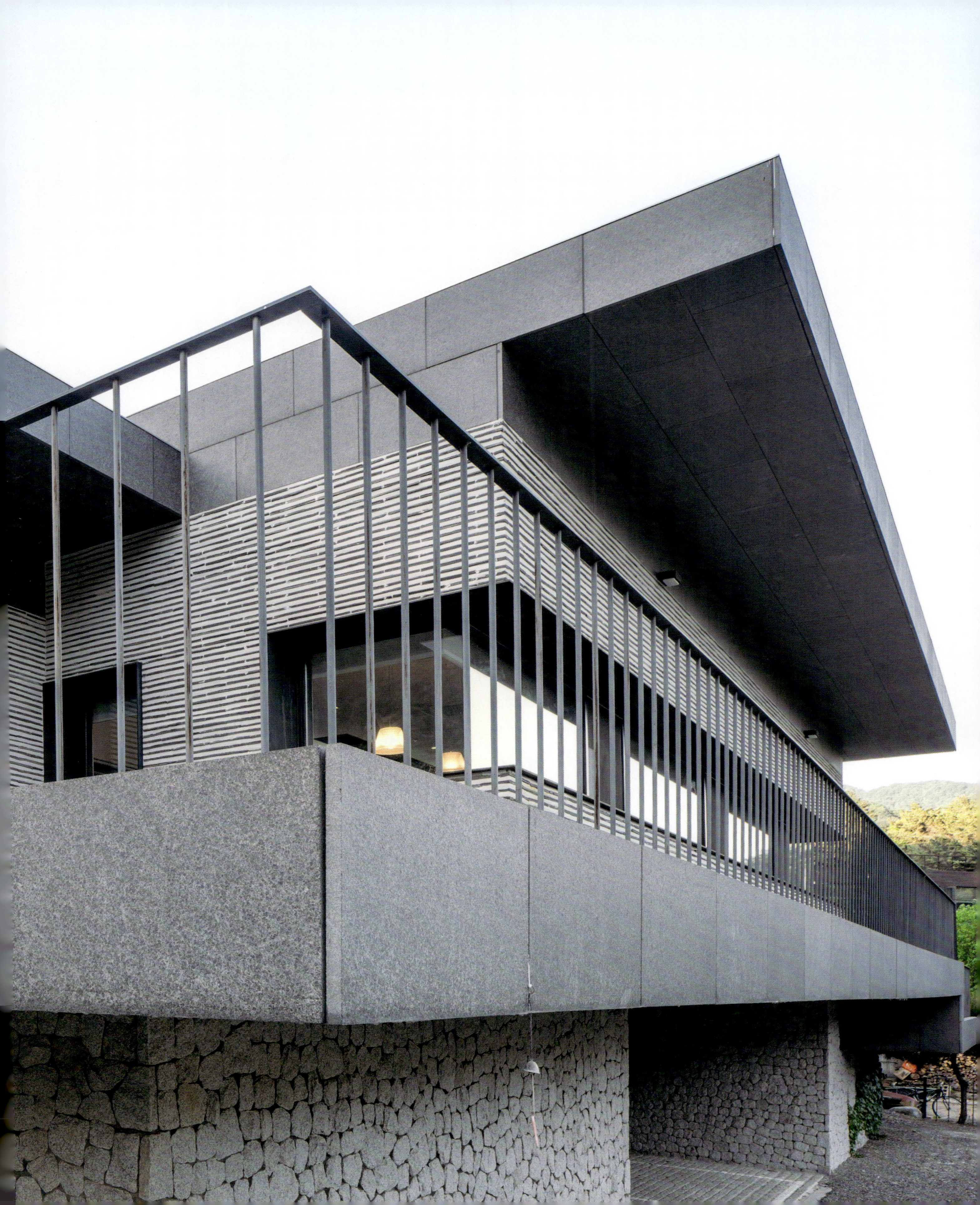

As with the Korean courtyard style, the use of the local and natural materials was cost-effective. The Korean giwa (a form of ceramic tile used in the old traditional roof construction) was applied in the wall construction and kneaded with a specially colored mortar to emphasize the horizontality of the façade along with the overhanging local granite stone roofs. While conceptually traditional, this project integrates various modern design practices like sustainable and passive design. Instead of using oil or LPG-generated heating, more efficient geothermal systems were implemented by digging down 505 feet (154 meters) into the ground. A grass rooftop was adapted as well to act as insulation and help negate heat build-up, substantially reducing the cost of energy and maintenance.

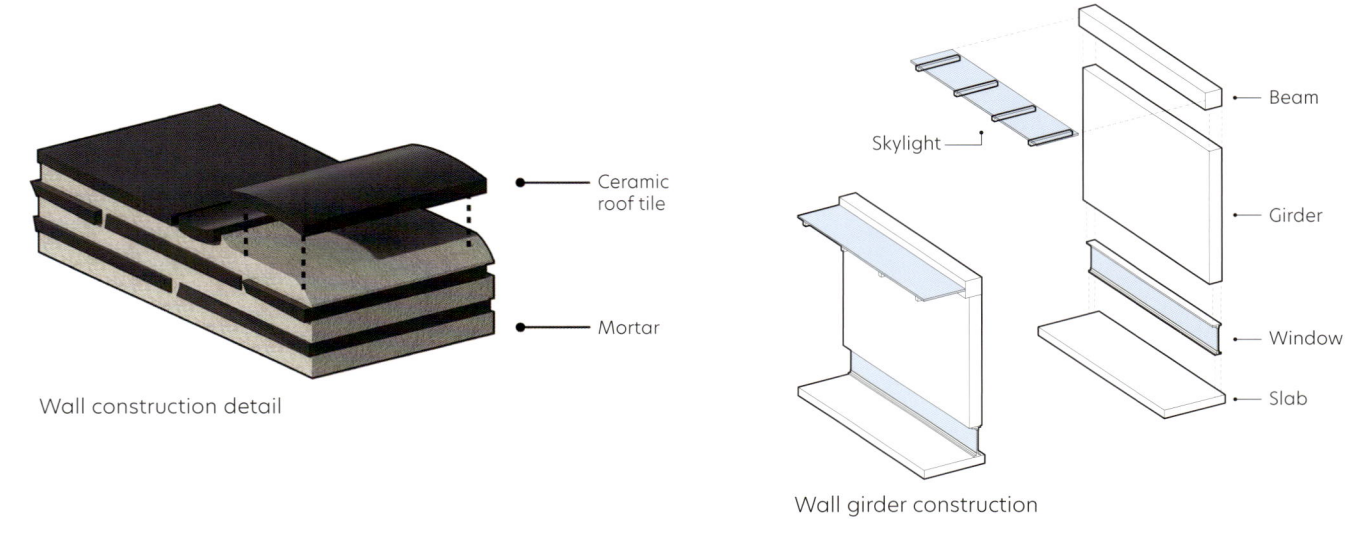

**Wall construction detail**
- Ceramic roof tile
- Mortar

**Wall girder construction**
- Skylight
- Beam
- Girder
- Window
- Slab

INJE RESIDENCE

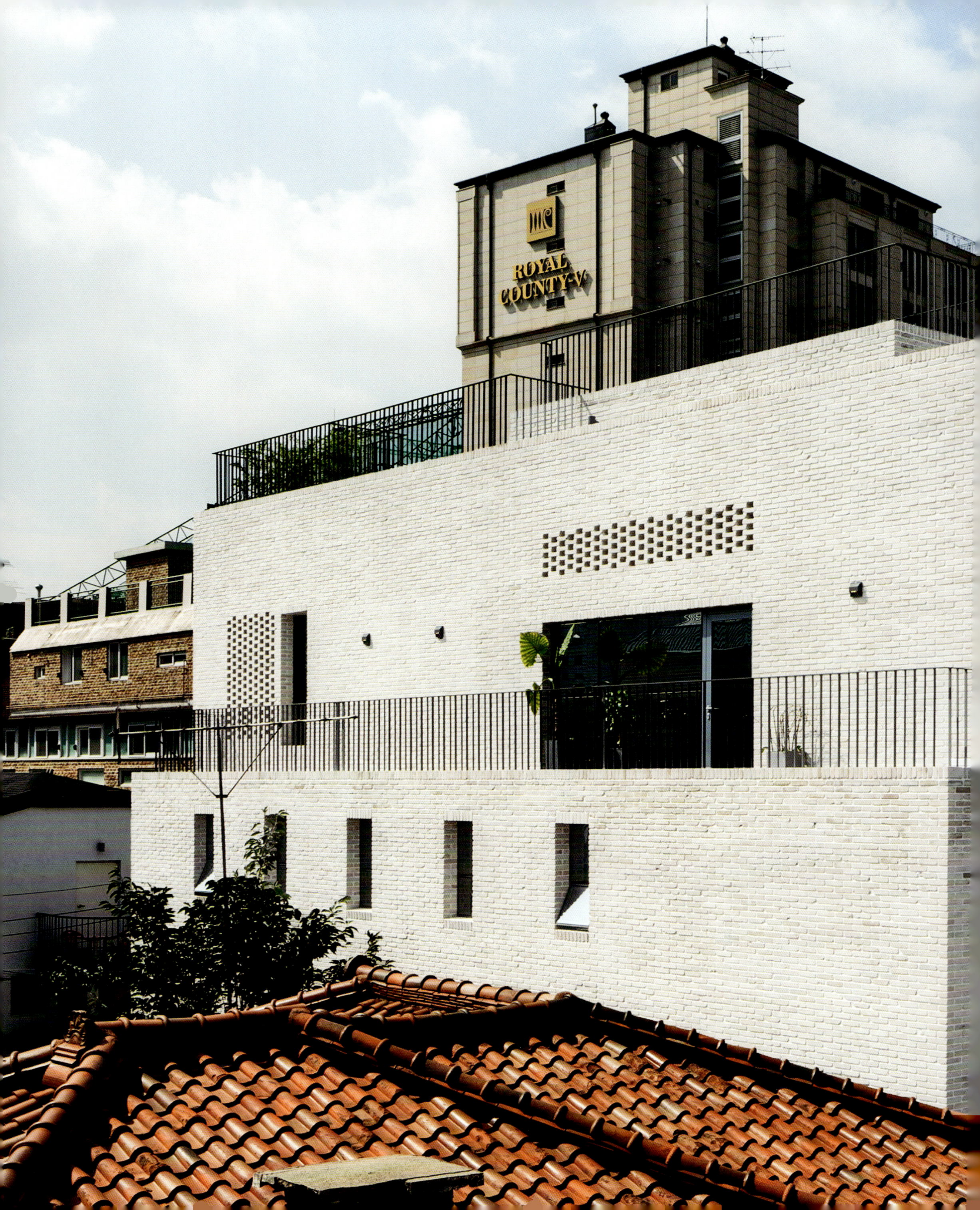
ROYAL
COUNTY-V

# YKH ASSOCIATES HEADQUARTERS

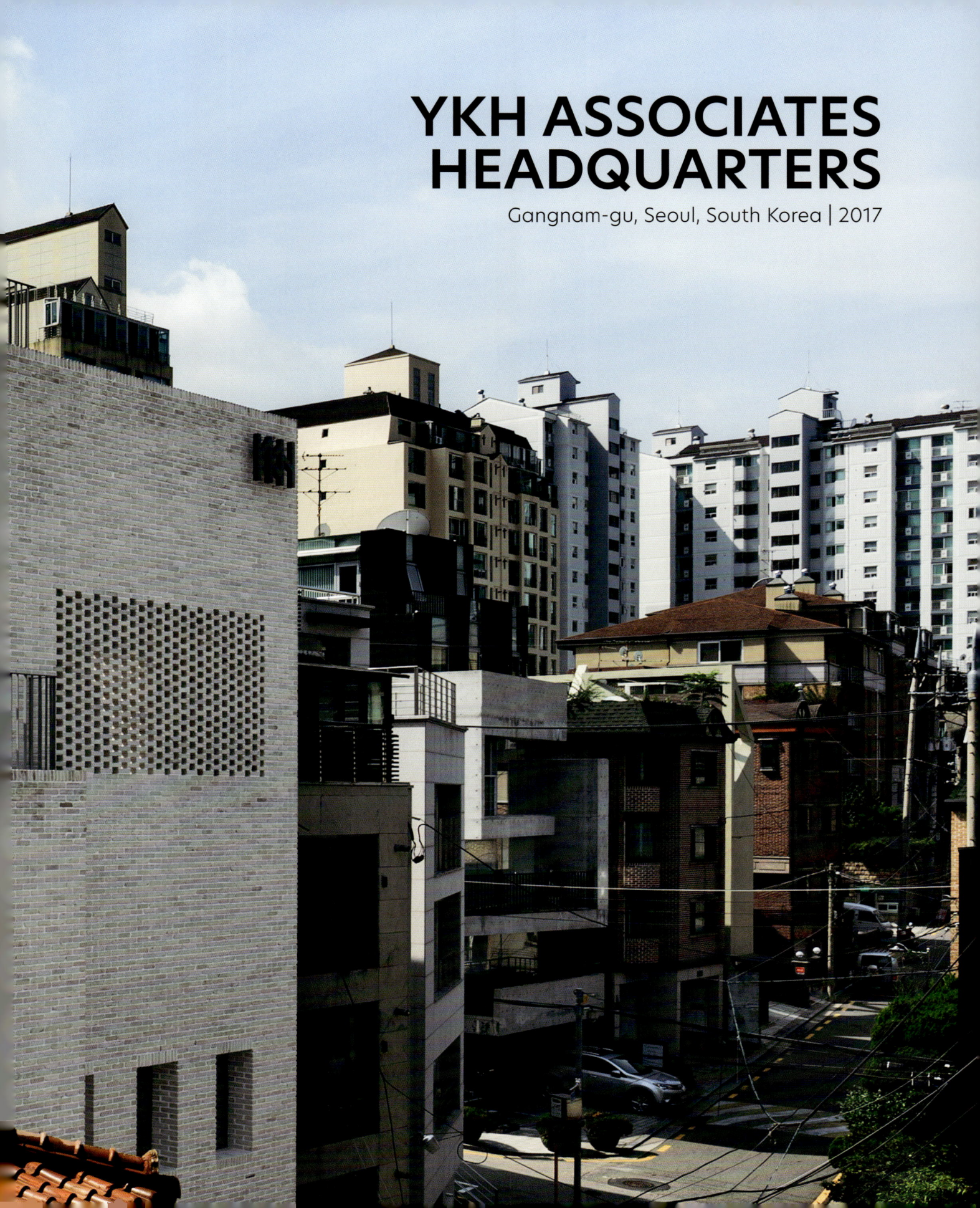

Gangnam-gu, Seoul, South Korea | 2017

Due to the growing size and portfolio of our firm, we began construction on a new headquarters in the Gangnam-gu district of Seoul. While the addition of space was necessary, the opportunity to showcase our firm's core design principles through our own building was palpable.

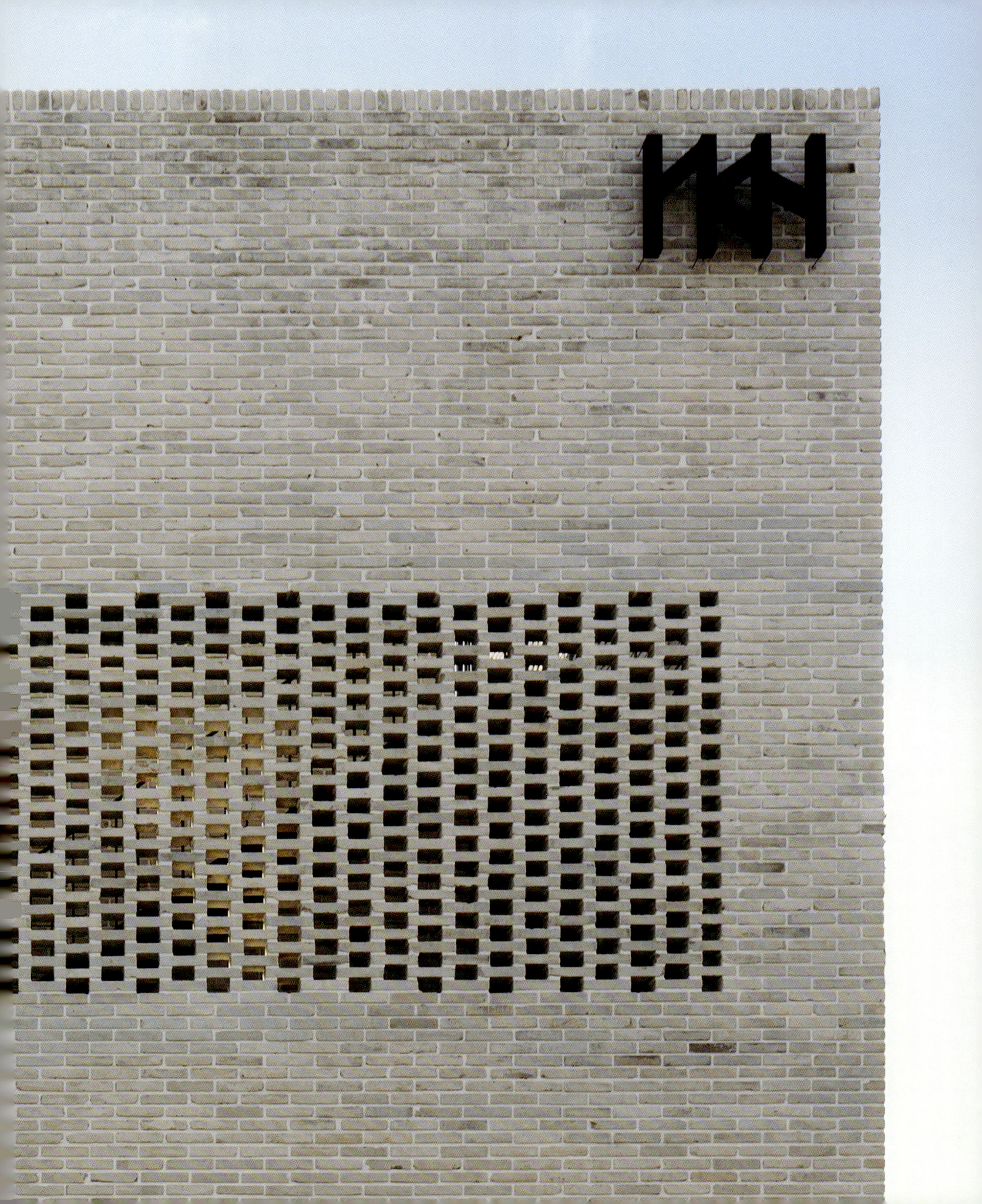

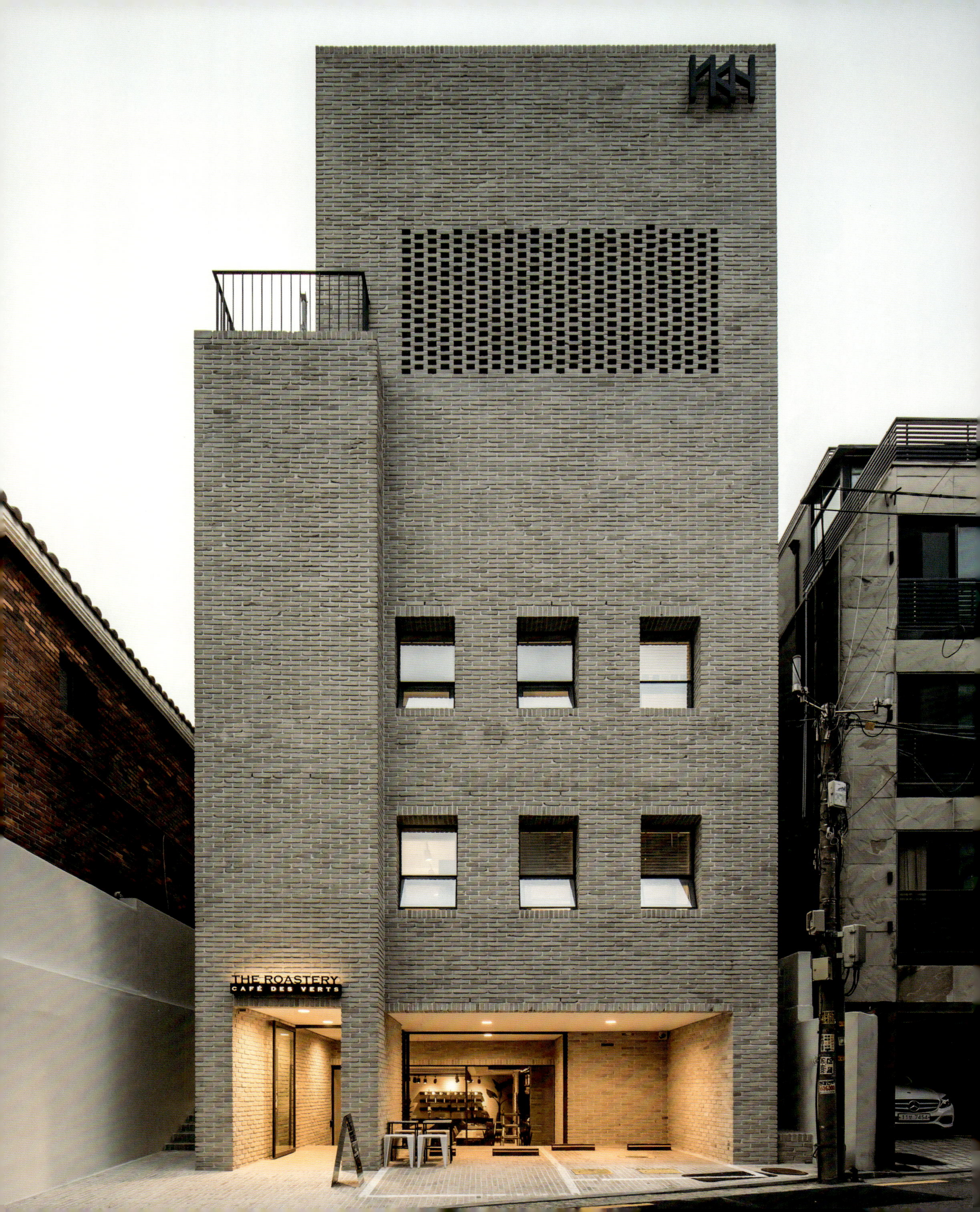
THE ROASTERY
CAFÉ DES VERTS

Like most urban design projects, spatial and economic optimization were paramount. Utilizing antique white brick for the façade allowed the project to reflect its material context while allowing its bold form to emerge from its environment. The resulting project is one that has a presence of maturity due to the age of its brick, yet also appears new because of the brick's modern formation. Additionally, the inclusion of solid-void brick formations allowed us to develop moments of overlap between the interior and exterior spaces.

While we chose the materials to express the timelessness of the project, the program and form were sculpted by the adaptations of restrictive urban zoning. This meant opening the space to provide the flow of required sunlight, pushing back the sides of the building for mandatory parking spaces, and dropping the project down to fit the height limit. This also included implementing a partially exterior wraparound staircase that would serve as a fire escape as well as a means by which our staff circulate through the building.

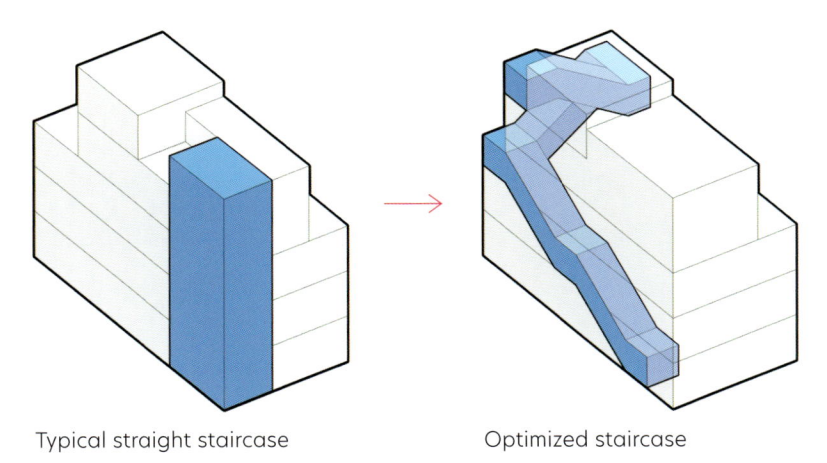

Typical straight staircase     Optimized staircase

**162**  VOID

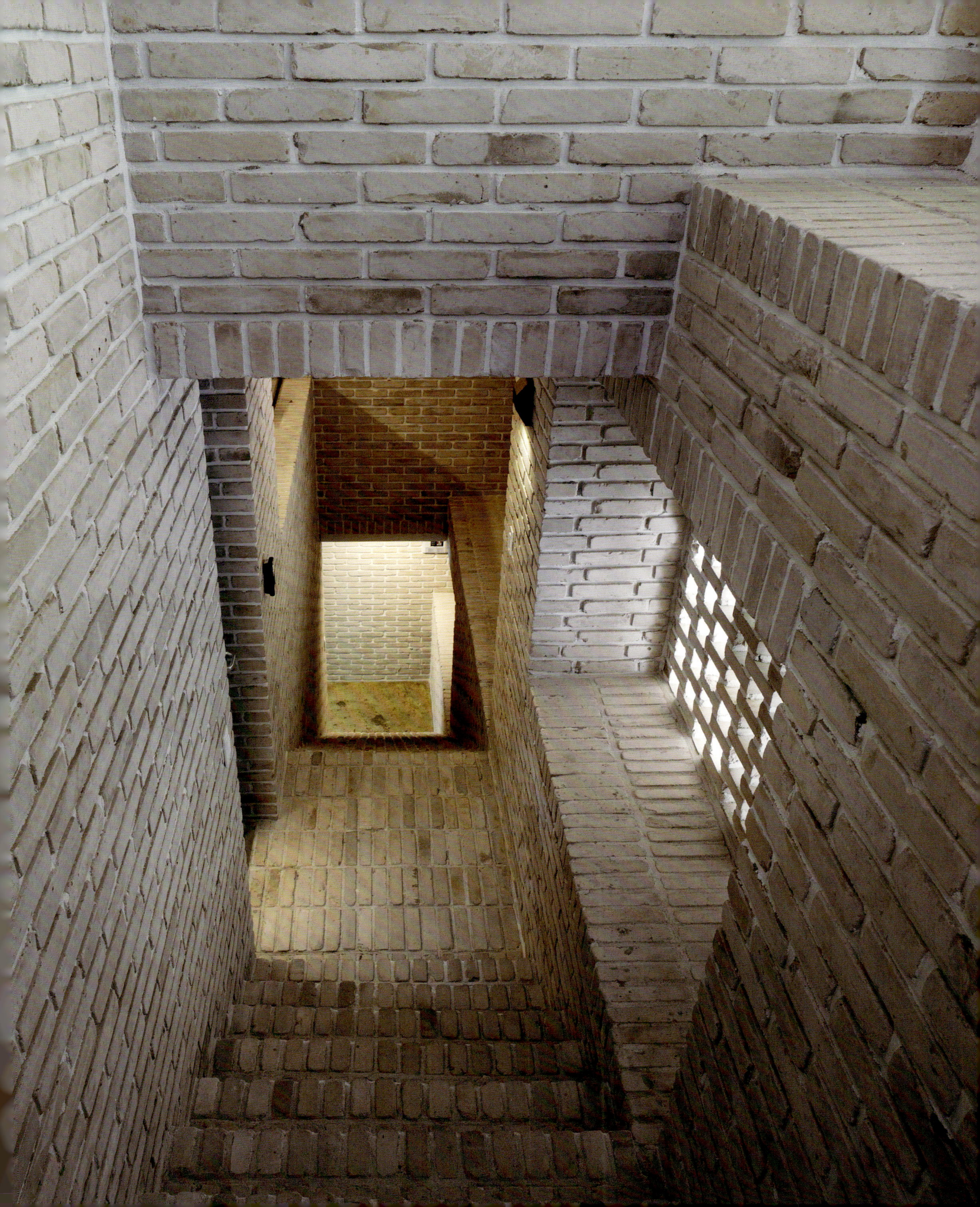

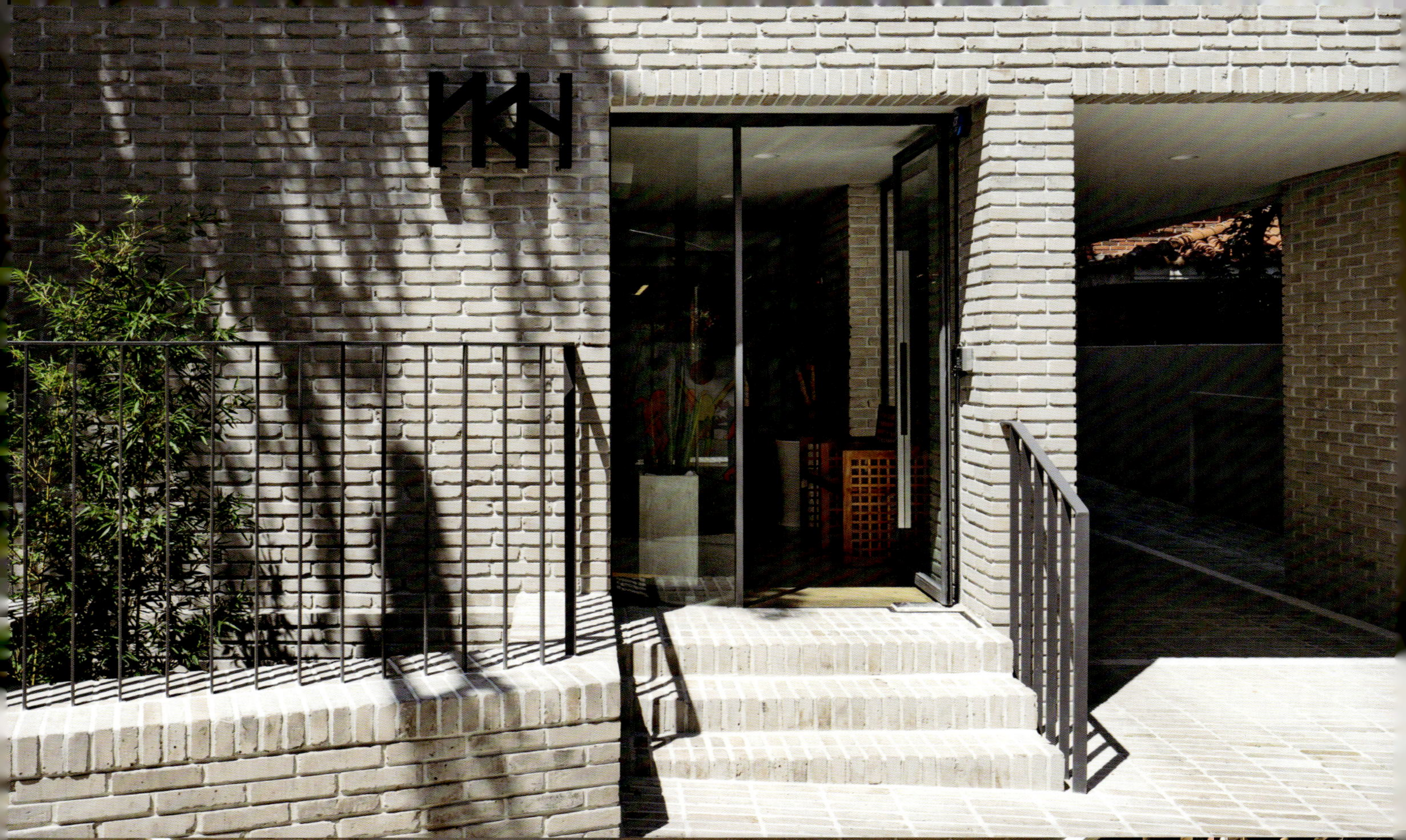

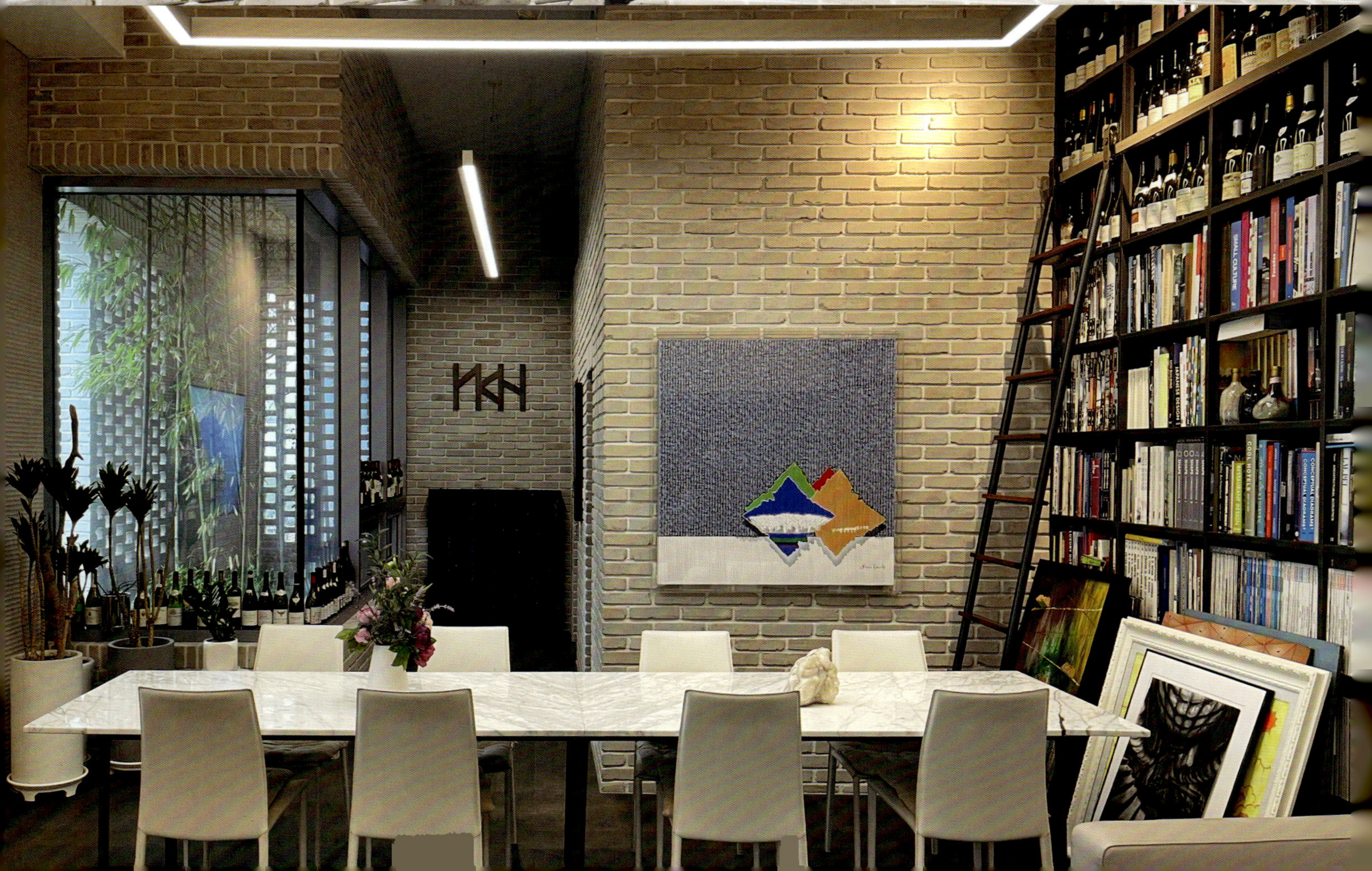

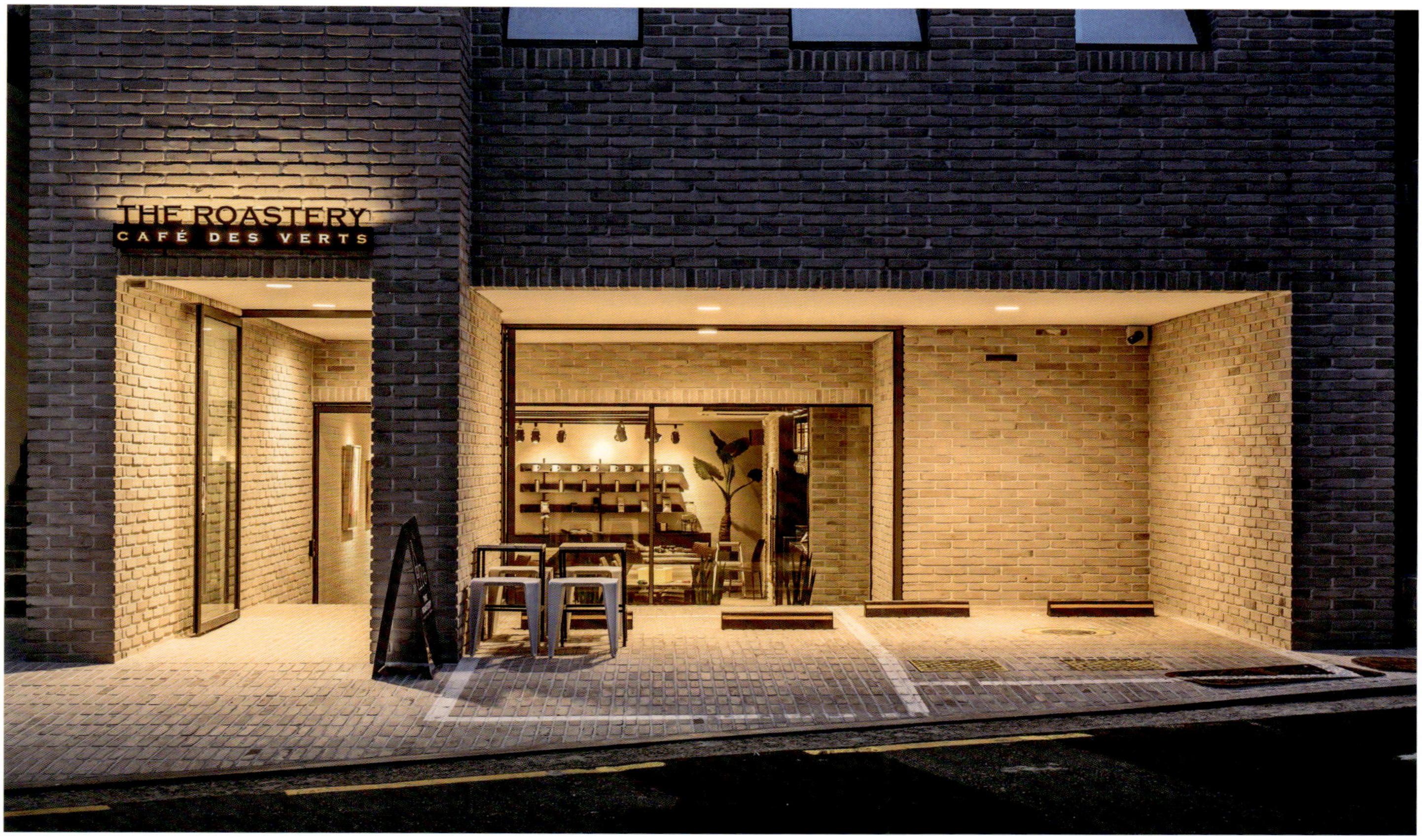
THE ROASTERY
CAFÉ DES VERTS

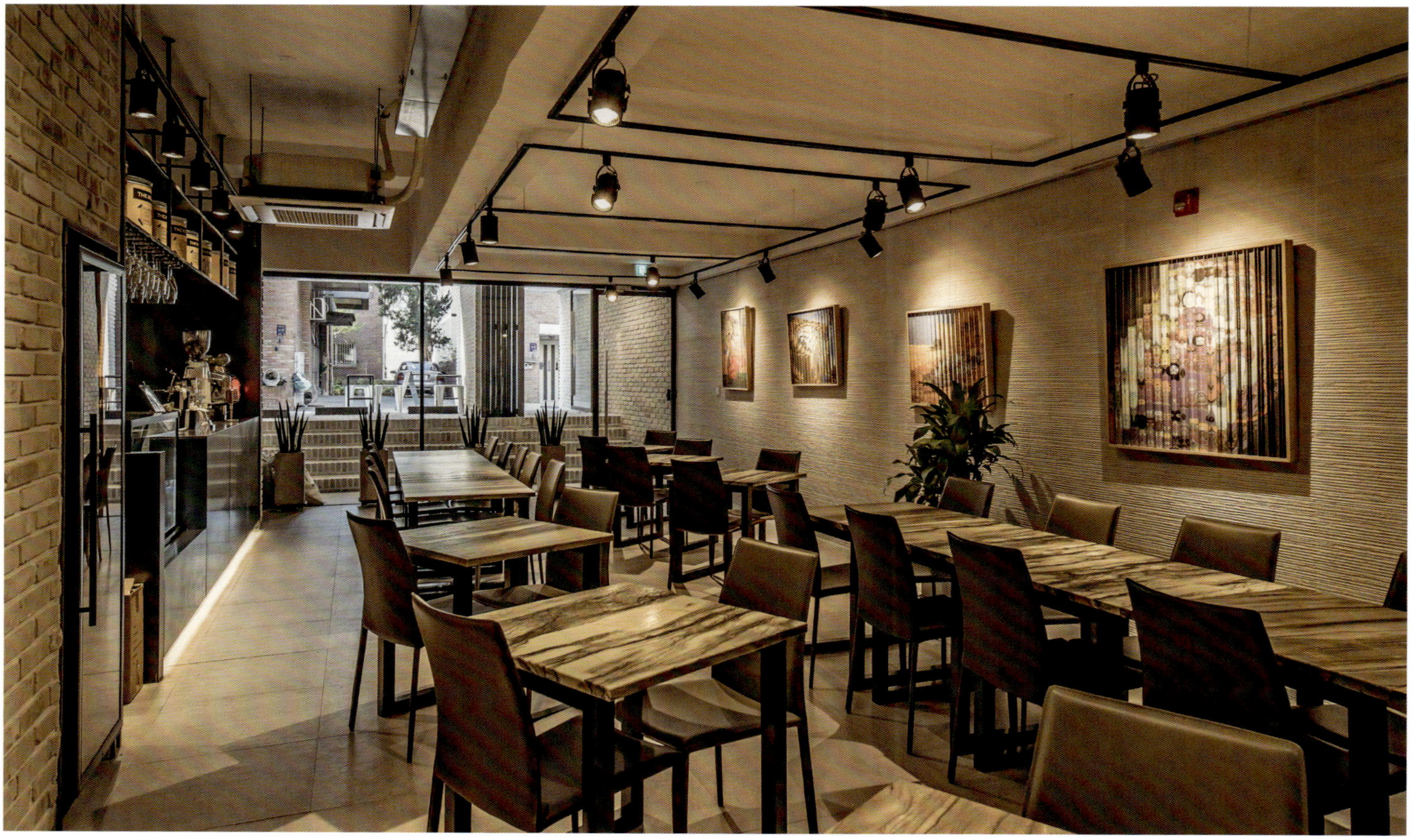

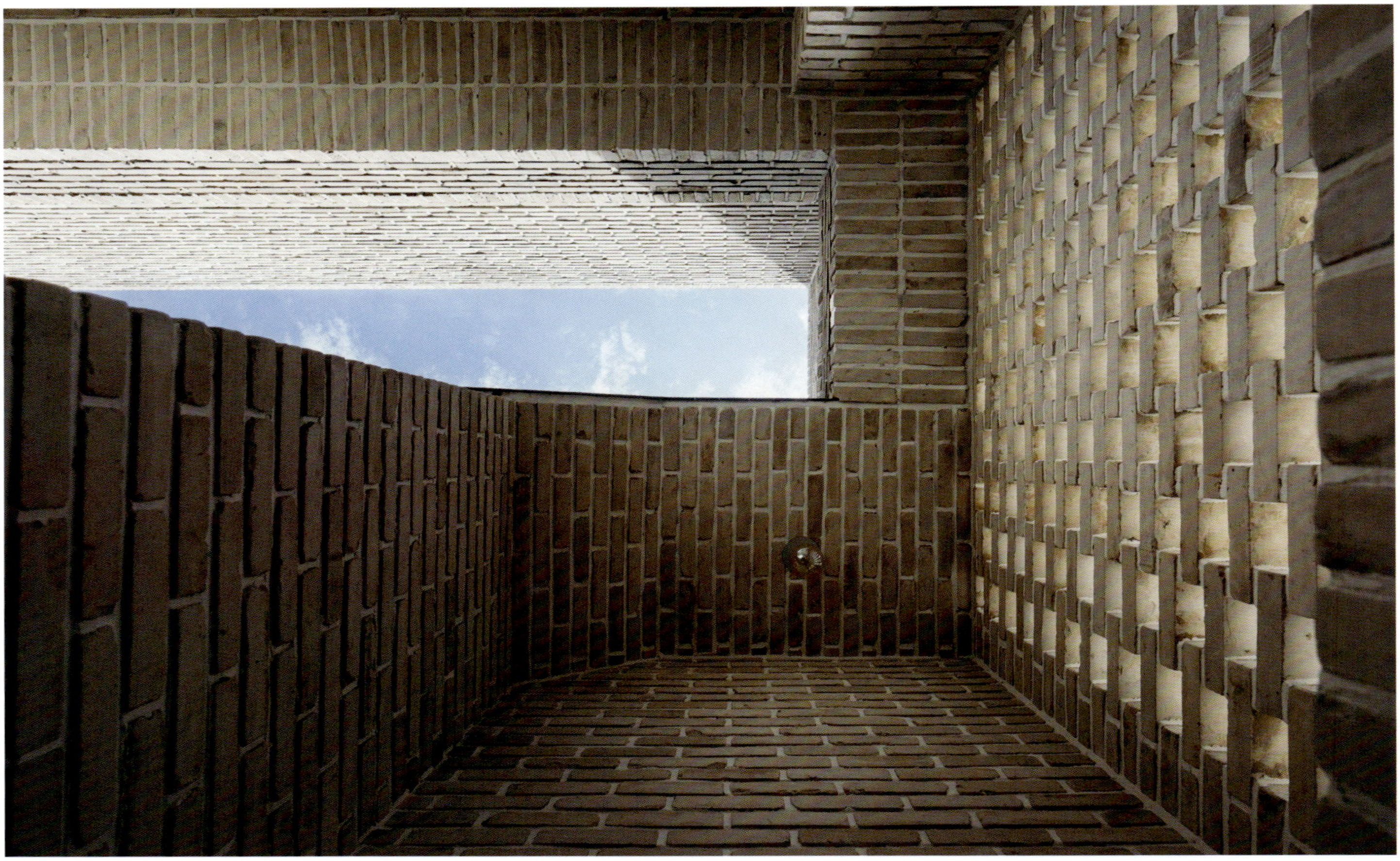

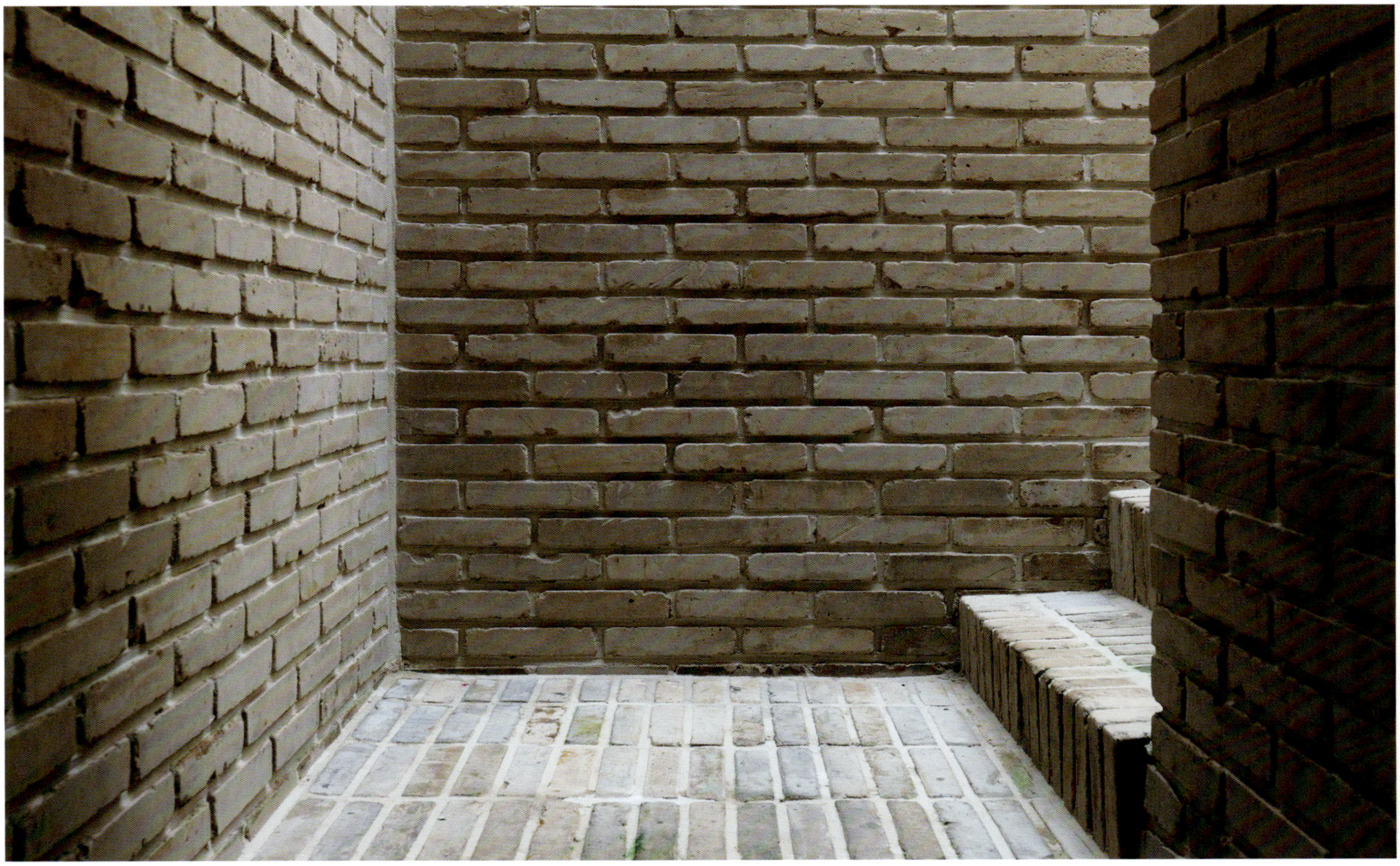

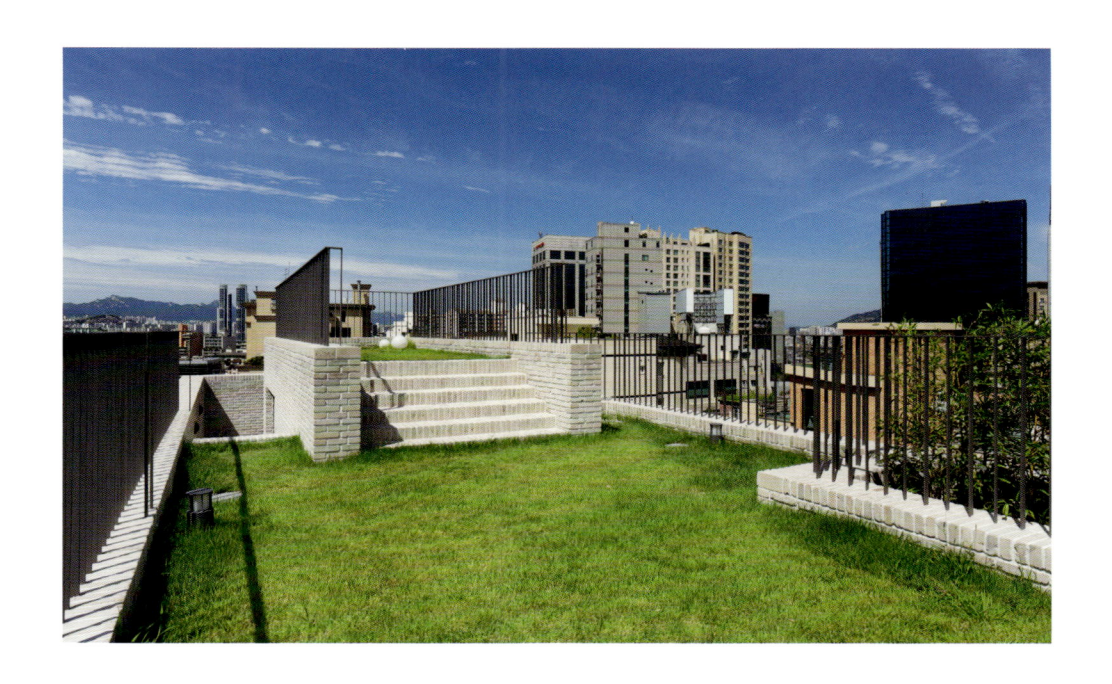

The building includes approximately forty workstations, multiple conference rooms, multiple offices for the principals, a public café, and a green space on the top level. Successfully implementing moments of green space throughout the project was essential in our attempt to create five expressive façades.

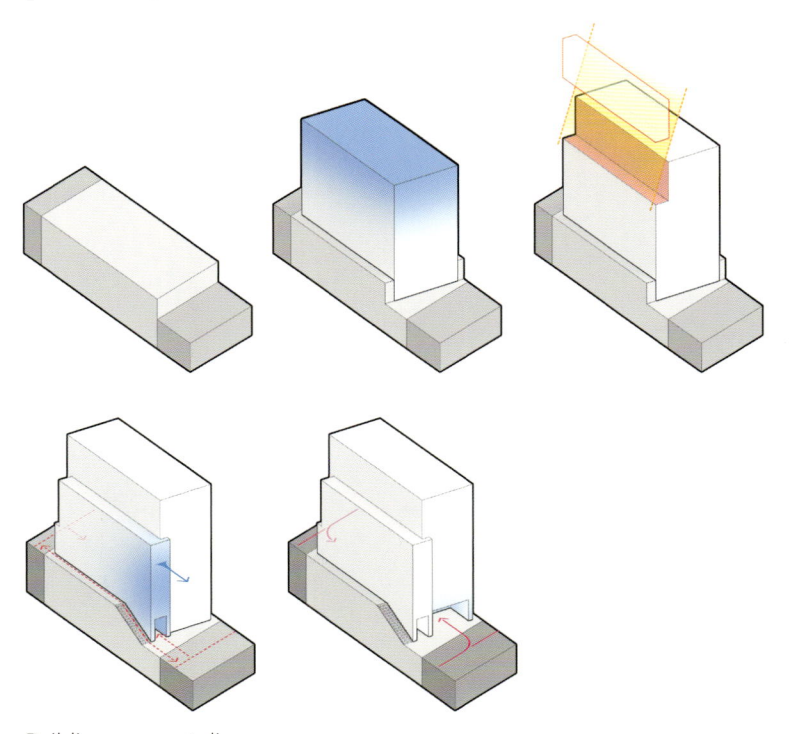

Building concept diagram

YKH ASSOCIATES HEADQUARTERS  **167**

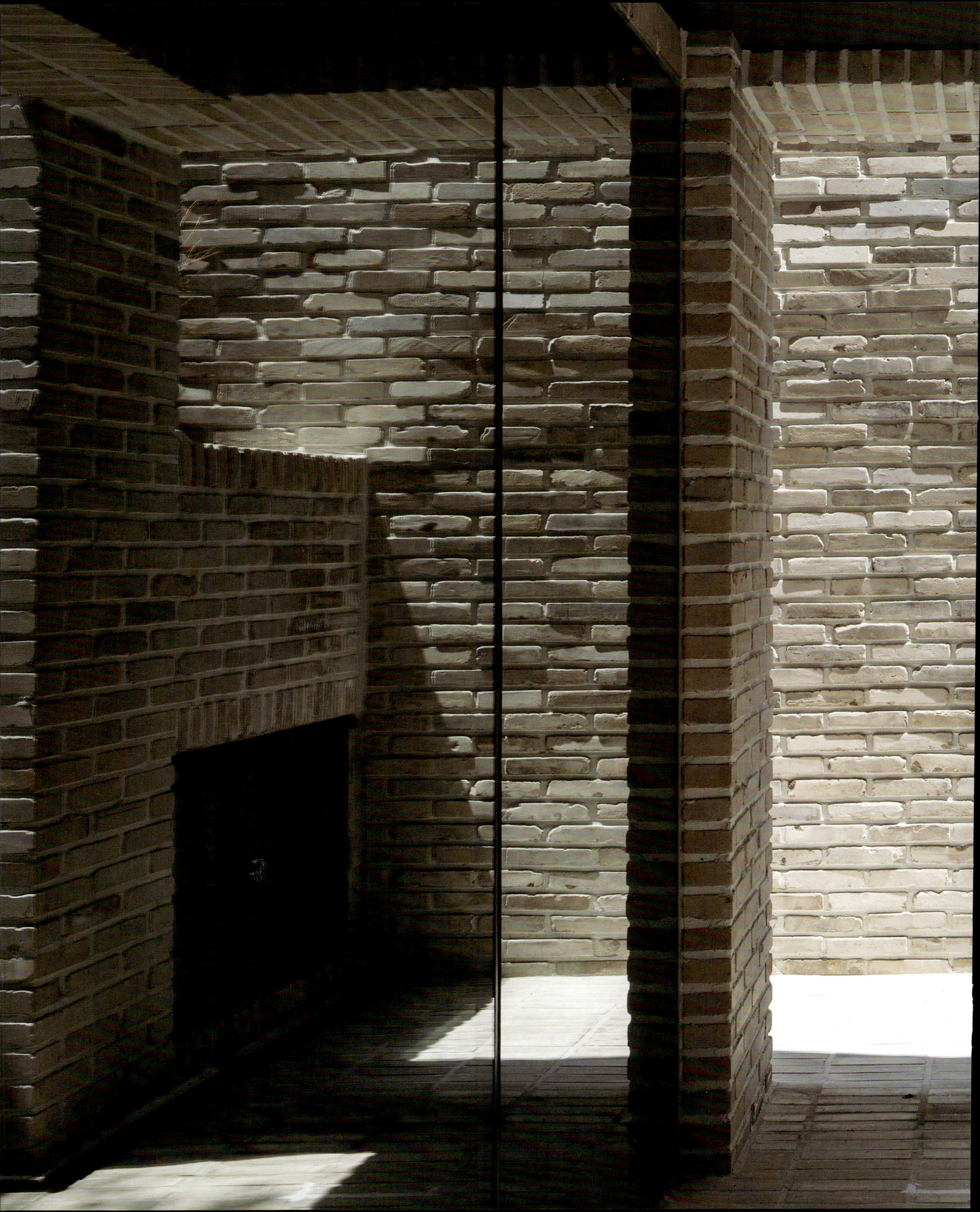

# VIXEN
# HEADQUARTERS
Gangnam-gu, Seoul, South Korea | 2018

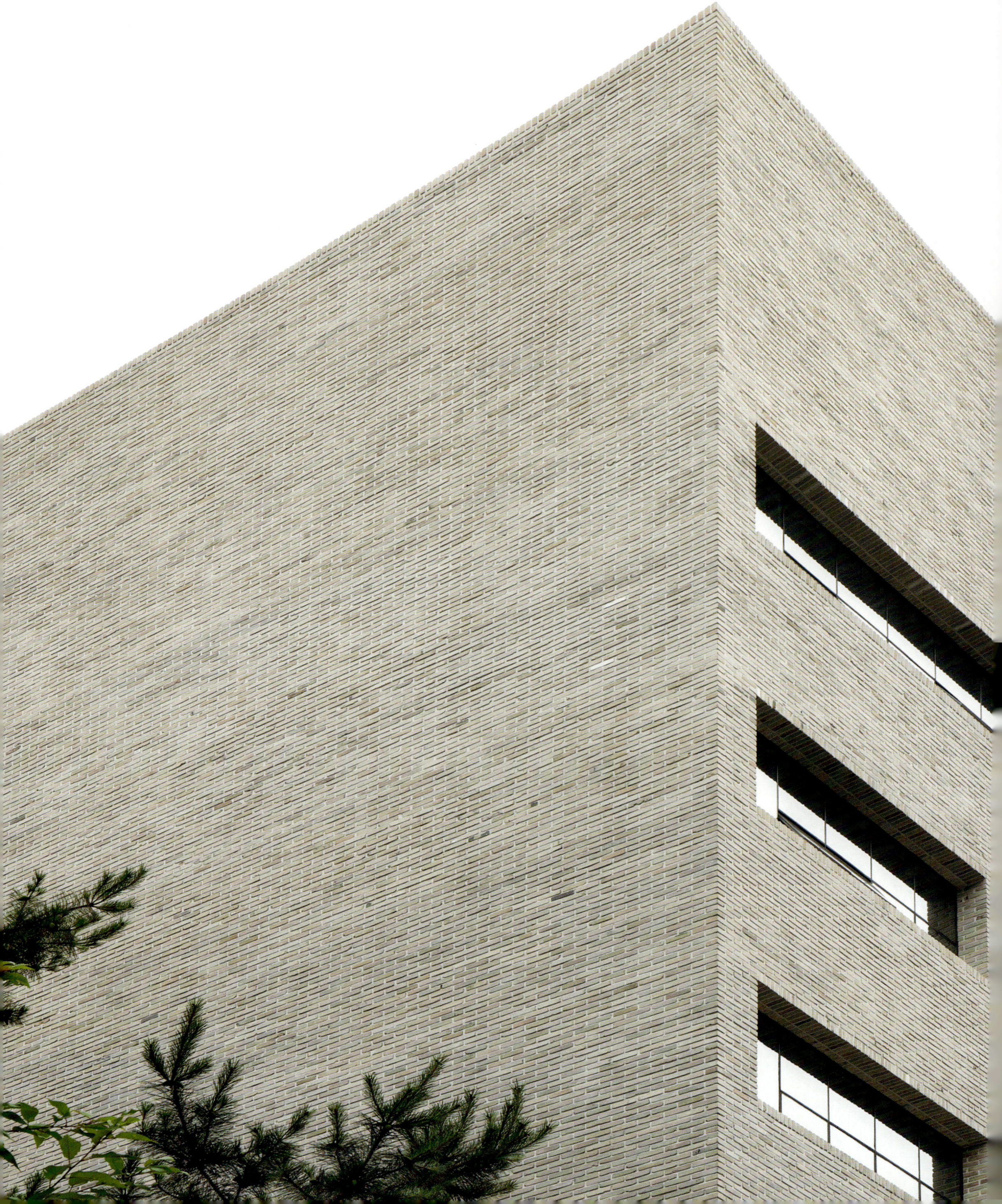

One of the crucial design challenges for the new headquarters of Vixen Studios, located in the Gangnam-gu district of Seoul, was to utilize the physical medium to faithfully represent the firm's vision. Vixen Studios has been growing as an internationally renowned advertising company by providing efficient and creative marketing insights since its founding in 1988. Accordingly, the owner wanted a new office space that would inspire creativity and maximize employee productivity in addition to communicating the philosophies of the firm. Based on the owner's needs analysis, we came up with a solution to accommodate multipurpose activities while also achieving a high degree of spatial and economic efficiency. Utilizing aged white brick and minimal ornamentation, a presence of maturity and timelessness emerges from the project. The voids created at the moments where the aged white brick meets the polished dark glass extenuates the building's relationship between timelessness and modernity.

Due to strict local zoning codes, encountering buildings with unnatural terraces or tapers is very common on the sloping back streets of Gangnam-gu. To avoid such design obstacles, Vixen's monolithic brick building is set back from the street. The principles of simplicity and efficiency also manifest in classification and organization of the project's space. An array of service spaces, including staircases, elevator core and restrooms, spans vertically throughout the building. Accordingly, open and closed workspaces are planned with consideration for security and types of work. Specifically, the office space on the second and third floors accommodates presentations and meetings with clients. Going upwards, the workspaces become more private.

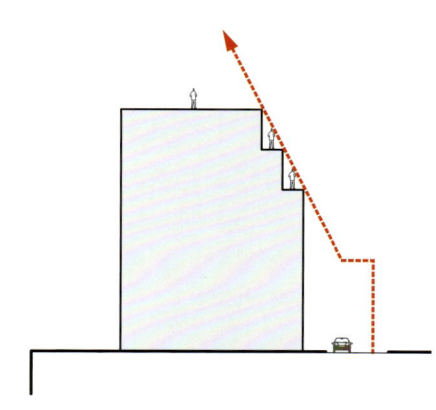

Typical multitiered form: building in tiers to meet the diagonal zoning regulation code for neighbors' daylight needs

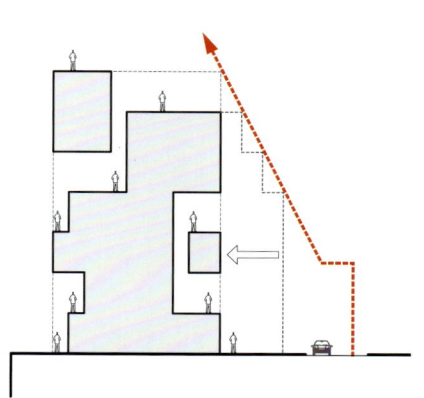

Our proposed form: slimmer and simpler box form positioned further south to play with inner voids and meet the maximum FAR requirements

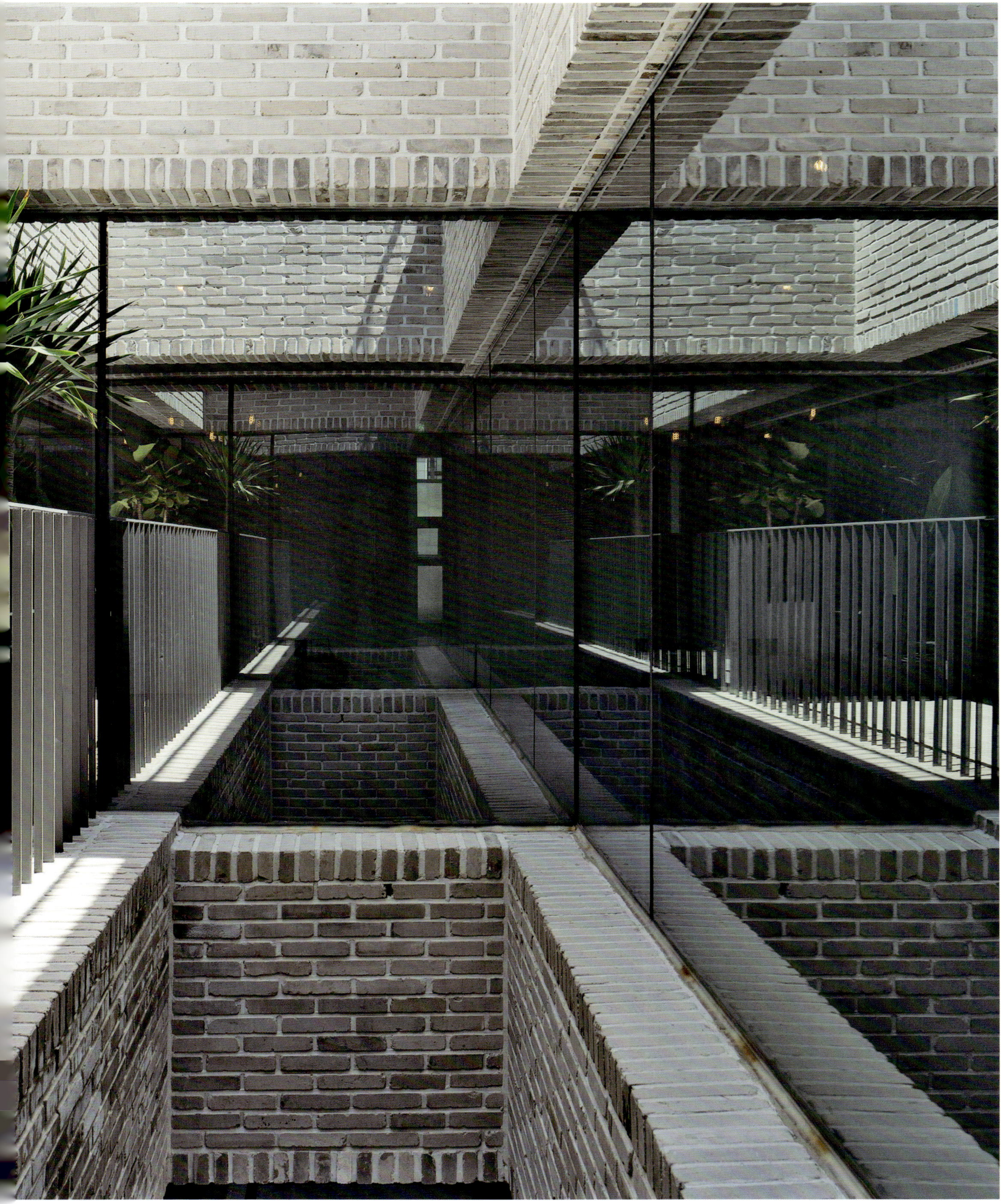

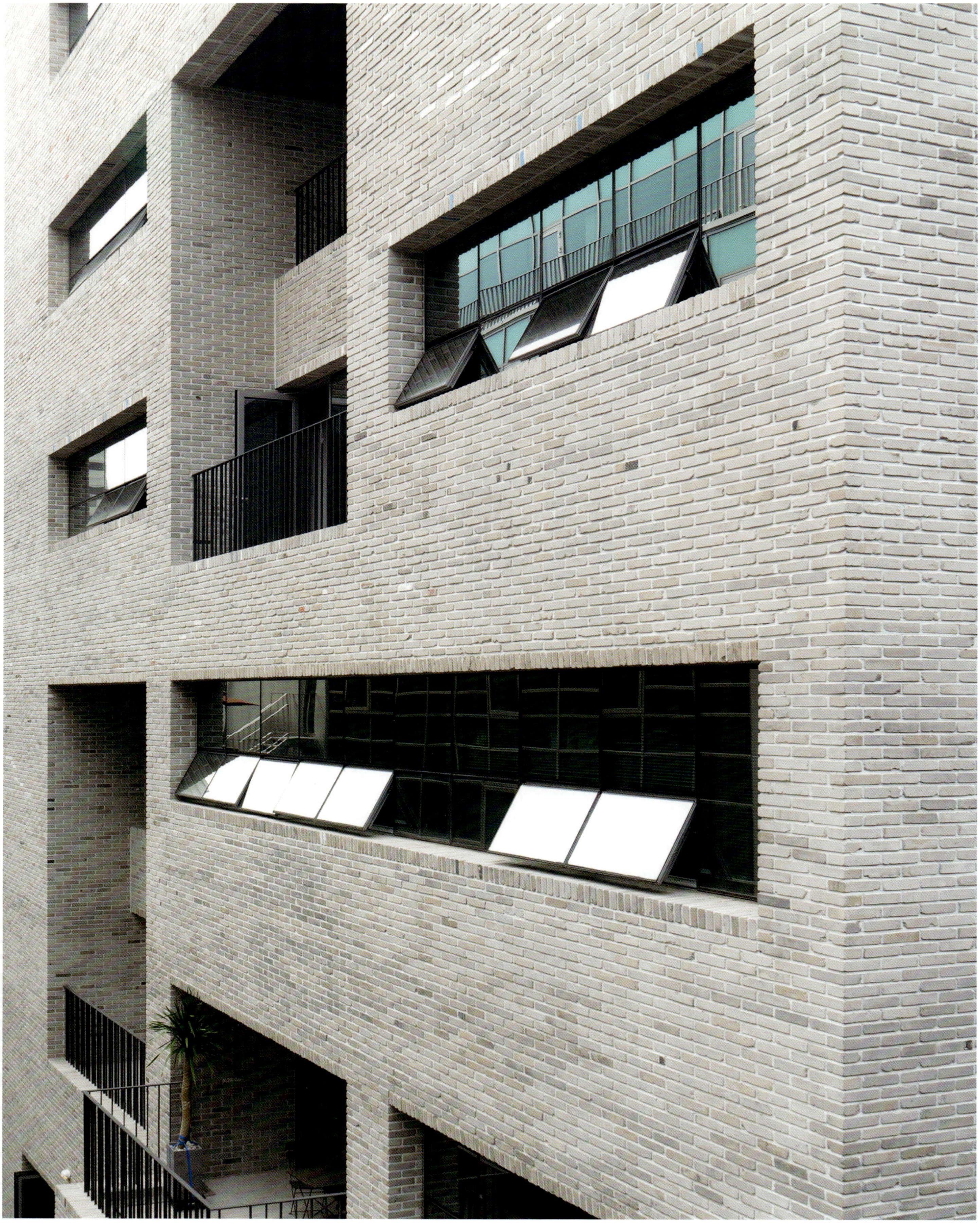

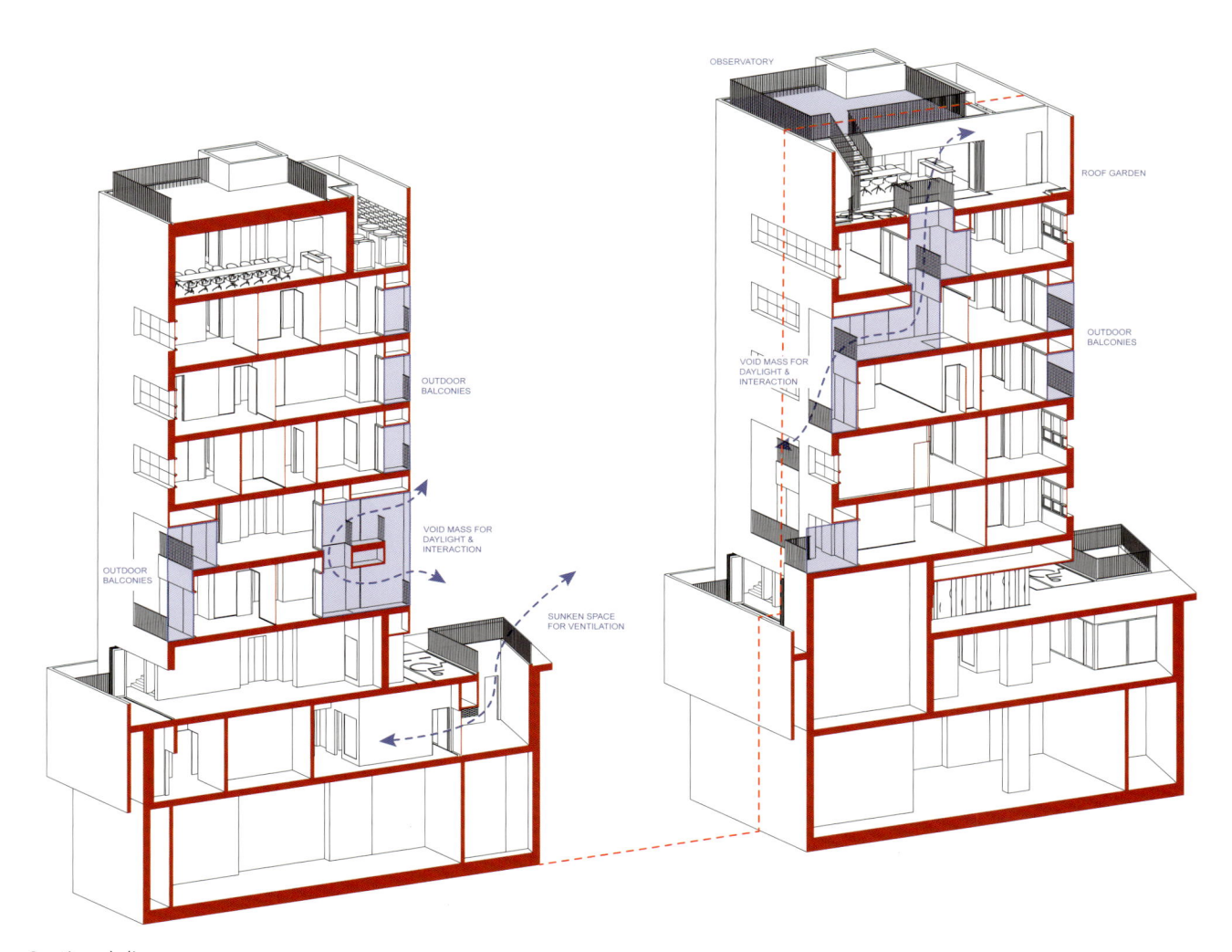

Sectional diagram

Within such a simple yet rigorous architectural plan, voids of different sizes create unique patterns on the brick façades and within the spatial depth of the building. Connecting the void space from the fourth floor and the roof plays a critical role in bringing sunlight and fresh air into the interior spaces. This empty space provides not only vertical connectivity and circulation, but it also opens spaces for employees to socialize.

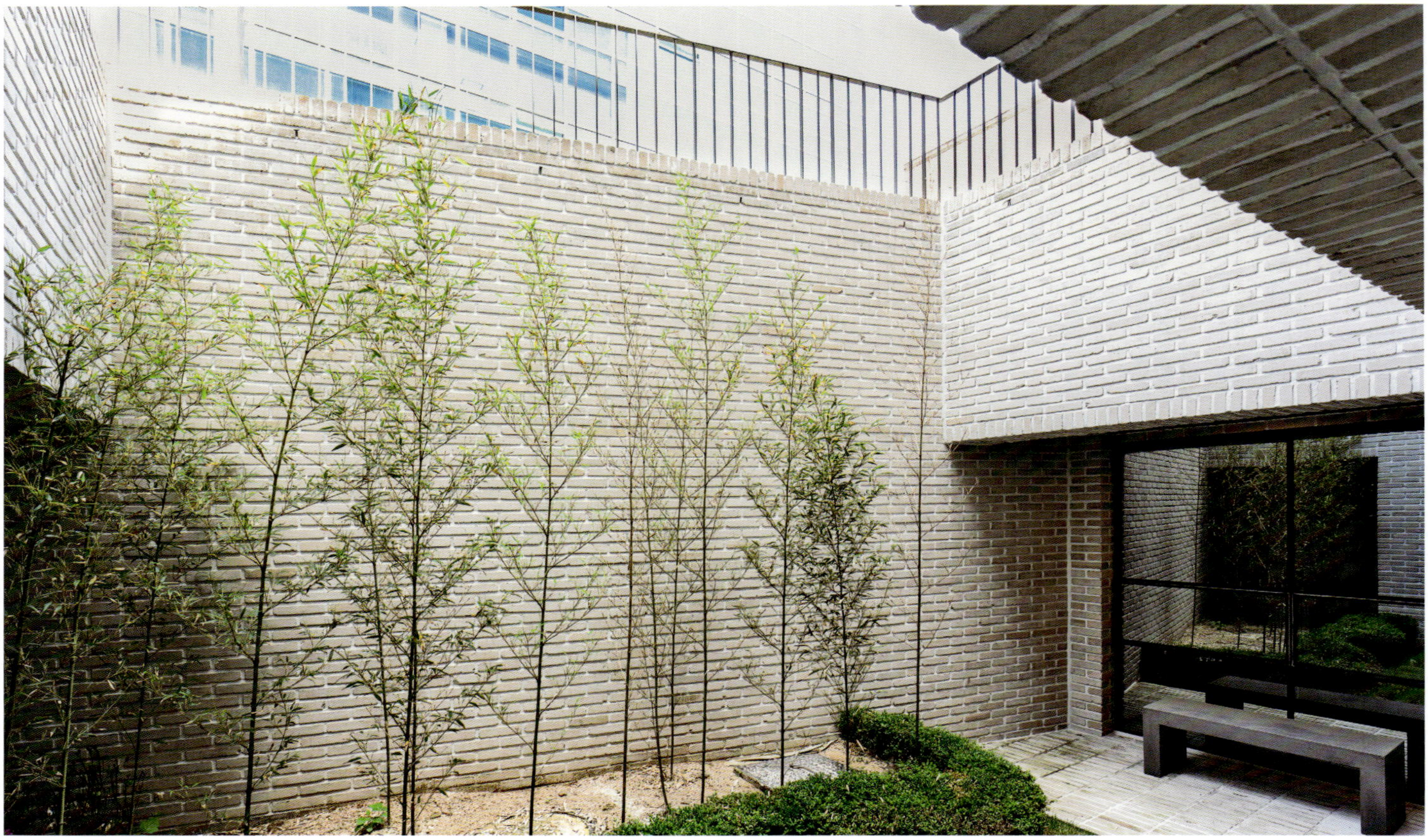

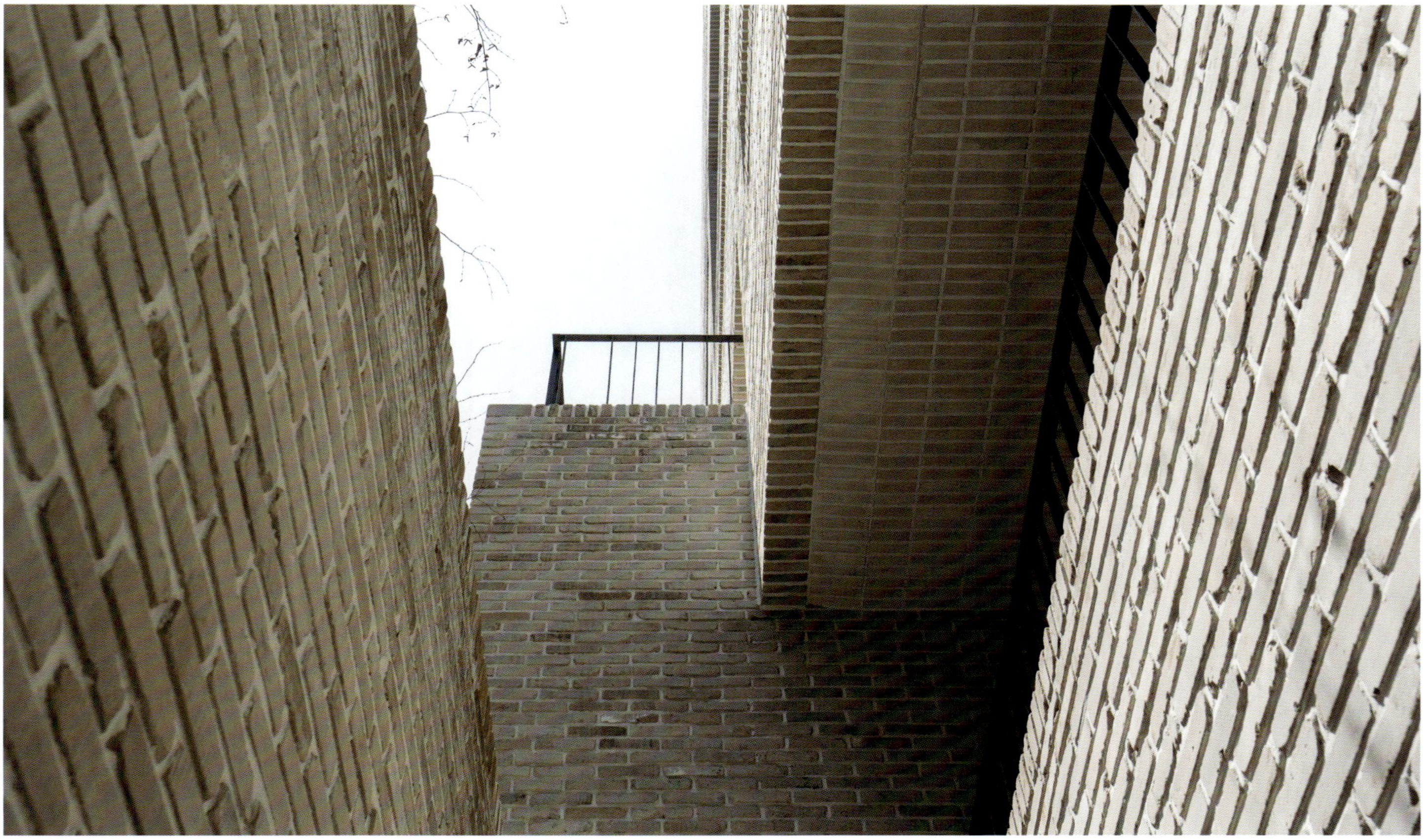

VIXEN HEADQUARTERS 177

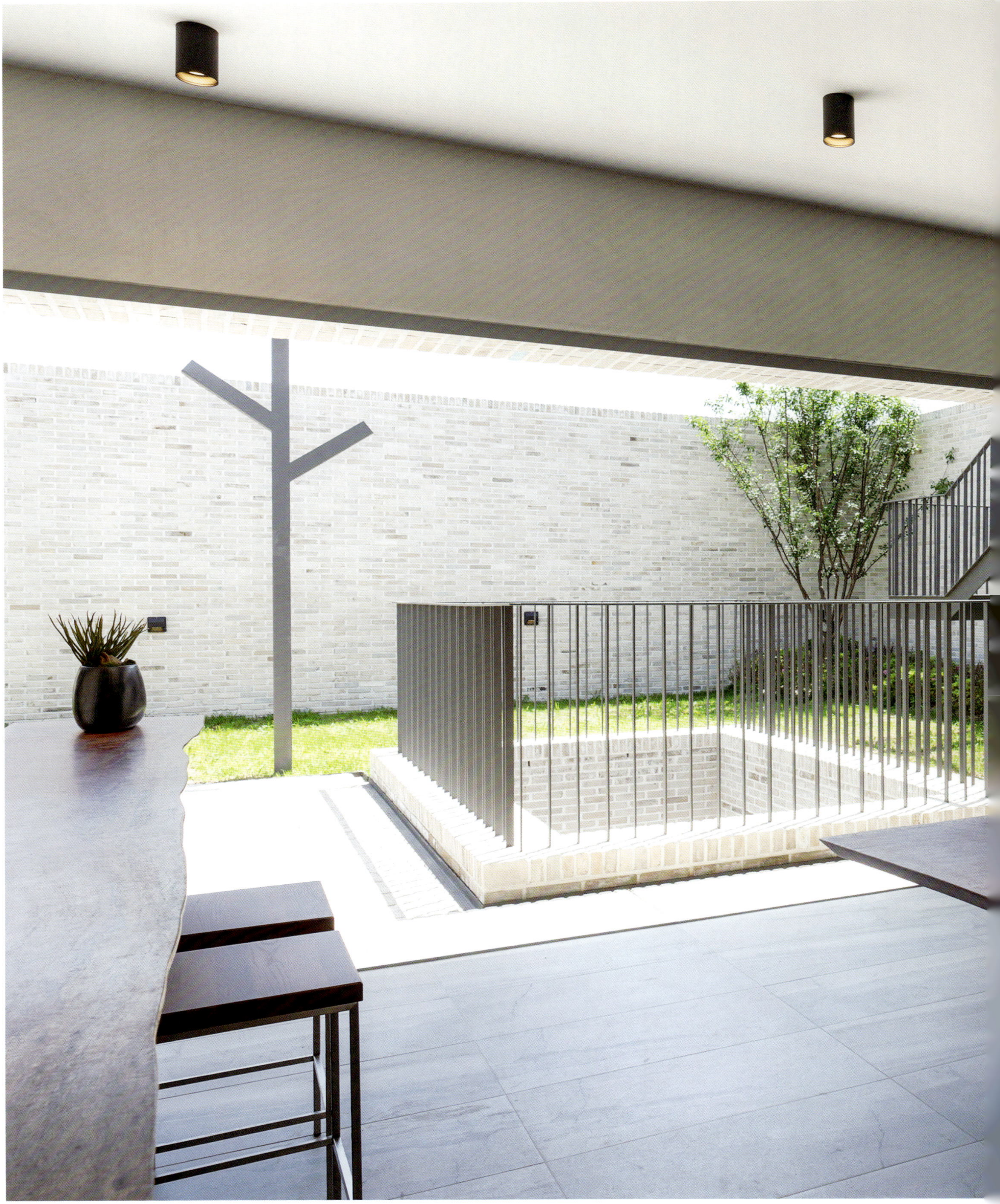

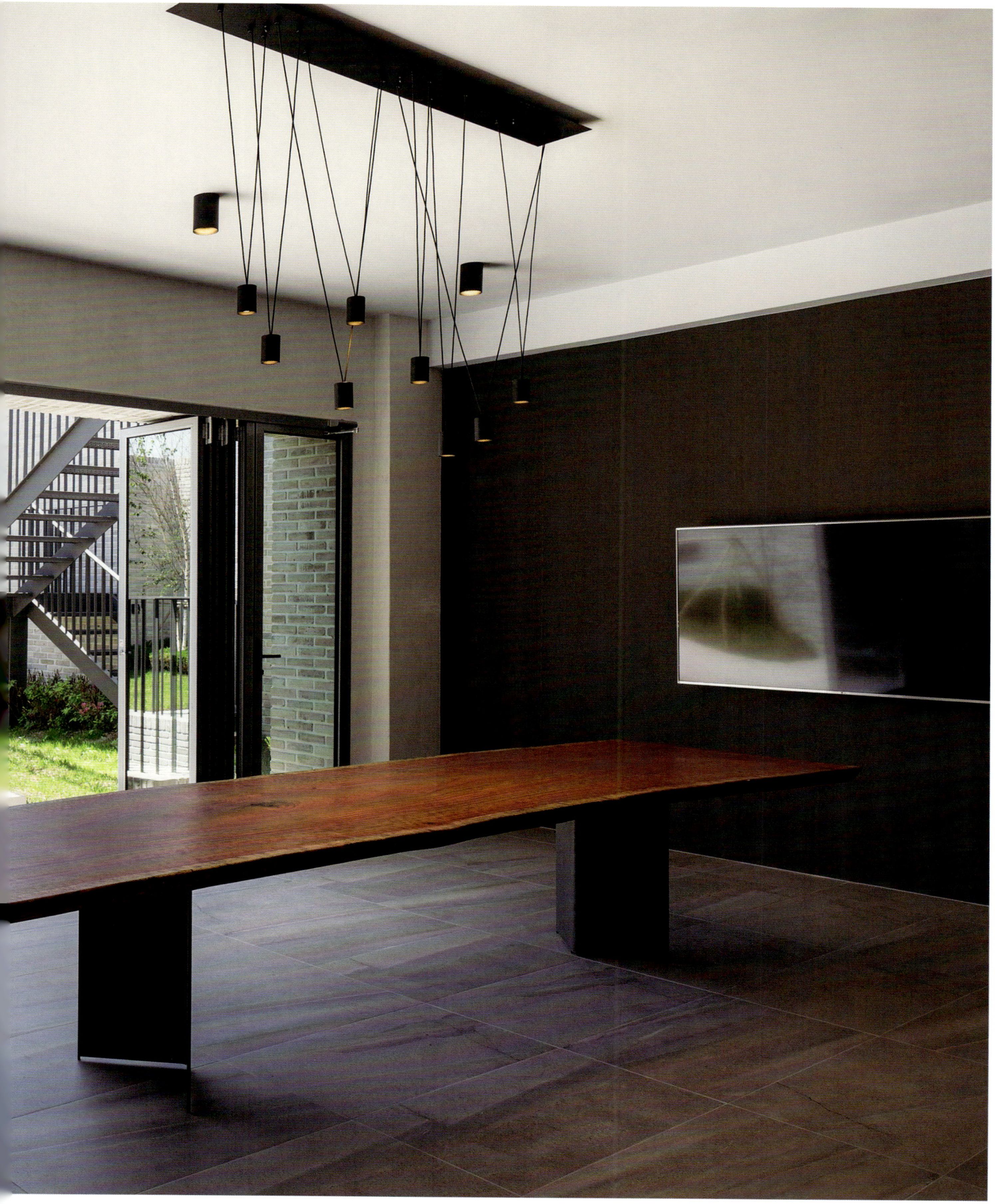

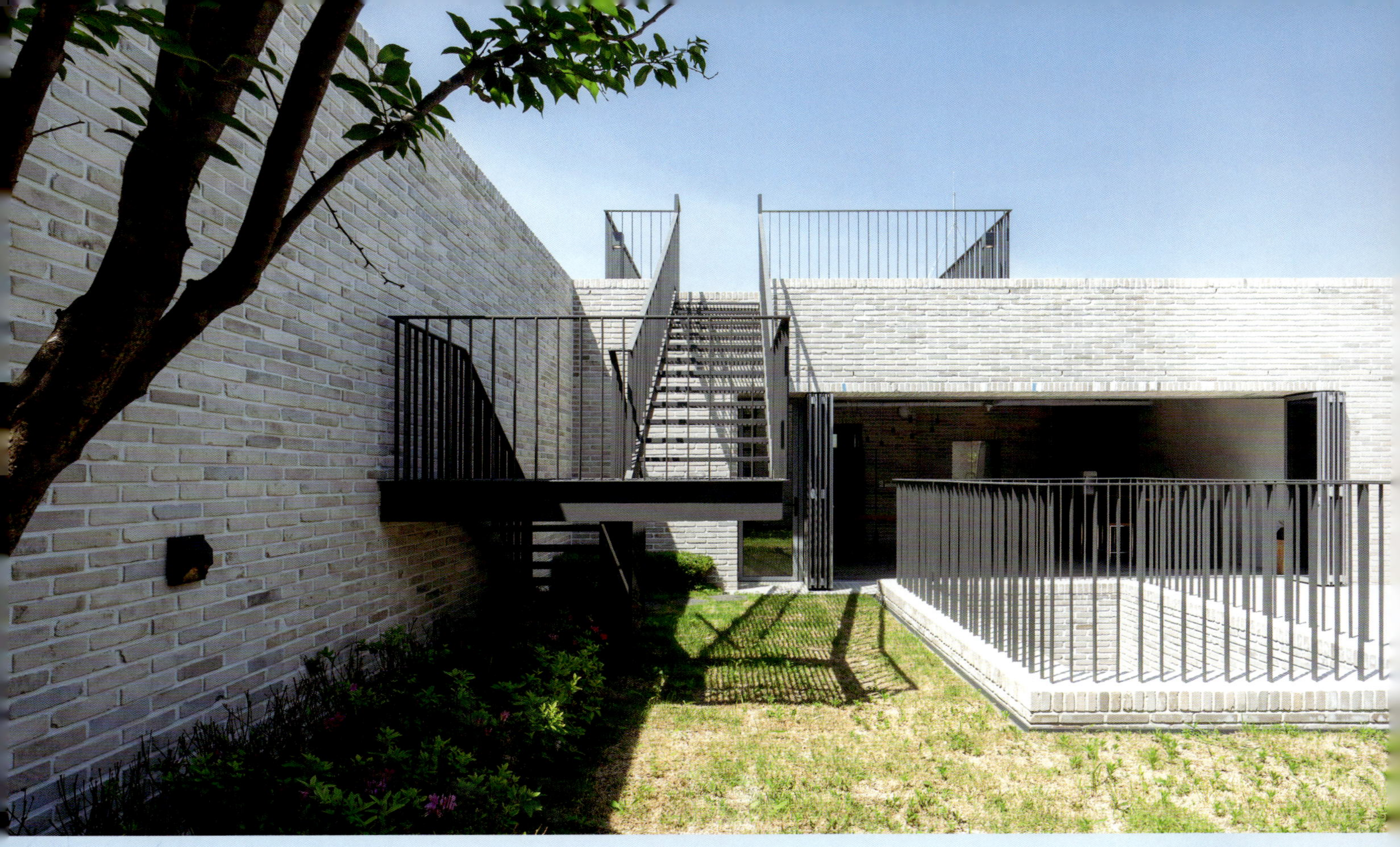

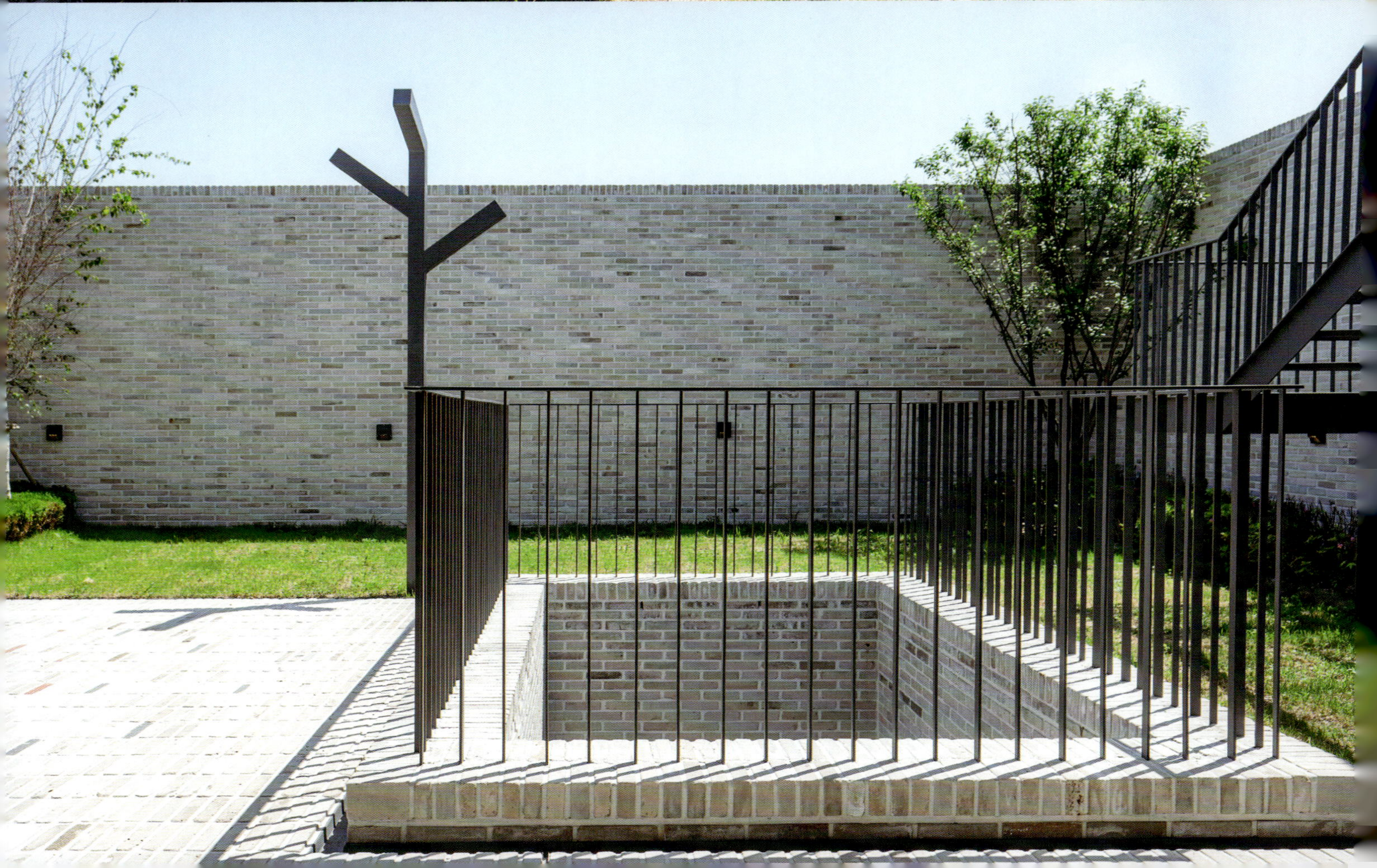

VIXEN HEADQUARTERS **181**

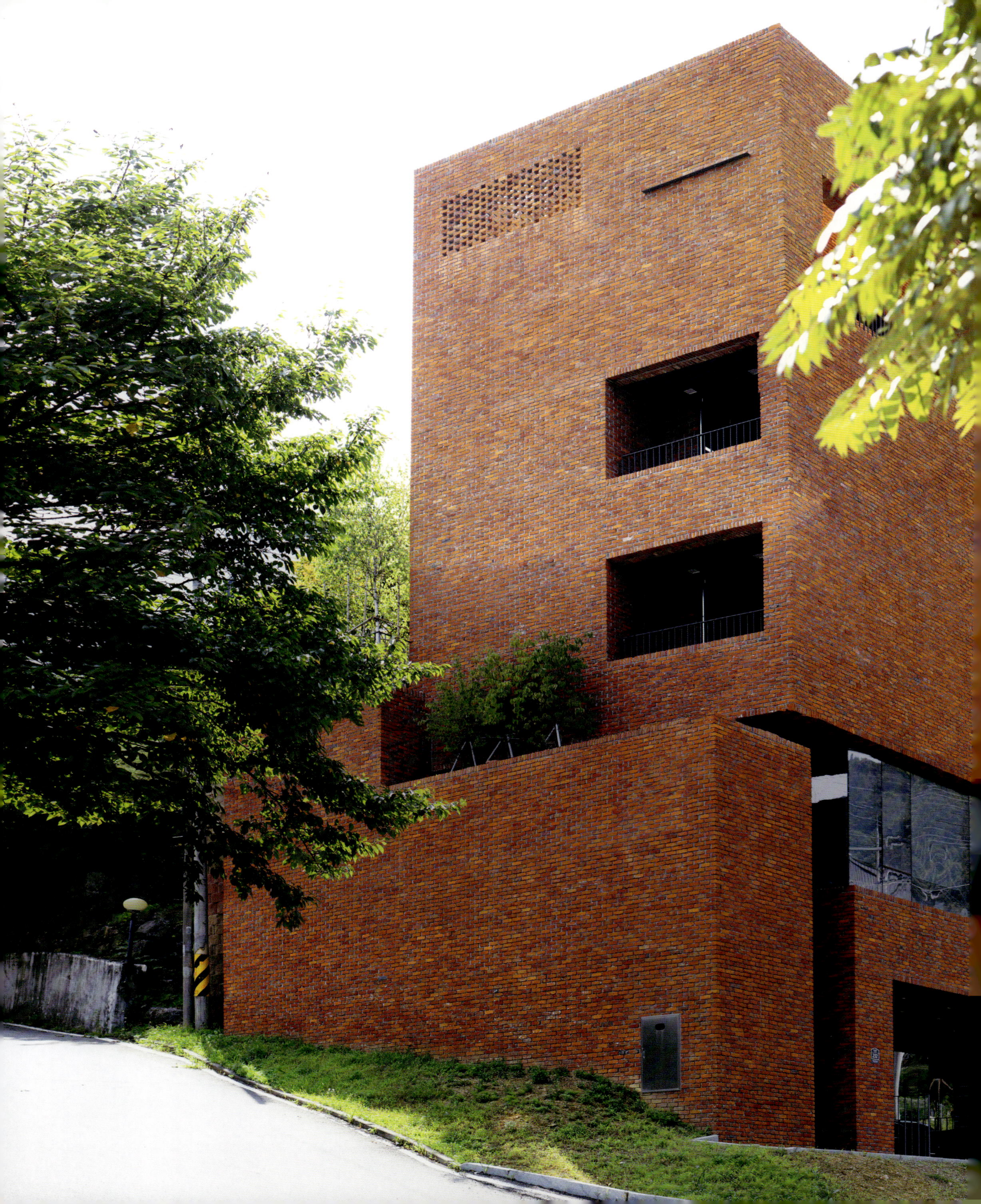

# TRENDEX HEADQUARTERS
Gwangju-si, Gyeonggi-do, South Korea | 2021

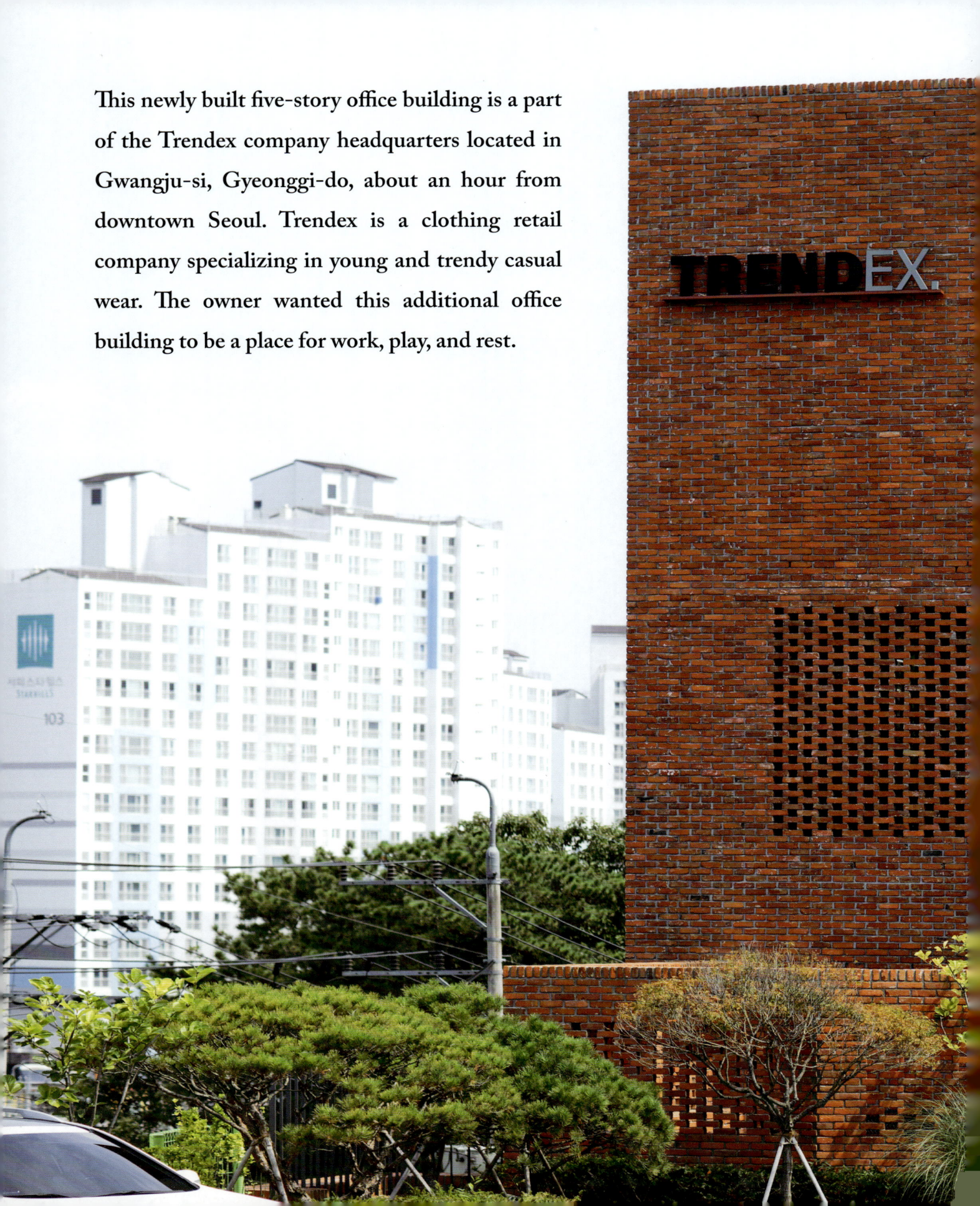

This newly built five-story office building is a part of the Trendex company headquarters located in Gwangju-si, Gyeonggi-do, about an hour from downtown Seoul. Trendex is a clothing retail company specializing in young and trendy casual wear. The owner wanted this additional office building to be a place for work, play, and rest.

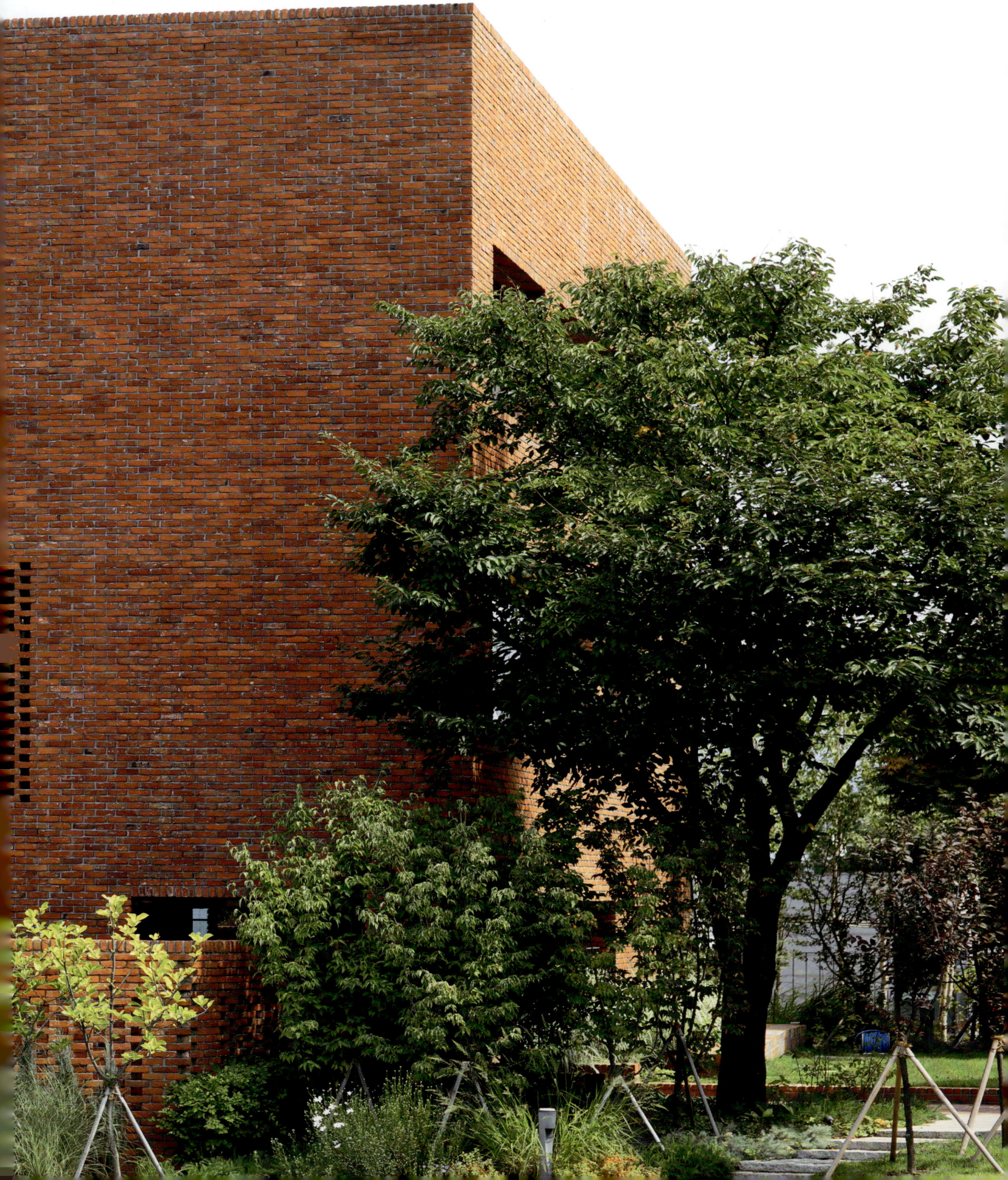

The street B2 level is dedicated to parking and a coffee bar area for employees, coworkers, and clients. The B1 level is where the creative workshop is located; it has an open landscaped plan for designers to gather, brainstorm, and create. The first level has a reception that can be approached directly from the parking lot of the adjacent warehouse and existing office structure. The second and third levels are dedicated to company management and administration personnel. The whole layout of the building is very similar to YKH Associates Headquarters in Seoul, utilizing the wrapping stairs idea. Users experience various spatial moments through the stairs surrounding the building; it was designed to provide a variety of experiences due to the succession of closed and partially opened spaces with views while climbing the stairs leading to the roof garden. This staircase connects the road and the warehouse lot levels, creating an interesting visual sequencing, as if climbing a mountain. We have used red bricks that were refurbished and cleaned to create a dated and renovated look instead of a newly built structure.

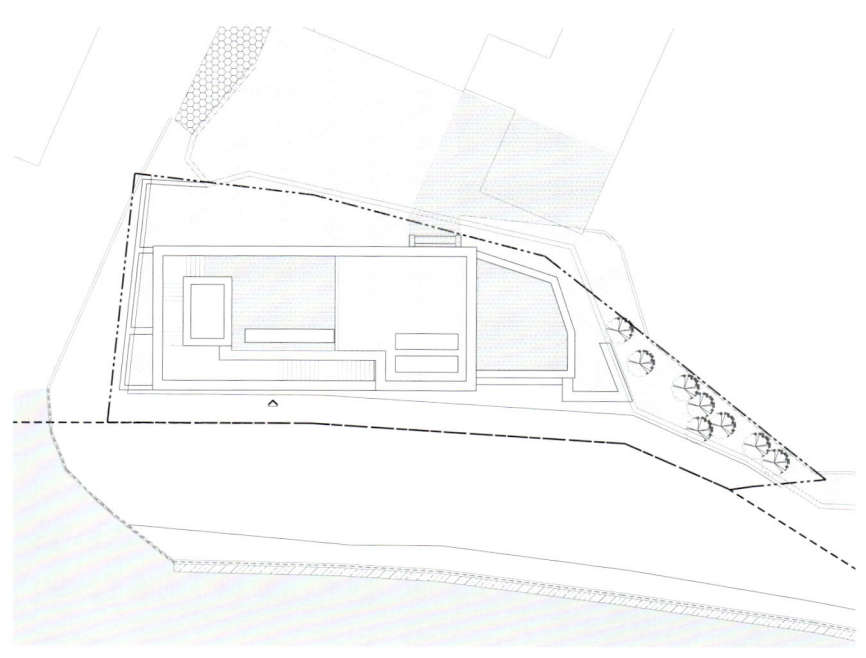

Site plan

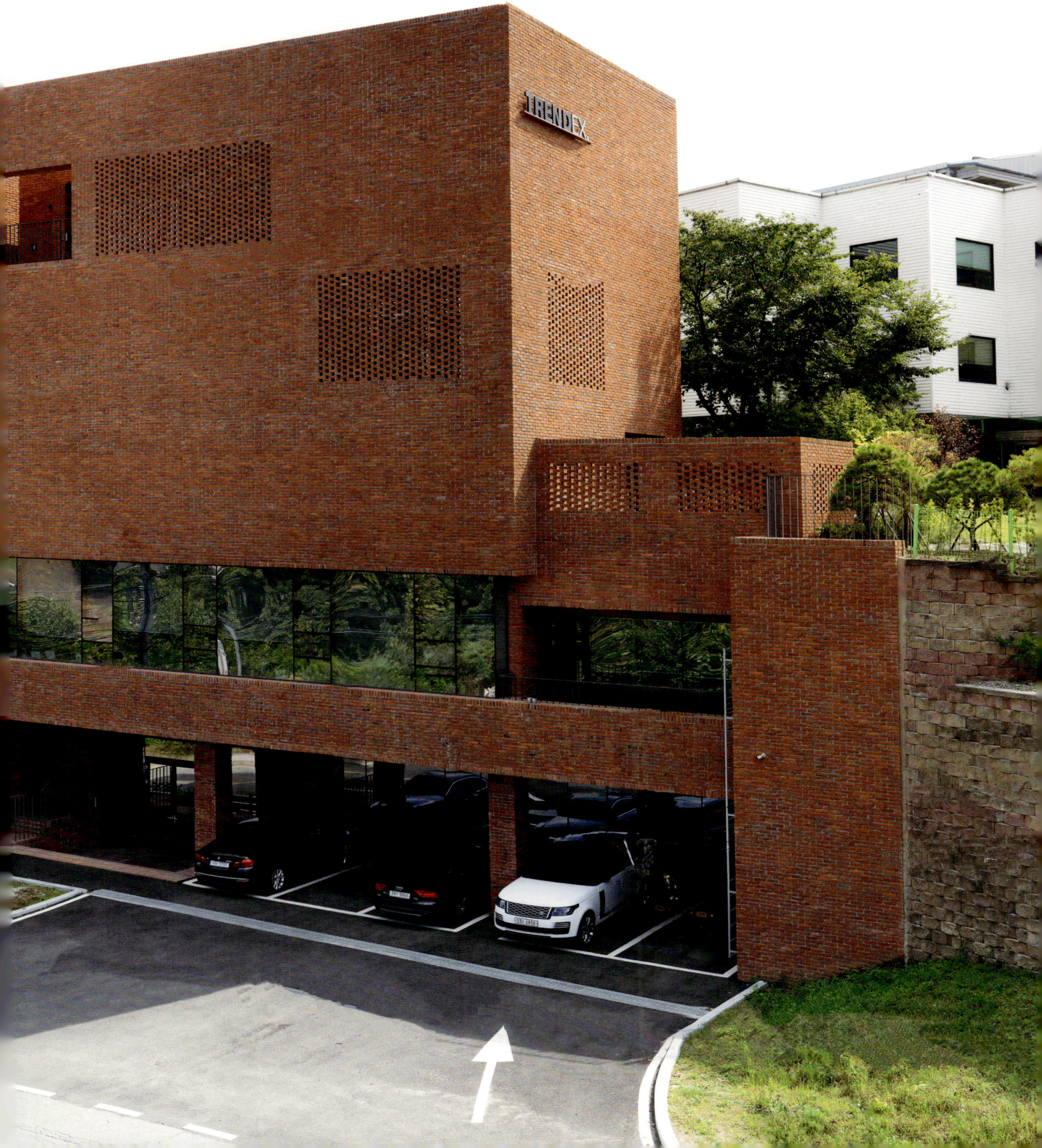
TRENDEX

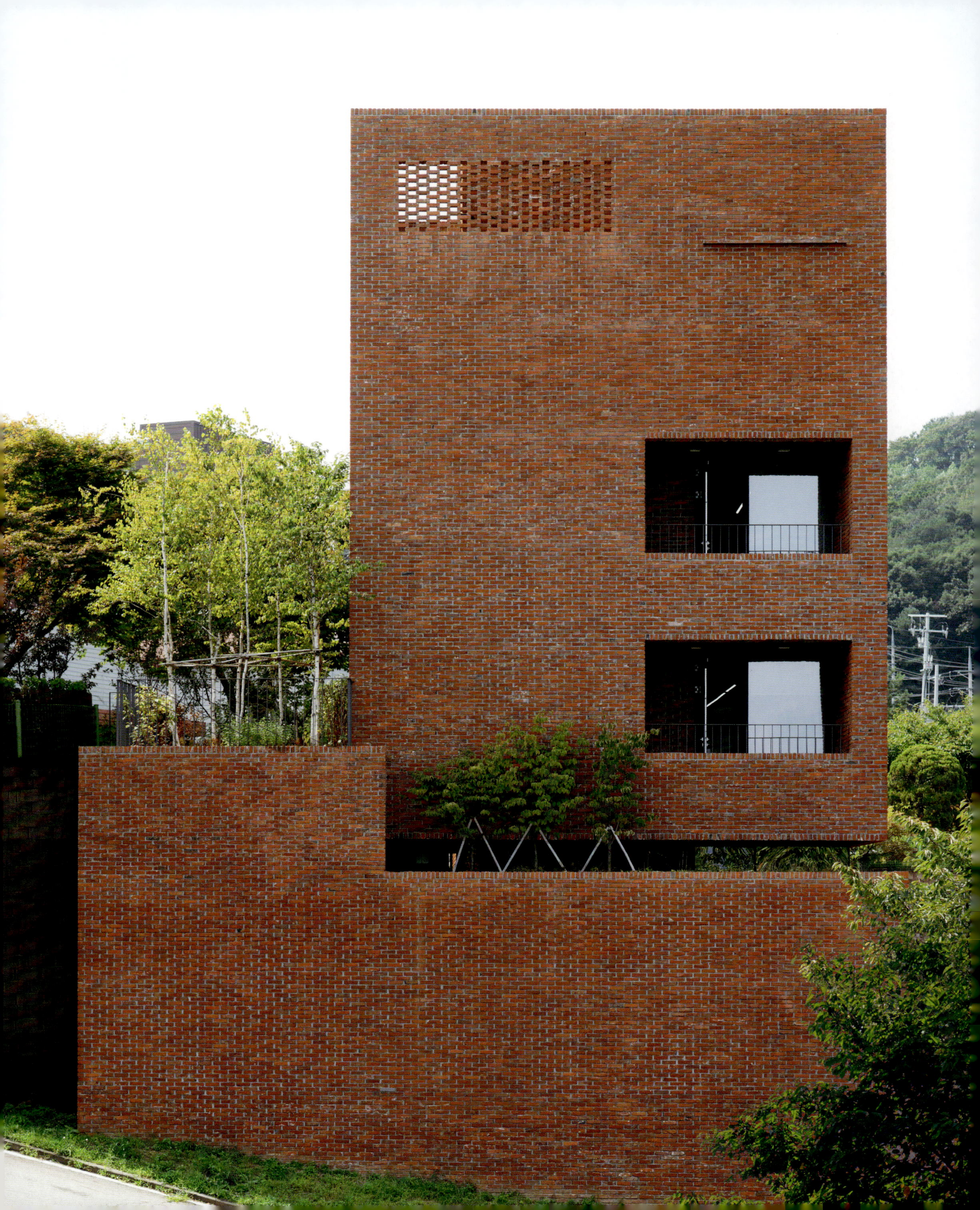

Sections

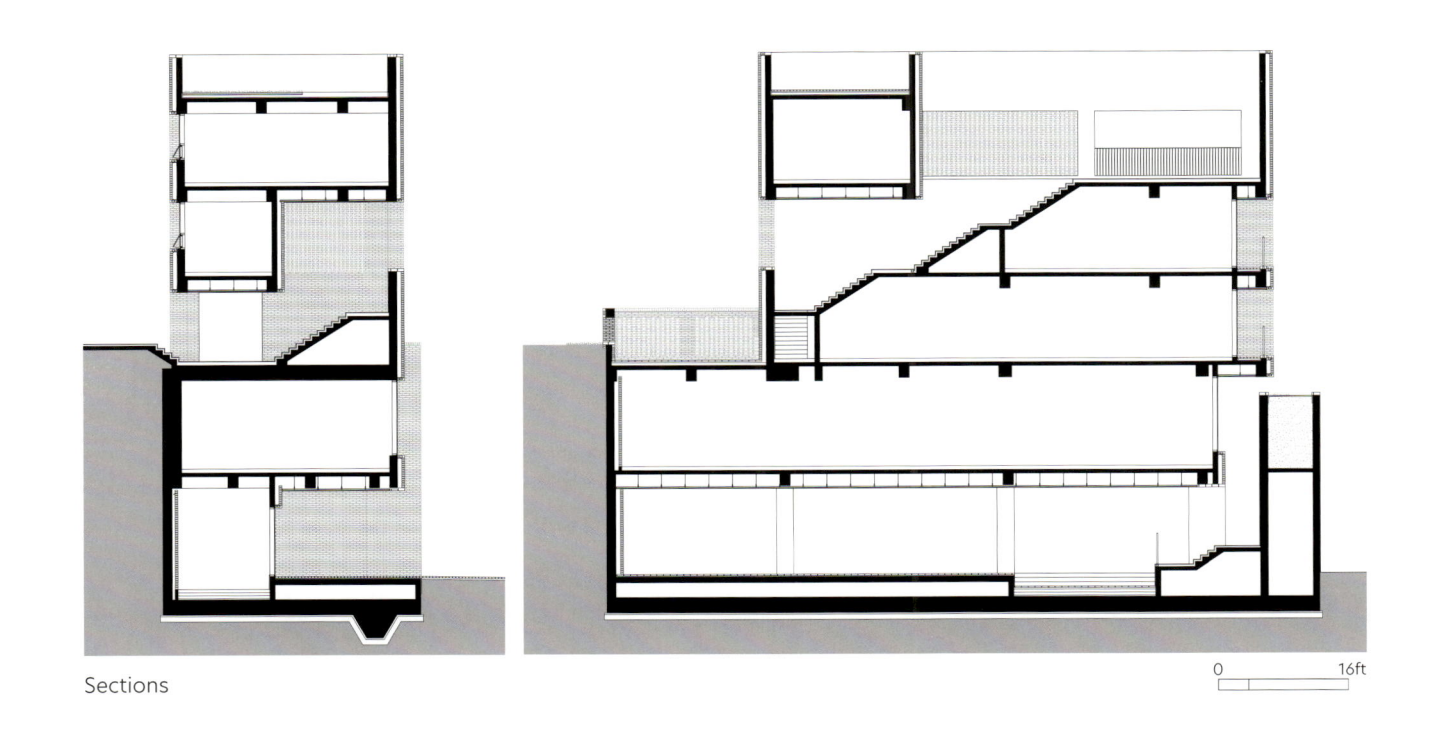

TRENDEX HEADQUARTERS

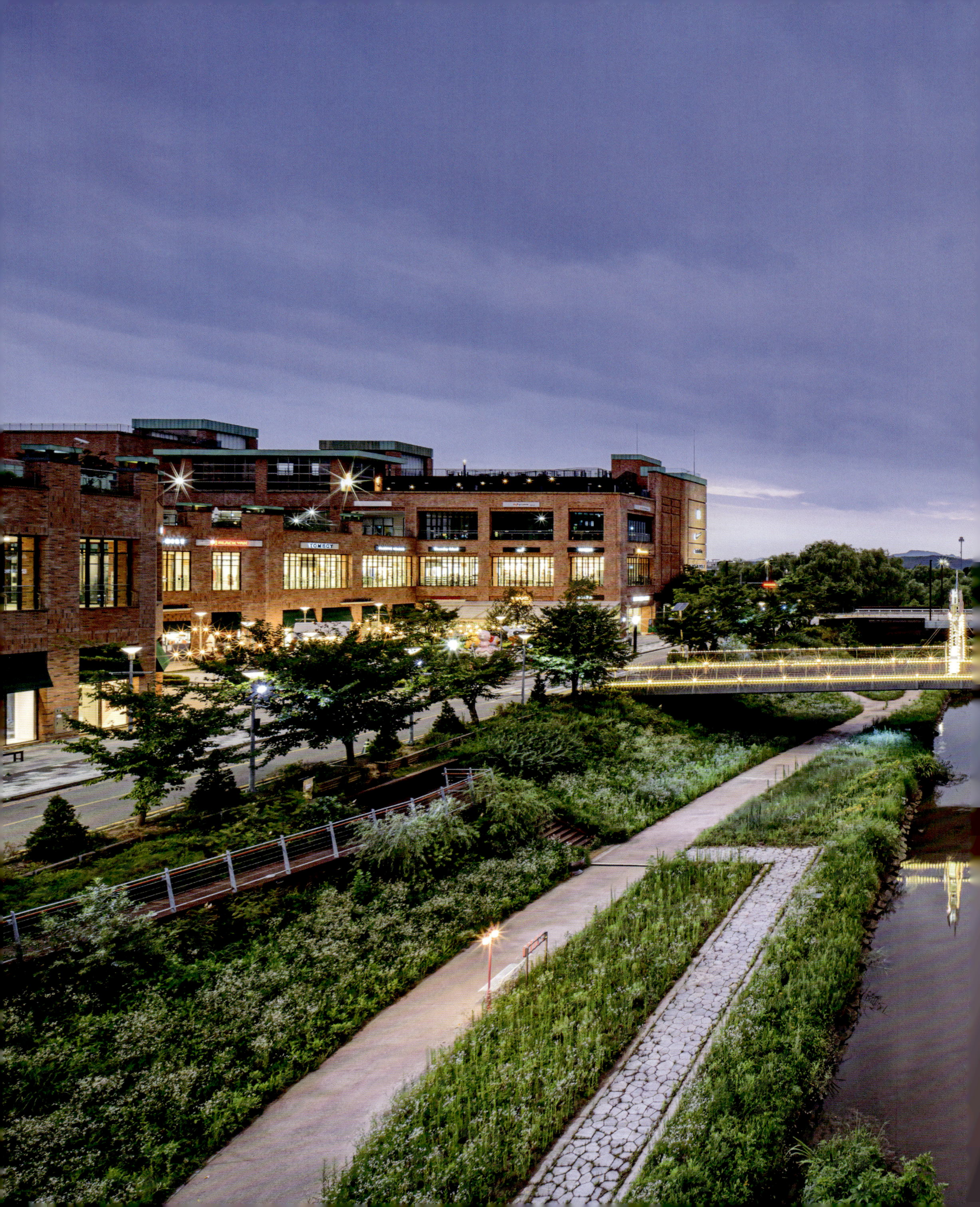
BLACKYAK
TOMBOY

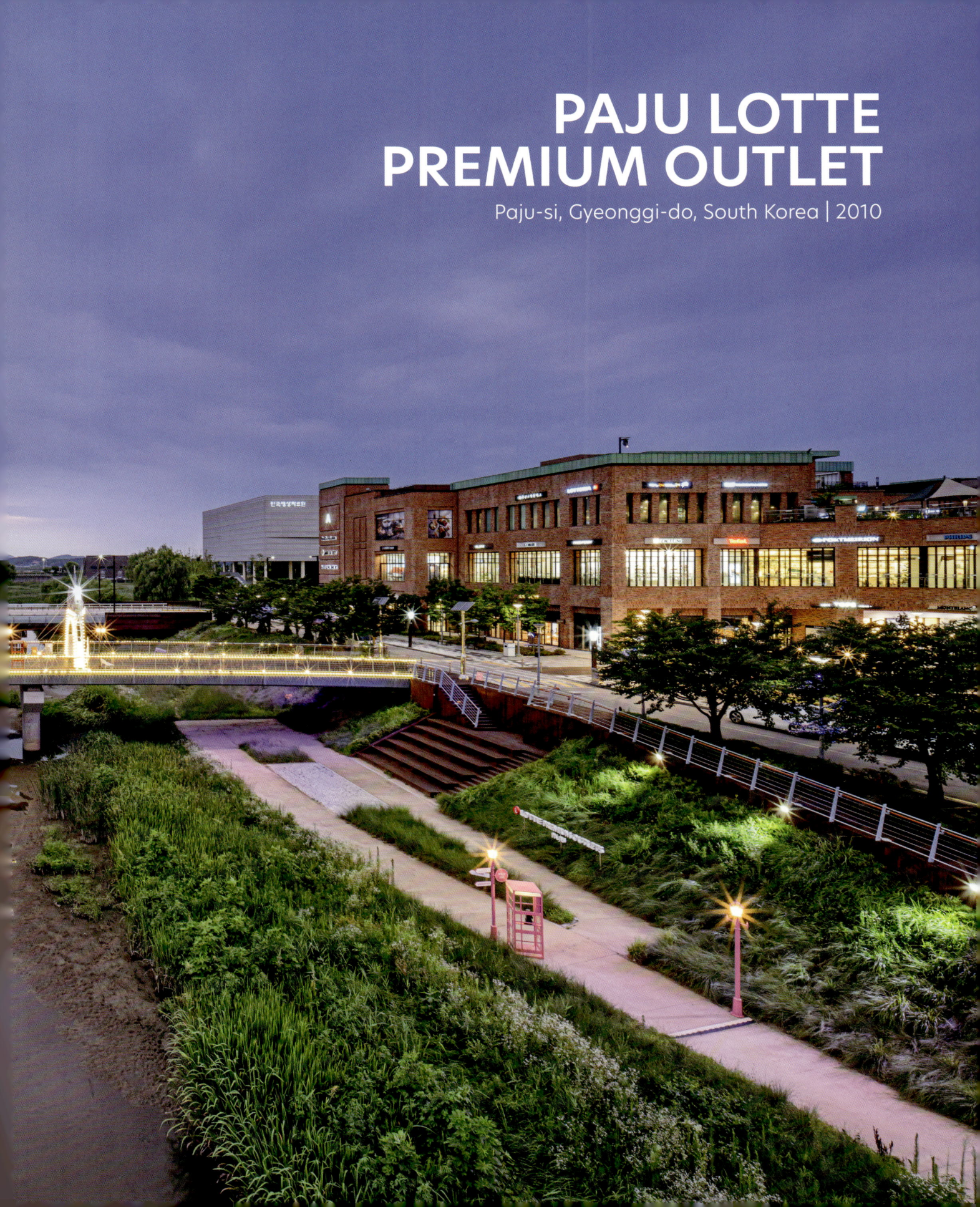

# PAJU LOTTE PREMIUM OUTLET

Paju-si, Gyeonggi-do, South Korea | 2010

The design for the Paju Lotte Premium Outlet was the winning entry for Lotte's invitational competition in 2010. Major requirements of the design competition included connecting four city blocks separated by various roads and rivulets, creating a next-generation commercial shopping center that operates in internal and external spaces simultaneously, and creating a landmark shopping experience in the metropolitan Seoul area.

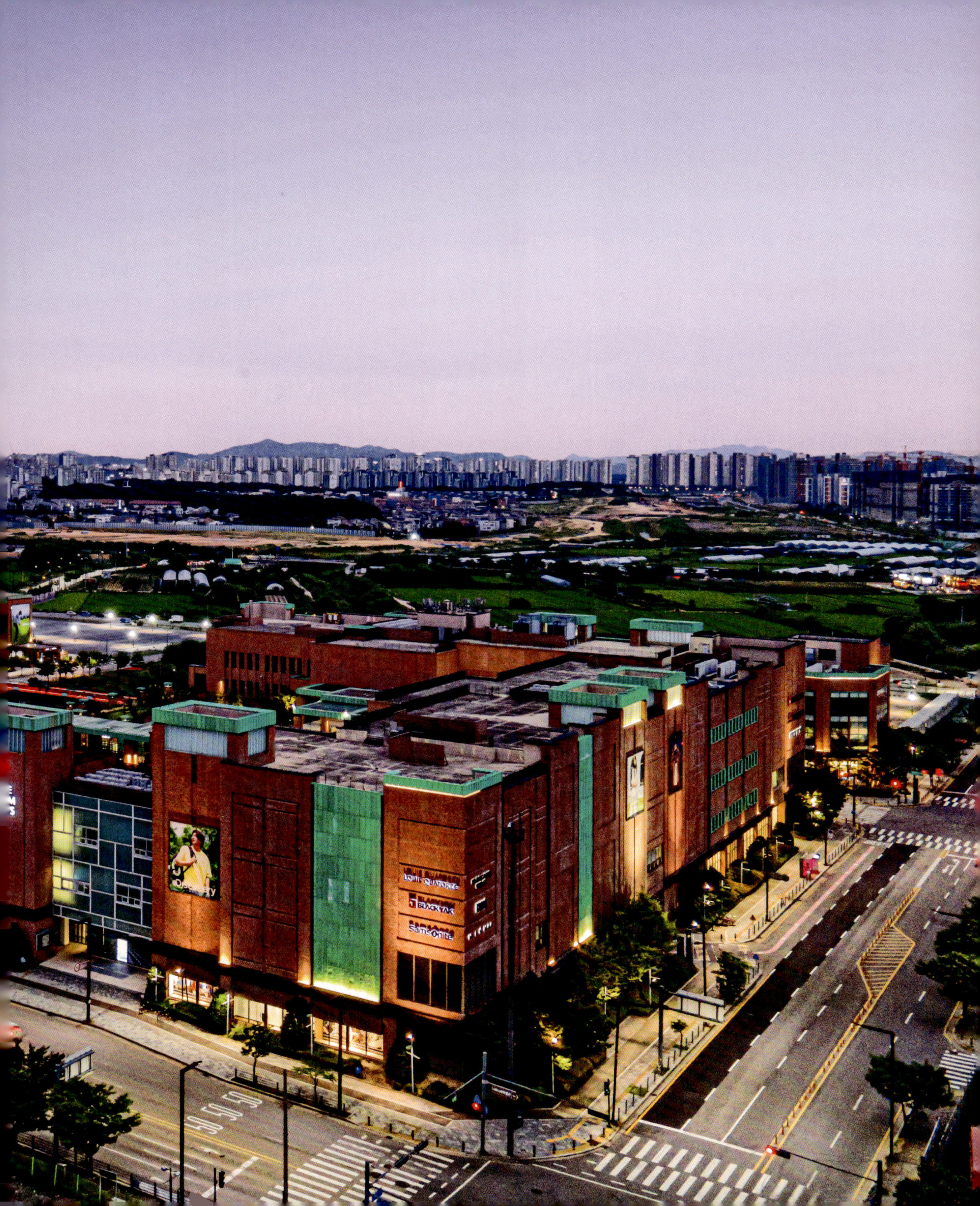
QUATORZE
BLACKYAK
Samsonite

The site is in an architecturally rich area in Paju-si, neighboring recent developments like Stan Allen's Paju Book-City—a cultural complex entirely devoted to the creation, publication, merchandising and sales of Korean books and home to 250 publishers with over 10,000 workers. As the site was a part of the Paju Book-City Neighborhood Association, we went through a rigorous review by the board of the association and had to comply with the architectural guidelines for Book-City.

Due to the nature of the outdoor shopping mall, we tried to create a variety of streets and squares so that customers can enjoy strolling and shopping as much as possible. We incorporated a pedestrian boardwalk that can be walked around, like an old European city scene, and a void-like square was created in the place where several streets meet. A bridge was created to connect two different blocks to each other. Front plazas facing the rivulet were placed in front of the entrance. All these gestures are the result of adopting a design methodology that creates voids from solid blocks. The "void" square is an essential wayfinding element and also provides an exciting sense of space in the shopping mall. To seamlessly connect these four blocks, we installed a series of bridges and boardwalks from the banks of the rivulets.

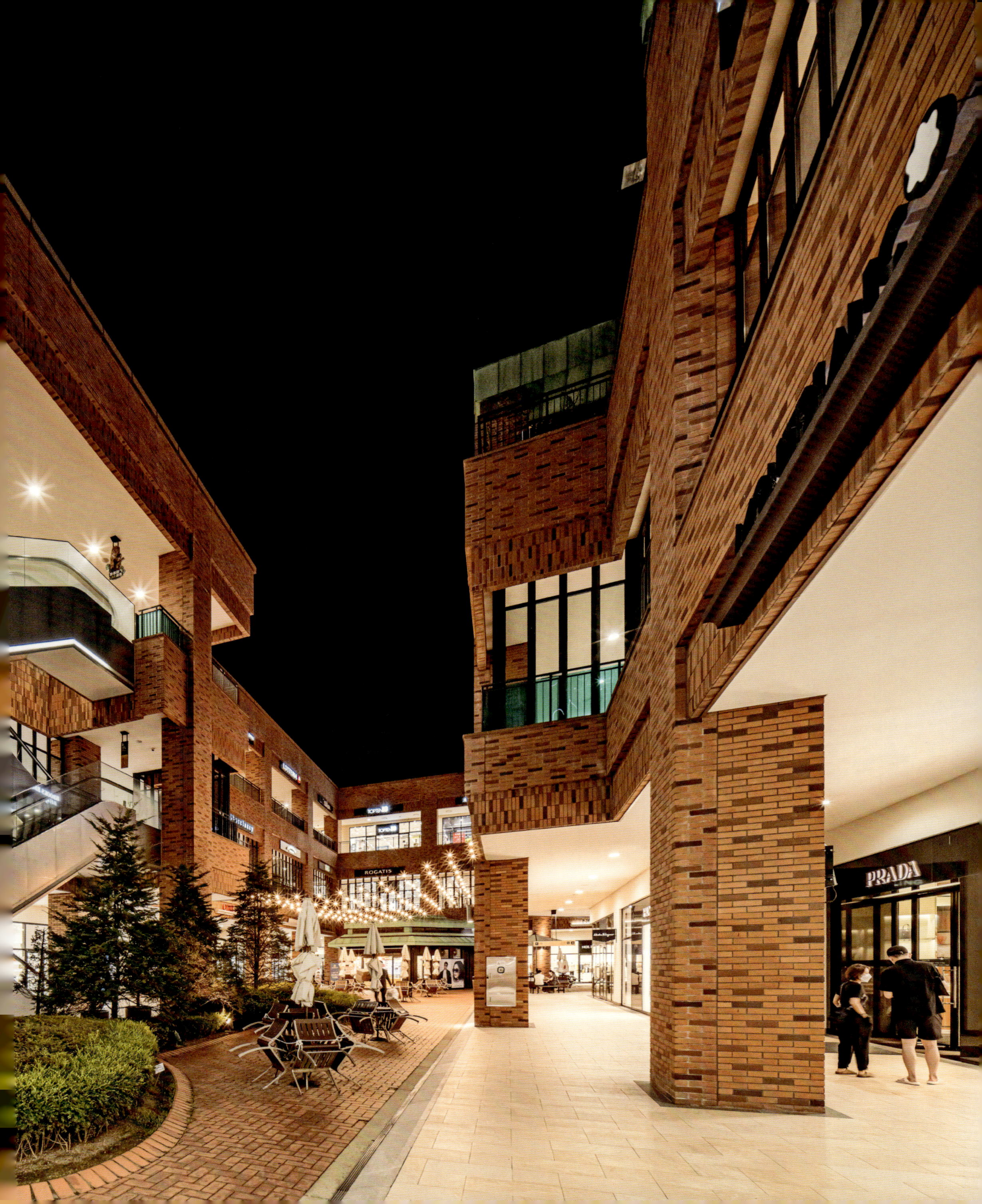
ROGATIS
PRADA

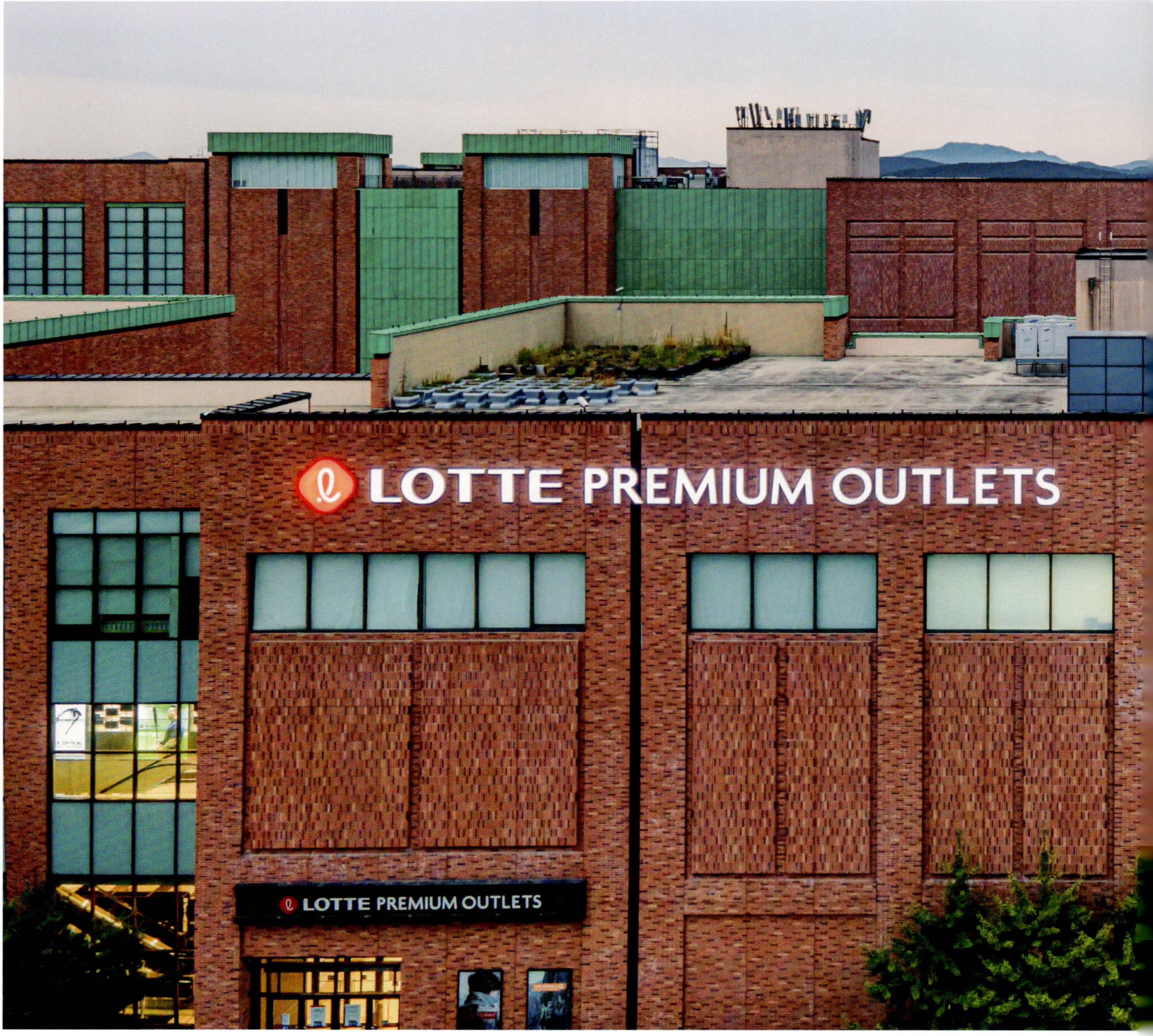
LOTTE PREMIUM OUTLETS
LOTTE PREMIUM OUTLETS

Our design aimed to effectively connect a densely urban commercial zone into its natural environment on a large scale, enhancing the usability of both spaces. To achieve a mature and timeless aesthetic, brick, copper, and glass were used for the materiality. The shopping center includes a variety of restaurants, high-end luxury brands, a cinema, and other recreational activities.

Taesun Hong, *City of Red Blue & Green* (1994), oil

In architecture, a **sense of surprise** articulates the impressive experience of moving from a narrow space to a wider space, much like the passage of music that incorporates the musical strengths of *piano* (soft) and *forte* (loud).

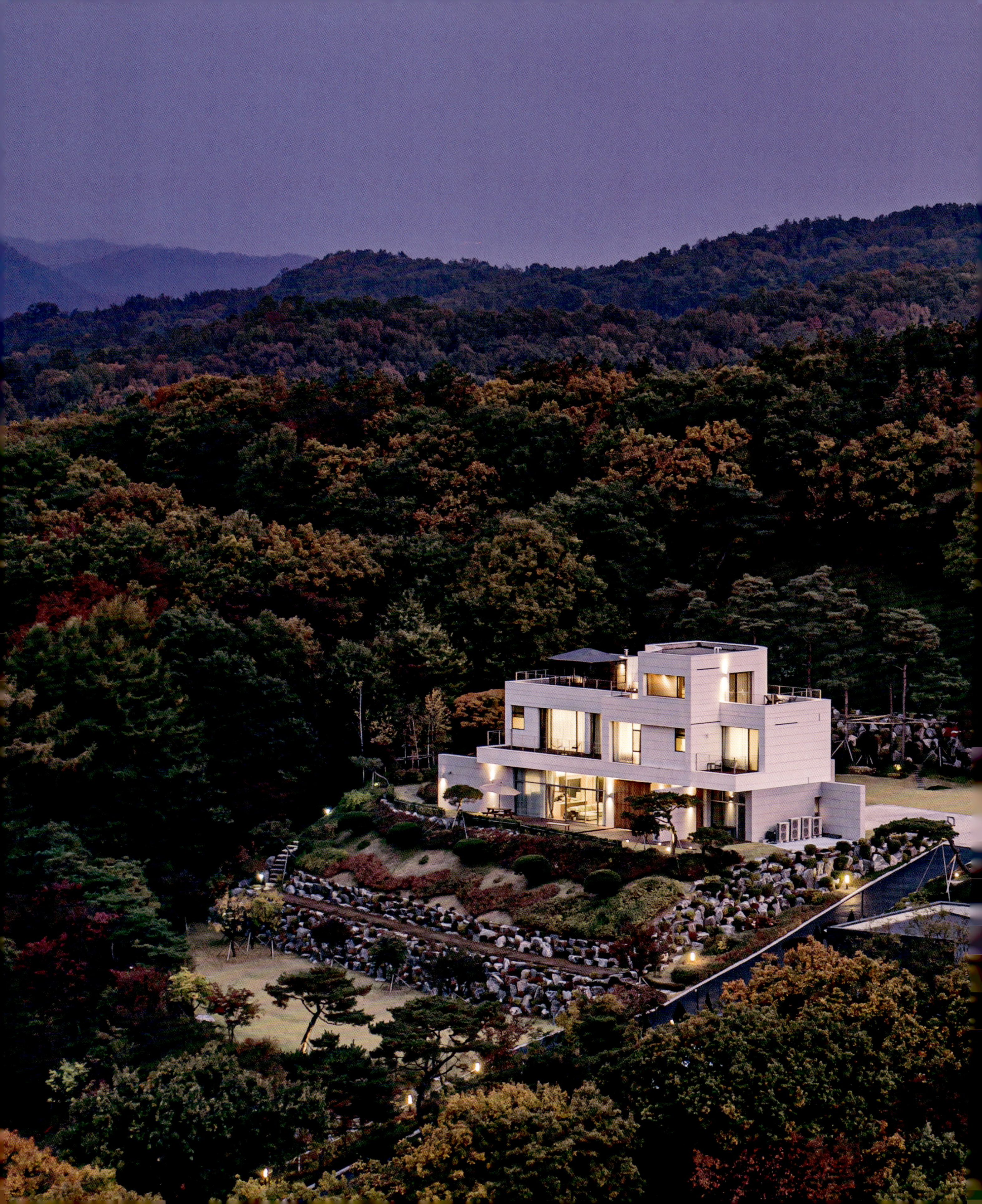

# YEOJU RESIDENCE

Yeoju-si, Gyeonggi-do, South Korea | 2016

This three-story retreat is in Yeoju-si, a suburban city of Seoul. The site sits on a remote hillside, overlooking a distant river and its surrounding plush landscape. Accordingly, the client sought to have a more open and spacious living/kitchen area that took advantage of the view. One obstacle that informed our design process was the strict programmatic zones as the project rose further from the ground. The design was initiated by juxtaposing all living spaces linearly in an east–west direction to maximize sunlight and curate the best views possible for every individual space. Having a materiality and general form that contrasts the project's environment allows both to become more independently striking.

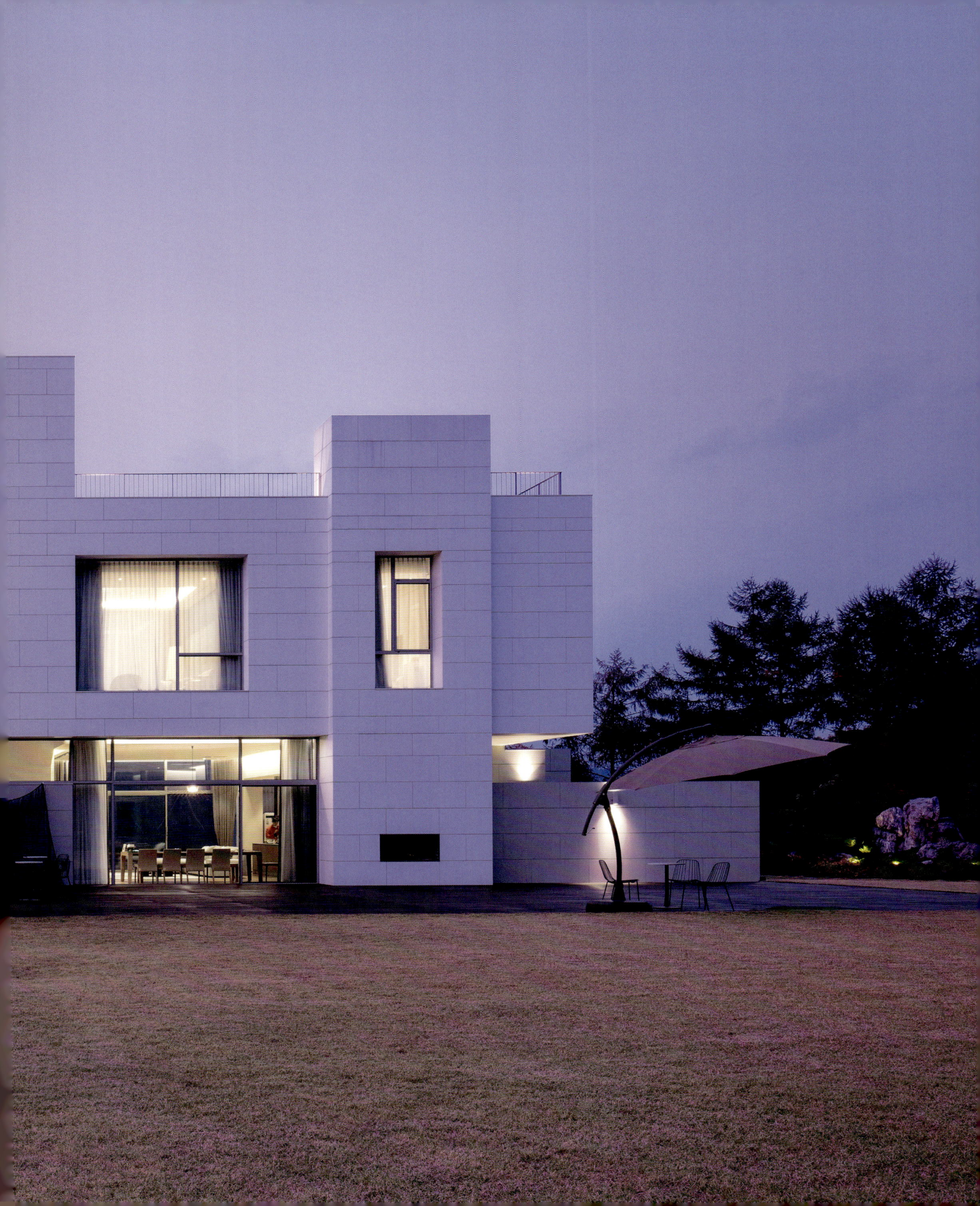

The design was developed to structure living spaces yet allow them to bend and flex enough to be partially ambiguous. The geometric composition of the project and its two-dimensional walls help to fix the volumes into their programmatic spaces, yet they remain unsecured enough to blur the demarcated boundaries of each space and to obtain a more autonomous living environment. Two outdoor decks lie outside of the north and south sides of the living/dining room area to allow the living space to extend outdoors.

Due to the importance of the entrance route to the client, the position of the car and the garage were thoughtfully considered throughout the design process. While storing the car in an indifferent parking zone near the house would have been sufficient, we decided to integrate the garage space with two discrete zones: the living room area and the guest bedroom suite. Thus, the entrance and car storage space became one of the more central and important spaces, as the driver experiences the view of the river as they step out of the car. Sliding and pivot doors also allow the space to operate as a porch and garden.

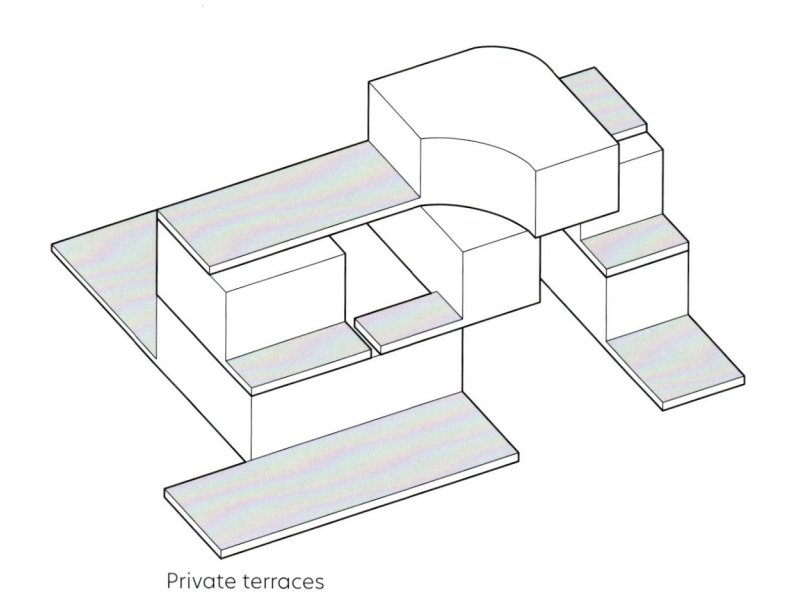

Private terraces

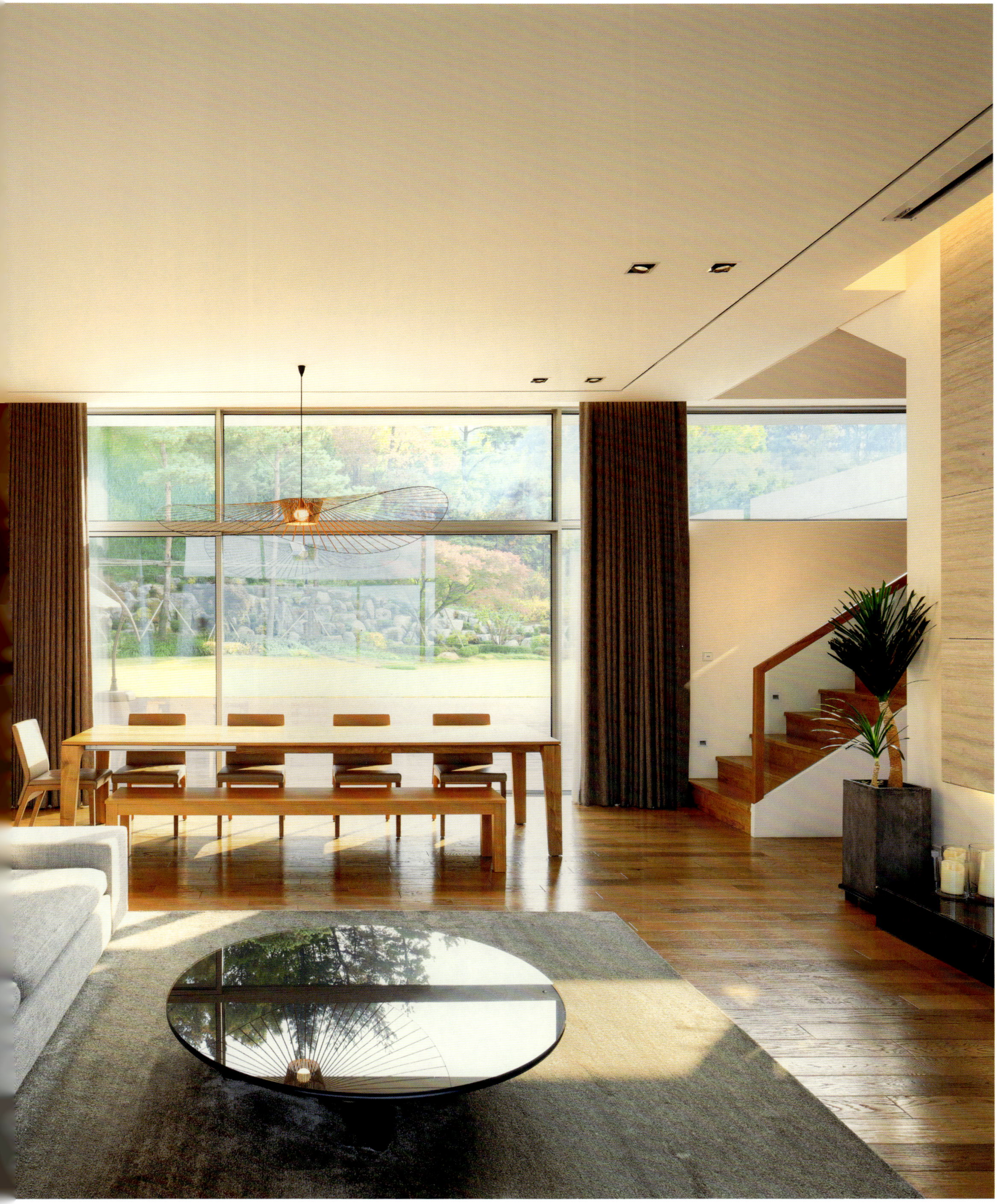

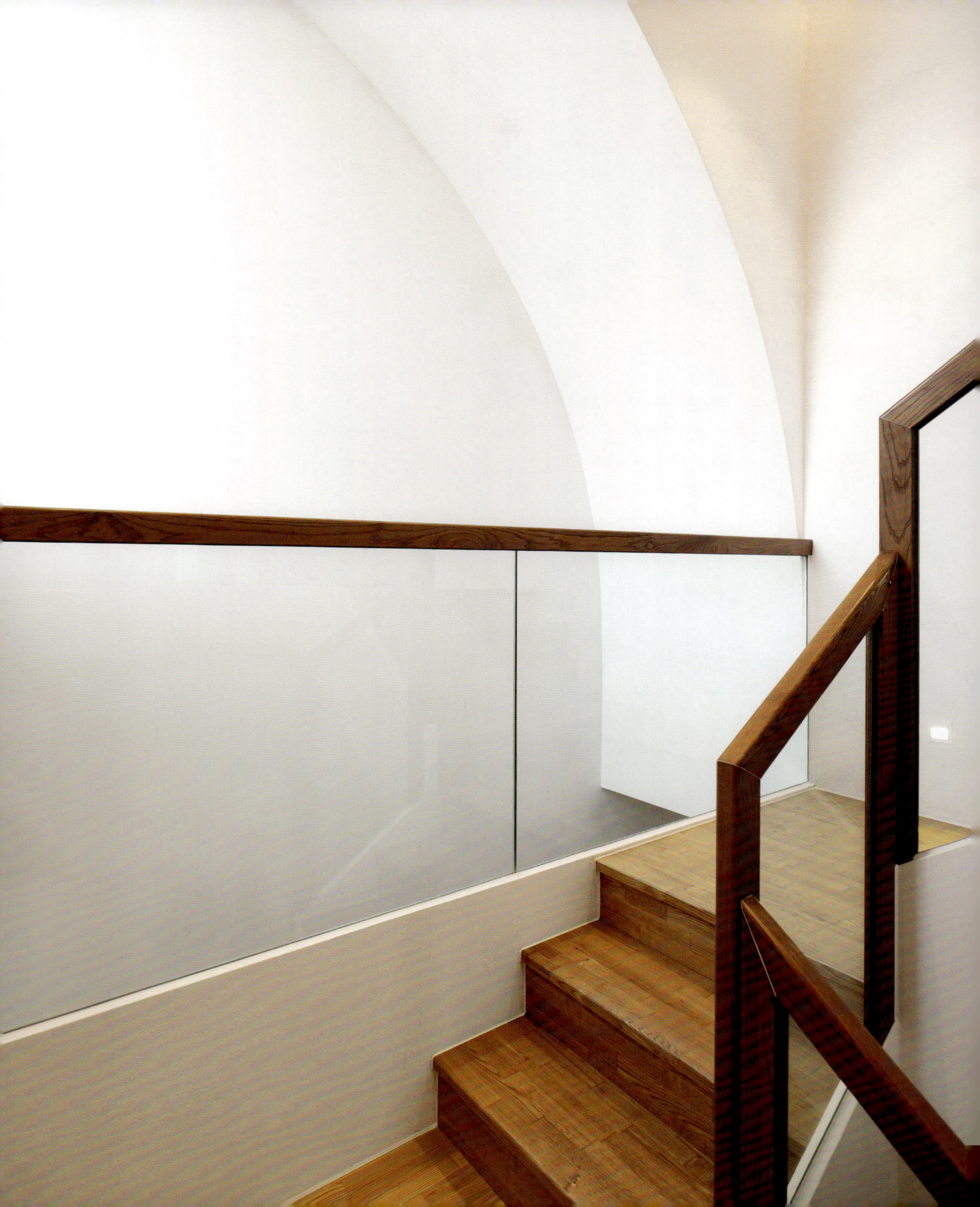

By strategically inserting and extending walls, exterior spaces and zones are distinguished to help define new living spaces. Extruding these walls on their original axis allows the boundaries of their respective space to be pushed outside, extending the border into abstract space. These rooms now extend to the grass or tree lines, or however far the user of this space can view. While these walls create physical boundaries for the spaces outside, they blur the boundary between interior and exterior space as the active living areas now fall between the two.

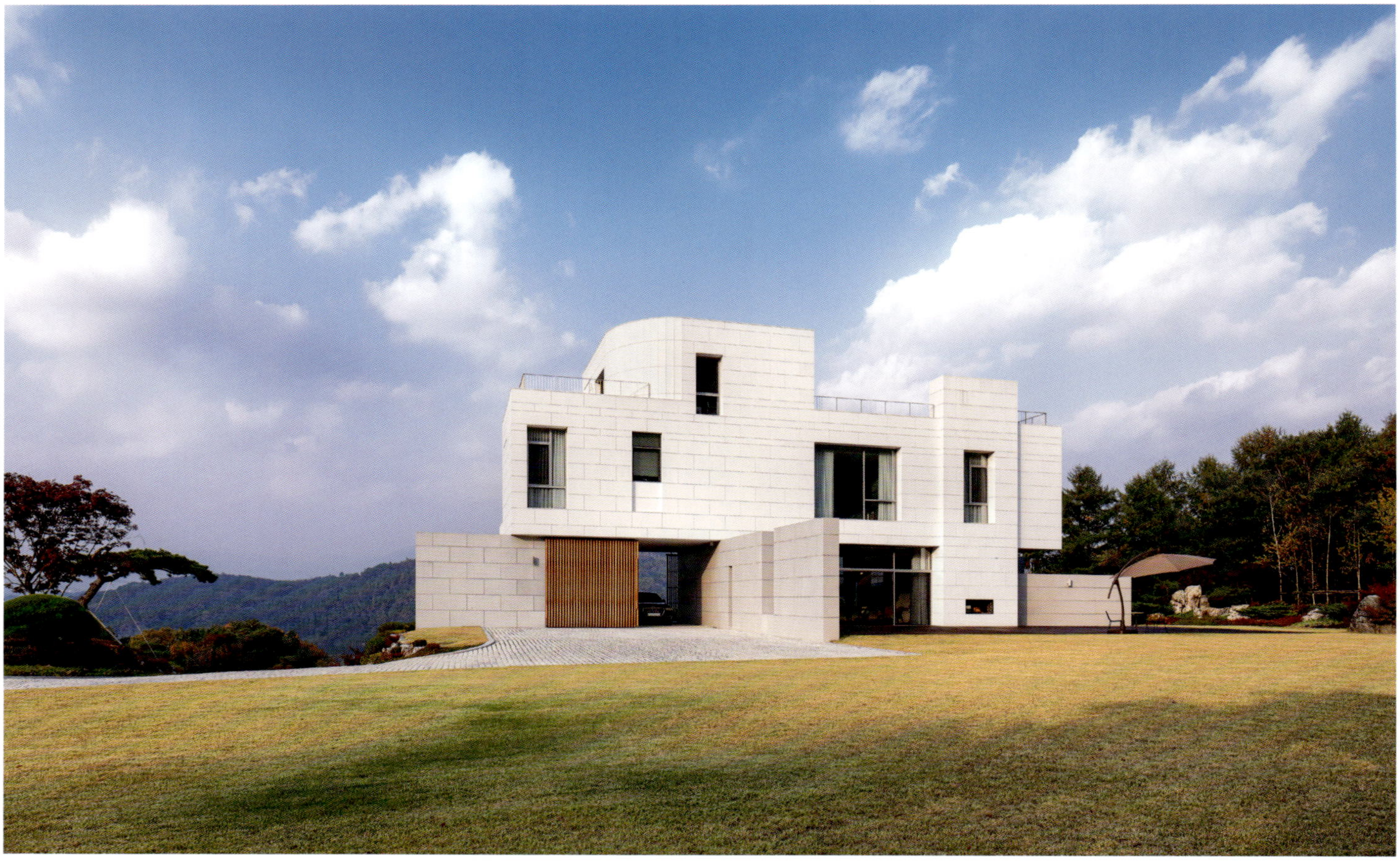

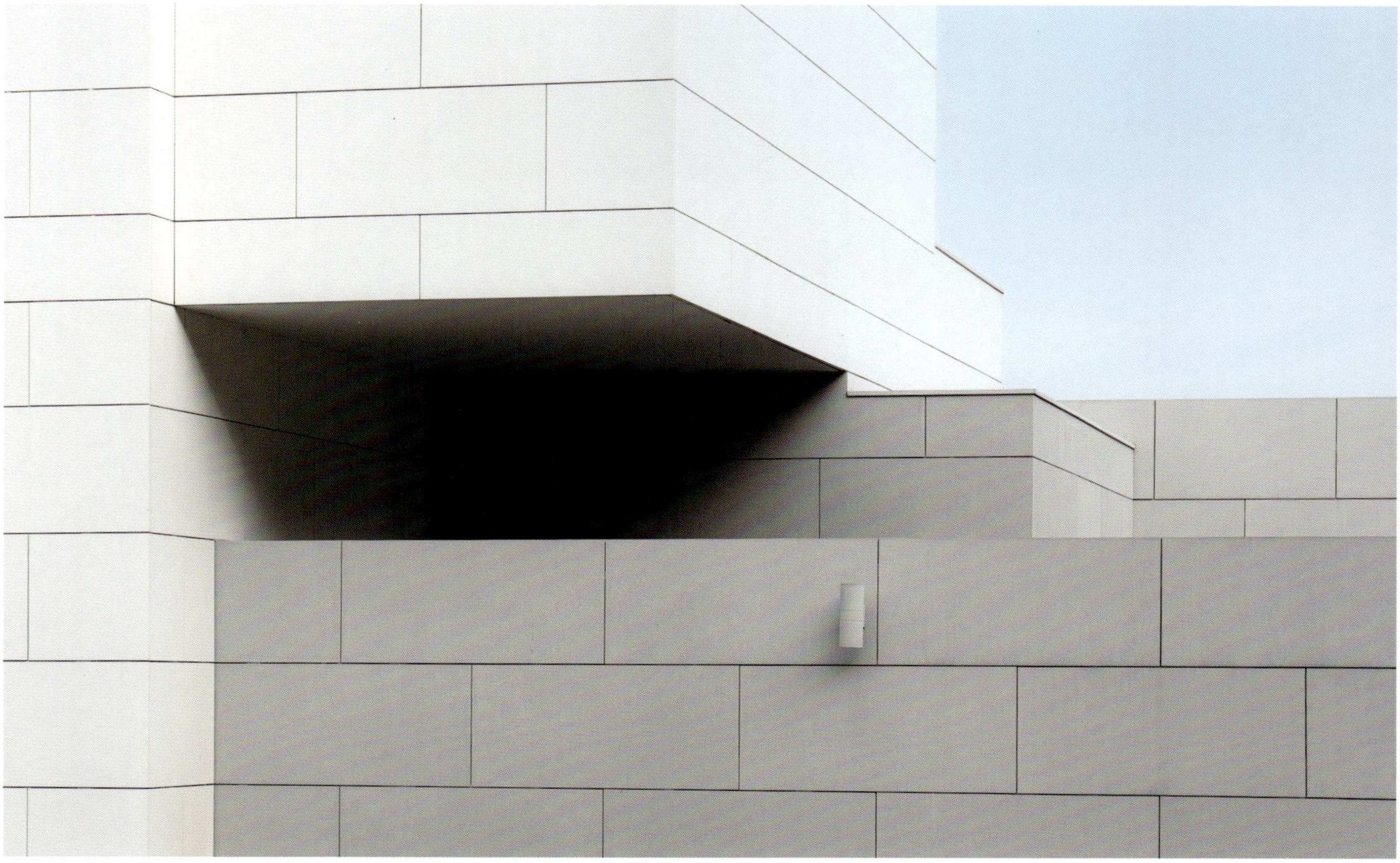

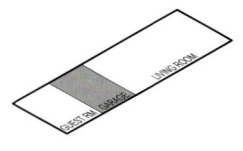

| Program requirement | Best views | Extended line as divider of space | Extruded |

| Punctured to allow views | Living spaces defined | Living blocks stacked | Final forms defined |

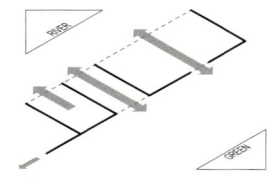

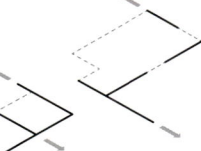

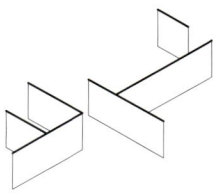

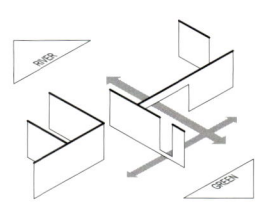

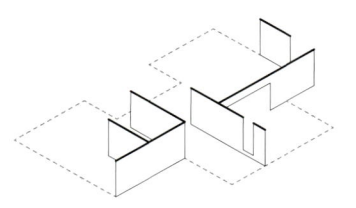

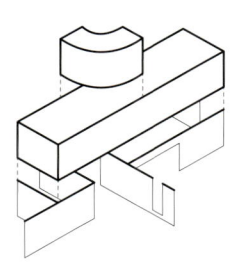

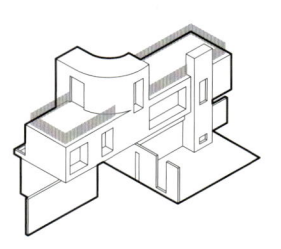

YEOJU RESIDENCE

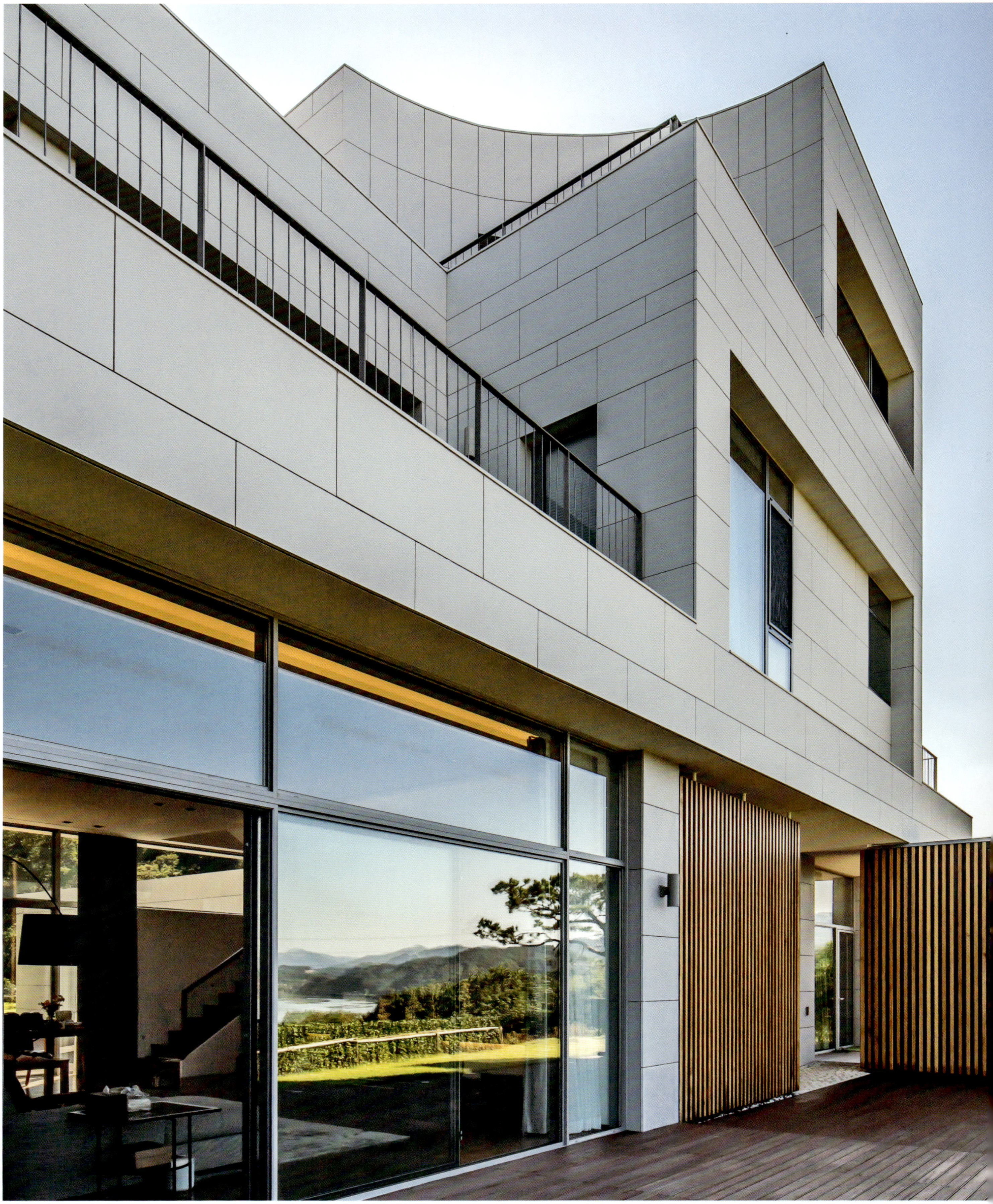

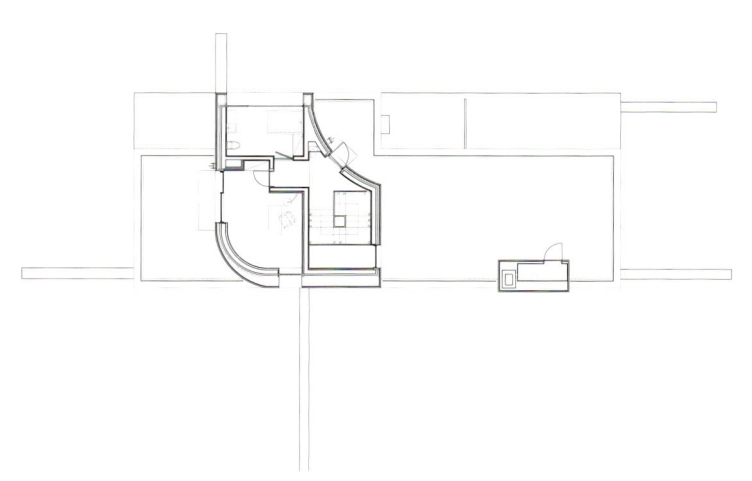

Third-floor plan

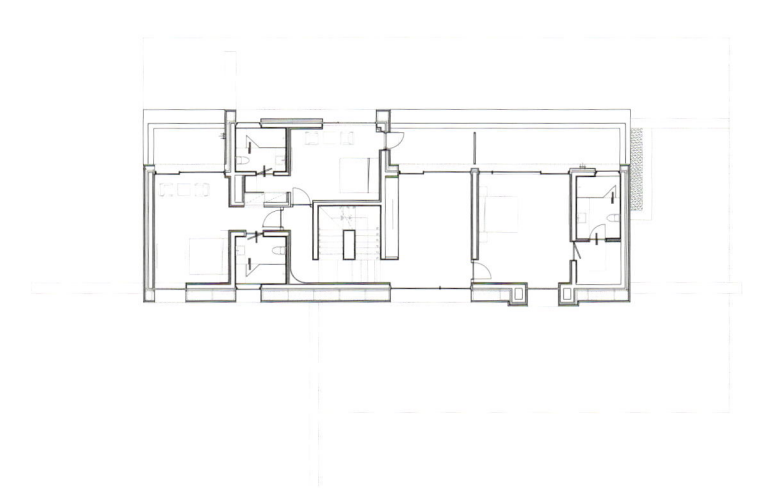

Second-floor plan

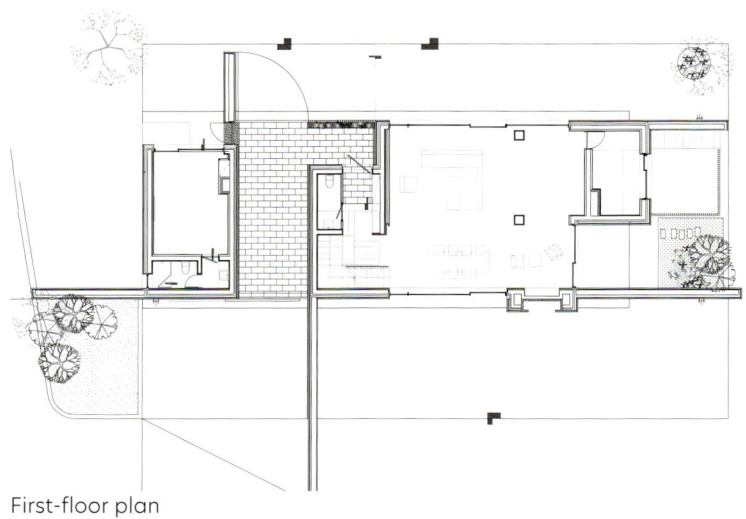

First-floor plan

YEOJU RESIDENCE

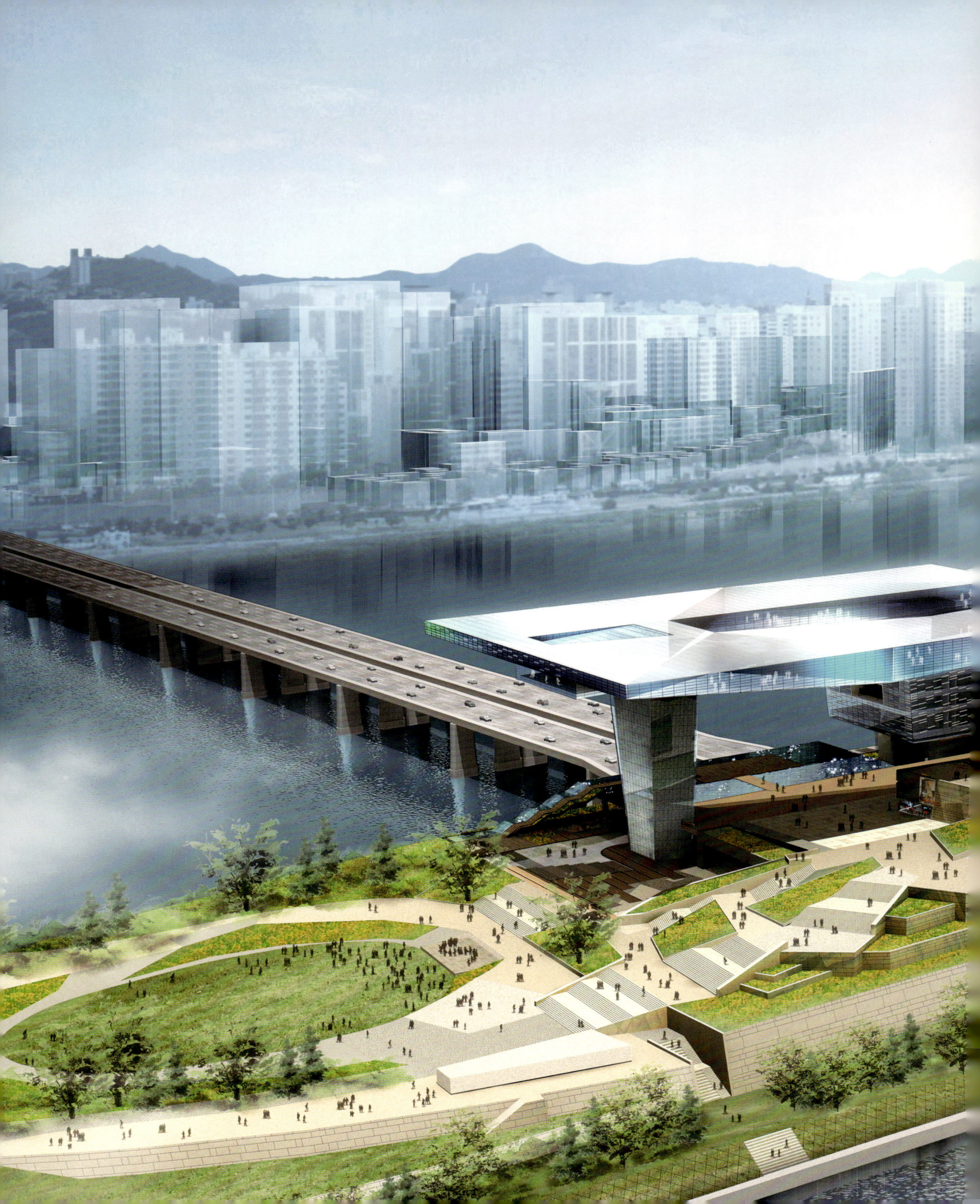

# SEOUL PERFORMING ARTS CENTER

Yongsan-gu, Seoul, South Korea | 2005

The Seoul Performing Arts Center (SPAC) design competitions were held in 2005 to determine the design of a major cultural arts center to be located on Nodul Island, a land mass in the center of the Seoul's Han River. The requested program included an opera house and symphony hall, an open-air performance space, and other related facilities and amenities.

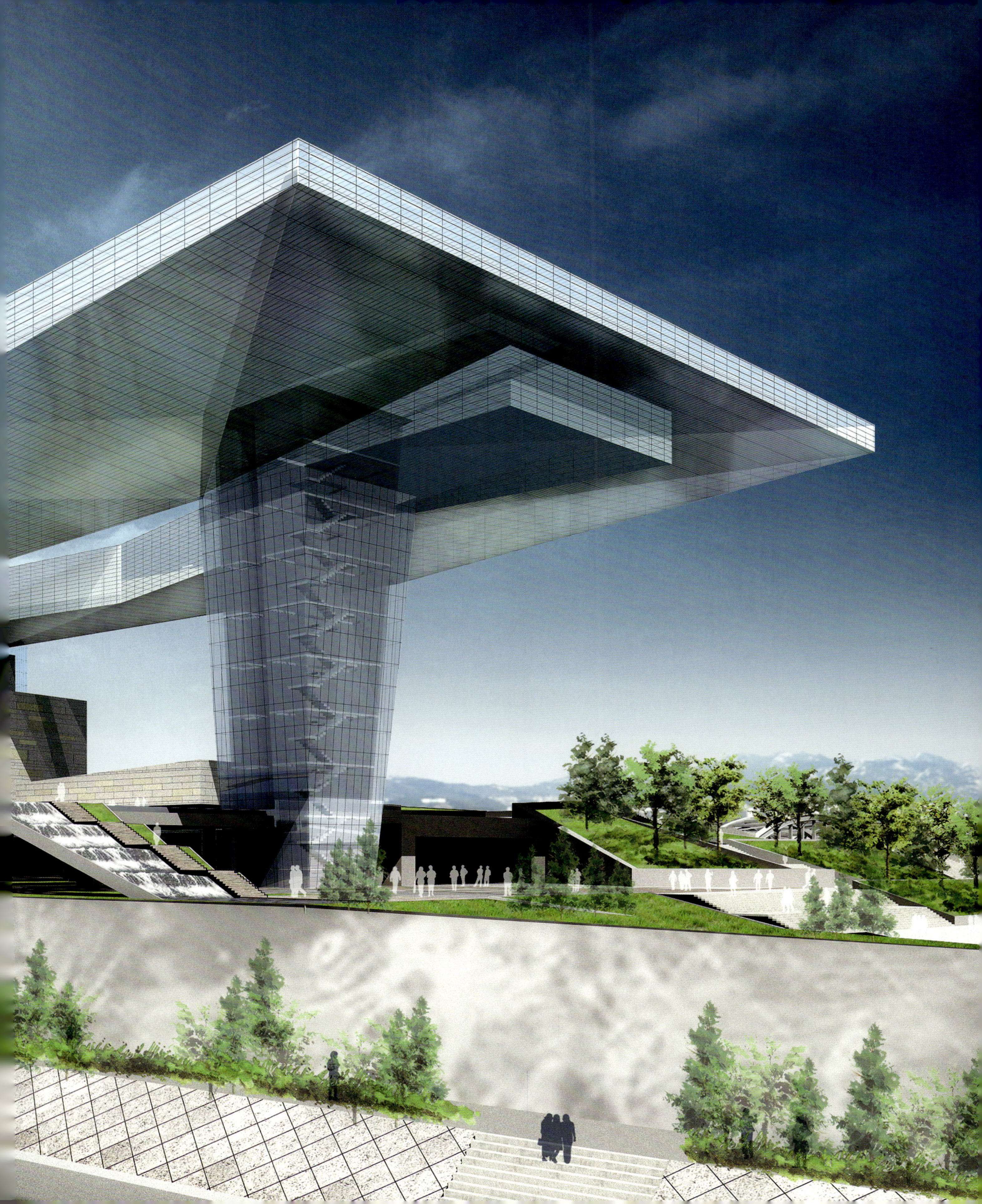

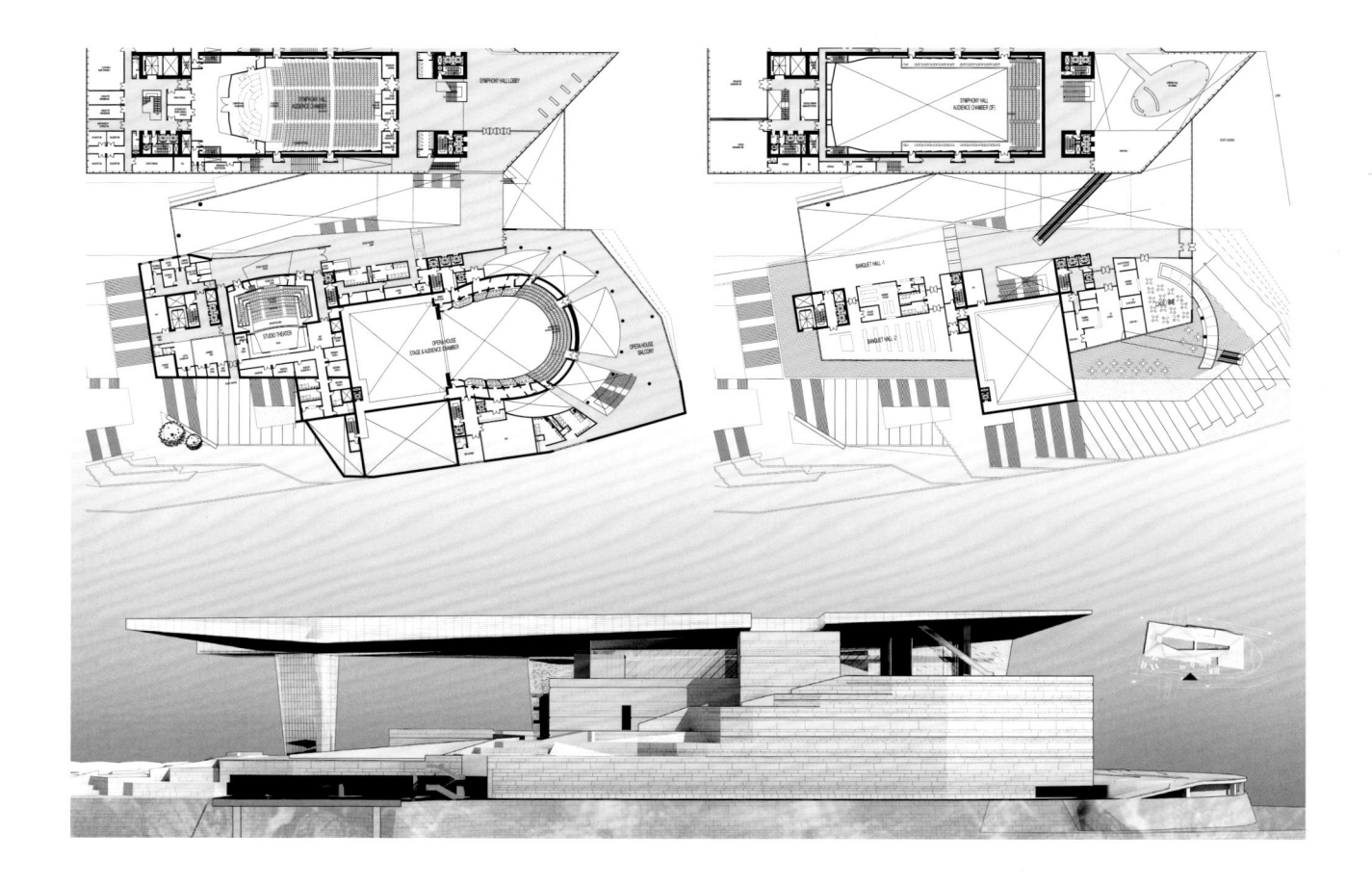

Our initial scheme—designed with Professor Junggon Kim—was selected as one of the five finalists in the first round. In the final round, our design won second place. Our design objective was to build a performing arts center not only for people who come to see a performance or for the cultural elite but a cultural center that is open year-round to everyone. Our design would have filled Nodul Island with a variety of spaces, such as open plazas, reflecting pools, naturally landscaped areas, open theaters, and a retail area so that people could come to relax and enjoy a day free from the traffic jams and the hustle and bustle of the city.

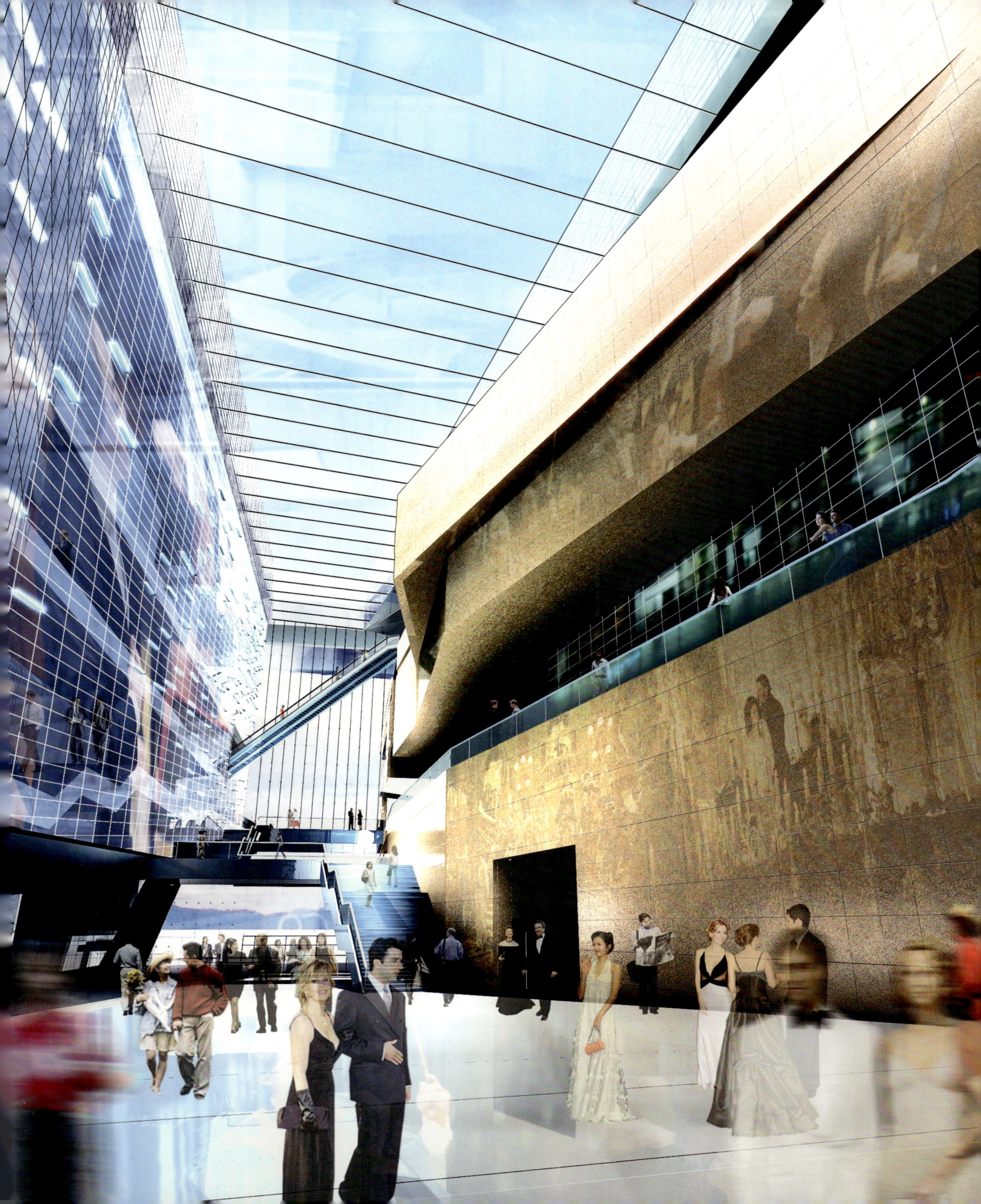

218  SENSE OF SURPRISE

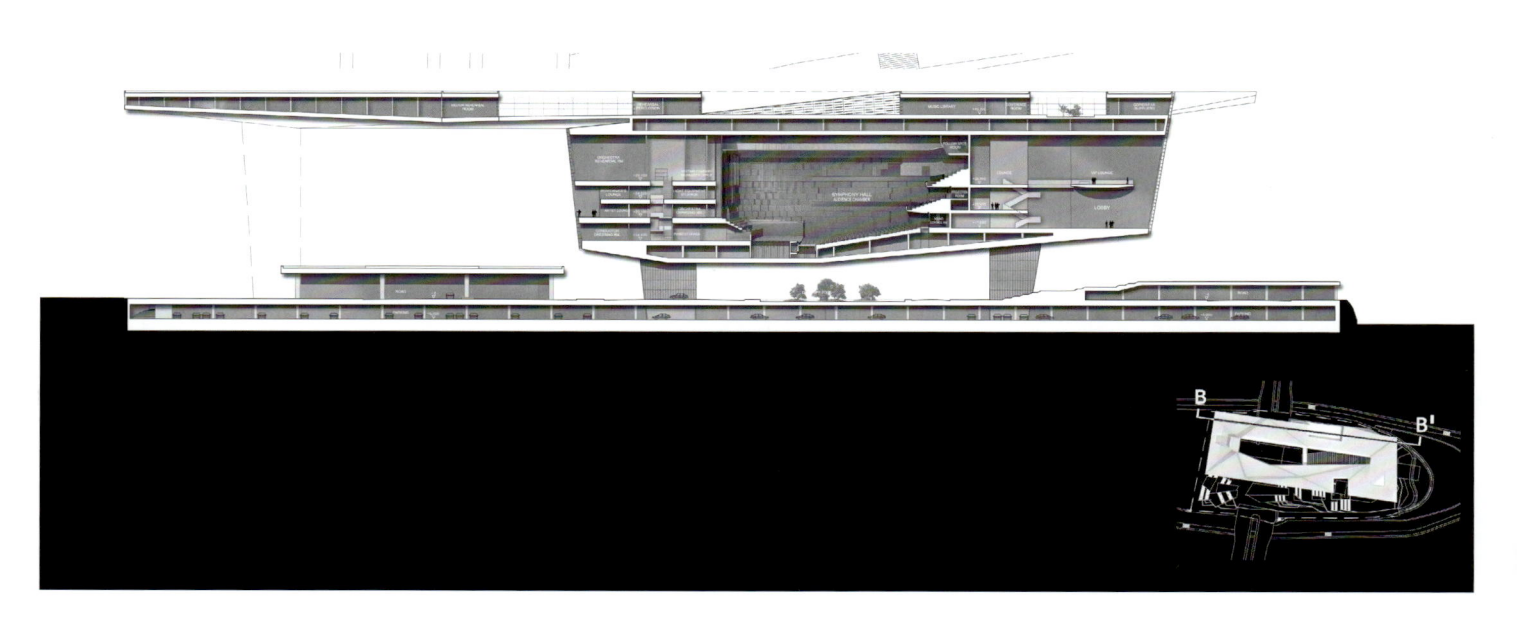

Nodul Island links the northern and southern regions of Seoul with highways that hold heavy commuter traffic. A bridge runs across the island, dividing it into two; the east and west flanks of the island each has a bridge also; the one on the western side serves as a bridge for the Seoul subway. SPAC's site is primarily on the eastern part of the island and stretches 230 feet (70 meters) beyond the bridge to the west. The bridge bisects the island, dividing the site, thus it was critical to link the site somehow. To solve this problem and link the island in a natural manner, we proposed a deck to be placed over the island, blocking views of the unattractive highway and the noise coming from the bridge. By covering the bridge and elevating the ground level one level higher, the deck would create a formal new open plaza for the public. It was crucial to use this deck cleverly to also insert the various programs. Splitting the deck and unfolding it would create voids into which we inserted the programs. The whole deck's landscaped surface could be used by the public. In addition to this new deck level, we would make use of the whole roof of the opera house to create a landscaped area where people could enjoy the series of intimate spaces, resulting in a dramatic increase in the amount of area that is available to the public.

SEOUL PERFORMING ARTS CENTER

SPAC's design was intended to both assimilate the site conditions and respect the city's history and heritage. Trying to keep the idea of the horizontal, together with the ideology of yin and yang forces, SPAC became a representation of the "mountain" and the "cloud." To emphasize these qualities, the opera house ("mountain") would be grounded to the earth, and from a distance its façade a rampart that would gradually rise up and surround Nodul Island. The symphony hall ("cloud") would be elevated and float above the island like a light cloud. We carefully considered the buildings' envelope materials selections to highlight the characteristics of each performance hall. We would have used stone, a heavy and solid material, for the opera house, while a lighter, more transparent material was the choice for the symphony hall. For the opera house, the material would have been organized as if slates of stones were layered one on top of the other. Trying to make it look as natural as possible, the façades' texture would be irregularly shaped. Like looking at sedimentary rocks, the texture of this "mountain" would appear to have been naturally shaped by the landscape and the surrounding environment; the skin an extroverted form that would absorb the influence of the elements and be eroded by them.

The void between these two performance halls would become the outer lobby, acting as the mediator between the two spaces. Placing the greatest importance on the people's experience of going to see a performance, the lobbies and VIP lounges of both symphony and opera halls would be positioned to face the island's outskirts. The organization of the two performing halls was simplified into three zones: lobby/public zone, performance hall zone, and service zone. The service zone would be placed closest to the main highway, for direct access to the service area. The public zone would provide the fullest waterfront enjoyment, away from the busy highway, and would offer amazing views of Seoul for people either during intermission or after the show from their respective lobbies.

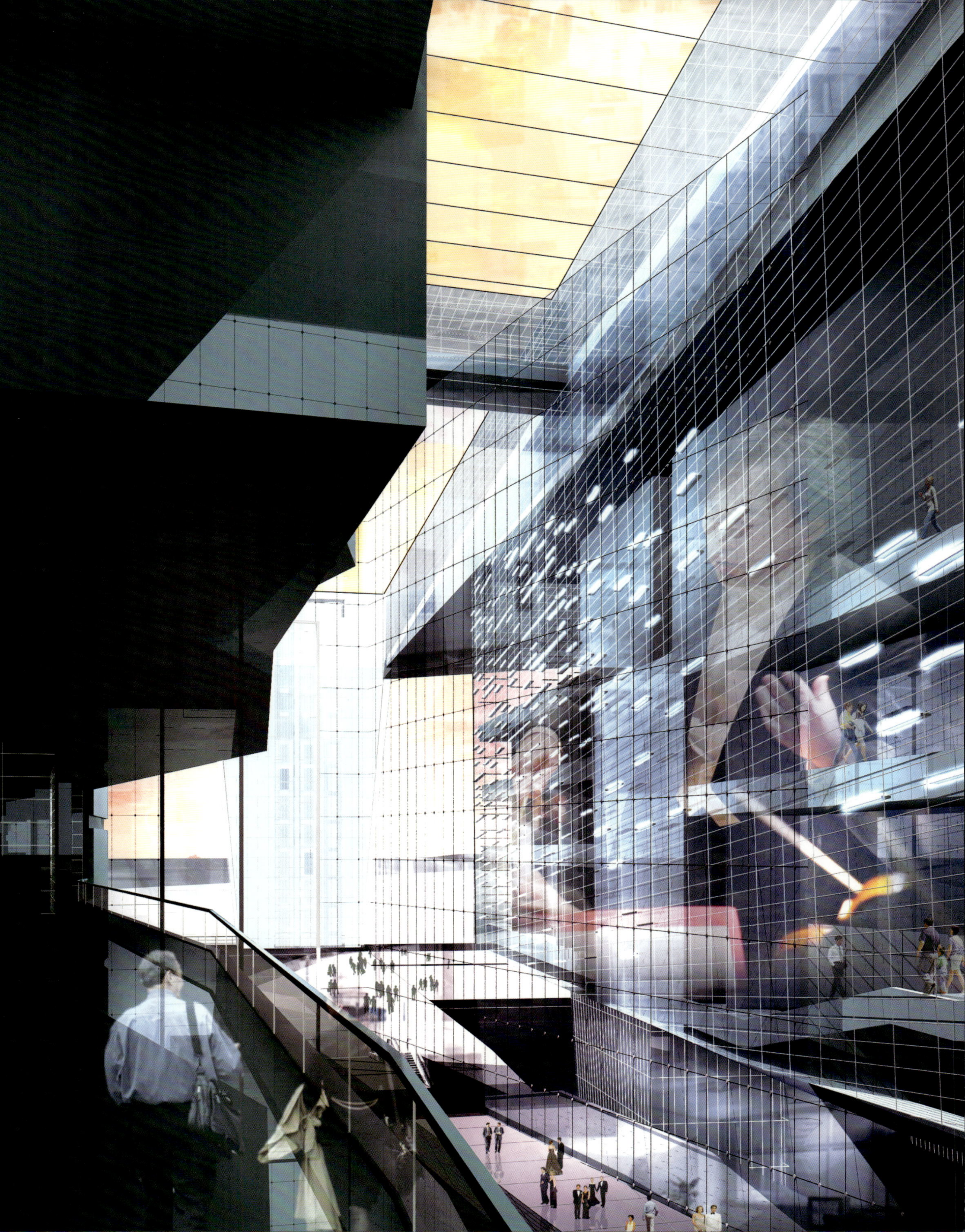

222  SENSE OF SURPRISE

The opera house would accommodate an audience of 1,740, comprising 1,490 fixed seats, 100 changeable seats, and 150 temporary seats. The opera house would be a modern reinterpretation of the traditional horseshoe-shaped hall (for best acoustics) with three tiers of balconies. The proscenium was set at 52 feet (16 meters) wide and 46 feet (14 meters) high. The audience chamber would be given a higher ceiling to impress upon the spectators the grand scale of the hall. Natural materials would be used to create a modern look, while also providing optimal acoustics.

The SPAC's symphony hall—a modern interpretation of the traditional shoebox-type hall, with two tiers of balconies—would accommodate an audience of 1,900 and 200 chorus seats. As home to the Seoul Philharmonic Orchestra, the acoustical aspects were given top priority.

The symphony hall's lobby would face the edge of the island, for clear views of Seoul's skyline. The VIP lounge would hang from the roof, above the main symphony hall lobby, offering VIP guests a unique experience along with use of the diverse facilities open to them, like the observatory, café, restaurant, gallery, performance at the reflecting pool island, and more. The program made use of the roof space above. The roof would be occupiable; performers and staff could walk on the roof and experience walking through this "cloud." Practice rooms, rehearsal rooms, music library, and administrative offices would be placed at roof level, offering performers and administrative staff their own space while being able to enjoy views of Seoul and the river through the structure's translucent skin; the inner opening would provide views toward the public plaza below, and an inner corridor would enable people to look down into the outer lobby.

A series of public outdoor stages would bring to life dynamic musical and theatrical performances, engaging spectators and the public year-round. Moreover, the landscape of SPAC would draw on the unique natural setting of Nodul Island. Bound by the ever-changing flow of Han River, the landscape itself would become a theatrical performance. A small outdoor theater would be located on the roof of the retail area, where on summery nights people could watch an outdoor movie projected on the wall of the opera house mass.

The "mountain" landscape would rise gradually from the east of the island to the west. The southern elevation of the landscape is exposed to the sun, wind, and water. With these external factors, the elevation would be carved playfully into irregularly shaped plateaus, paths, stairs, and overlooks. The various paths would lead to the roof garden. Each series of steps would break out to smaller more intimate plazas that become like a small outdoor stage. The different levels of the "mountain" would be activated by the various performances that occur on these intimate plazas.

The easternmost end of the landscape towers like a "cliff" over the river and provides great views over Seoul. This "cliff" would be lit at night, acting as a beacon that connects SPAC with the city. The "cliff" façade would include climbing walls, providing visitors with more recreational activities. The stairs would be steeper and punctuated by overlooks and stopping places to rest and view the city.

The "cloud" roof of the symphony hall would catch the eye of anyone driving along the highway(s) beside the river. Once on the island, visitors would gain access to the roof via three ways: Go directly up via the tower to the observatory and enjoy the sunset or view of Seoul. (The tower would not only act as a structure that holds the roof, but it would also hold the core that connects the public on the ground and deck level to the observatory and the other facilities available at roof level.) A grand escalator would run diagonally across between the opera house and the symphony hall. Taking the diagonal escalators up, the public would land on the roof of the opera house. From this level, they could access the public banquet halls or the café and have the option of going out to the sky garden. Another set of escalators at the sky garden level would lead directly to the "cloud." Once on the roof, people could enjoy eating at the sky lounge restaurant, which would include a landscaped balcony to be enjoyed on nice days. In addition to enjoying the views of Seoul from the restaurant, following the inner corridor, the public would also be able to look down toward the outer lobby and the formal plaza from above. From the highest level, visitors could choose to walk down, enjoying the entire landscape of the park.

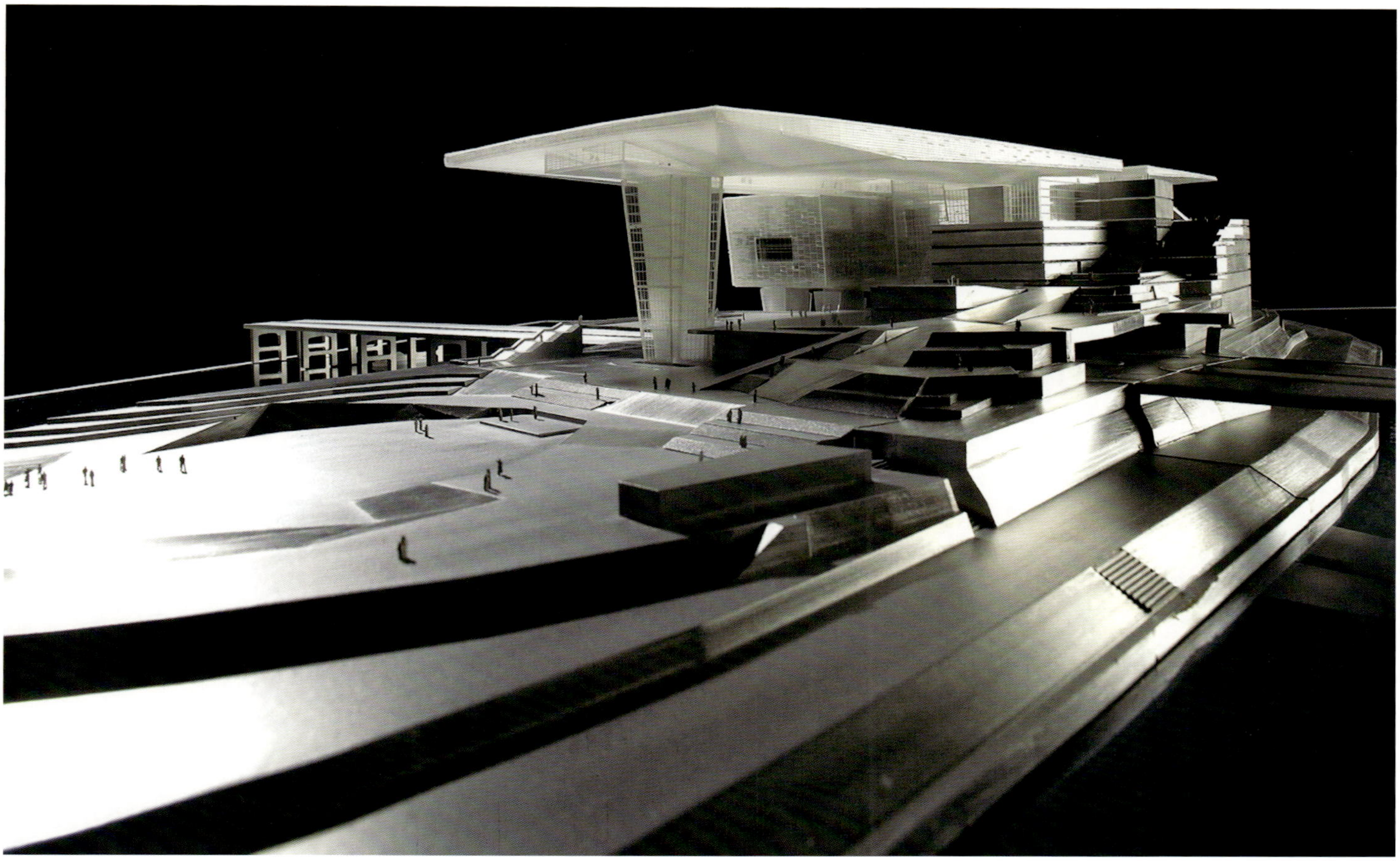

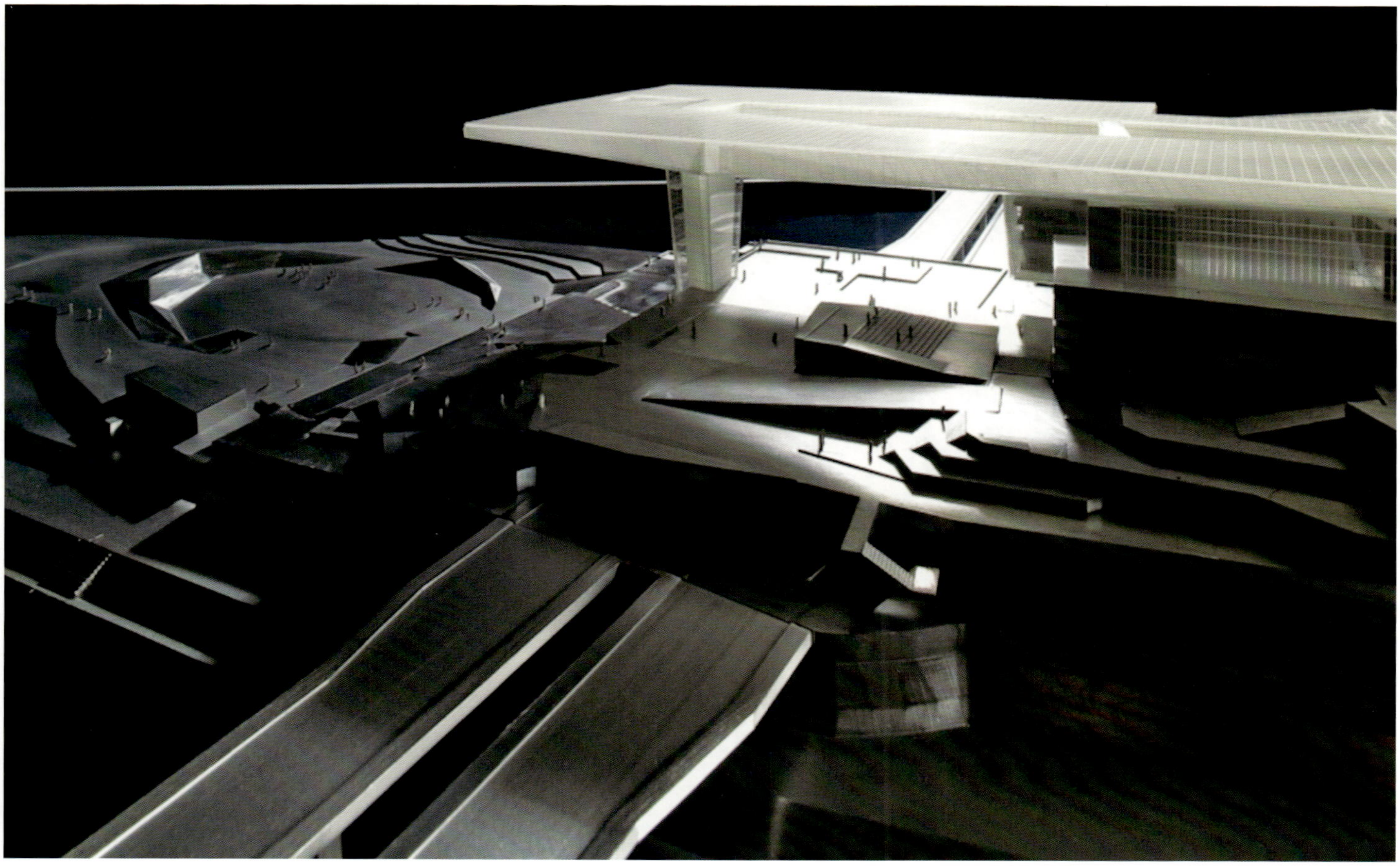

# LOTTE DEPARTMENT STORE ROOF GARDEN

Jung-gu, Busan, South Korea | 2010

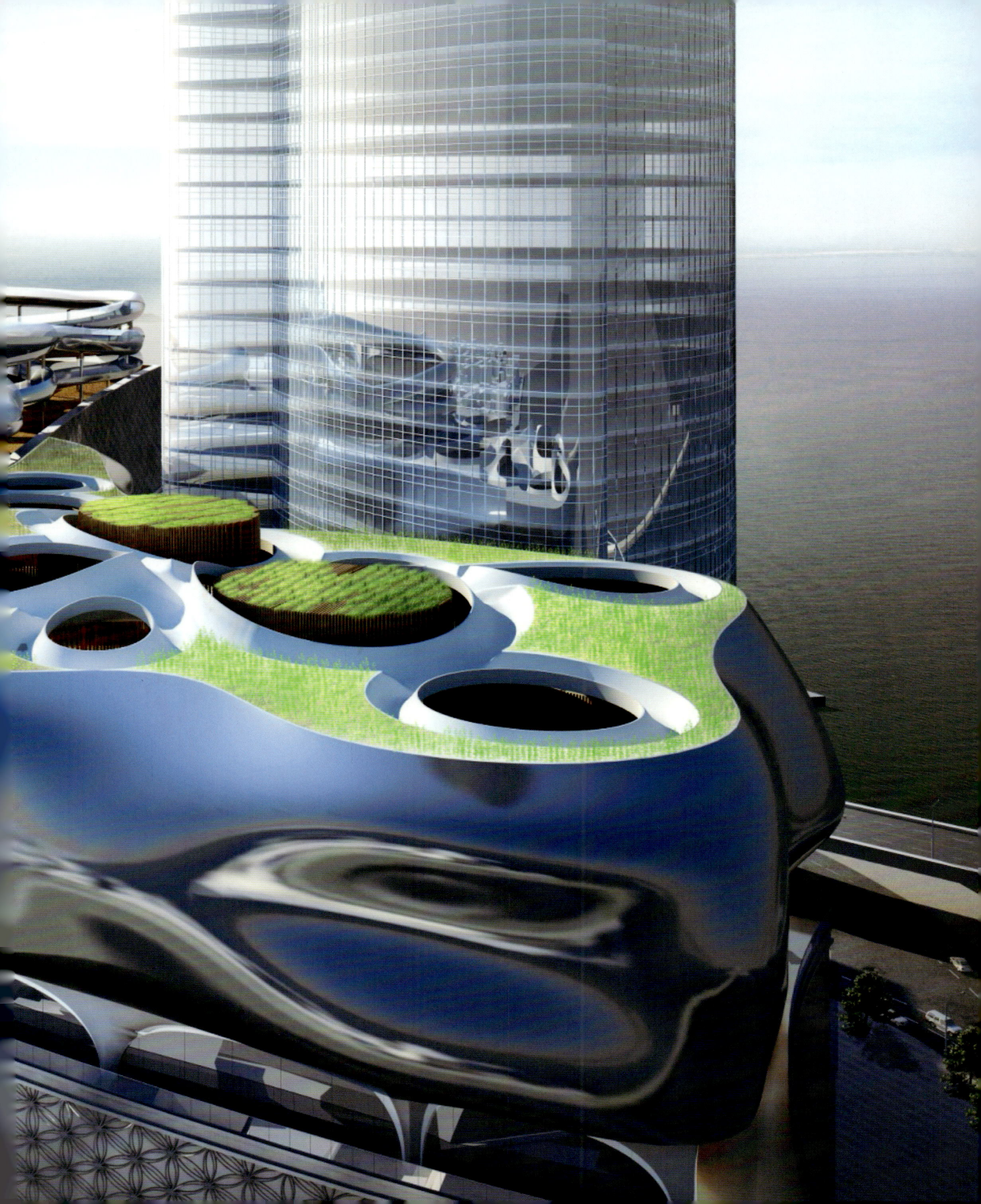

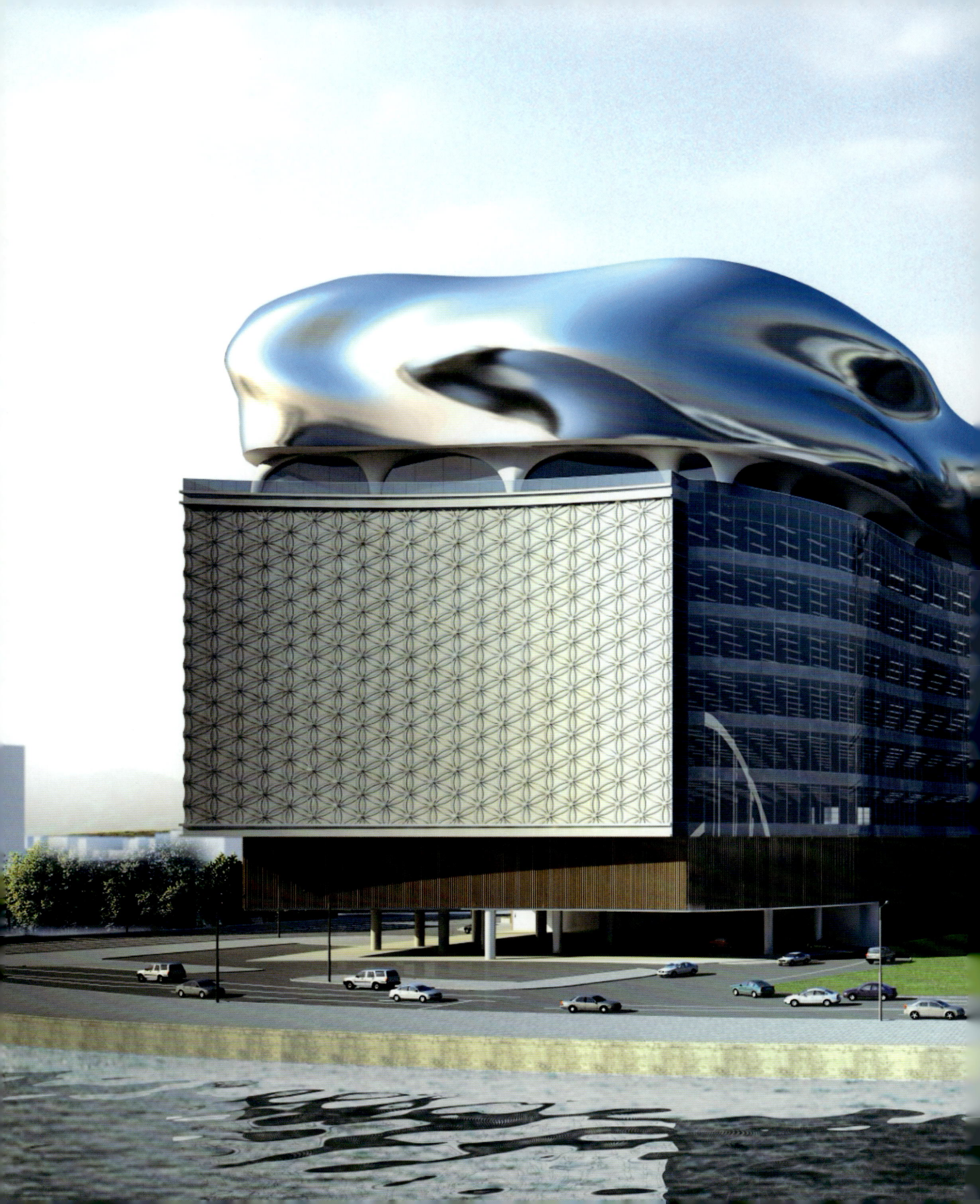

This proposal would not only provide a moment of tranquil urban green space, but also allow shoppers to experience the view of the ocean from an appropriately natural environment. The building's existing roof observatories were not effectively designed, as their limited points of connection within the building severely limited the potential of use by two additional floors of retail.

In this proposal we explored the "Way-Pod" design concept. The term is derived from I-Pod, creating a physical and digital hardware that could evolve with time. Way-Pod comprises the concepts of "Way," a free, elevated viewing corridor for the public, and "Pod," a private community center for entertainment, culture, and events.

"Way" is divided into six different sections: 1) Sol-way—a position on the roof with access to the western horizon view, including sunsets; 2) Heal-way—an area designed to promote healthier lifestyles by utilizing nearby jogging trails; 3) Art-way—an area allowing users to view exhibitions of art and media entertainment; 4) View-way—giving users a closer view of the bay and ocean; 5) EQ-way—allowing users to practice reflection and promote emotional intelligence (EQ); and 6) Tune-way—allowing users to enhance their sense of music.

"Pod," the name of the proposed new retail section, is divided into six different, functional sections: 1) Gig-pod—a performing arts area; 2) Foodie-pod—restaurant and café zone; 3) Kid-pod—a recreational area for children; 4) Gem-pod—a games area; 5) Edu-pod—educational shops and school supply area; and 6) Muse-pod—museums and art exhibition area.

The various programs of "Way" and "Pod" are inter-mixed, allowing users to experience an enhanced cultural, entertainment, retail, and observational experience. This fusion with hardware and software architecture would be a unique hybrid entertainment/observatory and will be a new prototype for retailers to mix shopping and culture together.

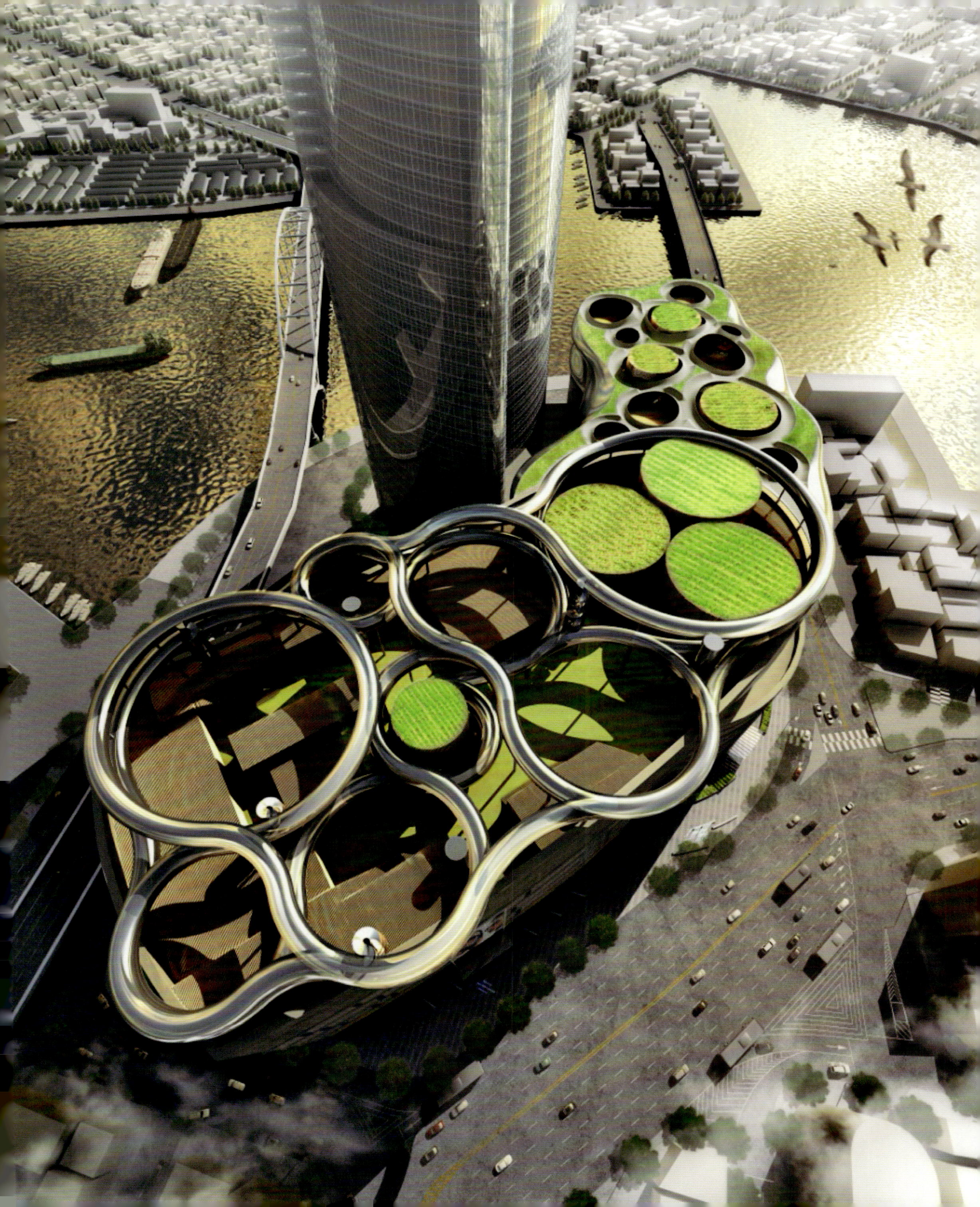

East elevation

West elevation

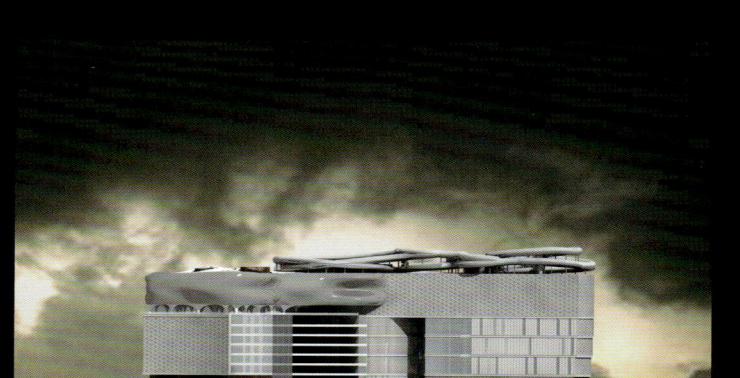

South elevation

North elevation

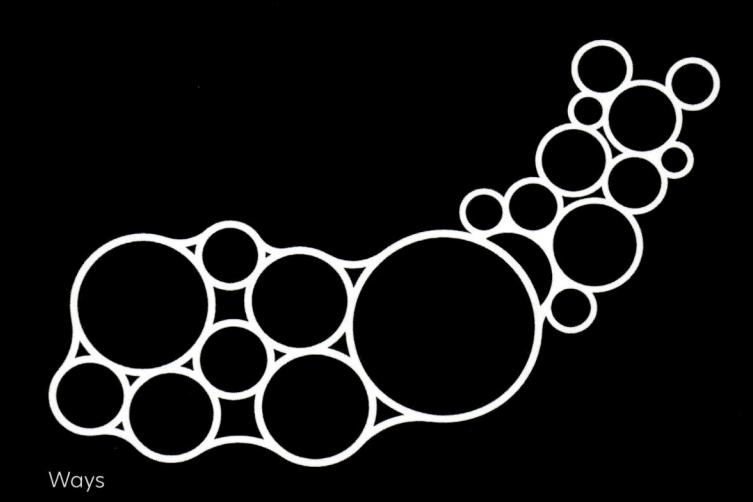

Ways

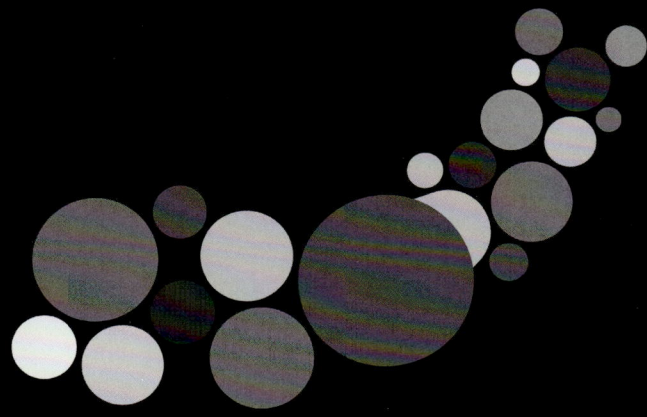

Pods

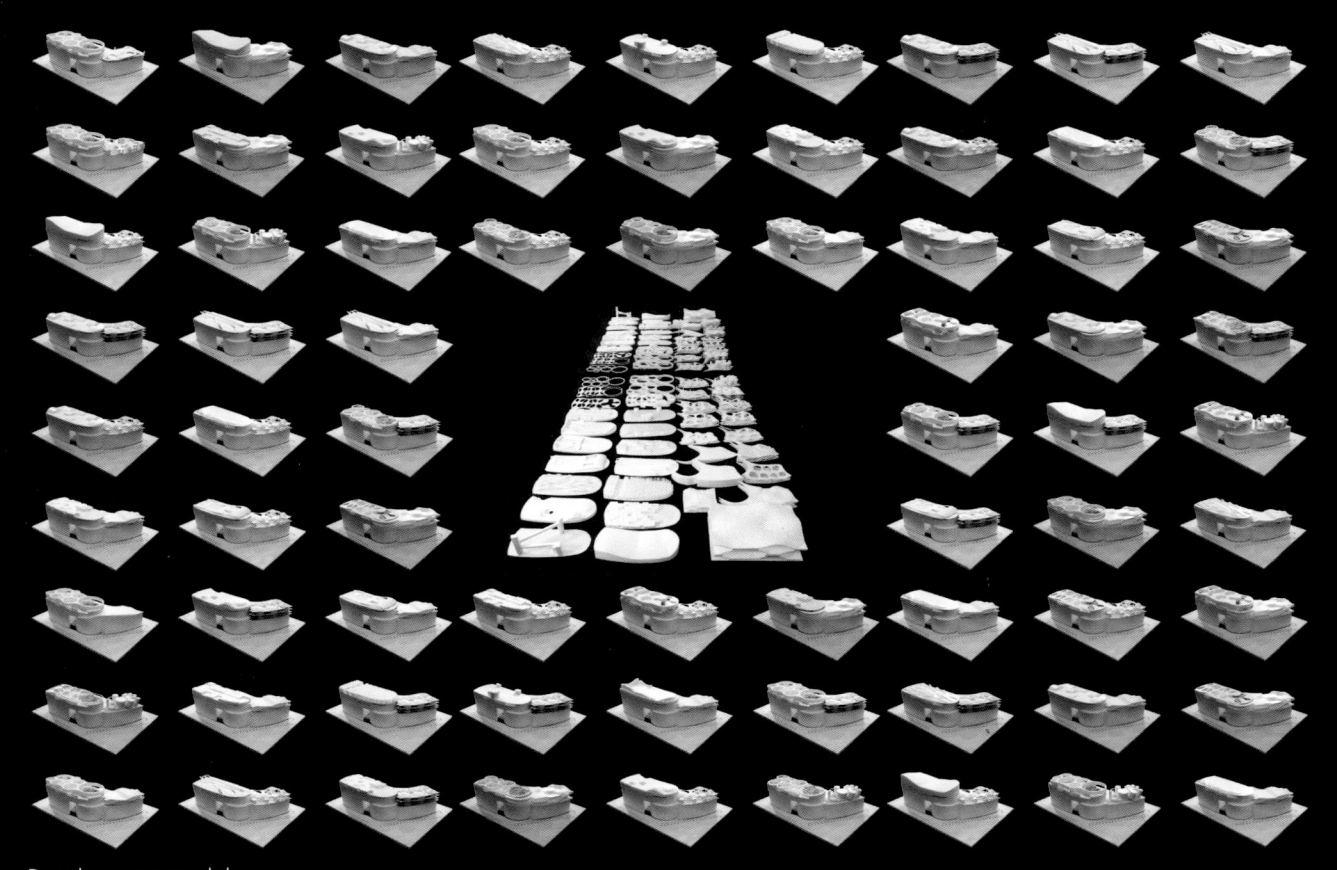

Development models

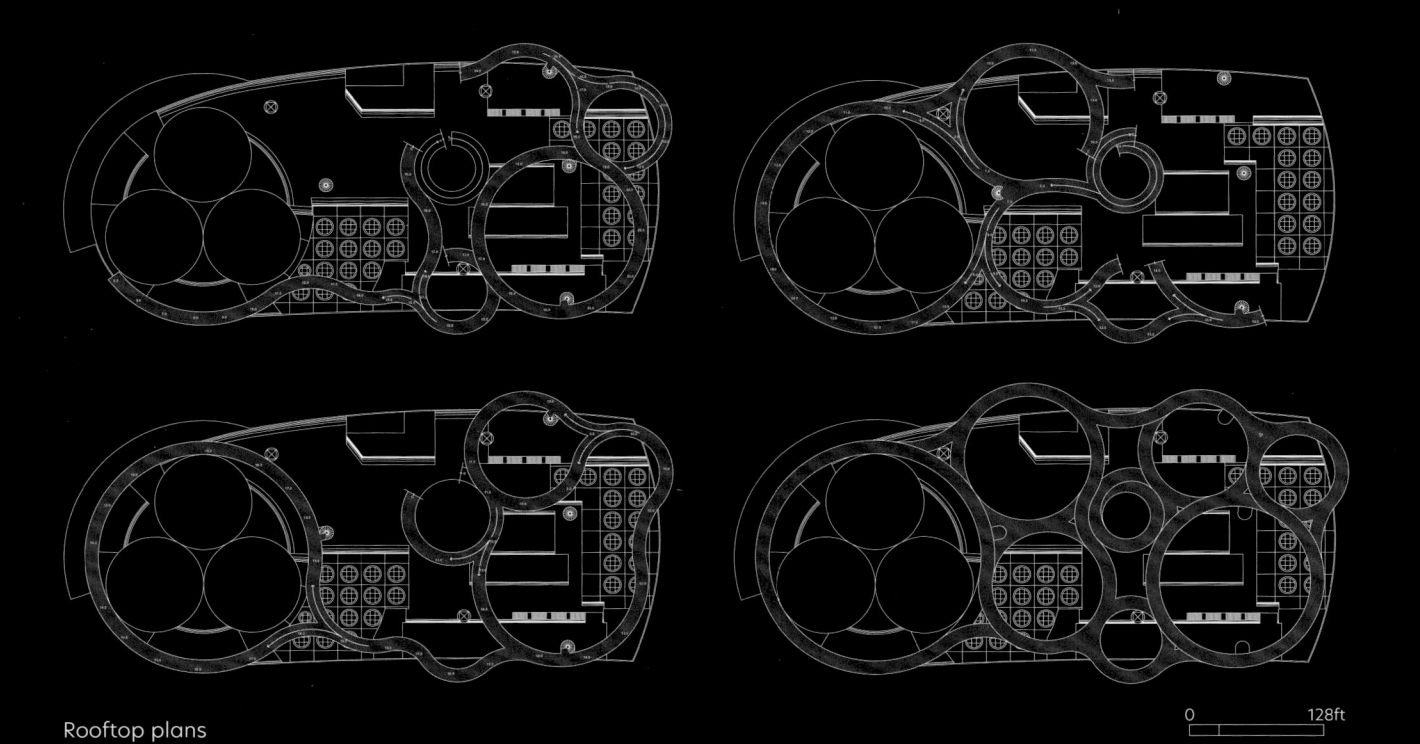

Rooftop plans

0   128ft

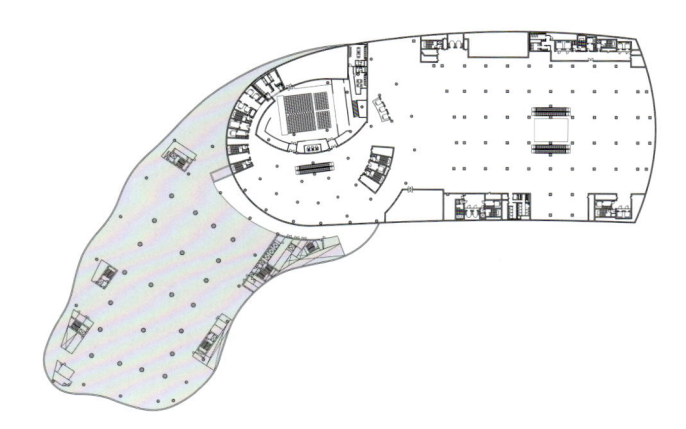

Tenth-floor plan (Museum)

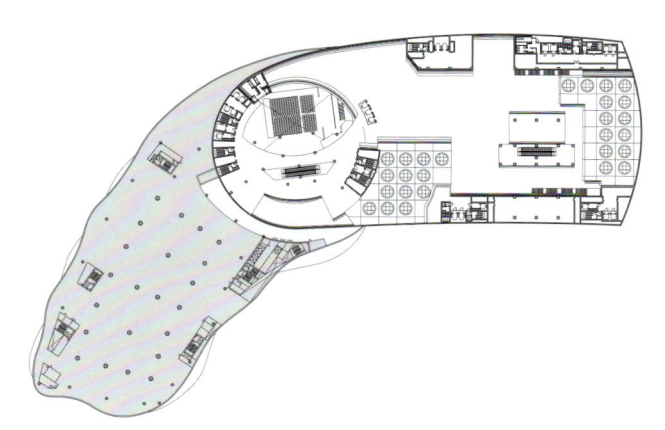

Eleventh-floor plan (Museum)

**234** SENSE OF SURPRISE

Rooftop plan (Garden)

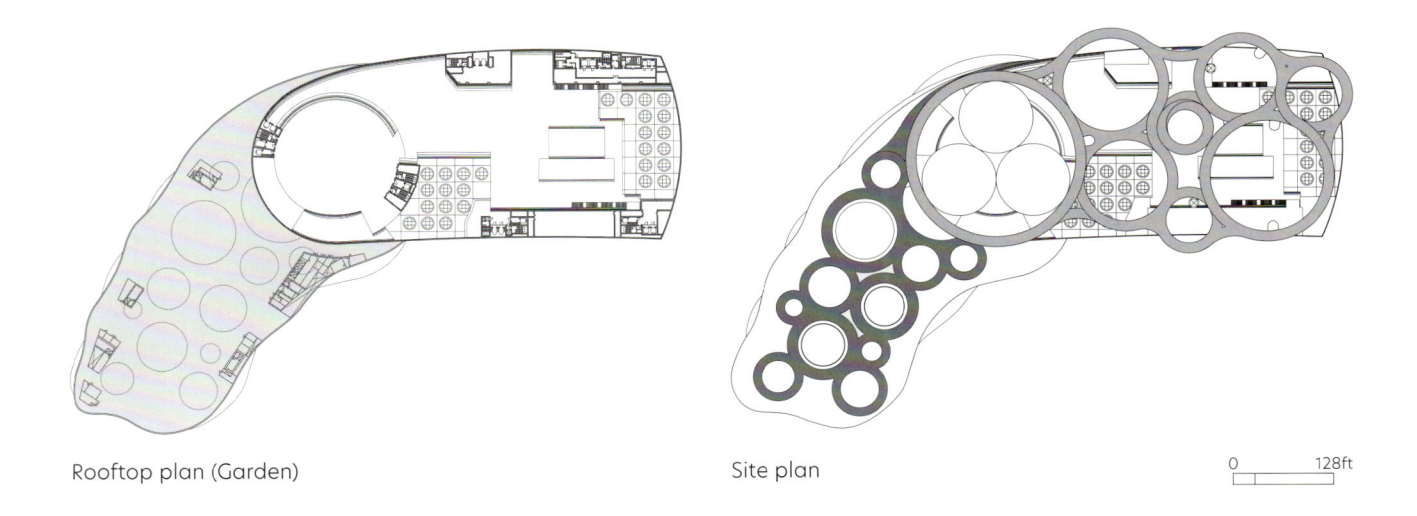

Site plan

0  128ft

LOTTE DEPARTMENT STORE ROOF GARDEN   235

# THE GREAT WALL APARTMENT FACTORY

Suizhong, Liaoning, China | 2012

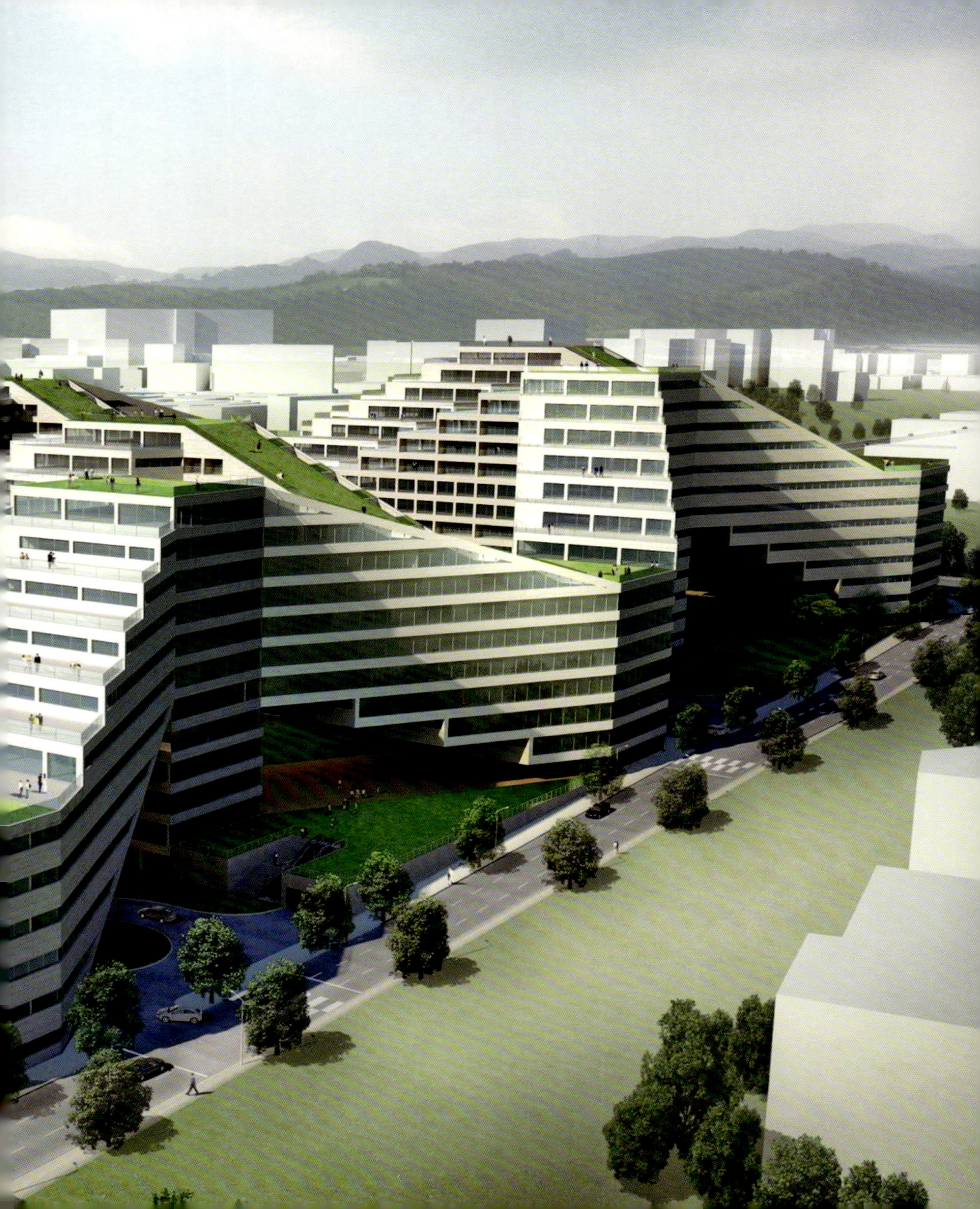

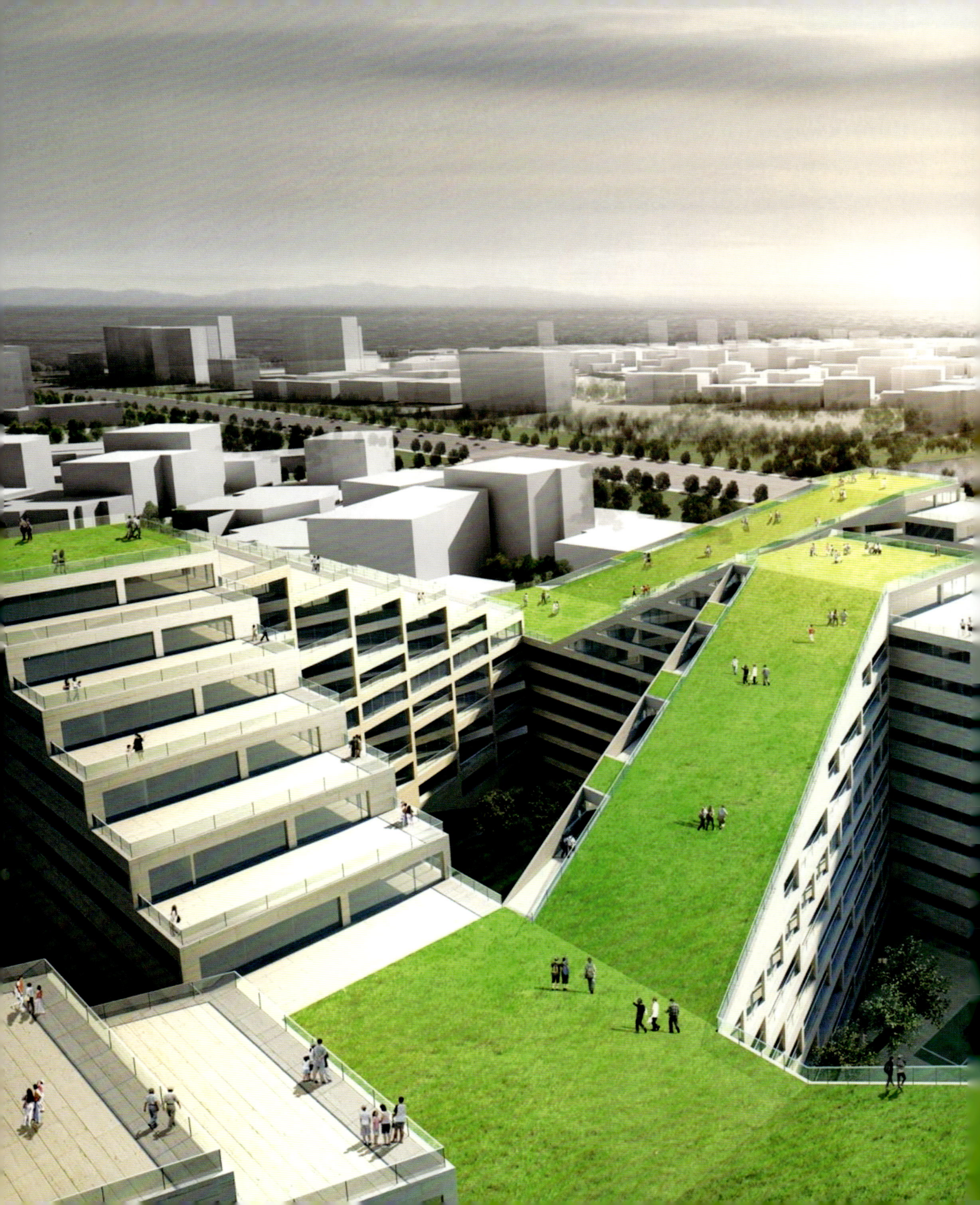

This mixed-use design aims to create a machine for living, combining office space with residential apartments that are anchored by a "retail podium," dubbed the hybrid apartment-factory. Despite it being a relatively experimental concept, many real estate developers in Korea have already found the design engaging and economically viable.

While the idea of adapting stacked, small-size factories in an urban residential layout has been received well, there have been some issues associated with poor working conditions and limited access to daylight. In the Suizhong Korea Town project, we attempted to develop the next generation "apt-factory" with improved ecological, economical, and social conditions.

Instead of developing a high-rise, a permeable "mat hybrid" layout with differentiated public outdoor courtyards is introduced. The residential "apt-factories" are flanked by two different types of commercial layouts: an entertainment-oriented program versus consumable fashion and electronics retail zones, creating a programmatic sandwich. This formation allows continuous and concentrated shopping experiences for both destination-oriented and incidental shoppers alike.

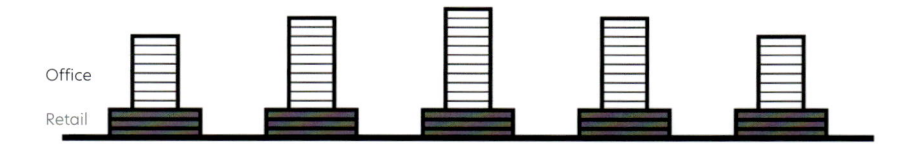

Conventional building spacing

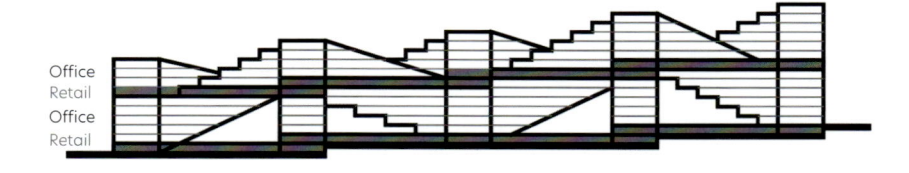

Integrated double-loaded spaces

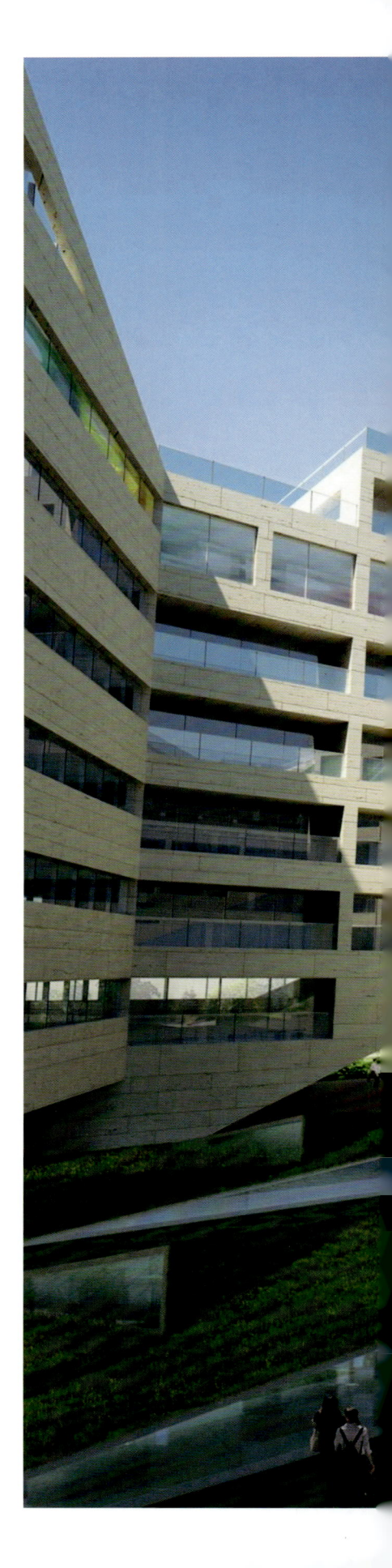

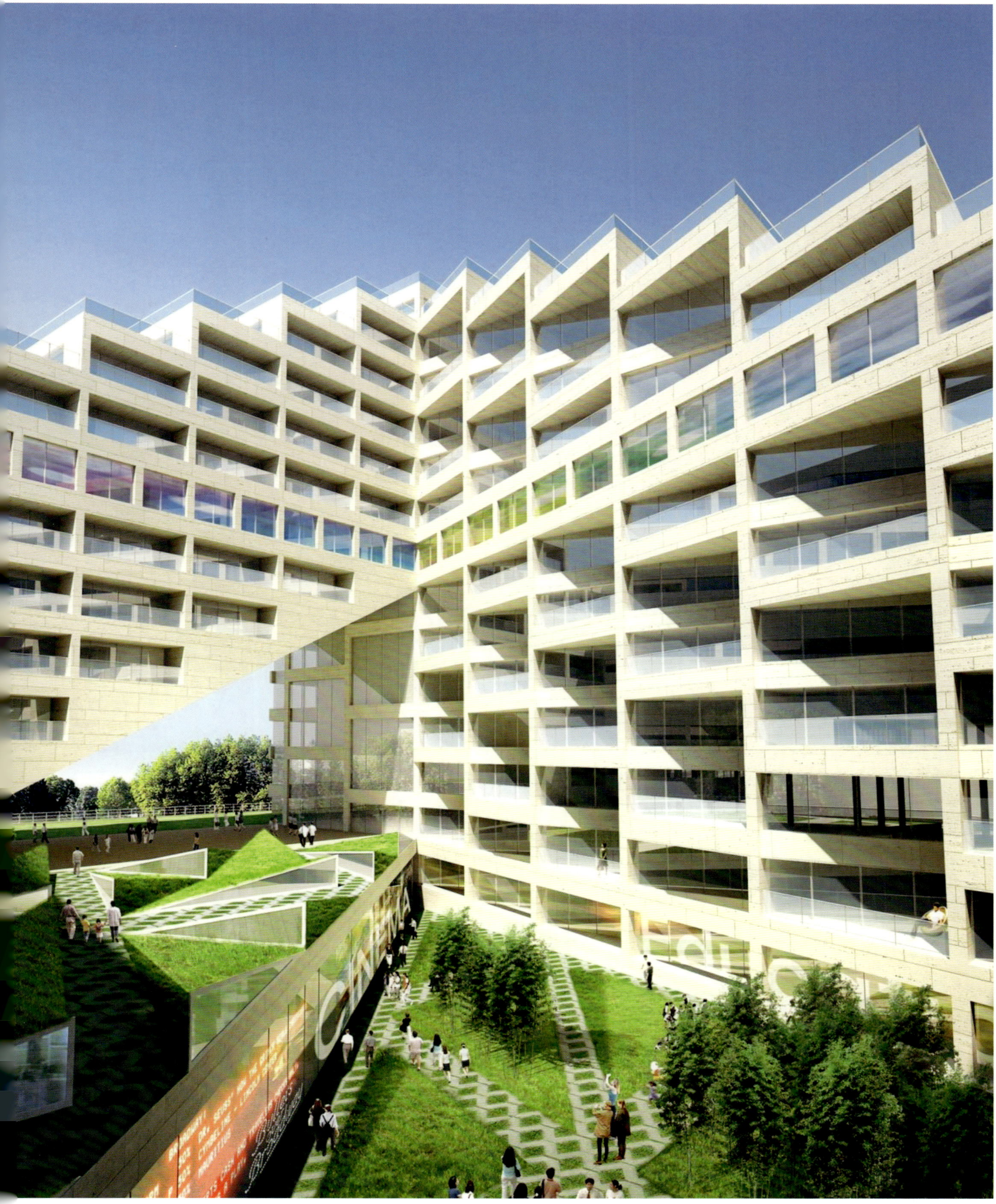
CINEMA

Site | Four towers | Conversion

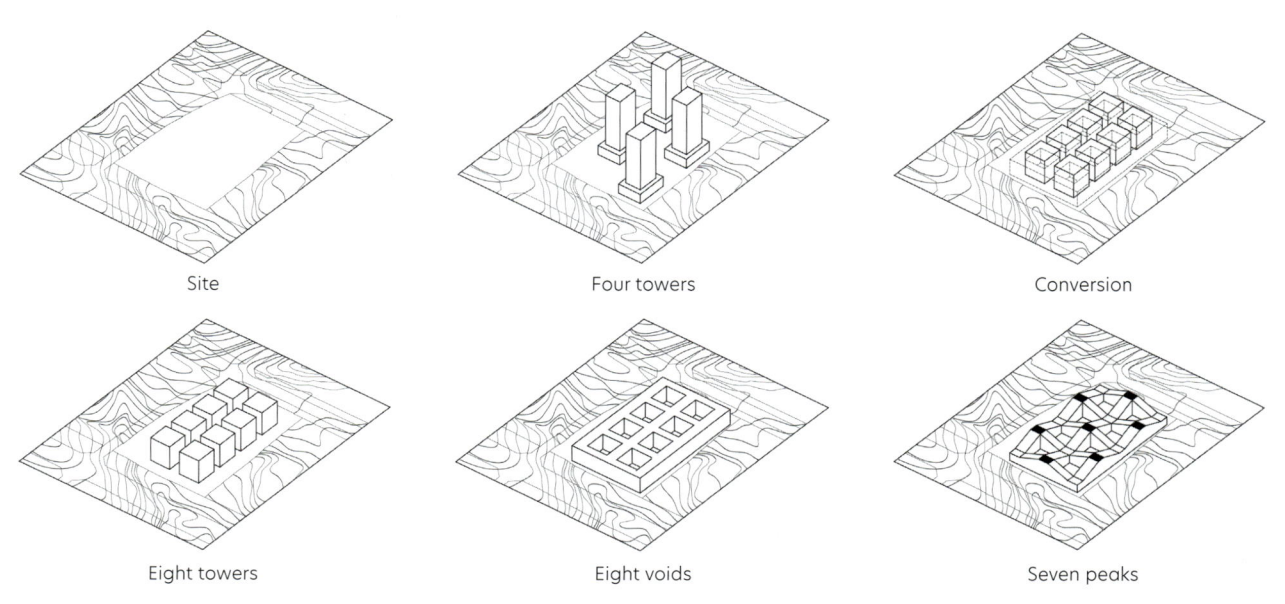

Eight towers | Eight voids | Seven peaks

242  SENSE OF SURPRISE

| Punctured | Elevated | Shifted |

| Leveled | Stepped | Walled |

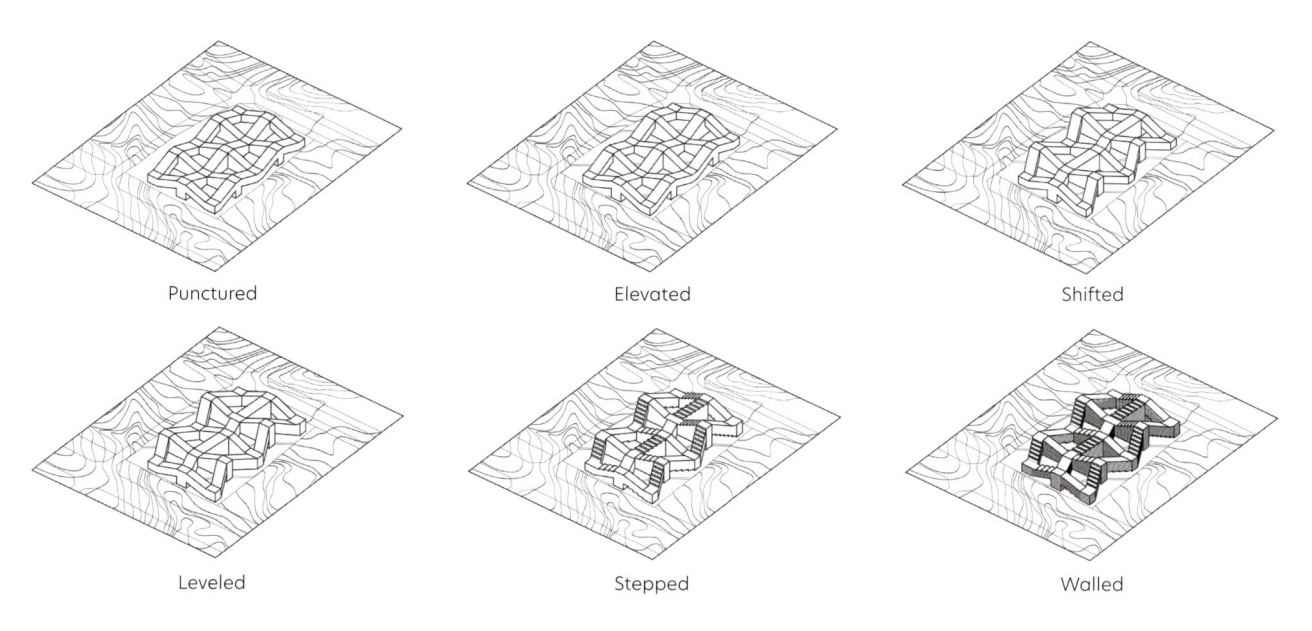

THE GREAT WALL APARTMENT FACTORY

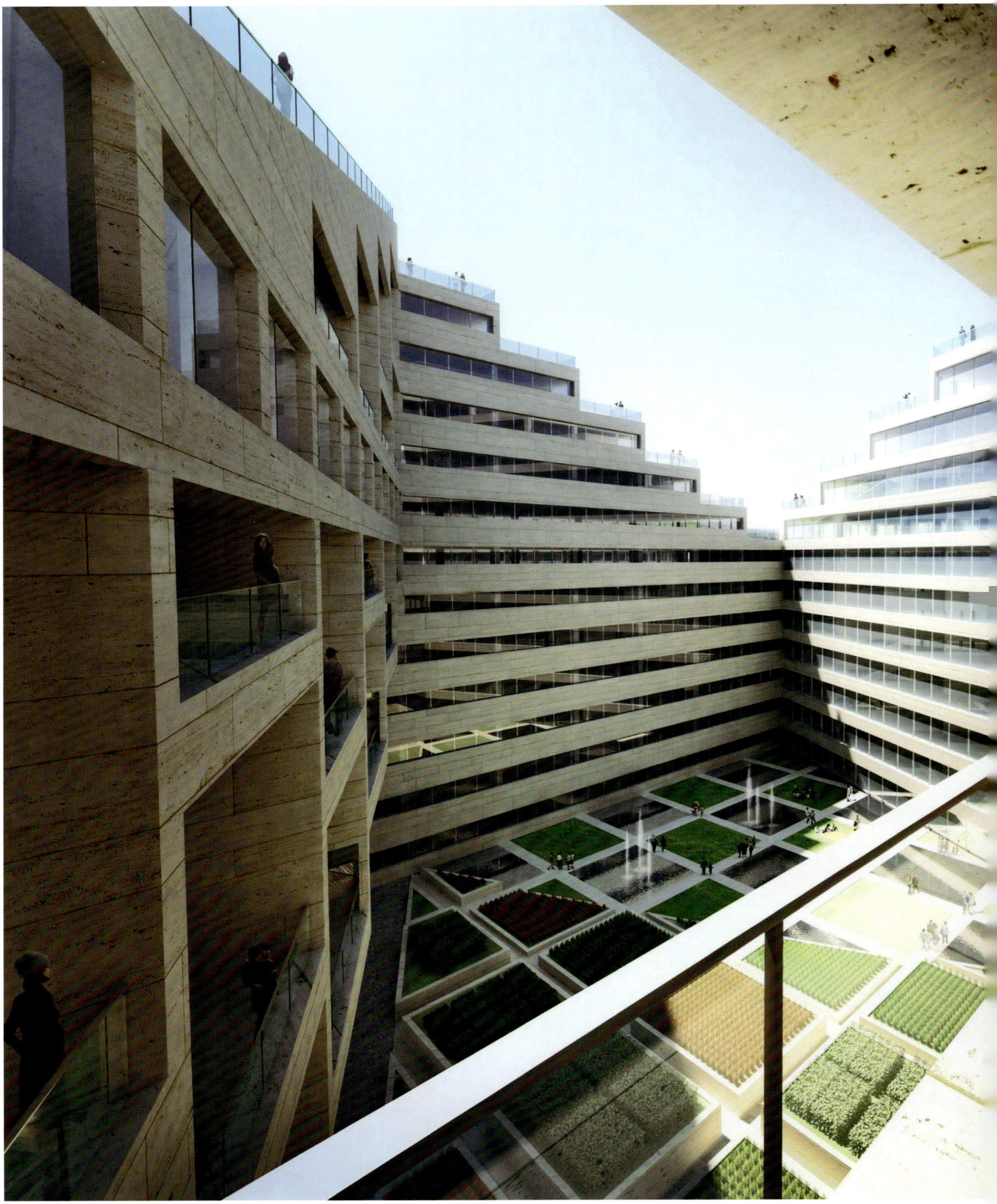

While the form of this horizontal skyscraper is geometric and contemporary, its materiality and programmatic function take inspiration from ancient Chinese precedents. Being influenced by elements of the infamous Hakka Walled Villages and the Great Wall of China, the resulting design has a snaking, coiled layout that creates voids of exterior courtyards from the dense, living wall. These eight plazas are filled with variety of entertainment and "green" venues, as well as bringing daylight and views into every pocket of the project. Additionally, this methodology elevates the seven cores that are created to formally represent the Sobaek mountain range of Korea. This allows users on the fifth floor, where a concentrated shopping area is located, to experience an "inside/shopping–outside/roof garden" concept. This interesting way of intertwining shopping and park spaces helps to make "shopping @ Korea Town" desirable. The roofs are partially stepped to not only provide additional resting decks for users of the apt-factories but to also create a multifaceted form that helps to create an optical-illusion-like form in the observer's mind.

By superimposing modern Korean real estate development practices with methodological themes derived from ancient Chinese structures, this next-generation design becomes an important cultural center and exciting gathering place.

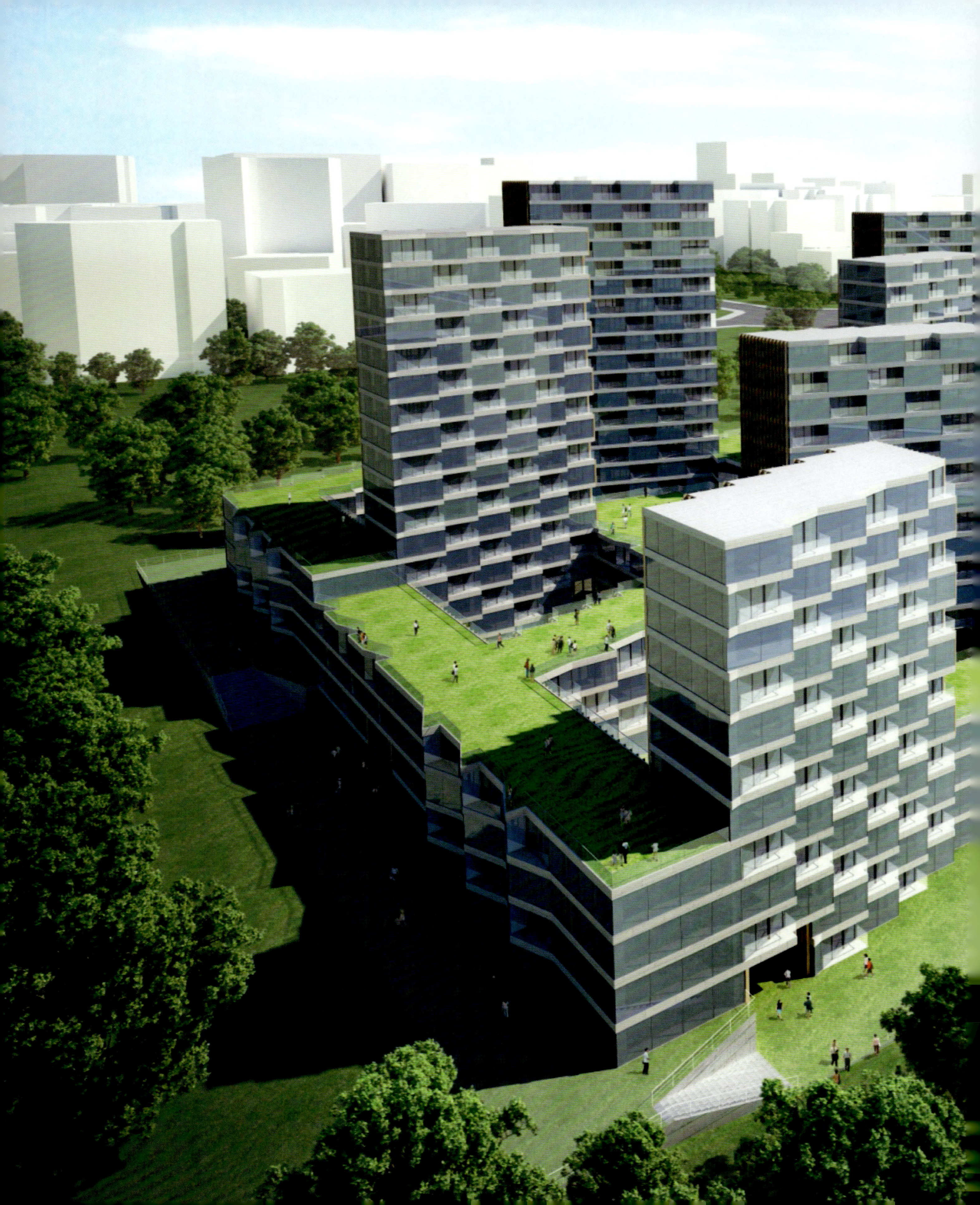

# NINE DRAGON HOUSING COMPLEX

Suizhong, Liaoning, China | 2011

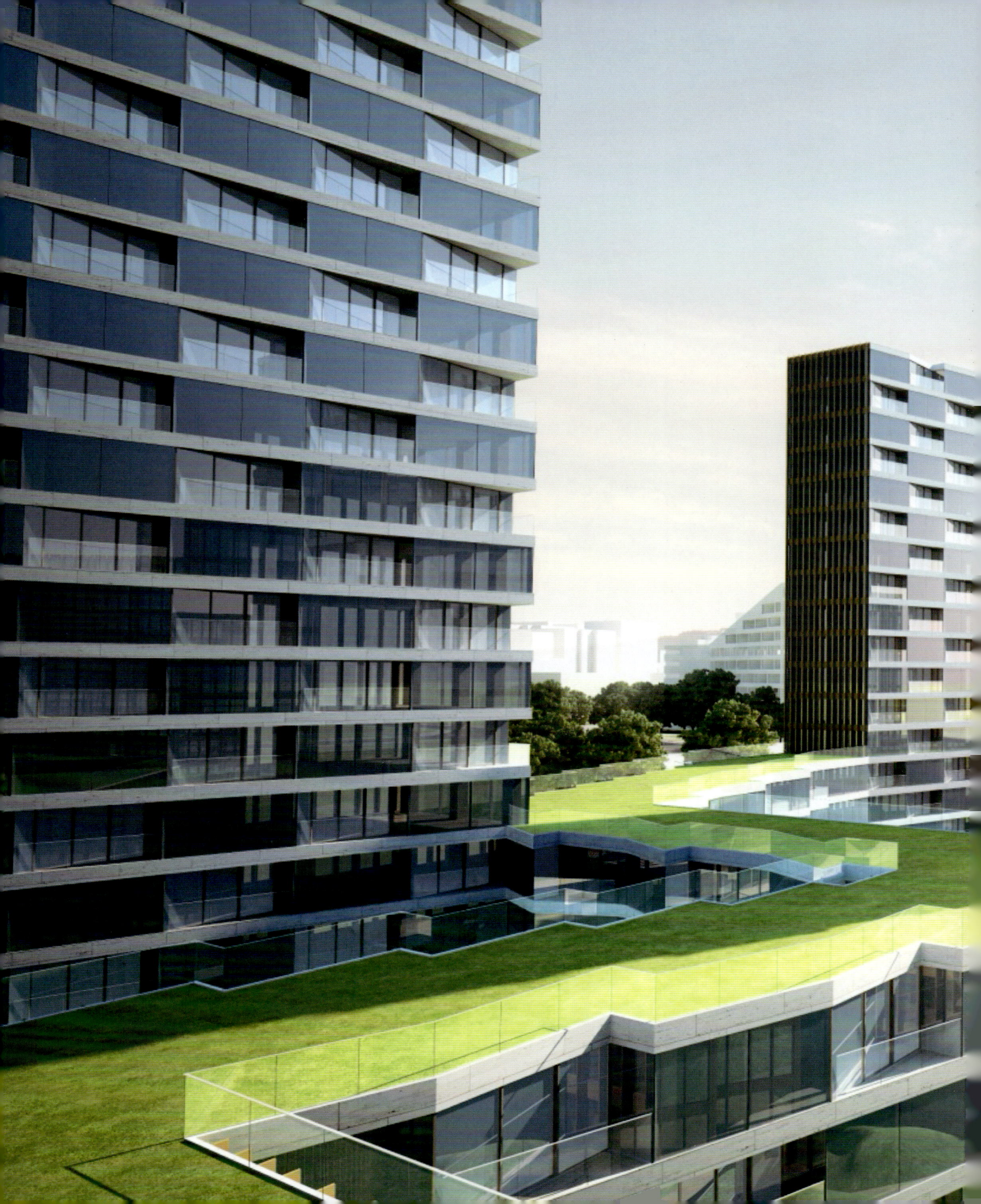

Located next to our proposed Great Wall Apartment Factory complex in Suizhong, China, this mixed-used development is a part of the same Korea Town development. The client's goal was to maximize usable space and generate unique yet marketable residential prototypes. Similar to our sister project, this conceptualization also utilizes distinct courtyards and roof gardens in response to the dense cluster of residential and commercial units.

A permeable "mat hybrid" format with differentiating public outdoor courtyards was applied to this site, as per our Great Wall concept. A grid-like base layer was created by spreading linear bar-type blocks in north–south and east–west directions. We then extruded specific sections of the linear block to increase the usable footprint of the total residential area. Finally, we optimized the interior and exterior spaces by adjusting the levels according to the best walkable routes and views possible for visitors and residents. The result is a next-generation housing typology that embraces (1) the courtyard apartment type (of the famed Eixample district in Barcelona, circa 1850s); (2) the linear row housing type (still the preferable residential type in Korea); and (3) the high-rise bar-type apartment (prevalent in Chicago's residential developments of the 1950s). This 362-unit housing complex was generated from a schematic combination of three apartment types with a practical response to meet programmatic, economic, and social needs.

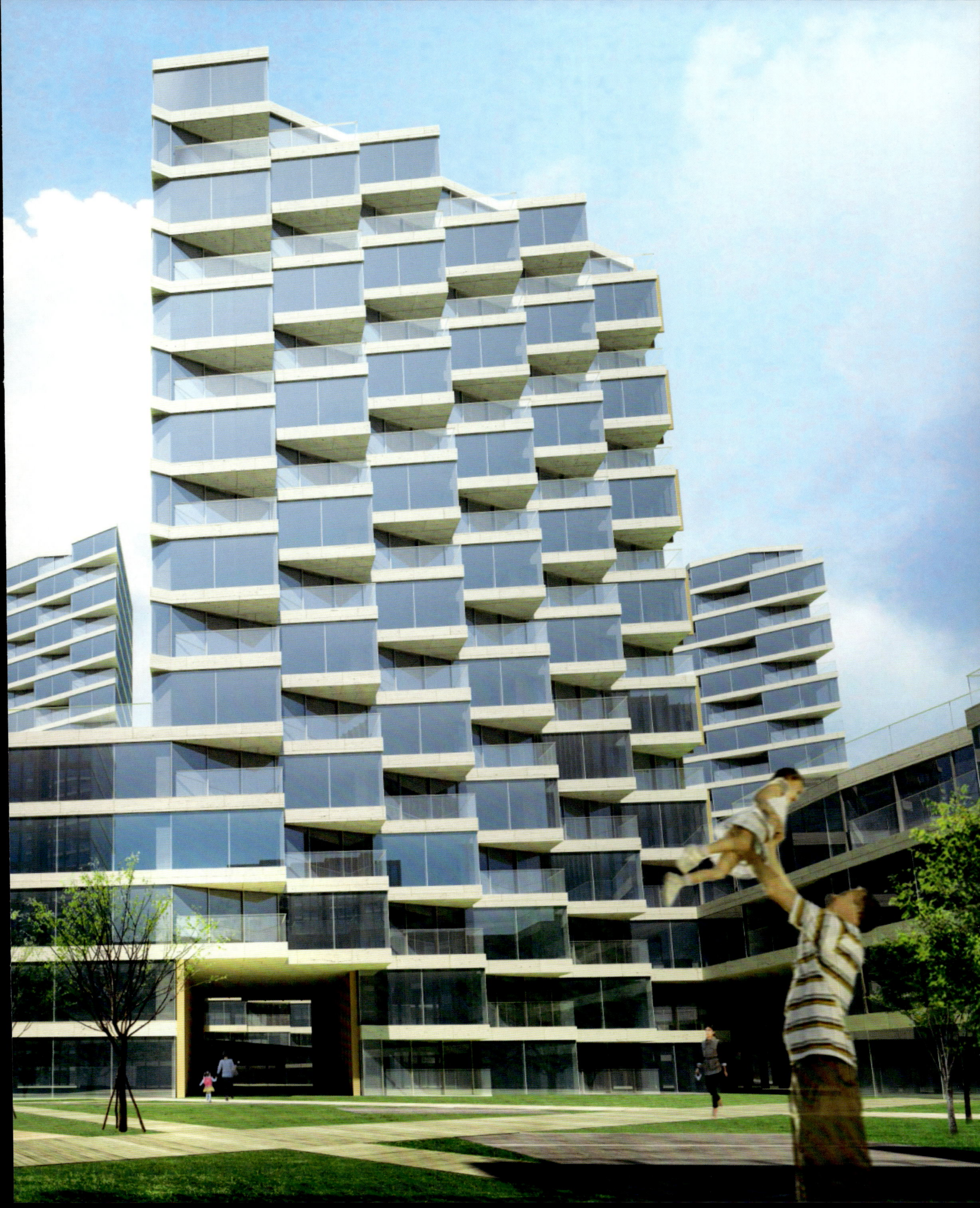

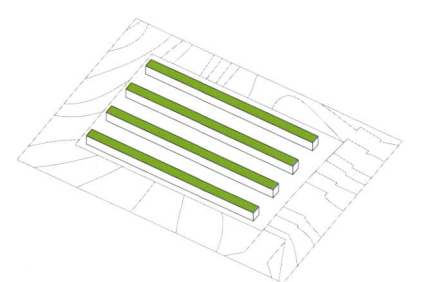

Linear block apartment type

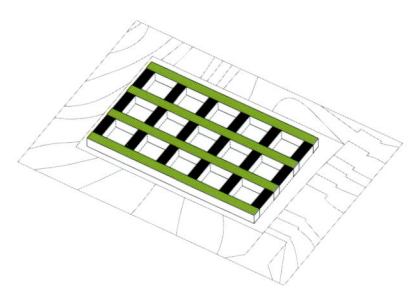

Intersecting linear block apartment courtyard spaces

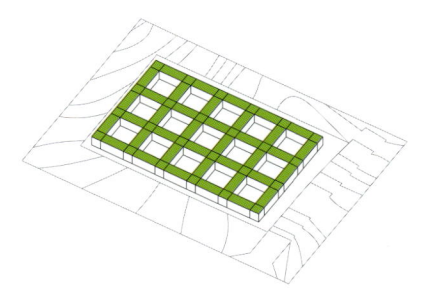

Courtyard apartment type

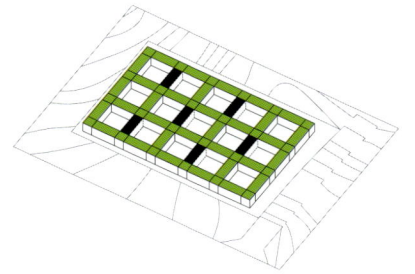

Linear block sections are extracted to respond to the program

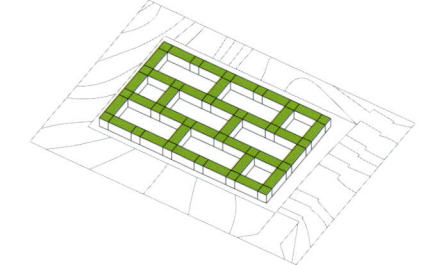

Shifted linear block section

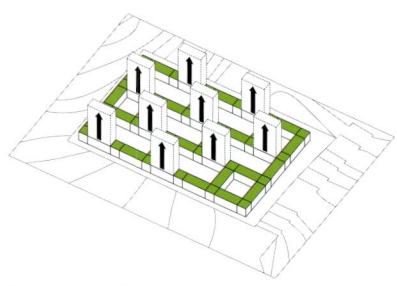

Extruding volumes create high-rise apartment type

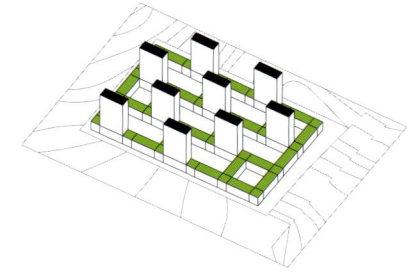

Hybrid apartment typology

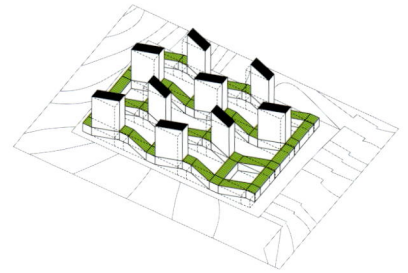

The system is shifted in response to view and daylight priorities

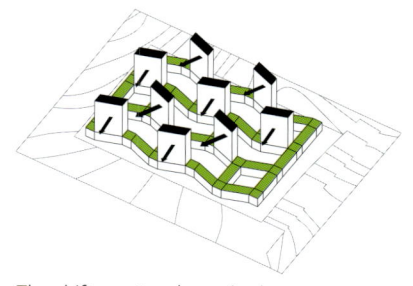

The shift creates dynamic views and exterior spaces

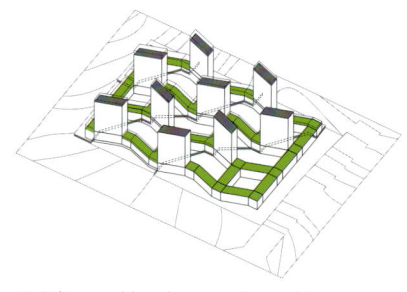

Heights and levels are adjusted to merge with the existing landform

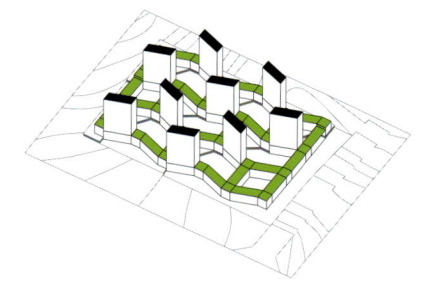

Final schematic design footprint

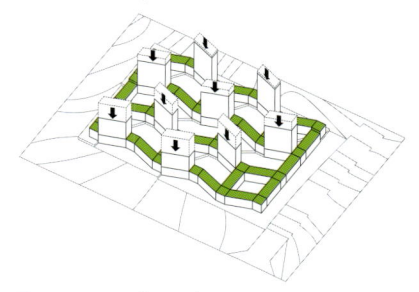

Towers are adjusted in response to shadow and daylight studies

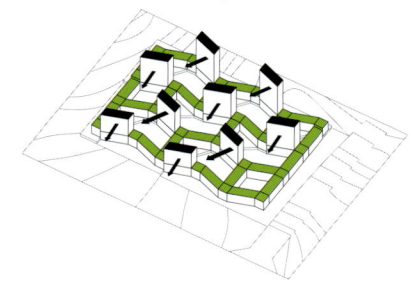

Adjusted heights provide for improved views of the landscape

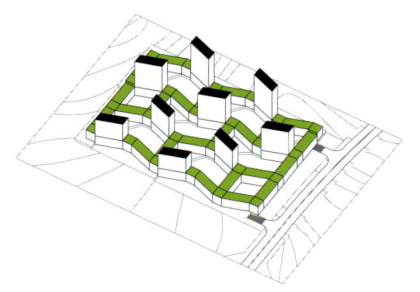

Final schematic design volume

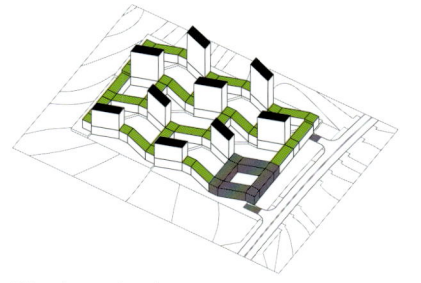

Mixed-use development: museum gallery allocation

Final museum schematic design volume

Access points and throughways

Final design

Connectivity: multilevel underground parking

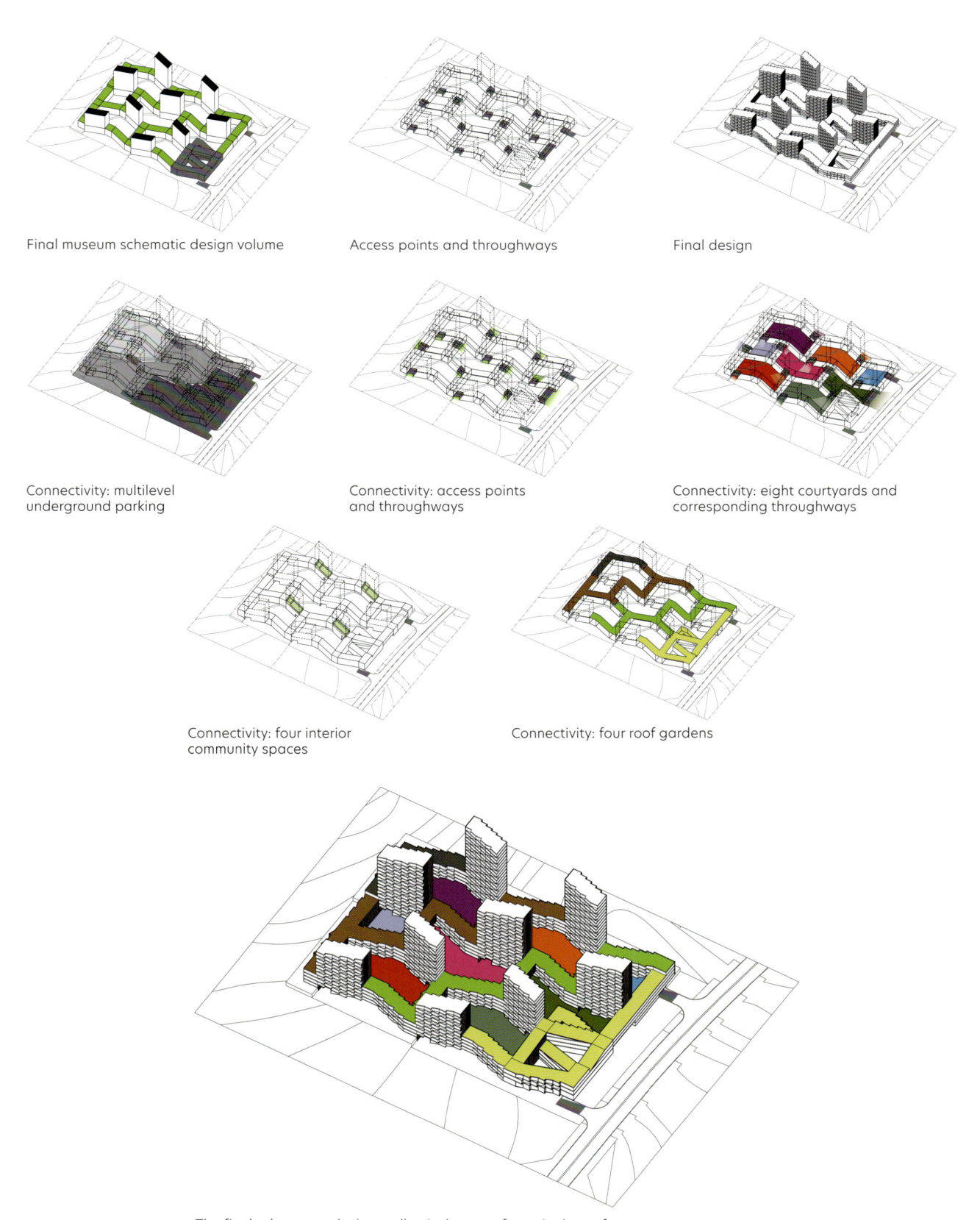

Connectivity: access points and throughways

Connectivity: eight courtyards and corresponding throughways

Connectivity: four interior community spaces

Connectivity: four roof gardens

The final scheme results in a collectively green footprint by surface area

NINE DRAGON HOUSING COMPLEX

SENSE OF SURPRISE

Throughout the complex, there is a fluid circulation between community centers, residential areas, gardens, courtyards, retail zones, and vehicle parking. In addition to building conventional entrances, there are a total of thirteen major passageways with six exterior access points and seven interior access points. In addition to two vehicular entrances and exits, the multilevel underground parking system has a series of inclining and declining ramps with convenient access points to various programs within the complex.

The tower heights and angles were adjusted to enhance natural lighting into the apartment and retail units. After several iterations of shadow studies, the position of the towers was adjusted so both high and low residential apartments had access to sufficient natural lighting. To optimize the project's open center with that location's best sun path, the complex's orthogonal grid system was horizontally rotated, resulting in positive and negative volumes that benefit the occupants' views and access to natural indoor lighting.

The mixed-use component of the project raises the issue of privacy as an important design challenge. Finding the balance between having fluid circulation between programs and maintaining a level of security and privacy for the residents within the complex was essential. Within the formal design of the overall housing complex, the surfaces and volumes of purely residential areas were shifted above and to the corners away from public access points to maximize privacy and safety. Additionally, the façade's multifaceted edges correlate with the boundaries of the nine unit types to create a visually closed unit-type system that increases the units' privacy.

Community spaces are interwoven throughout the housing complex to create a livable and safe environment. These spaces include eight courtyards, four connecting roof gardens, and four indoor community spaces whose programs can vary from cafés, library, health clubs, to event halls. Each courtyard holds different approaches to its landscape design and can be a place of rest or be activated as outdoor event spaces. These public spaces promote pedestrian life, physical activity, and a sense of community in this dense urban environment.

A gallery is located at the center of the project, itself acting as the complex's focal exhibition that establishes a connection to its surrounding programs and units. The intention of the gallery was to create a flexible exhibition-type program that stands out from the typical retail stores in the complex yet also seamlessly fits with the completed housing complex. The theme-and-variations concept established in the Korea Town Apt-Factory was reiterated in the design of the sales gallery and in the complex's elevations. The façade contains moments of duality when seen from different cardinal directions.

NINE DRAGON HOUSING COMPLEX 257

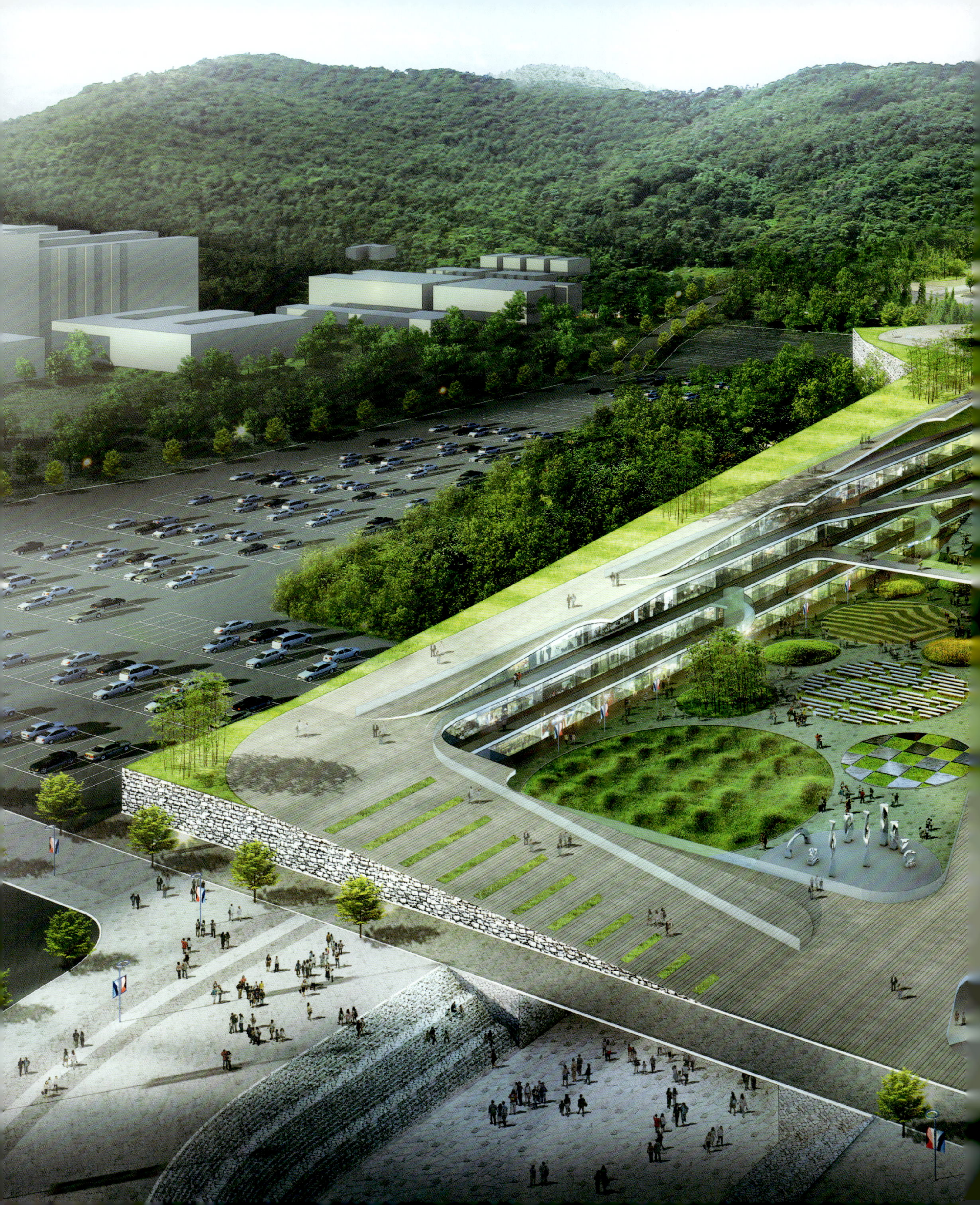

# BUYEO LOTTE PREMIUM OUTLET

Buyeo-gun, Chungcheongnam-do, South Korea | 2010

THE HEART OF AFRICA
CHANEL
NEW ARRIVALS
FRAGRANCE & BEAUTY
75%
INTRODUCING

The Buyeo Lotte Premium Outlet was awarded the prize of first place in the invitational design competition for Lotte's new landmark shopping center in Buyeo-gun, South Korea. The client's objective was to find a design that satisfied three goals: a new landmark for Buyeo-gun, the old capital of Korea; create a fun and attractive cultural center; and utilize eco design.

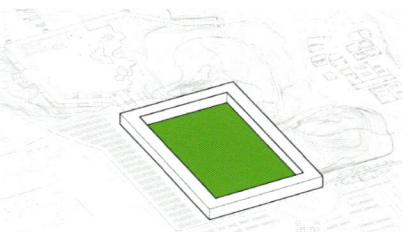

Typical "cluster" outlet form

Defined by external site forces

Defined by external site forces

Vertical leveling through programmatic juxtaposition

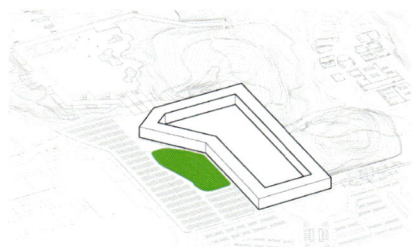

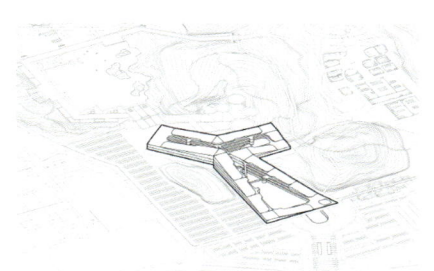

Insertion of vertical cores

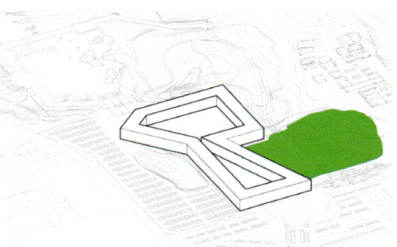

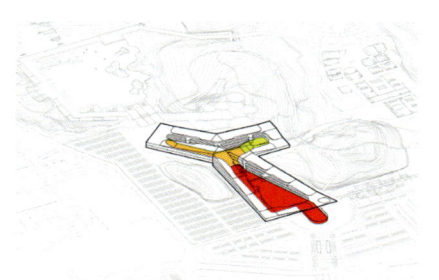

Three distinct courtyards

SENSE OF SURPRISE

Because the site is located next to an old palace of the Baekje Dynasty, a historic Korean landmark from the first century, we were trying to find a design solution that allows the "old" and "new" to coexist. Additionally, representing "landscape" as "architecture" was another theme we intended to bring to the project.

If the shopping center was constructed at the same elevation as the historic site, the latter would have inevitably been dwarfed due to the center's sheer scale. Instead, we opted to set the shopping center into the hill of the neighboring palace, allowing the visibility of the palace to remain unobstructed. Within the site, a band of shops is connected and fitted around the inside of the artificial canyon. This creates three distinct retail courts that have ramp access to multiple levels of commercial spaces.

By following the notion of "landscape" being a new form of "architecture" we were able to create an expressive and functional space by removing the environment. This duality satisfies a problem of mixing old and new—the roof garden and the exterior stone walls are to act as an old castle's remnants. In the case of eco design, this also succeeds, as the surrounding nature is preserved and remains the focus of the area while the environmental footprint is substantially less than it could have been.

The program of the retail center was designed to have three distinct courtyards, each with its own characteristics and function. The initial court closest to the entrance operates as the most typical retail area. However, the two courtyards that extend deeper into the hill and out of the view of the entrance space have a variety of restaurants, performance centers, and recreational activities. These are physical moments where the initial identity of a commercial zone begins to shift. Like the backstreets of a lively city or a populated market area, these set-back courtyards become centers for urban culture, entertainment, and life. The design of this layout is based on the notion that shopping is no longer a mere process of buying and selling, but of generating authentic cultural experiences.

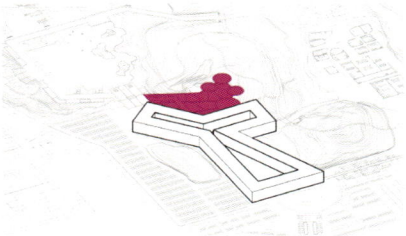

Defined by external programmatic forces

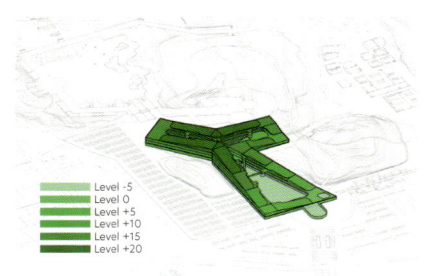

Grand roof garden

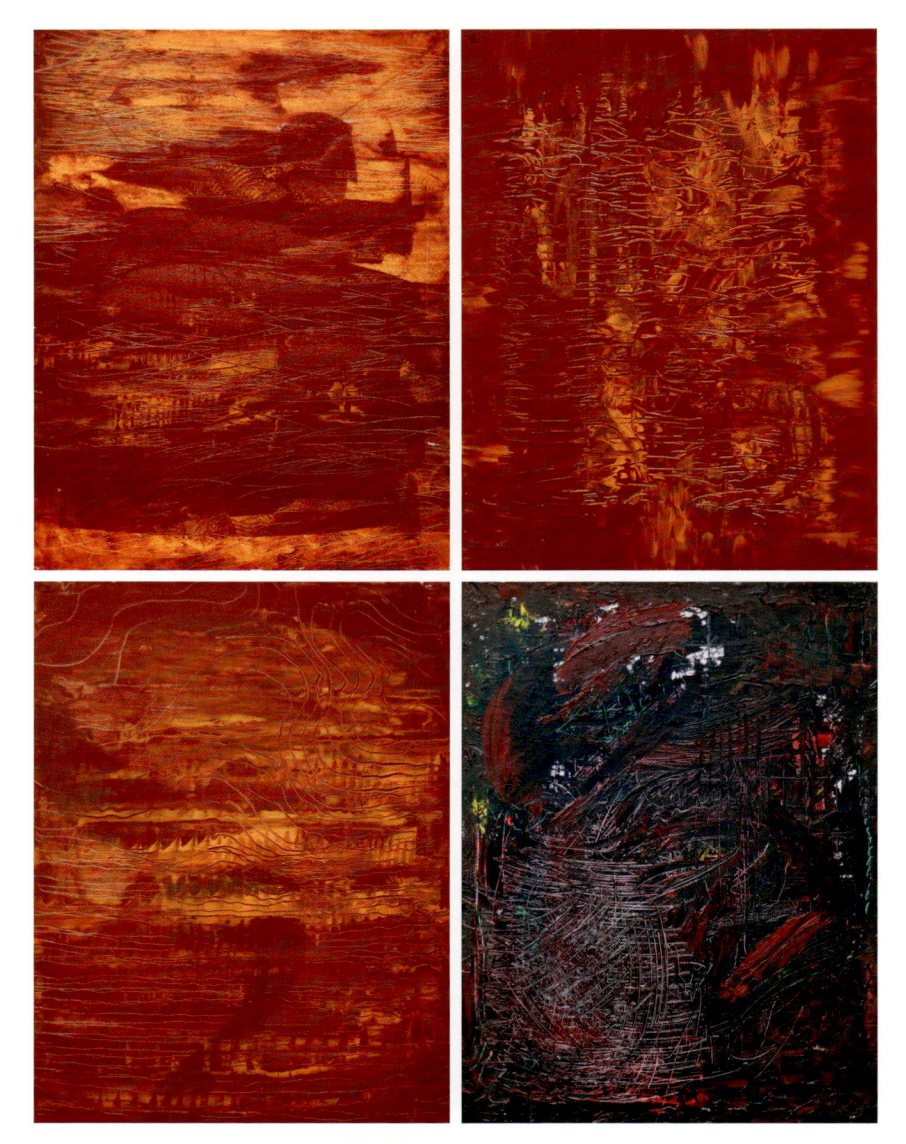

Taesun Hong, *Sunset 1, 2, 3, 4* (1992), oil

**Rhythm** is an arranged system of things that has a regulated pattern, generating an expression. Rhythm is most derived and constructed from a mathematical sequence as a strong, regularly repeated pattern—such as the pattern of sounds in relation to a beat. Repetition of elements, openings, shapes, or structural bays, establishes a regular or irregular rhythm in architecture.

The use of **dynamics** is the motivating or driving force—physical or moral. It is the quality of action in music. It means how loud or quiet the music is. Dynamics in architecture is expressed through a sense of energetic movement and action. It is best understood through the building's façade or mass.

# LOTTE UNDERGROUND PATH & PLAZA

Songpa-gu, Seoul, South Korea | 2011

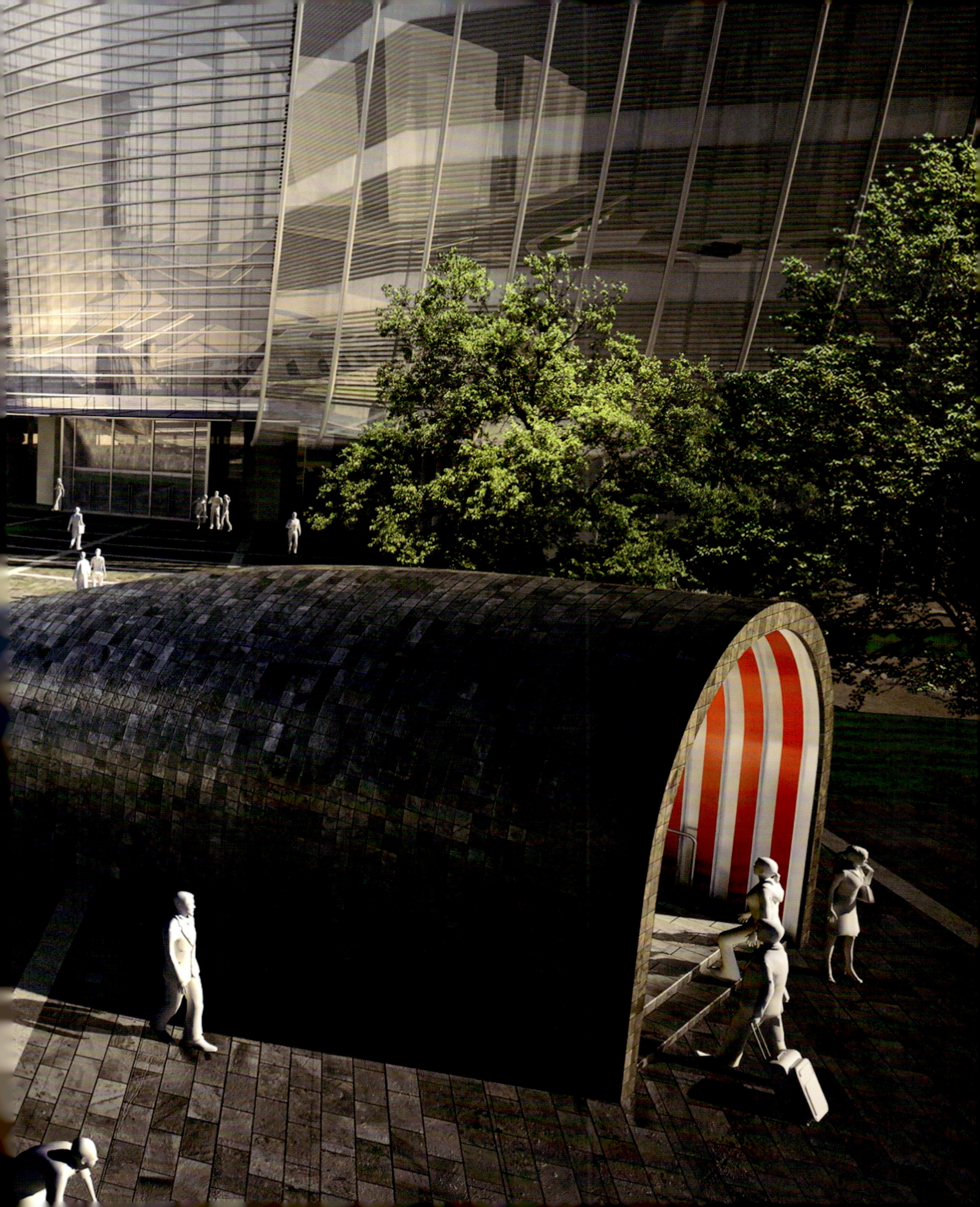

We were selected to design an underground transit system that would connect Lotte World (a recreation complex), Lotte's recent 120-story high-rise, and Seoul's Jamsil subway station. The goal of our path and plaza design was to create moments of urban life and interactivity. The entrance, exit, and ventilation areas are designed to create space for public events, exhibitions, performances, or relaxation. The color and design schemes are inspired from the surreal artwork and story beats from Lewis Carroll's *Alice in Wonderland*. Entering the underground space gives the users a sensation of entering another world—a new realm in the earth—instead of a constructed environment. The exterior design tries to work with organic forms.

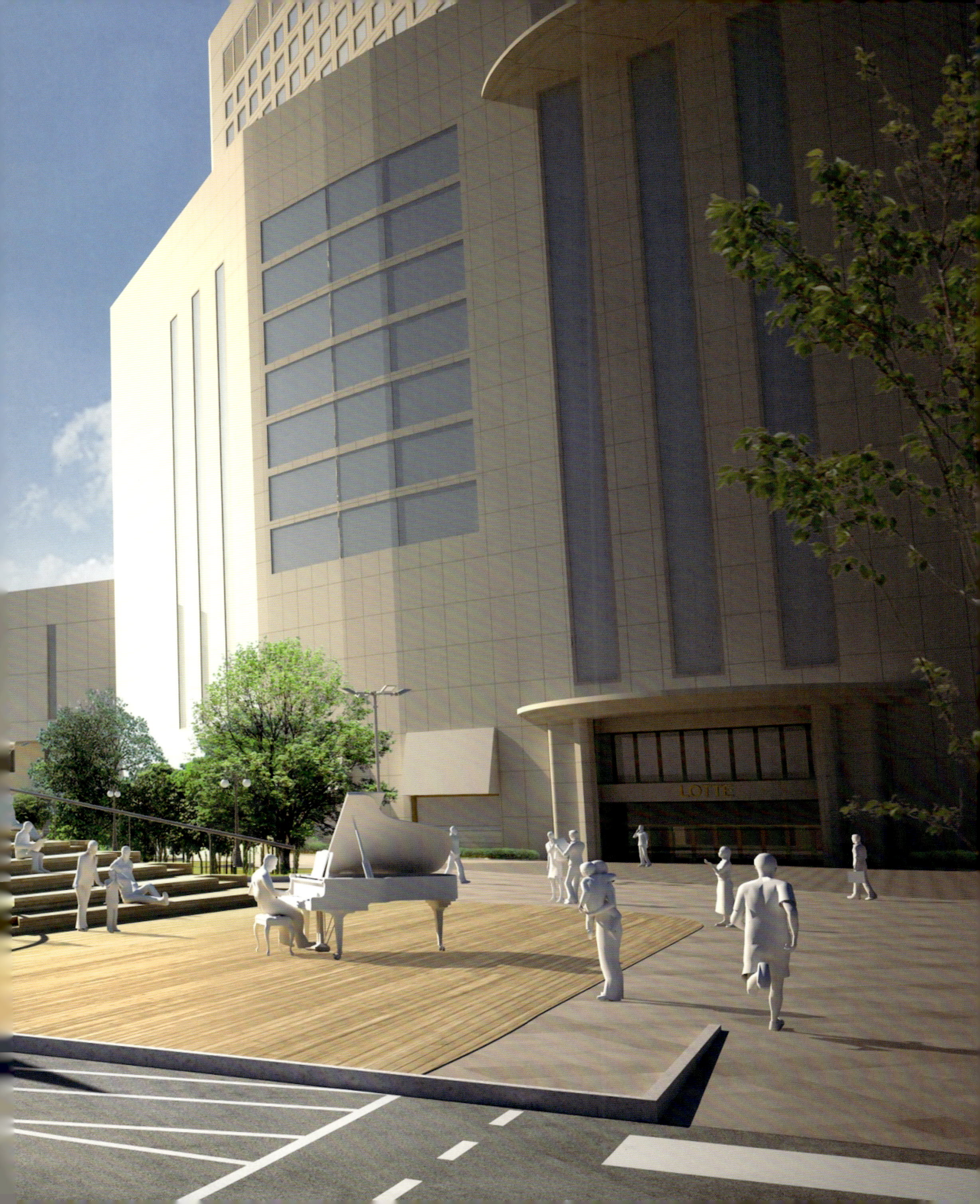
LOTTE

Eastern tunnel entrance concept process

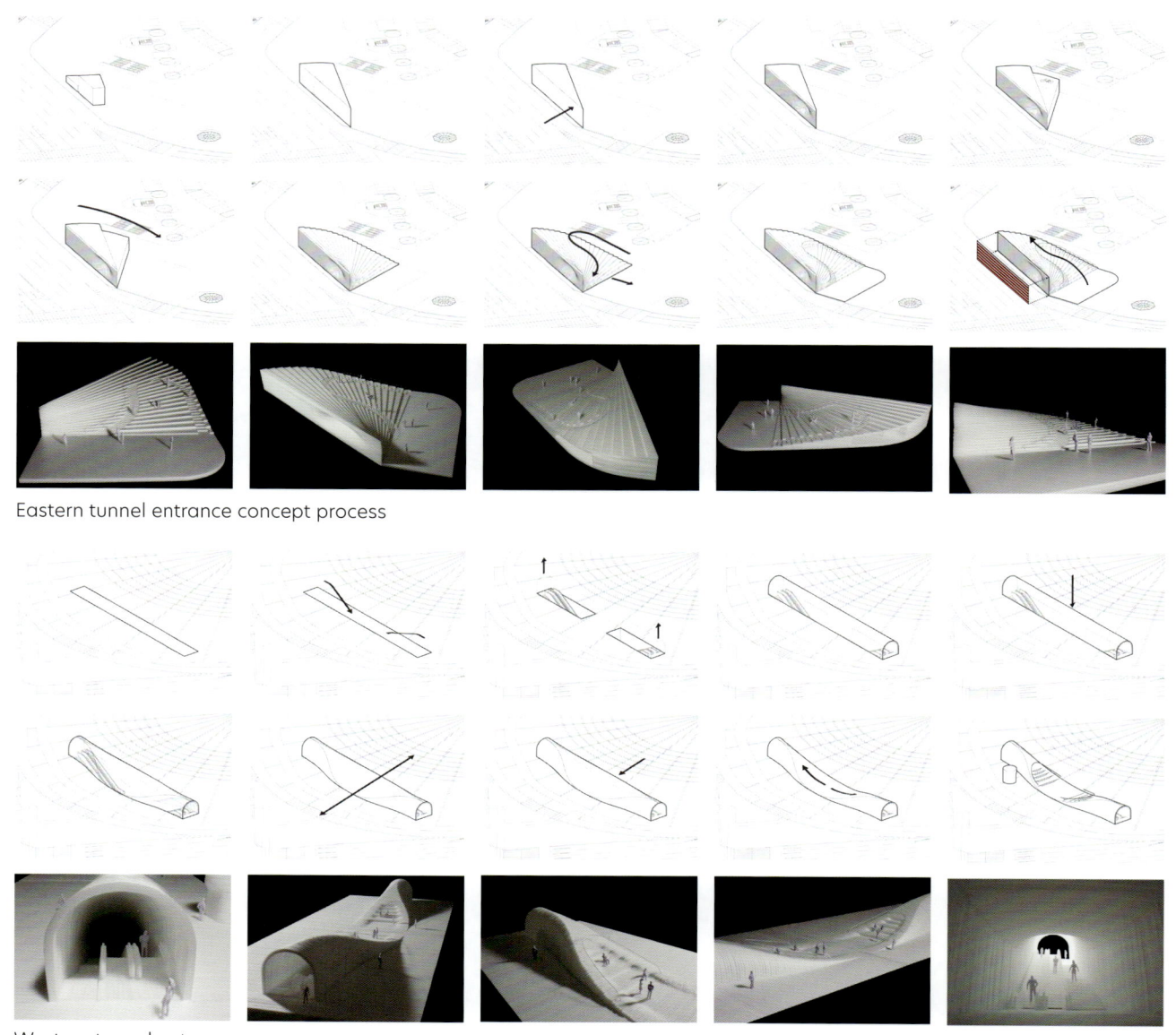

Western tunnel entrance concept process

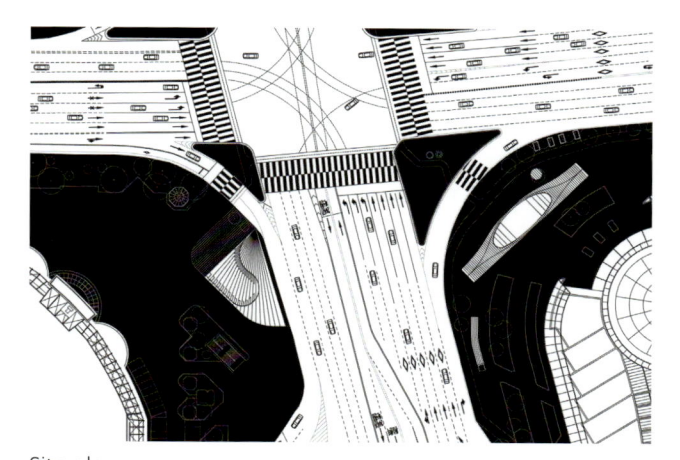

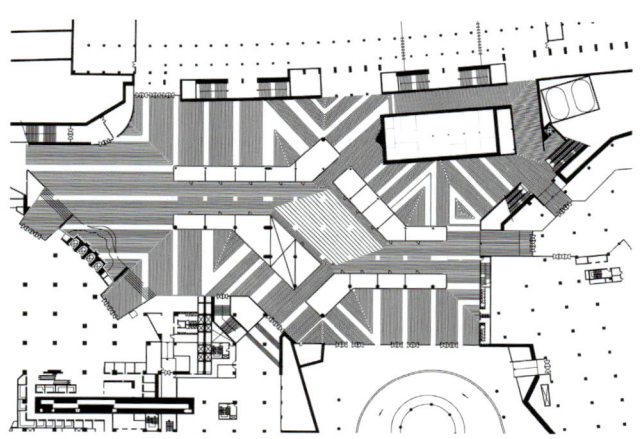

Site plan

Underground plan

270 RHYTHM AND DYNAMICS

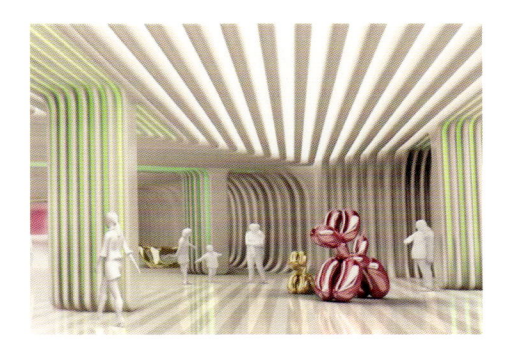

The underground path was designed to give people fundamental directions, utilizing the ceiling façade as a source of design and lighting. Lots of pattern studies were completed to accommodate this. In the center of the underground space lies event, exhibition, and performance arts areas.

LOTTE UNDERGROUND PATH & PLAZA

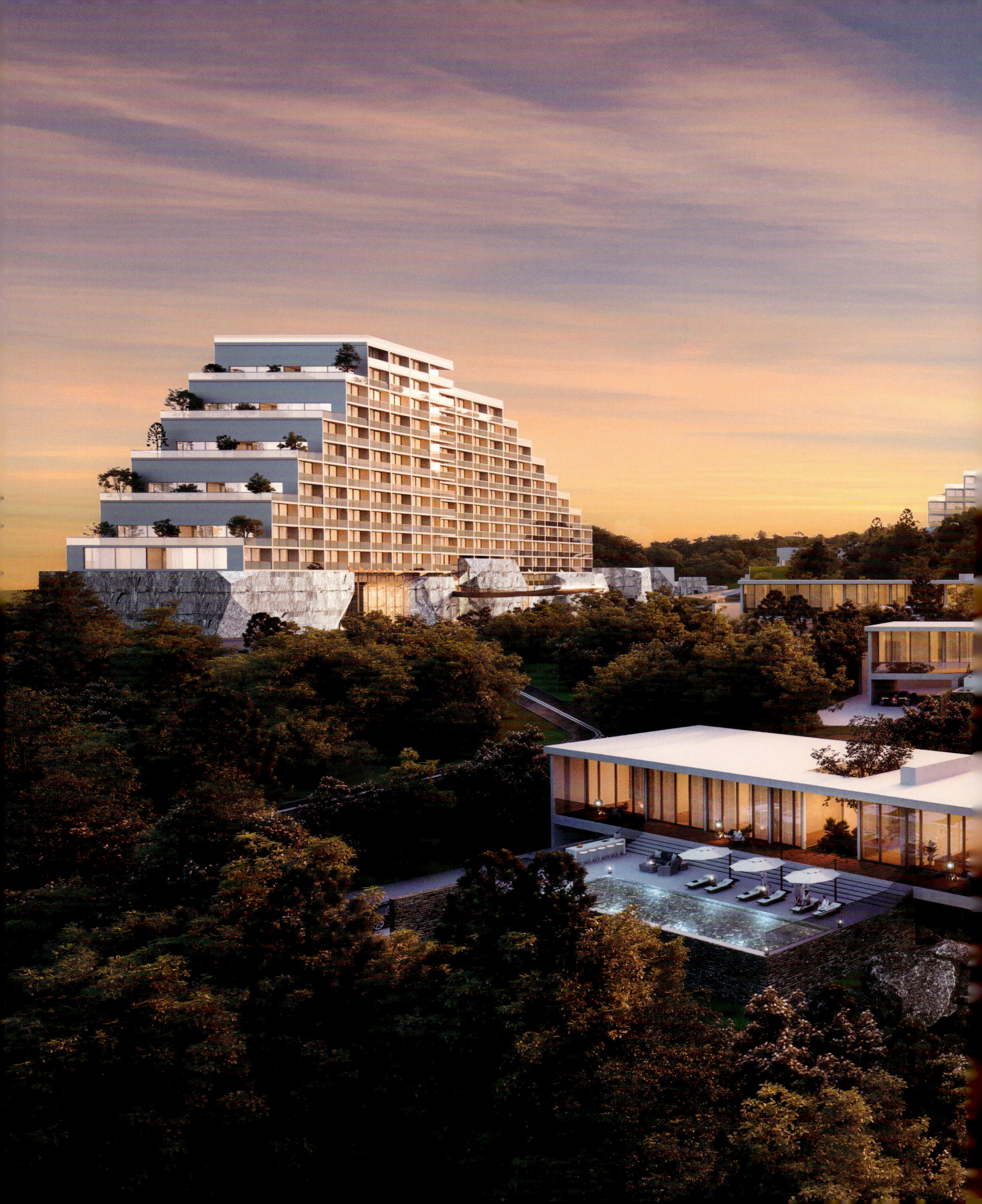

# OAK VALLEY RESORT
Wonju-si, Gangwon-do, South Korea | 2020

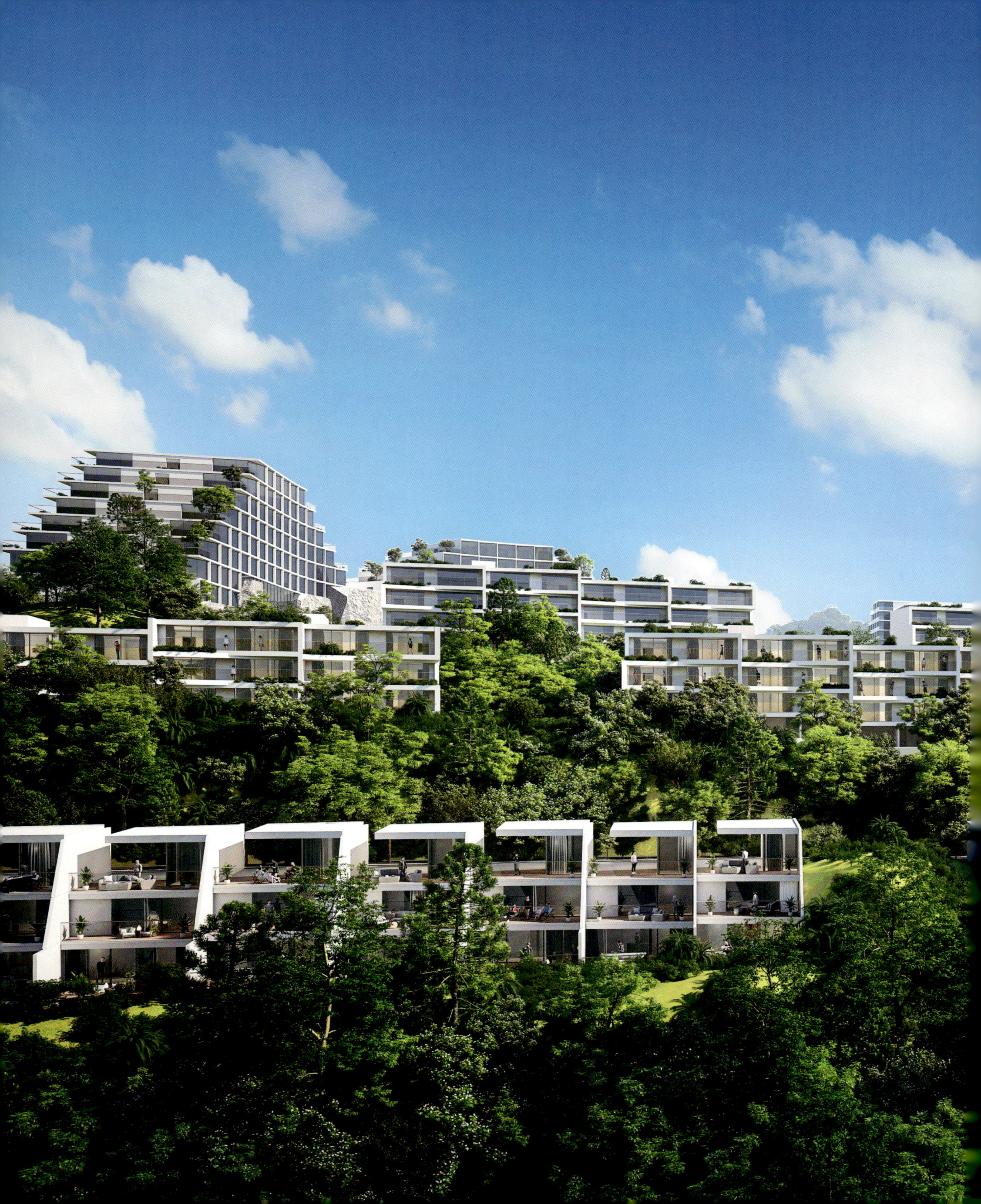

In 2020, a limited design competition was held to build an addition to the existing Oak Valley Golf Resort in Wonju-si. The vision of the new resort was a transformation of a legacy golf resort into a world-class integrated destination for all seasons and generations, offering experiential immersion into nature, adventure, and culture. We were chosen as the winner based on our initial scheme to provide a new solution to revitalize the existing resort complex. Our winning scheme calls for providing, firstly, a new prototype residential community where users can work/live/play in nature; secondly, an efficient structure that is both aesthetically pleasing and economically viable; and thirdly, phase-able development plans for the entire complex situated within the 600-acre (243-hectare) site.

Our scheme also tries to use all the natural materials readily available in the Wonju-si area; stone (Park Roche), wood (Park Bois) and Soil (Park Terre). We created a concept called *terrarium*: a new retail place where people can cure their own coffee, cheese, Korean traditional sauces, and charcuteries; this motivates the user to revisit the campus. We also added an educational program onto this new typology, including perfume, pottery, and cupping classes. Furthermore, we suggested various amenities to support the living structure, such as an observatory, tracking follies, yoga spaces, and other contemplation areas.

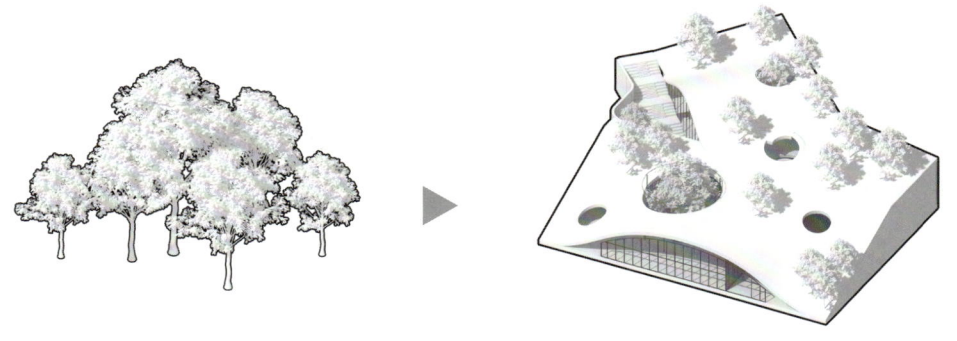

Natural elements are integrated into the built structures

OAK VALLEY RESORT 277

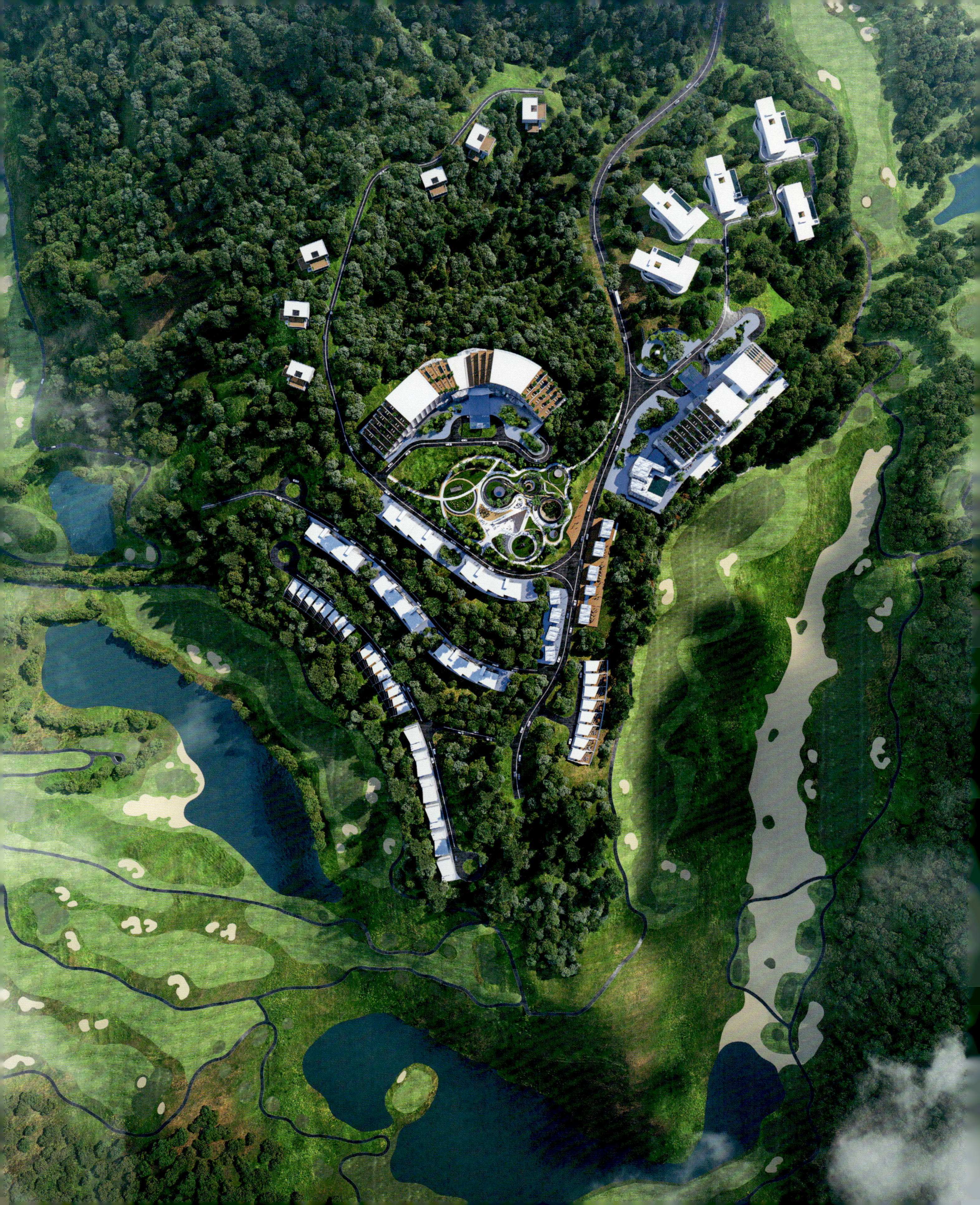

For the room design, our aim was for a new trend idea for placing the bathroom facilities on the façade side for people to enjoy the view of the site while showering or bathing.

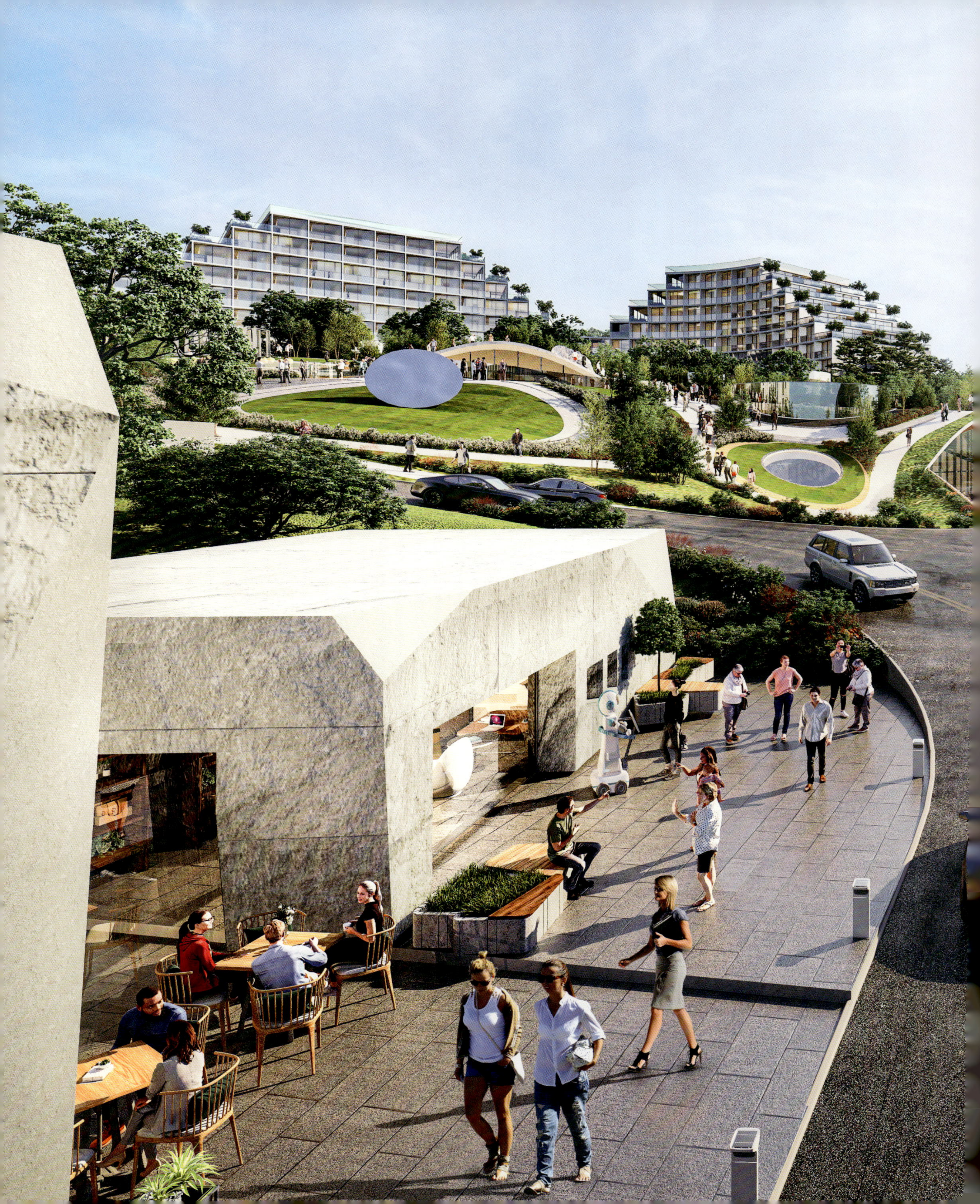

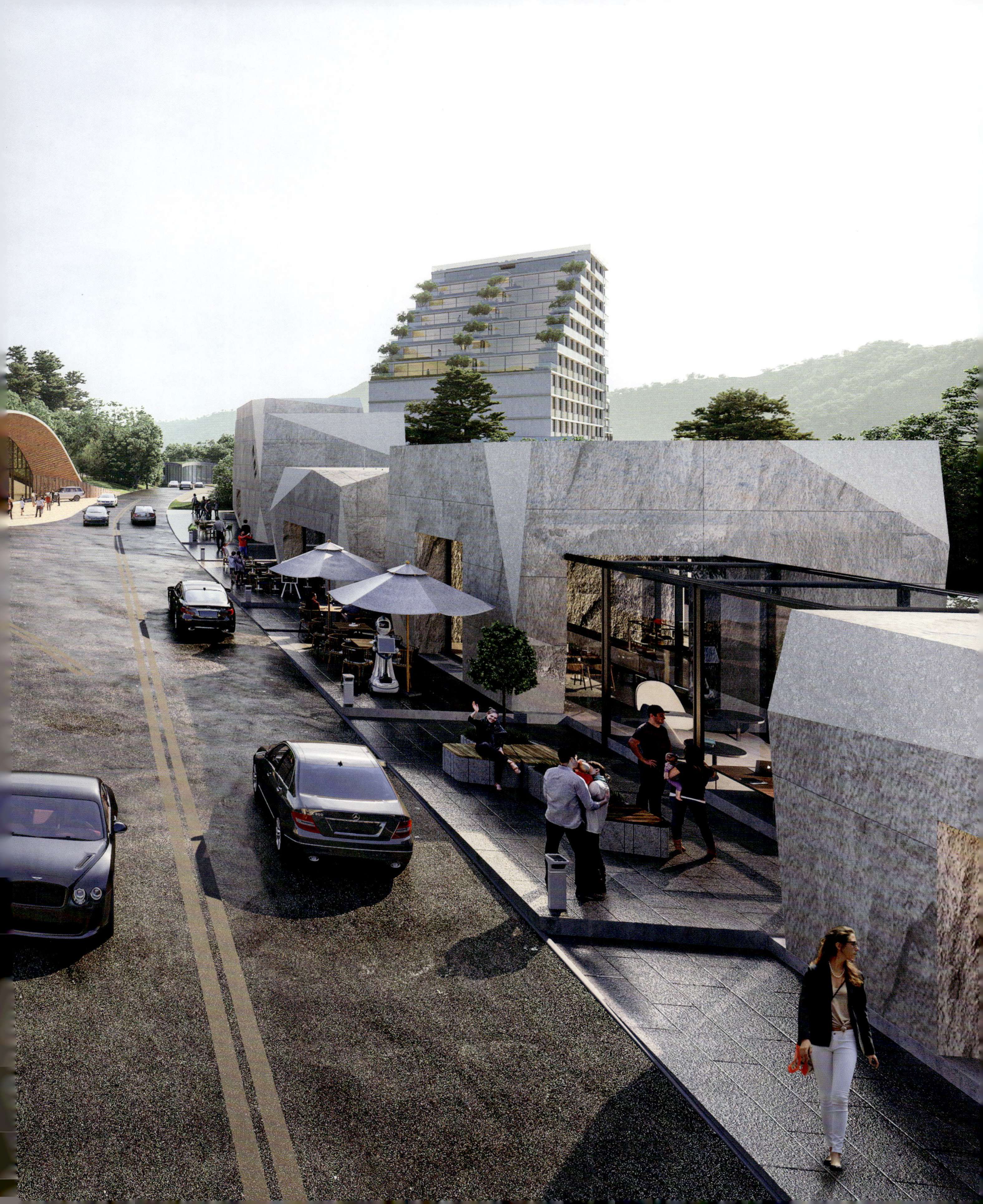

# JEJU SEOGWIPO VIP INSTITUTE HOTEL RESIDENCE

Seogwipo-si, Jeju-do, South Korea | 2015

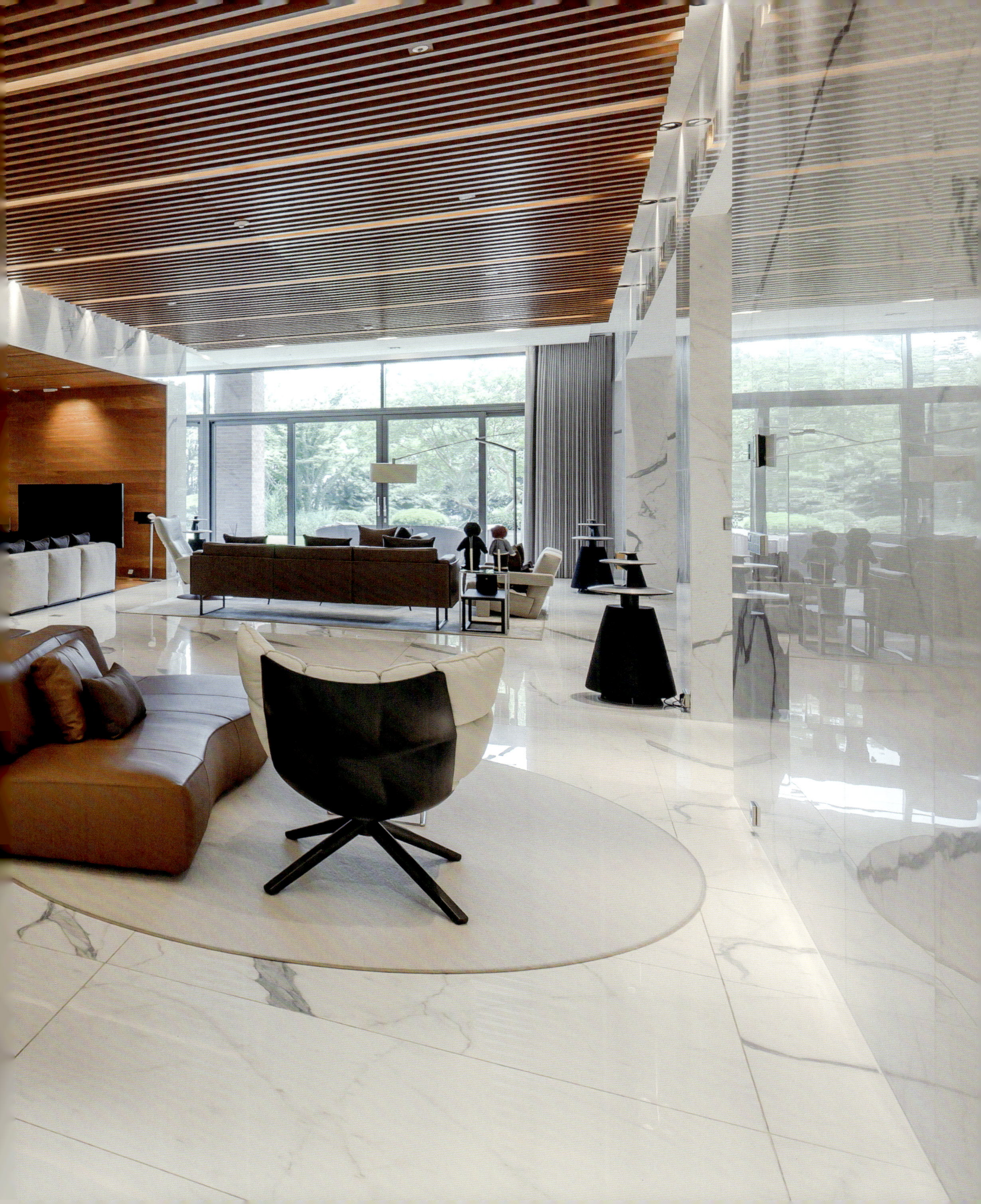

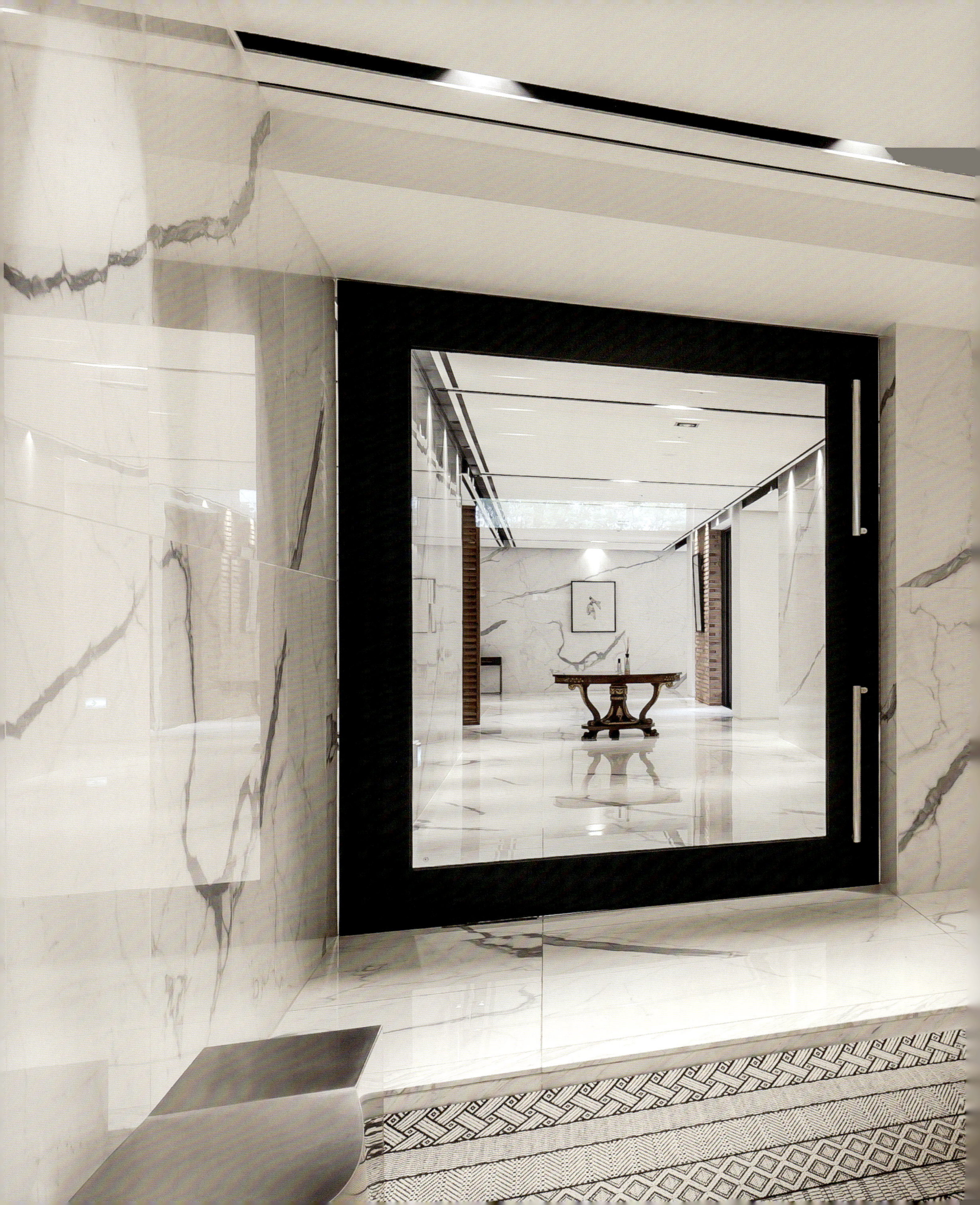

A part of the five-star luxury resort Jeju Shinhwa World, this 43,056-square-foot (4,000-square-meter) institute was intended to provide exclusive access for visiting VIPs. The site has approximately 3 acres (1.2 hectares) of land near the ocean. The island location's climate is prone to humidity but is mostly relatively temperate.

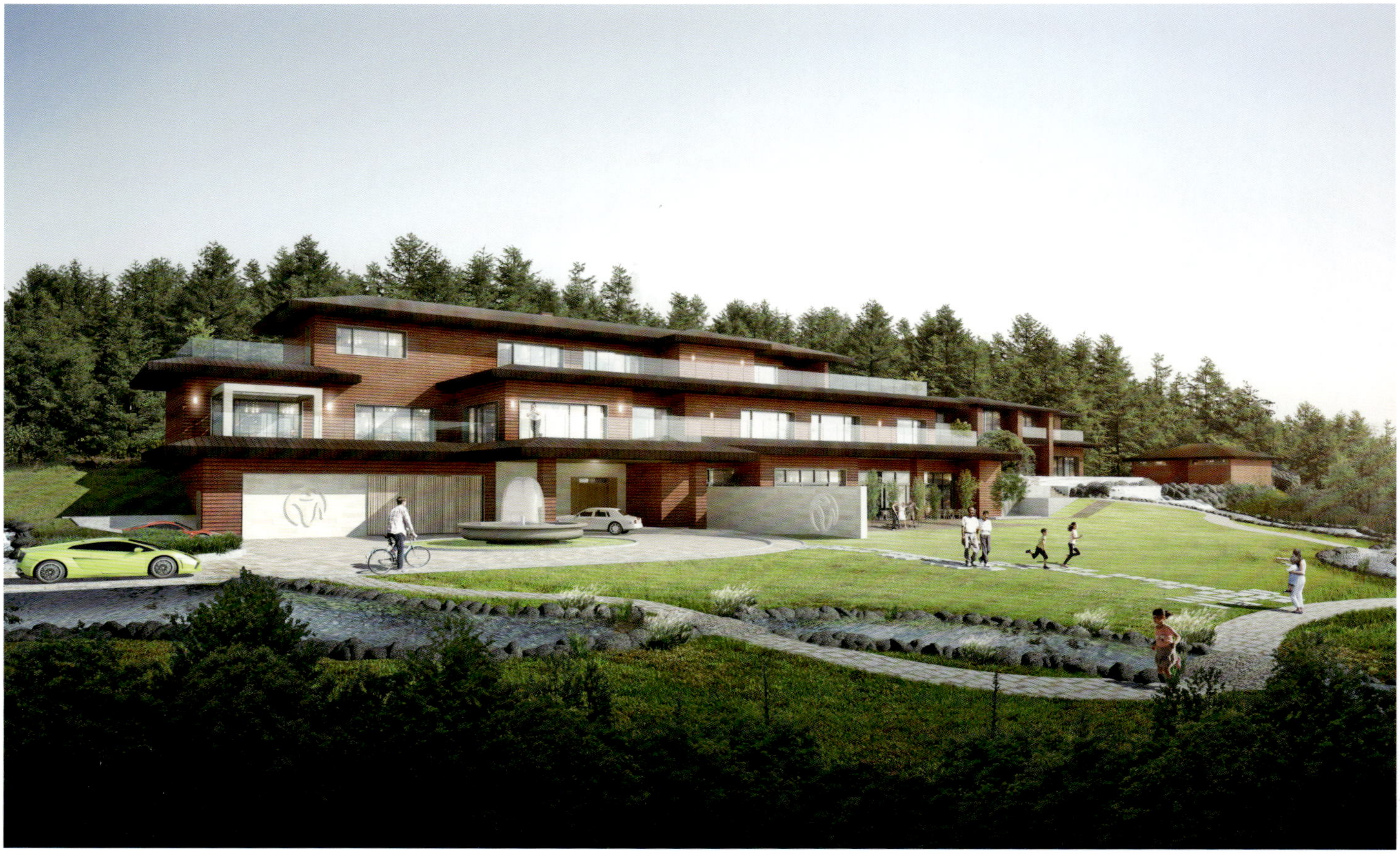
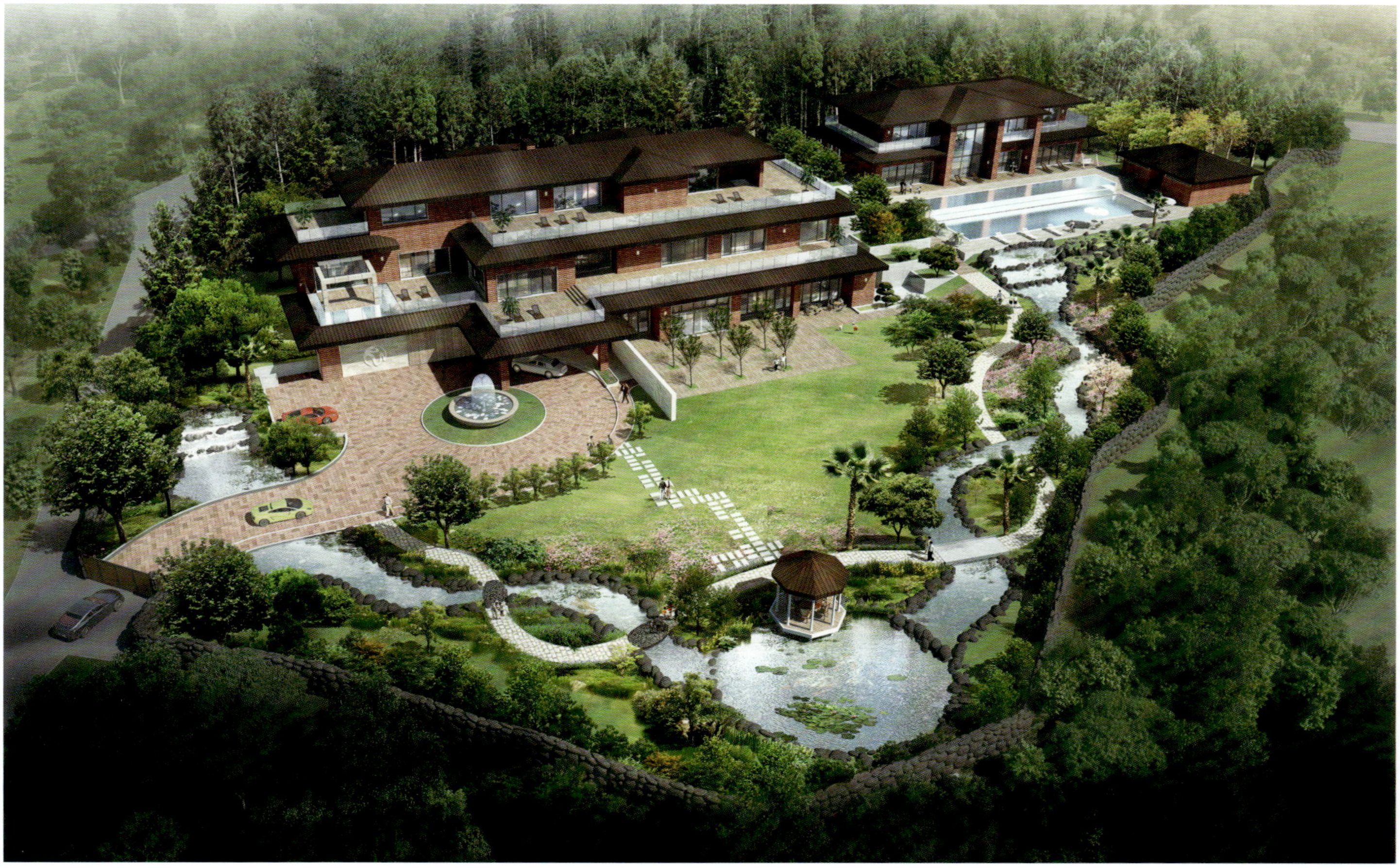

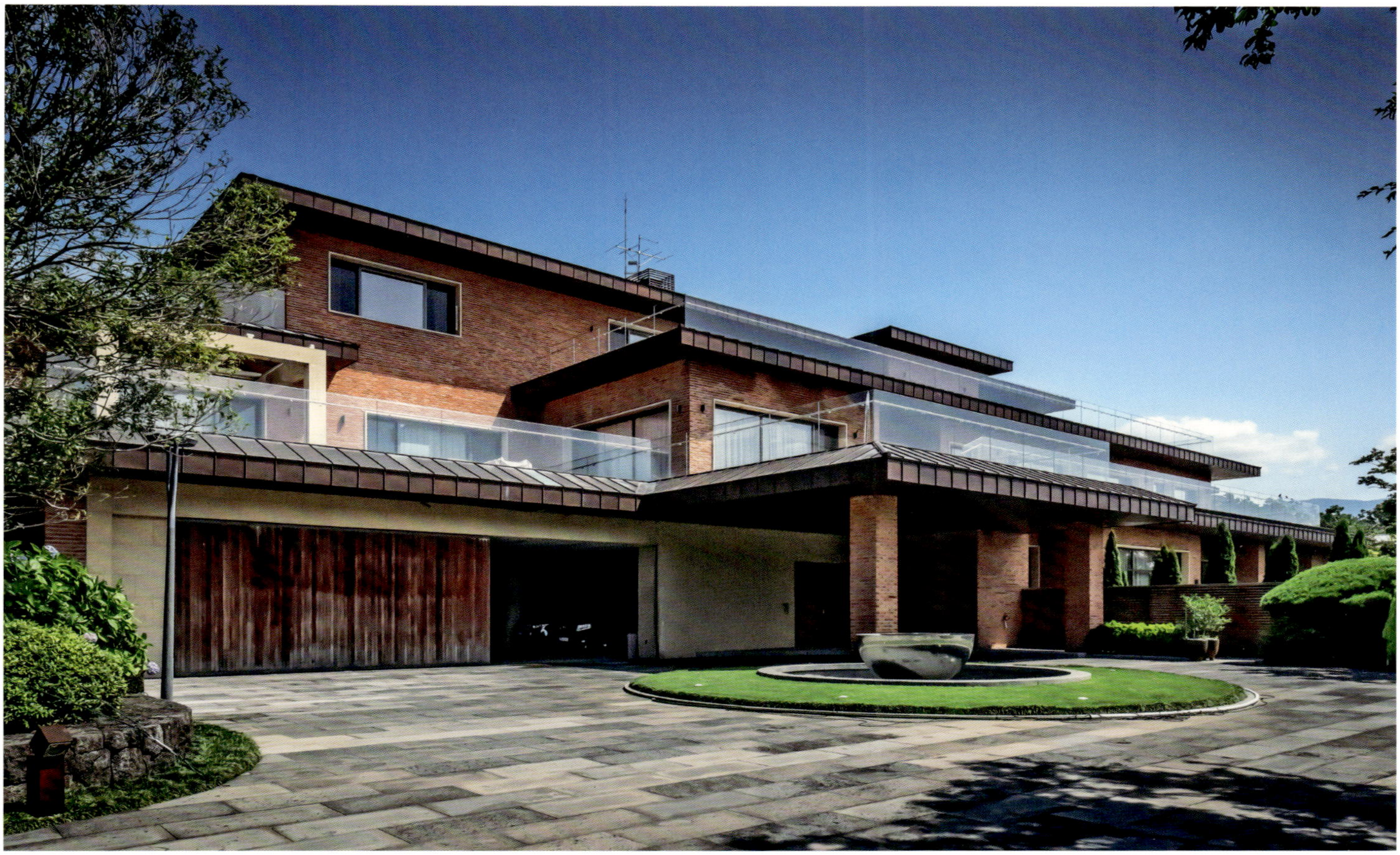

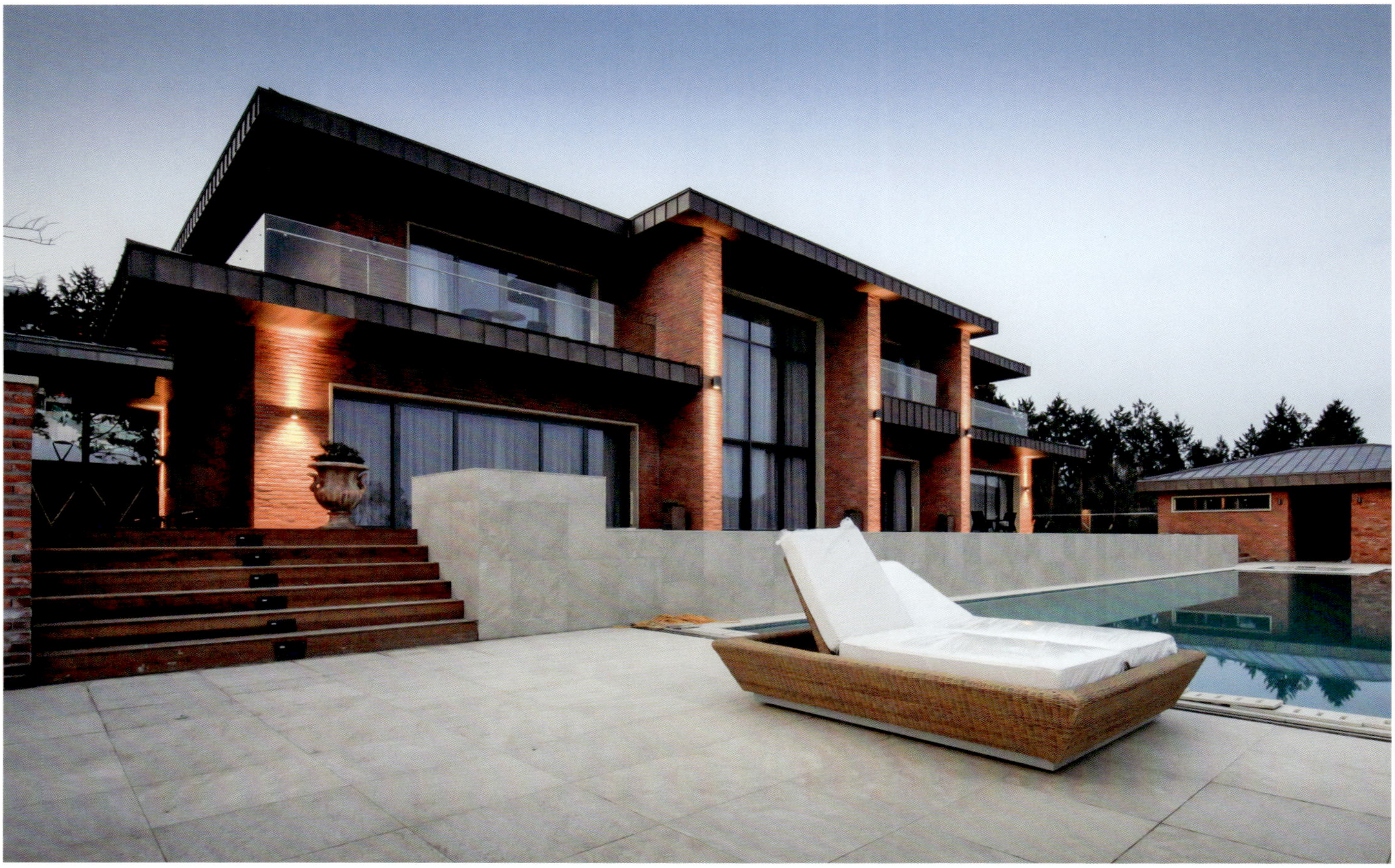

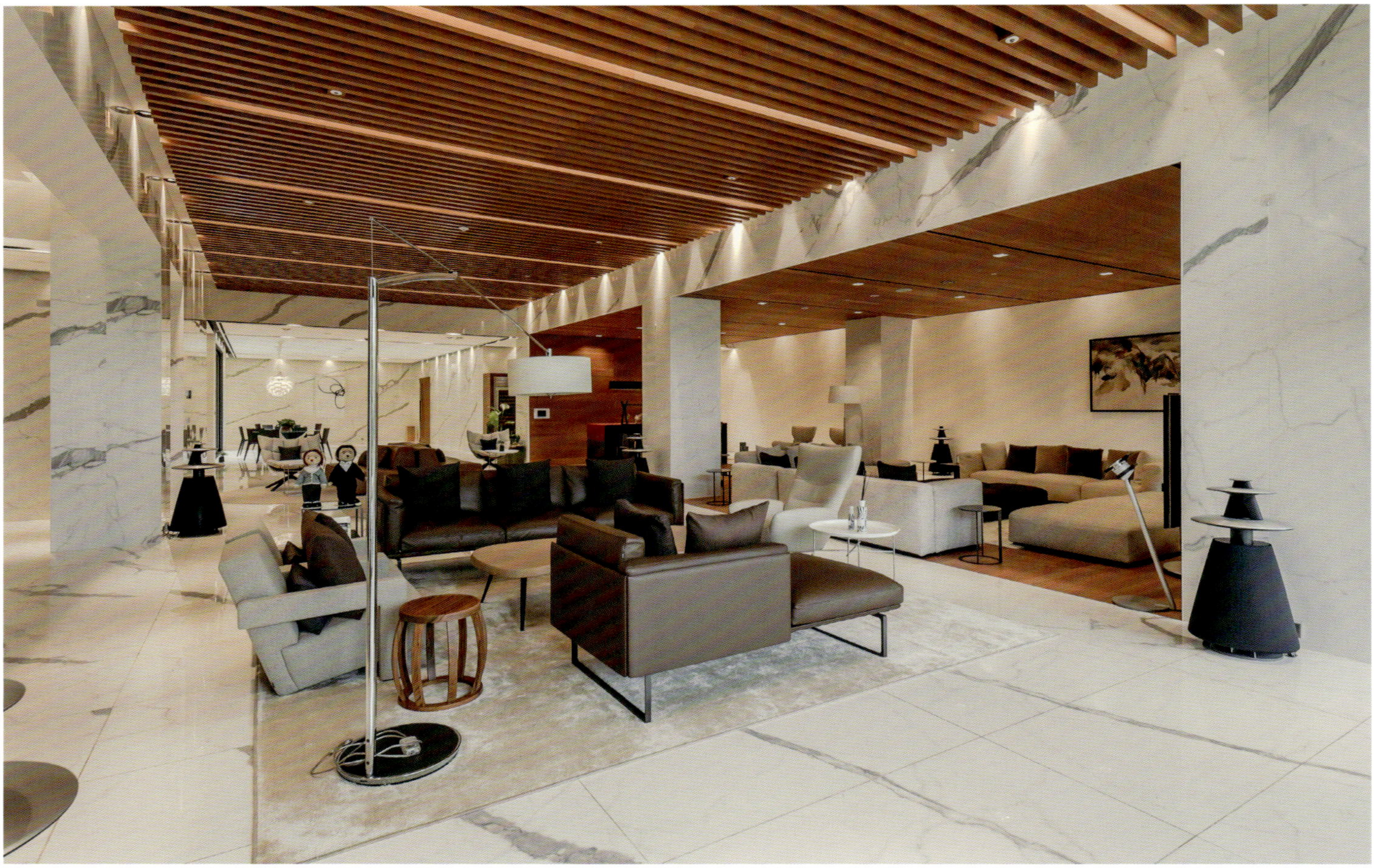

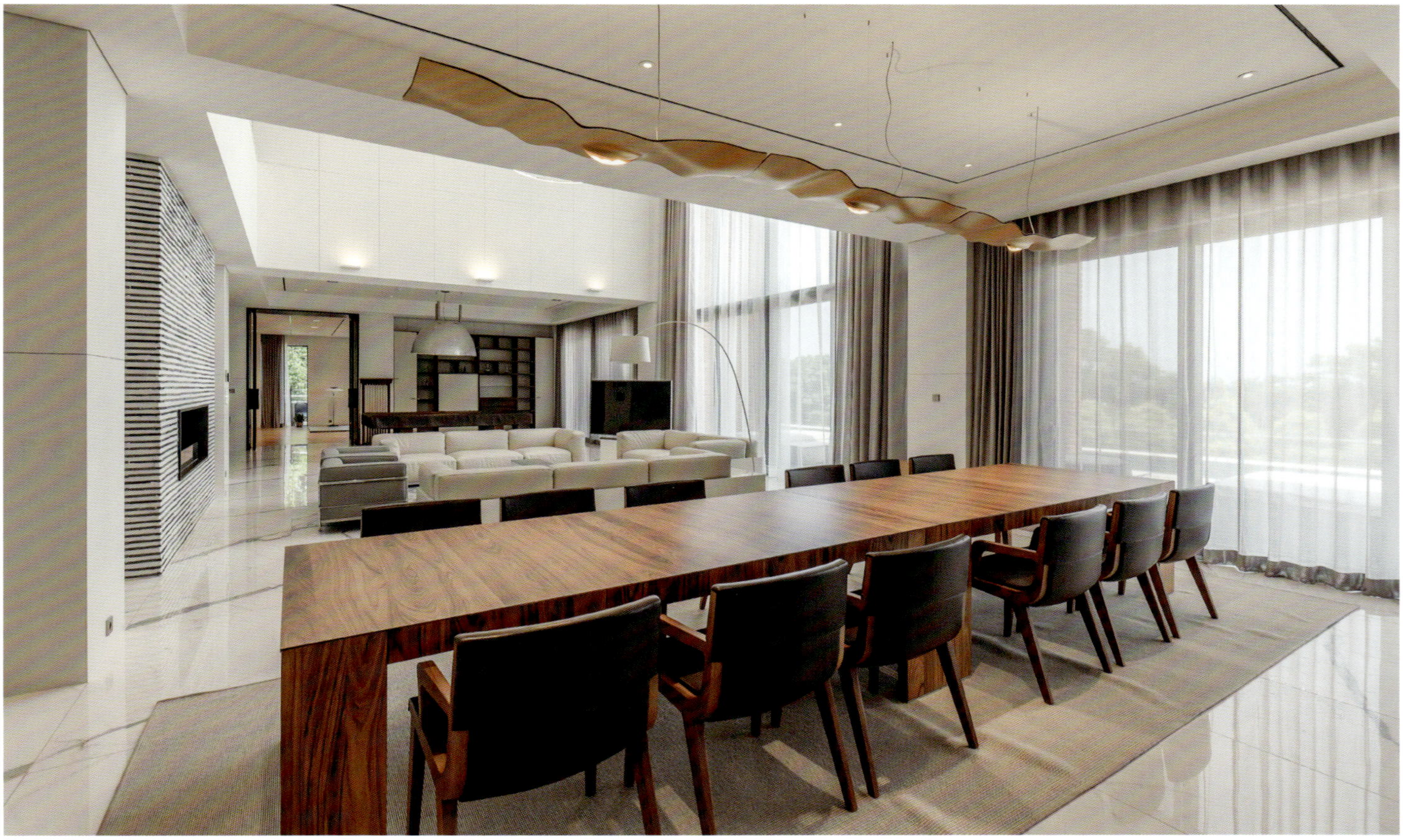

To fulfill the owner's intended program and feng shui requirements, we divided the entire structure into two different masses—a larger one emphasizing entertainment and dining experiences and a smaller one for relaxation.

The larger structure consists of three levels: on the second level there is a penthouse suite with a large outdoor ipe wood deck; on the first level there are four guest suites, a living room, a library, formal indoor and outdoor dining rooms (also with an ipe wood deck), a theater, bar, gym, and a large dining area; and on the basement level a professional kitchen capable of Chinese, Korean, and Western cuisines, and a large aquarium (32.8 feet wide by 13 feet high by 13 feet deep [10 meters wide by 4 meters high by 4 meters deep]) for visual interest.

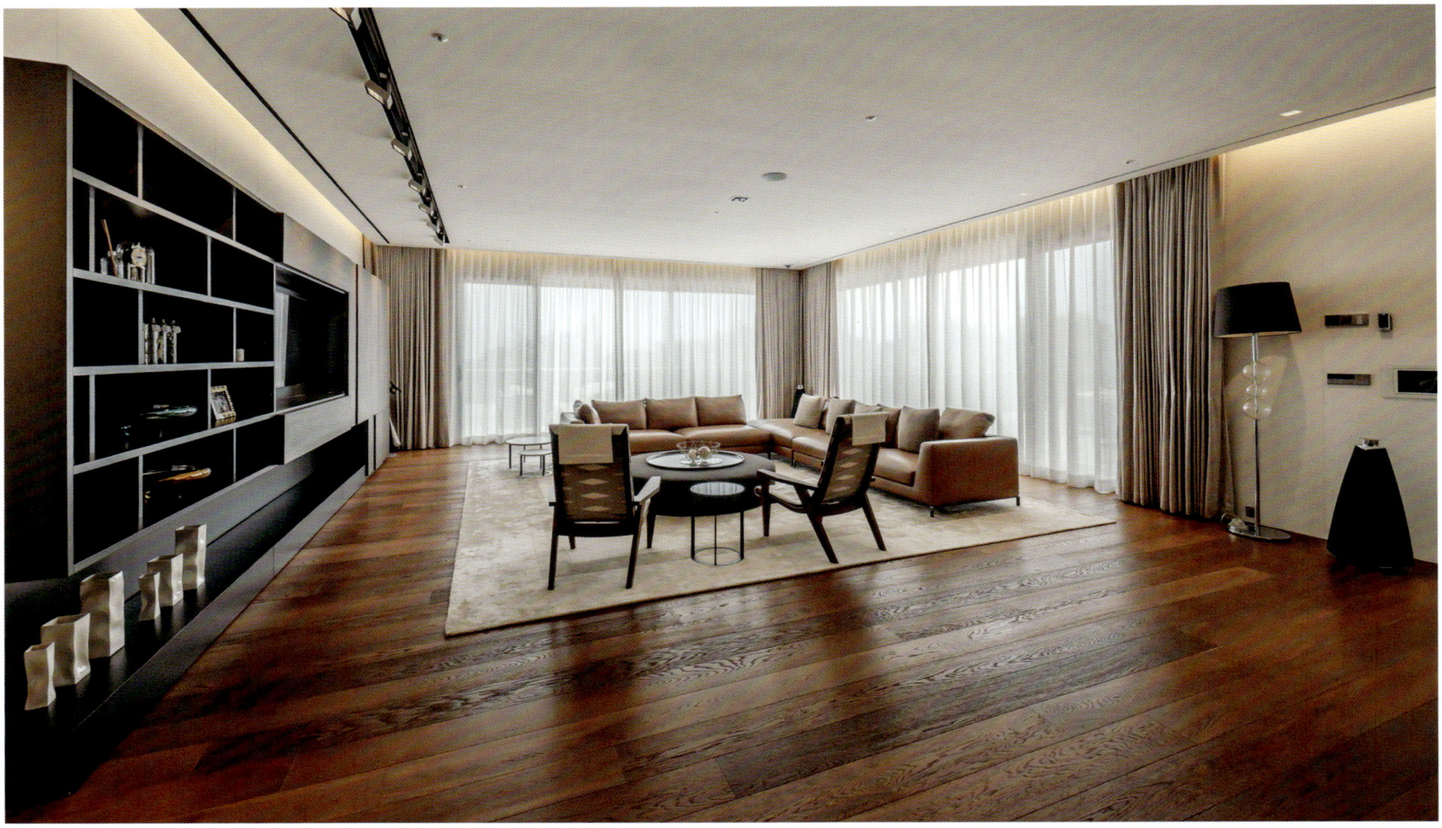

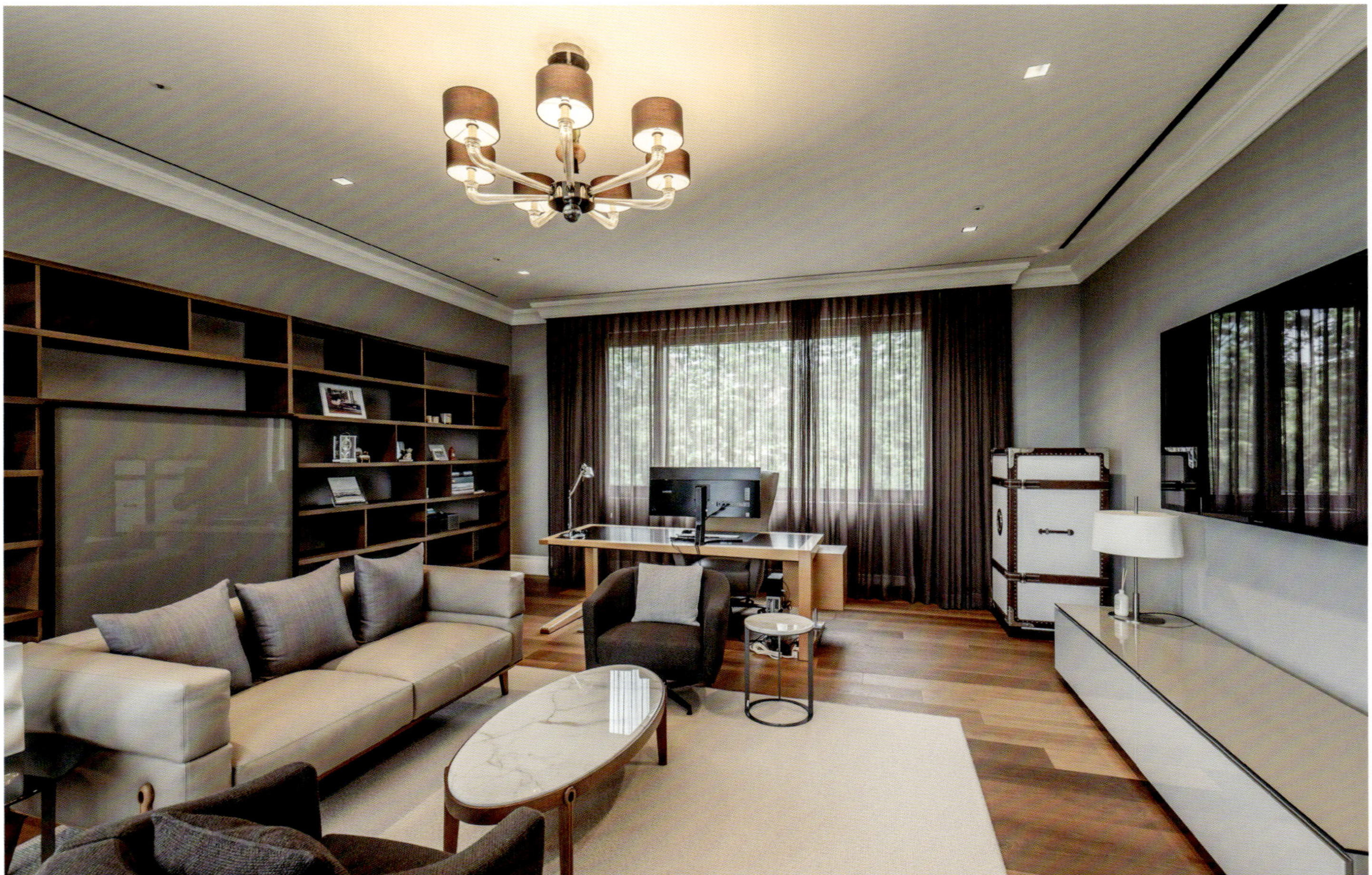

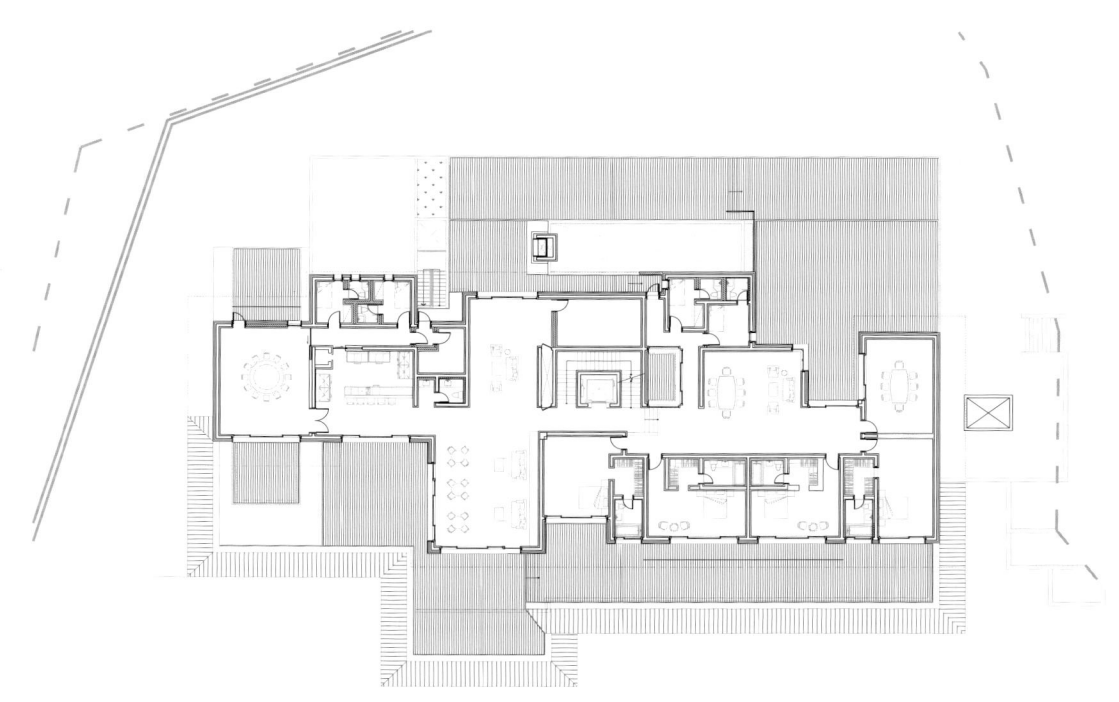

Larger accommodation second-floor plan

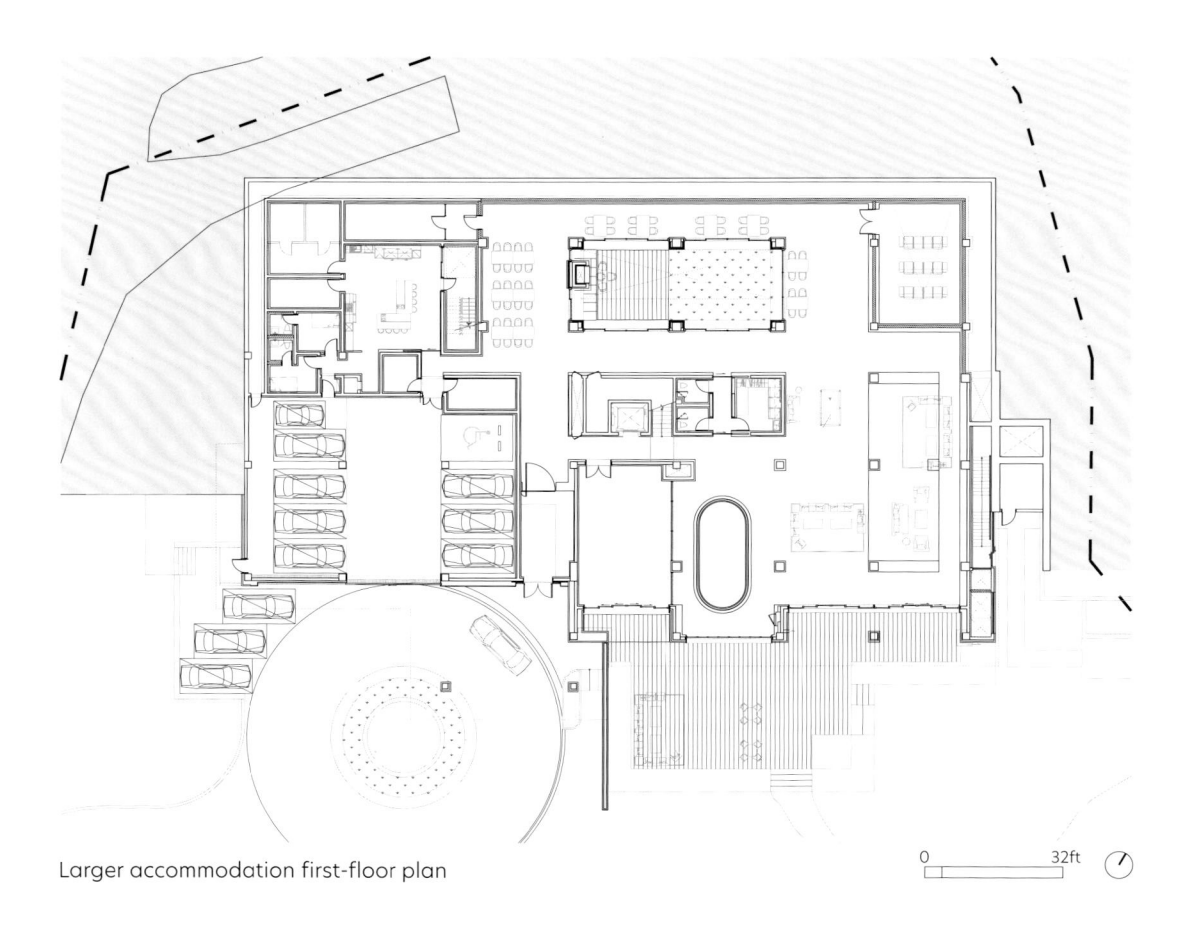

Larger accommodation first-floor plan

JEJU SEOGWIPO VIP INSTITUTE HOTEL RESIDENCE

The smaller mass includes on the second level three guest suites and a living room and on the first level a sushi bar counter, a large dining area, a two-story living area with a pool table bar, and a large gym area. On the first-level outdoor deck area we placed a two-tier heated infinity pool and sauna house.

The owner wanted a traditional, aged, comfortable, and relaxed atmosphere thus we chose a Frank Lloyd Wright architectural style, with dominant horizontal and vertical lines—for rhythm—and cantilevered broad eaves. For the building's materiality we used sand-blasted aged red brick to create a façade that expresses warmth and comfort. The final scheme came out of rigorous alternative studies of proportion and material details. In the main building, we inserted a sunken courtyard to bring in natural light and to create a small garden within the basement level. This gesture creates a sense of surprise and is a wayfinding device in this large 16,146-square-foot (1,500-square-meter) basement entertainment level. To alleviate the chronic problem of humidity on Jeju Island, we provided an air tunnel between the retaining wall and a separate wall.

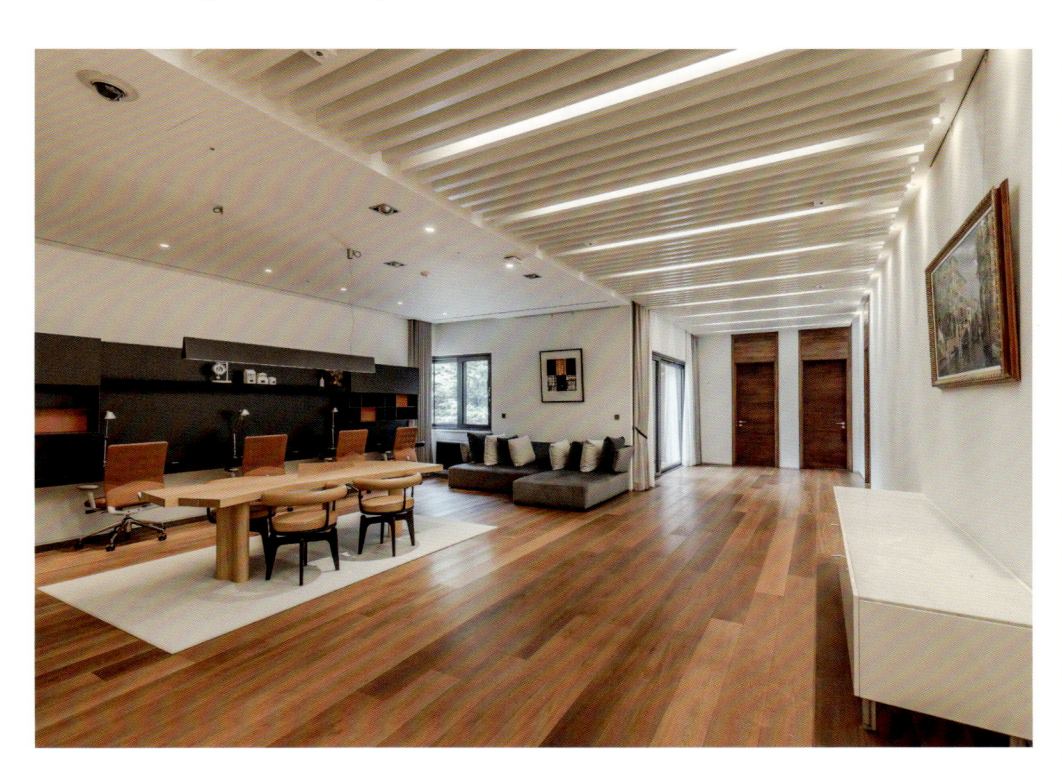

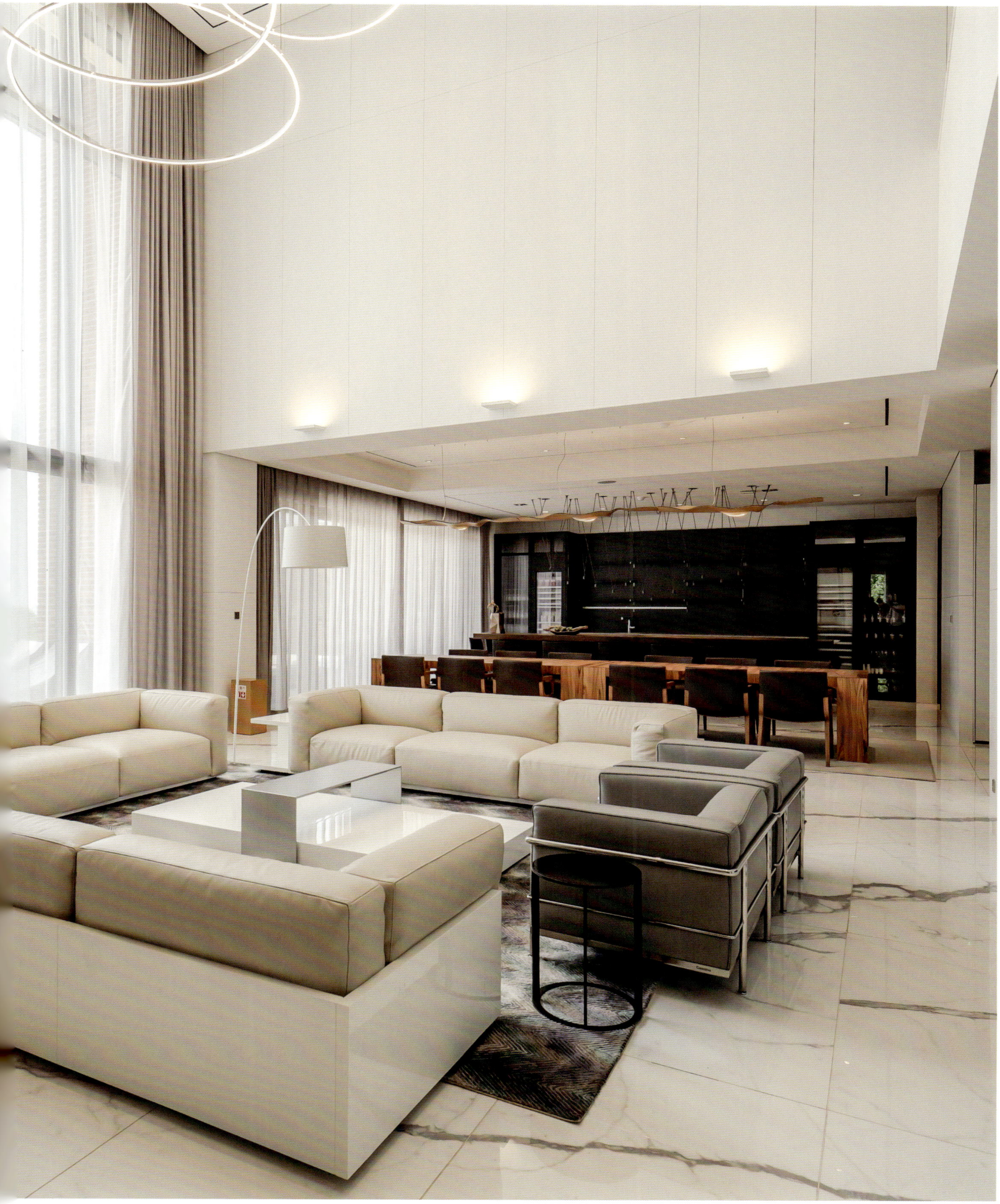

# OYALA CONVENTION & OBSERVATORY

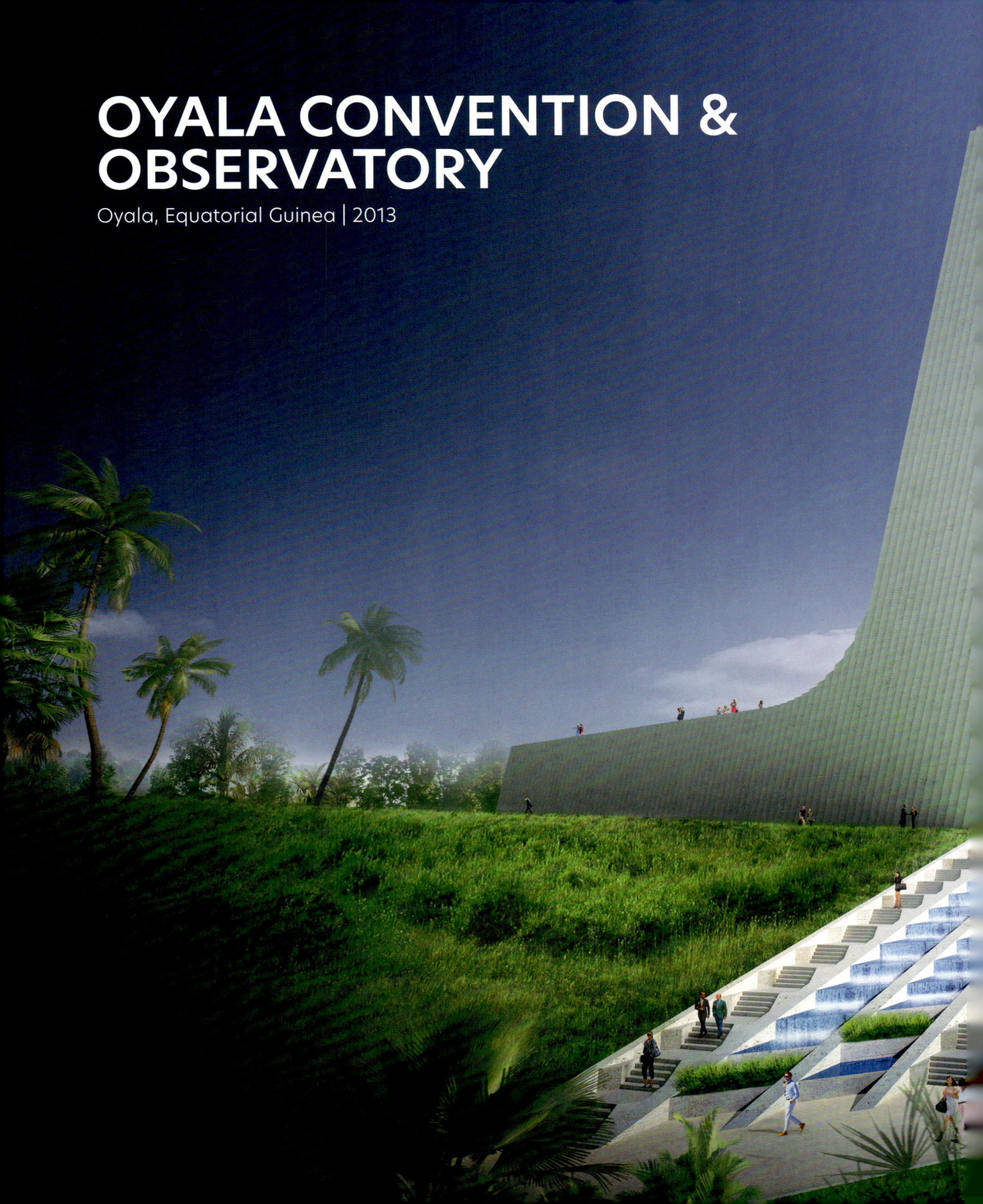

Oyala, Equatorial Guinea | 2013

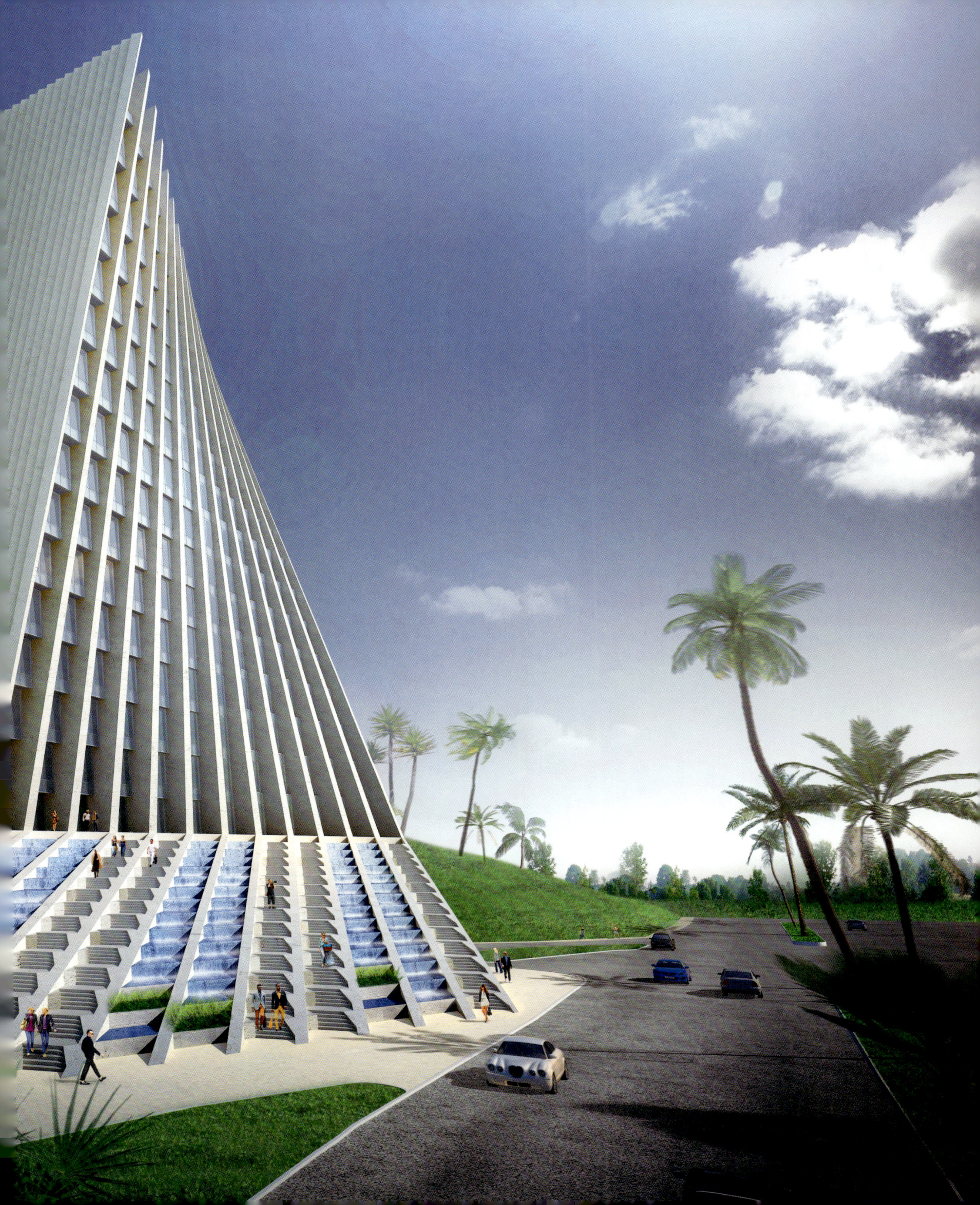

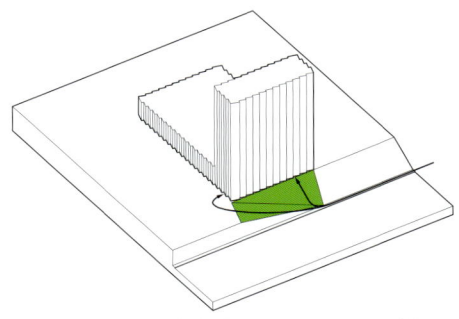

Direct access from main road: the landscape is carved for a smooth transition from the access road. Two slopes lead to two points of access.

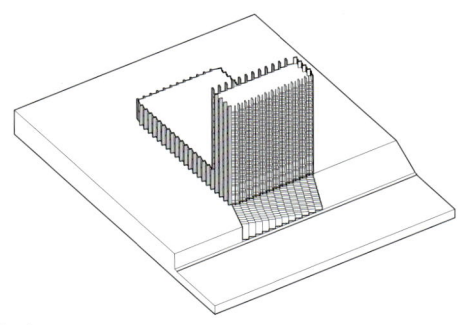

Finalized scheme

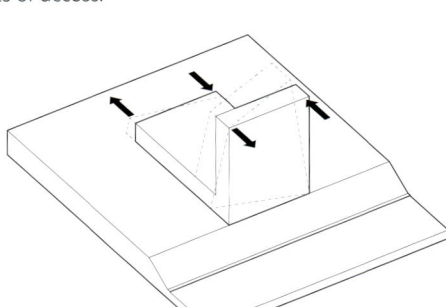

Pulling and pushing: a new form was derived from the original L-type volume while still maintaining the solid void experience

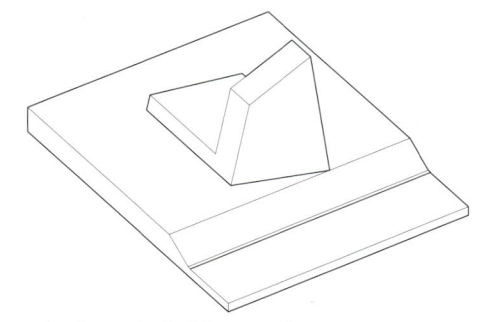

Transformed volume: the building transforms from static to dynamic

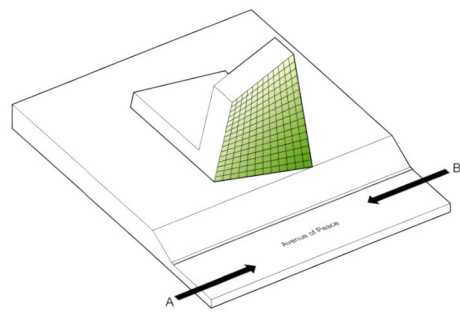

Evolved façade offers multifaceted views from the road: the transformed building's façade is dynamic in multiple dimensions

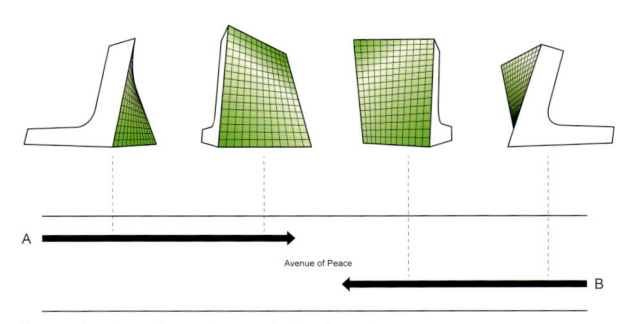

Dynamic views from the road: the façade provides unique views from both directions

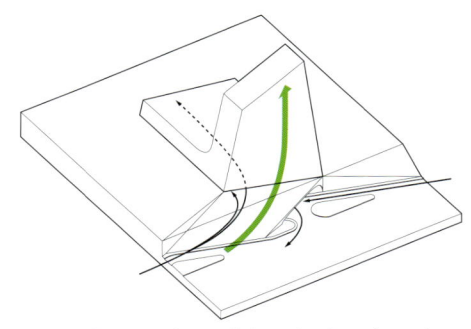

Grand stairs transform continuously into the façade and provide circulation paths: separate pedestrian circulation and underground vehicular area are accessed with one form

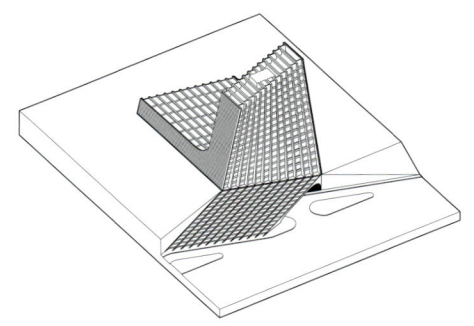

Scheme 1 evolved

RHYTHM AND DYNAMICS

The Oyala Convention & Observatory was designed for the Equatorial Guinean government as they began finalizing the plans and development of their capital city, Oyala. To facilitate city planning and growth in the city, Equatorial Guinea's government wanted to create a convention center and an observatory. We came up with a design that both effectively addresses these functions while also has an advanced form and aesthetic to represent its [then] newly founded home country. As such, the project has a rotating tower and an observation point to survey the real-time process of building a new capital city, while its materiality and form are contemporary and progressive. The project will include government offices in addition to the observatory and convention center.

The project is slightly elevated from the road. Initial iterations of the project played with stacked triangular shapes, seeing the form that was generated as they twisted in multiple directions. Finding this moment expressive, the next iteration included repetitive, fanning planes. Coupled with its fixed horizontal base mass, the project begins to visually communicate a sense of progressive, physical speed. Much like the young country itself, the aim was to generate a building that elicits a sense of curiosity, excitement, and admiration.

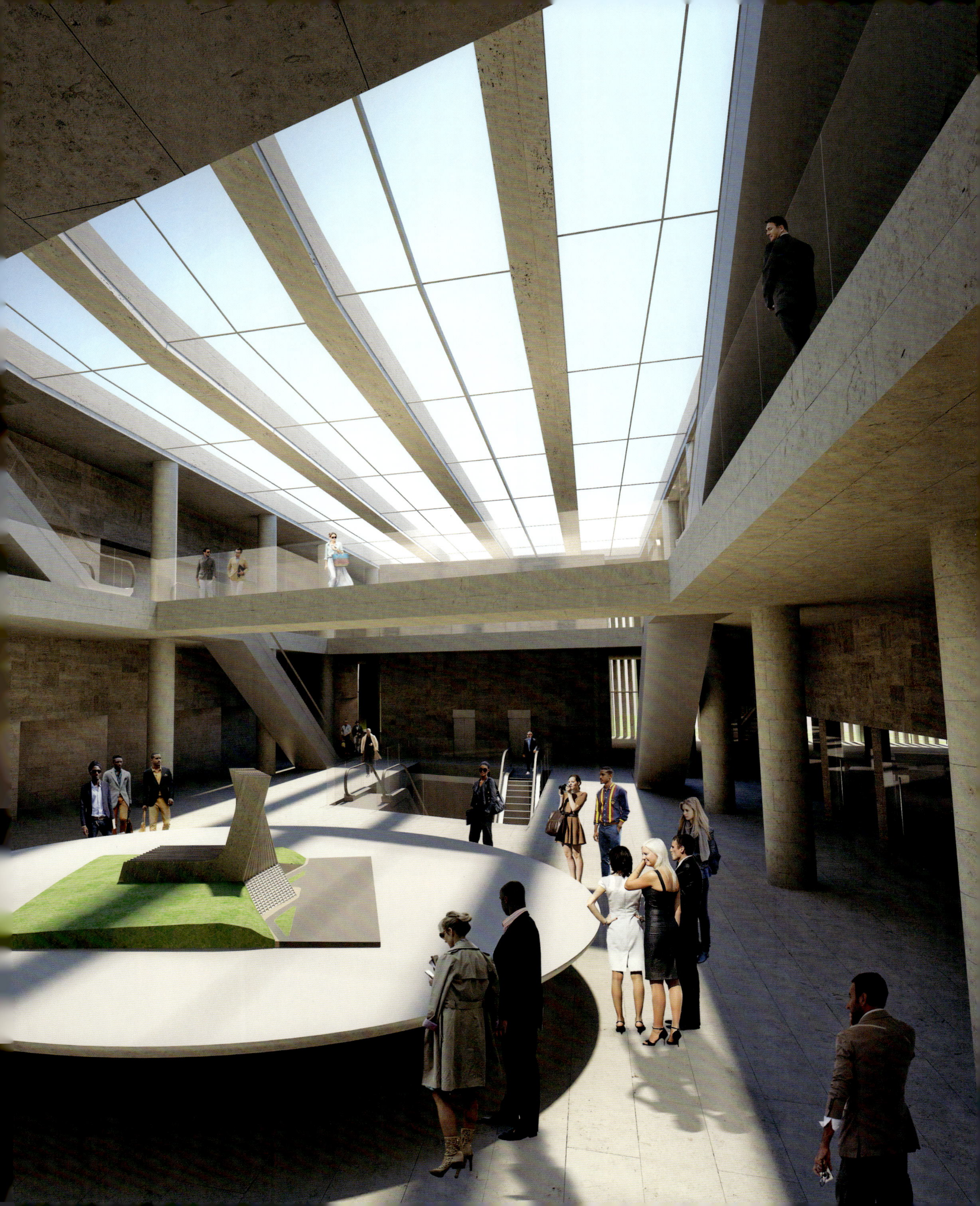

Taesun Hong, *City of Music 4* (1991), charcoal

**Circulation** and **connection** define the flows of movement through a system, how one space (or sound) connects to another.

# GYEONGHUI-DANG MIXED-USE

Jongno-gu, Seoul, South Korea | 2021

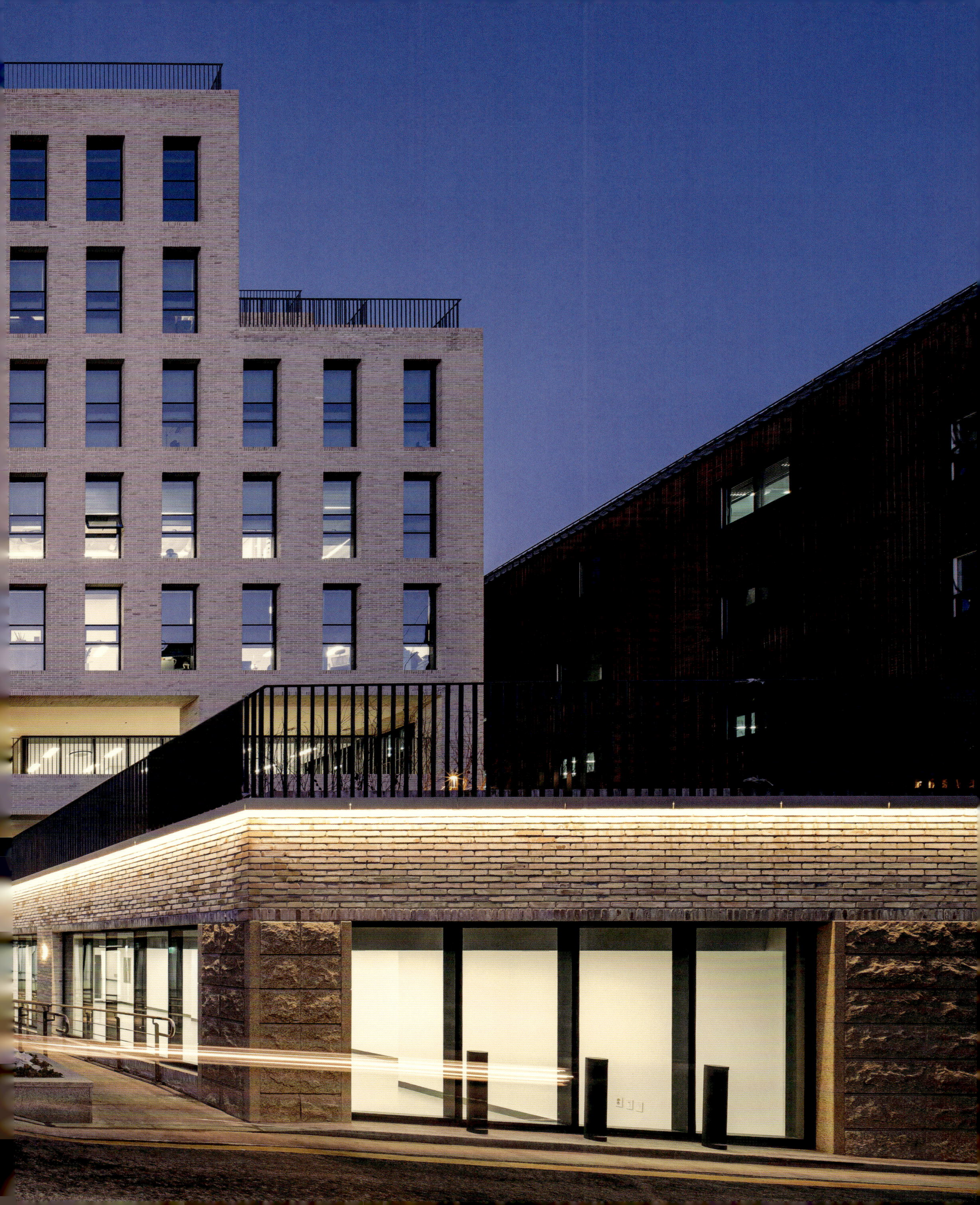

This project focuses on a space that engages with historical and cultural context. The site is in the middle of Seoul's historical city center, the Jongno-gu District, within a historical preservation area. During the Chosun Dynasty, the site was part of Gyeonghui Palace (since destroyed and mostly dismantled by the Japanese). However, as part of the site is in a historical preservation area, we investigated and excavated to uncover relics, including part of the palace's boundary wall and foundations. Thus, we developed our concept design to preserve the current condition of the site and adapt it to the owner's requirements. The Relics Exhibition Museum preserves the historical context and provides a place of culture and education for the community.

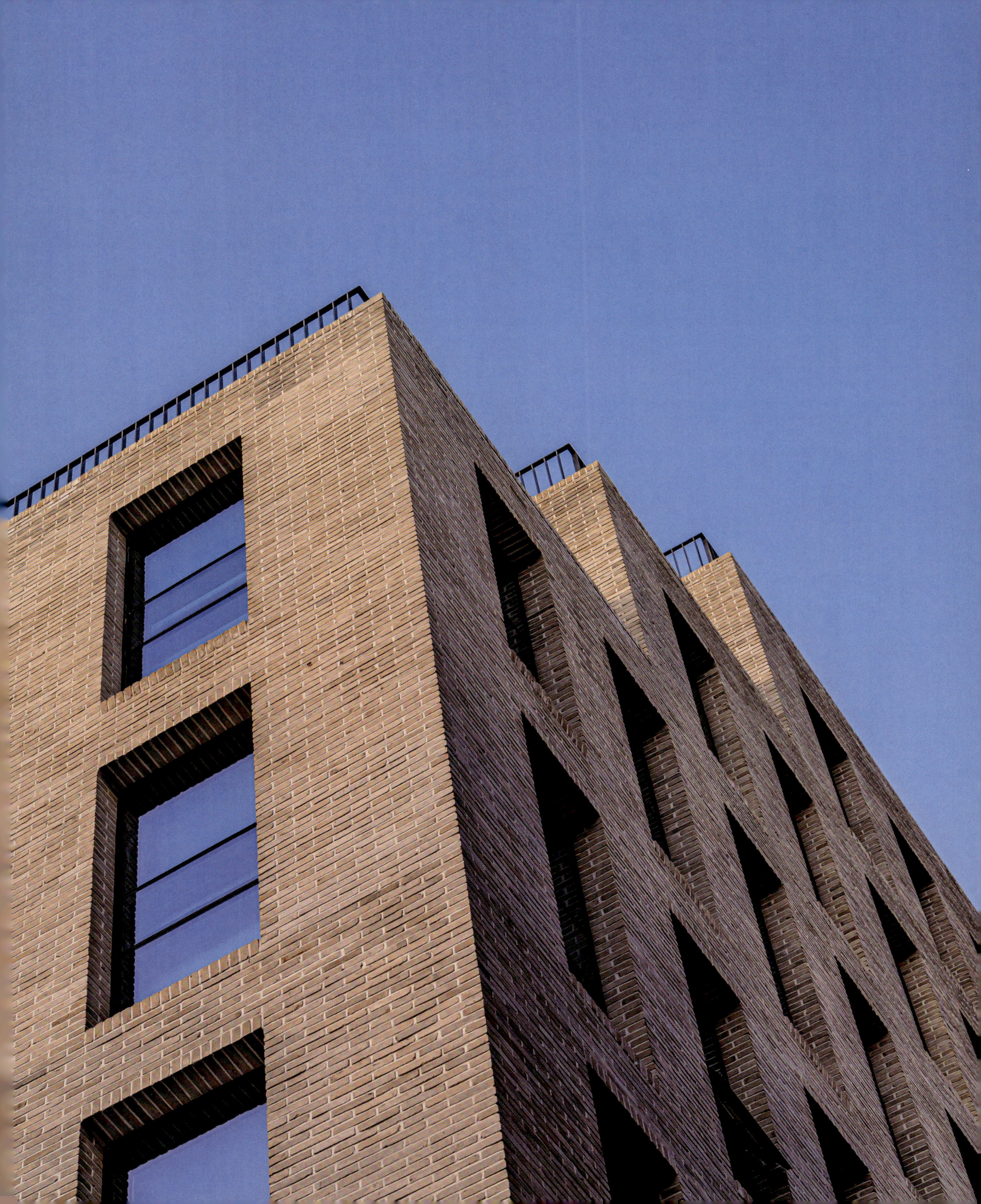

Since part of the site is severely sloped and the maximum aboveground level development guideline calls for a FAR of 200 percent, our team searched a way to increase the overall rentable areas by utilizing the average ground-level elevation point to be set at the middle of the slope; therefore, the abutting road level was established as a B2 level. After a series of calculations, we provided more than an 80 percent increase in the FAR. The local building regulations define the underground area as "the area that is more than 50 percent buried." We carved out a portion of the lower two floors to allow for a more open and pleasant retail shopping environment.

As the program requires connecting four levels of retail spaces above the road level, we inserted an outdoor stair connecting the road and the top retail space located on the adjoining wall of the Seonggok Art Museum. Since the long narrow shape of the site encounters a small area of street façade, we expanded four floors of the retail spaces to be vertically stacked along with our designed public staircase that penetrates the building; the five floors of office space juxtapose in a separate circulation system.

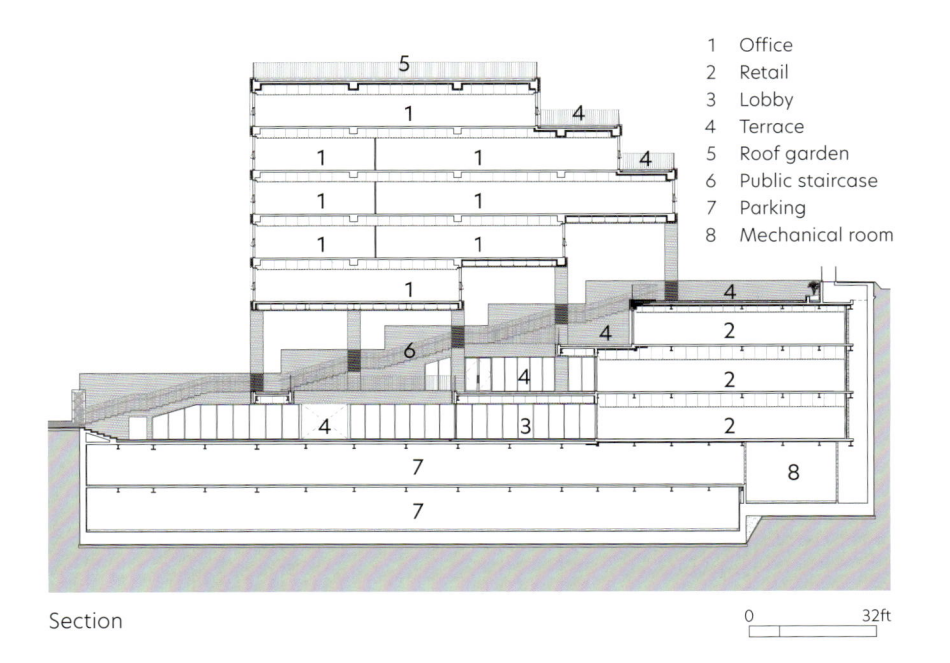

1. Office
2. Retail
3. Lobby
4. Terrace
5. Roof garden
6. Public staircase
7. Parking
8. Mechanical room

Section

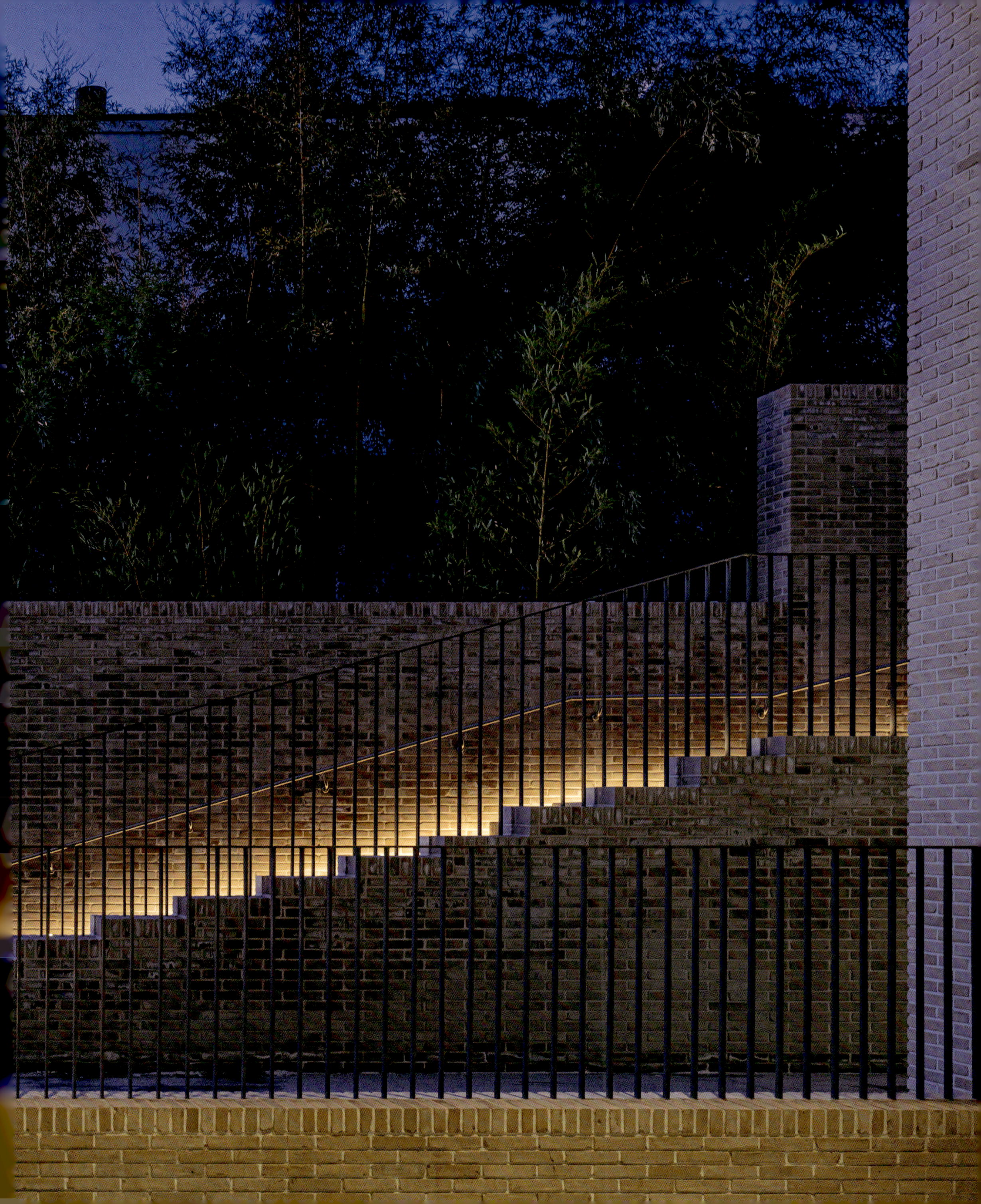

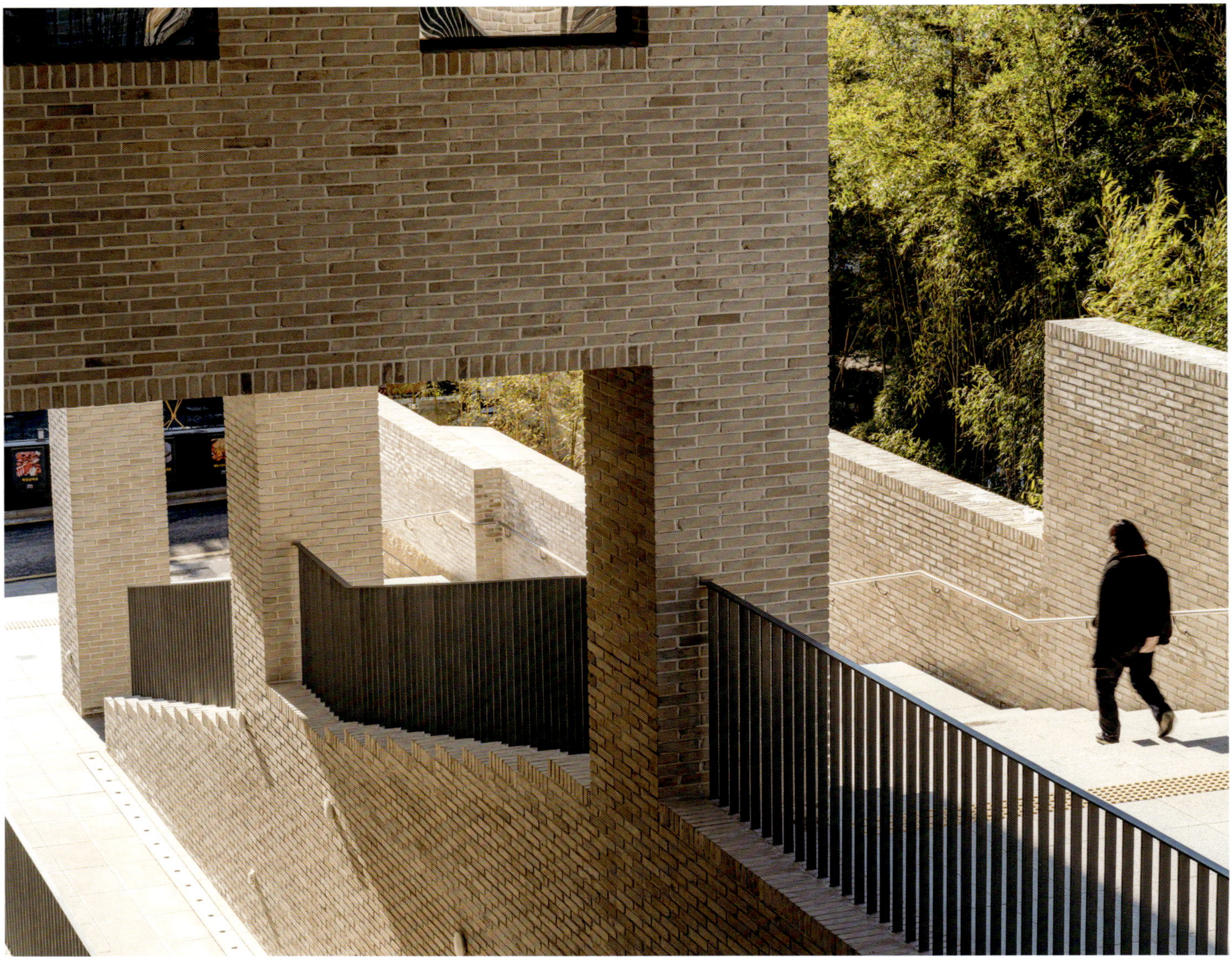

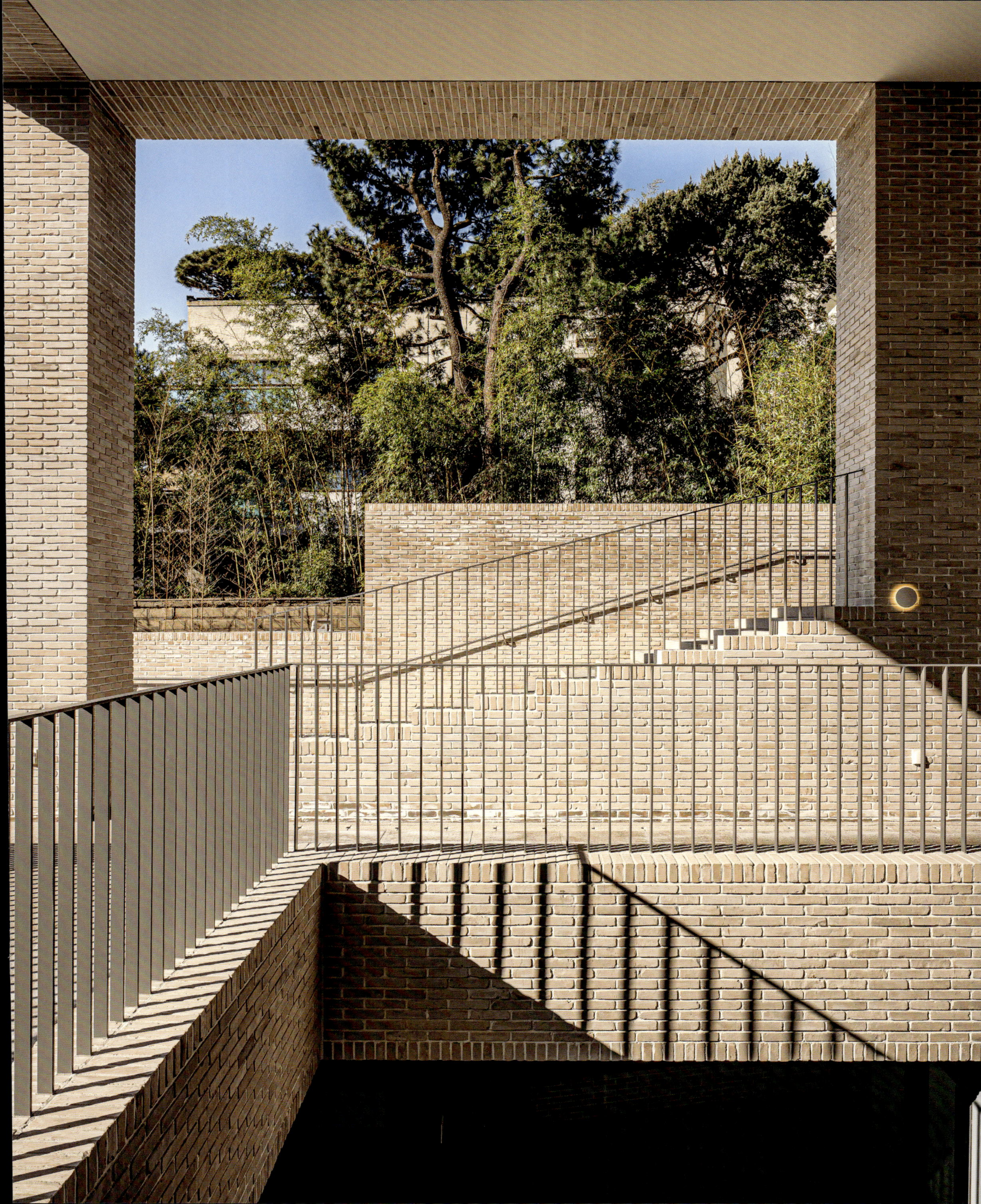

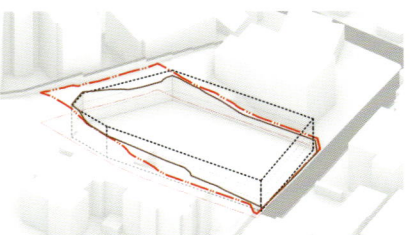

Existing site condition

Maximizing usable area by using site condition

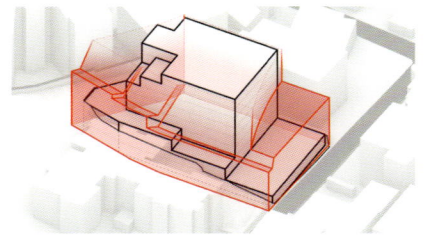

Maximizing volume created by zoning regulation

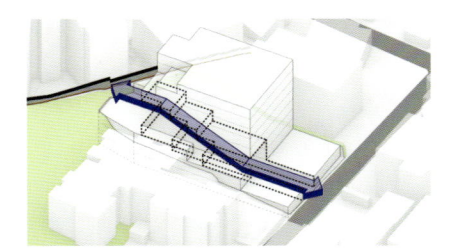

Interior void created for retail

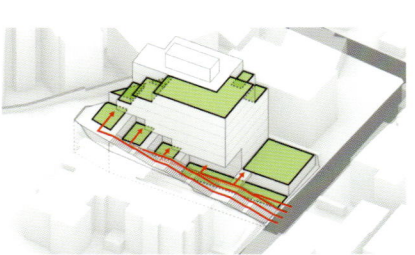

Created public rest zone by utilizing terraces

310  CIRCULATION AND CONNECTION

Despite the constraints of the local site condition and zoning regulations, our design solution was to trigger a design for a three-dimensional linear pathway from street level to the rooftop, where people can observe views of Gyeonghui Palace while taking in the journey of street experience within the building.

This approach resembles the open-air Spanish Steps located in Rome. At the same time, street events and experiences continue to the building with connecting gardens and retail areas. We hope this newly established step will become a feature as a designated rest stop for the neighborhood, thus attracting many visitors to the site. Once visitors reach the top of the stair, they experience a pocket garden and a plaza-like space. We have also provided a roof garden and terrace spaces for office users to enjoy. We chose reused brick (imported from China) as cladding, to harmonize with the surrounding materials.

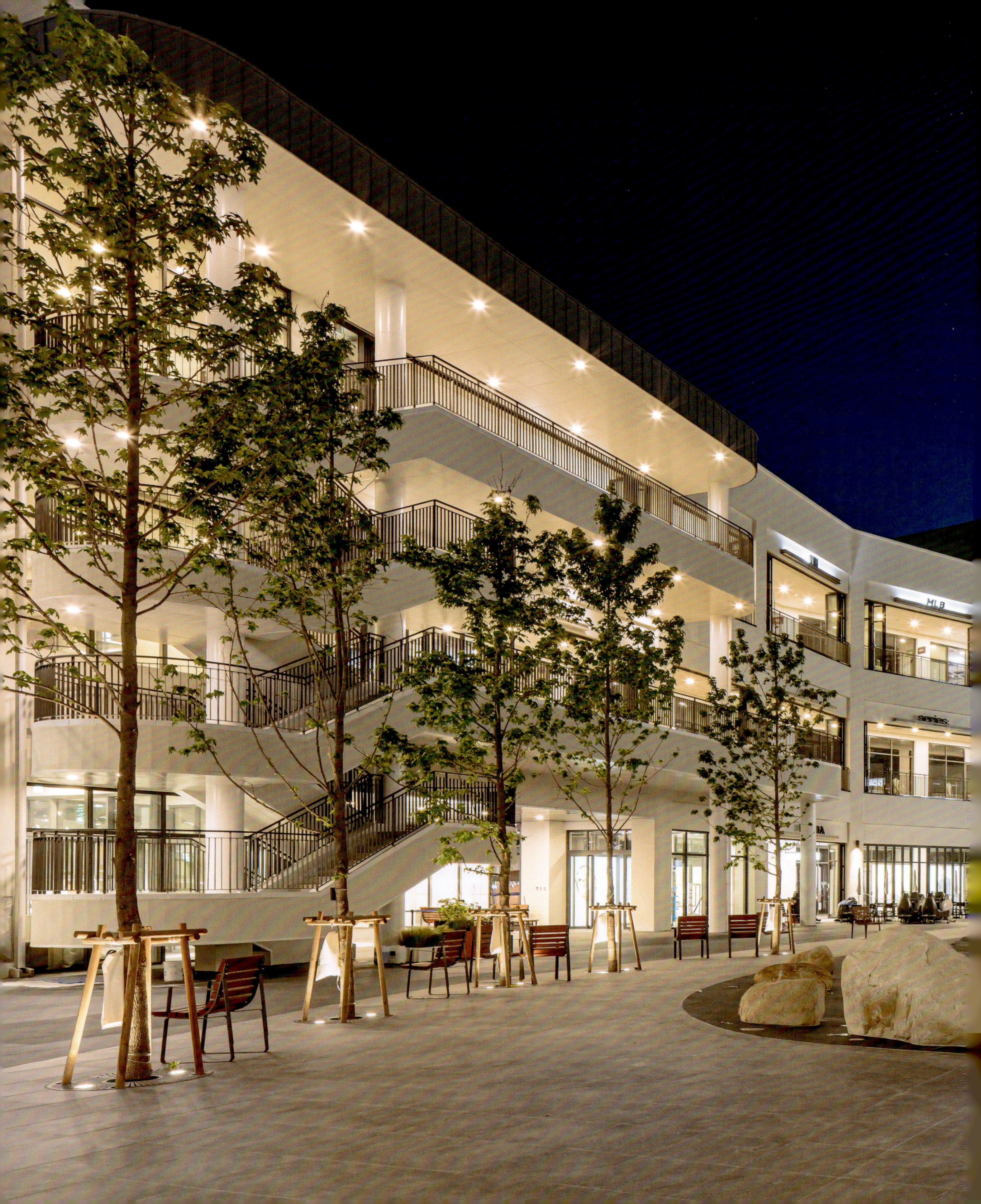
MLB
series:

# DAEJEON HYUNDAI PREMIUM OUTLET

Yuseong-gu, Daejeon, South Korea | 2019

A competition-winning entry from an invitational design competition, the Daejeon Hyundai Premium Outlet is an outdoor shopping center located in Daejeon, Korea. One of the focuses of this design was adapting to the various site and programmatic requirements, like the adjacent small creek park and open ground-level car park areas. Keeping a potential future expansion in mind, we have created a "court" scheme with various open volumes. The main pedestrian entries are accentuated with smaller, more private corridors that take the shoppers up into the commercial zone.

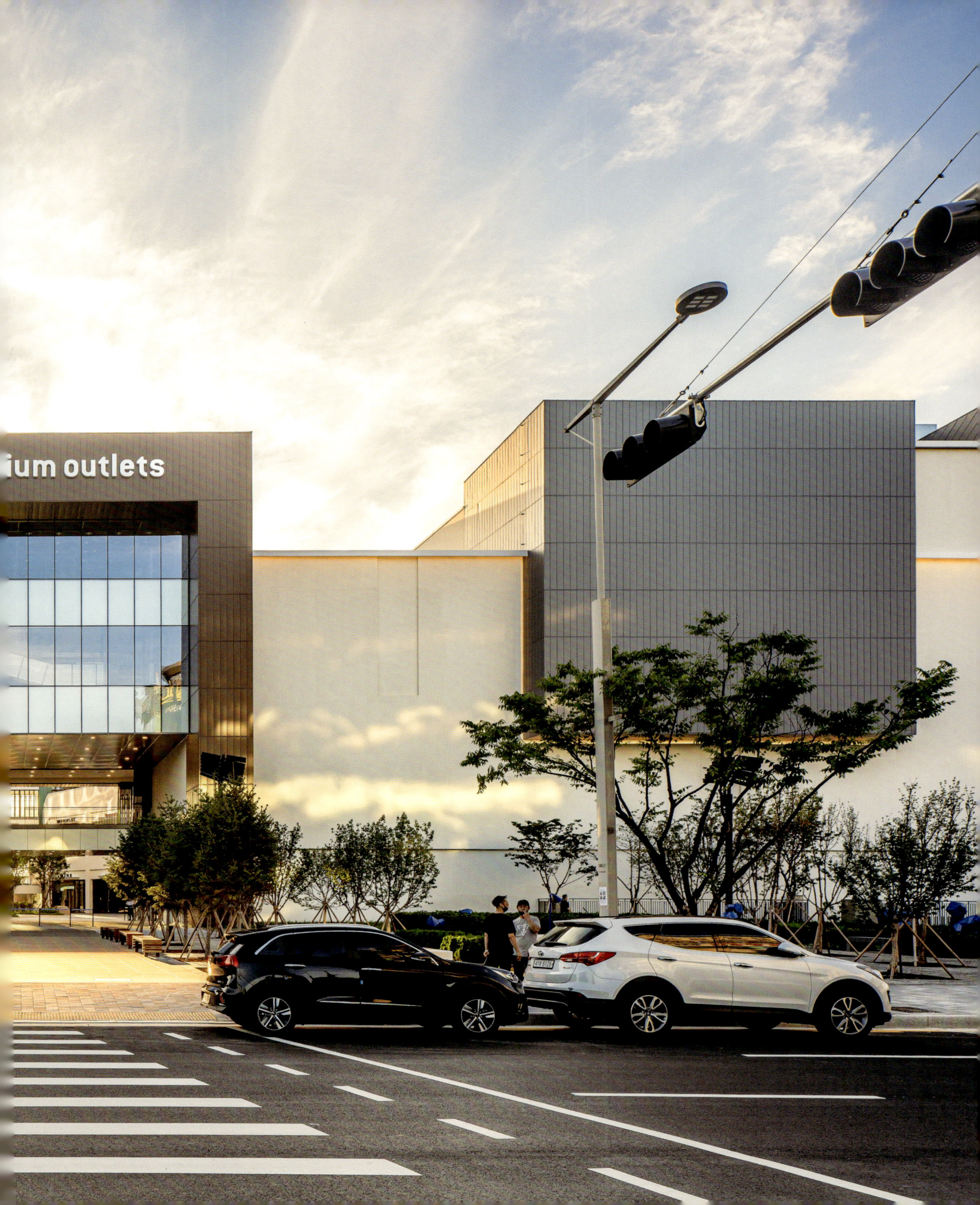
ium outlets

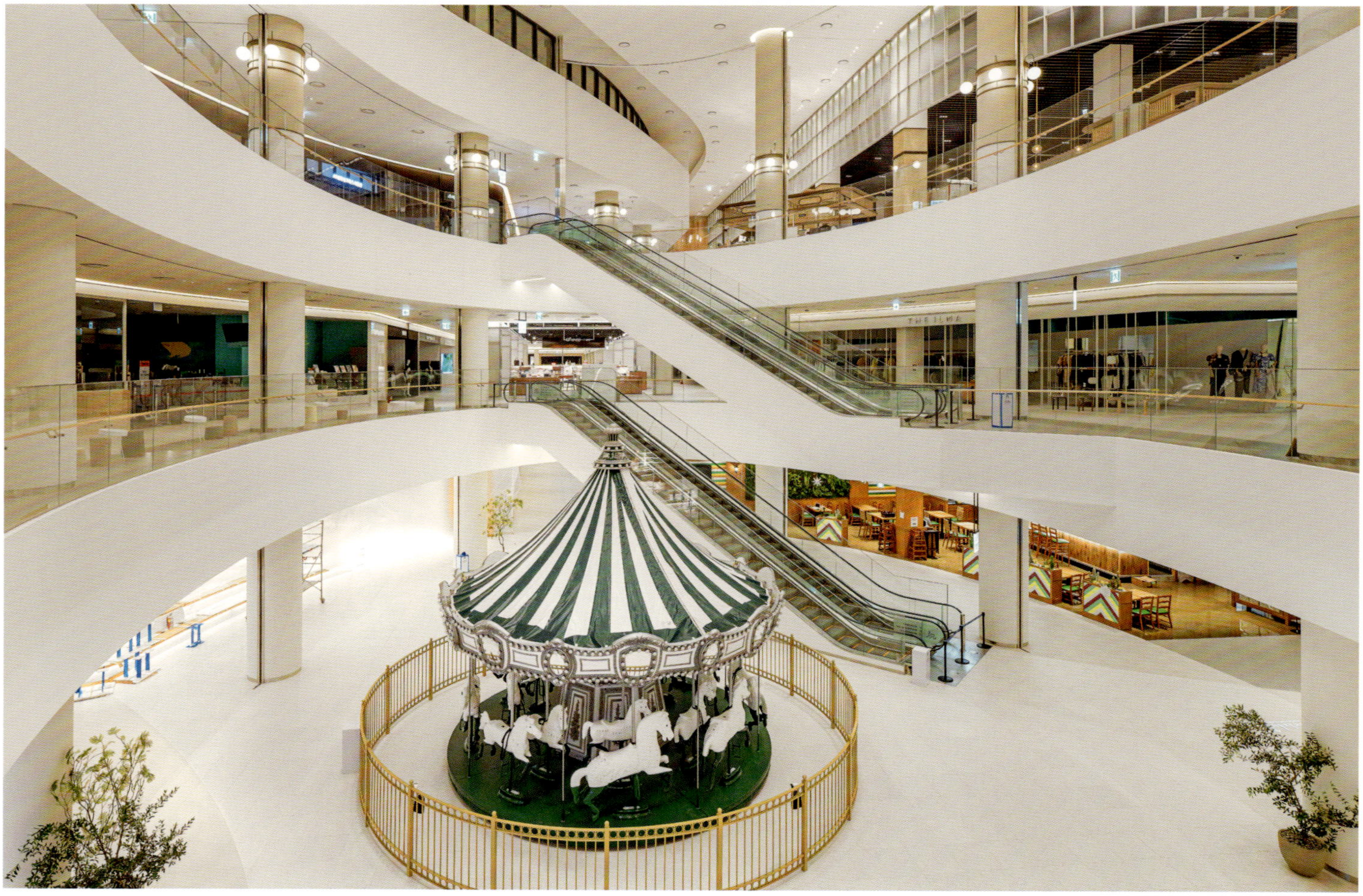

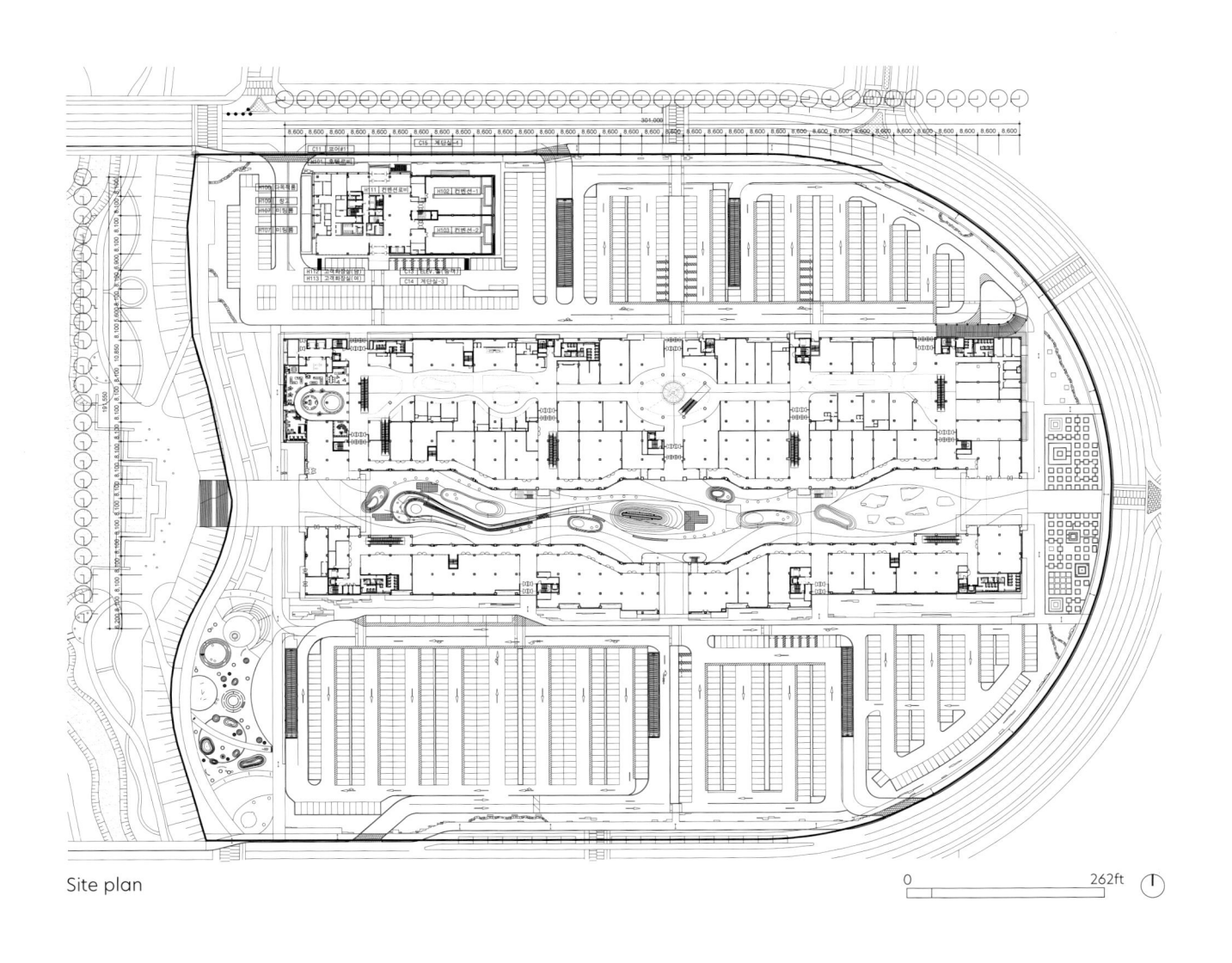

Site plan

DAEJEON HYUNDAI PREMIUM OUTLET

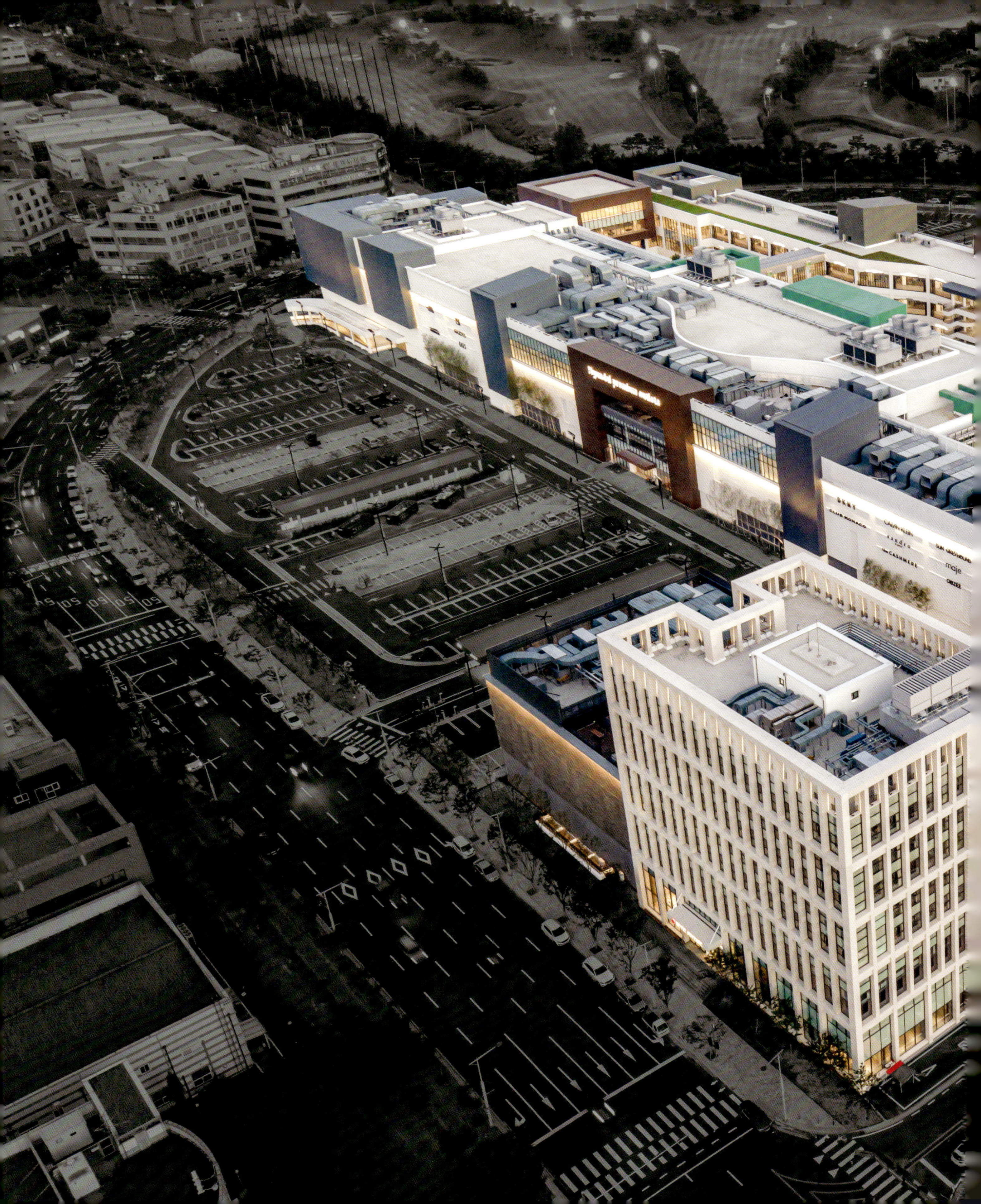
DKNY
CLUB MONACO
CALVIN KLEIN
sandro
CASHMERE
maje

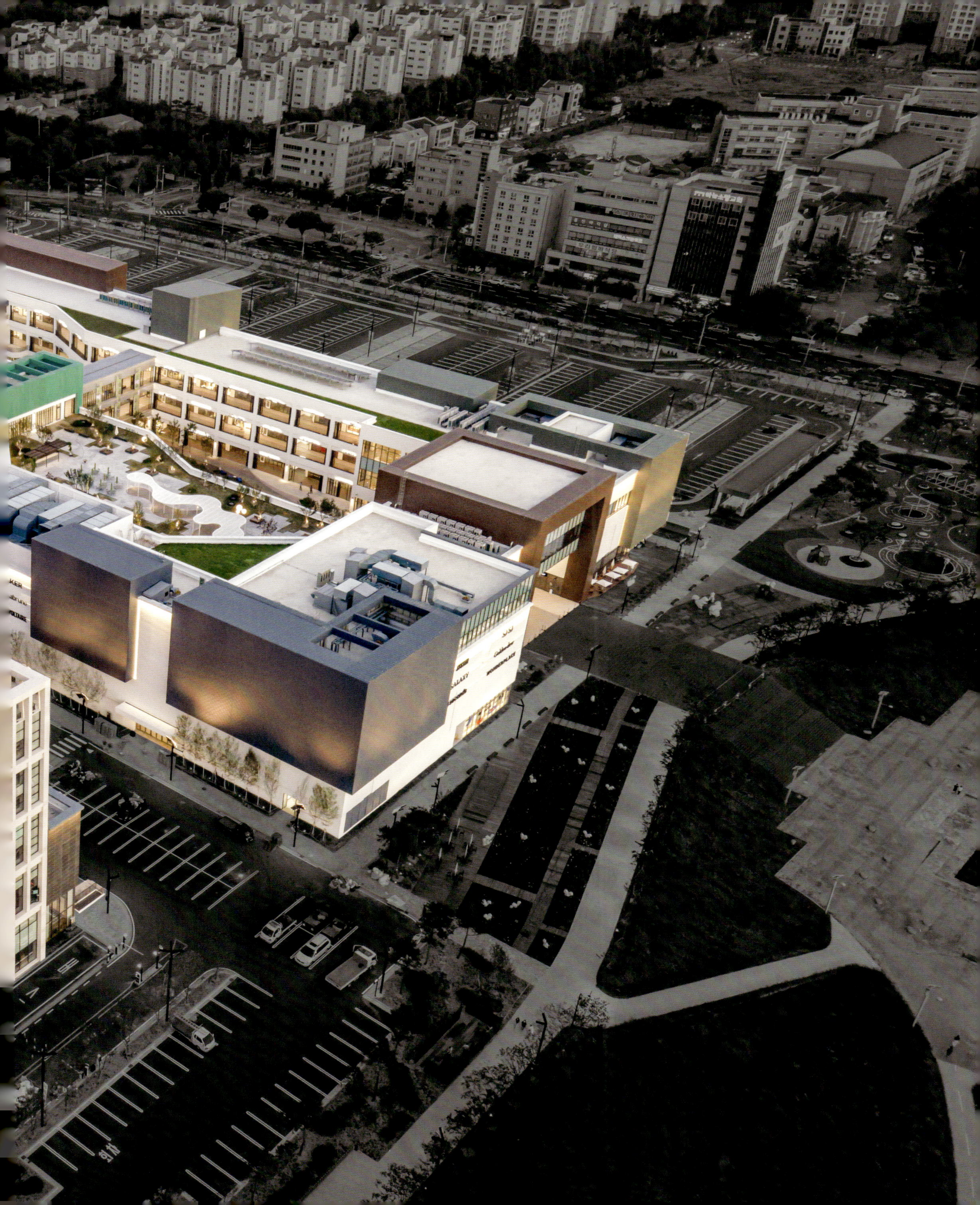

On the upper levels are open balconies that span the edges of each level, bringing fresh air and natural sunlight into the shopping areas. By implementing natural landscaping and sitting areas, the open exterior spaces become courtyards, recreational areas, and parks that can be activated adjacent to the bustling commercial zone. The final product is a new "urban" park where people can rest and be entertained as they shop throughout the day. These urban green cores connect each shopping center and quad throughout the outlet. Additionally, the corridors have adaptable capabilities throughout the year as their folding doors and windows insulate the building during the late fall and winter.

DAEJEON HYUNDAI PREMIUM OUTLET 321

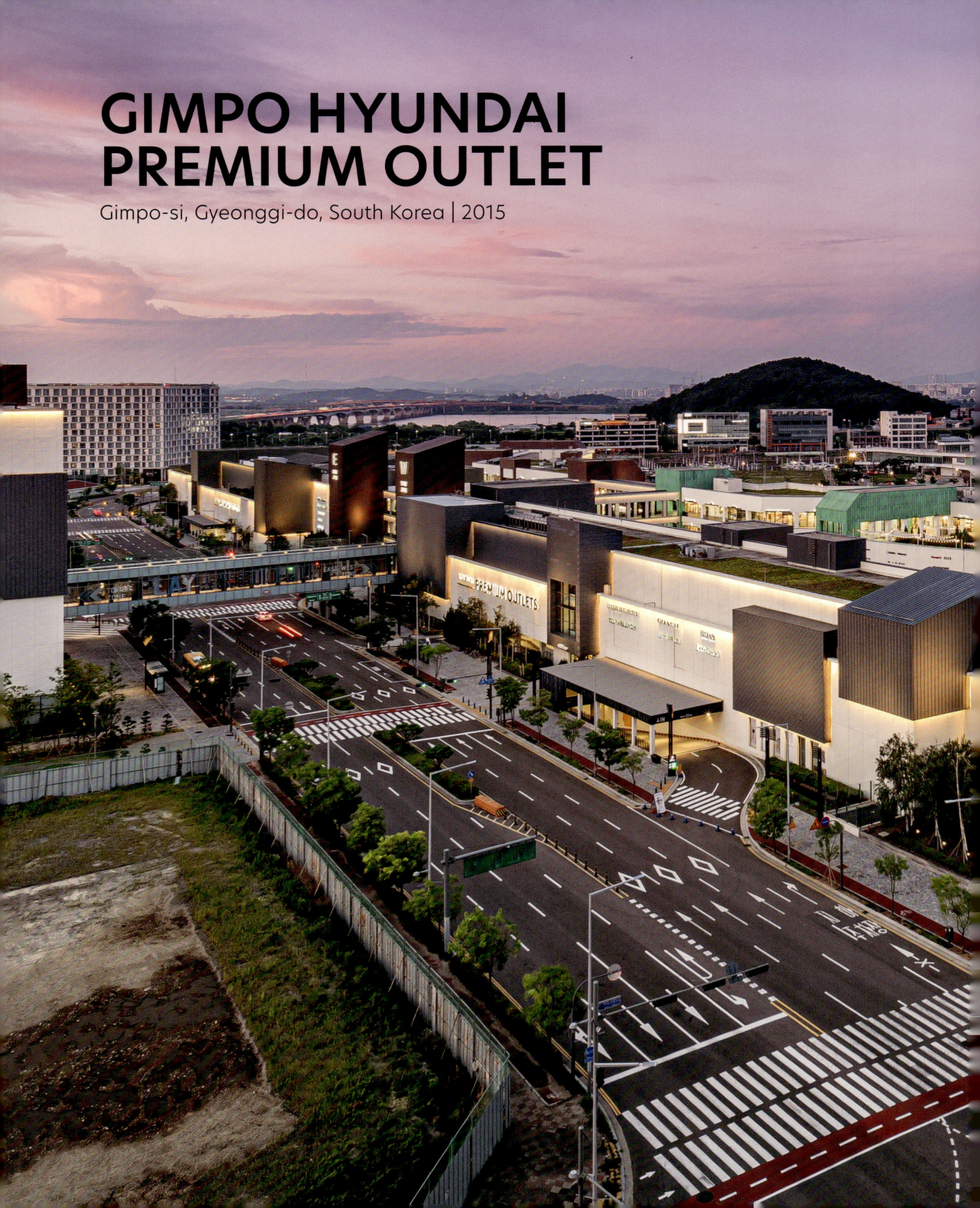

# GIMPO HYUNDAI PREMIUM OUTLET

Gimpo-si, Gyeonggi-do, South Korea | 2015

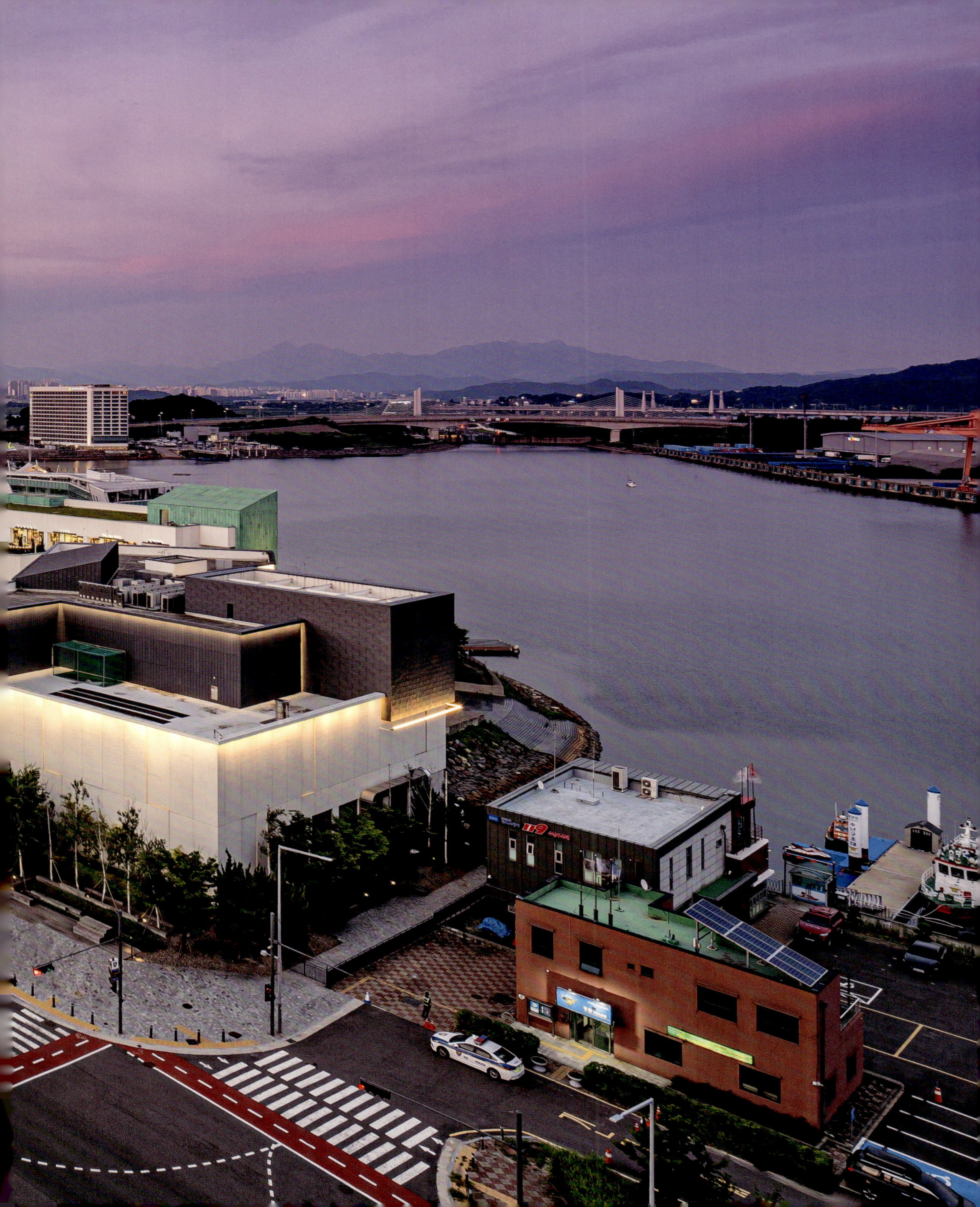

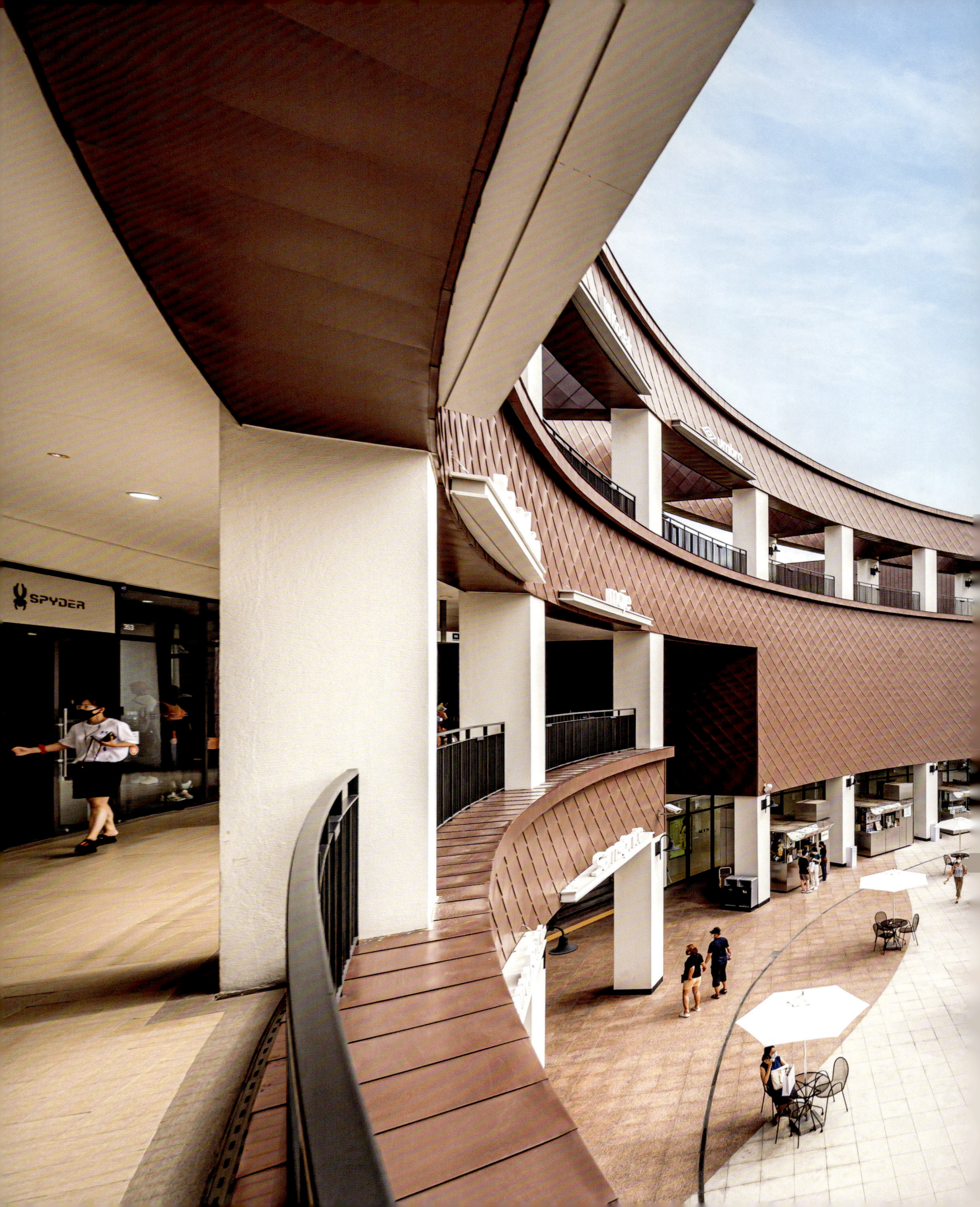
SPYDER

Our design for the Gimpo Hyundai Premium Outlet, a shopping center, is an invitational competition-winning entry. Major requirements of the design competition included successfully connecting five city blocks separated by various roads and a canal, creating a commercial center that operates in internal and external spaces simultaneously; inserting publicly engaging cultural and educational performance event areas; and creating a landmark shopping experience in the newly developing area of Gimpo-si.

We adapted European loggia rooms inside the shopping center to provide moments of transition to the shopping area from the exterior park and canal. We chose this precedent because it best allows the interior shopping space and the exterior recreational space to mix without defining clear barriers. From this, a series of areas, now undefined, leads a sort of "voyage" of shopping through these corridors, leading through four different plazas and ultimately arriving at the canal at the front.

ZWILLING
RAUM
CKCALVIN KLEIN
DKNY
LANVIN
MAGAZZINI
Salvatore Ferragamo
staub

# HEYRI "THE STEP" PLAZA

Paju-si, Gyeonggi-do, South Korea | 2003

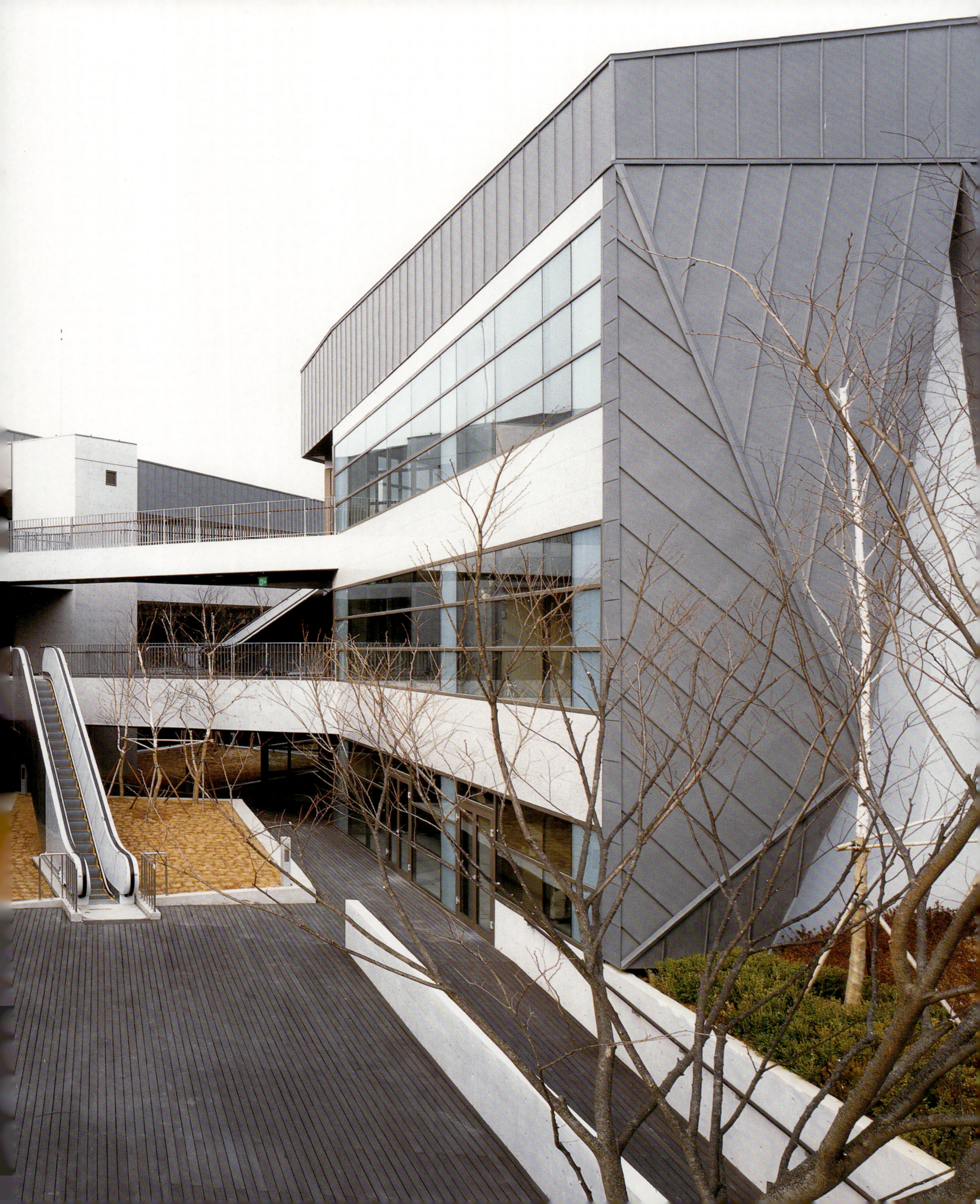

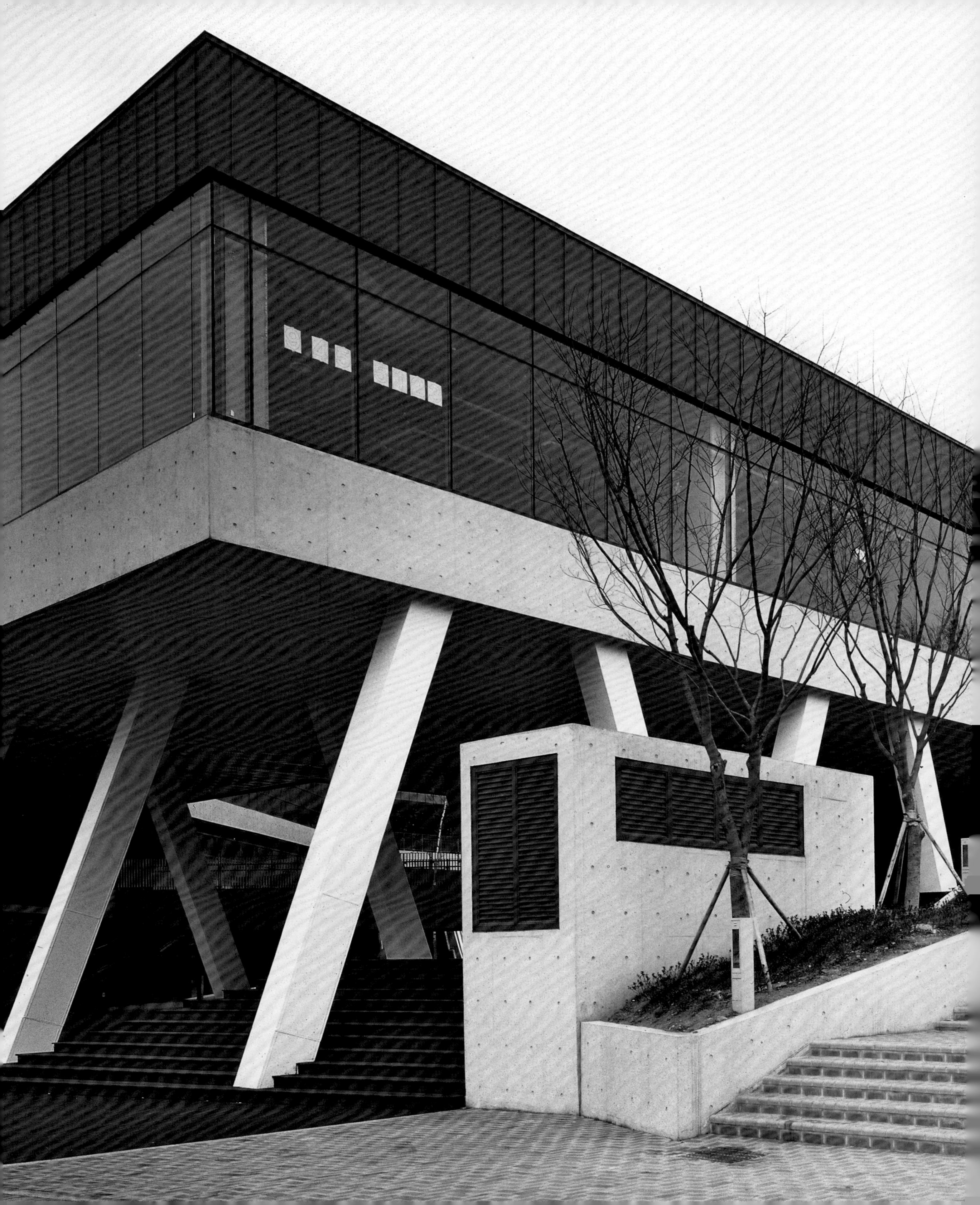

Heyri "The Step" Plaza is a mixed-use project that is part of the Heyri Art Valley Development Plan, a plan that aims to give Korea's largest art community a larger spatial footprint in which to thrive. Five blocks surround the central plaza, providing easy access to a variety of academic facilities, like libraries, classrooms, dormitories, a museum, galleries, a multipurpose hall, and a shopping mall.

The project contains two housing residences within the development: the first, consisting of thirty-eight dorm rooms and eighteen art studios, while the second contains twenty-four art studios and eight luxury-style apartments. Providing designers and scholars a place to live, work, and socialize encourages interactions and collaborations of professionals across disciplines. The "Big Steps" themselves lead to the central plaza, functioning as stages for various events and activities. The organization, circulation and materials used in this project all reflect the influences of art, culture, and people, and the present, in this unique semi-urban community.

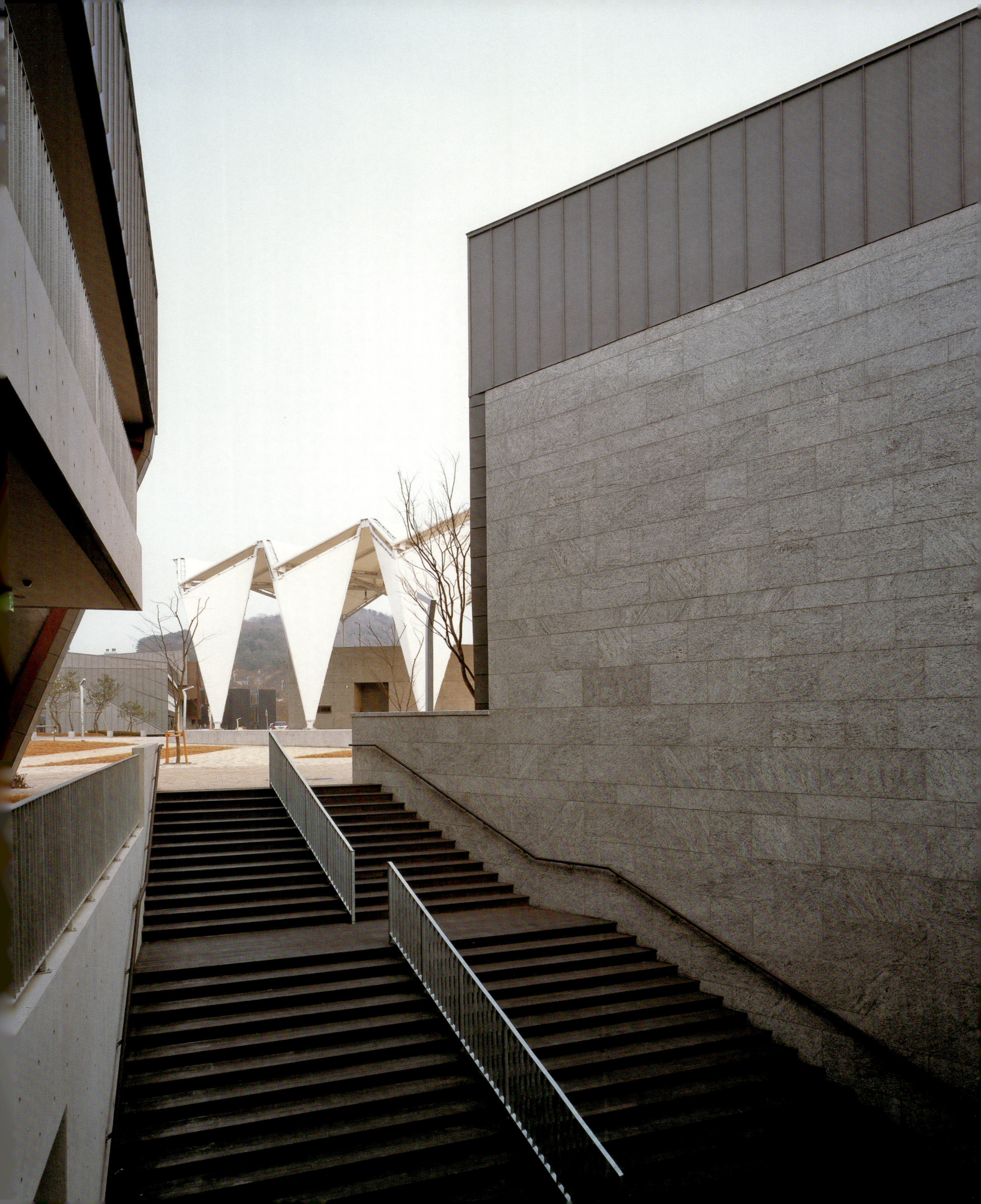

Taesun Hong, *After the War* (1980), pencil

**Scale** and **proportion** express the physical or auditory magnitude of a design. Scale is chosen to generate a contrast or reference between the volume of forms. Proportion is the dimensional relation of one with the other. It is also the relation of part with the whole. Proportion in music is distance between notes or intervals. Also, it is the relation between intensities of various sound frequencies. Proportion in architecture is meant to be the relationship between the elements together.

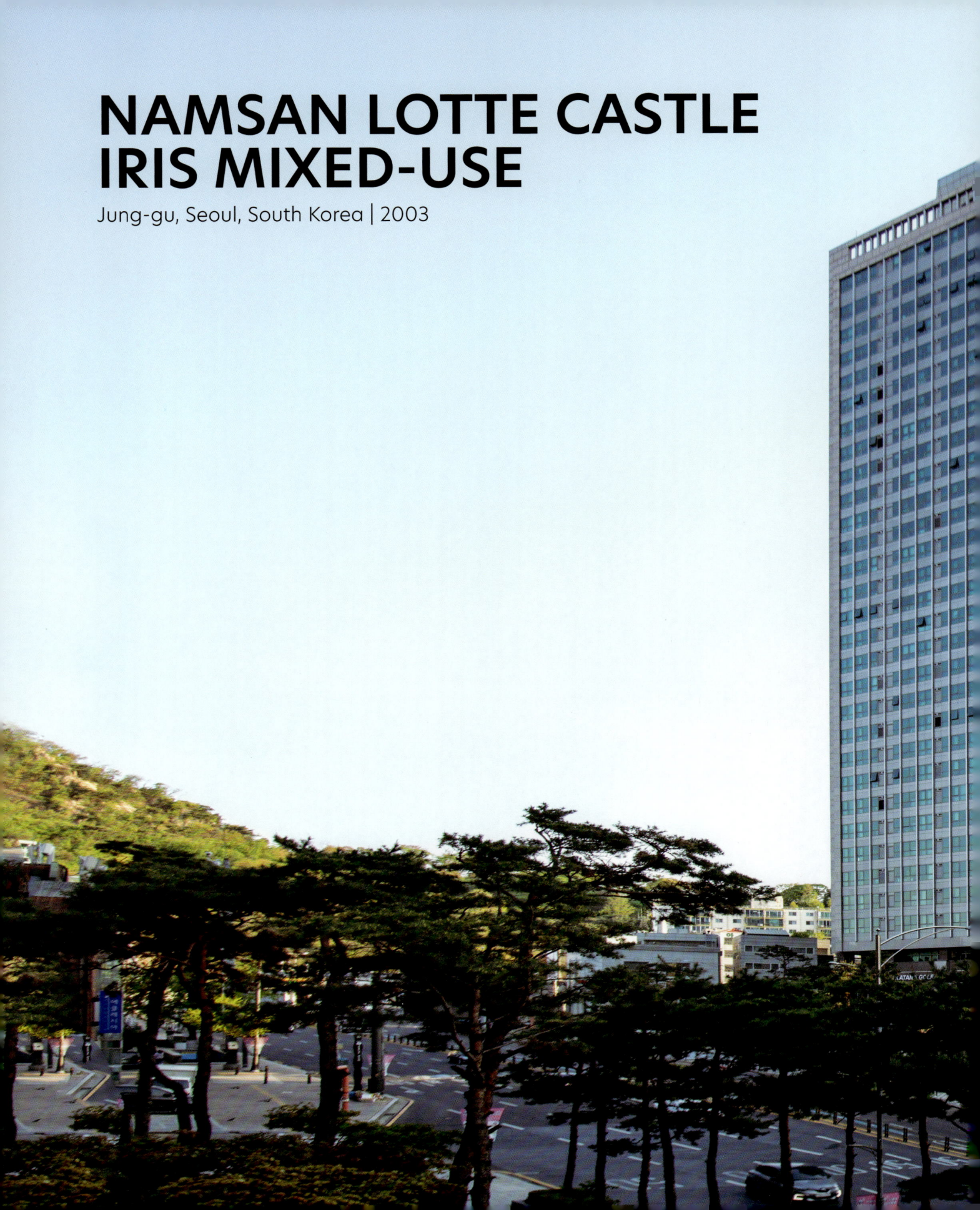

# NAMSAN LOTTE CASTLE IRIS MIXED-USE

Jung-gu, Seoul, South Korea | 2003

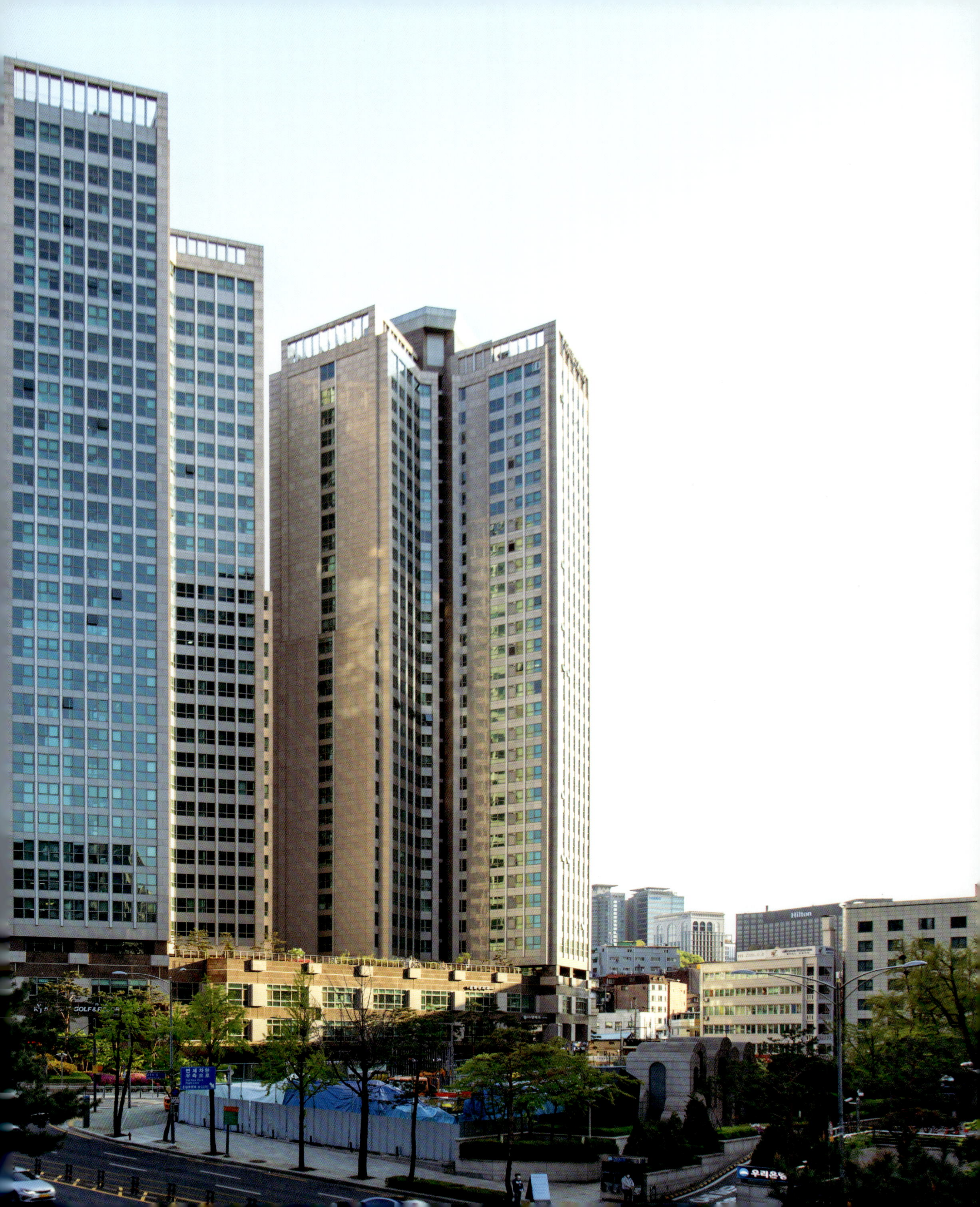
Hilton
우리은행

The Namsan Lotte Castle Iris mixed-use project consists of two thirty-two-story towers, a base platform of officetel and retail that connects the two towers and seven floors of basement levels of parking and residential amenities. This complex is in the central business district of Seoul, Korea. Our initial design approach was to maximize the breathtaking views of the adjacent Namsan Mountains while providing an appropriate number of apartments within the rules of Seoul's parking requirements.

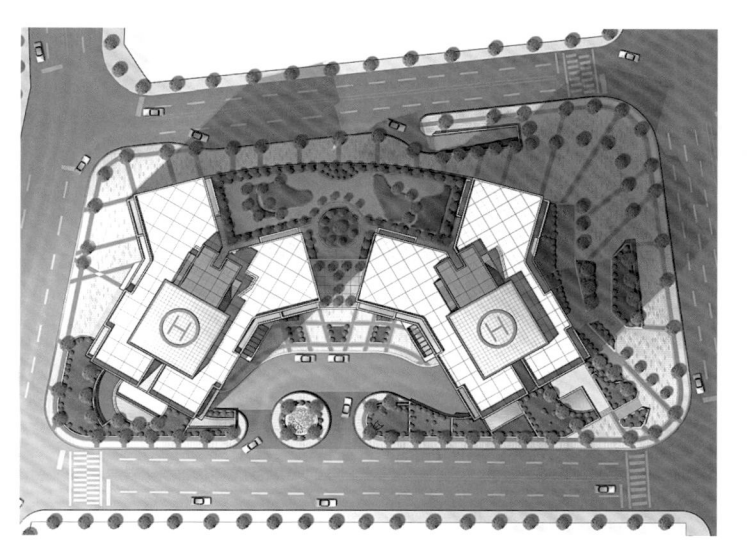

We arrived at numerous design alternatives for each tower to figure out the right footprint size. After a series of progress meetings with marketing experts and the owner, we chose two T-shaped tower schemes over a linear tower scheme. On this prominent avenue that connects the Namsan 3rd Tunnel and central business district of Seoul's old city, the proportion and the materiality of the twin towers were a key issue for this design exercise.

As per the strict building code restrictions and a programmatic requirement—typical of residential buildings of this type in Korea—all 386 units required southern exposure. The final tower's typical floor comprises four apartment units of varying sizes and views; the shape ensures that each unit receives a maximum amount of southern daylight. On the issue of construction costs, we considered the affordability of cladding materials, such as aluminum sheet metal; we ended up finding a low-cost granite stone that was within the budget. We accentuated the verticality of the building by framing the tower with a wider protruding stone and filling the body with narrower aluminum mullions.

# SK NAMSAN LEADERS' VIEW MIXED-USE

Jung-gu, Seoul, South Korea | 2005

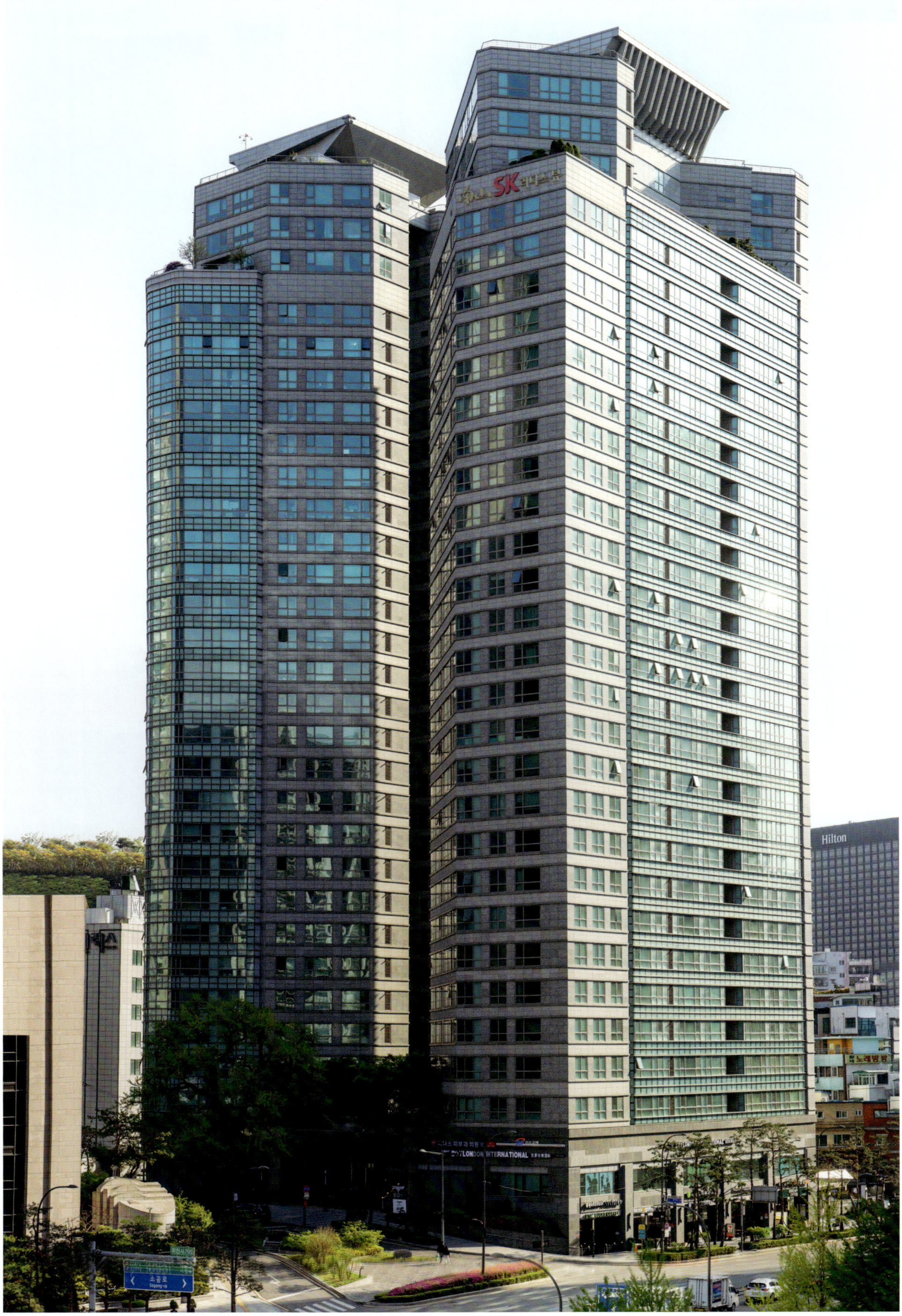
SK
LONDON INTERNATIONAL
Hilton

The aim of this residential/office/retail mixed-use complex was to create a balanced living and working community. To comply with the stringent set-back and building height requirements and to satisfy the owner's maximum area requirements, we chose an X-shaped massing, separated into two towers, and placed a core in the middle. This approach resulted in all four sides obtaining either views across the southern Namsan mountain or the northern city views.

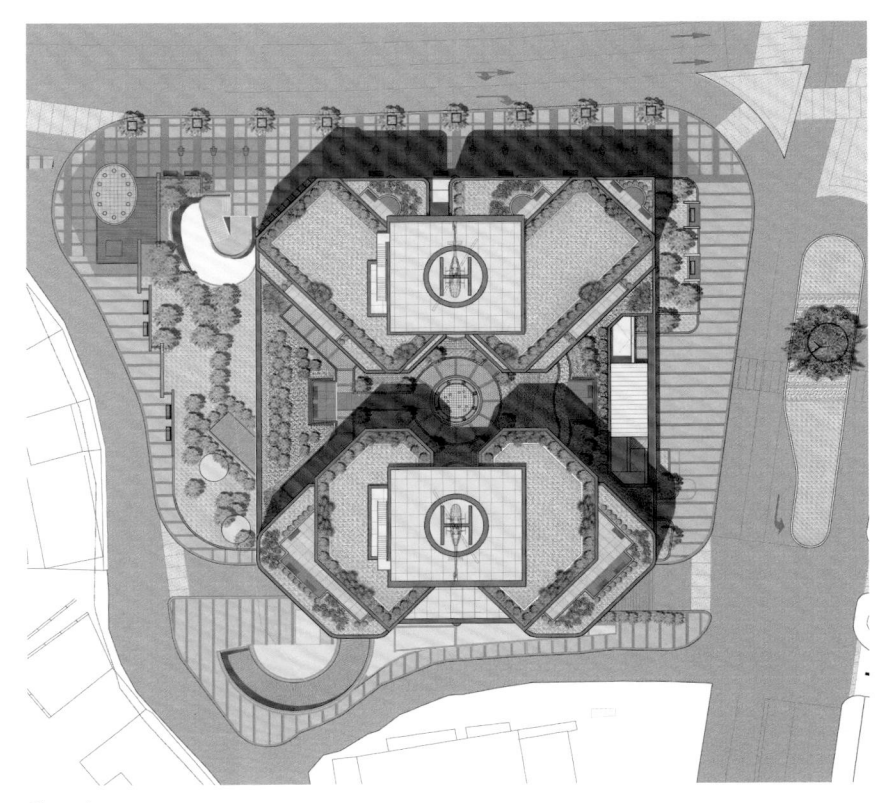

Site plan

The typical floor of the residential tower consists of five units—two larger units on the southern façade (with mountain views) and three smaller units (with city views). The lower retail platform is extended to the first basement level and this building is connected directly to the Seoul Subway line 4. The B1 retail level has a direct connecting walkway to the Shinsege Department store that is located across Hoihyun Avenue. Directly above the podium retail zone, we established a pocket park for use by the residents.

The design challenge was to organize the complex as a unified design but to express its different uses. A range of differently textured but same-color stones were used to unify the complex and an aluminum cladding was used to accentuate the roof and canopy design. Numerous shape studies were done to make sure that the scale of the towers did not overbear the adjacent Wooribank Headquarters building or the building we designed for the Namsan Lotte Iris mixed-use project nearby.

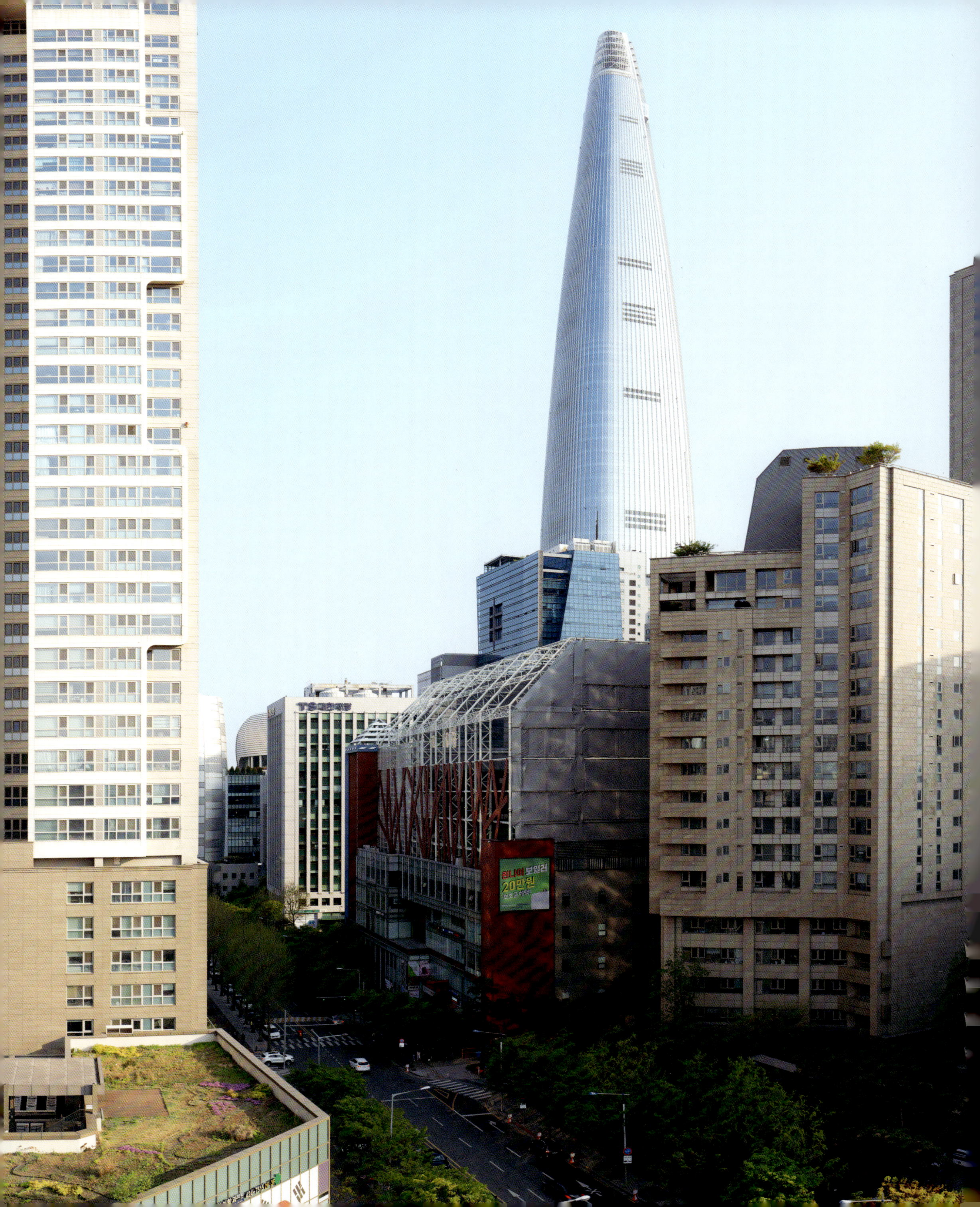

# JAMSIL POSCO THE STARPARK RESIDENCE

Songpa-gu, Seoul, South Korea | 2004

The site of the Posco Starpark residence is in a densely urban area of Seoul's Jamsil district. The aim of this mixed-use complex was to create a balanced living and working community. Because the site fell in a relatively restrictive building zone, we opted to design multiple towers connected by an open urban courtyard space instead of one solid mass. The height of each tower was staggered, increasing the quantity and quality of city views from each unit. Additionally, this allowed significantly more natural light to enter the lower levels and courtyard spaces.

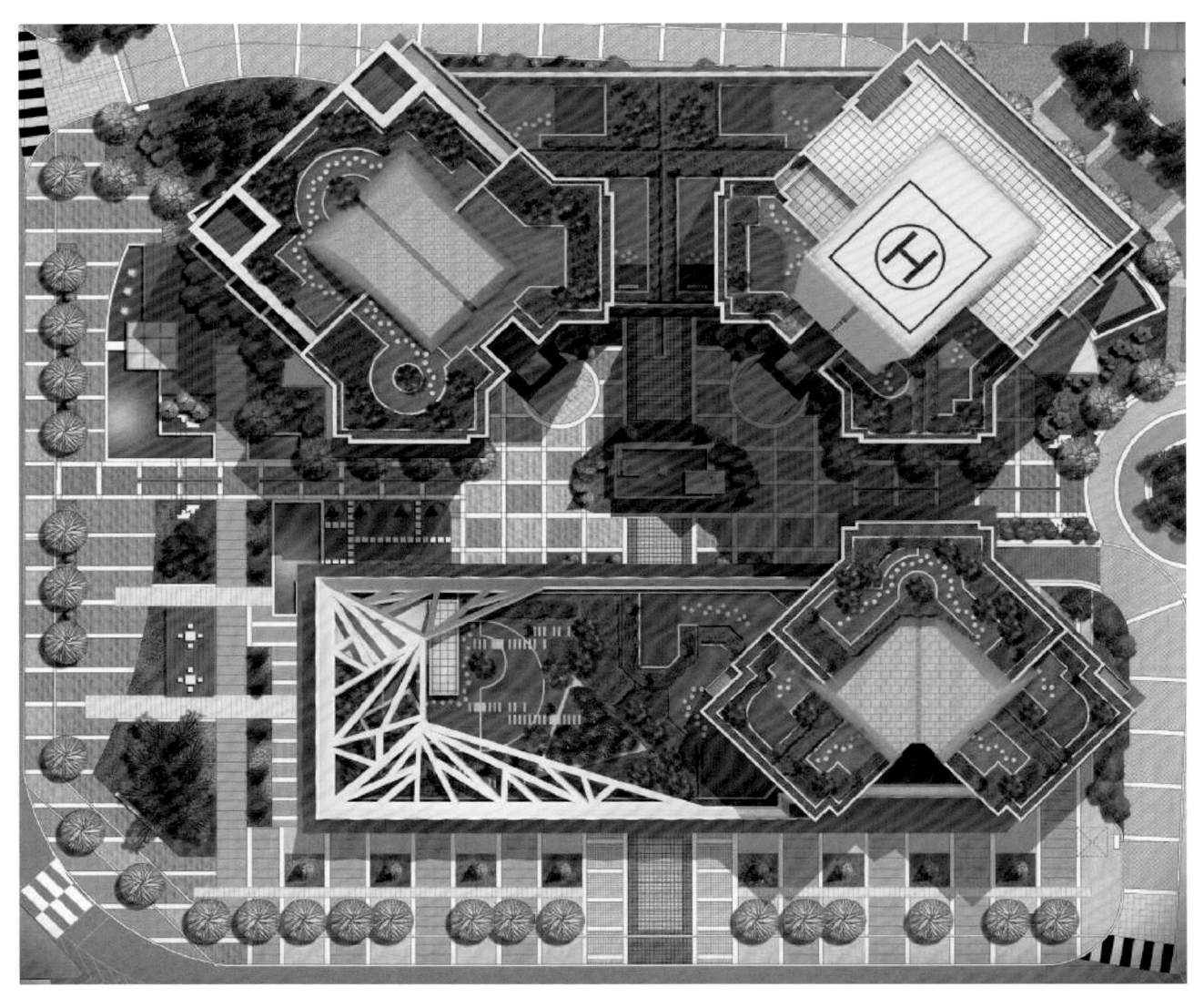

Site plan

By using contrasting materiality in specific areas of the complex, we can indicate at what point the courtyard spaces are unified with the buildings' interior spaces and at what point they branch off into their own entities. We used stone for the façades of the lower levels and courtyard floor and then used metal cladding for the exterior of the higher tower sections. The fifth façade of each tower, all urban green space, is now elevated to a level where it is functionally isolated from other spaces, increasing the sense of overall autonomy and tranquility to the design.

# YOIDO RICHENSIA MIXED-USE RESIDENCE

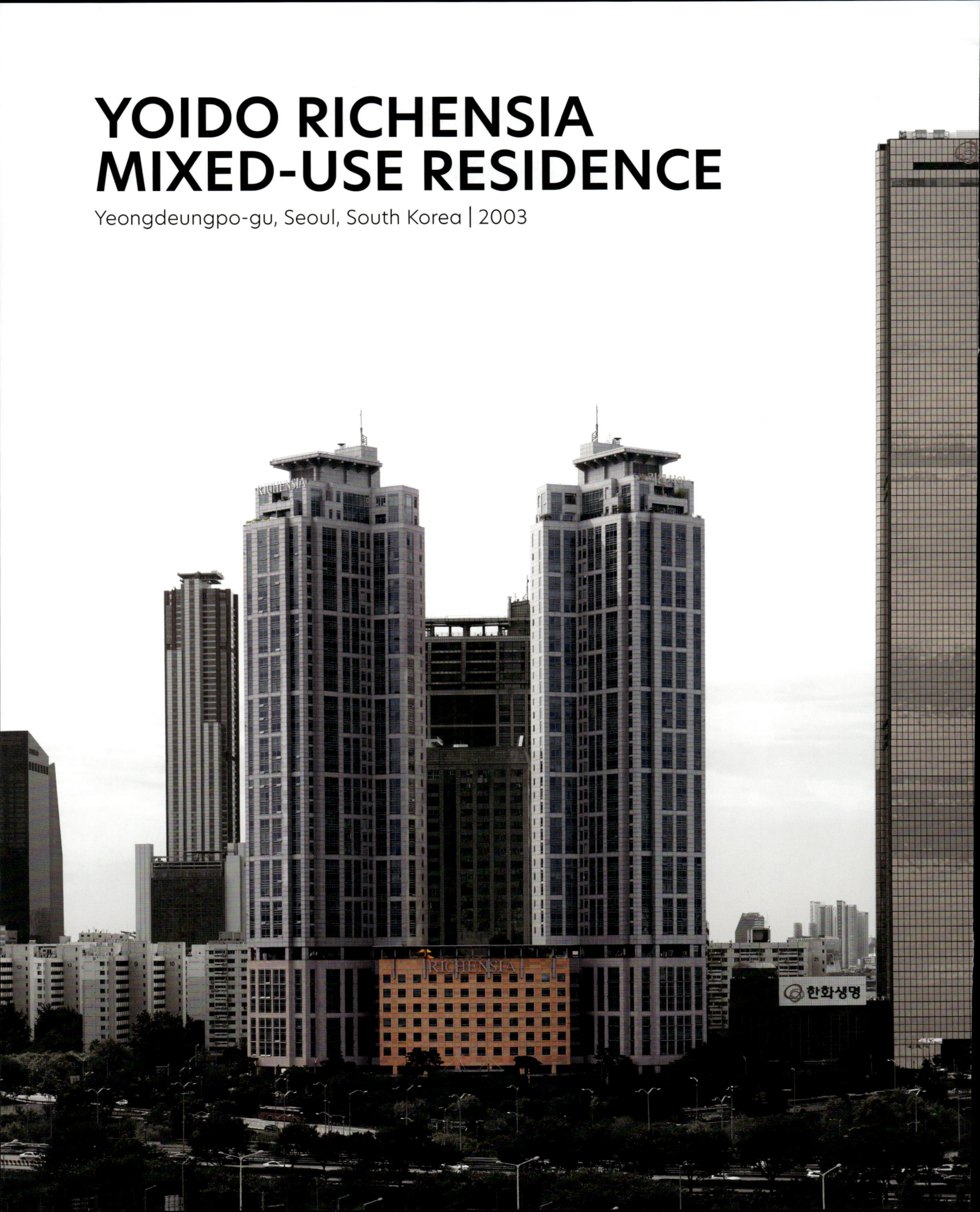

Yeongdeungpo-gu, Seoul, South Korea | 2003

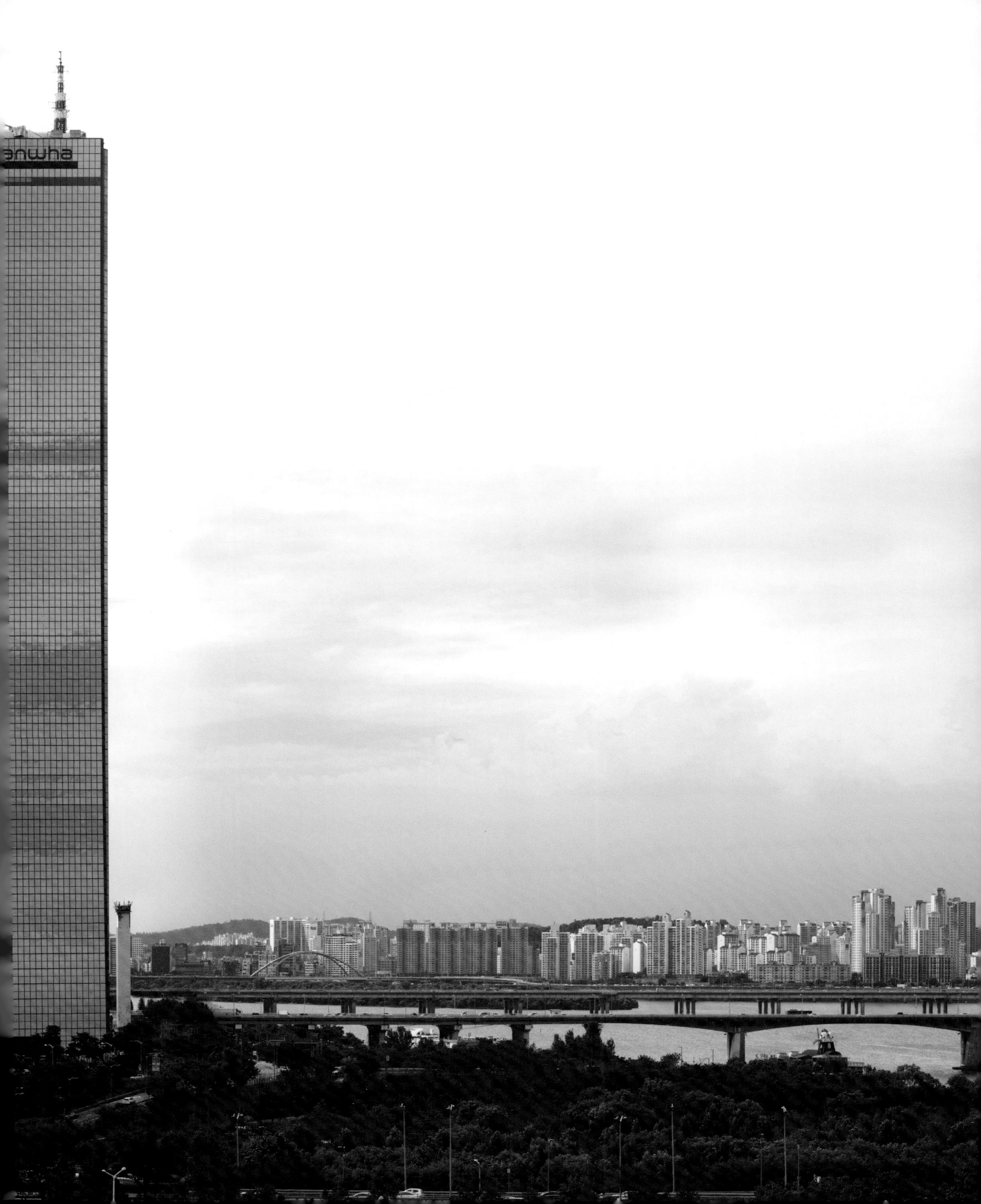

Yoido Richensia is a forty-story mixed-use officetel located in downtown Seoul along the scenic Han River and Olympic Highway. The project is situated next to the '63 Building, one of the oldest high-rise buildings in Korea in the heart of a historic downtown site. The challenge was to design a building with high visibility that would stand out among the other high-rises around it—yet would also not disrupt the visibility of the culturally significant '63 Building.

YOIDO RICHENSIA MIXED-USE RESIDENCE

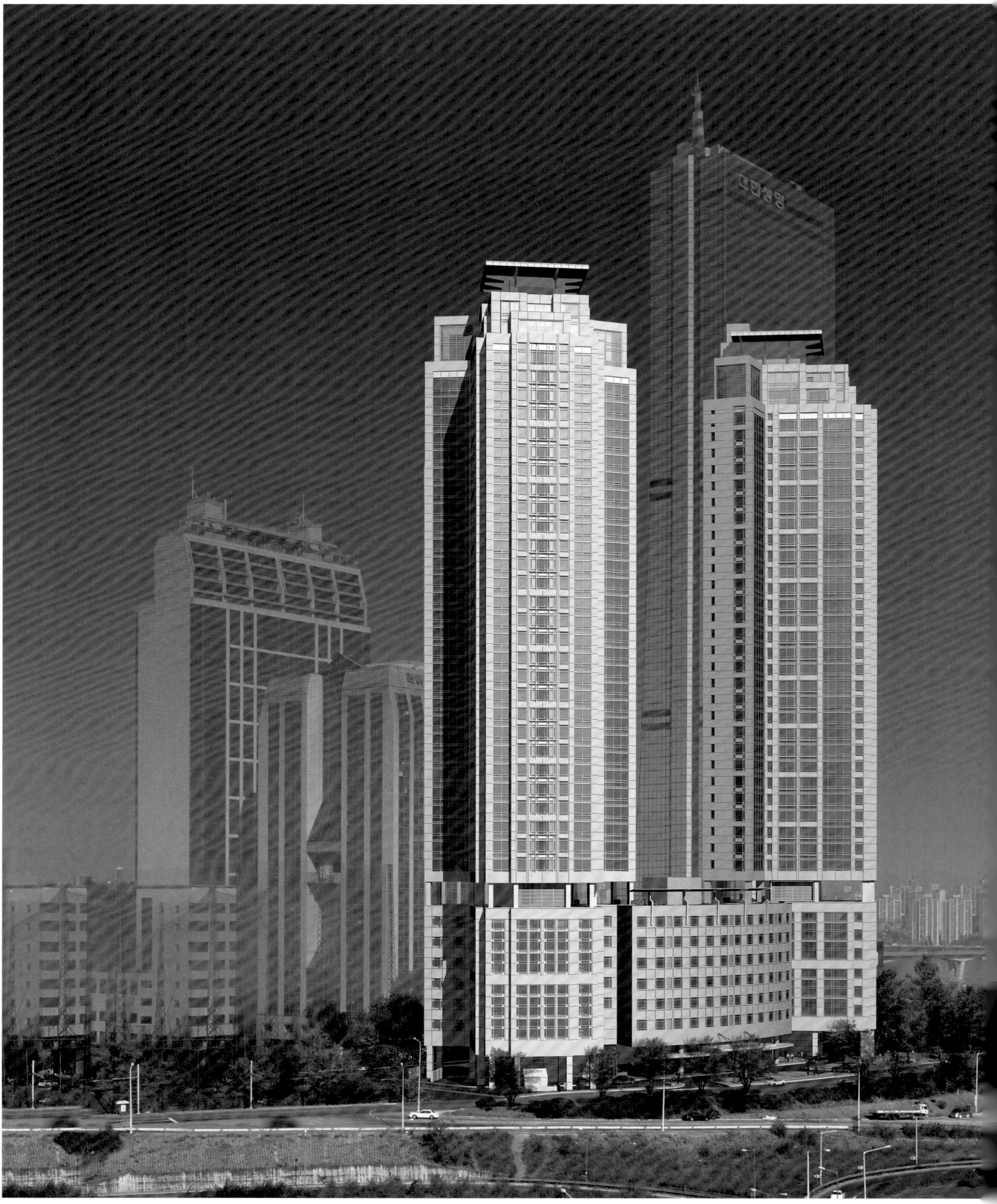

The mixed-use facility includes 235 upscale luxury apartments and 252 office suites. The form of the building was developed by finding ways to create visibility through the building while simultaneously maximizing views for residents. So, two thirty-two-story towers were designed to emerge out of the base office section, creating a viewing path and channel of light for neighboring buildings. The orientation of the two towers was positioned to maximize their exposure to southern natural light while helping provide visual privacy for the residential units. The residential space is divided into individually owned luxury housing units within the towers, each comprising approximately 2,000 square feet (21,528 square meters).

The lower section consists of six floors of office suites, which were primarily designed for business use and lodging purposes. The structure also includes a fitness facility, retail shops, a rooftop community area, and an underground parking lot.

Site plan

# GOHEUNG STELLA RESORT
Goheung-gun, Jeollanam-do, South Korea | 2018

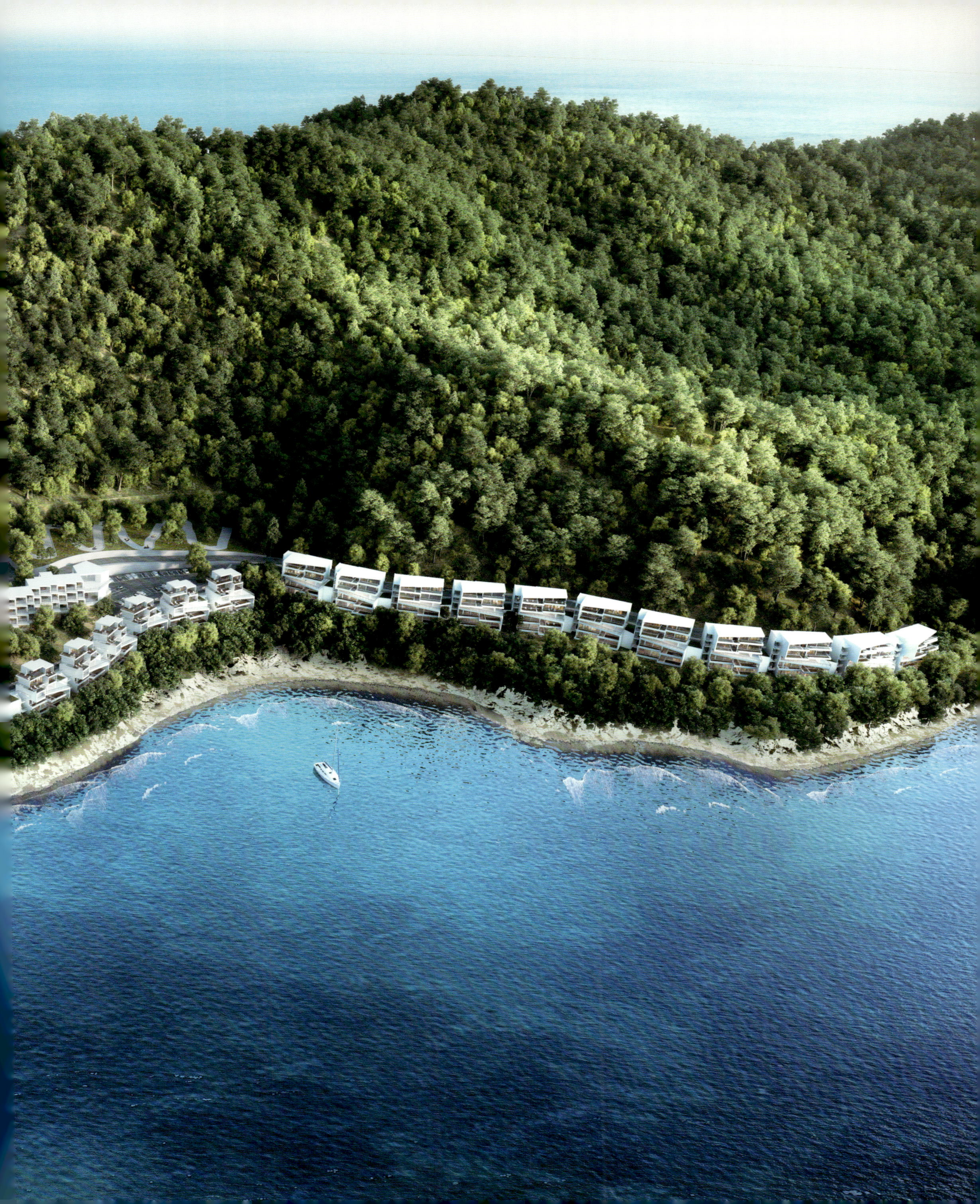

The site of Stella Resort is located on Oinaro Island, near Korea's Naro Space Station. The design is composed of private villas (151 units) and a large luxury hotel (about 100 units), with added activities like snorkeling, culinary classes, rooftop observatory, and a convention center. Because of its unique topography and position on the curving shoreline, the resort's site has the capacity to create landings with incredible views.

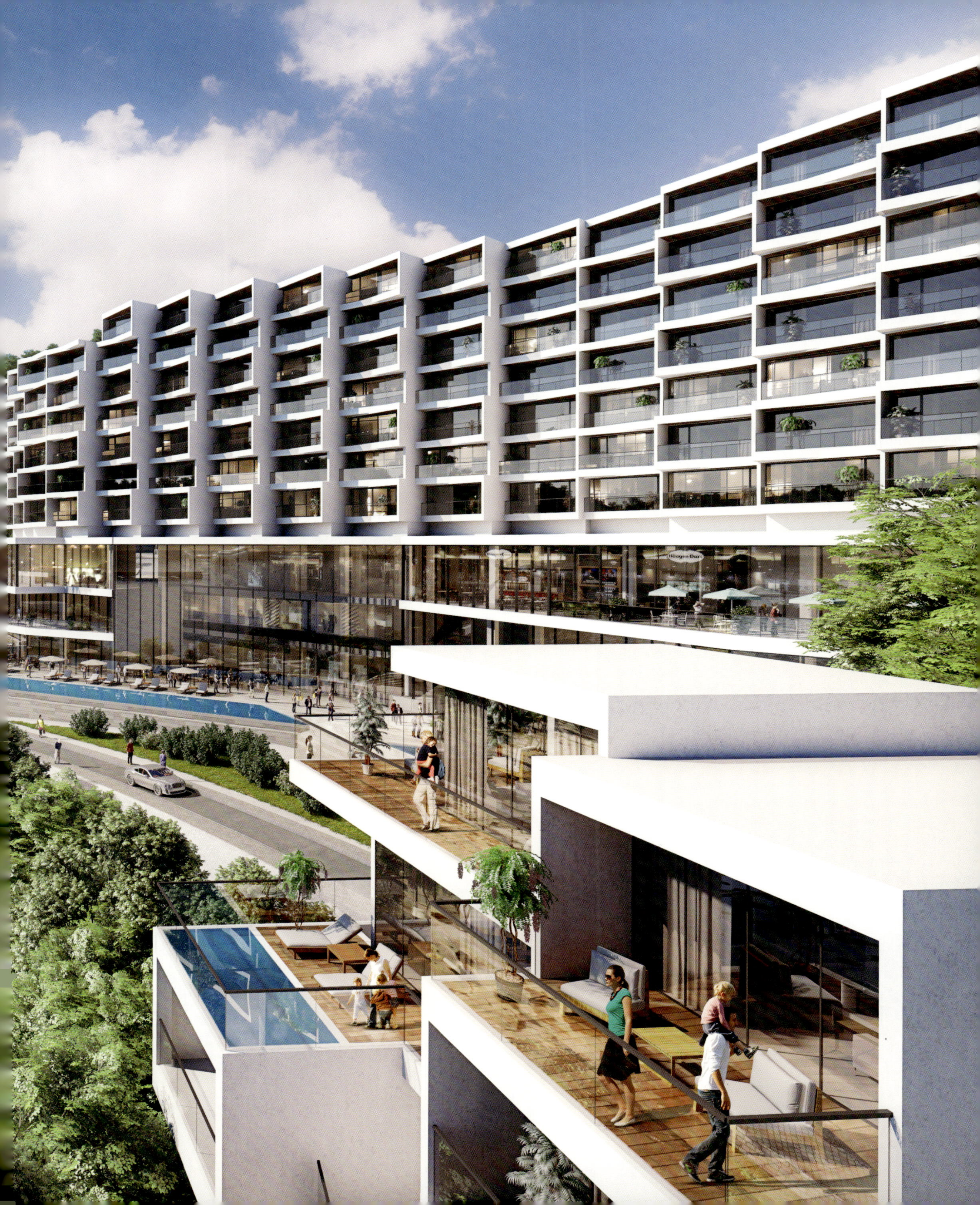

Village

Village

Hotel

Hotel

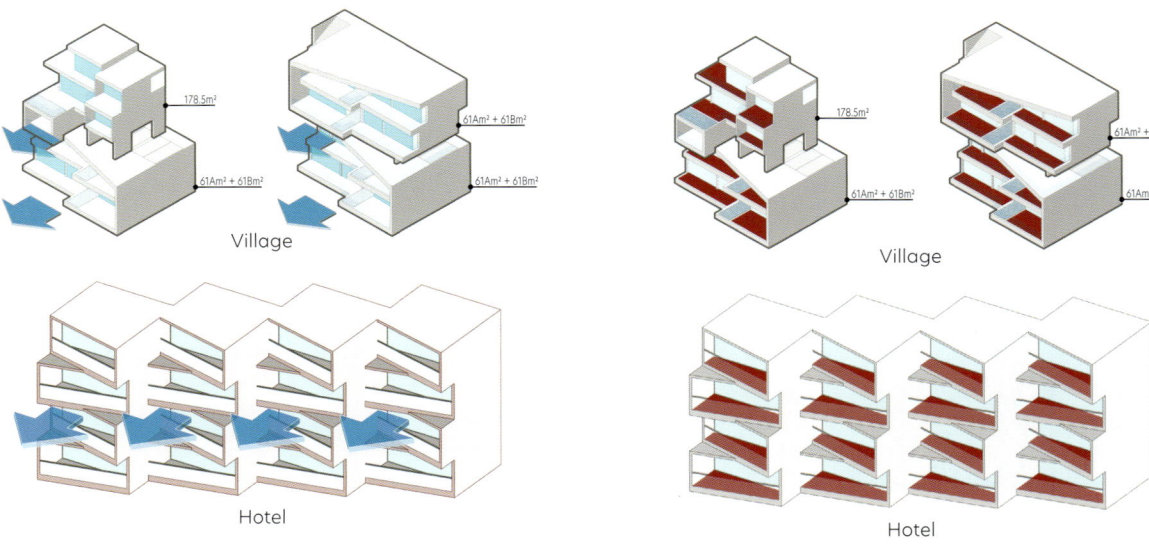

Ocean views from every room

Terraces with amazing ocean views

**358**   SCALE AND PROPORTION

GOHEUNG STELLA RESORT

Every unit has access to a private terrace and infinity pool, providing an environment where the visitor can have a private, intimate experience with nature. This experience is carried out on the other side of the site, as well, in the resort's luxury cabins. Separate from the more densely arranged villas and hotel rooms, these units are more immersed in nature. While they are within walking distance of the food court and recreational facilities, their isolation in the natural environment gives an authentic connection to the outdoors.

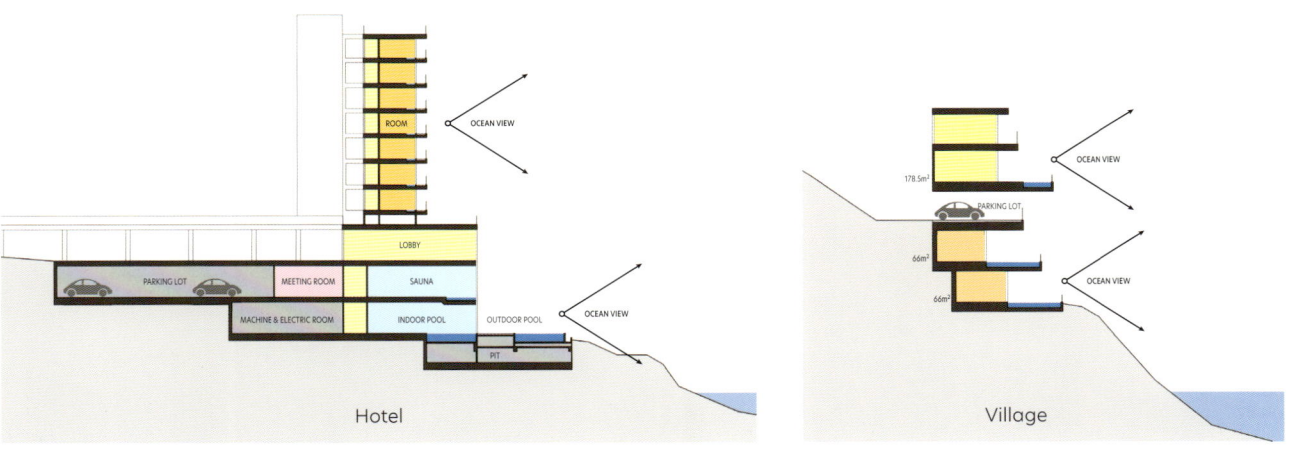

Views from the all-seasons infinity pools

GOHEUNG STELLA RESORT

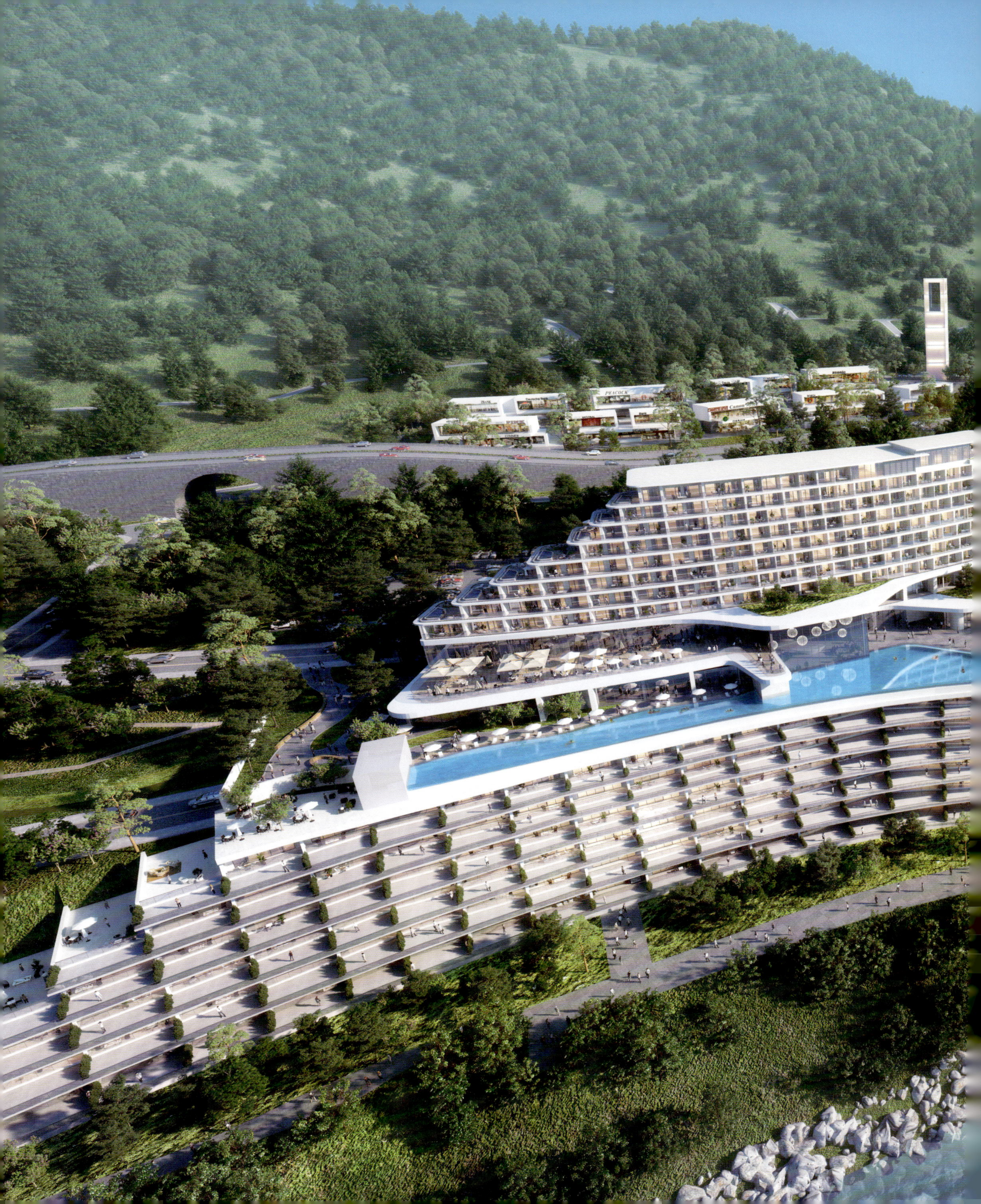

# YEOSU THE OCEAN RESORT

Yeosu-si, Jeollanam-do, South Korea | 2019

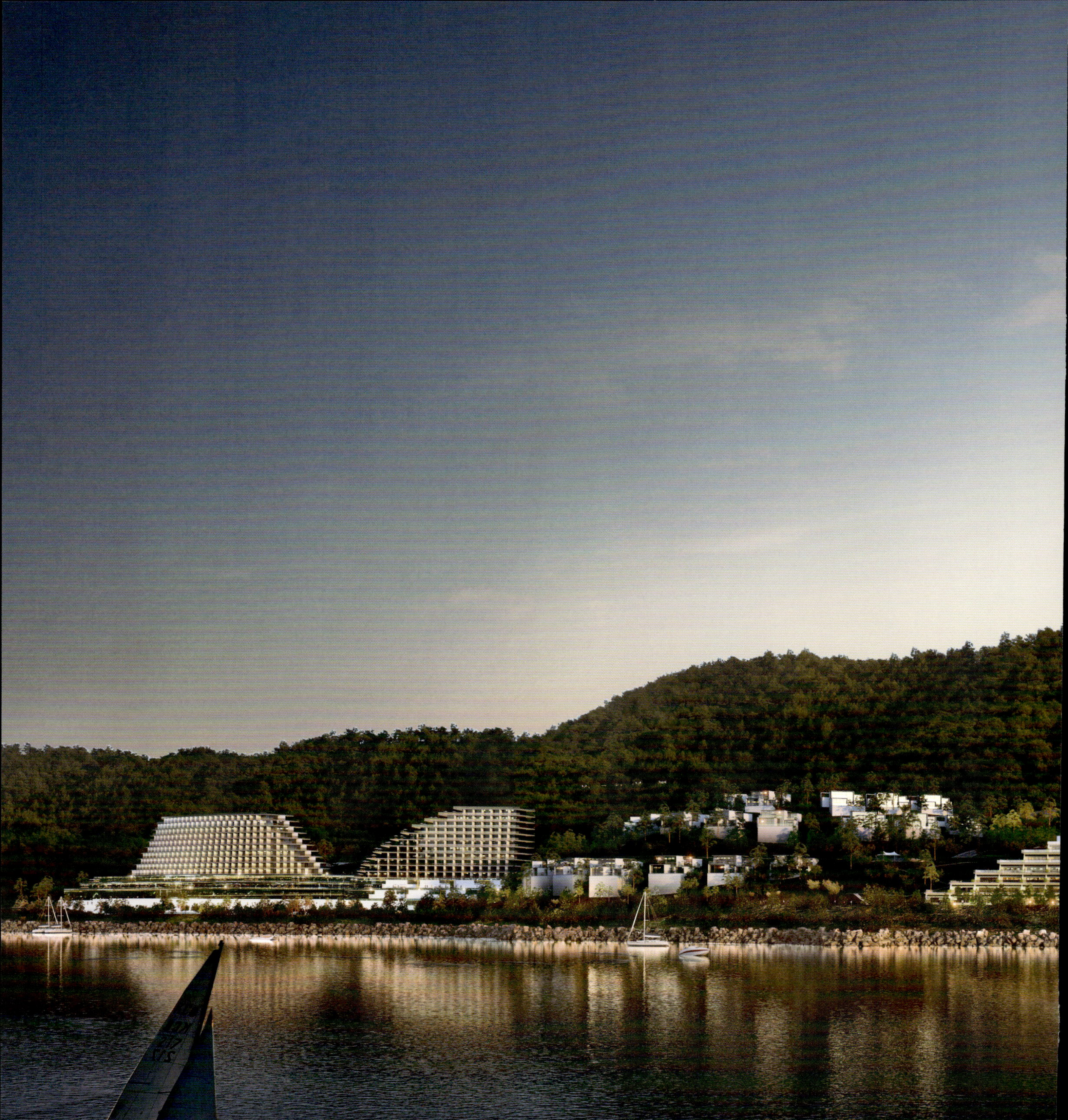

This ocean beach resort is a mixed-use complex located along the coast of Yeosu-si, South Korea. The complex is made up of 274 units, a large, 400-seat multipurpose banquet hall, and one of the world's longest infinity pools. The project's site is located along the top of a seaside cliff, providing an optimal 180-degree seaside view. This informed the complex's general form, becoming a terrace as it matched the decline of the site's sloping topography. This gave us the design challenge of creating dynamic views not only from every room, but from any location in the resort.

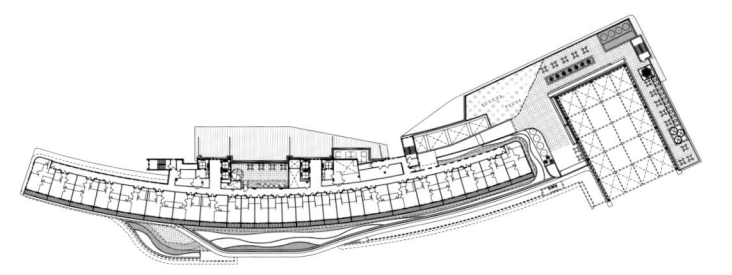

Third-floor plan (hotel)

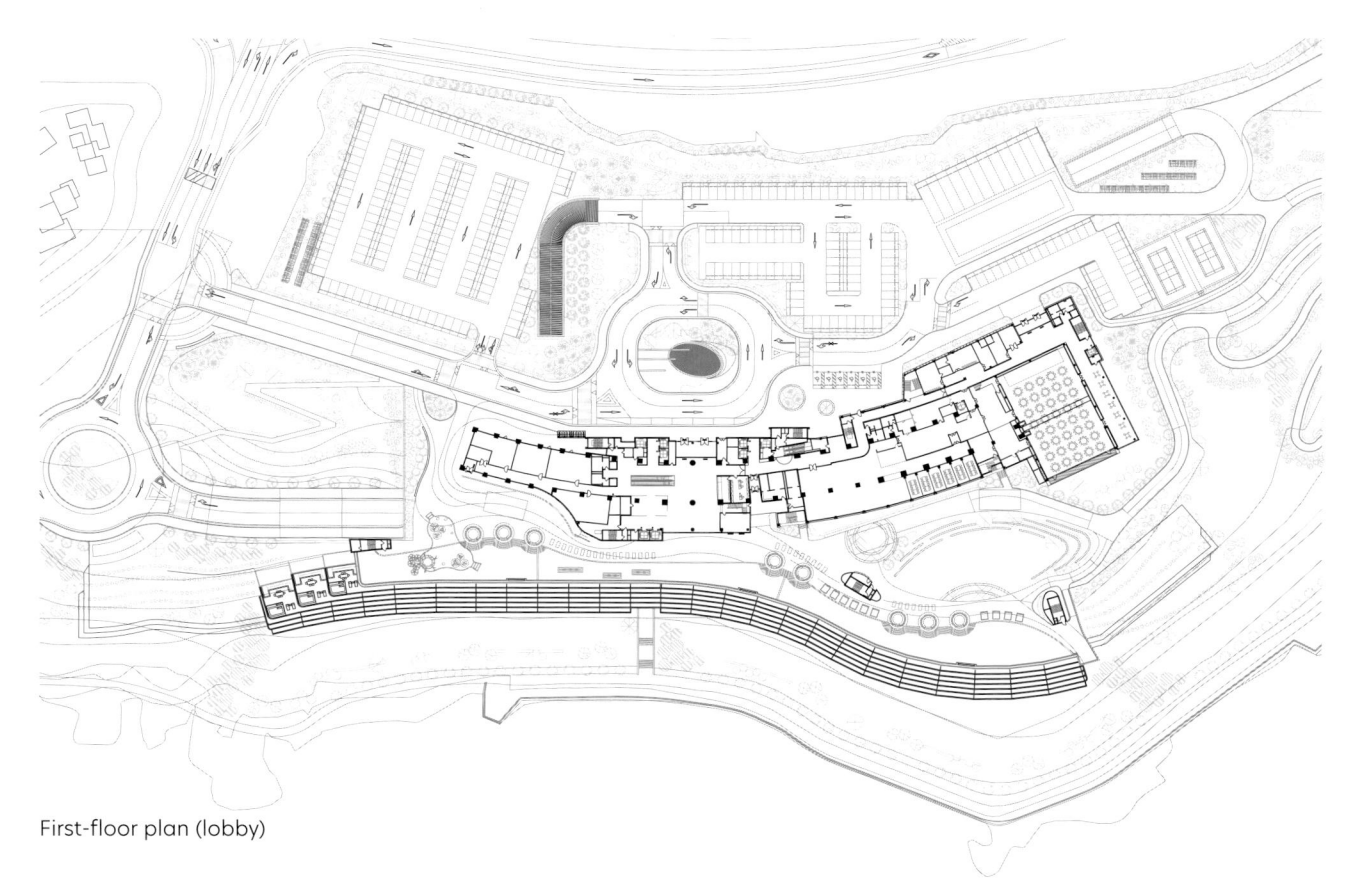

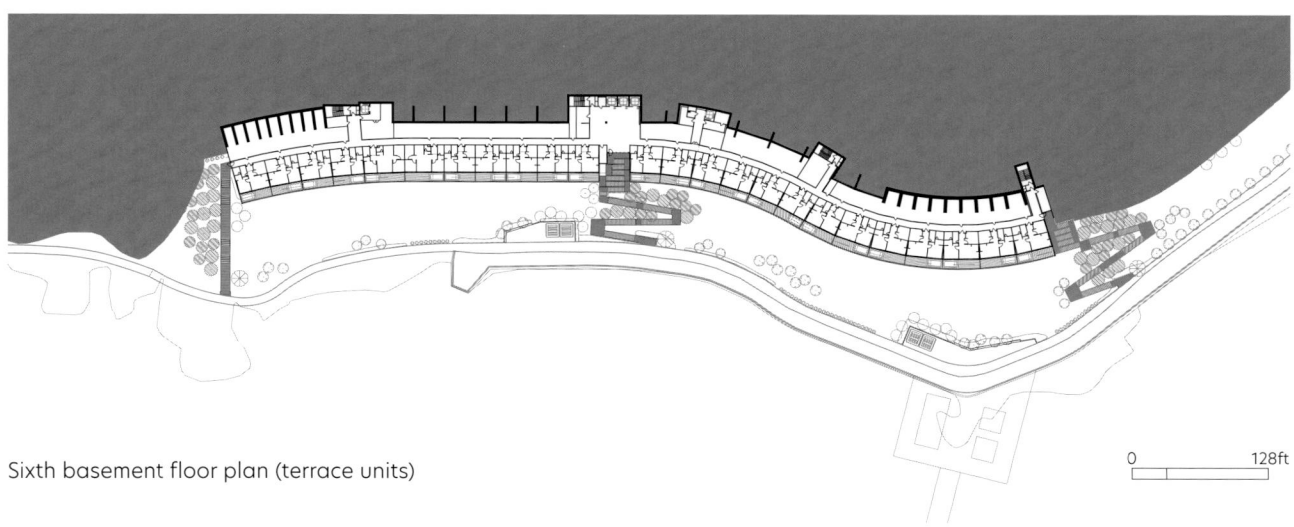

First-floor plan (lobby)

Sixth basement floor plan (terrace units)

0    128ft

**366**   SCALE AND PROPORTION

The exterior of the resort, reminiscent of a cruise ship, was designed naturally according to the flow of its surrounding land, wind, and water. From that design concept, we created a programmatic layout optimized for recreation and leisure.

The programmatic mixing of luxury hotels, condominium units, health-related support facilities, arts and leisure amenities, boutique shopping, entertainment, and marine nature provides a collection of desirable activities that engage this new community. The complex's advanced design allows its inhabitants to have a lifestyle that effectively integrates environment, health, and recreation.

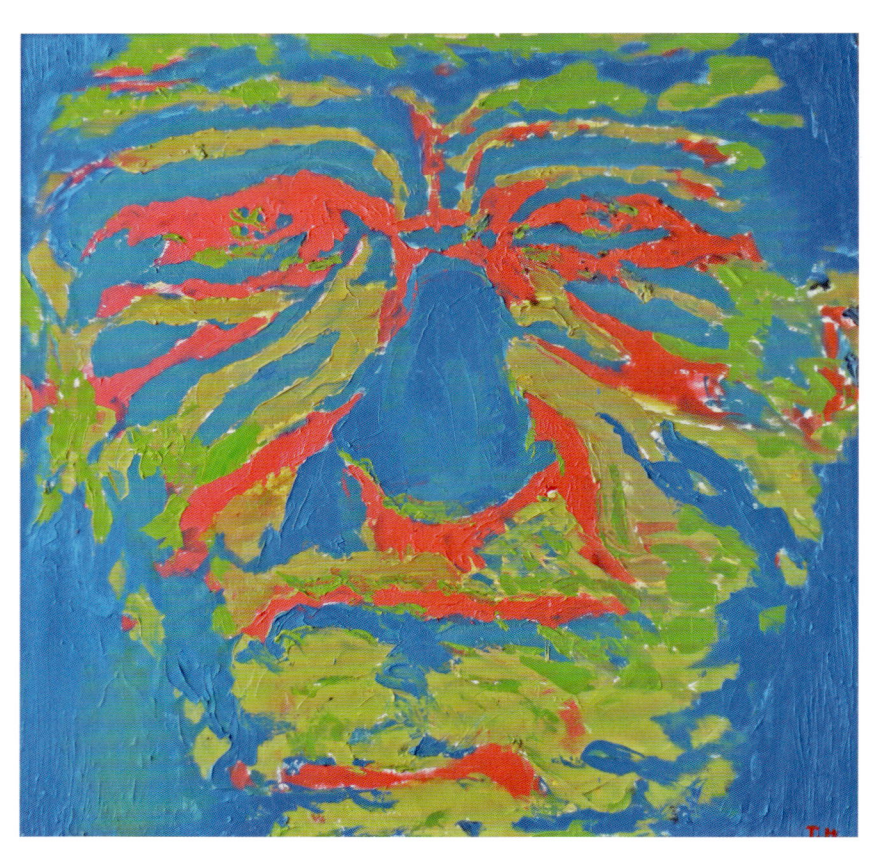

Taesun Hong, *Self-portrait* (1984), oil

# Appendix

**Chronological List of Other Works**

**YKH Associates Profile**

**Awards and Publications**

**Project Credits**

**Acknowledgments**

# Chronological List of Other Works

**1995**

**Beijing World Trade Center**
Beijing China
Design: 1995
Associate architect: Yamasaki Associates
Office, hotel, retail & exhibition, garden apartments
Total floor area: 5,381,955.20 ft² (500,000 m²)

**Dalian Xiwang Office Building**
Dalian, China
Design/completion: 1995/1999
Associate architect: Yamasaki Associates
Office, retail, exhibition facilities
Total floor area: 957,988 ft² (89,000 m²)

**Dongsuh Securities Headquarters**
Seoul, Korea
Design: 1995
Associate architects: Yamasaki Associates, Mooyoung A&E
Office, retail
Total floor area: 300,097.82 ft² (27,880 m²)

**1996**

**Beijing Millennium Tower**
Beijing, China
Design/completion: 1996/2000
Associate architect: Yamasaki Associates
Office, retail
Total floor area: 731,945.91 ft² (68,000 m²)

**1997**

**Gyeonggi Provincial Office Complex**
Suwon-si, Gyeonggi-do, South Korea
Design: 1997
Associate architects: Yamasaki Associates, Mooyoung A&E
Office, welfare facilities, media & communication facilities
Total floor area: 543,577.48 ft² (50,500 m²)

**Gyeonggi Small Business Foundation**
Suwon-si, Gyeonggi-do, South Korea
Design/completion: 1997/2001
Associate architects: Yamasaki Associates, Mooyoung A&E
South Korea Education & Research Centre
Total floor area: 513,406.23 ft² (47,697 m²)

**Incheon Kyeyang District Townhall**
Incheon, South Korea
Design/completion: 1997/2002
Associate architects: Yamasaki Associates, Mooyoung A&E
Office, congress hall, health clinic
Total floor area: 484,828 ft² (45,042 m²)

**MBC Ilsan Broadcasting Studio Complex**
Goyang-si, Gyeonggi-do, South Korea
Design: 1997
Associate architects: Yamasaki Associates, Mooyoung A&E
Office, retail, broadcast facilities
Total floor area: 675,726 ft$^2$ (62,777 m$^2$)

**1998**

**The National Grand Theater of China**
Beijing, China
Design: 1998
Associate architect: Yamasaki Associates
Opera house, concert hall, management, administration, theater, exhibition hall
Total floor area: 1,282,573.70 ft$^2$ (119,155 m$^2$)

**1999**

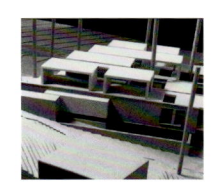

**Bloomfield Hills Residence**
Bloomfield Hills, Michigan, United States
Design: 1999
Associate architect: Zago Architecture
Residence
Total floor area: 8,008.35 ft$^2$ (744 m$^2$)

**2000**

**Bundang Park-View Mixed-Use**
Seongnam-si, Gyeonggi-do, South Korea
Design/completion: 2000/2004
Associate architects: Yamasaki Associates, Mooyoung A&E, Kunwon Architects, Myungin Architects
Residences (1,829), office, retail
Total floor area: 4,705,874 ft$^2$ (437,190 m$^2$)

**Chereville Mixed-Use**
Goyang-si, Gyeonggi-do, South Korea
Design: 2000
Associate architects: Yamasaki Associates, Heerim Architects
Residences (3,264), office, retail
Total floor area: 2,816,721.60 ft$^2$ (261,682 m$^2$)

**Fine Venture Tower**
Seoul, South Korea
Design/completion: 2000/2001
Associate architect: Zago Architecture
Office, retail
Total floor area: 158,035.73 ft$^2$ (14,682 m$^2$)

**Hong Residence**
Bloomfield Hills, Michigan, United States
Design: 2000
Residence
Total floor area: 5,005.22 ft$^2$ (465 m$^2$)

**Jeonnam Provincial Office Complex**
Muan-gun, Jeollanam-do, South Korea
Design: 2000
Associate architects: Yamasaki Associates, Mooyoung A&E
Government facilities, office, retail
Total floor area: 5,005.22 ft² (77,967 m²)

## 2001

**Andamiro Headquarters**
Seoul, South Korea
Design: 2001
Office, retail, fitness center
Total floor area: 374,594.85 ft² (34,801 m²)

**Hwanghakdong Mixed-Use Redevelopment**
Seoul, South Korea
Design: 2001
Residence, office, retail
Total building area: 3,756,561.70 ft² (348,996 m²)

**Incheon International Airport Hotel**
Incheon, South Korea
Design: 2001
Units (447), hotel, office, retail
Total building area: 1,252,359.40 ft² (116,348 m²)

**Oksu-dong Officetel**
Seoul, South Korea
Design/completion: 2001/2004
Residence, office, retail
Total building area: 172,782.29 ft² (16,052 m²)

## 2002

**Beijing Songlingri Mixed-Use**
Beijing, China
Design: 2002
Residences, office, hotel, retail, convention center
Total floor area: 3,937,277 ft² (365,785 m²)

**Doosan We've Pavilion Officetel**
Seongnam-si, Gyeonggi-do, South Korea
Design/completion: 2002/2005
Residences (1,519), office, retail
Total floor area: 2,091,341.70 ft² (194,292 m²)

**Oryukdo SK View Apartments**
Busan, South Korea
Design/completion: 2002/2005
Residences (3,000)
Total floor area: 2,091,341.70 ft² (666,124 m²)

**Sangam Digital Media Center**
Seoul, South Korea
Design: 2002
Office, retail
Total floor area: 217,291 ft² (20,187 m²)

## 2003

### Cheongdam Paragon Residence
Seoul, South Korea
Design/completion: 2003/2006
Residences (92)
Total floor area: 412,612.98 ft² (38,333 m²)

### Dongbinggo Sport Center
Seoul, South Korea
Design: 2003
Sports center, retail
Total floor area: 78,436.62 ft² (7,287 m²)

### Dongyang E&C Headquarters
Seoul, South Korea
Design: 2003
Office, retail, exhibition
Total floor area: 283,951.96 ft² (26,380 m²)

### Dubai Hotel & Office Tower
Dubai, United Arab Emirates
Design: 2003
Associate architect: Yamasaki Associates
Office, retail, hotel
Total floor area: 1,601,131.70 ft² (148,750 m²)

### Gasandong Byucksan Digital Valley
Seoul, South Korea
Design/completion: 2003/2005
Office, factory, retail
Total floor area: 652,239.15 ft² (60,595 m²)

### Mona Lisa Shopping Center
Seoul, South Korea
Design: 2003
Cultural facilities, retail
Total floor area: 243,748.75 ft² (22,645 m²)

### OSFE Shopping Plaza
Seoul, South Korea
Design/completion: 2003/2004
Retail
Total floor area: 271,928.67 ft² (25,263 m²)

### Sejin Techno Park
Seoul, South Korea
Design/completion: 2003/2005
Office, factory, retail
Total floor area: 1,074,475 ft² (99,822 m²)

### Sinsadong #647 Retail Complex
Seoul, South Korea
Design/completion: 2003/2004
Retail
Total floor area: 5,263.55 ft² (489 m²)

**Somerset Palace Hotel & Residence**
Seoul, South Korea
Design/completion: 2003/2005
Associate architect: Heerim Architects
Residences, retail
Total floor area: 551,069 ft² (51,196 m²)

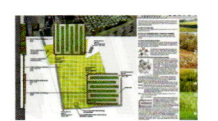

**World Trade Center Memorial Competition**
Memorial Park, New York, United States
Design: 2003
Total floor area: 635,070.71 ft² (59,000 m²)

**Yongpyong Greenpia Condominiums**
Pyeongchang-gun, Gangwon-do, South Korea
Design/completion: 2003/2006
Condominiums (334), retail
Total floor area: 642,648.51 ft² (59,704 m²)

## 2004

**Odaesan Resort Masterplan**
Pyeongchang-gun, Gangwon-do, South Korea
Design: 2004
Residences, hotel, condominiums, club house, cultural facilities
Site area: 120,994,533 ft² (11,240,760 m²)
Total floor area: 6,980,880.30 ft² (648,545 m²)

**Yongpyong Beache Palace Resort**
Boryeong-si, Chungcheongnam-do, South Korea
Design/completion: 2004/2008
Hotel rooms (287), retail
Total floor area: 521,554.51 ft² (48,454 m²)

**Yongpyong The Forest Phase 1**
Pyeongchang-gun, Gangwon-do, South Korea
Design/completion: 2004/2006
Single-family detached residences (106)
Total floor area: 272,165.47 ft² (25,285 m²)

**Yongsan Foreign School**
Seoul, South Korea
Design: 2004
Educational facilities
Total floor area: 282,875.57 ft² (26,280 m²)

## 2005

**Almaty Mixed-Use**
Almaty, Kazakhstan
Design: 2005
Residences, office, retail
Total floor area: 1,513,179.80 ft² (140,579 m²)

**IBIS Ambassador Hotel**
Suwon-si, Gyeonggi-do, South Korea
Design/completion: 2005/2008
Hotel rooms (237), retail
Total floor area: 427,477.94 ft² (39,714 m²)

### Nonhyun-Dong SK Apelbaum Apt.
Seoul, South Korea
Design: 2005
Residences (38)
Total floor area: 177,001.74 ft² (16,444 m²)

### Seoul City Hall Expansion Design Competition
Seoul, South Korea
Design: 2005
Government facility
Total floor area: 1,035,574.30 ft² (96,208 m²)

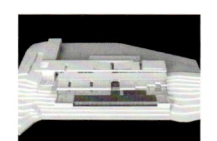

### Villa in Ras Al Khaimah
Ras Al Khaimah, United Arab Emirates
Design: 2005
Residences
Total floor area: 18,729.20 ft² (1,740 m²)

### Yongpyong The Forest Phase 2
Pyeongchang-gun, Gangwon-do, South Korea
Design/completion: 2005/2009
Residences (56)
Total floor area: 255,944.26 ft² (23,778 m²)

### YuYu Pharmaceutical Factory Extension
Jecheon-si, Chungcheongbuk-do, South Korea
Design/completion: 2005/2006
Factory
Total floor area: 89,189.76 ft² (8,286 m²)

## 2006

### Ahyun New Town 3rd District Redevelopment
Seoul, South Korea
Design: 2006
Associate architect: Yamasaki Associates
Residences (3,111), retail
Total floor area: 1,499,821.70 ft² (139,338 m²)

### Kolon Songdo Mixed-Use Complex
Seoul, South Korea
Design: 2006
Residences (552), amenities, retail
Total floor area: 1,544,416.60 ft² (143,481 m²)

### La Bella Verde Mixed-Use
Atlanta, United States
Design: 2006
Residences, retail, fitness center, community park
Total floor area: 97,790.13 ft² (9,085 m²)

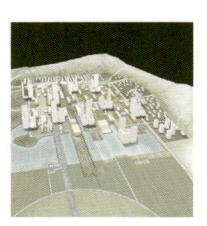

### Master Planning for Public Admin. Town Competition
Sejong, South Korea
Design: 2006
Associate architect: Studio_K_works
Convention center, office, support facilities
Site area: 29,746,163 ft² (2,763,509 m²)
Total floor area: 19,127,899 ft² (1,777,040 m²)

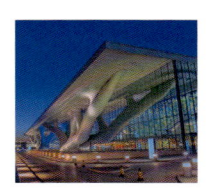

**Qatar Education City Convention Center**
Doha, Qatar
Design/completion: 2006/2011
Associate architects: Arata Isozaki, RHWL Architects, Yamasaki Associates
Convention center, education
Total floor area: 818,057.19 ft² (76,000 m²)

## 2007

**Ansan Posco 90BL Masterplan**
Ansan-si, Gyeonggi-do, South Korea
Design: 2007
Hotel, office, residences, retail
Total floor area: 9,326,551.60 ft² (866,465 m²)

**Daehakro Musical Theater**
Seoul, South Korea
Design: 2007
Associate architect: Studio_K_works
Theater
Total floor area: 61,117.48 ft² (5,678 m²)

**Danang D-City Masterplan**
Danang, Vietnam
Design/completion: 2007/2012
Associate architects: JinaArchitects, 153 Architects
Hotel, office, convention, cultural facilities, retail, golf course
Site area: 22,662,143 ft² (2,105,382 m²)
Total floor area: 28,613,186 ft² (2,658,252 m²)

**Incheon SongdoF8 Shopping Mall**
Incheon, South Korea
Design: 2007
Office, retail
Total floor area: 1,502,943.30 ft² (139,628 m²)

**International Bank of Qatar Headquarters**
Doha, Qatar
Design: 2007
Associate architect: Yamasaki Associates
Office
Total floor area: 243,748.75 ft² (22,645 m²)

**Lusail Marina Mixed-Use District 10**
Doha, Qatar
Design: 2007
Associate architect: Yamasaki Associates
Residences (155), office, retail, fitness center
Total floor area: 731,601.46 ft² (67,968 m²)

**Lusail Marina Office Complex 28**
Doha, Qatar
Design: 2007
Associate architect: Yamasaki Associates
Office, retail
Total floor area: 340,731.58 ft² (31,655 m²)

### Paju Castle Bridge Shopping Mall
Paju-si, Gyeonggi-do, South Korea
Design: 2007
Retail
Total floor area: 199,455.26 ft² (18,530 m²)

### Palm Jebel Ali Spine Precinct 3 Development
Dubai, United Arab Emirates
Design: 2007
Residences (902), town houses (66)
Total floor area: 3,427,336.70 ft² (318,410 m²)

### Samsung Thales LAB
Yongin-si, Gyeonggi-do, South Korea
Design: 2007
Laboratory
Total floor area: 97,348.81 ft² (9,044 m²)

### Sungwoo Ostar Resort Golf Villas
Hoengseong-gun, Gangwon-do, South Korea
Design: 2007
Associate architect: HIMMA
Residences (117), 36-hole golf course
Total floor area: 560,552.16 ft² (52,077 m²)

### Taeyoung Bloomore Resort
Gyeongju-si, Gyeongsangbuk-do, South Korea
Design/completion: 2007/2010
Associate architect: WondoshiArchitects
Condominiums (300), therapy center, cultural facilities, water park
Total floor area: 717,791.37 ft² (66,685 m²)

## 2008

### Hanoi Golf Resort Masterplan
Hanoi, Vietnam
Design: 2008
Hotel rooms (70), golf course
Total floor area: 490,834.31 ft² (45,600 m²)

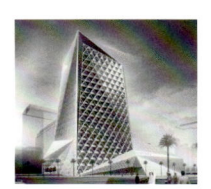

### Kahramaa Headquarters
Lusail, Qatar
Design: 2008
Associate architect: Yamasaki Associates
Office, retail
Total floor area: 484,203.75 ft² (44,984 m²)

### Ocean 9 Casino Hotel Resort
Subic Bay, Philippines
Design: 2008
Hotel, casino, retail
Total floor area: 1,200,423.60 ft² (111,523 m²)

### Seoul Performing Arts Center 2nd Competition
Seoul, South Korea
Design: 2008
Associate architects: Haeahn Architects, Changjo Architects, Junggon Kim
Cultural facilities, retail
Total floor area: 596,159.18 ft² (55,385 m²)

### Seoul Resort Masterplan
Seoul, South Korea
Design: 2008
Residences (319)
Total floor area: 1,100,954.30 ft² (102,282 m²)

### Shanghai Pos Plaza Remodeling
Shanghai, China
Design: 2008
Office, retail
Total floor area: 676,845.45 ft² (62,881 m²)

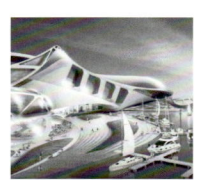

### SK Marina Resort Masterplan
Ansan-si, Gyeonggi-do, South Korea
Design: 2008
Residences (394), golf course, marina complex
Site area: 5,159,583.60 ft² (479,341 m²)
Total floor area: 2,692,161.60 ft² (250,110 m²)

### Youngjong Woonseo Hotel
Incheon, South Korea
Design: 2008
Hotel rooms (585)
Total floor area: 532,027.80 ft² (49,427 m²)

### Youngjong IBC-II Masterplan
Incheon, South Korea
Design: 2008
Associate architect: Arquitectonica Architecture
Golf course, condominiums, casino hotels, culture center, museum, government facilities, retail
Site area: 53,216,773 ft² (4,944,000 m²)
Total floor area: 21,151,084 ft² (1,965,000 m²)

### Youngjong Woonbuk Residential Complex
Incheon, South Korea
Design: 2008
Residences (1,273)
Total floor area: 3,344,347 ft² (310,700 m²)

## 2009

### Klahaus Villa Complex
Gapyeong-gun, Gyeonggi-do, South Korea
Design: 2009
Private residences (83)
Total floor area: 50,999.41 ft² (4,738 m²)

### Samchully LAB Competition
Osan-si, Gyeonggi-do, South Korea
Design: 2009
Laboratory
Total floor area: 148,821.83 ft² (13,826 m²)

### Subic Bay Casino
Subic Bay, Philippines
Design: 2009
Casino
Total floor area: 126,766.57 ft² (11,777 m²)

### Seongnam Sungho Market Redevelopment
Seongnam-si, Gyeonggi-do, South Korea
Design: 2009
Residences (412), officetels (400), retail
Total floor area: 1,630,108 ft² (151,442 m²)

## 2010

### Baikal Gardens Resort Masterplan
Irkutsk, Russia
Design: 2010
Villas (257), condominiums (120), golf course, hotel, academic institution
Site Area: 19,958,658 ft² (1,854,220 m²)
Total floor area: 1,934,382.30 ft² (179,710 m²)

### Cherish Furniture Headquarters
Goyang-si, Gyeonggi-do, South Korea
Design/completion: 2010/2012
Office, retail
Total floor area: 19,375 ft² (1,800 m²)

### Dow Corning Laboratory Expansion
Jincheon-gun, Chungcheongbuk-do, South Korea
Design/completion: 2010/2012
Laboratory
Total floor area: 18,083.37 ft² (1,680 m²)

## 2012

### Belize Resort Masterplan
Ambergris Caye, Belize
Design: 2012
Condominiums (4,500), villas (600), 54-hole golf course, hotels
Site area: 134,167,213 ft² (12,464,542 m²)
Total floor area: 16,267,164 ft² (1,511,269 m²)

### Hongmai Park City
Hanoi, Vietnam
Design: 2012
Residence, retail
Site area: 1,351,656.50 ft² (125,573 m²)
Total floor area: 3,889,711.20 ft² (361,366 m²)

### Huludao Convention Exhibition Center
Huludao, China
Design: 2012
Exhibition center, park, retail
Total floor area: 3,756,561.70 ft² (348,996 m²)

**2013**

**Don-Am Jang Residence Renovation**
Seoul, South Korea
Design/completion: 2013/2015
Residence
Total floor area: 4,068.76 ft² (378 m²)

**Jeju Marriott Hotel**
Jeju-si, Jeju-do, South Korea
Design: 2013
Hotel, convention center, retail, casino
Total floor area: 730,848 ft² (67,898 m²)

**2014**

**Jeju Residence**
Jeju-si, Jeju-do, South Korea
Design/completion: 2014/2015
Residence
Total floor area: 3,186 ft² (296 m²)

**2015**

**Asan Baebang Officetel**
Asan-si, Chungcheongnam-do, South Korea
Design/completion: 2015/2017
Residence, office, retail
Total floor area: 239,023.39 ft² (22,206 m²)

**Camkor City M6 Masterplan**
Phnom Penh, Cambodia
Design: 2015
Residence, office, clinic, amenities, retail
Total floor area: 1,055,164.60 ft² (98,028 m²)

**Giheung Lotte Premium Outlet**
Yongin-si, Gyeonggi-do, South Korea
Design/completion: 2015/2019
Shopping mall
Total floor area: 1,354,605.80 ft² (125,847 m²)

**Jeju Lotte Resort**
Seogwipo-si, Jeju-do, South Korea
Design: 2015
Condominium, villa, water park, retail
Total floor area: 523,470.49 ft² (48,632 m²)

**Wuhan VTP Development**
Wuhan, China
Design: 2015
Associate architect: MAA
Hotel, office, shopping mall, exhibition center
Total floor area: 4,843,759.70 ft² (450,000 m²)

**2016**

**Dongbinggo Villas**
Seoul, South Korea
Design/completion: 2016/2018
Residences
Total floor area: 21,818.45 ft² (2,027 m²)

### Ilsung Resort
Mungyeong-si, Gyeongsangbuk-do, South Korea
Design: 2014/under construction
Condominium, villa, water park, retail
Total floor area: condominiums 146,841.27 ft² (13,642 m²); villas 34,444.513 ft² (3,200 m²)

### Jeju Seohongdong Residence
Seogwipo-si, Jeju-do, South Korea
Design/completion: 2016/2017
Residence
Total floor area: 2,142 ft² (199 m²)

## 2017

### Myeongji International Business Complex
Busan, South Korea
Design: 2017
Residences, office, commercial, shopping mall, start-up
Site area: 970,754 ft² (90,186 m²)
Total floor area: 5,694,216.20 ft² (529,010 m²)

### Suncheon Lotte Shopping Mall
Suncheon-si, Jeollanam-do, South Korea
Design: 2017
Park, retail, parking
Total floor area: 860,327 ft² (79,927 m²)

### Yeoju Companiom Animal Theme Park
Yeoju-si, Gyeonggi-do, South Korea
Design: 2017
Hotel, pet facilities, retail
Site area: 754,550.12 ft² (70,100 m²)
Total floor area: 131,857.90 ft² (12,250 m²)

### Yongpyong 4-3 Resort Complex
Pyeongchang-gun, Gangwon-do, South Korea
Design: 2017
Condominiums, retail
Total floor area: 348,244.79 ft² (32,353 m²)

## 2018

### Geoje FestaVista City Resort
Geoje-si, Gyeongsangnam-do, South Korea
Design: 2018
Resort, Retail, Shopping Mall
Total floor area: 2,444,720.65 ft² (227,121.98 m²)

### Hue Hi-Tech Park
Hue, Vietnam
Design: 2018
Residence, hotel, office, retail, IT & VR center, convention center, education facilities, support facilities
Total floor area: 9,309,060.30 ft² (864,840 m²)

### Jeju English Village Masterplan
Seogwipo-si, Jeju-do, South Korea
Design: 2018
Residence, support facilities
Total floor area: 67,285.20 ft² (6,251 m²)

### Suseong Medical District Masterplan
Daegu, South Korea
Design: 2018
Medical hotel, hospital, educational center, retail
Total floor area: 559,486.53 ft² (51,978 m²)

## 2019

### Wakayama Casino Resort
Wakayama, Japan
Design : 2018
Resort, Hotel, Retail, Convention Center, Casino
Total floor area : 840,386.33 ft² (702,670 m²)

### Busan Daeyundong Retail
Busan, South Korea
Design/completion: 2019/2020
Office, retail
Total floor area: 47,554.96 ft² (4,418 m²)

### Daechidong Mixed-Use
Seoul, South Korea
Design: 2019
Office, retail
Total floor area: 40,935.15 ft² (3,803 m²)

### Haenam Osiano Resort & Hotel
Haenam-gun, Jeollanam-do, South Korea
Design: 2019
Hotel, condominium, convention center, retail
Total floor area: 165,333.66 ft² (15,360 m²)

### Sejong Town House B1 Block Development
Sejong, South Korea
Design: 2019
Residences (42)
Total floor area: 158,272.54 ft² (14,704 m²)

## 2020

### Ganghwa Resort Masterplan
Ganghwa-gun, Gyeonggi-do, South Korea
Design: 2020
Camping facility, swimming pool, retail
Total floor area: 33,368.12 ft² (3,100 m²)

### Gangneung "MerForet" Resort Design Competition
Gangneung-si, Gangwon-do, South Korea
Design: 2020
Condominiums, convention center, cultural facilities, retail
Total floor area: 2,029,772 ft² (188,572 m²)

### Hue Convention Center
Hue, Vietnam
Design: 2020
Convention center, retail
Total floor area: 180,047.93 ft² (16,727 m²)

### Jindo Harbor Masterplan
Jindo-gun, Jeollanam-do, South Korea
Design: 2020
Residence, office, retail, industrial facilities, commercial facilities
Total floor area: 83,433,405 ft² (7,751,217 m²)

### Siheung Apartment Factory
Siheung-si, Gyeonggi-do, South Korea
Design: 2020
Apartment factory, retail
Total floor area: 651,744 ft² (60,549 m²)

### Sound Museum
Seoul, South Korea
Design: 2020
Associate architect: Kengo Kuma Associates
Museum, cultural facilities
Total floor area: 113,236.34 ft² (10,520 m²)

### Ulideul Resort
Seogwipo-si, Jeju-do, South Korea
Design: 2020
Resort, retail
Total floor area: 156,851.70 ft² (14,572 m²)

## 2021

### Bucheon Sports Complex Development Masterplan
Bucheon-si, Gyeonggi-do, South Korea
Design: 2021
Residence, office, retail, industrial facilities, commercial facilities
Total floor area: 6,248,945 ft² (580,546 m²)

### Guuidong #640-6 Retail
Seoul, South Korea
Design: 2021
Office, retail
Total floor area: 6,017 ft² (559 m²)

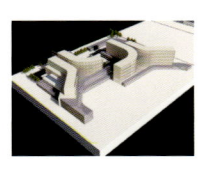

### Hajodae Resort
Yangyang-gun, Gangwon-do, South Korea
Design: 2021
Resort, retail
Total floor area: 1,150,468.30 ft² (106,882 m²)

### Hankook Tire Shopping Mall
Seongnam-si, Gyeonggi-do, South Korea
Design: 2021
Exhibition, commercial, retail
Site area: 43,647 ft² (4,055 m²)
Total floor area: 123,279 ft² (11,453 m²)

**Hannam 381 Mixed-Use**
Seoul, South Korea
Design: 2021
Office, retail
Total floor area: 12,206.27 ft² (1,134 m²)

**Janglimdong Warehouse**
Busan, South Korea
Design: 2021
Warehouse
Total floor area: 1,066,445.20 ft² (99,076 m²)

**Jindo Farmers' Housing Development**
Jindo-gun, Jeollanam-do, South Korea
Design: 2021
Residence
Total floor area: 84,098.43 ft² (7,813 m²)

**Masan One Island Masterplan**
Changwon-si, Gyeongsangnam-do, South Korea
Design: 2021
Associate architect: dA Architecture Group
Residence, office, hotel, retail
Total floor area: 4,699,674 ft² (436,614 m²)

**Miadong Mixed-Use Development**
Seoul, South Korea
Design: 2021
Residence, office, retail
Total floor area: 1,419,027.80 ft² (131,832 m²)

**Myungwon Royal Tea Museum**
Hadong-gun, Gyeongsangnam-do, South Korea
Design: 2021
Museum
Total floor area: 23,529.91 ft² (2,186 m²)

**Nonhyun 102-5 Mixed-Use**
Seoul, South Korea
Design: 2021
Residence, office, retail
Total floor area: 8,212.86 ft² (763 m²)

**Shin's Residence**
Seongnam-si, Gyeonggi-do, South Korea
Design: 2021
Residence
Total floor area: 3,229.17 ft² (300 m²)

**Sihwa MTV Mixed-use**
Siheung-si, Gyeonggi-do, South Korea
Design: 2021
Associate architect: A Group Associates
Apartments (400), officetels (596), retail
Total floor area: 1,920,862.90 ft² (178,454 m²)

**Yangpyeong Residence**
Yangpyeong-gun, Gyeonggi-di, South Korea
Design: 2021
Residence
Total floor area: 14,961.835 ft² (1,390 m²)

## 2022

**Yongpyong Resort 8th Condominiums**
Pyeongchang-gun, Gangwon-do, South Korea
Design: 2022
Condominiums, retail
Site area: 281,799 ft² (26,180 m²)
Total floor area: 681,334 ft² (63,298 m²)

**Yangyang Boutique Hotel**
Yangyang-gun, Gangwon-do, South Korea
Design: 2022
Hotel
Site area: 7,233 ft² (672 m²)
Total floor area: 5,468 ft² (508 m²)

**Jeju English Town Residences**
Seogwipo-si, Jeju-do, South Korea
Design: 2022
Residence
Site area: 81,117 ft² (7,536 m²)
Total floor area: 31,646 ft² (2,940 m²)

**Chuncheon Tram Car & Station Design**
Chuncheon-si, Gangwon-do, South Korea
Design: 2022
Public transportation
Station area: 41,355 ft² (3,842 m²)
Total floor area: 41,355 ft² (3,842 m²)

**XiGEIST Modular Homes Prototypes**
South Korea
Design: 2022
Residence
Building area: 1,883 ft² (175 m²)
Total floor area: 1755 ft² (163 m²)

DECONSTRUCTION
THE CREATIVE COMMUNITY
John Portman and Associates
Gwathmey Siegel Apartments
PIANO
ACTIVITY DIAGRAMS
INTERIOR DESIGN
MODERN ARCHITECTURE A-Z
99 Apartments II
ADVANCED ARCHITECTURE
ARCHITECTURE NOW!
A LIFE IN ARCHITECTURE
Zaha Hadid Architects
GUSTAV KLIMT
RETROSPECTA 08-09
THE COMPLETE ZAHA HADID
architecture
RICHARD KEATING
ITSUKO HASEGAWA
Norman Foster
STUDIOS
CESAR PELLI
MURPHY/JAHN
COX ARCHITECTS
TERRY FARRELL
CONCEPT
BUILDING A NEW MILLENNIUM
KRÁLOVSKÁ CESTA
Roman Architecture
Late Baroque and Rococo Architecture
The Fashion System
TASCHEN
ALESSI
Kim, Seok-chul
SHIGERU BAN
Landscape Architecture
OVER EUROPE
INTERIOR DESIGNERS OF THE UNITED STATES OF AMERICA
ARCHITECTS OF SOUTH AFRICA
MINI BUILDING
TYPE & IMAGE
JOHN UPDIKE
Graphic De
RETROSPECTA
VERSACE
BARTON MYERS
MANY MASKS
International Architecture Yearbook
Beautiful Beach Houses
FINN JUHL
ZEN INTERIORS
The Art of Drawing
AIRES MATEUS
COX ARCHITECTS
URBANISM
CONCEPT
c3

# YKH Associates Profile

### TAESUN HONG, AIA, NCARB

Taesun Hong was born in Seoul, Korea in 1964 and he moved to Michigan, United States, when he was fifteen years old. He studied fine arts at Cranbrook School, Bloomfield Hills, Michigan, prior to attending Oberlin College in Ohio for Piano, Fine Arts and Premedical Studies. He attended the "Career Discovery" program at the Graduate School of Design at Harvard University in 1987 and immediately after the introduction of architectural studies he began his internship at Leers, Weinzapfel Associates in Boston, Massachusetts. He then pursued his architecture studies at Yale University. He also studied at the Syracuse Universita, Florence, Italy, and had traveled Europe extensively before returning to Yale for his Master of Architecture degree in 1992. He joined as a partner and established Pallos & Hong Architects in Birmingham, Michigan, in 1992. After winning the Incheon Bus Terminal Design Competition in 1993 with Minoru Yamasaki Associates, he joined Minoru Yamasaki Associates as a senior designer. Taesun Hong won numerous international design competitions at Yamasaki Associates in Troy, Michigan, and served as CEO and design director. Taesun Hong established Yamasaki Associates Korea in Seoul, South Korea, in 2000, and in 2009 he changed the firm name to YKH Associates. For the last thirty years, Taesun Hong has received many awards for his designs, including the Honor Award of American Institute of Architects San Francisco in 2021. He has been lecturing and teaching at many institutions in Korea and he is now concentrating his design works in San Francisco and in Seoul with the philosophy that architecture is about creating a space of "timelessness" and "materiality."

### YKH ASSOCIATES

YKH is a United States/Korea/Vietnam–based design firm composed of architects, designers, builders, and thinkers operating within the fields of architecture, urban planning, and interior design. The office is currently involved in a large number of projects throughout Asia, the Middle East, the United States, and Central America. YKH is committed to providing architecture that responds appropriately to the functional criteria of a project while expressing the aesthetic qualities of the built form.

www.ykharch.com

## CURRENT PARTNERS

**Taesun Hong** AIA, NCARB
CEO / Design Director

**Soyeon Kim**
Partner

**Daejung Sang**
Partner

**Jaeho Shin**
Partner

**Keunho Kim**
Partner

**Wonjin Kim**
Partner

**Donghyun Yoon**
Partner

**Kiho Kim**
Partner

## CURRENT PRINCIPALS

**Heewon Kim**
Principal

**Seho Lee**
Principal

**Yongho Hwang**
Principal

**Nackkyung Lee**
Principal

**Wonhye Shin**
Principal

**Jongsoon Yun**
Principal

**Seongho Cha**
Principal

**Dongjae Kim**
Assoc. Principal

**Dongyoung Kim**
Assoc. Principal

**Jeongshik Gim**
Assoc. Principal

## CURRENT & PAST EMPLOYEES

Kiwan Ahn, Buyeon An, Heekyung An, Soyeon An, Yongjae Bae, Yeongmuk Bak, Eunji Bang, William Bingham, Jiae Byun, Bokhyung Cho, Juhee Cho, Kwangil Cho, Kyuyong Cho, Minju Cho, Songhyun Cho, Yunju Cho, Jaesung Choi, Kyungduk Choi, Motbi Choi, Piljae Choi, Bokhyung Chu, Kyungdon Chu, Minji Chu, Minjoo Chun, Euisung Chung, Namkyu Chung, Seunghoon Chung, Taekyung Chung, Pat Doyle, Hyein Goo, Jungwon Gwak, Jaewoo Ha, Joewoong Ha, Jinho Han, Jungwoo Han, Euinggi Hong, Inkyung Hong, Sangtaek Hong, Jinju Hwang, Junwon Hwang, Hyekyung Hyun, Dongsoo Jang, Minju Jeon, Sejin Jeong, Donghyun Ji, Eric Ji, Hajung Jin, Junhak Ju, Isaac Jung, Kooho Jung, Sunghoon Jung, Youjung Jung, Hansung Kang, Jiwon Kang, Jangdo Ki, Bongjin Kim, Byungsoo Kim, Chaewan Kim, Changhyun Kim, Daam Kim, Donghyun Kim, Dongwook Kim, Hyejung Kim, Hyunjae Kim, Insung Kim, Jaemin Kim, Jihwan Kim, Jisun Kim, Jongseok Kim, Junghyun Kim, Jungyoung Kim, Kwansuk Kim, Kyungok Kim, Kyungsoo Kim, Kyungwook Kim, Minho Kim, Sookyung Kim, Soomi Kim, Sungjun Kim, Sunmi Kim, Taegon Kim, Taekyung Kim, Wonjin Kim, Yongki Kim, Yongseok Kim, Youngmo Kim, Yunjung Kim, Youngsoo Ko, Hasun Kong, Jawon Koo, Seunghoi Koo, Joongwon Kwak, Byungkoo Kwon, Eunjung Kwon, Hwayong Kwon, Hyukki Kwon, Kyuseung Kyung, Donghwan Lee, Euisung Lee, Heejung Lee, Hyegyu Lee, Hyunjong Lee, Jihoon Lee, Jihwang Lee, Jihyun Lee, Jongmin Lee, Juheon Lee, Miji Lee, Minwoo Lee, Sangwook Lee, Seunghyeon Lee, Sooyeon Lee, Sub Lee, Youngjo Lee, Yunmi Lee, Heonman Lim, Hongryang Lim, Hoon Lim, Jaechan Lim, Jiyoung Lim, Jungyun Lim, Seungjae Lim, Taebyung Lim, Jongho Ma, Euijung Maeng, Hudson Matz, Kyungah Noh, Byungwon Oh, Dongjin Oh, Jaesuk Oh, Chan Park, Chansik Park, Chulhong Park, Chulhoon Park, Eunjoo Park, Hero Park, Jongsoo Park, Jungen Park, Kiho Park, Kyuho Park, Kyungran Park, Sangyul Park, Sunghoon Park, Sungshin Park, David Paterson, Mirolub Popov, Robert Rose Jr., Jaewoo Seok, Jaehyun Shim, Jaiseong Shim, Sohee Shim, Donghui Shin, Nahye Shin, Sooho Shin, Byungsik So, Sunghwan So, Yunhee So, Sanghyuk Son, Inha Song, Jaeho Song, Sumi Song, Younggil Song, Hyeyong Wang, Jungmi Won, Kyungsun Woo, Sangmin Yang, Sungwon Yang, Yungchul Yeom, Seunghyup Yoo, Jihee Yun, Nara Yun, Seongah Yun, Sungmin Yun, Yeojin Yun

# Awards and Publications

## AWARDS

**2022**
Yongpyong Resort 8th Condominiums Design Competition, First Place Winner
Pyeongchang-gun, Gangwon-do, South Korea

**2021**
AIA San Francisco Chapter Architecture Awards Competition, Honor Award
Sebyeol Brewery, Paju-si, Gyeonggi-do, South Korea

World Architecture Community Awards, Architecture—REALISED, 36th Cycle, First Place Winner
YKH Associates Headquarters, Gangnam-gu, Seoul, South Korea

**2020**
Gangnam-gu Building Awards Competition, Beautiful Building Award
YKH Associates Headquarters, Gangnam-gu, Seoul, South Korea

Hillmaru Country Club & Golf Hotel Design Competition, First Place Winner
Pocheon-si, Gyeonggi-do, South Korea

Korean Architecture Award, 2020
Excellence Award
Sebyeol Brewery, Paju-si, Gyeonggi-do, South Korea

Oak Valley Resort Design Competition, First Place Winner
Wonju-si, Gangwon-do, South Korea

**2019**
Yeosu The Ocean Resort Design Competition, First Place Winner
Yeosu-si, Jeollanam-do, South Korea

**2018**
Geoje FestaVista City Resort Design Competition, First Place Winner
Geoje-si, Gyeongsangnam-do, South Korea

**2017**
Yeoju-si Companion Animal Theme Park Design Competition, First Place Winner
Yeoju-si, Gyeonggi-do, South Korea

**2016**
Jeju Myth Theme Park Hotel & Villa Interior Design Competition, First Place Winner
Jeju-si, Jeju-do, South Korea

Cheongdam "Anobli" Hotel Interior Design Competition, First Place Winner
Seoul, South Korea

**2015**
Giheung Lotte Premium Outlet Design Competition, First Place Winner
Yongin-si, Gyeonggi-do, South Korea

Daejeon Hyundai Premium Outlet Design Competition, First Place Winner
Yuseong-gu, Daejeon, South Korea

Jeju Lotte Resort Design Competition, First Place Winner
Jeju-si, Jeju-do, South Korea

**2014**
Ilsung Mungyeong Resort & Spa Design Competition, First Place Winner
Mungyeong-si, Gyeongsangbuk-do, South Korea

Jeju Seogwipo VIP Institute Hotel Residence Design Competition, First Place Winner
Seogwipo-si, Jeju-do, South Korea

Samsung-dong Luxury Hotel Renovation Proposal Competition, First Place Winner
Seoul, South Korea

**2013**
Buphwajungsa Temple Design Competition, First Place Winner
Dongdaemun-gu, Seoul, South Korea

Nokburn-dong Hotel Design Competition,
First Place Winner
Seoul, South Korea

## 2012
Gimpo Hyundai Premium Outlet Design Competition,
First Place Winner
Gimpo-si, Gyeonggi-do, South Korea

Asan Baebang Officetel Design Competition,
First Place Winner
Daejeon-si, South Korea

## 2010
Buyeo Lotte Premium Outlet Design Competition,
First Place Winner
Buyeo-gun, Chungcheongnam-do, South Korea

Busan Marine Terrace Resort Design Competition,
First Place Winner, MA Prize
Nam-gu, Busan, South Korea

## 2009
Paju Lotte Premium Outlet Design Competition,
First Place Winner
Paju-si, Gyeonggi-do, South Korea

Sungho Market Redevelopment Design Competition,
First Place Winner
Seongnam-si, Gyeonggi-do, South Korea

Seoul Performing Arts Center Third Invited Design
Competition, Finalist
Yongsan-gu, Seoul, South Korea

Belize Green Paradise Resort Design Competition,
First Place Winner
Ambergris Caye, Belize

## 2008
IBC II Casino Resort Master Plan Design RFP Competition,
First Place Winner
Incheon, South Korea

IKOGest Ibis Hotel RFP Competition, First Place Winner
Seoul, South Korea

Subic Bay Casino Hotel Design RFP Competition,
First Place Winner
Subic Bay, Philippines

Yeongjong Woonseo Pheonix Hotel Design RFP Competition,
First Place Winner
Incheon, South Korea

Dubai Palm Jebal Ali Mixed-Use Invitational Design
Competition, Second Place Winner
Dubai, United Arab Emirates

## 2007
International Bank of Qatar Headquarters Building Design
RFP Competition, First Place Winner
Doha, Qatar

Gyeonggi-do Korea Design Awards, Bronze Winner
Heyri "The Step" Plaza, Paju-si, Gyeonggi-do, South Korea

## 2006
Ahyun 3rd District New Town Residential Development RFP
Competition, First Place Winner
Seoul, South Korea

Seoul Performing Arts Center Second Invited Design
Competition, Second Place Winner
Yongsan-gu, Seoul, South Korea

## 2005
Qatar Educational Convention & Conference Center RFP
Competition, First Place Winner
Doha, Qatar

Yongsan Foreign School Invited Design Competition,
Second Place Winner
Seoul, South Korea

Seoul Performing Arts Center Competition,
Grand Prize Winner
Yongsan-gu, Seoul, South Korea

Seoul City Hall Design Competition,
Second Place Winner
Seoul, South Korea

## 2004
Jamsil Posco the Starpark Residence Design RFP Competition, First Place Winner
Songpa-gu, Seoul, South Korea

Hyundai Sungwoo Ostar Resort Design RFP Competition, First Place Winner
Hoengseong-gun, Gangwon-do, South Korea

## 2003
Shinrim-Dong Hanwon Shopping Mall Invited Design Competition, First Place Winner
Seoul, South Korea

Chungdam Jinheung Villa Redevelopment Invited Design Competition, First Place Winner
Seoul, South Korea

## 2000
Asia Publication-Culture & Information Center Design Competition, First Place Winner
Paju-si, Gyeonggi-do, South Korea

Bundang Park-View Residential Development Invited Design Competition, First Place Winner
Seongnam-si, Gyeonggi-do, South Korea

Bundang Pantheon IV Residential Complex Design Competition, Second Place Winner
Seongnam-si, Gyeonggi-do, South Korea

Fine Venture Tower Design RFP Competition,
First Place Winner
Seoul, South Korea

Jeonnam Provincial Office Complex Design Competition,
Third Place Winner
Muan-gun, Jeollanam-do, South Korea

Ilsan Chereville Residential Complex Design Competition,
First Place Winner
Ilsan-si, Gyeonggi-do, South Korea

Korea Highway Corporation Training Institute Design Competition, Second Place Winner
Hwaseong-si, Gyeonggi-do, South Korea

## 1999
Beijing Opera House Invited Design Competition, Finalist
Beijing, China

## 1998
MBC Broadcasting Center Design Competition,
First Place Winner
Ilsan-si, Gyeonggi-do, South Korea

## 1997
Incheon Geyang District Office Design Competition,
First Place Winner
Incheon, South Korea

## 1995
Gyeonggi Small Business Association Office Design Competition, First Place Winner
Suwon-si, Gyeonggi-do, South Korea

Gyeonggi Provincial Office Design Competition,
First Place Winner
Suwon-si, Gyeonggi-do , South Korea

Dongsuh Security Office Design Competition,
Second Place Winner
Seoul, South Korea

## 1993
Incheon Bus Terminal Design Competition,
First Place Winner
Incheon, South Korea

# PUBLICATIONS

## 2022
Gyeonghui-dang Building (Seoul, South Korea), *Chosun Daily* "Real Estate Section," January 4, 2022

## 2021
Sebyeol Brewery (Paju-si, Gyeonggi-do, South Korea), *Chosun Daily* "Culture Section," August 13, 2021

Sebyeol Brewery 2021 AIASF Architecture Honor Award, June 30, 2021
(https://aiasf.org/architecture/design-awards/2021-honorees/sebyeol-brewery/)

## 2020
Yeoju Residence (Yeoju-si, Gyeonnggi-do, South Korea), *ArchDaily*, March 11, 2020
(https://www.archdaily.com/935203)

Sebyeol Brewery (Paju-si, Gyeonggi-do, South Korea), *ArchDaily*, January 3, 2020
(https://www.archdaily.com/931863)

## 2019
Inje Residence (Inje-gun, Gangwon-do, South Korea), *C3Korea Magazine*, December 10, 2019

Sebyeol Brewery (Paju-si, Gyeonggi-do, South Korea), *Chosun Biz Magazine*, October 23, 2019

Inje Residence (Inje-gun, Gangwon-do, South Korea), *ArchDaily*, August 14, 2019
(https://www.archdaily.com/922905)

Buphwajungsa Temple (Dongdaemun-gu, Seoul, South Korea), *Wallpaper*, May 28, 2019
(https://www.wallpaper.com/gallery/architecture/cutting-edge-religious-architecture-around-the-world#pic_267989)

## 2018
YKH Associates Headquarters (Gangnam-gu, Seoul, South Korea), *Mini Building 7*, A&C Publishing Co., Ltd

Vixen Headquarters (Gangnam-gu, Seoul, South Korea), *ArchDaily*, August 10, 2018
(https://www.archdaily.com/899726)

YKH Associates Headquarters (Gangnam-gu, Seoul, South Korea), *ArchDaily*, April 13, 2018
(https://www.archdaily.com/892332)

## 2011
Nine Dragon Housing Complex (Suizhong, Liaoning, China), *ArchDaily*, November 10, 2011
(http://www.archdaily.com/182446)

Buyeo Lotte Premium Outlet (Buyeo-gun, Chungcheongnam-do, South Korea), *Space Magazine*, August, 2011

Lotte Department Store Roof Garden (Jung-gu, Busan, South Korea), *ArchDaily*, July 15, 2011
(http://www.archdaily.com/150787)

The Great Wall Apartment Factory (Suizhong, Liaoning, China), *ArchDaily*, May 27, 2011
(http://www.archdaily.com/138949)

Buyeo Lotte Premium Outlet (Buyeo-gun, Chungcheongnam-do, South Korea), *ArchDaily*, May 10, 2011
(http://www.archdaily.com/133372)

Busan Marine Terrace Resort (Nam-gu, Busan, South Korea), *ArchDaily*, April 29, 2011
(http://www.archdaily.com/131147)

## 2006
Taesun Hong, Yamasaki Korea
*Hankyung News*, April 3, 2006

## 2005
Taesun Hong, Yamasaki Korea
*Sisa Magazine*, September 28, 2005

# Project Credits

All photography, renderings, diagrams, and plans are supplied courtesy YKH Associates. Photography exceptions are noted.

### Buphwajungsa Temple
Location: Dongdaemun-gu, Seoul, South Korea
Completion: 2013
Client: Buphwajungsa Temple
Lead architect: Taesun Hong
Design team: Soyeon Kim, Daejung Sang, Jeonggyu Lee, Yongho Hwang, Gungu Lee
Construction: Opus Born Construction, Donghoon DOS (Interior)
Site area: 9,256.96 ft² (860 m²)
Building footprint area: 5,406.6 ft² (502.29 m²)
Total floor area: 43,544.64 ft² (4,045.43 m²)
Photography: Dongwook Jung (Time of Blue)

### Busan Marine Terrace Resort
Location: Nam-gu, Busan, South Korea
Completion: 2010
Client: Poonglim Industrial Co, Ltd.
Lead architect: Taesun Hong
Design team: Wonjin Kim, Chan Park, Youngmo Kim, Jongseok Kim, Kiwan Ahn, Yeojin Youn, Dongsoo Jang, Junghwan Ko, Yaejin Kim, Jangdo Ki
Site area: 1,419 ft² (131,830 m²)
Building footprint area: 279,776 ft² (25,992 m²)
Total floor area: 1,279 ft² (118,823 m²)
No. of units: 117 (residences); 111/29 (hotel suites/terrace rooms)

### Buyeo Lotte Premium Outlet
Location: Buyeo-gun, Chungcheongnam-do, South Korea
Completion: 2010
Client: Lotte Shopping
Lead architect: Taesun Hong
Design team: Wonjin Kim, Chan Park, Jongseok Kim, Kiwan Ahn, Yeojin Youn, Dongsoo Jang, Eunjeong Kwon, Miji Lee, Jongnam Kim, Jangdo Ki
Site area: 804,042.58 ft² (74,698 m²)
Building footprint area: 267,778 ft² (24,877.40 m²)
Total floor area: 430,168.92 ft² (39,964 m²)

### Daejeon Hyundai Premium Outlet
Location: Yuseong-gu, Daejeon, South Korea
Completion: 2019
Client: Hyundai Department Store
Lead architect: Taesun Hong
Design team: Daejung Sang, Keunho Kim, Dongyoung Kim, Donghyun Ji, Jihwang Lee, Sanghyuk Son, Kyuseung Kyung, Seunghyeon Lee
Construction: Hyundai E&C
Site area: 1,073,063.90 ft² (99,690.90 m²)
Building footprint area: 321,451.91 ft² (29,863.86 m²)
Total floor area: 1,394,148.70 ft² (129,520.65 m²)
Photography: Dongwook Jung (Time of Blue)

### Gimpo BOHM Officetel
Location: Gimpo-si, Gyeonggi-do, South Korea
Completion: 2018
Client: Ilju Construction
Lead architect: Taesun Hong
Design team: Soyeon Kim, Daejung Sang, Jeonggyu Lee, Heewon Kim, Jinsuk Kim, Bongki Cho, Gungu Lee, Hero Park, Dongjin Lee, Jaemin Kim
Construction: Ilju Construction, Donghoon Dos
Site area: 19,929.38 ft² (1,851.50 m²)
Building footprint area: 11,805.86 ft² (1,096.80 m²)
Total floor area: 174,590.52 ft² (16,219.99 m²)
Photography: Dongwook Jung (Time of Blue); YKH Associates

### Gimpo Hyundai Premium Outlet
Location: Gimpo-si, Gyeonggi-do, South Korea
Completion: 2015
Client: Hyundai Department Store
Lead architect: Taesun Hong
Design team: Daejung Sang, Keunho Kim, Seho Lee, Dongyoung Kim, Dongwook Kim, Jongmin Lee
Construction: Hyundai E&C
Site area: 554,393 ft² (51,504.80 m²)
Building footprint area: 269,319.39 ft² (25,020.59 m²)
Total floor area: 1,655,252 ft² (153,777.95 m²)
Photography: Dongwook Jung (Time of Blue)

**Goheung Stella Resort**
Location: Goheung-gun, Jeollanam-do, South Korea
Completion: 2018
Client: Space Development Corporation
Lead architect: Taesun Hong
Design team: Daejung Sang, Heewon Kim, Dongjae Kim, Songhyun Cho, Yeongmuk Bak, Jaemin Kim, Motbi Choi, Chaewan Kim
Site area: 2,444,720.60 ft² (227,121.98 m²)
Building footprint area: 170,415.95 ft² (15,832.16 m²)
Total built area: 331,609.82 ft² (30,807.56 m²); hotel 142,193 ft² (13,210.17 m²); villa 134,730 ft² (12,516.83 m²); commercial 54,686.69 ft² (5,080.56 m²)
No of units: villa: 151; hotel: 100

**The Great Wall Apartment Factory**
Location: Suizhong, Liaoning, China
Completion: 2012
Client: Global Star Town, Inc.
Lead architect: Taesun Hong
Design team: Wonjin Kim, Sungsin Park, Eunjeong Kwon, Donghyun Ji, Whee Lee
Site area: 789,748 ft² (73,370 m²)
Building footprint area: 347,028 ft² (32,240 m²)
Total floor area: 3,261,626 ft² (303,015 m²)

**Gyeonghui-dang Mixed-Use**
Location: Jongno-gu, Seoul, South Korea
Completion: 2021
Client: Sungmoon Lee, Sungil Co.
Lead architect: Taesun Hong
Executive Architect: Ghowoo Architectural Design Group
Design team: Seungkwan Yang, Daejung Sang, Heewon Kim, Dongjae Kim, Jongwoo Kim, Chang Geun Jeong, Songhyun Cho, Yeongmuk Bak, Jaemin Kim, Motbi Choi, Chaewan Kim
Construction: Tracon E&C
Site area: 20,763.58 ft² (1,929 m²)
Building footprint area: 12,094.33 ft² (1,123.60 m²)
Total floor area: 93,678.31 ft² (8,703 m²)
Photography: Dongwook Jung (Time of Blue)

**Heyri "The Step" Plaza**
Location: Paju-si, Gyeonggi-do, South Korea
Completion: 2003
Client: Heyri Plaza
Lead architect: Taesun Hong
Design team: Daejung Sang, Youngjo Lee, Seunghoi Koo, Jungyoung Kim, Jisun Kim, Chansik Park, Kyungsoo Kim, Seongah Yun, Jaeseong Choi, Hanseong Kang, Yunju Cho, Jiwon Kang, Yeonggil Song, Taekyung Jung, Inseong Kim, Junwon Hwang, Seongwon Yang
Construction: Bomi E&C
Site area: 253,347.90 ft² (23,536.79 m²)
Building footprint area: 83,925.13 ft² (7,796.90 m²)
Total floor area: 300,843.12 ft² (27,949.24 m²)
Photography: YKH Associates

**Hillmaru Country Club & Golf Hotel**
Location: Pocheon-si, Gyeonggi-do, South Korea
Completion: 2015
Client: Donghoon Co., Ltd
Lead architect: Taesun Hong
Design team: Soyeon Kim, Daejung Sang, Jeonggyu Lee, Heewon Kim, Yongho Hwang, Dongjae Kim, Bongki Cho, Gungu Lee, Heejeong Jeong, Yeongmuk Bak, Jaemin Kim, Motbi Choi, Chaewan Kim, Minyoung Park, Joewoong Ha, Isaac Jung
Construction: Youngjin E&C, Seogwang E&C, Dawon Company, Donghoon Dos
Site area: 30,846,256 ft² (2,865,711 m²)
Building footprint area: 174,021.22 ft² (16,167.10 m²)
Total floor area: 381,975.55 ft² (35,486.69 m²); clubhouse 149,859.25 ft² (13,922.38 m²); tower condo 76,513.43 ft² (7,108.33 m²); villa condo 18,981 ft² (1,763.40 m²); dormitory 78,650.60 ft² (7,306.88 m²); teehouse 2,446.42 ft² (227.28 m²); management facilities 55,524.77 ft² (5,158.42 m²)
Photography: Blumer Lehmann (Martin Eggenberger, Simon Huber); YKH Associates

**Ilyang DHL Korea Headquarters**
Location: Mapo-gu, Seoul, South Korea
Completion: 2019
Client: Ilyanglogis
Lead architect: Taesun Hong
Design team: Daejung Sang, Seho Lee, Sangmin Yang, Minju Cho, Jongmin Lee, Yongki Kim, Sungmin Yun, Junhak Ju
Construction: Baeksang E&C
Site area: 18,116.74 ft² (1,683.10 m²)
Building footprint area: 8,306.62 ft² (771.71 m²)
Total floor area: 53,194.17 ft² (4,941.90 m²)
Photography: Dongwook Jung (Time of Blue)

### Inje Residence
Location: Inje-gun, Gangwon-do, South Korea
Completion: 2014
Client: Pyungan L&C
Lead architect: Taesun Hong
Design team: Wonjin Kim, Daejung Sang
Construction: Yiinsigak, Inc.
Site area: 12,066 ft² (1,121 m²)
Building footprint area: 4,306 ft² (400 m²)
Photography: Dongwook Jung (Time of Blue); YKH Associates

### Jamsil Posco the Starpark Residence
Location: Songpa-gu, Seoul, South Korea
Completion: 2004
Client: POSCO Engineering & Construction Co., Ltd
Lead architect: Taesun Hong
Design team: Daejung Sang, Hyukki Kwon, Changhyun Kim, Sunghwan So, Chansik Park, Jaechan Lim, Yongjae Bae, Jungyoung Kim
Construction: POSCO Engineering & Construction Co., Ltd
Site area: 124,754 ft² (11,590 m²)
Building footprint area: 47,738 ft² (4,435 m²)
Total floor area: 1,074,540 ft² (99,828 m²)
No. of units: 213
Photography: Junghwan Lee

### Jeju Seogwipo VIP Institute Hotel Residence
Location: Seogwipo-si, Jeju-do, South Korea
Completion: 2015
Client: Landing Jeju Dev. Co., Ltd
Lead architect: Taesun Hong
Design team: Soyeon Kim, Daejung Sang, Jeonggyu Lee, Seho Lee, Yongho Hwang, Dongyoung Kim
Construction: Poston Construction, Donghoon DOS
Site area: 74,626.19 ft² (6,933 m²)
Building footprint area: 10,764 ft² (1,228.47 m²)
Total floor area: 32,088.40 ft² (2,981.11 m²)
Photography: Jeonggyu Lee

### Lotte Department Store Roof Garden
Location: Jung-gu, Busan, South Korea
Completion: 2010
Client: Lotte Shopping
Lead architect: Taesun Hong
Design team: Wonjin Kim, Jeongyeon Lim, Dongsoo Jang, Jihyang Lee, Nara Youn
Building footprint area: 213,502 ft² (19,835 m²)
Total floor area: 320,248 ft² (29,752 m²)

### Lotte Underground Path & Plaza
Location: Songpa-gu, Seoul, South Korea
Completion: 2011
Client: Lotte Shopping
Lead architect: Taesun Hong
Design team: Wonjin Kim, Jeongyeon Lim, Dongsoo Jang, Jihyang Lee, Nara Youn
Site area: 119,253.36 ft² (11,079 m²)
Total floor area: 170,166.66 ft² (15,809 m²)

### NEFS Headquarters
Location: Gangnam-gu, Seoul, South Korea
Completion: 2020
Client: NEFS
Lead architect: Taesun Hong
Design team: Jaeho Shin, Daejung Sang, Heewon Kim, Dongjae Kim, Songhyun Cho, Yeongmuk Bak, Jaemin Kim, Motbi Choi, Chaewan Kim
Construction: Dosi Construction
Site area: 10,406.55 ft² (966.80 m²)
Building footprint area: 4,844.23 ft² (450.05 m²)
Total floor area: 52,515.18 ft² (4,878.82 m²)
Photography: Dongwook Jung (Time of Blue)

### Namsan Lotte Castle Iris Mixed-Use
Location: Jung-gu, Seoul, South Korea
Completion: 2003
Client: Military Mutual Aid Association
Lead architect: Taesun Hong
Executive architect: Baum Architects
Design team: Jaiseong Shim, Daejung Sang, Changhyun Kim, Heewon Kim, Junghyun Kim
Construction: Lotte Engineering & Construction Co., Ltd
Site area: 80,460 ft² (7,475 m²)
Total floor area: 1,242,338 ft² (115,417 m²)
No. of units: 386
Photography: Junghwan Lee

### Nine Dragon Housing Complex
Location: Suizhong, Liaoning, China
Completion: 2011
Client: Global Star Town, Inc.
Lead architect: Taesun Hong
Design team: Wonjin Kim, Kiwan Ahn, Eunjeong Kwon, Donghyun Ji, Ingrid Kong, Eunsong Jung
Site area: 281,770.11 ft² (26,177.30 m²)
Building footprint area: 114,318.11 ft² (10,620.50 m²)
Total floor area: 997,935.16 ft² (92,711.21 m²)

### Oak Valley Resort
Location: Wonju-si, Gangwon-do, South Korea
Completion: 2020
Client: HDC
Lead architect: Taesun Hong
Design team: Daejung Sang, Seho Lee, Kiwan Ahn, Jongmin Lee, Motbi Choi, Sungmin Yun, Junhak Ju, Piljae Choi, Inkyung Hong
Construction: HDC
Site area: 2,025,445 ft² (188,170 m²)
Building footprint area: 449,339.44 ft² (41,745 m²)
Total floor area: 1,381,332.60 ft² (128,330 m²); tower 913,177.87 ft² (84,837 m²); terrace village 62,215.40 ft² (5,780 m²); commercial village 69,125.83 ft² (6,422 m²); raw house village 165,333.66 ft² (15,360 m²); mountain village 171,469.09 ft² (15,930 m²)

### Oyala Convention & Observatory
Location: Oyala, Equatorial Guinea
Completion: 2013
Client: Government of Equatorial Guinea
Lead architect: Taesun Hong
Design team: Wonjin Kim, Byungsik So, Donghyun Ji, Chan Park
Building footprint area: 38,455.15 ft² (3,572.60 m²)
Total floor area: 248,492.41 ft² (23,085.70 m²)
No. of parking bays: 151

### Paju Lotte Premium Outlet
Location: Paju-si, Gyeonggi-do, South Korea
Completion: 2010
Client: Lotte Shopping
Lead architect: Taesun Hong
Design team: Daejung Sang, Keunho Kim, Seunghoi Koo, Yunhee So, Heonman Lim, Kyungran Park, Kiwan Ahn, Hyejung Kim, Junghyun Lim, Miji Lee, Jihwang Lee, Changhyun Kim
Construction: Lotte Engineering & Construction Co. Ltd
Site area: 432,806 ft² (40,208.03 m²)
Building footprint area: 292,359.75 ft² (27,161.11 m²)
Total floor area: 1,601,558.50 ft² (148,789.65 m²)
Photography: Dongwook Jung (Time of Blue)

### Sebyeol Brewery
Location: Paju-si, Gyeonggi-do, South Korea
Completion: 2019
Client: Seungwon Park, Sebyeol Brewery
Lead architect: Taesun Hong
Design team: Jaeho Shin, Heewon Kim, Dongjae Kim, Songhyun Cho, Yeongmuk Bak, Jaemin Kim, Motbi Choi, Chaewan Kim
Construction: Dosi Construction
Site area: 40,074 ft² (3,723 m²)
Building footprint area: 14,285.86 ft² (1,327.20 m²)
Total floor area: 24,533.11 ft² (2,279.20 m²)
Photography: Dongwook Jung (Time of Blue); YKH Associates

### Seoul Performing Arts Center
Location: Yongsan-gu, Seoul, South Korea
Completion: 2005
Client: Seoul Metropolitan Government
Lead architects: Taesun Hong, Junggon Kim
Design team: Peter Choi, Daejung Sang, Youngjo Lee, Seunghoi Koo, Kooho Jung, Youngmo Kim, Jungyoung Kim
Site area: 563,932 ft² (52,391 m²)
Building footprint area: 304,415.66 ft² (28,281.14 m²)
Total floor area: 596,163.70 ft² (55,385.42 m²)

### SK Namsan Leaders' View Mixed-Use
Location: Jung-gu, Seoul, South Korea
Completion: 2005
Client: Makers Holdings Co., Ltd
Lead architect: Taesun Hong
Design team: Daejung Sang, Seunghoi Koo, Jaiseong Shim, Changhyun Kim, Heewon Kim, Junghyu Kim
Construction: SK Construction & Engineering
Site area: 54,601 ft² (5,072.60 m²)
Building footprint area: 28,930.27 ft² (2,687.71 m²)
Total floor area: 853,516 ft² (79,294.23 m²)
No. of units: 233
Photography: Junghwan Lee

### Trendex Headquarters
Location: Gwangju-si, Gyeonggi-do, South Korea
Completion: 2021
Client: Trendex Co.
Lead architect: Taesun Hong
Design team: Jaeho Shin, Daejung Sang, Heewon Kim, Dongjae Kim, Songhyun Cho, Yeongmuk Bak, Jaemin Kim, Motbi Choi, Chaewan Kim
Construction: Dosi Construction
Site area: 4,789.94 ft² (445 m²)
Building footprint area: 1,665.49 ft² (154.73 m²)
Total floor area: 8,371.2 ft² (777.71 m²)
Photography: Junghwan Lee

### Vinyl C Headquarters
Location: Gangnam-gu, Seoul, South Korea
Completion: 2021
Client: Youngmin Park
Lead architect: Taesun Hong
Design team: Daejung Sang, Yongho Hwang, Kiwan Ahn, Jihoon Lee, Kyungwook Kim, Byeongsu Kim
Construction: Gadam Construction
Site area: 5,850.19 ft² (543.50 m²)
Building footprint area: 3,172.99 ft² (294.78 m²)
Total floor area: 16,791 ft² (1,559.94 m²)
Photography: Dongwook Jung (Time of Blue)

### Vixen Headquarters
Location: Gangnam-gu, Seoul, South Korea
Completion: 2018
Client: Vixen Communications
Lead architect: Taesun Hong
Design team: Jaeho Shin, Daejung Sang, Yongho Hwang, Youngsoo Ko, Jihoon Lee
Construction: Dosi Construction
Site area: 5,430.40 ft$^2$ (504.50 m$^2$)
Building footprint area: 2,643.72 ft$^2$ (245.61 m$^2$)
Total floor area: 21,504.36 ft$^2$ (1,997.82 m$^2$)
Photography: Jaechul Yu

### Yangpyeongdong Mixed-Use Building
Location: Yeongdeungpo-gu, Seoul, South Korea
Completion: 2020
Client: SJ. Lab Corp.
Lead architect: Taesun Hong
Design team: Daejung Sang, Heewon Kim, Dongjae Kim, Yeongmuk Bak, Jaemin Kim, Motbi Choi
Construction: Dosi Construction
Site area: 6,237.69 ft$^2$ (579.50 m$^2$)
Building footprint area: 3,258.13 ft$^2$ (302.69 m$^2$)
Total floor area: 28,931.85 ft$^2$ (2,687.86 m$^2$)

### Yeoju Residence
Location: Yeoju-si, Gyeonggi-do, South Korea
Completion: 2016
Client: Jongyun Cheon
Lead architect: Taesun Hong
Design team: Soyeon Kim, Daejung Sang, Jeonggyu Lee, Dongyoung Kim, Juhee Cho
Construction: Donghoon DOS
Site area: 10,656.27 ft$^2$ (990 m$^2$)
Building footprint area: 2,081.96 ft$^2$ (193.42 m$^2$)
Total floor area: 4,222.25 ft$^2$ (392.26 m$^2$)
Photography: Dongwook Jung (Time of Blue)

### Yeosu The Ocean Resort
Location: Yeosu-si, Jeollanam-do, South Korea
Completion: 2019
Client: HJ Magnolia Yongpyong Hotel & Resort Corp
Lead architect: Taesun Hong
Design team: Daejung Sang, Keunho Kim, Nackkyung Lee, Dongyoung Kim, Kyungsoo Kim, Yeongmuk Bak, Sanghyuk Son, Jaemin Kim, Dukjin Kim, Minwoo Lee, Seunghyeon Lee, Soomi Kim, Donghui Shin, Hyegyu Lee
Site area: 815,032.53 ft$^2$ (75,719 m$^2$)
Building footprint area: 109,688.66 ft$^2$ (10,190.41 m$^2$)
Total floor area: 584,922.52 ft$^2$ (54,341.08 m$^2$); hill condo 384,104.87 ft$^2$ (35,684.51 m$^2$); terrace condo 200,817.65 ft$^2$ (18,656.57 m$^2$)

### YKH Associates Headquarters
Location: Gangnam-gu, Seoul, South Korea
Completion: 2017
Client: YKH Associates
Lead architect: Taesun Hong
Design team: Soyeon Kim, Jaeho Shin, Daejung Sang, Seho Lee, Jongmin Lee, Yeongmuk Bak, Yongki Kim
Construction: Dosi Construction, Donghoon DOS
Site area: 2,355.14 ft$^2$ (218.80 m$^2$)
Building footprint area: 1,362.71 ft$^2$ (126.60 m$^2$)
Total floor area: 6,159.76 ft$^2$ (572.26 m$^2$)
Photography: Jeonggyu Lee, Jaechul Yu, YKH Associates

### Yoido Richensia Mixed-Use Residence
Location: Yeongdeungpo-gu, Seoul, South Korea
Completion: 2003
Client: Military Mutual Aid Association
Lead architect: Taesun Hong
Associate architect: Gowoo Architects
Design team: Jaiseong Shim, Daejung Sang, Changhyun Kim, Heewon Kim, Junghyun Kim
Construction: Kumho E&C
Site area: 74,744.59 ft$^2$ (6,944 m$^2$)
Building footprint area: 27,960.23 ft$^2$ (2,597.59 m$^2$)
Total floor area: 935,170.90 ft$^2$ (86,880.22 m$^2$)
No. of units: apartments: 235; office suites: 252
Photography: Junghwan Lee

# Acknowledgments

Thank you to all of my music and architecture teachers and colleagues for allowing me to create the body of works that I present in this book. Many thanks to Jaemin Kim, Hudson Matz, and Hannah Ou for your efforts in organizing this book. Thank you, Dr. Menas Kafatos, Prof. Junggon Kim, Prof. Paul Lim, and Bill Bingham for your wonderful words of encouragement. I am indebted to all of my current and previous colleagues at YKH Associates. Thank you Mom and Dad, and Jhuree and Ahree, for your endless support.

Published in Australia in 2022 by
The Images Publishing Group Pty Ltd
ABN 89 059 734 431

Offices

*Melbourne*
Waterman Business Centre
Suite 64, Level 2 UL40
1341 Dandenong Road
Chadstone, Victoria 3148
Australia
Tel: +61 3 8564 8122

*New York*
6 West 18th Street 4B
New York, NY 10011
United States
Tel: +1 212 645 1111

*Shanghai*
6F, Building C, 838 Guangji Road
Hongkou District, Shanghai 200434
China
Tel: +86 021 31260822

books@imagespublishing.com
www.imagespublishing.com

Copyright © YKH Associates 2022
The Images Publishing Group Reference Number: 1626

All photography is attributed in the Project Credits on pages 394–98 unless otherwise noted.
Endpapers: Dongwook Jung (Time of Blue); Buphwajungsa Temple

All rights reserved. Apart from any fair dealing for the purposes of private study, research, criticism or review as permitted under the Copyright Act, no part of this publication may be reproduced, stored in a retrieval system or transmitted in any form by any means, electronic, mechanical, photocopying, recording or otherwise, without the written permission of the publisher.

A catalogue record for this book is available from the National Library of Australia

Title: Taesun Hong: YKH Associates // The Master Architect Series
ISBN: 9781864709230

This title was commissioned in IMAGES' Melbourne office and produced as follows: *Editorial* Georgia (Gina) Tsarouhas, *Graphic design* Ryan Marshall, *Art direction/production* Nicole Boehringer *Thanks to* Jeanette Wall (proofing)

Printed on 157gsm Chinese OJI FSC® matt art paper, by Artron Art (Group) Co., Ltd, in China

IMAGES has included on its website a page for special notices in relation to this and its other publications.
Please visit www.imagespublishing.com

Every effort has been made to trace the original source of copyright material contained in this book.
The publishers would be pleased to hear from copyright holders to rectify any errors or omissions.

The information and illustrations in this publication have been prepared and supplied by Taesun Hong and YKH Associates and the contributors. While all reasonable efforts have been made to ensure accuracy, the publishers do not, under any circumstances, accept responsibility for errors, omissions and representations express or implied.